Baby Names
for Australians

ANNE MATTHEWS

ACKNOWLEDGMENTS

Many thanks to the following people for their assistance and suggestions: Jill Varley, Ainslie Cahill, Di Robinson and Paul Andrew (Indonesian names), Judy and Tashi Tenzing and Pem Pem Tshering (Tibetan and Sherpa names), David Watts (Aboriginal names) and Sandra Thompson (Maori names).

Published in 2012 by New Holland Publishers
Sydney

Level 1, 178 Fox Valley Road, Wahroonga, NSW 2076, Australia

newhollandpublishers.com

First published in 1998
Reprinted 1998, 1999
New edition published in 2001
Expanded edition published in 2007.
Reprinted 2022.

Copyright © 2012 New Holland Publishers
Copyright © 2012 in text Anne Matthews

All rights reserved. No part of this publication may be reproduced, stored in a retrieval system or transmitted, in any form or by any means, electronic, mechanical, photocopying, recording or otherwise, without the prior written permission of the publishers and copyright holders.

National Library of Australia Cataloguing-in-Publication entry:
    Matthews, Anne.
    Baby names for Australians / Anne Matthews.
    3rd ed.
ISBN: 9781742572222 (pbk.)

Subjects: Names, Personal--Australia--Dictionaries.
    English language--Australia--Etymology--Names.
929.440994

Group Managing Director: Fiona Schultz
Publishing Manager: Lliane Clarke
Project editor: Jodi De Vantier
Designer: Kimberley Pearce
Cover design: Yolanda La Gorcé
Production Director: Arlene Gippert

10 9 8 7 6 5

Keep up with New Holland Publishers:
 NewHollandPublishers
 @newhollandpublishers

In memory of my parents, George and Christina, who named me, somewhat optimistically, 'graceful follower of Christ'.

And with special thanks to Geoff – the (occasionally) divinely peaceful one – for his suggestions and support.

Contents

Preface	6
Introduction	7
Features	
21st-century names	14
Names for Australians	16
First Fleet names	18
Celebrity kids' names–boys	20
Celebrity kids' names–girls	22
Unisex names	24
Alternative spellings	25
Astrological names–fire signs	26
Astrological names–earth signs	28
Astrological names–air signs	30
Astrological names–water signs	32
20th-century names	34
Surnames as first names	36
'Noun' names	38
Shakespearean names	40
Biblical names	42
Astronomy and 'star' names	44
Girls' names	45
Boys' names	329
Names by ethnic origin	586

PREFACE

I have long been fascinated by names. At primary school in England in the late 1950s, it occurred to me that I had a rather unexciting name: other girls were labelled, far more imaginatively I thought, Donna, Cheryl, Wendy, Lindsey, Nicola and Yvonne. It could have been worse, however: Cynthia, Ernest, Gloria, Samson, Rodney and Priscilla – names that seemed old-fashioned even then.

During the 1960s and early 1970s, however – when most of my earlier contemporaries bore traditional names like David, Christine, Elizabeth, Mary, Richard, Susan, Philip, Jane and Alan – I came across far more interesting names: males called Barry, Hamish, Scott, Evan and Glenn; and girls labelled Tracey, Jessica, Olivia, Rowena, Jacqueline, Karen and Lucy.

Then I began travelling in Europe and another, unimaginably rich, world of names opened up to me. Where, I wondered, had all of these names come from? What did they mean? How many different appellations could a person come across in a lifetime? My interest in the subject was further fuelled by Dr Basil Cottle, my most venerable English lecturer, who was somewhat of an expert on etymology in general, and the meaning of surnames in particular.

My move to Australia at the end of the 1970s, and a long period of working as an adventure travel guide in Asia, South America, Africa and other parts of the world, brought me into contact with yet more intriguing and downright exotic 'people labels'. I spent many months with people called Sonam and Dechen, Emilio and Rosita, Chen and Lee, Salim and Amira. And back home in Australia there were always names like Shane, Kerry, Narelle, Wayne, Leanne and Bradley – titles I had rarely come across in the UK – to wonder at.

As its own title implies, *Baby Names for Australians* is designed particularly for Australians. Its 50,000 or so entries include names that range from Aboriginal to Zimbabwean, and the publication is intended for Australians of all ethnic backgrounds.

Those of you who are curious about names and their origins will find this book enlightening. It is, however, primarily intended for parents who are searching for a meaningful or attractive name for their child, and I hope this publication proves to be a source of inspiration.

Anne Matthews

Introduction

I suppose it sounds obvious, but naming began as a means of distinguishing one person from another. Personal names generally came first, followed by surnames (family names). If there were ten Williams, Gastons or Wolfgangs living in a village, it was decidedly less confusing to distinguish them by adding something – a surname – that perhaps defined what they looked like, who their father was, or whether they lived at the top of the hill or down by the river.

In that same area, many decades later, there might have been several William Reads, all bearing the distinguishing family name of the original Read, 'the red-haired one'. Middle names thus came into being, with the various William Reads described as William Henry, William Edmund, William Ralph and so on. Names are essentially 'people labels' and a form of description – someone might be described as 'tall, with dark hair', but that person is more often defined as David Evans, or David John Evans.

There are many factors involved in selecting a 'label', and some of these are discussed below. Christian, given, personal or first names, call them what you like, remain with a person for life, and this is one of the most important decisions that a parent has to make for their child.

Choosing a Name for Your Child

Naming for Sound

Does the name sound feminine enough for a girl or masculine enough for a boy? Or does this matter, particularly in the 21st century when unisex names are increasingly common.

The sound of names in combination, especially with the family name, should also be considered. A short first name often complements a long surname: for example, Alice Warburton, rather than Jacqueline Warburton. Conversely, you could combine a long first name with a one-syllable family name: Alexander Dale, rather than Jake Dale.

We all tend to make judgments about a name, based on its sound as well as associations with people we have known. Here are a few examples of my own 'associations'.

Regal, important-sounding names

Boys:
Alexander, Charles, David, Edward, George, Henry, Hugo, Jacob, James, Justin, Leo, Louis, Marcus, Max, Nicholas, Oscar, Rex, Samuel, William, Xavier.
Girls:
Alexandra, Alexis, Anastasia, Audrey, Charlotte, Claudia, Cleo, Edwina, Elizabeth, Eve, Frances, Imogen, Isabella, Julia, Olivia, Phoebe, Rowena, Stephanie, Victoria, Zara.

Names with Attitude

Boys:
Angus, Caleb, Chase, Cody, Darcy, Fergus, Hunter, Jack, Jackson, Jake, Jasper, Jed, Jett, Kurt, Leon, Leroy, Nate, Phoenix, Tyson, Zac.

Girls:
Amber, Chelsea, Coco, Courtney, Georgia, Jade, Layla, Lola, Lorelei, Mackenzie, Maddison, Maxine, Natasha, Rochelle, Roxanne, Ruby, Samantha, Scarlett, Sienna, Zoë.

Ultra-Feminine Names for Girls

Abbey, Alice, Allegra, Anna, Ava, Bella, Chiara, Emily, Emma, Isla, Laura, Lily, Mia, Molly, Natalie, Poppy, Sarah, Sienna, Sophie, Willow.

'Softer' Names for Boys

ARCHIE, AUSTIN, BAILEY, BEAU, BLAKE, DYLAN, ELI, GABRIEL, HARRY, HUGH, JESSE, JOEL, KAI, LIAM, LUKE, MICHAEL, NOAH, OLIVER, SAM, TOBY.

Naming for Meaning

Many people choose a name for its meaning, such as 'beautiful', 'strong', 'gentle' or 'good'. Despite their recent popularity, some names have rather unfortunate meanings – examples are Courtney (the short-nosed one) and Brodie (a ditch) – so it's worth checking.

Naming after Places and 'Things'

You might like to name your child after something or somewhere that is particularly relevant or close to your heart. There are, for example, names from the world of astronomy; animal and bird names (Leon, Marlon, Melissa and Jemima); flower and plant names (Willow, Poppy, Ashley and Myall); names of gemstones (Amber, Jet, Jade, Ruby and Garnet); and 'colour names' that describe hair or skin colouring, such as Blake and Jennifer ('fair'), Tynan and Leila ('dark'), and Flynn and Scarlett ('fiery').

- **Places:** You could also consider the name of a favourite town, city, country or other geographical feature. You might have grown up in Tully or Bronte, for example, lived in Dakota or Siena, and spent your honeymoon in India or Paris.

- **Astrological names:** If you have an interest in astrology, why not give your child a name that is appropriate for his or her zodiac sign. An Aries child for example, could be named Aidan (little fiery one) or Marcella (belonging to Mars) to suit this fire sign and its ruler, Mars, while Dylan and Nerina would be suitable names for water-sign Pisceans.

Naming after a person

There may be a particular given name that is passed down through the generations, or a surname, perhaps the mother's maiden name, could be incorporated as a middle name.

- **Celebrities:** these might be a favourite actor, sporting star or well-known personality. The past popularity of names like Audrey (Hepburn), Ava (Gardner) (incidentally, both currently very popular), Marilyn (Monroe), Gary (Cooper) and Wayne (John Wayne) can be attributed to the celebrity factor – as can modern names such as Ashlee, Charlize, Khloe, Miley, Reese, Scarlet, Sienna and Harlow (from 1930s actress Jean Harlow) for girls, and Ashton, Cruise, Harry, Jude, Orlando and William for boys.

- **Children of celebrities:** Although celebrities are notorious for giving their kids unusual (and sometimes unfortunate) names, many of these are popular with Australian parents. Names such as Mia (Kate Winslet and the Hewitts), Ava (Reese Witherspoon), Kalan (the Murdochs), Jaden/Jayden (Andre Agassi and Britney Spears) and Cruz (David Beckham and the Hewitts) have certainly caught on.

- **Historical characters:** This includes names from the Bible and other religious texts, or historical personalities – Lincoln (Abraham), Florence (Nightingale), and Amelia (Earhart) are examples from the past. You could also choose a truly Australian 'label', such as Macquarie, Tasman, Flinders, Banjo, Alice or Melba, or even a First Fleeter's name.

- **Fictitious characters:** taken from Greek, Roman, Sanskrit and Norse mythology, or from novels, plays, films or television programs. Shakespearean names such as Miranda and Olivia have long been popular, while other examples are Rhett and Scarlett from *Gone with the Wind*, Arwen from *The Lord of the Rings* and, of course, the very Australian Matilda and Clancy.

Middle names

You may find it difficult to decide between a classical name such as William or Charlotte; going 'modern' with Kai, Ryder, Harper, Savannah or Willow; or 'ethnic' with something like Luca or Gabriella. In this instance, choosing two names is a good solution. You could give your baby a more conventional first name and an unusual middle name (Bella Swan, Matilda Sunshine and Benjamin Blue for example), or the reverse (Jericho James, Emerson Rosa and Indigo Helen).

Interestingly, many 'old-fashioned' names are making a comeback for this role. Rose has been popular as a middle name for over a decade but Anne, Christine, Dorothy, June, Helen, Susan and, particularly, Elizabeth and Margaret are on the rise. Andrew, Christopher, Brian, Michael, Phillip,

Peter, Robert and Thomas are increasingly popular middle names for boys.

Modern trends

The 21st century has seen some significant trends in baby naming – including the following.

- **Classic names:** traditional, often biblical, names such as Charlotte, Sophie, Olivia, Elizabeth, Hannah, Joshua, Edward, Christopher, Samuel and Adam have made a comeback in recent years.

- **Ethnic names:** names from cultures and languages as varied as Gaelic, Arabic, Aboriginal, Hebrew and Italian are also popular. Examples include Declan, Jarrah, Rafael, Rocco, Xavier, Amelie, Caitlin, Isabella, Isla, Layla and Samira.

- **Unisex names:** In some cultures – Tibetan, for example – it is common for boys and girls to share names such as Nima or Tashi, and this concept is becoming more popular in western society. Male/female variations (Francis/Frances and Leslie/Lesley) have been around for a long time, but there are now dozens of genuinely unisex names such as Charlie, Riley, Noa, Kyle, Drew, Harper and Tyson. I have even seen Felix, Pierre, Rex and Rory in birth announcements for girls.

- **Surnames as first names:** both boys and girls now have names such as Cameron, Clooney, Finlay, Maddox, Walker and Weston. Interestingly, many of these are 'occupation names' like Cooper, Hunter, Mason, Miller and Tyler. Celebrity surnames and brand names are popular too, including Jagger, Ledger, Presley, Aniston, Armani and Chanel.

- **'Noun' names:** this trend, almost certainly established by celebrities, means names such as Affinity, Blessing, Button, Cedar, Chardonnay, Holiday, Mystique, Reef, Spark and Summer are not uncommon. Some of these are attractive and unusual but it can be taken too far – consider Bandit, Danger, Martyr, Trick and Wraith.

- **Made-up names:** another major trend is to make up names. Famous authors of the past created Vanessa (Jonathan Swift), Dorian (Oscar Wilde), Wendy (J M Barrie) and Lorna (R D Blackmore), but today's parents are perhaps going overboard. A New Zealand couple, for example, received a court order to allow their nine-year-old daughter to change the name she understandably hated – 'Talula Does The Hula From Hawaii'. Other names that have been officially 'blocked' include 4real, Fat Boy, and Fish and Chips for twins (although Benson and Hedges *was* allowed!).

Made-up names can be created by dropping or adding letters – Mackenzie to Kenzie, Ava to Avah and Max to Maxx. A popular trend in the USA is to add La, Ta, Tal or Tan to female names, creating concoctions such as Lakeisha and

Takeisha (from Keisha) and Talaine (from Elaine). There are also many boys' names with D or De prefixes, including DeMarcus, Dwayne and DeReese.

Other examples of adapting an existing name are Jayden and Jaylen (from Jay), Zacoda (from Zac), Jarilyn (from Marilyn) and Jelissa (from Melissa). You could even change the order of the letters, whereby Mary becomes Ryma and Liam becomes Mial. Other examples are Etan and Neveah, Nate and Heaven respectively, in reverse.

If you need inspiration, many baby name websites scramble letters in anagram style to make up a possibly unique name on your behalf.

- **Combining names:** there are two major options: from two full names – for example, Amalia-Rose, Marie-Claire, Giancarlo and Kobe-Lee – or from parts of two names. Examples of these are Alexavier (Alexander and Xavier), Jaleb (Jay and Caleb), Sacharias (Sacha and Zacharias), Alexanna (Alex and Anna), Jaslyn (Jasmine and Lynn) and Sarahanna (Sarah and Hannah).

- **Alternative spellings:** many parents like to distinguish a popular name by spelling it differently, so that Jacob becomes Jaykeb, Jackson to Jaxxon, Olivia to Alivyah and Georgia to Jorja. There is nothing essentially wrong with this, but imagine the inconvenience of your child having to constantly spell out his or her name in the future.

WHAT TO AVOID

Virtually everyone can recall a few name disasters. Although these can be amusing, it isn't wise to land your child with something along the lines of Crispin Bacon, Ida Down, Harley Davis, Wanda Farr, Ophelia Dickey or Jack Daniel. Although not 'disasters' as such it's also probably best to avoid combinations such as Jane Lane, Harry Barry, David Davidson and William Williams.

DIMINUTIVES

In Australia especially, the shortening and familiarising of names is almost inevitable, but think carefully about this practice, and consider your surname in particular. Here are some diminutives of Patricia, Richard, Alexander, Christine, John and Timothy respectively – Pat Lamb, Rick Shaw, Sandy Banks, Chris Cross, Jack Frost and Tim Tam. If you're keen to avoid a diminutive, go for short names like Jack, Mia, Anna, Ryan, Jade, Jai, Lara, Tom and Zac. But some of these can still be familiarised by adding a 'y' or 'o' at the end.

INITIALS

And, finally, think about the initials formed by given and family names. Initials can create some not particularly desirable 'words' that may well cause embarrassment in the future. Real-life examples are JAP, DOB, GAB, KAK, FAB, PAW, LOB, BAK, LEAP, IMP and ODD.

ORIGINS OF NAMES

Following are brief descriptions of some of the less obvious 'origin of name' categories that are used throughout the book. Note that names of modern English origin are not designated as 'English' in the text.

Aboriginal: not necessarily traditional Indigenous Australian names, but rather Aboriginal words from various parts of the continent.
Ancient Egyptian: names from the language of the Egyptians of antiquity, as opposed to modern-day Arabic.
Aramaic: a Semitic language, related to Hebrew.
Babylonian: the language of the ancient region of Babylon, located in Mesopotamia (present-day Iraq).
Baha'i: a religious faith, founded in Persia in the 19th century. The religion has its own calendar, consisting of nineteen months.
Basque: from the western Pyrenees region of Spain and France.
Breton: Celtic names from Brittany in north-western France.
Catalan: the language of Andorra and Catalonia, a region of north-east Spain.
Celtic: Breton, Cornish and Welsh names from the Celtic (Indo-European) languages of extreme-west Europe. Some Gaelic names are similar and may also be included.
Cornish: Celtic names from Cornwall, the most south-westerly English county.
Flemish: from a form of Dutch, used mainly in northern Belgium.
Gaelic: names that originate from the Gaelic (a form of Celtic) languages of Ireland, the Isle of Man and Scotland. The definitions 'Irish' and 'Scottish' generally indicate Gaelic names that have been anglicised.
Gypsy: names from the language of Europe's gypsy people, sometimes known as Romany.
Hindi: essentially Sanskrit names, but these are specifically from northern India.
Israeli/Jewish/Modern Jewish: Hebrew, but generally popular modern names rather than ancient names from the Bible and other sources.
Mayan: the language of the Mayan people of Mexico.
Middle English: from the form of English used from approximately AD 1100–1400.
Native American: names from the many languages of the Indigenous peoples of North America.
Nepali: from the language of Nepal, similar to Hindi.
Old English: names from the form of English (Anglo-Saxon) that was in use prior to AD 1100.
Old French: from the form of French used prior to approximately AD 1400.
Old Norse: from the pre-AD 1400 language of Scandinavia and Iceland.
Persian: names from the ancient language of Persia, now Iran.

Sanskrit: the classical language of India, covering names given to Hindus, Buddhists and other groups of the Indian subcontinent.
Sherpa/Tibetan: from the Sino-Tibetan language. Names that are used in Tibet, Bhutan, Ladakh (India) and by the Sherpa people of Nepal.
Sikh: a religious sect, founded in the 16th-century in north-western India. Their main language, Punjabi, is of Indo-Aryan origin.
Slavic: from the Indo-European languages of Russia, the Czech Republic, Slovakia, Poland, Serbia, Croatia, Bosnia, Bulgaria and other eastern European countries.
Swahili: from an eastern African language that has its origins in Arabic.
Teutonic: of Germanic origin, including names that are (or were) used in Germany, Holland, Scandinavia and Britain.
Urdu: a language derived from Hindustani (Hindi), used primarily in Pakistan and parts of northern India.
Yiddish: a form of Hebrew that has incorporated German and Slavic words.

USING THIS BOOK

Here are some pointers for using *Baby Names for Australians*.

- **Meaning:** when known, the name's meaning is included.
- **Ethnic origin and usage:** in many instances, names of a particular ethnic or linguistic origin – for example, Abigail (Hebrew) and Andrew (Greek) – are not necessarily in modern usage in their country of origin (Israel and Greece respectively for the above examples).
- **Variations and diminutives:** not all variations and diminutives of a name are listed separately within the A–Z format. With Jordan under 'Boys', for example, some variations (such as Jordaan, Jorden and Jordon) do not have their own separate entry, and these are therefore included only under Jordan. If you think a particular name might be a variation of another – or a name does not seem to be included – you should scan the page for the closest spelling.
- **Unisex names:** many names are now being used for both sexes, so if you are interested in a unisex name, look under both Girls and Boys!

21ST-CENTURY NAMES

Some of the most popular baby names of recent years are listed below. The top Australia-wide names in 2010 were:

William	Ruby
Jack	Chloe
Oliver	Charlotte
Cooper	Isabella
Noah	Mia

BOYS

The boys' list has changed little over the past few years, although newer inclusions are Archie, Chase, Elijah, Hamish, Hunter, Jett, Kai, Levi, Owen, Toby and Tyson. Several 'old-fashioned' names such as Andrew, Anthony and Christopher are making a comeback, and biblical names like Benjamin, Ethan, Joshua and Samuel are still popular.

Aaron	Cooper	Jake	Mitchell
Adam	Daniel	James	Nathan
Aidan/Aiden	Darcy	Jasper	Nate
Alex	David	Jayden	Nicholas
Alexander	Declan	Jesse	Noah
Andrew	Dylan	Jett	Oliver
Angus	Edward	Jonathan	Oscar
Anthony	Eli	Jordan	Owen
Archer	Elijah	Joseph	Patrick
Archie	Ethan	Joshua	Riley
Ashton	Finn	Kai	Ryan
Bailey	Gabriel	Lachlan	Ryder
Beau	George	Leo	Sam
Benjamin	Hamish	Levi	Samuel
Blake	Harrison	Liam	Sebastian
Brodie	Harry	Lincoln	Seth
Caleb	Hayden	Logan	Taj
Callum	Henry	Louis	Thomas
Cameron	Hudson	Lucas	Toby
Charles	Hugo	Luke	Tyler
Charlie	Hunter	Marcus	Tyson
Chase	Isaac	Mason	William
Christian	Jack	Matthew	Xavier
Christopher	Jackson/Jaxon	Max	Zac
Connor	Jacob	Michael	Zachary

GIRLS

The formerly 'hot' Caitlin, Lauren, Madeline and Rose are currently less popular for girls, while newer list entries include Addison, Audrey, Bella, Eva, Isla, Paige, Scarlett, Stella, Summer, Tahlia and Willow. Also on the rise are Elizabeth and the typically 1970s–80s Amber, Jade and Skye.

Abbey/Abby	Coco	Ivy	Paige
Abigail	Ebony	Jade	Phoebe
Addison	Eliza	Jasmine	Piper
Alana	Elizabeth	Jessica	Poppy
Alexandra	Ella	Kayla	Rose
Alexis	Ellie	Kiara	Ruby
Alice	Eloise	Lara	Samantha
Alyssa	Emily	Lauren	Sarah
Amber	Emma	Layla	Saskia
Amelia	Eva	Leah	Savannah
Amelie	Eve	Lilly/Lily	Scarlett
Amy	Evie	Lola	Sienna
Anna	Gabriella	Lucy	Skye
Annabelle	Gemma	Mackenzie	Sofia/Sophia
Ashley	Georgia	Madison	Sophie
Audrey	Grace	Madeline	Stella
Ava	Hannah	Matilda	Stephanie
Bella	Harper	Maya	Summer
Caitlin	Hayley	Megan	Tahlia
Charli	Heidi	Mia	Tayla/Taylor
Charlotte	Holly	Mikayla	Victoria
Chelsea	Imogen	Mila/Milla	Violet
Chloe	Isabella	Molly	Willow
Claire	Isabelle	Natalie	Zara
Claudia	Isla	Olivia	Zoë

NAMES FOR AUSTRALIANS

The following are truly 'dinky di' Australian names – from Aboriginal words, Australian icons, historical figures, celebrities, places, rivers, valleys, mountains, lakes, islands, birds, plants and more. For more attractive and unusual Australian names, see the Aboriginal section of *Names by ethnic origin* (pages 587–588).

BOYS

ALBURY	Burnu	Giles	Leeuwin	Richmond
Angas	Burnum	Gordon	Lindeman	Rowley
Anzac	Byron	Gough	Lindfield	Ross
Araluen	Cairns	Gwydir	Lindsay	Seymour
Argyle	Carnarvon	Hamilton	Logan	Shackleton
Arnhem	Cazaly	Hawke	Lorne	Shane
Arthur	Chifley	Hawkesbury	Lowan	Simpson
Arunta	Christmas	Heron	Macarthur	Stirling
Ashmore	Clancy	Hobart	MacDonnell	Stradbroke
Atherton	Clyde	Hogan	Mackay	Strahan
Austral	Cooper	Holt	Macquarie	Stuart
Avon	Courtenay	Howard	Mallee	Sturt
Banjo	Cowan	Howe	Mawson	Sydney
Banjora	Daly	Hume	Menzies	Tambo
Barrington	Darwin	Hunter	Miles	Taree
Barton	Dawson	Huon	Mitchell	Tasman
Barwon	Deakin	Jabiru	Monash	Tempe
Bass	Denmark	Jackson	Monti	Torrens
Bathurst	Derwent	Jacob	Morant	Torres
Benaud	Drysdale	Jardine	Moreton	Tuart
Berrigan	Durack	Jarrah	Mulga	Tully
Blaxland	Errol	Jervis	Murray	Tweed
Bourke	Farnham	Jirra	Myall	Warrigal
Bowen	Fitzroy	Kami	Nardoo	Wentworth
Bowral	Flinders	Kerry	Norfolk	Wirrin
Boyd	Flynn	Kieren	Orpheus	Wills
Brisbane	Forbes	Kulan	Oxley	Windsor
Brolga	Franklin	Lachlan	Paterson	Winton
Buckley	Fraser	Latrobe	Perth	Yarran
Burke	Gibson	Lawson	Phillip	York

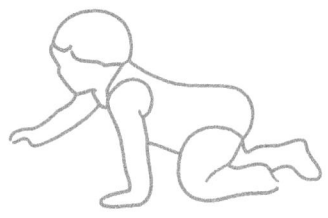

GIRLS

Acacia	Carina	Indigo	Lyndal	Raelene
Adelaide	Carpentaria	Isa	Mareeba	Rata
Agnes	Casey	Jedda	Margaret	Robina
Ainslie	Cassia	Julia	Maria	Roma
Airlie	Cate	Junee	Marion	Rosella
Akala	Charlotte	Kadina	Matilda	Rozelle
Alexandrina	Clare	Kaleen	Melaleuca	Sarah
Alice	Coral	Kallista	Melba	Sarina
Allora	Corella	Karri	Merinda	Shiralee
Anka	Darwinia	Karuah	Mimosa	Sofala
Arafura	Dawn	Katherine	Miranda	Swan
Arinya	Diamantina	Keira	Mona	Sydney
Arora	Dianella	Kelly	Moree	Sylvania
Arundel	Dryandra	Kembla	Myndee	Tamar
Augusta	Eden	Kiama	Naretha	Tasma
Australia	Elanora	Kilda	Narelle	Tatya
Avalon	Eliza	Killara	Narooma	Telopea
Avoca	Elizabeth	Kimberley	Nellie	Temora
Babinda	Elouera	Kirra	Nerida	Thea
Banksia	Elle	Koolyn	Nicole	Toni
Barossa	Emerald	Korra	Niley	Torah
Bega	Evonne	Kyeema	Olga	Victoria
Berri	Florey	Kylie	Olinda	Vivonne
Berry	Ghera	Laura	Olivia	Wanda
Bindi	Greta	Leena	Oola	Waratah
Boronia	Grevillea	Lemana	Opal	Wilga
Brindabella	Gumnut	Leura	Parmelia	Yamba
Bronte	Gymea	Lorrae	Pentecost	Yara
Capricornia	Helena	Lucia	Peta	Yarra
Cardinia	Hibiscus	Lucinda	Quentin	Yindi

First Fleet Names

Australia's first European settlers – the 1400 or so men, women and children of the 1788 First Fleet – bore, by today's standards, a limited range of first names. The original 775 convicts (those that survived the journey) included just 190 women, and there were few females among the other voyagers, most of whom were marines, the ships' crews, and civil and military officers. The 'First Fleeters' were overwhelmingly English, but the ships also brought people of Irish, Welsh, Scottish, French, West Indian and other origins.

These are the names of most of the First Fleeters.

MALES

The 10 most common names:
1 John (over 220)   6 Edward
2 William (over 160) 7 George
3 Thomas (almost 100) 8 Richard
4 James (almost 100) 9 Robert
5 Joseph (around 50) 10 Samuel

Aaron	Cornelius	Henry
Abraham	Curtis	Hilton
Alexander	Daniel	Hobson
Allen	David	Hugh
Ambrose	Dennis	Humphrey
Andrew	Donald	Isaac
Anthony	Duncan	Ishmael
Archibald	Edmund	Jacob
Arthur	Edward	James
Augustus	Elias	Jeremiah
Barnaby	Ferdinand	Jesse
Barney	Francis	Job
Bartholomew	Frederick	John
Benjamin	Furzey	Jonathon
Bernard	Gabriel	Joseph
Charles	Gavin	Joshua
Christopher	George	Laurence
Cooper	Hardwicke	Lawrence

Leonard	Oten	Rupert
Luke	Ottiwell	Samuel
Mark	Owen	Simon
Martin	Patrick	Stephen
Mathew	Paul	Terrance
Matthew	Peter	Thom
Micah	Philip	Thomas
Michael	Phillip	Timothy
Morris	Ralph	Tobias
Mortimore	Redmund	Walter
Moses	Richard	Walton
Nathaniel	Robert	Watkin
Newton	Robinson	William
Nicholas	Rodney	Yorgan
Noah	Roger	Zachariah

FEMALES

The 10 most common names:

1 Mary (over 65) 6 Susannah
2 Elizabeth (over 40) 7 Catherine
3 Ann (over 30) 8 Margaret
4 Jane (over 15) 9 Martha
5 Sarah (over 10) 10 Rebecca

Agnes	Flora	Mary
Alice	Frances	Nancy
Amelia	Hannah	Olive
Ann	Henrietta	Olivia
Betty	Isabella	Phebe
Caroline	Jane	Phoebe
Catherine	Jenny	Rachel
Charlotte	Johanna	Rebecca
Deborah	Judah	Rosanna
Dorothy	Judith	Rose
Eleanor	Laura	Ruth
Elizabeth	Lydia	Sarah
Ellen	Lucy	Sophia
Ester	Margaret	Susanna
Esther	Maria	Susannah
Fanny	Martha	Tamasin

CELEBRITY KIDS' NAMES — BOYS

Celebrity kids sometimes have very strange names. It all started back in the 1960s and 1970s – consider David Bowie's son Zowie, Mia Farrow's boy Satchel and, probably the craziest of all, Frank Zappa's Dweezil and Ahmet Emuukha Rodan (as well as his girls Moon Unit and Diva Thin Muffin Pigeen).

More recent unusual boy's names include Pilot Inspektor and even Audio Science (actors Jason Lee and Shannyn Sossamon respectively), while Angelina Jolie and Brad Pitt have also come up with some unusual, although far more appealing, names – such as Maddox Chivan and Pax Thien.

Abraham	Ziggy Marley	Chester	Tom Hanks
Aidan Patrick	Lachlan Murdoch	Christian	Princess Mary
Aleph	Natalie Portman	Cornelis	Jana Rawlinson
Alexander	Naomi Watts	Cristiano	Cristiano Ronaldo
Amadeus	Boris Becker	Cruz	David Beckham
Angus	Melanie Howard	Dashiell	Cate Blanchett
Archie	Adam Gilchrist	David	Madonna
Arpad Flynn Alexander	Elle MacPherson	Deacon	Reese Witherspoon
		Dexter	Elvis Costello
Atlas	Anne Heche	Dylan	Catherine Zeta-Jones
Augustin	Linda Evangelista		
Aurelius Cy Andrea	Elle MacPherson	Eddy	Celine Dion
		Egypt Daoud	Alicia Keys
Axel	Will Ferrell	Elijah Blue	Cher
Banjo	Rachel Griffiths	Ethan	Dannii Minogue
Barron William	Donald Trump	Enzo	Patricia Arquette
Beau	Emma Bunton	Ever Imre	Alanis Morrisette
Beckett	Stella McCartney	Finn	Christy Turlington
Benjamin	Gisele Bündchen	Flynn	Miranda Kerr
Bob	Charlie Sheen	Frank	Elvis Costello
Brendan Joseph	Mark Wahlberg	Gideon	Ziggy Marley
Bronx Mowgli	Ashlee Simpson	Hamish	Antonia Kidman
Brooklyn Joseph	David Beckham	Harrison	Adam Gilchrist
Bruno	Nigella Lawson	Hayes Logan	Kevin Costner
Bryce Maximus	LeBron James	Henry	Rachel Weisz
Buddy Bear Maurice	Jamie Oliver	Homer James Jigme	Richard Gere
Caspar Matthew	Claudia Schiffer	Hopper	Sean Penn
Cayden Wyatt	Kevin Costner	Ignatius	Cate Blanchett
Chance	Nathan Bracken	Indhi	Brett Kirk
Charles	Russell Crowe	Indiana August	Casey Affleck

Jack	Johnny Depp	Otis	Tobey Maguire
Jackson	James Packer	Pax Thien	Angelina Jolie
Jaden	Andre Agassi	Phinnaeus Walter	Julia Roberts
Jagger Jonathan	Lindsay Davenport	Presley	Cindy Crawford
James	Antonia Kidman	Preston	Brett Lee
Jarvis	Damien Leith	Prince Michael	Michael Jackson
Jayden James	Britney Spears	Raphael	Richard Roxburgh
Jett	John Travolta	Robert Ford	Owen Wilson
Joshua	Pat Rafter	Rocco	Madonna
Kaiis Steven	Geena Davis	Roman Robert	Cate Blanchett
Kalan Alexander	Lachlan Murdoch	Romeo	Jon Bon Jovi
Kian William	Geena Davis	Rowan Francis	Brooke Shields
Kingston James McGregor	Gwen Stefani	Ryder Russell	Kate Hudson
		Samuel	Naomi Watts
Klaus	Eric Bana	Seargeoh	Sylvester Stallone
Knox Léon	Angelina Jolie	Sean Preston	Britney Spears
Kyah	Tim Cahill	Seven Sirius	Erykah Badu
Laken James	Morgan Spurlock	Shae	Tim Cahill
Lennon	Liam Gallagher	Sindri Eldon	Björk
Leo	Penelope Cruz	Slater Joseph	Angela Bassett
Levi	Matthew McConaughey	Sparrow James Midnight	Nicole Richie
Levon Green	Uma Thurman	Story Elias	Jenna Elfman
Liam	Calista Flockhart	Taylor	Harry Kewell
Louis Bardo	Sandra Bullock	Tennyson	Russell Crowe
Maddox Chivan	Angelina Jolie	Track	Sarah Palin
Mason Dash	Kourtney Kardashian	Trig	Sarah Palin
Matteo	Ricky Martin	Truman	Tom Hanks
Max	Christina Aguilera	Tyler	Paul Roos
Memphys	Brett Kirk	Valentine	Ricky Martin
Miguel	Mike Tyson	Vincent	Princess Mary
Miller	Stella McCartney	Walker	Cindy Crawford
Milo William	Liv Tyler	Weston	Nicholas Cage
Moroccan	Mariah Carey	Winston	Billie Piper
Morocco Elijah	Mike Tyson	Wolfe	Merrick Watts
Moses	Gwyneth Paltrow	Wyatt Steven	Cheryl Crow
Nathan	Jon Stewart	Xavier	Joe Hockey
Nayib	Gloria Estefan	Yeshna	Sinead O'Connor
Nelson	Celine Dion	Zachary Jackson Levon	Elton John
Ocean Alexander	Forest Whitaker		
Oscar	Hugh Jackman	Zuma Nesta Rock	Gwen Stefani

Celebrity Kids' Names – Girls

Unusual names from the past include Bob Geldof's Peaches Honeyblossom, Fifi Trixibelle and Little Pixie, Michael Hutchence's Heavenly Hiraani Tiger Lily, and Demi Moore's Scout LaRue, Tallulah Belle and Rumer Glen. Jamie Oliver is a modern-day 'serial weird-namer', with Daisy Boo Pamela, Petal Blossom Rainbow, Poppy Honey Rosie (and his son – Buddy Bear Maurice!).

Other odd modern names include Apple, Exodus and Mars Merkaba, but perhaps the craziest of all is actor Rob Morrow's name for his daughter – Tu (say it with the surname). What was he thinking?

Adelaide	Joe Hockey	**Cosima**	Nigella Lawson
Aerin Elisabeth	Lachlan Murdoch	**Danielle Riley**	Lisa Marie Presley
Agnes Lark	Jennifer Connelly	**Dannie-Lynn Hope**	Anna Nicole Smith
Ali-Rose	Justin Langer		
Alisia	John Aloisi	**Destry**	Stephen Spielberg
Alizeh Keshvar	Geena Davis	**Deva**	Monica Belluci
Allegra Penelope	Jessica Rowe	**D'Lila Star**	Sean Combs
Amandine	John Malkovich	**Ella Bleu**	John Travolta
Amaya	John Aloisi	**Emerson Rose**	Teri Hatcher
Anais	Noel Gallagher	**Emme**	Jennifer Lopez
Annie	Adam Gilchrist	**Emmy Charlotte**	Ricky Ponting
Apple Blythe	Gwyneth Paltrow	**Eden**	Marcia Cross
Aquinnah	Michael J Fox	**Estella**	Collette Dinnigan
Audrey Mae	Greg Kinnear	**Exodus**	Mike Tyson
Ava	Hugh Jackman	**Faith Margaret**	Nicole Kidman
Avalon	Patrick Keating	**Finley Aaron**	Lisa Marie Presley
Bailey	Stella McCartney	**Gaia**	Emma Thompson
Bluebell Madonna	Geri Halliwell	**Gianna Maria**	Kobe Bryant
Bristol	Sarah Palin	**Giselle Charlotte**	Jessica Rowe
Bronwyn Golden	Angela Bassett	**Grace**	Kevin Costner
Brooke	Shane Warne	**Grier Hammond**	Brooke Shields
Calico	Alice Cooper	**Haile Jade**	Eminem
Carys	Catherine Zeta-Jones	**Harlow**	Patricia Arquette
Chance	Sean Combs	**Harper Vivienne**	Lisa Marie Presley
Charlene Riva	Roger Federer	**Hazel Patricia**	Julia Roberts
Charlotte	Todd McKenny	**Holly**	Glenn McGrath
Chastity	Cher	**Honor Marie**	Jessica Alba
Chloe	Danny Green	**India**	Pat Rafter
Clementine	Rachel Griffiths	**Indigo**	James Packer
Coco Riley	Courtney Cox-Arquette	**Ireland**	Kim Basinger
		Iris	Jude Law

Isabella	Princess Mary	Olive	Isla Fisher
Isadora Barney	Björk	Olivia	Lance Armstrong
Jada	Kim Clijsters	Paris Michael Katherine	Michael Jackson
Jaz Elle	Andre Agassi		
Jazz	George Gregan	Piper	Gillian Anderson
Jessica	Justin Langer	Puma	Erykah Badu
Jessie James	Sean Combs	Ramona	Maggie Gyllenhaal
Johnnie Rose	Melissa Etheridge	Reiley Dilys Stella	Stella McCartney
Josephine	Princess Mary		
Judah	Ziggy Marley	Ripley	Thandie Newton
Katia	John Aloisi	Roisin	Sinead O'Connor
Kimber	Clint Eastwood	Ruby	Cathy Freeman
Leni	Heidi Klum	Sadie	Christina Applegate
Léonie	Monica Belluci	Sage Florence	Toni Collette
Lilly-Sue	Brian McFadden	Sailor Lee	Christie Brinkley
Lily-Rose Melody	Johnny Depp	Sam	Charlie Sheen
Locklyn Kyla	Vince Vaughn	Sasha	Barack Obama
Lola	Charlie Sheen	Savannah	Marcia Cross
Lou	Heidi Klum	Scarlet	Sylvester Stallone
Louisanna Ray	Leelee Sobieski	Schuyler	Michael J Fox
Lourdes	Madonna	Seraphina Rose	Ben Affleck
Louise	Prince Edward	Shiloh Nouvel	Angelina Jolie
Lucia	Mel Gibson	Sophia	Erica Bana
Mabel	Tracey Ullman	Sophie	Justin Langer
Maggie Rose	Jon Stewart	Stella	Matt Damon
Makani Ravello	Woody Harrelson	Summer	Shane Warne
Malia	Barack Obama	Sunday Rose	Nicole Kidman
Marion Loretta	Sarah Jessica Parker	Sunny Madeline	Adam Sandler
Mars Merkaba	Erykah Badu	Suri	Tom Cruise
Matilda Rose	Heath Ledger	Sybella	Antonia Kidman
Matisse	Wendell Sailor	Tabitha Hodge	Sarah Jessica Parker
Mattea	Mira Sorvino	Taylor	Jamie Durie
Mearah Sanaa	Shaquille O'Neal	Valentina Paloma	Salma Hayek
Mia	Lleyton Hewitt	Vida	Matthew McConaughey
Milan	Mike Tyson		
Mirage	Eric Burdon	Violet	Ben Affleck
Molly	Brian McFadden	Vivienne Marcheline	Angelina Jolie
Monroe	Mariah Carey		
Myla Rose	Roger Federer	Willow	Will Smith
Nahla Ariela	Halle Berry	Zahara Marley	Angelina Jolie
Natashya Lorien	Tori Amos	Zahra Savannah	Chris Rock
Nico	Thandiwe Newton	Zola Ivy	Eddie Murphy

Unisex Names

Unisex naming is increasingly common in the 21st century. The following list reveals many possibilities for names to suit both boys and girls.

Addison	Darby	Kyle	Ripley
Aidan	Darcy	Leith	Ronan
Ainslie	Delaney	Leroy	Rory
Archer	Derryn	Linton	Roshan
Ariel	Dexter	Lorne	Rowan
Arran	Dion	Luca	Royal
Ashleigh	Doone	Lyle	Ryan
Aspen	Drew	McKenna	Ryder
Aubrey	Dylan	Mackenzie	Sasha
August	Eden	Mallee	Seven
Avery	Emerson	Mallory	Shannon
Bailey	Erin	Marlon	Shay
Blaine	Ezra	Memphis	Shelby
Blair	Farran	Merlin	Sheldon
Blake	Felix	Montana	Sheridan
Blaze	Garnet	Morgan	Sidney
Bodie	Greer	Murphy	Skylar
Brady	Gryffyn	Myall	Slaney
Brodie	Harley	Myron	Sonam
Brooklyn	Harper	Nevada	Sorrell
Bryce	Harris	Nima	Storm
Cairo	Hartley	Ninja	Sweeney
Caley	Hayden	Noa	Tashi
Carey	Indiana	Paige	Tate
Carson	Jamieson	Parker	Tierney
Casey	Jarrah	Perry	Tobie
Cassidy	Jay	Phoenix	Trilby
Charleston	Jazz	Pierre	Tully
Charlie	Jesse	Piper	Tulsa
Chase	Jett	Quentin	Tyler
Claude	Johnnie	Quincy	Tynan
Cody	Jordan	Rebel	Tyson
Corey	Judah	Regan	Utah
Corin	Jude	Reilly	Whitney
Curtis	Keeley	Rémy	Wylie
Dacey	Kelsey	Renny	Yael
Dakota	Kendall	Rex	Zen
Daley	Kirby	Rhys	Zenith
Dallas	Krishna	Riley	Zola

ALTERNATIVE SPELLINGS

Here are alternative spellings of popular names – some inventive and others just plain bizarre. In addition to these, which I have seen and are therefore all 'real', there are rumours of names such as Linkin, Decklyn, Jaymz, Harisyn, Jeni-Fa, Bhronty, Payshance, Antwonet and even Kdn (Kaden) and XTina (Christina)!

BOYS

Aleczander	Jaemes	Kaspa	Mytchel
Ashtyn	Jaspah	Kayleb	Ondray
Auskar	Jaxxyn	Kupah	Oska
Bodhi	Jaykeb	Leihem	Phlyn
Danyall	Jezzee	Lockelin	Rhauri
Dhillan	Jhette	Maks	Rhly
Exavier	Jhyimy	Maysen	Ryhen
Feenix	Joesph	Mykle	Tohbee

GIRLS

Abbegael	Cheltzee	Jazzmyne	Roenah
Alivyah	Ebbani	Jeorgiah	Saphyre
Aleesha	Emmalee	Klohe	Sayla
Alys	Fhebee	Lusi	Soffea
Ambeur	Gessicah	Makaelah	Summah
Ashlygh	Huntah	Mekenzee	Tayla
Awdree	Imijin	Phyper	Tcharli
Cerenitee	Jaklynn	Rhubee	Tilah

Astrological Names

Fire signs

The three fire signs – Aries, Leo and Sagittarius – are considered 'masculine' and are characterised by energy, warmth and enthusiasm, passion, intuition and impulsiveness. The following names relate to the signs' symbols, qualities, ruling planets, relevant gods and goddesses, and other associations.

Aries

21 March–19 April*

Symbol: ram
Planet: Mars (the red planet), named after the Roman god of war
Day: Tuesday
Associations: Ares (Greek equivalent of Mars)

Boys:
Aidan, Ares, Arien, Atish, Bharat, Bobo, Brander, Chait, Clancy, Deimos, Ebo, Eden, Flannery, Fudo, Furnell, Hamal, Jumane, Keegan, Kenneth, Kuja, Loki, Mangal, Marcus, Mardi, Mark, Mars, Martin, Mawrth, Mingma, Nisan, Quirinus, Ramsden, Rhys, Rory, Tagu, Tuesday, Tyr, Tyson, Viking, Zamael.

Girls:
Akako, Alala, Ardelle, Ariesca, Avice, Bellona, Blaze, Brenda, Drupadi, Ember, Enyo, Garnet, Hilda, Hjördis, Humayra, Kalama, Kimba, Kobla, Kura, Lamesha, Louise, Mahira, Malawi, Mangala, Marcella, Marcia, Mardi, Marta, Martelle, Martina, Mesha, Neith, Omaira, Rory, Scarlett, Sharatan, Talata, Tuesday, Triti, Xaviera.

Leo

23 July–22 August*

Symbol: lion
Planet: the Sun
Day: Sunday
Associations: the Greek gods Apollo and Phoebus

Boys:
Ahad, Apollo, Ari, Ariel, Artan, Aru, Asad, Aslan, Atar, Avi, Babar, Boseda, Cymbeline, Danladi, Dinko, Gurion, Haidar, Helios, Itvar, Kamal, Leander, Leo, Leon, Levent, Lionel, Llewellyn, Nedelko, Nima, Raviwar, Ruslan, Sabiti, Sef, Sher, Simha, Singh, Sisi, Sul, Surya, Usama, Zondag.

Girls:
Adya, Akosua, Alinga, Apolline, Ariella, Arilda, Awusi, Cyriaca, Eileen, Eithne, Eleanor, Esi, Fire, Helen, Helia, Hestia, Kalinda, Leandra, Leona, Leonarda, Leoene, Leontine, Levana, Lionelle, Neda, Nima, Phoebe, Quashi, Quiric, Ravia, Savitri, Sekhmet, Solana, Sorina, Sula, Sunniva, Sunny, Vesta, Xanthe, Zahava.

SAGITTARIUS

22 NOVEMBER–21 DECEMBER*

Symbol: archer (a centaur)
Planet: Jupiter (or Jove), after the Roman god of the heavens
Day: Thursday
Associations: Zeus (Greek equivalent of Jupiter), lightning

Boys:
Agni, Alhamisi, Archdale, Archer, Athos, Barak, Belen, Blaze, Bogart, Bow, Centauri, Chiko, Dhanu, Edan, Fletcher, Gurwar, Hamis, Ibsen, Ives, Jove, Jueves, Jumala, Jupiter, Kaho, Khamisi, Kislev, Mackay, Monsa, Motega, Phurba, Sachiel, Saeth, Sagittarius, Sarngin, Terrell, Tetsuya, Thor, Thursday, Vander, Zeus.

Girls:
Aba, Abina, Adrastea, Alhamisi, Amalthea, Ananke, Ayao, Baba, Brihspati, Carmé, Dhanu, Edana, Elara, Elektra, Evette, Flame, Himalia, Indred, Io, Jeudi, Jueva, Jupitra, Lakya, Lavonne, Lysithea, Pasiphae, Poloma, Sagitta, Sarnga, Sinope, Thursday, Torsta, Toshi, Vonda, Vonetta, Ya, Yumi, Yumiko, Yvette, Yvonne.

* Dates are approximate as there is a slight annual variation.

Aries　　　　Leo　　　　Sagittarius

Earth Signs

The three earth signs – Taurus, Virgo and Capricorn – are considered 'feminine' and are characterised by practicality, patience, persistence, stability and sensation. The following names relate to the signs' symbols, qualities, ruling planets, relevant gods and goddesses, and other associations.

Taurus

20 April–20 May*

Symbol: bull
Planet: Venus, named after the Roman goddess of love and beauty
Day: Friday
Associations: Aphrodite (Greek equivalent of Venus), fertility

Boys:
Adonis, Alan, Amor, Anteros, Azriel, Beau, Beltane, Byron, Carey, Cavan, Cupid, Darwin, David, Eros, Friday, Hussain, Jabuk, Jamal, Jimoh, Jumah, Kadi, Kalon, Kami, Kason, Keane, Keeley, Kevin, Kofi, Mackenzie, Milan, Milos, Nandi, Pasang, Patek, Prem, Shakil, Taurean, Terran, Vesak, Vrisha.

Girls:
Anata, Aphrodite, Astarte, Beltane, Demetria, Efia, Erda, Europa, Flora, Freya, Friday, Fulla, Gaia, Guri, Gwener, Hathor, Hero, Ijumaa, Inanna, Indara, Ishtar, Isis, Jamal, Jord, Jumah, Lada, Lakshmi, Maia, Malara, Milda, Nahid, Pasang, Pateka, Pomona, Rati, Tanith, Taurea, Terra, Venus, Vesaka.

Virgo

23 August–22 September*

Symbol: virgin
Planet: Mercury, after the Roman messenger of the gods
Day: Wednesday
Associations: Hermes (Greek equivalent of Mercury), angels, youth, purity

Boys:
Adam, Angelo, Bersh, Braden, Budhvar, Cahil, Dale, Dean, Denver, Elul, Enki, Gabriel, Garuda, Hamaliel, Hermod, Izzat, Javan, Kanku, Keiki, Ketah, Kumar, Kwako, Lhakpa, Mercredi, Mercury, Michael, Mladen,

Raphael, Revie, Sheldon, Slade, Streda, Tama, Tamaiti, Tarun, Thoth, Virgo, Wednesday, Yerin, Yukio.

Girls:
Adara, Agnes, Aku, Aludra, Aluma, Angela, Arbiya, Asma, Astrea, Azalea, Azra, Bethulah, Caloris, Chavi, Colleen, Dhara, Eartha, Elula, Fauna, Idona, Imogen, Kanya, Karida, Kumari, Lhakpa, Lowanna, Mercredi, Mercuria, Miko, Narada, Onata, Parthenia, Rhea, Rochelle, Streda, Talitha, Tellus, Wednesday, Virginia, Virgo.

CAPRICORN

22 DECEMBER–19 JANUARY*

Symbol: goat
Planet: Saturn, after the Roman god of agriculture and vegetation
Day: Saturday
Associations: Kronos (Greek equivalent of Saturn), mountains (mountain goat)

Boys:
Ashton, Bakri, Barden, Bartholomew, Barton, Blair, Bokah, Bolton, Capricorn, Cavill, Dalton, Demetrius, Denton, Fielding, George, Giles, Hendra, Hilton, Hutton, Kelby, Kidd, Kingston, Kronos, Leighton, Makar, Mimas, Pemba, Riley, Ruston, Sacheverell, Sadwyn, Sani, Satordi, Saturn, Satyr, Saxton, Shavato, Titan, Warwick, Zadornin.

Girls:
Adama, Aja, Ama, Amalthea, Arwa, Auriga, Bakri, Capella, Capra, Cassiel, Ceres, Danu, Georgia, Georgina, Hayley, Inari, Keira, Kimberley, Kona, Kronia, Kwame, Makara, Montana, Nashira, Payton, Pausa, Peta, Sadwyn, Samedi, Sania, Sanivara, Saturday, Saturnia, Sierra, Sita, Sobota, Teresa, Tethys, Teveta, Yael.

* Dates are approximate as there is a slight annual variation.

Taurus   Virgo   Capricorn

AIR SIGNS

The air signs – Gemini, Libra and Aquarius – are considered 'masculine' and are characterised by communication and eloquence, ideas, thought, knowledge and reason. The following names relate to the signs' symbols, qualities, ruling planets, relevant gods and goddesses, and other associations.

GEMINI

21 MAY–20 JUNE*

Symbol: TWINS
Planet: Mercury, the Roman messenger of the gods
Day: Wednesday
Associations: Hermes (Greek equivalent of Mercury), angels

Boys:
Alber, Amphion, Angelo, Azriel, Budhvar, Castor, Enki, Faris, Gabriel, Garuda, Gefell, Gemini, Hariel, Hermes, Hermod, Jeth, Juriel, Kato, Lhakpa, Maslin, Mercredi, Mercury, Michael, Odion, Para, Raphael, Raziel, Revie, Sandalfon, Sivan, Streda, Taiwo, Tavish, Thomas, Twain, Ulan, Uriel, Yamal, Zachriel, Zethus.

Girls:
Aku, Alhena, Ambriel, Anael, Angela, Angelica, Anihera, Arael, Arbiya, Arcangela, Caloris, Dabria, Dina, Gabrielle, Gemina, Hasana, Hermia, Hermione, Kakra, Lhakpa, Malak, Melek, Mercuria, Miri, Mithuna, Narada, Nariel, Nashota, Nitika, Nuria, Oriel, Sarea, Sivanah, Streda, Taiwo, Tameka, Tamsin, Thomasina, Wednesday, Xingxing.

LIBRA

23 SEPTEMBER–22 OCTOBER*

Symbol: scales
Planet: Venus, after the Roman goddess of love and beauty
Day: Friday
Associations: Aphrodite (Greek equivalent of Venus), justice, balance

Boys:
Adil, Adonis, Ajmal, Alan, Anteros, Baris, Clorian, Concord, Cosmo, Cupid, Damir, Duffy, Friday, Gwener, Halcyon, Hugh, Jimoh, Jonah, Jumah, Jun, Justin, Kadi, Kami, Kazumi, Libra, Ludomir, Manoj, Miles,

Miran, Nasim, Pasang, Patek, Pax, Tishri, Ved, Venerdi, Vidya, Yestin, Zadok, Zaniel.

Girls:
Afi, Airlia, Anemone, Anila, Aphrodite, Astarte, Aura, Breeze, Efia, Freya, Friday, Gwener, Hathor, Hero, Ijumaa, Inanna, Ishtar, Jumah, Kofi, Kopu, Kuan-Yin, Lada, Lakshmi, Libra, Malara, Milda, Nahid, Pallas, Pasang, Pateka, Rati, Shukra, Sylph, Tanith, Tishra, Tula, Veda, Venisa, Venus, Zazel.

AQUARIUS

20 JANUARY–18 FEBRUARY*

Symbol: water bearer
Planet: Uranus, after a Greek god of the heavens
Day: Saturday
Associations: Saturn (sub-ruler), Zeus, Kronos, the sky

Boys:
Akash, Ambar, Aquarius, Athos, Atlas, Celestine, Darel, Darshan, Gwydion, Hara, Indra, Kalani, Konol, Kronos, Kumbha, Langi, Lani, Mahendra, Namgyal, Nirvan, Ouranus, Pemba, Rudra, Sadwyn, Sani, Satordi, Saturn, Shavato, Shevat, Sobota, Sultan, Taran, Titan, Umbriel, Uranius, Varuna, Warrun, Yakez, Zadornin, Zeus.

Girls:
Akasha, Alkira, Ambar, Aolani, Aquaria, Azura, Cassiel, Celeste, Ciel, Dione, Hara, Ira, Juno, Kalani, Kaloni, Kilia, Kimiko, Kona, Kronia, Kwame, Lali, Lani, Magha, Maweke, Mingara, Moneta, Nepelle, Olympia, Ourania, Sadwynne, Sania, Sanivara, Saturday, Saturnia, Shevat, Sky, Sobota, Tethys, Urania, Varuna.

* Dates are approximate as there is a slight annual variation.

Gemini　　　　Libra　　　　Aquarius

WATER SIGNS

The water signs – Cancer, Scorpio and Pisces – are considered 'feminine' and are characterised by imagination, spirituality, sensitivity, mystery and the emotions. The following names relate to the signs' symbols, qualities, ruling planets, relevant gods and goddesses and other associations.

CANCER

21 JUNE–22 JULY*

Symbol: crab
Planet: the Moon
Day: Monday
Associations: moon gods and goddesses

Boys:
Alako, Artemas, Badar, Bailly, Chandra, Chubie, Dawa, Hurley, Jacey, Jericho, Jojo, Kaa, Kappa, Karem, Karkat, Kedjo, Keeden, Kekra, Kenn, Kojo, Lundy, Macalla, Manuel, Marama, Miki, Mitiaro, Monday, Noko, Ocean, Pondeli, Qamar, Seger, Shashi, Somavar, Tadzi, Tai, Tammuz, Timin, Varick, Zaniel.

Girls:
Adzo, Ajua, Alkina, Amaris, Arianrhod, Artemis, Ashada, Ayla, Candi, Chandra, Cynthia, Dalit, Dawa, Delia, Diana, Endora, Iloura, Jacey, Kamaria, Karkata, Keina, Kekra, Kolora, Kwabena, Levana, Lona, Lucina, Lundi, Mahina, Marina, Merlyn, Monday, Quilla, Rhiannon, Selena, Samundra, Sheni, Tallulah, Tanisha, Yara.

SCORPIO

23 OCTOBER–21 NOVEMBER*

Symbol: scorpion
Planet: Pluto, named after the Roman god of the underworld and the dead
Day: Tuesday
Associations: Mars (sub-ruler), rivers

Boys:
Akar, Almo, Antares, Anubis, Bardo, Bobo, Carey, Caspian, Charon, Clyde, Colorado, Daven, Derwent, Ebo, Huon, Jumane, Kano, Kartik, Kelsey, Kuja,

Lachlan, Mangal, Marcus, Mardi, Mark, Marlow, Milu, Mingma, Mortimer, Munro, Murphy, Osiris, Rio, Scorpius, Shannon, Tiki, Tuesday, Tyne, Vrischik, Zamael.

Girls:
Ammut, Ara, Beltana, Beverley, Binda, Boann, Brook, Broula, Calleen, Clytie, Colenso, Eurydice, Hela, Inari, Jordan, Kali, Kartika, Kelda, Kerith, Kobla, Mangala, Marcella, Mardi, Martina, Michal, Morana, Nepa, Nixie, Omaka, Paringa, Persephone, Plutia, Proserpina, Sarasvati, Scorpia, Shaula, Talata, Tuesday, Triti, Vrischika.

PISCES

19 FEBRUARY–20 MARCH*

Symbol: fishes
Planet: Neptune, after the Roman god of the oceans, water and rain
Day: Thursday
Associations: Poseidon (Greek equivalent of Neptune), Jupiter (sub-ruler)

Boys:
Adar, Adrian, Alhamisi, Conway, Derya, Dylan, Hamis, Ikan, Jumala, Jumarat, Jupiter, Kai, Kala, Kanaloa, Khamisi, Kosi, Machanu, Maren, Marlin, Moana, Nalu, Neifion, Neptune, Nereus, Njord, Phurba, Poseidon, Proteus, Qudrat, Rinjin, Sachiel, Samaki, Samani, Styx, Tambo, Tarki, Thursday, Torstai, Triton, Varuna.

Girls:
Abina, Adara, Adriana, Alá, Anka, Armorel, Asera, Baba, Calypso, Ceto, Cordelia, Cybele, Derya, Dolphina, Doris, Gemalla, Jala, Jeudi, Kenda, Lakya, Layaleta, Lorelei, Magura, Mary, Meena, Moana, Naida, Neptunia, Nerina, Oceana, Pacifica, Piscea, Rosemary, Sagara, Sakana, Salacia, Sirena, Tara, Thursday, Torsta.

* Dates are approximate as there is a slight annual variation.

Cancer   Scorpio   Pisces

20TH-CENTURY NAMES

The following lists contain some of the most popular Australian boys' and girls' names throughout the various decades of the 20th century.

BOYS

GIRLS

1990s

Adam	Joshua	Alexandra	Jasmine
Alexander	Lachlan	Amy	Jessica
Benjamin	Liam	Ashleigh	Lauren
Cameron	Luke	Brooke	Madeleine
Daniel	Matthew	Caitlin	Maddison
Dylan	Mitchell	Courtney	Olivia
Edward	Nathan	Emily	Rachel
Jake	Nicholas	Emma	Samantha
James	Ryan	Georgia	Sarah
Jordan	Thomas	Hannah	Sophie

1970s–80s

Adam	Luke	Amanda	Laura
Andrew	Mark	Belinda	Lisa
Benjamin	Matthew	Clare	Melanie
Christopher	Michael	Danielle	Melissa
Craig	Nicholas	Fiona	Michelle
Daniel	Peter	Joanne	Natalie
David	Scott	Jodie	Nicole
James	Shane	Kate	Rebecca
Jason	Simon	Kelly	Sharon
John	Timothy	Kylie	Stephanie

BOYS GIRLS

1950s–60s

Alan	Ian	Catherine	Karen
Anthony	John	Christine	Leanne
Brett	Kevin	Deborah	Linda
Brian	Michael	Denise	Lynette
Colin	Paul	Dianne	Maria
Darren	Peter	Elizabeth	Robyn
David	Richard	Helen	Sharon
Gary	Robert	Jacqueline	Suzanne
Graeme	Stephen	Jennifer	Tracey
Gregory	Wayne	Julie	Wendy

1930s–40s

Alan	John	Barbara	Lorraine
Barry	Keith	Beverley	Margaret
Brian	Kenneth	Carol	Marjorie
Bruce	Leslie	Janice	Mary
Colin	Michael	Jean	Maureen
David	Peter	Joan	Pamela
Donald	Raymond	Joyce	Patricia
Francis	Robert	Judith	Sandra
George	Ronald	June	Shirley
James	William	Kathleen	Valerie

Early 1900s

Albert	Leonard	Alice	Florence
Alfred	Michael	Annie	Gladys
Arthur	Norman	Beryl	Irene
Charles	Peter	Bridget	Ivy
Douglas	Reginald	Doris	Joan
Ernest	Robert	Dorothy	Lilian
Frederick	Stanley	Edith	Lily
George	Thomas	Eileen	Margaret
Harold	Walter	Elizabeth	Rose
Jack	William	Elsie	Winifred

Surnames as First Names

A popular trend is to use surnames as first names, so here is a selection (some suitable for both boys and girls). Interestingly, many of these are 'occupation names', such as Butler, Cooper, Deacon, Fletcher, Hunter, Mason, Painter, Taylor, Thatcher and Tyler.

Brand names like Armani, Chanel and Dyson are on the rise, as are the surnames of celebrities past and present – including Aniston, Arquette, Beckham, Brando, Cruise, Harlow, Jagger and Ledger.

With a few exceptions, the meanings can be found in the Boys A–Z.

Adamson
Anderson
Aniston
Arden
Armani
Arquette
Asher
Ashford
Ashley
Ashton
Atherton
Austin
Bailey
Bardot
Baxter
Beale
Becket
Beckham
Benson
Blake
Boston
Brando
Brock
Bronson
Brooks
Brosnan
Bryden
Bryson
Burton
Butler

Byrne
Callaghan
Cameron
Campbell
Carmichael
Caron
Carter
Cartier
Cash
Chanel
Chaplin
Clayton
Clooney
Cole
Coleman
Connor
Cooper
Copeland
Corley
Corrigan
Cruise
Cruz
Dali
Davenport
Deacon
Denver
Dior
Dorsey
Driscoll
Driver

Duffy
Dundee
Dyson
Easton
Edison
Einstein
Elliott
Ellis
Ennis
Everton
Ferguson
Finlay
Fletcher
Ford
Fox
Fraser
Garner
Garrett
Garrison
Gere
Gilroy
Goldwin
Gregan
Grosvenor
Guthrie
Hammond
Harlow
Harrison
Hartley
Hayes

Heath	McGregor	Rix
Hendrix	Mackinley	Robinson
Heston	McLaren	Roper
Hilton	Maclean	Rowell
Hobson	McMahon	Ruston
Holden	Maddox	Rylan
Holland	Major	Sagan
Hopper	Mansell	Sailor
Hudson	Marley	Sawyer
Hunter	Marlow	Segovia
Hurley	Mason	Sheehan
Ibsen	Miller	Sheraton
Innes	Mirren	Sinclair
Ireland	Molloy	Slater
Jagger	Mondrian	Snape
Jameson	Monet	Spencer
Jardine	Moreau	Sullivan
Jarvis	Mortimer	Tallis
Jefferson	Mountfort	Taylor
Jensen	Nash	Teague
Jovi	Nelson	Tennyson
Judd	Nichols	Terrell
Johnson	Nolan	Thatcher
Kafka	Ogilvie	Travers
Keating	O'Shea	Trudeau
Keaton	Painter	Truman
Kelby	Payton	Trump
Kennedy	Penrose	Tyler
Kiernan	Petrie	Varley
Kingsley	Phelps	Vennard
Kingston	Phillips	Villiers
Kipling	Porter	Walker
Kirkland	Presley	Washington
Knox	Preston	Wesley
Kressley	Quinn	Weston
Ledger	Rafferty	Wilder
Lennon	Ravel	Wills
Leyland	Reeves	Wyatt
Lincoln	Rendell	Wycliff
Lockyer	Richmond	Wynter
Logan	Rider	Yardley
London	Ridley	Yates
Loren	Rivers	Zidane

'NOUN' NAMES

A growing trend is to name children after things, so here is a list of 'noun' names, all of which are real. Although most are first names, some have been given as a second name – such as (Taj) Storm, (Jaya) Jungle, (Matilda) Sunshine and (April) Rain.

BOYS

Afro
Armature
Armour
Badge
Bandit
Banjo
Barley
Beaver
Blade
Blue
Button
Cannon
Cedar
Census
Chilli
Chivas
Curio
Danger
Dare
Denim
Deuce
Diesel
Druid
Equinox

Flame
Forest
Fountain
Garrison
Genesis
Granite
Gunner
Hammer
Hawk
Haze
Heron
Holden
Holiday
Hurricane
Icon
Jet
Journey
Jungle
Juke
Lark
Lawn
Leaf
Leopard
Limerick

Link
Maroon
Matrix
Maverick
Meadows
Midnight
Morocco
Ocean
Orchard
Phrase
Pirate
Polo
Prince
Quest
Radar
Reef
Revel
River
Rock
Rocket
Rover
Sage
Sailor
Saviour

Seal
Sequoia
Shadow
Snare
Soul
Spark
Sparrow
Speck
Spike
Sprig
Squire
Stack
Star
Storm
Story
Teak
Team
Tiger
Track
Treat
Tribe
Trick
Zealot
Zenith

Some modern names are from brands or proper nouns – such as Chivas, Cartier, Holden, India, Memphis and Sistine – as well as 'adjective' and other unusual names such as Dax, Kalm, Sinn and Tiga for boys, and Nevaeh (heaven spelt backwards!), Chic, Golden, Precious, Shine, True and Ultra for girls.

Although listed separately, many of these names are suitable for both boys and girls.

GIRLS

Affinity	Epiphany	Love	Providence
Alchemy	Eternity	Magenta	Puma
Allure	Exodus	Mandolin	Rain
Amour	Fairy	Mantra	Rainbow
Angel	Fawn	Martyr	Rebel
Apple	Fedora	Mascot	Satin
Armistice	Fig	Medley	Scout
Autumn	Finesse	Minx	Season
Beauty	Flair	Mirage	Shade
Blessing	Flax	Mystique	Shiraz
Bliss	Gunnel	Navy	Sierra
Bluebell	Halo	Nebula	Silk
Breeze	Haze	Orange	Sky
Butterfly	Heaven	Painter	Song
Calico	Hope	Patience	Sonnet
Cartier	Illusion	Peach	Summer
Chablis	Indigo	Pepper	Sunshine
Chai	Jetty	Petal	Swan
Chardonnay	Jewel	Pine	Tigerlily
Charisma	Jubilee	Pink	Vine
Clarity	Kite	Pleasance	Vogue
Destiny	Lake	Poet	Willow
Dove	Liberty	Praise	Wraith
Eclipse	Lotus	Prize	Zephyr

Shakespearean Names

These names are from many of William Shakespeare's plays – from tragedies and historical dramas such as *Hamlet*, *Romeo and Juliet* and *Henry V*, to comedies like *A Midsummer Night's Dream*, *Much Ado About Nothing* and *As You Like It*.

BOYS

Aaron	Caesar	Eros	Laurence
Abraham	Caius	Fabian	Lawrence
Abram	Caliban	Fenton	Lear
Achilles	Camillo	Ferdinand	Lennox
Adam	Cassio	Flavius	Leonardo
Adrian	Cassius	Florizel	Leonato
Aeneas	Cato	Francis	Leontes
Agamemnon	Charles	Francisco	Lewis
Agrippa	Chiron	Frederick	Lodovico
Ajax	Christopher	Geffrey	Lorenzo
Alexander	Cicero	George	Lucentio
Alexas	Claudio	Gonzalo	Lucio
Alonso	Claudius	Gregory	Lucius
Andrew	Cleon	Griffith	Lysander
Angelo	Conrade	Hamlet	Macbeth
Angus	Corin	Hector	Malcolm
Antonio	Cornelius	Henry	Malvolio
Antonius	Cromwell	Horatio	Marcellus
Antony	Curan	Hortensio	Marcius
Archibald	Curtis	Hubert	Marcus
Arthur	Cymbeline	Hugh	Mark
Balthasar	Davy	Humphrey	Martius
Banquo	Demetrius	Iago	Matthew
Basset	Dennis	Jack	Menelaus
Bates	Dick	James	Mercutio
Benedick	Dion	Jaques	Michael
Benedict	Donalbain	John	Montague
Benvolio	Duncan	Julius	Nathaniel
Bernardo	Edgar	Junius	Nestor
Bertram	Edmund	Launce	Nicholas
Brutus	Edward	Launcelot	Oberon

Octavius	Philip	Rogero	Taurus
Oliver	Philo	Romeo	Theseus
Orlando	Pierce	Ross	Thomas
Orsino	Pompey	Sampson	Timon
Osric	Priam	Saturninus	Titus
Oswald	Prospero	Saunder	Toby
Othello	Proteus	Sebastian	Troilus
Owen	Quintus	Sextus	Tybalt
Paris	Ralph	Shadow	Ulysses
Pedro	Reynaldo	Silvius	Valentine
Percy	Richard	Simon	Vernon
Pericles	Robert	Stephano	Vincentio
Peter	Robin	Stephen	Walter
Philemon	Roderigo	Tarquin	William

GIRLS

Adriana	Doll	Julia	Octavia
Aemilia	Dorcas	Juliet	Olivia
Alice	Eleanor	Juno	Ophelia
Andromache	Elinor	Katharina	Patience
Anne	Elizabeth	Katherine	Paulina
Ariel	Emilia	Lavinia	Perdita
Audrey	Francisca	Luce	Phebe
Beatrice	Gertrude	Lucetta	Portia
Bianca	Goneril	Luciana	Regan
Blanche	Helen	Lucretia	Rosalind
Calphurnia	Helena	Lychorida	Rosaline
Cassandra	Hermia	Margaret	Silvia
Celia	Hermione	Margery	Tamora
Ceres	Hero	Maria	Thaisa
Charmian	Hippolyta	Mariana	Timandra
Cleopatra	Imogen	Marina	Titania
Constance	Iris	Meg	Ursula
Cordelia	Isabel	Miranda	Valeria
Cressida	Isabella	Mopsa	Viola
Desdemona	Jaquenetta	Nan	Violenta
Diana	Jessica	Nell	Virgilia
Dionyza	Joan	Nerissa	Volumnia

BIBLICAL NAMES

Biblical names such as Benjamin, Daniel, Ethan, Abigail, Hannah and Rebecca are always popular, so here is an extensive list of personal names and placenames from the Bible. Note that many are anglicised versions of the original Hebrew (and other) names.

BOYS

Aaron
Abaddon
Abel
Abner
Abraham
Absalom
Adam
Adlai
Ahab
Alexander
Amos
Andrew
Asa
Asher
Azriel
Balthasar
Barnabas
Bartholomew
Baruch
Benjamin
Boaz
Cain
Caleb
Canaan
Caspar
Cornelius
Cyrus
Daniel
Darius
David
Ebenezer
Eden
Ehud
Eli
Elijah
Elisha
Enoch
Enos
Ephraim
Esau
Ethan
Exodus
Ezekiel
Ezra
Felix
Gabriel
Gaddiel
Galahad
Gamaliel
Gera
Gershom
Gideon
Gilead
Goliath
Herod
Hillel
Hiram
Hosea
Ira
Isaac
Isaiah
Ishmael
Israel
Jacob
Jadon
Jairus
James
Japhet
Jared
Javan
Jedidiah
Jeremiah
Jericho
Jesse
Jesús
Jethro
Joachim
Job
Joel
John
Jonah
Jonas
Jonathan
Jordan
Joseph
Joshua
Josiah
Judah
Judas
Jude
Laban
Lamech
Lazarus
Lemuel
Levi
Luke
Malachi
Mark
Matthew
Melchior
Menachem
Micah
Michael
Mordecai
Moses
Nahum
Naphtali
Nathan
Nathaniel
Nehemiah
Nekoda
Nicodemus
Nicolas
Nimrod
Noah
Obadiah
Omar
Paul
Peter
Philemon
Philip
Phineas
Raphael
Reuben
Samson
Samuel
Saul
Seth

Shadrach	Simon	Timothy	Zachary
Shem	Solomon	Titus	Zadok
Shiloh	Stephen	Tobias	Zebedee
Silas	Thaddeus	Uri	Zebulun
Silvanus	Thomas	Uriah	Zechariah
Simeon	Timon	Uzziel	Zephaniah

GIRLS

Abigail	Edna	Leah	Salome
Abijah	Elizabeth	Lois	Samaria
Abilene	Esther	Lydia	Sapphira
Adah	Eunice	Magdalene	Sarah
Adina	Eve	Mara	Sela
Ariel	Exodus	Martha	Seraphina
Asenath	Ezra	Mary	Sharon
Atarah	Galilee	Mehitabel	Sheba
Athalia	Hadassa	Memphis	Shifra
Bathsheba	Hagar	Merab	Shiloh
Bernice	Hannah	Michal	Shulamit
Bethany	Hebron	Miriam	Susannah
Bethel	Hepzibah	Moriah	Syntyche
Bethesda	Hulda	Myra	Tabitha
Beulah	Jemima	Naomi	Talitha
Candace	Jesse	Nazareth	Tamar
Carmel	Jezebel	Orpah	Tarah
Chloe	Joanna	Persis	Tirzah
Claudia	Jordan	Phoebe	Tryphena
Damaris	Judith	Prisca	Vashti
Deborah	Junia	Priscilla	Yael
Delilah	Keren	Rachel	Zillah
Dinah	Kerith	Rebecca	Zilpah
Drusilla	Keturah	Rhoda	Zion
Eden	Keziah	Ruth	Zippora

ASTRONOMY AND 'STAR' NAMES

These mostly rather unusual names are derived from the names of planets, stars and other aspects of astronomy.

BOYS

Apus
Aquila
Ara
Arcas
Arcturus
Arietis
Ashwin
Astaire
Astron
Caelum
Calca
Cetus
Chiron
Columba
Corvus
Cosmo
Cygnus
Dara
Derrrilin
Dorado
Draco
Fetu
Galileo
Hamal
Hercules
Hespero
Hoku
Hute
Indra
Indus
Jewang
Kahoku
Kalani
Kalbar
Kami
Karma
Kootingal
Lepus
Lynx
Merak
Mirrabook
Namgyal
Nirvan
Noga
Orion
Pavo
Pegasus
Perseus
Phoenix
Pinon
Pinterry
Polaris
Rehua
Rigel
Seren
Shavar
Shihab
Sirius
Star
Sterling
Tuldar
Whetu
Wilari
Zeus
Zodiac
Zoroaster

GIRLS

Altair
Alula
Alzubra
Andromeda
Antlia
Ariel
Arundhati
Ashwina
Asta
Astral
Astrea
Auriga
Auristela
Aurora
Callisto
Carina
Celeste
Danika
Elara
Eos
Esta
Estelle
Esther
Estrella
Galaxy
Garma
Hera
Hesper
Hoshi
Juno
Kaniva
Kulka
Lacerta
Lyra
Malara
Meissa
Miranda
Miriyan
Najam
Nebula
Nepelle
Noelani
Olympia
Quarallia
Raja
Rehua
Sadira
Satarah
Serena
Sidra
Sirios
Sitara
Soraya
Starla
Stella
Swati
Tara
Tarika
Ularit
Urania
Ursa
Vega
Vela
Vespera
Xingxing
Yildiz

Girls' names

A

Aamor Breton: a sunbeam.
Aana *See* Anne.
Aandi Nepali: thunder.
Aashlee/Aashleigh/Aashlie
  See Ashleigh.
Aasta/Aastah *See* Asta.
Aba Ghanaian: born on a Thursday.
Abagael/Abaigh *See* Abigail.
Abayomi African: one who brings joy.
Abbe/Abbey/Abbi/Abbie/Abby
  Diminutives of Abigail.
Abbegael/Abbigail/Abegail
  See Abigail.
Abelia Hebrew: breath. The feminine form of Abel.
  Abela, Abella, Abellia.
Abena *See* Abina.
Abeo Nigerian: happy she was born.
Abequa Native American: home-loving.
  Abequah.
Abera/Aberah *See* Avera.
Abey *See* Abigail.
Abia Arabic: great.
Abigail Hebrew: father's joy.
  Abagael, Abaigh, Abbegael, Abbigael, Abbigail, Abbigail, Abegael, Abegail, Abigael, Abigale.
  Diminutives: Abbe, Abbey, Abbi, Abbie, Abby, Abey, Gael, Gail, Gale, Gayle.
Abijah Hebrew: God is my father. A name from the Old Testament.
Abija, Abisha.
Abilene Hebrew: a biblical placename. Also the name of a city in Texas.
  Abiline, Aibileen, Aibilene.
Abina Ghanaian: born on a Thursday.
  Abena, Abenah, Abinah.
Abir Arabic: the fragrant one.
Abira *See* Adira.
Abisha *See* Abijah.
Abra Hebrew: the father of many. The feminine form of Abraham.
  Abrah, Abriana, Abrianah.
Abriella/Abrielle/Abril *See* April.
Acacia Greek: thorny, as in the acacia tree.
Acantha Greek: a legendary nymph.
Accalia Latin: the foster mother of Romulus and Remus, the founders of Rome.
  Acca.
Acey The feminine form of Ace, meaning unity.
  Ace, Acee, Aci, Acie, Acy.
Achilla Greek: the feminine form of Achilles.
  Achillea.
Aconia The name of a 4th-century Roman aristocrat.
Acqua Italian: water.
  Aqua.
Ada Teutonic: prosperous and joyful.
  Adah, Adda, Aida, Ajda (Turkish), *Ayda, Aydah.*
  Diminutives: Addi, Addie, Addy.
Adabelle From Ada and Belle:

joyous and beautiful.
Adabela, Adabell, Adabella.
Diminutive: Ada.

Adah Hebrew: adornment or an ornament. A biblical name. *See also* Ada.

Adair Scottish Gaelic: from the oak tree near the ford. Also a boy's name.

Adalia Hebrew: God is my refuge. *Adali, Adalie.*

Adalita *See* Adèle.

Adalyn A combination of Ada and Lynn.
Adalin, Adalinn, Adalinne, Adalynn, Adalynne.

Adama Hebrew: of the red earth. The feminine form of Adam.
Adamah, Adamina, Adaminah.

Adan *See* Aidan.

Adana A city in Turkey.

Adara From Adar, the twelfth lunar month of the Hebrew calendar, which begins in February/March and is the equivalent of Pisces. Arabic: a virgin. Greek: beauty.
Adar, Adarra, Adarrah, Addara.

Adarna A magical bird in Philippine mythology.

Adda *See* Ada.

Addi/Addie/Addy *See* Ada and Adelaide.

Addison Old English: the son (or daughter) of Adam. Generally a boy's name.
Addisyn, Addyson, Adison,
Adisyn, Adyson.

Addolorata Italian: one who is sorrowful.

Adel/Adela/Adelah *See* Adèle.

Adelaide Old German: noble and kind. *See also* Adèle.
Adelaida, Adelais, Adelheid (German, Swiss), *Adelia, Adélie, Adelice, Adelicia, Adelina, Adelind, Adeline, Adella* (Spanish), *Adline, Alina, Aline, Alyna, Edeline* (German).
Diminutives: Addi, Addie, Addy, Dell, Della, Heidi.

Adèle French: noble; a saint's name. *See also* Adelaide.
Adalita, Adel, Adela, Adelah, Adelia, Adeliah, Adelita, Adell, Adella, Adelle, Adellya, Adelya.
Diminutives: Dell, Della.

Adelfa/Adelfia *See* Adelpha.

Adelheid German and Swiss forms of Adelaide.

Adelia/Adeliah/Adelice *See* Adèle and Adelaide.

Adelicia Old English form of Adelaide and Alice.
Adelice.

Adélie A type of penguin. Also a form of Adelaide.

Adelina/Adelind/Adeline *See* Adelaide.

Adelinda From Adelaide and Linda. *Adelinde.*

Adelita *See* Adèle.

Adella/Adelle *See* Adelaide and

Adèle.
Adellya/Adelya *See* Adèle.
Adelong Aboriginal: a creek that runs through a plain.
Adelpha Greek: sisterly.
Adelfa, Adelfia, Adelphia.
Adena/Adene *See* Adina.
Adenia *See* Adina.
Adeola Nigerian: a crown.
Aderyn Welsh: a bird.
Aderna.
Adia Swahili: a gift from God.
Adiah.
Adiba Arabic: cultured.
Adiel Hebrew: an ornament of God.
Adiella.
Adila Arabic: equal, like.
Adilah.
Adima Teutonic: noble, famous.
Adin *See* Adina.
Adina Hebrew: slender and delicate. A biblical name.
Adena, Adene, Adenia, Adin, Adine, Idina.
Diminutives: Dena, Dina.
Adira Hebrew: strong.
Abira.
Adison/Adisyn *See* Addison.
Adiva Arabic: gentle.
Adivah.
Adline *See* Adelaide.
Adolpha Teutonic: a noble she-wolf. The feminine version of Adolf.
Adolfa, Adolfina, Adolfine, Adolphina, Adolphine.
Adoncia Spanish: sweet.
Adonia Greek: a beautiful goddess. The feminine form of Adonis.
Adora Latin: the adored one.
Adorah, Adorée.
Adorabelle A combination of Adora and Belle.
Adorabella.
Adorée *See* Adora.
Adorna Latin: adorned with jewels.
Adraine/Adrana/Adrea *See* **Adriana.**
Adrastea Greek: a satellite of the planet Jupiter.
Adrasteia.
Adriana Latin: a dark woman from the sea. The feminine form of Adrian and generally an Italian name.
Adraine, Adrana, Adrea, Adria, Adriane (German), *Adrianna, Adrianne, Adriella, Adrielle, Adrienne* (French), *Hadria.*
Adrienne French form of Adriana.
Advent Latin: the arrival. Suitable for a child born during Advent, starting on the last Sunday in November and leading up to Christmas.
Adventa, Adventia, Adventina, Aventia, Aventina.
Adya A name used in south-east India for girls who are born on a Sunday.
Adyson *See* Addison.
Adzo Ghanaian: born on a Monday.
Aëdon Greek: a mythological

maiden who was changed into a nightingale by the god Zeus.
Aegea Greek: of the Aegean.
Aemilia *See* Amelia.
Aerin/Aerrin *See* Erin.
Aerlia/Aerliah *See* Airlia.
Aerona Welsh: a berry.
Aeron, Aeronah, Aeronwy.
Affinity Middle English: a natural liking or attraction.
Affinité.
Affrica Celtic: pleasant. Also from the name of a continent.
Afric, Africa, Africah, Afrika, Afrikah.
Afi Ghanaian: born on a Friday.
Afua.
Afifa Arabic: one who is chaste.
Afifah.
Afina Hebrew: a young deer.
Afinah, Aphina.
Afra *See* Aphra.
Afraima Arabic/Hebrew: fruitful.
Afrika/Afrikah *See* Affrica.
Afrodite/Afroditi *See* Aphrodite.
Afua *See* Afi.
Agafia/Agafya Russian forms of Agatha.
Agapé Greek: love.
Agata *See* Agatha.
Agate French: a precious stone.
Agatha Greek: good, kind, honourable. St Agatha was a 3rd-century Sicilian martyr.
Agafia (Russian), *Agafya* (Russian), *Agata* (Italian, Polish),
Agathe (French, German), *Agathy, Agda* (Swedish), *Agueda* (Spanish).
Diminutives: Ag, Aggie, Aggy.
Agda Swedish form of Agatha.
Aglaia Greek: splendour, splendid beauty. The goddess of harmony.
Agnes Greek: pure, chaste. The name of a saint of the Middle Ages.
See also Annice.
Agnella, Agnese (Italian), *Agnessa* (Russian), *Agneta* (Danish), *Agnethe* (German, Scandinavian), *Agneza, Agnies* (French), *Agnieska* (Polish), *Agnieszka* (Polish), *Agnita, Agnola* (Italian), *Agnus, Agynes, Agyness, Aigneis* (Irish), *Akenehi* (Maori), *Akinehi* (Maori), *Anaïs, Anay, Anezka* (Czech), *Annais, Annis, Annys* (Greek), *Ines, Inese, Inessa, Inez, Nesta* (Welsh), *Ynes* (Spanish), *Ynez* (Spanish).
Diminutives: Aggie, Gosia (Polish), Ina, Nessa, Nessi, Nessie, Neysa, Neza.
Agnola Italian form of Agnes.
Agostina Italian form of Augusta.
Agrafena/Agrafina *See* Agrippina.
Agrippina Latin: the feminine form of Agrippa.
Agrafena (Russian), *Agrafina* (Russian), *Agripina.*
Agueda Spanish form of Agatha.
Aguila Spanish: like an eagle.
Agynes/Agyness *See* Agnes.

Aharona *See* Arona.
Ahawi Native American: a deer.
Ahimsa Hindi: the peaceful or virtuous one.
Ahimsah.
Ahlia *See* Aliya.
Ahorangi Maori: the enlightened teacher.
Ahuda Hebrew: sympathetic.
Ahuva Hebrew: beloved.
Ahava, Ahuda.
Ai Japanese: love.
Aibileen/Aibilene *See* Abilene.
Aida *See* Ada.
Aidan Irish Gaelic: the little fiery one. Ideal for a girl with red hair. *See also* Edana.
Adan, Eidan.
Aideen *See* Etain.
Aigneis Irish form of Agnes.
Aija Latvian: a melody.
Aikaterini Greek form of Catherine.
Aiki A Japanese name of uncertain meaning.
Aiko Japanese: the little loved one, the beloved.
Ailani Hawaiian: a high chief. Also a boy's name.
Aileen/Ailene *See* Eileen.
Aili A popular Finnish name. *See also* Eileen.
Ailis Irish Gaelic form of Alice.
Ailise, Ailish, Alish, Eilish.
Ailisha *See* Alicia.
Aillee *See* Eileen.
Ailsa Scottish: after a rocky inlet known as Ailsa Craig.
Ailwyn/Ailwynn/Ailwynne *See* Alwin.
Aimée French: beloved. A form of Amy.
Aindrea *See* Andrea.
Aine Irish Gaelic: brightness, radiance. The queen of the fairies in Celtic mythology.
Aithne, Eithne, Ena, Ethene.
Aingeal Irish Gaelic form of Angela.
Aino A figure from Finnish mythology.
Ainsley Old English/Scottish: a wood or clearing. Also a boy's name.
Ainslea, Ainslee, Ainsleigh, Ainslie, Ainsly, Anslea, Ansley, Aynslea, Aynslee, Aynslie, Aynsley.
Aireen/Airene *See* Irene.
Airlia Greek: ethereal.
Aerlia, Aerliah, Aira, Airlea, Airlee, Airley, Airlie, Airly.
Aisha Arabic: life. The name of Mohammed's third and favourite wife.
Ayesha, Ayisha, Ayse (Turkish), *Yaisha.*
Aisleen *See* Eileen.
Aisling/Aislinn *See* Ashling.
Aithne *See* Aine.
Aivah *See* Ava.
Aiveen An Irish Gaelic name of uncertain meaning.
Aja Hindi: a goat.
Ajah.

Ajala Sanskrit: the earth. Tibetan: an older sister.
Ajay A modern name, probably from the initials A and J. Also a Sanskrit boy's name.
Ajae, Ajai.
Ajaya Sanskrit: the feminine form of Ajay, meaning invincible.
Ajda *See* Ada.
Ajla Slavic form of Ayla.
Ajua Ghanaian: born on Monday.
Aka Hawaiian: a shadow. Also a boy's name.
Akako Japanese: red.
Akala Aboriginal: a parrot.
Akalah, Akalia, Akaliah.
Akamai Hawaiian: the clever one.
Akana A mountain in Papua New Guinea.
Akasha Hindi: the feminine form of Akash, meaning the sky.
Akee *See* Aki.
Akeela/Akeelah *See* Akila.
Akela Hawaiian: noble or wise. *See also* Akila.
Akelah.
Akenehi A Maori form of Agnes.
Akesa Greek: an area of ancient Greece.
Akgul An unusual name from Uzbekistan.
Aki Japanese: born in the autumn.
Akee.
Akiko Japanese: a shining light.
Akila Arabic: wise. Nigerian: a heroine.
Akeela, Akeelah, Akela, Akelah, Akilah.
Akilina Russian form of Aquilina.
Akina Japanese: a spring flower.
Akinehi A Maori form of Agnes.
Akira Japanese: intelligent.
Akosua Ghanaian: born on Sunday.
Aku Ghanaian: born on Wednesday.
Akua, Ekua.
Alá Loftiness: the name of the Baha'i month that encompasses 2–20 March, so a suitable name for a Pisces girl.
Alabama The name of a US state.
Alacoque From St Marguerite Marie Alacoque, a 17th-century French nun.
Alahna *See* Alana.
Alaia Basque: joyful
Alaya, Aleya.
Alain *See* Alana.
Alaina/Alaine *See* Alana and Elaine.
Alainya *See* Elena.
Alaitz *See* Alice.
Alaka Sanskrit: one who has curly hair.
Alakah, Alakka, Alakkah.
Alala Greek: a mythological war goddess.
Alamea Hawaiian: precious.
Alameah.
Alameda Spanish: a poplar tree.
Alana Hawaiian: awakening. Irish Gaelic: the bright fair one, the beautiful child. Derived from a

word that is used as a term of endearment by the Irish and the feminine form of Alan.
Alahna, Alain, Alaina, Alaine, Alanah, Alanda, Alanis, Alanna, Alannah, Alanya, Alarna, Alayne, Aleina, Aleyna, Aliana, Alianna, Aliene, Alina, Allana, Allanah, Allene, Alleyna, Allyn.
Diminutives: Lana, Lane, Lanna.

Alani Hawaiian: an orange tree.

Alanis *See* Alana.

Alaqua Native American: a sweet gum tree.

Alarice Teutonic: the ruler of all. The feminine form of Alaric.
Alarica, Alarise, Alarissa, Alaryse.

Alarna *See* Alana.

Alaska A state of the USA.
Alaskah.

Alastrina Greek: the protector of mankind. The feminine form of Alastair.
Alastrine, Alastriona.

Alatea Spanish from Greek: truth.

Alauda Gaelic: a lark.

Alaula Hawaiian: the dawn.

Alaya *See* Alaia.

Alayne *See* Alana.

Alba Aboriginal: a sandhill. *See also* Albina.

Albeenia/Albena/Albenia *See* Albina.

Alberta Teutonic: noble and illustrious; the feminine form of Albert. Also the name of a Canadian province. *Alberdina, Alberdine, Alberte, Albertina, Albertine, Albrette, Alverta, Elberta, Elbertina* (Spanish), *Elbertine* (French).
Diminutives: Ali, Allie, Berta, Berte, Bertie.

Albina Latin: a white lady, someone of very fair hair and colouring.
Alba (Italian), *Albeenia, Albena, Albenia, Albine, Albinia, Alvina, Aubina, Aubine.*
Diminutive: Bina.

Albrette *See* Alberta.

Alcestis The name of a loving wife in Greek mythology.
Alceste.

Alchemy Middle English: one with magical powers.
Alcamie, Alcamy, Alcemy, Alchamy, Alchemie, Alchemye, Alkamie, Alkamye.

Alcina Greek: strong-minded. A sorceress in Greek mythology.
Alzina.

Alcyon/Alcyone *See* Halcyone.

Alda Teutonic: wise and rich.
Aldah.

Aldabella From Alda and Bella, Italian for beautiful.
Aldabelle, Aldahbella, Aldahbelle.

Aldara Greek: a winged gift.

Aldith Old English: a fighter.
Alditha, Aldithe, Aldyth, Aldytha, Aldythe.

Aldona Lithuanian: the name of a 14th-century Polish queen.

Aldonza Spanish: sweet.
Aldonzah.
Aldora Old English: of noble rank.
Aldrey Old English: from the alder tree. Also a boy's name.
Aldree, Aldrie, Aldry, Oldree, Oldrie, Oldrey, Oldry.
Aldyth/Aldytha/Aldythe *See* Aldith.
Aleasa/Alecia *See* Alicia.
Aleata/Aleda *See* Alida.
Aledis *See* Aleydis.
Aleece *See* Alice.
Aleen *See* Eileen.
Aleesha/Aleisha *See* Alicia.
Aleeza *See* Aliza.
Aleida *See* Alida.
Aleina *See* Alana.
Alejandra *See* Alexandra.
Aleka/Alekna *See* Alexandra.
Aleks/Aleksandra/Aleksia/ Aleksija *See* Alexandra and Alexis.
Alena Czech/German: a diminutive of Magdalena (*see* Madeline). Lithuanian: a form of Helen. *See also* Alhena.
Diminutive: Alenka (Slavic).
Alene *See* Eileen.
Alenka Slavic: a diminutive of Alena. *See also* Madeline.
Aleria Latin: like an eagle.
Alesana/Alesanna *See* Alexanna.
Alese *See* Alice.
Alesha/Aleshia *See* Alicia.
Alesia A form of Alicia.
Diminutive: Lesia.

Alessandra/Alessandria Italian forms of Alexandra.
Alesson/Alessyn *See* Alison.
Aleta/Aletta/Alette *See* Alida.
Aletha/Alethe *See* Alice, Alida and Althea.
Alethea Greek: truthful. *See also* Alice.
Aletea, Alethe, Alethia, Aletia, Alithea, Alithia, Eletha, Elethea. Diminutive: Thea.
Alex A short form of Alexandra, but also an independent name.
Aleks, Alix, Allix, Alyks, Alyx. Diminutives: Lex, Lexa, Lexey, Lexi, Lexie, Lexy.
Alexa *See* Alexis.
Alexandra Greek: the defender, or helper of mankind, the feminine form of Alexander. *See also* Alexis and Zena.
Alejandra (Spanish), *Aleka* (Greek), *Alekna, Aleksandra* (Russian), *Aleksia* (Danish, Norwegian), *Aleksija* (Slavic), *Alessandra* (Italian), *Alessandria, Alexanderina, Alexandria, Alexandrina, Alexandrine* (French), *Alexanria, Alexdra* (Russian), *Alexena, Alexia, Alexina* (Scottish), *Alexsia, Aliaksandra* (Russian), *Alisandra, Alissandra, Alixandra, Alixia, Allixandra, Allixia, Alyksandra, Alyxandra, Elisandra, Elissandra. Diminutives:* Aleks, Alex, Ali,

Alix, Alixa, Alla (Russian), Allie, Allix, Alyks, Alyx, Drina, Leksi, Lex, Lexa, Lexi, Lexie, Lexine, Lexy, Sacha, Sandi, Sandie, Sandra, Sandy, Sascha, Sasha, Xandra, Zandra, Zena (Scottish), Zina.

Alexanna A combination of Alex (the defender) and Anna (grace). *Alesana, Alesanna, Alexana, Alexzana, Alexzanna, Alezana, Alezanna.*

Alexdra A Russian form of Alexandra.

Alexia/Alexina See Alexandra and Alexis.

Alexis A form of Alexandra. *Aleksija* (Slavic), *Alexa, Alexia, Alexina, Alexine.*

Aleya See Alaia.

Aleyce See Alice.

Aleydis Greek: a patient friend. *Aledis, Alidis.*

Aleyna See Alana.

Aleyscha/Aleysha See Alicia.

Alezana/Alezanna See Alexanna.

Alfa See Alpha.

Alfhild Scandinavian: a battle elf. *Alfhilda, Alvild, Alvilda.*

Alfia A feminine form of Alfred, meaning a wise counsellor. See also Alfreda. *Alfea, Alfera, Alfira.*

Alfonsa Teutonic: noble and ready. The feminine form of Alphonse. *Alfonsine, Alonsa, Alonza, Alphonsa, Alphonsina, Alphonsine.*

Alfreda Teutonic: a wise counsellor. The feminine form of Alfred. See also Alfia. *Alfrida, Alfrieda, Elfreda, Elfreida, Elfrida, Elfrieda, Elfriede* (German), *Elva.* *Diminutives:* Alfie, Allie, Freda, Frida, Frieda.

Algerine A woman from Algeria.

Algita Aboriginal: a crocodile.

Alhamisi Swahili: Thursday's child.

Alhena Arabic: a ring. A star in the constellation of Gemini. *Alena.*

Ali Diminutive of Alberta, Alexandra, Alice and Alison.

Alia See Aliya.

Aliaksandra A Russian form of Alexandra.

Aliana/Alianna See Alana.

Alice Greek: the wise counsellor, or the truthful one. Teutonic: noble. The name became popular after the publication of Lewis Carroll's *Alice in Wonderland* books. See also Ailis, Alicia and Alison. *Adelice, Adelicia, Ailis* (Irish Gaelic), *Alaitz, Aleece, Alese, Aletha, Alethea, Aleyce, Alicea, Alicia, Aliciedik* (Breton), *Alicja* (Polish), *Aliki* (Greek), *Alis, Alisa* (Italian), *Alisha, Aliss, Alissa, Alisse, Alithia, Alletta* (Dutch), *Allys, Allysa, Allyse, Alodia* (Breton), *Alyce, Alys, Alyssa, Aylce* (Irish), *Aylice* (Irish), *Elyse.*

Diminutives: Ali, Allie, Ally, Elli, Ellie, Elly, Ellye, Elsa, Elsie, Elza, Ilsa.

Alicen/Aliceson *See* Alison.

Alicia Originally a form of Alice, but now a popular name in its own right. *See also* Licia.
Ailisha, Aleasa, Alecia, Aleesha, Aleisha, Alesha, Aleshia, Alesia, Aleyscha, Aleysha, Alicea, Alicha, Alicja, Alisha, Alisia, Alissha, Alissia, Allecia, Allisha, Allissa, Allysha, Allyssa, Alycia, Alysa, Alyse, Alysha, Alysia, Alyssa, Elecia, Eleesha, Elicia, Elisha, Ellecia, Ellicia, Ellisha, Elysha, Elyshia, Ilisha.

Alida Latin: the little winged one.
Aleata, Aleda, Aleida, Aleta, Aletha, Aletta (Italian, Spanish), *Alette* (French), *Alita, Allida, Alouetta, Alouette, Alyda, Elida, Elita.*
Diminutives: Leda, Lida, Lita.

Alidis *See* Aleydis.

Aliene *See* Alana.

Aliikai Hawaiian: the queen of the sea.

Alika Hawaiian: truthful. Nigerian: very beautiful.

Aliki Greek form of Alice.

Alima Arabic: skilled in dancing and music.
Alimah.

Alina/Aline *See* Adelaide, Alana, Eileen and Helen.

Alinga Aboriginal: the sun.

Alis/Alisa/Alisha/Alisia *See* Alice and Alicia.

Alisandra/Alissandra *See* Alexandra.

Alish *See* Ailis.

Alison Originally a diminutive of Alice.
Alesson, Alessyn, Alicen, Aliceson, Alisson, Allison, Allson, Allsun (Irish), Allyson, Alson, Alsoun, Alyson, Alysoun, Arihana (Maori).
Diminutives: Alee, Ali, Alie, Allee, Allie, Ally, Lissie, Lisy.

Aliss/Alissa/Alissha/Alissia *See* Alice and Alyssa.

Alithia *See* Alethea and Alice.

Alivia/Alivyah *See* Olivia.

Alix/Alixa/Alixandra/Alixia *See* Alex and Alexandra.

Aliya Arabic: sublime, exalted. Hebrew: to ascend.
Aalia, Aaliah, Aaliyah, Ahlia, Alia, Aliyah.

Aliza Jewish: joy.
Aleeza, Alizah, Alize (French), *Alizée* (French), *Alizeh.*

Alkamie/Alkamye *See* Alchemy.

Alkina Aboriginal: the moon.

Alkira Aboriginal: the sky.

Alla *See* Alexandra.

Allana/Allanah *See* Alana.

Allecia *See* Alicia.

Allegra Italian/Spanish: cheerful, joyous.
Alegra, Alegria (Spanish),

Allegria.
Allene/Alleyna *See* Alana.
Alli Aboriginal: a dog.
Allida *See* Alida.
Allie Diminutive of Alberta, Alexandra, Alice and Alison.
Allirea Aboriginal: quartz.
Allira, Allirra, Allyra, Allyrra.
Allison *See* Alison.
Allix/Allixandra/Allixia *See* Alexandra.
Allona/Allonah *See* Alona.
Allora Aboriginal: the place of the swamp. The name of a town in Queensland.
Allorah.
Alloula/Allula *See* Alula.
Allson/Allsun *See* Alison.
Allunga Aboriginal: the sun.
Allure Middle English: one who attracts or charms.
Alure.
Allyn *See* Alana.
Allyra/Allyrra *See* Allirea.
Allys/Allysa/Allyse *See* Alice.
Allysha/Allyssa *See* Alicia.
Allyson *See* Alison.
Alma Celtic: good. Latin: of the soul. Turkish: an apple.
Almah.
Almada A city in Portugal.
Almasi Swahili: a diamond.
Almas, Almaz, Almazi.
Almeda *See* Almedha and Almeta.
Almedha Welsh: shapely.
Almeda, Almida.
Almena A Spanish placename.
Almina.
Almera/Almeria *See* Almira.
Almeta Latin: ambitious.
Almeda.
Almida *See* Almedha.
Almira Arabic: truth without question.
Almera, Almeria, Almerinda, Almiria.
Almond Middle English: a plant name.
Almonde.
Alodia Breton form of Alice.
Alodie Old English: wealthy, prosperous.
Elodia, Elodie.
Aloha Hawaiian: greetings.
Alohi Hawaiian: brilliant.
Aloisa/Aloise *See* Aloysia and Louise.
Aloma The name of an American actress (Aloma Wright).
Alomah.
Alona Hebrew: from the oak tree.
Alonah, Allona, Allonah.
Alondra Spanish: a lark.
Alonsa/Alonza *See* Alfonsa.
Alouetta/Alouette *See* Alida.
Aloysia The feminine form of Aloysius. *See also* Louise.
Aloisa, Aloise, Aloisia, Aloysa, Aloyse, Aloyza (Polish).
Aloyza *See* Aloysia and Louise.
Alpha Greek: the first one. The first letter of the Greek alphabet.

Alfa.
**Alphonsa/Alphonsina/
Alphonsine** *See* Alfonsa.
Alsace The name of a French province.
Alson/Alsoun *See* Alison.
Alta Latin: tall.
Altair From the Arabic word for a bright star, or an eagle.
Altamira Spanish: a high view.
Althea Greek: the healer, or wholesome.
Aletha, Alethe, Althee, Altheta, Althia.
Diminutive: Thea.
Altheda Greek: flower-like.
Aludra Greek: a virgin.
Alula Arabic: the first or firstborn. Latin: a star in Ursa Major.
Alloula, Allula, Aloula, Alulah.
Aluma Hebrew: a girl.
Alva Latin: the white or blonde one. Also a diminutive of Alvina.
Alvah.
Alvara German: from the army of elves.
Variation: Elvara.
Alvera *See* Elvira.
Alverta *See* Alberta.
Alvild/Alvilda *See* Alfhild.
Alvina Teutonic: a beloved and noble friend; the feminine form of Alvin. *See also* Albina and Elvina.
Alveena, Alvine, Alvinia.
Diminutives: Alva, Alvah.
Alvira *See* Elvira.

Alvita Latin: vivacious, full of life.
Alwin Welsh: beloved by all.
Ailwyn, Ailwynn, Ailwynne, Alwen, Alwyn, Alwynn, Alwynne.
Alyce *See* Alice.
Alyda *See* Alida.
Alyks/Alyksandra *See* Alexandra.
Alyna *See* Adelaide.
Alyona Russian diminutive of Yelena. *See* Helen.
Alys/Alyse *See* Alice.
Alysa/Alysha *See* Alicia.
Alysia Greek: possessive. *See also* Alicia.
Alycia.
Alyson/Alysoun *See* Alison.
Alyssa Greek: the sane one; the name of a herb with yellow or white flowers. Also a form of Alicia.
Alissa, Alyssia, Alyssum.
Alyx/Alyxandra *See* Alexandra.
Alzena Arabic: a woman.
Alzina *See* Alcina.
Alzubra Arabic: a star.
Am Vietnamese: a child of the moon.
Ama Ghanaian: born on Saturday. Sanskrit: a mother.
Amah, Amma, Ammah.
Amabel Latin: lovable, the sweet one. *See also* Mabel.
Amabella, Amabelle.
Amadea Latin: beloved of God.
Amadika Zimbabwean: the beloved

A – GIRLS

one.
Amadora Italian: the gift of love.
Amadore.
Amala Arabic: hope. Tibetan: a mother. *See also* Amelia.
Amal.
Amalea/Amali/Amalia/Amalie *See* Amelia.
Amalia-Rose An attractive 'combination name', from Amelia (industrious) and Rose.
Amelia-Rose.
Amalina/Amalita *See* Amelia.
Amalinda *See* Amelinda.
Amalthea Greek: the nourisher. The she-goat nurse of the god Zeus in Greek mythology and a satellite of the planet Jupiter.
Almathea.
Amana Hebrew: faithful or loyal.
Amanah.
Amanda Latin: worthy of being loved.
Amanada, Amandah, Amandine (French), *Amantha.*
Diminutives: Manda, Mandi, Mandie, Mandii, Mandy.
Amandine French form of Amanda.
Amani Arabic: an aspiration, a desire.
Amany.
Amantha *See* Amanda.
Amara Greek: unfading or eternal beauty. Sanskrit/Thai: eternal. *See also* Amare.
Amaranth Greek: an eternal flower.

Amaranta (Spanish), *Amarantha.*
Amare Italian: to love.
Amara.
Amaril/Amarill/Amarilla/Amarillis *See* Amaryllis.
Amarina Aboriginal: rain.
Amarinah, Amarine.
Amaris Hebrew: God has promised. Sanskrit: a child of the moon.
Amari.
Amarli *See* Amelia.
Amarna Arabic: the name of an Egyptian archaeological site.
Amarni.
Amaryllis Greek: a shepherdess. Also a 'flower name'.
Amaril, Amarill, Amarilla, Amarillis, Amaryll, Amarylla.
Amata Italian and Spanish forms of Amy. *See also* Amice.
Amatista Spanish form of Amethyst.
Amaya Japanese: night rain.
Amazonia Greek: warlike. Also after the Amazon River.
Amazona.
Amba/Ambah *See* Ambaa, Amber and Ambika.
Ambaa Nepali: a guava.
Ambaah, Amba, Ambah.
Ambar Sanskrit: of the sky. *See also* Amber.
Ambara Arabic: the perfumed one.
Ambarah, Ambarin, Ambarina, Ambarine.
Amber Arabic: a gemstone. This

name became popular in the 1940s, after the publication of the novel *Forever Amber*. See also Ember.
Amba, Ambah, Ambar (Hindi), *Amberr, Ambeur, Ambr* (Welsh), *Ambra* (Italian), *Ambre* (French), *Ambur, Amipa* (Tongan), *Emba* (Swahili), *Embah*.

Amberley A modern made-up name.
Amberlee, Amberleigh, Amberlie, Amberly.

Ambika Hindi: a mother.
Amba.

Ambra Italian form of Amber.

Ambriel The angel of the month of May.
Ambriele, Ambriell, Ambrielle.

Ambrosine Greek: the divine immortal one. The feminine form of Ambrose.
Ambrosetta, Ambrosette, Ambrosia, Ambrosina.

Ambur See Amber.

Ame/Amee See Amy.

Ameena See Amina.

Ameera/Ameerah See Amira.

Ameika See Amice.

Amelia Teutonic: industrious, striving. See also Emily.
Aemilia, Amala, Amalea, Amali, Amalia (Scandinavian), *Amalie* (German), *Amalina* (Italian, Spanish), *Amalita* (Spanish), *Amarli, Amealia, Amela, Amelea, Amelee, Amélie* (French), *Amelinda, Ameline, Amelita, Amielia, Amilee, Amilia, Amilie, Amily, Amiria* (Maori), *Amylee, Amylia, Amylie, Emelia, Emmelia*.
Diminutives: Amy, Mell, Melli, Mellie, Melly, Milli, Millie, Milly.

Ameliarose An attractive 'combination name'.
Amelia-Rose.

Amelinda From Amelia and Linda.
Amalinda, Amelinde.

Amena Celtic: pure.
Amene, Amina.

America Italian: a country, named in honour of the Italian explorer Amerigo Vespucci.
Americah, Ameriga, Amerigah, Amerika, Amerikah.

Amethyst Greek: the name of a semi-precious stone.
Amatista (Spanish), *Amethyste*.

Ami/Amia/Amie/Amiee/Amii See Amy.

Amice Latin: friendship. See also Amity.
Amata, Amecia, Ameika, Amica, Amicia, Amika, Amikka.

Amielia/Amilee/Amilia/Amily See **Amelia**.

Amika/Amikka See Amice.

Ami-Leigh Either a modern form of Amelia or Amelie, or a combination of Amy (beloved) and Leigh (a meadow or clearing).
Amilea, Ami-Lea, Amilee, Ami-

Lee, Amileigh, Amy-Lea, Amy-Lee, Amy-Leigh.
Amina Arabic: honest, faithful. See also Amena.
Ameena, Aminah.
Aminatta An African name of uncertain meaning.
Aminta Greek: the protector.
Amintha, Aminthe.
Amipa The Tongan form of Amber.
Amira Arabic: a princess. Hebrew: speech.
Ameera, Ameerah, Amirah.
Amiria Maori form of Amelia.
Amirtha Sanskrit: probably meaning invisible.
Amisha A Sanskrit name of uncertain meaning.
Ameesha.
Amita Hebrew: truth. See also Amity.
Amity Latin: friendship. See also Amice.
Amita, Emita, Emity.
Amma/Ammah See Ama.
Ammut The crocodile-headed Ancient Egyptian goddess of the underworld.
Amora Hebrew: a speaker or interpreter.
Amorah.
Amoretta/Amorette See Amorita.
Amori A kangaroo in the mythology of west New Guinea.
Amorie.
Amorita Latin: the little beloved one.
Amoretta, Amorette (French).
Amour French: love.
Ampelia Spanish: the feminine form of Ampelio (from Ampelius, a 7th-century saint).
Amrita Sanskrit: immortal.
Amy Old French: beloved. Also a diminutive of Amelia.
Aimee, Aimée (French), *Amata* (Italian, Spanish), *Ame, Amee, Ami, Amia, Amie, Amiee, Amii, Amye, Aymee, Aymi, Aymie.*
Amy-Lea/Amy-Lee/Amy-Leigh See Ami-Leigh.
Amylee/Amylia/Amylie See Amelia.
An Chinese: peace. Vietnamese: safety.
Ana See Anastasia and Anne.
Anada/Anadah See Ananda.
Anael The angel of the air.
Anahera See Anihera.
Anaïs See Agnes.
Anala Hindi: fire.
Analena/Analyn See Annalynn.
Anamae/Anamay See Annamay.
Anamari/Anamaria/Anamarie See **Annamaria**.
Anan Arabic: of the clouds.
Ananda Sanskrit: joyful.
Anada, Anadah, Anandah, Anandalila, Anandani, Anandi, Anandini.
Anani Hawaiian: an orange tree.
Ananke Greek: necessity. A goddess

of fate and a satellite of the planet Jupiter.
Anagke.
Ananya Sanskrit: unique.
Anastasia Russian from Greek: she who will rise again. The name of a 4th-century saint.
Anastacia, Anastacie, Anastase, Anastasie (French), *Anastasija* (Slavic), *Anastasiya* (Russian), *Anastassia, Anastazia* (Slavic), *Anastazie* (Czech), *Anastazja* (Polish), *Anasthasia, Anstice. Diminutives:* Ana, Nastasia (Russian), Nastia (Russian), Nastya (Russian), Stacee, Stacey, Stacia, Stacie, Stacy, Stasya (Russian), Tasoula (Greek).
Anat Israeli: a singer.
Anata Babylonian: the goddess of the earth.
Anatola Greek: from the east. The feminine form of Anatole.
Anatholia, Anatolia.
Anay *See* Agnes.
Anca/Ancika *See* Anne.
Ancela *See* Angela.
Ancelin Old French: a spear attendant. The feminine form of Lancelot.
Ancelot.
Anchala Sanskrit: unshaken.
Anchoret *See* Angharad.
Ancilla Latin: a handmaiden.
Anceilea, Anceilia, Ancillea, Ancillia.

Anda/Andah *See* Andrea.
Andea A woman of the Andes.
Andeah, Andeana, Andia, Andiah.
Andela *See* Angela.
Andi/Andie *See* Andrea.
Andia/Andiah *See* Andea.
Andine A feminine form of Andrew, meaning strong. *See also* Andrea.
Andena, Andene, Andina.
Andorra A small principality in Europe, located between France and Spain.
Andora, Andorah, Andorrah.
Andra/Andre *See* Andrea.
Andras Norwegian: breath.
Andrea Greek: strong, a feminine form of Andrew or Andreas.
See also Andine and Andrewina.
Aindrea, Anda, Andah, Andra, Andranela, Andranella, Andranelle, Andre, Andreana, Andreanna, Andrée (French), *Andreea, Andreena, Andreja* (Slavic), *Andreya, Andria, Andriana, Andriea, Andriella, Andrielle, Andrija, Andrina, Andrine. Diminutives:* Andi, Andie, Andy.
Andrewina Another feminine form of Andrew (*see also* Andrea).
Andrewine.
Andria/Andriana *See* Andrea.
Andriea/Andriella/Andrina/ Andrine *See* Andrea.
Andromache Greek: the wife of

Hector in mythology.

Andromeda Greek: a ruler of men; a heroine of Greek legend, who was rescued from a sea monster by Perseus. Also the name of a constellation.

Andy *See* Andrea.

Aneeka/Aneka/Anekah *See* Anne.

Aneesha/Aneysha *See* Anisha.

Aneira Welsh: truly golden. The feminine form of Aneurin.

Aneko Japanese: an older sister.

Anela/Anella *See* Angela and Anne.

Anemone Greek: a wind flower. A mythological nymph who turned into a flower.

Aneta/Anett/Anette *See* Anne.

Anezka Czech form of Agnes.

Angarua Polynesian: a legendary figure.

Angel *See* Angela.

Angela Greek: a heavenly messenger, an angel. *See also* Angelica.
Aingeal (Irish), *Ancela* (Polish), *Andela* (Czech), *Anela* (Hawaiian), *Anella, Ange* (French), *Angel, Angèle* (French), *Angelina* (Italian), *Angeline, Angella, Angiola* (Italian), *Angiolina* (Italian), *Angyl, Angyll, Aniela* (Italian, Polish), *Aniella, Anjela* (Bohemian), *Anjelina, Anjeline, Annella.*
Diminutives: Angelita (Spanish), Angie, Anjee, Anji, Anjie.

Angelica Latin: the angelic one. A form of Angela and also a plant name.
Angelika (Swedish), *Angeliki* (Greek), *Angelique* (French), *Anjelica.*
Diminutives: Anjee, Anji, Anjie.

Angelina/Angeline/Angelita *See* Angela.

Angelique French form of Angelica.

Angerona The Roman goddess of secret sorrow, whose rites were celebrated on 21 December. Suitable for a Sagittarian child.

Angharad Welsh: free from shame, or much loved.
Anchoret.

Angiola/Angiolina Italian forms of Angela.

Angioletta Italian: a little angel.
Angiolette.

Angwen Welsh: very handsome. *See also* Anwen.
Angwenn, Angwenne.

Angyl/Angyll *See* Angela.

Anh Vietnamese: a flower.

Ani Tibetan: a nun. *See also* Anne.
Aniy.

Anica *See* Anne.

Anice *See* Annice.

Aniek Dutch form of Anne.

Aniela/Aniella *See* Angela.

Anihera Maori: an angel.
Anahera.

Anika/Aniko *See* Anne.

Anila Sanskrit: of the wind. The feminine form of Anil.

Aniqa *See* Anne.
Anique/Annique *See* Annice.
Anisha Sanskrit: lordly.
Aneesha, Aneysha, Anishah.
Aniston The surname of a famous US actress (Jennifer Aniston). *Anniston.*
Anita/Annita *See* Anne. *Diminutive:* Nita.
Anitra A name created by Norwegian playwright Henrik Ibsen for his play *Peer Gynt*.
Aniwaniwa Maori: a rainbow.
Aniza *See* Annissa.
Anja German and Scandinavian diminutives of Anna (*see* Anne). *Anjah.*
Anjali Sanskrit: an offering; homage. *Anjalee, Anjouli, Anjuli.*
Anjee/Anji/Anjie *See* Angela and Angelica.
Anjela/Anjelina/Anjeline *See* Angela.
Anjelica *See* Angelica.
Anjouli/Anjuli *See* Anjali.
Anka Aboriginal: a barramundi. Turkish: a phoenix. *See also* Anne.
Ankine An Armenian name of uncertain meaning.
Ankita Sanskrit: possibly meaning one who is marked.
Ann/Anna *See* Anne.
Annabel A combination of Anna (grace) and Belle (beautiful).
Anabel (Spanish), *Anabela, Anabelle, Annabel, Annabell,*
Annabella, Annabelle, Annabellina, Annahbella.
Diminutives: Bella, Belle.
Annagret/Annagrete *See* Annegrete.
Annais *See* Agnes.
Annali *See* Anne.
Annalice/Annaliesje/Annalisa/ Anna-Lisa *See* Anneliese.
Annalouise A delightful 'combination name'.
Annalouisa, AnnaLouisa, Anna-Louisa, AnnaLouise, Anna-Louise.
Annalyce/Annalyse *See* Anneliese.
Annalynn A combination of Anna (grace) and Lynn (a waterfall).
Analena, Analyn, Annalena, Annalyn, AnnaLynn, Annalynne, AnnaLynne.
Annamaria From Anna and Maria.
Anamari, Anamaria, Anamarie, Annamari, Anna Maria, Annamarie, Annemarie, Anne Marie.
Annamay A combination of Anna (grace) and May.
Anamae, Anamay, Annamae.
Annata Italian form of Anne.
Anne From the Hebrew name Hannah, meaning grace, or favoured by God. *See also* Annabel, Annamaria, Anneliese, Hannah and Nancy.
Aana, Ana (Samoan, Slavic, Spanish), *Anca* (Bohemian),

Ancika (Bohemian), *Ane* (Lithuanian, Maori), *Aneeka, Aneka, Anekah, Anela, Anella, Aneta* (Serbian), *Anett, Anette, Ani* (Maori), *Anica* (Spanish), *Aniek* (Dutch), *Anika, Aniko* (Hungarian), *Anina, Aniqa, Anita* (Spanish), *Anka* (Serbian), *Anke* (German), *Ann, Anna, Annah, Annaka, Annali* (Swiss), *Annata* (Italian), *Anneka* (Dutch), *Anneke* (Dutch), *Anneli, Annelie, Annella* (Scottish), *Annelle, Annerl* (Bavarian), *Annett, Annetta* (French), *Annette, Annica* (Italian), *Annick, Annika* (Swedish), *Annike, Annita, Annot* (Scandinavian), *Annuschka* (Russian), *Anouska* (Swedish), *Antje* (Dutch), *Anu* (Finnish), *Anusia* (Greek, Polish), *Anya* (Hebrew), *Anysia, Hanna, Hannah, Ona* (Lithuanian), *Panna* (Hungarian). *Diminutives:* Anja (German, Scandinavina), Anjah (German, Scandinavian), Anni, Annie, Anninka (Russian), Ans (Dutch), Nan, Nana, Nanci, Nancy, Nanette (French), Nanine, Nanna, Nanon (French), Nina (Russian), Ninette, Ninon (French), Nita (Spanish), Vanka (Russian), Vanni (Italian).

Annecy *See* Annice.

Annegrete German: a combination of Anne and Grete, a diminutive of Margaret.
Annagret, Annagrete, Annegret.

Anneli/Annelie *See* Anne.

Anneliese German/Scandinavian: from Anne and Liese (*see* Elizabeth).
Analise, Anlise, Annalice, Annalicia, Annaliese, Annaliesje, Annalisa, Anna-Lise, Anna-Lisse, Annalyce, Annalyse, Anneliis, Annelisa, Annelise.
Diminutive: Anneli.

Annella *See* Angela and Anne.

Anneloes Dutch: a combination of Anne and Louise.

Annetta/Annette *See* Anne.

Anni/Annie *See* Anne.

Annica Italian form of Anne.

Annice Old English form of Agnes.
Anice, Anique, Annecy, Annique, Annis, Annise, Annys, Annyse.

Annick/Annika/Anninka *See* Anne.

Annis/Annise *See* Agnes and Annice.

Annissa Arabic: charming, gracious.
Anissa, Aniza, Anniza, Annyssa, Anyssa.

Ann-Margret From Anne and Margaret.
Ann-Margaret, Anne-Margaret, Anne-Margret.

Annot *See* Anne.

Annunziata Italian: the bearer of news.
Annonciada (Spanish),

Annonziata, Annunciata, Nonziata, Nunziata.
Annuska/Anouska/Anouskh *See* Anushka.
Annwen/Annwynne *See* Anwen.
Annys/Annyse *See* Agnes and Annice.
Anona Latin: of the harvest or the ninth, as in the ninth child.
Annona, Anonna.
Anoush Armenian: sweet.
Anousha.
Ans Dutch diminutive of Anna.
Anschau The name of a German town.
Ansca.
Anselma Teutonic: a divine helmet. The feminine form of Anselm.
Anselmah, Anselme (French), *Anzelma, Anzelmah.*
Diminutives: Selma, Selmah, Zelma, Zelmah.
Ansha Sanskrit: a portion
Anslea/Ansley *See* Ainsley.
Anstice *See* Anastasia.
Ansuya Sanskrit: a learned woman.
Antara Sanskrit: a musical note.
Antares The brightest star in the constellation of Scorpius.
Anteia Greek: a mythological figure.
Anthea Greek: flower-like.
Anthee, Anthia, Anthie.
Diminutives: Thea, Thia.
Anthela Greek: like a flower.
Anthoula.
Anthonia *See* Antonia.

Antigone Greek: a name featured in mythology and implying strength of character.
Antigoni.
Antionette *See* Antonia.
Antje Dutch form of Anne.
Antlia The name of a southern constellation.
Antoenia/Antoenella *See* Antonia.
Antoinetta/Antoinette *See* Antonia.
Antonia Latin: beyond price, praiseworthy. The feminine form of Anthony.
Anthonia, Antoenella, Antoenia, Antoinette (French), *Antoinietta, Antonella* (Italian), *Antonetta* (Slavic), *Antonietta, Antonette, Antonea, Antonett, Antonette, Antoni, Antonica* (Italian), *Antonie* (German), *Antonietta* (Italian), *Antonija, Antonina, Antonine, Antonya* (Lithuanian).
Diminutives: Netta, Nette, Nettie, Netty, Nina (Russian), Toinette (French), Toni, Tonia, Tonie, Tonya.
Anu Finnish form of Anne or Anna.
Anudhi A Sanskrit name of uncertain meaning.
Anuradha Sanskrit: the name of a goddess.
Anushka Sanskrit: a term of endearment.
Annuska, Annuskha, Anouska, Anouskh, Anusha, Anuska.

Anusia Greek and Polish forms of Anne.
Anwen Celtic: very beautiful. *See also* Angwen.
Annwen, Annwyn, Annwynne, Anwyn, Anwynne.
Anya/Anysia *See* Anne.
Anyssa *See* Annissa.
Anzelma/Anzelmah *See* Anselma.
Anzu Japanese: an apricot.
Aoife Irish Gaelic: life.
Aolani Hawaiian: a heavenly cloud.
Apakura Polynesian: a legendary figure.
Apanie Aboriginal: water.
Apara Nigerian: one who comes and goes.
Aperira Maori form of April.
Aphina *See* Afina.
Aphra Hebrew: dust, or a female deer. A saint's name.
Afra, Aphrah, Ayfara.
Aphrodite Greek: the mythological goddess of beauty, love and fertility.
Afrodite, Afroditi, Aphroditi.
Apolline Greek: the sun, sunlight.
Apollena, Apollene, Apollina.
Apollonia Greek: belonging to Apollo. The name of a saint.
Aponi Native American: a butterfly.
Apple An unusual modern name, made famous by actress Gwyneth Paltrow's daughter.
April Latin: the first month in the Roman calendar, and the beginning of spring. *See also* Avril.
Abriella, Abrielle, Abril (Spanish), *Aperira* (Maori), *Aprila, Aprile, Aprilee, Aprilette, Aprill, Aprille, Aprillee, Apryl, Avril* (French), *Avrilette* (French), *Ebrel* (Cornish), *Ebril* (Welsh), *Ebrill* (Welsh).
Apsara Sanskrit: a beautiful supernatural being in Hindu mythology.
Apsarah.
Aquamarine Latin: a gemstone and a 'colour name'.
Diminutive: Aqua.
Aquaria Latin: after the zodiac sign and constellation of Aquarius.
Aquarian, Aquarien, Aquarienne.
Aqueena Native American: the peaceful one.
Aqueen, Aqueenah, Aquene, Aquinna, Aquinnah.
Aquilina Latin: like an eagle. The feminine form of Aquila.
Akilina (Russian), *Aquila.*
Aquitaine A region of France.
Aquitain, Aquitane, Aquitania (Latin), *Aquitayn, Aquitayne.*
Ara Greek: an altar, or the goddess of destruction.
Arah.
Arabella Latin: a beautiful altar. Teutonic: an eagle heroine.
Arabel, Arabela (Spanish), *Arabelle, Arrabella, Arrabelle.*
Diminutives: Bel, Bella, Belle.
Arabia A region of the Middle East.
Arabiah, Araybia, Araybiah.

Arachne Greek: a mythological maiden who was turned into a spider.
Arael The angel of the birds.
Arafura The name of a northern Australian sea; probably of Portuguese origin.
Araluen Aboriginal: the place of waterlilies.
Araminta Greek: a beautiful fragrant flower.
Aramanta, Aramintha.
Arancia Italian: orange.
Aranka Hungarian: golden.
Arantxa Spanish: possibly a form of Arancia.
Arancha.
Aravane A Persian name of uncertain meaning.
Araxia Armenian: of the river.
Araxie.
Araybia/Araybiah *See* Arabia.
Arbiya Arabic: Wednesday.
Arcadia Greek: after Arcady, a mountainous region of Greece.
Arcangela Italian: an archangel.
Arcangele, Arcangelina, Arcangeline.
Archer Old English: a bowman.
Arda Hebrew: bronze. *See also* Ardath and Ardelle.
Ardah.
Ardan *See* Arden.
Ardath Hebrew: a field of flowers.
Arda.
Ardelle Latin: warm and enthusiastic.
Arda, Ardeen, Ardelia, Ardelis, Ardell, Ardella, Ardene, Ardine, Ardis.
Arden Old English: the valley of the eagles.
Ardan.
Ardene/Ardine/Ardis *See* Ardelle.
Arduina A hunter-goddess in Celtic mythology.
Arduenna, Arduenne, Arduinna.
Areeta/Areetah *See* Areta.
Arella *See* Ariella.
Arena Latin: a sandy place.
Aresca *See* Ariesca.
Areta Greek: virtuous, one of untarnished reputation.
Areeta, Areetah, Arete, Aretha, Areti, Aretta, Arette (French), Arieta, Arietha, Arita, Aritah.
Aretha *See* Areta.
Arethusa Greek: a mythological nymph who was changed into a fountain.
Arethousa.
Arezou Persian: wishful.
Argenta Latin: the silvery one.
Argentia, Argentina.
Argiro Greek: silver.
Argira, Argirea, Argiria, Argirio, Argyrea, Argyro.
Aria Latin: a beautiful melody.
Ariah, Arija, Arijah, Arya.
Ariadne Greek: the holy one. The daughter of King Minos of Crete in Greek mythology.
Ariadna, Ariana, Ariane, Ariann,

Arianne.
Ariana/Ariane/Ariann
See Ariadne.
Arianrhod Welsh: silvery. The Celtic goddess of the moon.
Arianrod.
Arianwen Welsh: like silver.
Arian, Arianwenn, Arianwenne, Arianwyn, Arianwynn, Arianwynne.
Arie/Arien/Ariene See Ariesca.
Ariel See Ariella.
Ariella Hebrew: God's lioness.
Aariel, Arella, Arieal, Ariel, Ariela, Ariella, Arielle.
Ariesca A feminine form of Ares/Aries, the Greek god of war (the equivalent of Mars) and a zodiac sign and constellation.
Aresca, Arie, Arien, Ariene, Aries.
Arieta/Arietha See Areta.
Arietta A little lioness.
Ariette.
Arihana Maori form of Alison.
Arija/Arijah See Aria.
Arika Aboriginal: a waterlily.
Arilda German: a hearth maiden.
Arina Romanian and Russian forms of Irina (see Irene).
Arinya Aboriginal: a kangaroo.
Arish An Egyptian placename.
Arista Greek: the best.
Aristea.
Arita/Aritah See Areta.
Ariza Hebrew: a cedar tree.
Arja See Irja.

Arkina Armenian: priceless.
Arkeena, Arkinah.
Diminutive: Arkie.
Arlene A modern name of uncertain origin.
Arleen, Arlena, Arlenis, Arline, Arlise, Arlyne.
Arlette Teutonic: an eagle.
Arletta.
Arlie See Harley.
Arline/Arlise/Arlyne See Arlene.
Armada Spanish: the armed one.
Armanda A feminine form of Armand. See Herman.
Armani After the Italian fashion designer, Giorgio Armani.
Armanee, Armanie, Armany.
Armelle French Celtic: a princess.
Armella.
Armida Italian: one who is not fit.
Armilla Latin: a bracelet.
Armina Teutonic: a warrior maid; a feminine form of Herman. *See also* Erma.
Armine, Arminia, Arminie.
Armistice English from Latin: a truce.
Armystice.
Armonia See Harmony.
Armorel Gaelic: the one who lives by the sea.
Armorell, Armorelle.
Armynel French: a woman of the army. A feminine form of Armand.
Arna Hebrew: a cedar tree. Also a form of Arnalda.

Arnah.
Arnalda Teutonic: strong as an eagle. A feminine form of Arnold.
Arna, Arnelle, Arnette, Arnolda, Arnoldine.
Arnette *See* Arnalda.
Arnica A medicinal plant.
Arnika (German), *Arnijka.*
Arnice A modern invention; a feminine form of Arnold.
Arnise.
Arnurna Aboriginal: a blue waterlily.
Aroha Maori/Polynesian: love.
Arona Hebrew: exalted. The feminine form of Aaron.
Aharona, Aronah.
Aroona Aboriginal: running water. Also a boy's name.
Aroonah.
Arora Aboriginal: a cockatoo.
Arquette The surname of a well-known family of American actors (Rosanna, David, etc).
Arquet, Arquett.
Arrabella/Arrabelle *See* Arabella.
Artemis Greek: perfect. The name of the Greek goddess of the moon and hunting.
Artema, Artemas, Artemi, Artemie, Artemisa, Artemisia.
Arthura A female form of Arthur, a Celtic name meaning as strong as a bear, or strong as a rock.
Artha (Welsh), *Arthah, Arthurah, Arthure, Arthuria, Arthuriah, Arthurina, Arthurine, Artura, Arturah, Arture, Arturia, Arturina, Arturine.*
Arti Indonesian: a popular girl's name.
Artis Icelandic: thunder, or a follower of Thor.
Aruna Sanskrit: the dawn.
Aruni.
Arundel Old English: one who dwells with the eagles. Originally a boy's name.
Arundale, Arundell, Arundelle.
Arundhati Sanskrit: the morning star.
Arusha Sanskrit: red.
Arva Greek: an eagle.
Arwa Arabic/Sanskrit: a female mountain goat.
Arwen Welsh: a muse.
Arwenn, Arwenne, Arwyn, Arwynn, Arwynne.
Arya *See* Aria.
Asa Japanese: the morning.
Asada *See* Ashada.
Asahi Japanese: the morning sun.
Asch/Ascher *See* Asher.
Asela Spanish: like an ash tree.
Asella After St Asella, who was described as 'a flower of the Lord'.
Asenath Hebrew: a name from the Old Testament.
Asera Arabic/Hebrew: the queen of the sea.
Aseri An Estonian placename.
Asha Sanskrit: hope.
Ashana, Ashia.

Ashada Sanskrit: the Hindu month of June/July, which corresponds to Cancer.
Asada, Asalha, Ashala.

Ashanti African: the name of a people in Ghana.
Ashante.

Asher Hebrew: the fortunate one. More commonly a boy's name.
Ascher.
Diminutives: Asch, Ash, Ashe.

Ashima Sanskrit form of Asima.

Ashira Hebrew: wealthy.

Ashleigh Old English: an ash tree meadow or wood.
Aashlee, Aashleigh, Aashli, Aashlie, Ashlea, Ashlee, Ashlei, Ashley, Ashli, Ashlie, Ashly, Ashlygh.

Ashling Irish Gaelic: a vision or dream.
Aisling, Aislinn, Ashlen, Ashleyne, Ashlin, Ashlinn, Ashlinne, Ashlyn, Ashlynn, Ashlynne.

Ashna Sanskrit: a friend.

Ashni A contemporary name of uncertain meaning.
Ashnee, Ashnie, Ashnii.

Ashwina Sanskrit: a child of the stars. The feminine form of Ashwin.
Ashwini.

Asia Latin: the name of a continent.
Asiah.

Asima Arabic: a protector.
Ashima (Sanskrit), *Asimah.*

Asira Arabic: the honoured or chosen one.

Asisa Hebrew: ripe.

Asiya Arabic: powerful.

Asli Turkish: genuine.

Asma Arabic: beautiful or sublime. The name of the Baha'i month that encompasses 20 August– 7 September, so an appropriate name for a Virgo baby.
Asmah.

Asmara An Ethiopian city.

Asmodel The angel of April.
Asmodell, Asmodelle.

Aspasia Greek: welcome.

Aspen Old English: the aspen tree, a type of poplar.
Aspenn, Aspenne, Aspin, Aspyn, Aspynn, Aspynne.

Asphodel Greek: a lily or a daffodil.
Asphodell, Asphodelle.

Asprey An English surname, the name of British luxury brand.

Asra Arabic: one who travels by night.

Asri An Indonesian name of uncertain meaning.

Assia The name of a German-born poet, the lover of British poet Ted Hughes (Assia Wevill).

Assunta Italian: from the Assumption of the Virgin Mary.
Assumpta.

Asta Greek/Old Norse: a star. Also a short form of Astrid.
Aasta, Aastah, Astah, Astra,

Astrah.
Astaire Greek: a star. The surname of a famous actor and dancer (Fred Astaire).
Astair, Asther (Scandinavian).
Astarte The Phoenician goddess of love and fertility, the equivalent of the Greek Aphrodite and the Roman Venus.
Astella/Astelle *See* Estelle.
Aster Greek: after the flower.
See also Astral.
Astera, Asteria.
Asther *See* Astaire.
Astra/Astrah *See* Asta and Astral.
Astral Latin: a star.
Aster, Astra, Astrah, Astrella, Astri, Astro.
Astrea Greek: innocence. The Greek goddess of justice, who left earth and became a constellation.
Astraea, Astri.
Astri/Astro *See* Astral and Astrea.
Astrid Old Norse: divine strength.
Astred, Astrida, Astride, Astrud.
Diminutive: Asta.
Asucena/Asusena/Asuzena *See* Azucena.
Asuka Japanese: a combination of words meaning tomorrow and perfume.
Asvina Sanskrit: the Hindu month that corresponds to September/October.
Aszura/Aszure *See* Azura.
Ataahua Maori: beautiful.

Atalanta Greek: the name of a swift runner in classical mythology.
Atlanta.
Atalia *See* Athalia.
Ata Marama Maori: moonlight.
Atanua Polynesian: a goddess of the dawn.
Atarah Hebrew: a crown. A name from the Old Testament.
Atara.
Atarapa Polynesian: of the dawn.
Atarau Maori: moonlight or a moonbeam.
Ateca/Atecah *See* Atika.
Atena *See* Athena.
Athalia Hebrew: God is exalted. A name from the Bible.
Atalia, Athalea, Athalee, Athali, Athalie (French), *Athelie.*
Athanasia Greek: immortal.
Athea The name of an Irish village.
Athia.
Athela Old English: noble.
Athena Greek: a wise woman. After Athene, the Greek goddess of wisdom.
Atena, Athenaios (Greek), *Athenais* (French), *Athene, Athène* (French), *Athenee, Athina, Athine, Atina.*
Atherine Either a feminine form of Arthur, or from Catherine.
Athereen, Atherene.
Atholene The feminine form of Athol, a Scottish placename.
Atholeen, Atholine, Athollene.

Athor *See* Hathor.
Atika Arabic/Indonesian: pure or clear.
Ateca, Atecah, Atica, Aticah, Atikah.
Atin Indonesian: a common girl's name.
Atiqa Arabic: noble.
Atira Hebrew: a prayer.
Atiya Arabic: a gift.
Atlanta *See* Atalanta.
Atsumi Japanese: warm and beautiful.
Attica Greek: the feminine form of Atticus, a man of Athens.
Attika.
Ature Polynesian: a fish.
Aubina/Aubine *See* Albina.
Aubrey Teutonic: the golden-haired ruler of the elves. Generally a boy's name.
Aubra, Aubrah, Aubree, Aubrian, Aubrianna, Aubrianne, Aubrie.
Audette Possibly a modern form of Audrey.
Audetta.
Audine Probably another modern form of Audrey.
Audean, Audeane, Audeen, Audeene, Audene, Audyne.
Audra *See* Audrey.
Audrey Old English: strong and noble, regal. *See also* Odrey.
Audey, Audra, Audray, Audree, Audrée (French), *Audri, Audrie, Audrienne, Audrina, Audry, Audrye, Awdree, Awdrey, Awdrie, Awdry.*
Diminutives: Aud, Audie, Dee.
Augusta Latin: majestic, or revered. The feminine form of Augustus.
Agostina (Italian), *August, Auguste* (French, German), *Augusteen* (Irish), *Augustina, Augustine, Augustyna, Awsta* (Welsh).
Diminutives: Gussie, Gusta, Tina.
Aura Greek: of the air. Latin: a gentle breeze.
Aure (French), *Aurea, Auria.*
Aurea *See* Aura and Aurelia.
Aurelia Latin: golden.
Aurea, Aurel, Aurela, Aurélie (French), *Aureol, Aureole, Auriel, Auriol, Auriole, Aurnia* (Irish), *Oralee, Oralia, Oralie, Orelia, Oriel, Orla* (Irish Gaelic).
Auria *See* Aura.
Auriga Babylonian: a constellation of the northern sky, representing a charioteer accompanied by goats.
Auristela Chilean: a golden star.
Aurnia *See* Aurelia.
Aurora Latin: daybreak. The goddess of the dawn and also an astronomical term.
Aurore (French).
Ausma Latvian: a suitable name for a girl born in the month of June.
Ausmah.
Austine A feminine form of Austin.
Austin, Austina, Austinia, Austyna, Austyne, Austynia.

Australia From the Latin word australis, meaning southern.
Austra, Austral, Australe, Australie.

Autumn Like Summer, a popular 'season name', particularly in the USA.
Autum.

Ava Greek: an eagle.
Aiva, Aivah, Avah, Ayva, Ayvah.

Avalina/Avaline *See* Aveline.

Avalon The legendary island where King Arthur is supposedly buried. Also a Sydney placename.
Avala, Avalah, Avalona, Avalonia, Avilion, Avilon.

Avan The name of an Armenian town and district.

Avani Sanskrit: of the good earth.

Avanti Italian: before or forward.
Avantie.

Avara Sanskrit: the youngest.

Avel Hebrew: breath.

Aveline Old French: from a placename. *See also* Evelyn.
Avalina, Avaline, Avelaine, Avelina, Aveling.

Avena Latin: from the oat field.
Avene.

Aventia/Aventina *See* Advent.

Avera Hebrew: a transgressor.
Abera, Aberah, Averah.

Averil Old English: the slayer of the boar.
Averel, Averell, Averill, Averyl, Avyril, Everil, Everild, Everilda, Everill.

Avery Old English: the ruler of the elves. Also a boy's name.
Averey, Averi, Averie.

Aveza *See* Avice.

Avia From Av, the fifth lunar month of the Hebrew calendar, encompassing July/August and corresponding to the astrological sign of Leo.
Aviana, Aviela.

Avice French: warlike.
Aveza, Avicia, Avis, Avisa.

Avilion/Avilon *See* Avalon.

Avirit Hebrew: of the air.

Avis Latin: a bird. Also a form of Avice.

Aviva Jewish: of the springtime.
Avivah.

Avoca Irish: a sweet valley.
Avoka.

Avonia The feminine form of Avon, the name of an English river.
Avona, Avonah, Avoniah.

Avril The French form of April.
Avrilette, Avryl, Avyril.

Avyril *See* Averil and Avril.

Awanata Native American: a turtle.

Awandela Native American: born at dawn.

Awatea Maori: daylight.

Awdree/Awdrey/Awdrie/Awdry *See* Audrey.

Awena/Awenia *See* Owena.

Awenita Native American: a fawn.

Awhina Maori: to embrace.

A – GIRLS

Awsta Welsh form of Augusta.
Awusi Ghanaian: born on a Sunday.
Axelle Teutonic: the father of peace. The feminine form of Axel.
Axella.
Aya Japanese: probably meaning colour or colourful.
Ayala Modern Hebrew: a deer.
Ayame Japanese: like an iris (the flower).
Ayanna African: a beautiful flower.
Ayaan, Ayann, Ayannah.
Ayao Ghanaian: born on a Thursday.
Ayda/Aydah *See* Ada.
Ayelet Hebrew: a gazelle.
Ayesha/Ayisha *See* Aisha.
Ayfara *See* Aphra.
Aygul Turkish: a moon rose.
Ayla Hebrew: an oak tree. Turkish: moonlight.
Ajla (Slavic), *Aylah.*
Aylce/Aylice *See* Alice.
Ayleen/Aylene *See* Eileen.
Aylin Turkish: the halo of the moon.
Aylwen Welsh: a fair brow.
Aymee/Aymi/Aymie *See* Amy.
Aynslea/Aynsley *See* Ainsley.
Ayoka Nigerian: one who brings joy.
Ayse Turkish form of Aisha.
Aysel Turkish: moonlight.
Aysen.
Aysu Turkish: moon water.
Aysun Turkish: as beautiful as the moon.
Ayumi Japanese: she who walks beautifully.
Ayushi A Sanskrit name of uncertain meaning.
Ayva/Ayvah *See* Ava.
Azalea Latin: dry earth. Teutonic: noble cheer. A 'flower name'.
Azalia, Azaliea, Azelia.
Azami Japanese: a thistle flower.
Azaria Hebrew: helped by God. Also a boy's name.
Azara, Azariah, Azeria, Zaria. Diminutive: Aza.
Azelias Hebrew: aided by God.
Azima Arabic: the feminine form of Azim (grand or glorious).
Aziza Arabic: the cherished one.
Azize.
Azora The name of the Aztec king Montezuma's daughter. *See also* Azura.
Azra Arabic: virginal.
Azucena Spanish from Arabic: a lily.
Asucena, Asusena, Asuzena, Azusena, Azuzena.
Azura Old French: from the Persian word for blue sky. Also after the gemstone, azurite.
Aszura, Aszure, Azora, Azure, Azuria, Azurina, Azurine, Azurite, Azzura, Azzure, Azzurra.
Azusa Arabic: a lily. Also a Japanese name of uncertain meaning.

B

Baadal *See* Badal.
Baadar *See* Bandar.
Baalu *See* Balu.
Baba African: born on a Thursday.
Babah.
Babara Hungarian form of Barbara.
Babette/Babita *See* Barbara.
Babinda Aboriginal: a mountain.
Badal Nepali: a cloud.
Baadal.
Badriyah Arabic: like the full moon.
Badra, Badria, Badriah, Badriya, Badriyya, Badriyyah.
Baha Splendour. The name of the Baha'i month encompassing 21 March–8 April, so a suitable name for an Aries girl.
Bahaa.
Bahara Sanskrit: springtime.
Bahaar (Arabic), *Bahar* (Arabic), *Baharah, Bahareh.*
Bahari Swahili: the sea.
Bahareh.
Bahati Swahili: good fortune.
Bai Chinese: pure, or white.
Baiba A Latvian name of uncertain meaning.
Baibre/Bairbre Irish Gaelic forms of Barbara.
Bailey Old French: a bailiff or administrative official. Also a boy's name.
Baila, Bailea, Bailee, Baileigh, Bailie, Bailiegh, Baillea, Baillee, Bailley, Baillie, Bailly, Baily,
Baylee, Bayley, Bayly.
Bailly The name of a crater on the moon. *See also* Bailey.
Bailley.
Baini Nepali: a younger sister.
Bahini.
Baka Sanskrit: a crane, implying longevity.
Bakah.
Bakana Aboriginal: a lookout.
Bakri Nepali: a female goat.
Baku The capital of the republic of Azerbaijan, on the Caspian Sea.
Bala Sanskrit: a young girl.
Bali The name of an Indonesian island.
Balu Nepali: a bear.
Baalu.
Bambalina Italian: a little girl.
Bambi.
Bambi *See* Bambalina.
Bambra Aboriginal: a mushroom.
Bami Aboriginal: a girl.
Banaz A region of Turkey.
Bandar Hindi: a monkey.
Baadar (Nepali).
Bandera Aboriginal: a reed.
Banksia A genus of Australian plants, named after botanist Sir Joseph Banks.
Banksea.
Banu Persian: a lady.
Baptista Latin: the baptised one.
Baptiste (French), *Batista* (Italian), *Bautista* (Spanish).
Barbara Latin: the foreigner or

stranger.
Babara (Hungarian), *Babette, Babita, Baibre* (Irish Gaelic), *Bairbre* (Irish Gaelic), *Barabal* (Scottish Gaelic), *Barabara, Barba* (Spanish), *Barbary, Barbe* (French), *Bärbel* (German), *Barbera, Barbetta, Barbette, Barbica* (Slavic), *Barbora* (Czech), *Barbra, Barbro* (Swedish), *Varvara* (Russian).
Diminutives: Babs, Barb, Barbi, Barbie, Basia (Polish), Biba.

Bärbel German form of Barbara.

Barbica *See* Barbara.

Bardot The surname of a legendary French actress (Brigitte Bardot).
Bardeau, Bardeaux, Bardo, Bardoe, Bardow.

Barika Swahili: successful.

Barina Aboriginal: the summit.

Barkha Nepali: summer.

Barossa Spanish: the name of a South Australian valley and wine region.
Barrosa.

Bartholomea Dutch: the feminine form of Batholomeus (*see* Bartholomew).
Bartholomia.
Diminutives: Barta, Bartha.

Basak Turkish: wheat.

Basanta Nepali: springtime.

Basema *See* Basimah.

Basia Polish diminutive of Barbara.

Basilia Greek: queenly, regal. The feminine form of Basil.
Basella, Basellia, Basile, Basilla, Basillia, Bosiljka (Slavic).

Basimah Arabic: the smiling one.
Basema, Basima, Basma, Bassema, Bassima, Bassimah.

Bathilde Teutonic: the commanding maiden of war.
Bathilda, Batilda, Batilde.

Bathsheba Hebrew: the daughter of the oath, or the seventh daughter. The wife of King David in the Bible.
Bathshira (Arabic), *Batsheva* (Jewish).

Bato Japanese: a mythological horse-headed goddess.

Batyah Modern Hebrew: the daughter of God.
Batya.

Baviera A Spanish surname.

Baylee/Bayley/Bayly *See* Bailey.

Bearnas *See* Berenice.

Beata Latin: blessed. *See also* Beatrice.
Beate.

Beatrice Latin: the blessed one; she who brings joy. Beatrix was the name of a 4th-century saint.
Beata, Beatrisa, Beatrise, Beatrix (German), *Beatriz* (Spanish), *Beitris* (Scottish Gaelic), *Betrice, Betrise, Betrize, Betrys* (Welsh), *Bicetta* (Italian), *Peata* (Maori).
Diminutives: Bea, Bee, Bice, Cettina (Italian), Trix, Trixey, Trixi,

Trixie, Trixy.
Beau French: beautiful.
Beaux, Bo.
Beauty One who is a delight to behold.
Beauté (French).
Bebel A diminutive of Isabel.
Bec *See* Bic. Also a diminutive of Rebecca.
Becca/Beck/Beckie/Becky *See* Rebecca.
Beda Old English: a warrior maiden.
Bedelia Old English: strength.
Beela Aboriginal: a black cockatoo.
Variation: Beelah.
Beena *See* Bina.
Beeree Aboriginal: a lagoon.
Bega Aboriginal: beautiful; a town in New South Wales. Also the name of a saint.
Begonia A 'flower name'.
Begona, Begonah, Begoniah.
Behira Hebrew: the brilliant one.
Beila Yiddish form of Bella and Belle.
Beith A form of Beth (*see* Elizabeth).
Beitris Scottish form of Beatrice.
Bek/Bekki/Bekkie/Bekky Diminutives of Rebecca.
Bel/Bela *See* Belle.
Belana/Belanna/Belanne *See* Bellanna.
Belda French: a beautiful lady.
Belém The Portuguese name for Bethlehem.
Belgin Turkish: clear.
Belgium A 'country name'.
Belina French: a goddess.
Beline.
Belinda Italian: beautiful.
Belindah, Bellinda, Bellynda, Belynda, Bilinda, Billinda, Billynda.
Diminutives: Bella, Belle, Linda, Lindy.
Belita Spanish: the beautiful one.
Belize Spanish: a Central American country.
Bella *See* Belinda and Belle.
Bellanna A combination of Belle and Anna.
Belana, Belanna, Belanne, Bellana, Bellanne.
Belle French: beautiful. Also a diminutive of Annabel, Arabella, Belinda, Isabel and Isabella.
Beila (Yiddish), *Bel, Bela, Bell, Bella, Bellana, Bellina, Bello* (Italian), *Bellino* (Italian), *Bellva, Bellve, Belva, Belvane, Belvia.*
Bellona Latin: the Roman goddess of war.
Belloma.
Bellynda/Belynda *See* Belinda.
Belmina A form of Belle.
Bellmina, Bellmine, Belmine.
Beltana Aboriginal: running water.
Beltane Celtic: the name of an ancient festival, held on 1 May, which celebrated the beginning of summer. Suitable for a Taurus

child.
Beluka Nepali: evening.
Belva/Belvane/Belvia *See* Belle.
Bena Hebrew: the wise one. Native American: a pheasant.
Benazir Arabic: unique.
Benazeer.
Benedicta Latin: blessed. The feminine form of Benedict.
Benedetta (Italian), *Benedikta* (Dutch, German), *Benedikte* (Danish), *Benicia* (Spanish), *Benita* (Italian), *Benite* (Spanish), *Benoite* (French), *Bente* (Danish).
Benicia Spanish form of Benedicta.
Benigna Spanish: the kind or benevolent one. The feminine form of Benigno.
Benilda Latin: benign; of good intentions.
Benita/Benite/Benoite *See* Benedicta.
Benvinda The feminine form of Benvindo, a Brazilian name of uncertain meaning.
Beoline An African name of uncertain meaning.
Bercu Turkish: sweet smelling.
Berdine Teutonic: a glorious maiden.
Berendena/Berendiena/Berendina *See* **Bernadette.**
Bérengère French: possibly meaning a glorious spear.
Berengar, Berengaria.
Berenice Greek: the bringer of victory. *See also* Veronica.
Bearnas (Scottish Gaelic), *Bereniece, Berice, Bernice, Berniece, Bernyce, Berrice, Burnice, Fereniki* (Greek), *Nicetta* (Italian), *Pherenike* (Greek).
Diminutives: Berni, Bernie, Berny, Berri, Berrie, Berry, Burni, Burnie, Cettina (Italian).
Berga Teutonic: from the mountain.
Bergia.
Beril *See* Beryl.
Berimilla Aboriginal: a kingfisher.
Bermilla.
Berit A Scandinavian form of Birgit (*see* Bridget).
Berle *See* Beryl.
Berlina Either a variation of Beryl, or after the German city of Berlin.
Berlyl *See* Beryl.
Berna Turkish: young. *See also* Bernadette.
Bernadette French from Teutonic: as brave as a bear. The feminine form of Bernard and the name of a saint.
Berendena, Berendene Berendiena, Berendina, Berendine, Berna, Bernadene, Bernadina, Bernadine, Bernarda, Bernardetta (Italian), *Bernardette, Bernardica, Bernardika, Bernardina, Bernardine, Berneen* (Irish), *Bernetta, Bernita, Burnadette.*
Diminutives: Bern, Bernie, Berri, Berrie, Berry, Burni, Burnie.

Bernia Old English: a maiden of battle.
Bernice/Bernyce *See* Berenice.
Bernina A peak in the Swiss Alps.
Bernita *See* Bernadette.
Berrel/Berrell *See* Beryl.
Berri Aboriginal: a bush; the name of a town in South Australia. Also a short form of Berenice and Bernadette.
Berrie, Berry.
Berrice *See* Berenice.
Berry Old English: a fruit or berry. Also a diminutive of Berenice and Bernadette.
Berri, Berrie.
Berta/Berte *See* Bertha and Gilberta.
Bertana Aboriginal: the day.
Bertha Teutonic: bright and shining. *See also* Roberta.
Berta (German, Polish), *Berte, Berthe* (French), *Berther, Bertia, Bertina, Bertine.*
Diminutives: Bertie, Berty.
Berthilda Old English: a shining warrior maid.
Berthilde, Bertilda, Bertilde, Bertilla.
Bertia/Bertina/Bertine *See* Bertha.
Bertrude Teutonic: the name a 7th-century Frankish queen.
Berwyn Welsh: fair-haired, or a bright friend.
Berwin, Berwinn, Berwinne, Berwynn, Berwynne.

Beryan Cornish: the name of a saint.
Beryl Greek: a precious green jewel.
Beril, Berle, Berlina, Berlyl, Berrel, Berrell, Berylda, Beryle, Berylida, Berylyn.
Besa Albanian: faith or faithful.
Bess/Bessie/Bessy *See* Elizabeth.
Beth A diminutive of Elizabeth and names beginning with Beth.
Bethan Welsh diminutive of Elizabeth.
Diminutive: Beth.
Bethany Hebrew: a house of poverty. A placename from the New Testament.
Bethanie, Bethannie, Bethanny, Bethenie, Bethennie, Bethenny, Betheny.
Diminutive: Beth.
Bethel Hebrew: the house of God.
Bethell, Bethelle.
Diminutive: Beth.
Bethesda Hebrew: a house of mercy. A place mentioned in the Bible.
Bethia Hebrew: a daughter of God.
Bethulah Hebrew: an abundant harvest. An alternative name for Virgo, the Roman goddess of justice.
Bethula, Betula, Betulah.
Bethwynn An unusual 'combination name'. From Beth (*see* Elizabeth) and Wynn, meaning the fair or blessed one.
Bethwin, Bethwinn, Bethwinne, Bethwyn, Bethwynne.

B – Girls

Diminutive: Beth.
Beti *See* Elizabeth.
Betina/Betine/Bettina/Bettine
See Elizabeth.
Diminutive: Tina.
Betna The name of a river in Bangladesh.
Betrice/Betrise/Betrize
See Beatrice.
Betrys Welsh form of Beatrice.
Betsey/Betsi/Betsy Diminutives of Elizabeth.
Bette/Bettie/Betty/Bettye
See Elizabeth.
Betula/Betulah *See* Bethulah.
Beulah Hebrew: the married one. A biblical placename.
Beula.
Beverley Old English: from the stream of the beaver. Originally a surname.
Beverlea, Beverlee, Beverleigh, Beverli, Beverlie, Beverly.
Diminutive: Bev.
Bevin Irish Gaelic: sweet-voiced, melodious.
Beyoncé The name of a popular American singer and actor.
Bhadra Nepali: the gentle one.
Bhura Hindi: brown.
Bian Vietnamese: secretive, or hidden.
Bianca Italian form of Blanche. Used by Shakespeare for characters in two of his plays. *See also* Blondelle.
Biancah, Bianka, Biankah.
Biara Aboriginal: the moon.
Biarah.
Biba A diminutive of Barbara.
Bibi Arabic: a lady.
Bibiana Italian: to live.
Bic Chinese: green, like jade.
Bec.
Bice *See* Beatrice.
Bicetta Italian form of Beatrice.
Biddy Irish diminutive of Bridget.
Biddie.
Bihana Nepali: of the morning.
Bijana A Slavic name of uncertain meaning.
Bijou French: a jewel.
Bijoux.
Bilge Turkish: the wise one.
Bilinda/Billinda/Billynda
See Belinda.
Billa Aboriginal: a fish.
Billi Hindi: like a cat. *See also* Billie.
Billie Teutonic: a wise ruler or protector. The feminine form of Billy and William, and also a diminutive of Wilhelmina.
Bille, Billee, Billi, Billy, Billye.
Billiejo A combination of Billie and Jo (*see* Joanne). Also a boy's name.
Billeejo, Billee-Jo, Billeejoe, Billee-Joe, Billie-Jo, Billijo, Billi-Jo, Billijoe, Billi-Joe, Billyjo, Billy-Jo, Billyjoe, Billy-Joe.
Bina Hebrew: intelligence, understanding. Sanskrit: a musical instrument. Also a diminutive of

Albina and Sabina.
Beena.
Binda Aboriginal: deep water.
Bindi From an Aboriginal word, meaning a plant with burrs.
Bindea, Bindee, Bindey, Bindie, Bindy.
Bingarra Aboriginal: a creek.
Binita *See* Vinita.
Binnie Celtic: a wicker basket.
Binney, Binni, Binny.
Binya Aboriginal: a mountain.
Bipasha *See* Vipasha.
Birdie Modern English/American: a little bird.
Birdette, Birdey, Birdy.
Birgit/Birgitta/Birgitte Scandinavian forms of Bridget.
Birkita Basque form of Bridget.
Birra Aboriginal: a whitewood tree.
Bira.
Birte Danish diminutive of Birgitta (*see* Bridget).
Bisera Slavic: a pearl.
Biserka.
Björk Icelandic: a birch tree.
Byerk.
Blaike *See* Blake.
Blaine Irish Gaelic: thin, slender.
Blain, Blainey, Blane, Blaney, Blayne, Blayney.
Blair Scottish Gaelic: from the plain. Also a boy's name.
Blaire, Blayr, Blayre.
Blaise Latin: she who stammers.
Blaize, Blasa, Blasia, Blayz, Blayze, Blaze, Blazena (Slavic).
Blaize *See* Blaise and Blaze.
Blake Old English: fair-haired.
Blaike, Blayke.
Blanche Old French: fair-haired, or of a fair complexion. *See also* Bianca and Blondelle.
Bianca (Italian), *Blanca* (Spanish), *Blanch, Blanchard, Blancharde, Blanka* (Czech, Polish), *Blinnie* (Irish).
Blandina French: the name of an early saint.
Blandine.
Blane/Blaney *See* Blaine.
Blanka *See* Blanche.
Blasa/Blasia *See* Blaise.
Blayke *See* Blake.
Blayne/Blayney *See* Blaine.
Blayr/Blayre *See* Blair.
Blaze Old English: a bright fire or flame. Also a form of Blaise.
Blaize, Blayz, Blayze, Blazey, Blazie.
Blazena Slavic form of Blaise.
Blenn Welsh: a hill.
Blen, Blenne.
Blessing Middle English: one who brings happiness.
Bless, Blesse.
Bleu French form of Blue.
Bliss Old English: joy, gladness.
Blisse, Blyss, Blysse.
Blith/Blithe *See* Blythe.
Blodwen Welsh: a white flower, or blessed flower.

Blodwyn.
Blondelle French: the little blond or fair one. *See also* Bianca and Blanche.
Diminutives: Blondie, Blondine.
Blossom Old English: a flower or bloom.
Blue A modern 'colour name'.
Bleu (French), *Blu.*
Bluebell An unusual 'flower name'.
Blythe Old English: joyous and cheerful.
Variations: Blith, Blithe, Blyth.
Bo Chinese: precious. *See also* Beau.
Boadee/Boadie/Boady *See* Bodie.
Boann Irish Gaelic: the name of a Celtic water goddess.
Boanna, Boanne.
Bobbi/Bobbie/Bobby *See* Roberta.
Bodi Hungarian: God protects. *See also* Bodie.
Bodie A modern name, more commonly given to boys but now popular for girls.
Boadee, Boadi, Boadie, Boadey, Boady, Bode, Bodee, Bodeen, Bodene, Bodey, Bodhi, Bodi, Bodine, Bowdee, Bowdey, Bowdi, Bowdie.
Bodil Old Norse: a battle maiden.
Bogdana Slavic: the feminine form of Bogdan, meaning a gift from God.
Bogna.
Diminutive: Dana.
Bojana Slavic: the feminine form of Bojan, a warrior.
Bombala Aboriginal: a place where the waters meet. Can also be a boy's name.
Bona Latin: good.
Bonne (French).
Boni/Bonni/Bonnie/Bonny English/Scottish: fine, pretty. *See also* Bonita.
Bonita Spanish: pretty.
Diminutives: Boni, Bonni, Bonnie, Bonny, Nita.
Bonne *See* Bona.
Bonnieanna A combination of Bonnie and Anna (grace).
Bonnieanne, Bonnyanna, Bonnyanne.
Boo Generally a nickname, but an official name of one of chef Jamie Oliver's daughters.
Boorah Aboriginal: a kite or hawk.
Boora.
Borislava Russian: the feminine form of Borlslav (a famous warrior).
Boronia A 'plant name'.
Boshra An Arabic name of uncertain meaning.
Bosiljka Slavic form of Basilia.
Bowdee/Bowdey/Bowdi/Bowdie *See* Bodie.
Bozena Slavic: the favoured one.
Bozenah, Bozenka, Bozenna, Bozennah.
Diminutive: Bozica.
Bozka Slavic: a divine gift.

Brabazon Old French: a surname, probably meaning from the wooded land.
Brady Irish Gaelic: from an old surname.
Bradea, Bradee, Bradie, Braydea, Braydee, Braydie, Braydy.
Brandice/Brandie *See* Brandy.
Brandy Dutch: brandy, fine wine. Also a feminine form of Brandon.
Brandea, Brandee, Brandi, Brandice, Brandie.
Branislava/Branislawa *See* Bronislava.
Branka A diminutive of Bronislava.
Branwen Welsh: beautiful, or a holy raven.
Brangwen, Brangwyn, Brangwynne.
Braydee/Braydie *See* Brady.
Bre/Brea/Breah *See* Bree and Briana.
Brean/Breane See Bryn.
Breanah/Breanna/Breanne/ Breannon *See* Briana.
Brearne *See* Briana.
Breda A city in the Netherlands. Also a form of Bridget.
Breeda.
Bree A diminutive of Bridget and Briana, but also an independent name.
Bre, Brea, Breah, Brei, Brie.
Breean/Breeanen/Breeanna/ Breearna *See* Briana.
Breen/Brene *See* Bryn.
Breena *See* Brina.
Breeze English from Spanish: a light wind, implying someone who is carefree. Also a boy's name.
Breese, Breez, Breeza, Breezah, Briza, Brizah.
Brei *See* Bree.
Brenda Irish Gaelic: a raven. Old Norse: a flaming sword.
Brendah, Brinda, Brindah.
Brenley Old Norse: burning wood.
Brenlea, Brenlee, Brenleigh, Brenly, Brinlea, Brinlee, Brinleigh, Brinley, Brinly, Brynlea, Brynlee, Brynley, Brynlie.
Brenna Irish Gaelic: raven-haired.
Breta *See* Bridget.
Brettelle A feminine form of Brett, meaning a Breton.
Bretell, Bretella, Bretelle, Brettell, Brettella.
Briallen Welsh: a primrose.
Briella, Brielle, Brijelle, Bryallen, Bryella, Bryelle.
Briana Celtic: noble, honourable. The feminine form of Brian.
Breanah, Breanna, Breanne, Breannon, Brearne, Breeama, Breean, Breeanen, Breeanna, Bree-Anna, Breearna, Briahna, Briahne, Briann, Brianna, Brianne, Briarna, Brieana, Brieann, Brieanna, Brieanne, Brienna, Brina, Bryana, Bryanah, Bryann, Bryanna,

Bryannah, Bryanne.
Diminutives: Bre, Brea, Bree, Bria, Brie.
Briar Middle English: a thorny plant.
Briare, Bryar, Bryare.
Briar-Rose A pretty 'flower name', meaning a thorny rose.
Brice *See* Bryce.
Bríd/Bridey *See* Bridget.
Bridget Irish Gaelic/Celtic: strong, spirited; an ancient Celtic goddess. St Brigid is one of Ireland's patron saints.
Berit (Scandinavian), *Birgit* (Scandinavian), *Birgitta* (Scandinavian), *Birgitte* (Scandinavian), *Birkita* (Basque), *Breda* (Irish), *Bríd* (Irish Gaelic), *Bridged, Bridgenia, Bridgid, Brigett, Brigette, Brighid* (Irish Gaelic), *Brigid* (Irish), *Brigida* (Italian, Spanish), *Brigidine, Brigit, Brigitta* (Scandinavian), *Brigitte* (French, German), *Brita, Britt* (Swedish), *Brygida* (Polish), *Piritta* (Estonian, Finnish), *Pirkko* (Finnish).
Diminutives: Biddie, Biddy, Birte (Danish), Bree, Breta, Bridey (Irish), Bridgie, Bridie (Irish), Brie, Briege (Irish Gaelic), Brydie, Pirjo (Estonian, Finnish).
Bridie *See* Bridget.
Brie *See* Bree, Briana and Bridget.
Brieana/Brieanna/Brienna *See* Briana.
Briege Irish Gaelic diminutive of Brighid and Brigid.
Briella/Brielle *See* Briallen.
Brigantia Celtic: a mythological goddess who was associated with water, healing, prosperity and war. Her festival was held from 31 January to 2 February each year.
Brigette/Brigid/Brigidine/Brigitte *See* Bridget.
Brihspati A Sanskrit name for the planet Jupiter.
Brispati.
Brijelle *See* Briallen.
Brilea/Brilee/Brileigh/Briley *See* **Brylie.**
Brin/Brinn/Brinne *See* Bryn.
Brina Hebrew: the seventh. *See also* Briana and Bryna.
Breena.
Brinda/Brindah *See* Brenda.
Brindabella Possibly from an Aboriginal word; the name of a New South Wales mountain range.
Brinlee/Brinleigh/Brinley/Brinly *See* Brenley.
Briolette French: a pear-shaped gemstone.
Brioletta.
Briony *See* Bryony.
Briot The name of a village in France.
Brishti Sanskrit: rain.
Bristol Old English: the site of a fort. The name of a British city.

Bristole, Bristoll, Bristolle.
Britney *See* Brittany.
Britt A Swedish form of Bridget.
Brita, Britelle, Britta, Brittelle.
Brittany Latin: Britain. Also the name of a French province.
Britnee, Britney, Britnie, Brittania, Britteny, Brittnee, Brittney, Brittni.
Briza *See* Breeze.
Brodie Irish Gaelic: a ditch. Also a boy's name.
Brodea, Brodee, Brodey, Brody.
Brodie-Lee A combination of Brodie and Lee (a meadow or clearing).
Brodee-Lea, Brodee-Lee, Brodee-Leigh, Brodey-Lea, Brodey-Lee, Brodey-Leigh, Brodie-Lea, Brody-Lea, Brody-Lee, Brody-Leigh.
Brohnwyn *See* Bronwen.
Bromwyn *See* Bronwen.
Brona Irish: sorrow.
Brongwen/Brongwyn/ Brongwynne *See* Bronwen.
Bronislava Slavic: the feminine form of Bronislav, meaning glorious protection.
Branislava, Branislawa, Bronislawa.
Diminutive: Branka.
Bronnen Cornish: a rush.
Brontë English: from the surname of the Brontë sisters, novelists Anne, Charlotte and Emily.
Bronte, Brontee, Brontey, Brontie, Bronty.
Bronwen Welsh: white- or fair-breasted.
Brohnwyn, Brohnwynn, Brohwynne, Bromwyn, Bromwynn, Bromwynne, Brongwen, Brongwyn, Brongwynn, Brongwynne, Bronwenn, Bronwenne, Bronwyn, Bronwynn, Bronwynne.
Diminutives: Bron, Bronnie.
Brony Possibly a form of Bryony.
Bronee, Bronie, Broney.
Bronya Slavic: armour, protection.
Brook Old English: at the brook.
Brooke.
Brooklyn The name of a New York suburb.
Brooklin, Brooklinn, Brooklinne, Brooklynn, Brooklynne.
Broula Aboriginal: trickling water. A New South Wales placename.
Bruella/Bruelle *See* Brunella.
Bruna Teutonic: brown, or dark-haired. The feminine form of Bruno. *See also* Brunella.
Brunetta (French), *Brunette, Brunia, Bruno, Brunon, Burnetta.*
Brunella Teutonic/Italian: brown-haired. *See also* Bruna.
Bruella, Bruelle, Brunelle, Brunil, Brunila, Brunile, Brunill, Brunilla, Brunille.
Brunhilde Teutonic: an armed

warrior maiden. A warrior queen in Germanic legend.
Brunhild, Brunhilda, Brynhild, Brynhilde, Brynhildur (Icelandic).

Bryallen/Bryella/Bryelle *See* Briallen.

Bryana/Bryann/Bryannah/Bryanne *See* Briana.

Bryar/Bryare *See* Briar.

Bryce Celtic: the freckled one.
Brice, Bryz, Bryze.

Brydie *See* Bridget.

Brygida *See* Bridget.

Bryher Celtic: the name of one of the Isles of Scilly, off the coast of Cornwall.

Brylie Possibly a combination of Bryony and Lee.
Brilea, Brilee, Brileigh, Briley, Brylea, Brylee, Bryleigh, Bryley.

Bryn Welsh: a hill.
Brean, Breane, Breen, Brene, Brin, Brinn, Brinne, Brynn, Brynne.

Bryna Irish: strength.
Brina.

Brynhild/Brynhildur *See* Brunhilde.

Brynlea/Brynlee/Brynley/Brynlie *See* Brenley.

Bryony Greek: a vine-like plant.
Brihoney, Briohny, Brionee, Brioney, Brionie, Briony, Bryonee, Bryonia, Bryonie.

Bryz/Bryze *See* Bryce.

Buena Spanish: good.
Bueno, Buona.

Buffy Native American: a buffalo. Also a diminutive of Elizabeth.

Bunda Aboriginal: a mountain.

Bundarra Aboriginal: a kangaroo or wallaby.
Bunderra.

Bunjil Aboriginal: a falcon.

Bunny English: a little rabbit.
Bunnie.

Bunty English: originally a pet name, perhaps meaning a lamb.
Buntee, Buntie.

Buona *See* Buena.

Burilda Aboriginal: a black swan.

Burnadette/Burni/Burnie *See* Berenice and Bernadette.

Burnetta *See* Bruna.

Burnice *See* Berenice.

Buttercup A flower name.

Butterfly Old English: a brightly coloured insect.

C

Cacelie *See* Cecilia.

Cacilda A Brazilian name of uncertain meaning.

Caddie/Caddy *See* Cadence.

Cadence Latin: rhythmic.
Cadena, Cadenza (Italian), *Caydance, Caydence, Kadence, Kaidance, Kaidence, Kaydance, Kaydence.*
Diminutives: Caddie, Caddy.

Cadi Welsh form of Catherine.
Caecilia *See* Cecilia.
Cael *See* Cale.
Caelan/Caelen/Caelyn *See* Kalan.
Caelin *See* Caillin.
Caesaria/Caesarina/Caesarine *See* Cesarina.
Cagla Turkish: like an almond.
Cahaya Indonesian: like a light.
Cahill/Cail *See* Cale.
Cai Vietnamese: a woman.
Cailee/Caileigh/Cailey/Cailie *See* Caley.
Cailin *See* Caillin and Colleen.
Caillin Welsh: the peacemaker.
Caelin, Cailin, Cailinn, Caillyn, Cailyn, Caylin, Cayllin, Caylyn, Caylynn.
Cairine *See* Catherine.
Cairistìona Scottish Gaelic form of Christina.
Cairo From Arabic: the capital of Egypt. Also a boy's name.
Kairo.
Cait Irish Gaelic form of Kate.
Caitlin Irish Gaelic form of Catherine. *See also* Kathleen.
Caitlan, Caitlyn, Catlan, Catlin, Catlyn, Catlynn, Kaitlin, Kaitlinn, Kaitlyn, Katelin, Katelinn, Katelinne, Katelyn, Kate-Lynn, Katelynn, Katelynne.
Caja Cornish: a daisy.
Caya, Cayah, Kaia, Kaiah, Kaiya, Kaja, Kaya, Kayaa, Kya, Kyah, Kyha.

Calais The name of a French seaport.
Kalais.
Calan/Calen *See* Kalan.
Calandra Greek: a lark. *See also* Kalli.
Calandre (French), *Calandria* (Spanish), *Kalandra.*
Calantha Greek: a beautiful blossom.
Calanthe (French), *Kalantha.*
Calca Aboriginal: a star.
Cale Probably from Caley, an Irish name meaning slender.
Cael, Cahill, Cail, Kael, Kail, Kale.
Caleda *See* Calida.
Caledonia Latin: a woman from Scotland.
Caledonie.
Caley Irish Gaelic: slender; also a boy's name. *See also* Kayley.
Cailee, Caileigh, Cailey, Cailie, Calee, Calie, Caly, Caylee, Cayley.
Calico A cotton fabric.
Calicoh, Caliko, Calikoh, Callico, Kalico, Kallico.
Calida Latin: warm and loving.
Caleda, Callida.
California The name of an American state. Also a boy's name.
Calipso *See* Calypso.
Calista Greek: the most beautiful one.
Calise, Caliste, Callise, Callista, Calliste, Callyce, Callyse, Kalista,

Kallista.
Calla Greek: beautiful.
Calleen Aboriginal: fresh water.
Callia *See* Calliope.
Callidora Greek: the gift of beauty.
Calliope Greek: a beautiful voice. The muse of poetry in Greek mythology.
Callia, Calliopi, Kalliope (Greek), *Kalliopi.*
Callise/Callista/Calliste *See* Calista.
Callisto Greek: a mythological nymph.
Kallisto.
Callula Latin: the beautiful little one.
Callyce/Callyse *See* Calista.
Calogera Italian: the feminine form of Calogero, a 5th-century saint.
Caloris Greek: a geographical feature of the planet Mercury.
Calpurnia Latin: one of the wives of Julius Caesar.
Calphurnia, Kalpurnia.
Caly *See* Caley.
Calyn *See* Kalan.
Calypso Greek: a legendary sea nymph. Also a West Indian style of music.
Calipso, Kalipso, Kalypso.
Cam Vietnamese: sweet.
Cambelle A feminine form of Campell, meaning a crooked mouth.
Cambell, Cambella, Campbella, Campbelle.
Cambria Latin: an ancient name for Wales.
Camella *See* Camilla.
Camellia A flower name.
Camelia.
Cameo Italian: an engraved gem.
Kameo.
Cameron Scottish Gaelic: a crooked nose.
Camren, Camron, Camryn, Kameron, Kamryn.
Diminutives: Cam, Camm, Cammie.
Camilla Latin: from a Roman family name, possibly meaning noble.
Camella, Camila (Spanish), *Camilia, Camille* (French), *Kamila* (Czech, Polish).
Diminutives: Milli, Millie, Milly.
Camira Aboriginal: of the wind.
Campbella/Campbelle *See* Cambelle.
Camren/Camryn *See* Cameron.
Canace Greek: the daughter of the wind.
Kanace.
Canada A 'country name'.
Canan Turkish: beloved.
Cana.
Candace Possibly meaning brilliant white. The name of several queens of Ethiopia, and mentioned in the Bible.
Candice, Candis, Candiss,

Candus, Canduss, Candyce, Candyse, Chandace, Chandice, Kandace, Kandice, Kandyce.
Diminutives: Candi, Candie, Candy, Kandi, Kandie, Kandy, Khandi, Khandy.
Candi The female equivalent of the Hindu moon god, Chandra. Also a diminutive of Candace and Candida.
Candia Greek: an ancient placename.
Candida Latin: white.
Candide (French).
Diminutives: Candi, Candie, Candy.
Candis/Candiss *See* Candace.
Candra Latin: luminescent. *See also* Chandra.
Candus/Canduss *See* Candace.
Candy English: the sweet one. Also a diminutive of Candace and Candida.
Candi, Candie, Kandi, Kandie, Kandy, Khandi, Khandy.
Candyce/Candyse *See* Candace.
Canna Latin: a reed. A 'plant name'.
Cansu Turkish: the water of life.
Caoimhe Irish Gaelic: lovely.
Capella Latin: from capra, meaning a she-goat. Suitable for a Capricorn child.
Capelle.
Capra Latin: a she-goat. *See also* Capella and Caprice.
Caprah.
Capri An Italian island.

Capril.
Caprice Italian: unpredictable, whimsical.
Capra, Kapra, Kaprice.
Capricornia An ideal name for a Capricorn girl.
Capricorna.
Cara Cornish: love. Irish Gaelic: a friend. Italian: the beloved one.
Carah, Caralie, Careen, Carina, Carine, Carinna, Carinne, Carita, Caro, Cartia, Carylee, Carylie, Kara, Karah, Karalee, Karalie.
Carabella Italian: the beautiful beloved one.
Carabelle.
Caragh Irish: love.
Caralie *See* Cara.
Caralyn A combination of Cara and Lynn.
Cara-Lyn, Caralynn, Cara-Lynn, Caralynne, Cara-Lynne.
Caramella Italian: sweet. *See also* Carmel.
Caran *See* Karen.
Carden Irish Gaelic: from the black fortress. Also a boy's name.
Cardene, Cardin, Cardine.
Cardinia Aboriginal: the dawn.
Careen A character in Margaret Mitchell's *Gone with the Wind*. *See also* Cara.
Careena/Careenah *See* Carina.
Carel *See* Carol.
Caren/Carin *See* Karen.

Carensa/Carenza *See* Kerensa.
Caressa *See* Caresse and Carissa.
Caresse French: an embrace.
Caress, Caressa, Carezza (Italian).
Carey Celtic: from the river. Irish: the name of a castle. Also a boy's name.
Caree, Carie, Karee, Karey, Karie.
Cari Turkish: flowing like water.
Carice *See* Carissa.
Caridad *See* Charity.
Carilla *See* Carla and Carol.
Carina Aboriginal: a bride. The name of a southern constellation. *See also* Cara.
Careena, Careenah, Carinah, Carinna, Carinne.
Carine/Carinne *See* Cara and Carina.
Carinthia A region of Austria.
Carisma *See* Charisma.
Carissa Latin: the most beloved one.
Caressa, Carice, Carisa, Carise, Cariss, Carisse, Carisso, Carita, Karis, Karisa, Karise, Karissa.
Carita/Caritas *See* Cara, Carissa and Charity.
Carla A feminine form of Charles, meaning a free man. *See also* Carol, Caroline and Charlotte.
Carilla (Spanish), *Carlah, Carlee, Carleen* (Irish), *Carleigh, Carlene, Carletta, Carlin, Carlita, Kaarla, Kaarle, Karla, Karlah, Kharla. Diminutives:* Carley, Carlie, Carly, Karlee, Karley, Karly.

Carlan *See* Carlin.
Carlee/Carleen *See* Carla and Carlin.
Carleen A form of Carla or Carlin.
Carlene, Karleen, Karlene.
Carletta *See* Carla.
Carley/Carlie/Carly *See* Carla, Caroline and Charlotte.
Carlin Cornish: from the fort by the pool. Irish Gaelic: the little champion. *See also* Carla and Caroline.
Carlan, Carleen, Carlene, Carlyn.
Carlina/Carline Italian forms of Caroline.
Carlita *See* Carla.
Carlota/Carlotta *See* Charlotte.
Carlyn *See* Carlin.
Carlyon Cornish: from the slate works. Also a boy's name.
Carleon.
Carma *See* Karma.
Carman *See* Carmel.
Carmé Greek: one of Jupiter's satellites.
Karmé.
Carmel Hebrew: a garden or orchard. The name of a mountain in the Bible.
Caramella, Carman, Carmela (Italian), *Carmelina* (Italian), *Carmeline, Carmelita* (Spanish), *Carmella, Carmellao, Carmen* (Spanish), *Carmena, Carmencita, Carmenita, Carmia, Carmiel, Carmilla, Carmita, Karmel,*

Karmen.
Diminutives: Melina, Mell, Melli, Mellie, Melly.
Carmella *See* Carmel.
Carmen/Carmena/Carmencita *See* Carmel and Carmine.
Carmia/Carmiel/Carmilla/ Carmita *See* Carmel.
Carmine Spanish: crimson.
Carmena, Carmene, Carmina, Carmyne, Karmene, Karmina, Karmine.
Carna Hebrew: a horn.
Carnation A 'flower name'.
Carnelian A 'gemstone name'.
Variation: Cornelian.
Caro Spanish: the dear or beloved one. *See also* Cara and Caroline.
Carro.
Carol A feminine form of Charles, meaning a free man. *See also* Carla, Caroline and Charlotte.
Carel, Carilla (Spanish), *Carola, Carole* (French), *Caroll, Carroll, Carryl, Caryl, Karel, Karol, Karola, Karyl, Karyle.*
Carol-Lea A combination of Carol and Lea (a meadow or clearing).
Carol-Lee, Carol-Leigh.
Caroline A feminine form of Charles, a free man. *See also* Carla, Carol, Carrie and Charlotte.
Carlin (Italian), *Carlina* (Italian), *Carline, Carolan, Carolann, Caroleen, Carolen, Carolina* (Italian), *Carollyne, Carolyn, Carolyne, Carylin, Caryline, Carylon, Carylyn, Carylyne, Charlaine, Charleen, Charlene, Charline, Charlyne, Kararaina* (Maori), *Karleena, Karlena, Karlene, Karolen, Karolin, Karolina* (Polish, Scandinavian), *Karoline* (German), *Karolyn, Karolynn, Karolynne, Sharleen, Sharleine, Sharlene.*
Diminutives: Carleigh, Carley, Carlie, Carly, Caro, Carri, Carrie, Karrie, Lena, Lina, Lyn, Lynn.
Carollyne/Carolyn/Carolyne *See* Caroline.
Caron An unusual girl's name, derived from the surname of actress Leslie Caron.
Carone, Caronn, Caronne.
Carpentaria A northern Australian gulf.
Carrie Originally a diminutive of Caroline.
Carri, Kaari, Kaarie, Kari, Karri, Karrie.
Carro *See* Caro.
Carrol *See* Carol.
Carryl Welsh: love. *See also* Carol.
Caryl.
Carson Old English: the son or daughter of the marsh dweller.
Carrsen, Carrson, Carsen.
Carter Old English: a cart maker or driver. More commonly a boy's name.
Cartia *See* Cara.

Cartier A famous French jewellery company.
Carullo An unusual name from the Philippines.
Carylee/Carylie *See* Cara.
Carylin/Caryline/Carylon/Carylyne *See* Caroline.
Caryn *See* Karen.
Carys Welsh: the beloved one.
Cerys.
Casey Irish Gaelic: the vigilant one. Also a boy's name.
Casee, Casie, Kacee, Kacie, Kaisee, Kaisey, Kaisie, Kasey, Kasie, Kaycee, Kayci, Kaycie.
Cashmira *See* Kashmira.
Cass/Cassie *See* Cassandra.
Cassandra Greek: in legend, a Trojan princess with the gift of prophecy.
Casandra, Cassandre (French), *Kasandra, Kassandra.*
Diminutives: Cass, Cassie, Kass, Kassie.
Cassia Hebrew: the cassia tree, a variety of cinnamon. *See also* Kezia.
Cassidy Irish Gaelic: the clever one.
Kassidy.
Cassiel The angel of Saturday.
Cassina The name of several Italian towns.
Casina, Casintha, Cassintha.
Casta Latin: pure and modest.
Castalia Greek: a mythological figure.
Caster Old English: a Roman site. *Kaster.*
Catalina/Catarina *See* Catherine.
Catalonia Spanish: a region of Spain.
Cate/Catena/Caterina/Cath *See* Catherine.
Cathay An archaic name for China.
Cathee/Cathie Diminutives of Catherine.
Catherine Greek: pure. A 4th-century saint who was martyred on a wheel. *See also* Catrice, Kate, Katherine and Kathleen.
Aikaterini (Greek), *Cadi* (Welsh), *Cairine* (Gaelic), *Caitlin* (Irish Gaelic), *Caitrin* (Irish Gaelic), *Catalina* (Spanish), *Catarina* (Portuguese), *Caterina* (Italian), *Catharina, Catharine, Catherina, Catheryn, Catheryne, Cathrine, Cathriona, Cathro, Cathryn, Catrenia, Catrien, Catrin* (Welsh), *Catrina, Catriona* (Gaelic), *Cattarina* (Italian), *Ekaterina* (Russian), *Ekaterini* (Greek).
Diminutives: Cait, Cate, Catena, Catey, Cath, Cathee, Cathie, Cathy, Catina (Spanish), Cato (Dutch), Caty, Cayt, Cayte, Kate, Kerry, Treena, Trina, Triona.
Cathleen/Cathlene *See* Kathleen.
Cathlyn A combination of Catherine and Lynn.
Cathlin, Cathlinn, Cathlinne, Cathlynn, Cathlynne.

Cathlyn-Rose An unusual 'combination name'.
Cathrine/Cathro *See* Catherine.
Cathy *See* Catherine.
Catina Spanish diminutive of Catalina (*see* Catherine).
Catlan/Catlin/Catlyn/Catlynn *See* Caitlin.
Cato Dutch diminutive of Catherine.
Kato.
Catrenia *See* Catherine.
Catrice A modern form of Catherine.
Catrece, Katrece, Katrice.
Catrin/Catrina *See* Catherine.
Catriona Gaelic form of Catherine.
Cawana Aboriginal: a turtle.
Caya *See* Caja.
Cayam Hebrew: like the sea, or existence.
Caydance/Caydence *See* Cadence.
Cayla Hebrew: a crown of laurel.
Caylee/Cayley *See* Caley.
Caylin/Cayllin/Caylynn *See* Caillin.
Cayt/Cayte Diminutives of Catherine.
Ceara Irish Gaelic: a spear. *See also* Chiara.
Cearah.
Cecilia Latin: the blind one, or the sixth. The feminine form of Cecil and the patron saint of music. *See also* Sheila.
Cacelie (German), *Caecilia,*
Cecelia, Cecelie, Cecelle, Cecely,
Cécile (French), *Cecilie, Cecilija*
(Slavic), *Cecily, Cecilya, Ceclia,*
Cecylia (Polish), *Celia, Célie*
(French), *Cicely, Cielia, Cilicia,*
Cilka (Slavic), *Ciselina, Hihiria*
(Maori), *Hiria* (Maori), *Secilia,*
Selia, Sheila (Irish), *Síle* (Irish Gaelic), *Síleas* (Scottish Gaelic),
Silje (Norwegian), *Silke* (German),
Sisilia (Fijian).
Diminutives: Cele, Cissie, Sissey, Sissie, Sissy.
Cecily *See* Cecilia.
Cedar Middle English: a coniferous tree. Also a boy's name.
Cedarr, Cedarre, Ceder, Cederr.
Ceilidh Gaelic: a social gathering, involving music and dancing.
Ceinwen Welsh: blessed and fair.
Celandine A 'flower name'.
Celena/Celene *See* Selena.
Celeste Latin: heavenly.
Celesta, Celestina (Italian),
Celestine, Celina, Céline (French),
Seleste.
Diminutives: Celia, Célie.
Celia/Célie *See* Cecilia and Celeste.
Celina/Celine/Céline *See* Celeste and Selena.
Cella A modern name, perhaps derived from Ella (a fairy maiden).
Chella.
Celli Italian: the plural of cello.
Celosia Greek: flame-like.
Celtee/Celti/Celtie/Celty

See Keltie.
Celyn/Celyna/Celyne *See* Selena.
Cerelia Latin: spring flowers.
Cerella *See* Cyrilla.
Ceren Turkish: a young gazelle.
Cerena/Cerene/Cerenna *See* Serena.
Cerenitee/Cerenitie/Cerenity *See* Serenity.
Cerentha An unusual name, possibly derived from Ceres.
Cerenthia.
Ceres Latin: the Roman goddess of corn and tillage.
Cerelia, Cerella.
Ceridwen Welsh: fair poetry.
Ceridwyn, Cerridwen, Cerridwyn.
Diminutive: Ceri.
Cerilla *See* Cyrilla.
Cerina/Cerine *See* Serina.
Cerise French: cherry-red.
Cerrise, Cherise, Cherrise.
Cerys *See* Carys.
Cesarina Latin: a queen or empress. The feminine form of Caesar.
Caesaria, Caesarina, Caesarine, Cesaria, Cesarina, Cesarine.
Ceto A Greek goddess of the sea.
Keto.
Cettina Italian: a diminutive of Bicetta (Beatrice) and Nicetta (Berenice).
Chabeli A Spanish name of uncertain meaning.
Chabelli.

Chablis French: a type of white wine.
Chablee, Chabli, Chablie.
Chace *See* Chase.
Chadia The feminine version of Chad, an African country.
Chaddea, Chaddia, Chadea, Chadiya.
Chae *See* Shay.
Chaelen *See* Shaylen.
Chai Hindi: tea.
Chae, Chi, Chih.
Chaise *See* Chase.
Chaitra Sanskrit: the month of March/April, corresponding to the zodiac sign of Aries.
Chaja *See* Chaya.
Chaka/Chakka *See* Shaka.
Chakra Sanskrit: a wheel. A centre of spiritual power in the body.
Chalinda A Sri Lankan name of uncertain meaning.
Chalindah, Chalinder.
Challis Old French: a ladder or stairs. More commonly a boy's name.
Chalice, Chalis, Challys, Chalys.
Diminutives: Chali, Challie, Chally.
Chamba Sherpa/Tibetan: the loved one.
Chameli Hindi: jasmine.
Chamelli.
Chamonix The name of a French ski resort.
Chamonee, Chamonie, Shamonee,

Shamonie.
Chan Cambodian: a sweet-smelling tree.
Chanda American: possibly a form of Chandra.
Chandah, Chandani, Chandi, Chandice, Chandie, Chandy.
Chandace/Chandice *See* Candace.
Chandell/Chandelle *See* Chantal.
Chandra Sanskrit: the shining moon. *See also* Candi.
Candra.
Chanel French: a famous perfume and fashion label, created by Frenchwoman Coco Chanel.
Chanell, Chanelle, Channel, Channelle, Chenel, Chenell, Chenelle, Chennelle, Shanel, Shanell, Shanelle, Shannele, Shannelle.
Channette A modern American name.
Chanetta, Chanette, Channetta.
Chantal French: a stone or boulder. The name has also come to mean a little singer.
Chandel, Chandell, Chandelle, Chantale, Chantalle, Chantel, Chantele, Chantelle, Chauntel, Chauntell, Chauntelle, Chontal, Shantal, Shantel, Shantelle, Shentel, Shentell, Shentelle.
Chapa Native American: a beaver.
Chappa.
Chara *See* Charis.
Chardonelle Probably a variation of Chardonnay.
Chardonel, Chardonnel, Chardonell, Chardonnell, Chardonnelle.
Chardonnay French: a type of white wine.
Chardonae, Chardonai, Chardonay, Chardonnae, Chardonnai.
Charel/Charell/Charelle *See* Cheryl.
Charina Spanish: a diminutive of Rosario.
Charis Greek: grace, the graceful one.
Chara, Charice, Charise, Charissa, Charisse, Sharis, Sharris, Sharrise.
Charisma Greek: a gift, or healing power. The personification of grace and beauty in Greek mythology.
Carisma, Charis, Karisma, Kharis, Kharisma.
Charity Latin: loving and benevolent. One of the three Graces in Greek mythology.
Caridad (Spanish), *Carita* (Italian), *Caritas, Charita, Karita* (Scandinavian).
Diminutives: Cherrie, Cherry.
Charla/Charlee/Charleigh *See* Charlie.
Charlaine *See* Caroline.
Charlee-Jo A modern 'combination name'.
Charleigh-Jo, Charley-Jo, Charli-

Jo, Charlie-Jo.
Charleen/Charlene/Charline *See* Caroline.
Charlesetta A feminine form of Charles, meaning a free man. *See also* Charlotte.
Charleseta, Charleszeta, Charleszetta, Charleszita.
Charleston A modern form of Charles; more commonly a boy's name.
Charlie A diminutive of Charlotte, but used increasingly as an independent name. *See also* Sharlie.
Charla, Charlah, Charlee, Charleigh, Charley, Charli, Charlise, Charlize, Charly, Charlyse, Charlyze, Tcharli, Tcharlie.
Charli-Rose A modern 'combination name'.
Charlee-Rose, Charleigh-Rose, Charley-Rose, Charlie-Rose.
Charlise/Charlize *See* Charlie.
Charlotte A feminine form of Charles, a free man. *See also* Carla, Carol, Caroline and Charlie.
Carlota (Spanish), *Carlotta* (Italian), *Charlotta, Harata* (Maori), *Hariata* (Maori), *Karlotte* (German), *Sharlot, Sharlott, Sharlotte.*
Diminutives: Carleigh, Carley, Carlie, Carly, Lotta, Lottie, Lotty, Tottie, Totty.

Charlyne *See* Caroline.
Charlyse/Charlyze *See* Charlie.
Charmaine Greek: delightful.
Charmain, Charmayne, Charmian, Charmion, Sharmaine, Sharman, Sharmayne.
Charmian/Charmion *See* **Charmaine**.
Charna Yiddish: black.
Charnee/Charney/Charnie *See* Sharney.
Charo Spanish: a diminutive of Rosario.
Charon/Charonne/Charron *See* Sharon.
Charona *See* Sharona.
Chasca Incan: the goddess of the dawn.
Chase Old French: a hunter. More commonly a boy's name.
Chace, Chaise, Chayse.
Chaseley A modern name, probably derived from Chase.
Chaselee, Chaseleigh.
Chastity Latin: pure and chaste.
Chau Vietnamese: a pearl. Also a boy's name.
Chauntel/Chauntelle *See* Chantal.
Chava Hebrew: a form of Eve.
Chavaun/Chavaune *See* Siobhán.
Chavi Gypsy: a young girl.
Chavie.
Chay/Chaye *See* Shay.
Chaya Hebrew: life.
Chaja.
Chayanna/Chayanne

See Cheyenne.
Chayelen/Chaylen *See* Shaylen.
Chayse *See* Chase.
Cheeta/Cheetah *See* Chita.
Chella *See* Cella.
Chelle *See* Michelle.
Chelsea A fashionable London suburb.
Chelse, Chelsee, Chelsey, Chelsi, Chelsie, Chelsy, Cheltzee, Cheltzi, Cheltzie.
Chelsea-May A modern 'combination name'.
Chelsea-Mae, Chelsea-Mai.
Chen Chinese: the dawn.
Chenaide/Chenayde *See* Sinéad.
Chenell/Chennelle *See* Chanel.
Chenoa Native American: a white dove.
Cher French: the beloved one. *See also* Cheryl.
Chere, Cherelle, Cherene, Cheri, Cherice, Cherida, Cherie, Cherina, Cherien, Cherine, Cherise, Cherita, Cherri, Cherrie, Cherry, Cheryth, Sharee, Shareen, Shareena, Sharene, Sharina, Sharine, Sharini, Sher, Sheree, Sherica, Shericka, Sherika, Sherree, Sherri, Sherrie, Sherry, Sheryl.
Cheray A modern form of Cher or Cherie.
Cherae, Sherae, Sheray.
Cheri/Cherie/Cherien *See* Cher.
Cherilyn English: derived from Cher or Cheryl and Lynn.
Cheralyn, Cheralynn, Cheralynne, Cherilynn, Cherilynne, Cherlin, Cherlinn, Cherlinne, Cherlyn, Cherlynn, Cherlynne, Cherylene, Sheralyn, Sherilyn.
Cherina/Cherine *See* Cher.
Cherise/Cherrise *See* Cerise and Cher.
Cherish Old French: the treasured one.
Cherlin/Cherlyn *See* Cherilyn.
Cherona/Cheronne *See* Sharona.
Cherry *See* Charity and Cher. Also a 'fruit name'.
Cherri, Cherrie, Cherye.
Cheryl From Cher, the beloved one.
Charel, Charell, Charelle, Cherel, Cherrel, Cherrell, Cherrelle, Cheryle, Cheyrl, Cheyrle, Chryl, Chryle, Chryll, Chrylle, Scheryl, Sherril, Sherrill, Sheryl, Sheryll, Sherylle.
Cherylene *See* Cherilyn.
Chesna Slavic: peaceful.
Chezna.
Diminutive: Chez.
Chevonne *See* Siobhán.
Cheyenne A Native American tribe, and the name of a US city.
Chayanna, Chayanne, Cheyanne, Shaiann, Shaianna, Shaianne, Shayahn, Shayenne, Sheyana, Sheyane, Sheyanna, Sheyanne.
Cheylen *See* Shaylen.
Cheyrl/Cheyrle *See* Cheryl.

Chez A French word meaning at. Also possibly a variation of Shay.
Chezna *See* Chesna.
Chi/Chih *See* Chai.
Chiara The Italian form of Clare.
Ceara, Cearah, Ciara, Ciarah, Ciarra, Kiara, Kiarah, Kiarra.
Chic French: attractive and stylish.
Chique.
Chie Japanese: wisdom.
Chiffon French: a sheer fabric, implying delicacy.
Chiffonn, Chiffonne, Chifon, Chifonn, Chifonne.
Chihiro Japanese: a thousand riches or a thousand gains.
Chika Japanese: near.
Chilli From a Native American word meaning spicy.
Chilee, Chili, Chilie, Chillee, Chillie.
Chima A modern American name of uncertain meaning.
Cheema.
Chimena/Chimene *See* Ximena.
China A 'country name'.
Chinah, Chyna, Chynah.
Ching *See* Qing.
Chique *See* Chic.
Chiquita Spanish: the little one.
Chira Kurdish: probably meaning a light or lantern.
Chirsty *See* Kirstie.
Chiru Tibetan: coral.
Chita Sanskrit: a cheetah, panther or tiger.
Cheeta, Cheetah, Chitah.
Chitra Sanskrit: a portrait.
Chivon/Chivonn/Chivonne *See* Siobhán.
Chiyo Japanese: eternal.
Chiyoko Japanese: a child of eternity.
Chizu Japanese: a thousand storks. A name that implies longevity.
Chizuko A diminutive of Chizu, implying a child or little one.
Chloe Greek: a fertile young maiden. A New Testament name.
Cloe, Cloee, Cloey, Clohe, Khloe, Kloee, Klohe.
Chloris Greek: green; a plant lover.
Cloris, Khloris, Kloris.
Cho Japanese: a butterfly. Korean: beautiful.
Choden Sherpa/Tibetan: the devout one.
Chontal *See* Chantal.
Chora *See* Cora.
Chota Hindi: small, the little one.
Chow Chinese: summer.
Chris/Chrissie *See* Christina.
Chrisanne A combination of Chris and Anne (grace).
Chrisann, Chrisanna, Chrysann, Chrysanna, Chrysanne.
Chrisanthy/Chrissanth *See* Chrysantha.
Chriselee A combination of Chris and Lee (a meadow or clearing).
Chrisalea, Chrisalee, Chrisaleigh, Chrislea, Chrislee, Chrisleigh.

Chrishna *See* Krishna.

Chrislyn A combination of Chris (a Christian) and Lynn (a waterfall). *Chrisalin, Chrisalinn, Chrisalyn, Chrisalynne, Chrislynn, Chrislynne, Chrysalin, Chrysalinn, Chrysalyn, Chyrsalynn, Chryslynn, Chryslynne.*

Chrisoula Greek form of Chrysilla. *Chrysoula.*

Christabel English: a beautiful Christian. A combination of Christina and Belle. *Christabell, Christabella, Christabelle, Christobella, Christobelle, Cristabel, Kristabel, Kristabella, Kristabelle.*

Christal/Christalla/Christelle *See* Christina and Crystal.

Christanta *See* Chrysantha.

Christee/Christie/Christy Diminutives of Christina, but also used as independent names.

Christeen/Christena/Christene *See* Christina.

Christina Latin: a follower of Christ, a Christian. *Cairistìona* (Scottish Gaelic), *Chrisha, Christa, Christal, Christan, Christeen, Christel, Christelle* (French), *Christen, Christena, Christene, Christiana, Christiane, Christianna, Christine, Christyna, Christyne, Chrysstina, Chrysstine, Chrystina,* *Chrystine, Cristin, Cristina* (Italian, Portuguese), *Cristine, Crístíona* (Irish Gaelic), *Cristyna, Kerstin* (Swedish), *Kerstyn, Kirsten* (Scandinavian), *Kirstin, Kirstyn, Kjersti* (Norwegian), *Krisstine, Kristain, Kristan, Kristeen, Kristel* (German), *Kristen* (Danish), *Kristene, Kristern, Kristiani, Kristiann, Kristianna, Kristianne, Kristien, Kristiina, Kristina* (Swedish), *Kristine, Kristyn, Krysia, Krystena, Krystene, Krystina, Krystine, Krystyna* (Polish). *Diminutives:* Chris, Chrissi, Chrissie, Chrissy, Christie, Christy, Chrys, Chryss, Chryssa, Crissie, Crissy, Cristee, Cristi, Cristie, Cristy, Khrista, Kirstie (Scottish), Kirsty (Scottish), Kris, Kriss, Krissie, Krista, Kristee, Kristi, Kristie, Kristy, Stina, Tina.

Christmas Old English: born at Christmas time.

Christobelle *See* Christabel.

Christophina The feminine form of Christopher. *Christofina, Christofine, Christophine, Cristofina, Cristofine, Cristophina, Cristophine.*

Chryle/Chryll/Chrylle *See* Cheryl.

Chrys/Chryss Diminutives of Christina.

Chrysalin/Chrysalyn/Chryslynn

See Chrislyn.
Chrysann/Chrysanna
See Chrisanne.
Chrysantha Greek: a golden flower.
*Chrisanthy, Chrissanth,
Christanta, Chrysanthe, Chryseis,
Crisantha, Crisanthe, Crissantha.*
Chrysilla Greek: golden-haired.
Chrisoula (Greek), *Chrysoula,
Chryssa.*
Chrysoula *See* Chrisoula and Chrysilla.
Chryssa *See* Christina and Chrysilla.
Chrysstina/Chrysstine/Chrystina
See Christina.
Chrystal *See* Crystal.
Chu Chinese: a pearl. Native American: a rattlesnake.
Chun Chinese: spring.
Chyna *See* China.
Ciana/Cianna/Cianne *See* Kiana.
Ciara *See* Chiara and Kiera.
Ciarna/Ciarni *See* Kiana.
Cibele *See* Cybele.
Cicely *See* Cecilia.
Cidney *See* Sidney.
Cidonie *See* Sidonie.
Ciel French: the sky.
Ciella, Cielle.
Cielia *See* Cecilia.
Cilicia *See* Cecilia.
Cilka Slavic form of Cecilia.
Cilla A diminutive of Priscilla.
Cillah, Cylla, Cyllah, Silla, Sillah, Sylla, Syllah.
Cincelia A modern name, probably from Cynthia and Celia.
Cinderella French: a maiden of the cinders or ashes.
Diminutives: Cindi, Cindie, Cindy.
Cindy A diminutive of Cinderella, Cynthia and Lucinda (*see* Lucy).
Cindi, Cindie, Sindy.
Cindylou From Cindy and Louise.
Cinnabar Greek: red. A 'colour name' and also the name of a mineral.
Cinnamon Hebrew: a 'spice name'.
Cintia/Cinzia *See* Cynthia.
Cintra *See* Cyntra.
Circe An enchantress in Greek mythology.
Cirilla/Cirille *See* Cyrilla.
Ciselina/Cissie *See* Cecilia.
Citrine Middle English: a pale-yellow gem, a form of quartz.
Claerwen A Welsh placename.
*Claerwenn, Claerwenne,
Claerwyn, Claerwynn,
Claerwynne.*
Claire/Claireece/Clairette/Clairon *See* Clare.
Clancy Irish Gaelic: a red or ruddy warrior. More commonly a boy's name.
Clancee, Clancey, Clanci, Clancie.
Clara *See* Clare and Clorinda.
Clarabelle French: bright and beautiful. From Clara and Belle.
Clarabella, Claribel.
Clare Latin: bright and famous. The

name of an Irish county. *See also* Chiara, Clarice and Clarity.
Chiara (Italian), *Clair, Claire* (French), *Claireece, Clairette, Clairon, Clara, Clareen, Clarenza, Claresta, Clareta, Claretta, Clarette, Clarina, Clarinda, Clarine, Clarista, Clarona, Klara* (German, Scandinavian).
Diminutive: Clarrie.
Claribel *See* Clarabelle.
Clarice French from Latin: the little brilliant one. *See also* Clare and Clarity.
Clarisa (Spanish), *Clariss, Clarissa, Clarisse, Clerissa, Klarice, Klarise, Klarissa* (German), *Klarisse*.
Diminutive: Clarrie.
Clarinda/Clarine *See* Clare and Clorinda.
Clarista/Clarita *See* Clare and Clarity.
Clarity English from Latin: clearness. *See also* Clare and Clarice.
Clarita (Spanish), *Claritas, Claritee, Claritie*.
Clarona *See* Clare.
Claude/Claudette *See* Claudia.
Claudia Latin: the lame one. The feminine form of Claude.
Claude (French), *Claudetta, Claudette* (French), *Claudina, Claudine* (French), *Cloudia, Cloudina, Cloudine, Klaudia* (Polish).
Diminutives: Claud, Claude, Claudie.
Clea/Cleapatra *See* Cleopatra.
Cleantha Greek: a glorious flower.
Cleanthe (French), *Cleanthy, Cliantha, Clianthe, Clianthy, Kleantha, Kleanthe, Kleanthy*.
Clelia Italian: from Cloelia, a figure in Roman legend.
Clematis Greek: a climbing plant. A 'flower name'.
Clemence Latin: mild, merciful.
Clemencia, Clemency, Clementia, Clementina (Spanish), *Clementine, Clemenza* (Polish), *Klemence, Klemencia, Klementia, Klementine, Klementyna* (Polish), *Klimentina* (Slavic).
Diminutives: Clem, Clemmie.
Clementina/Clementine/Clemenza *See* Clemence.
Cleo/Cleone/Cleotha *See* Cleopatra and Clio.
Cleofa A 15th-century Italian noblewoman.
Cleofe.
Cleopatra Greek: glory of the father. The queen of Egypt from 47–30 BC.
Cleapatra, Cleopatrah, Cleotha, Cliopatra, Kleopatra, Kleopatrah, Kliopatra.
Diminutives: Clea, Cleo, Clio, Kleo, Klio.
Clerissa *See* Clarice.

Cleva Old English: from the cliff. The feminine form of Clive.
Clianicantha/Clianthe/Clianthy See Cleantha.
Clio Greek: the glorious one; the muse of history in Greek mythology. See also Cleopatra.
Cleo, Cleone, Clione.
Cliopatra See Cleopatra.
Clodagh Irish: the name of a river.
Cloda, Clodah, Clodina, Clodine.
Cloe/Cloee/Cloey/Clohe See Chloe.
Cloneen Irish Gaelic: an Irish placename.
Clonine.
Clorinda Persian: of renowned beauty.
Clarinda, Clorina.
Cloris See Chloris.
Clotilda Teutonic: a famous battle maiden.
Clothilda, Clothilde (French), *Clotilde.*
Cloudia/Cloudina/Cloudine See Claudia.
Clova Middle English from Latin: from clove, a spice.
Clovah, Clove.
Clover Old English: a flower name.
Clymene Greek: renowned.
Clytie Greek: famous. A water nymph who fell in love with the sun god Apollo. He changed her into a sunflower.
Clyte, Clytee, Clyti, Clytia.

Coco The first name of the famous fashion designer, Chanel.
Koko.
Coda Italian: a musical passage.
Codah, Koda, Kodah.
Cody Old English: a pillow or cushion. Also a boy's name.
Codee, Codey, Codi, Codie, Cohdee, Cohdi, Cohdie, Kodee, Kodi, Kodie, Kody, Kohdee, Kohdi, Kohdie, Kohdy.
Cola African: a type of nut.
Colah, Kola, Kolah.
Coleen/Colene See Colleen.
Colenso Cornish: from the dark pool.
Coleta/Colette/Colletta/Collette See Nicola.
Colina Spanish: a hill. Also a female form of Colin, meaning victory of the people.
Colinah, Collina (Italian), *Collinah, Collyna, Collynah, Colyna, Colynah.*
Colleen Irish Gaelic: a girl.
Cailin (Gaelic), *Coleen, Colene, Coline, Collene, Colline, Collyne.*
Collina/Collyna/Colyna See Colina.
Colombia A South American country.
Columba Latin: dove-like.
Colombe (French), *Columbia, Columbina, Columbine.*
Columbine A 'flower name'.
See also Columba.

Columbina.
Comfort A Puritan 'characteristic name'.
Concepción Latin: the beginning. A Spanish name that relates to the Virgin Mary's Immaculate Conception.
Concepta, Conception, Concetta (Italian), *Concettina* (Italian). *Diminutives:* Concha, Conchita.
Concha/Conchita *See* Concepción.
Concordia Latin: the harmonious one.
Condoleezza The name of the former US Secretary of State, Condoleezza Rice. It is believed to be derived from a musical term meaning 'with sweetness'.
Condola, Condoleesa, Condolesa, Condoleeza, Condolezza, Condolisa.
Conni/Connie/Conny *See* Constance.
Consolata *See* Consuela.
Constance Latin: steadfast, constant.
Constancia, Constancy, Constantia, Constantina, Constatina (Greek), *Contstance, Costantza, Konstandina, Konstantina, Konstanze* (German). *Diminutives:* Con, Conni, Connie, Conny.
Consuela Latin: the consoler or comforter. Generally a Spanish name.
Consolata (Italian), *Consuelo.*

Diminutive: Suela.
Content A Puritan 'characteristic name'.
Contstance *See* Constance.
Coolah Aboriginal: a tree.
Coorah Aboriginal: a woman, or a kangaroo.
Coora.
Copper Old English: a reddish-brown metal.
Copor (Welsh), *Copra, Coprah, Cupra, Cuprah, Cupria.*
Cora Greek: a maiden.
Chora, Corah, Coranna, Coranne, Coreen, Corella, Corena, Corene, Coretta, Corette, Corina, Corinda, Corinee, Corinna, Corinne, Corissa, Corisse, Correna, Corrin, Corrine, Corryn, Coryn, Corynna, Kora, Korina, Korinna, Korinne, Korryn, Korryne.
Corabelle A combination of Cora and Belle, meaning a beautiful maiden.
Corabell, Corabella.
Corah Hindi: the unchanging one. Also a form of Cora.
Coral Latin: from the sea.
Corale, Coralee, Coralie, Coralina, Coraline.
Coralie *See* Coral.
Coranna/Coranne *See* Cora.
Corazón Spanish: the heart. Often used in the Philippines.
Cordelia Celtic: a jewel of the sea.

A Shakespearean character in *King Lear*.
Cordélie (French), *Cordella, Cordellia, Cordelya, Kordelia, Kordellia, Kordelya.*
Diminutive: Delia.

Coreen Aboriginal: the end of the hills. *See also* Cora.

Corella Aboriginal: a type of parrot. *See also* Cora.

Corena/Corene *See* Cora.

Coretta/Corette *See* Cora.

Corey Celtic/Gaelic: dweller in the hollow. Also a boy's name.
Coree, Cori, Corie, Correy, Corry, Cory, Koree, Korey, Kori, Korie.

Corin Cornish: from the corner. Latin: the name of a Roman deity, possibly meaning a spear.
Corrin, Coryn, Korin, Korrin, Koryn.

Corina/Corinee/Corinna/Corinne *See* Cora.

Corissa/Corisse *See* Cora.

Corky A nickname, but sometimes used as a proper name.
Corkee, Corkey, Corki, Corkie.

Corlette A Manx Gaelic surname, possibly meaning of Thor's people.
Corlet, Corlett.

Corliss Old English: the cheerful one.
Corlissa, Corlisse.

Cornelia Latin: a horn. The feminine form of Cornelius.
Cornela, Cornelie, Cornelietta (Dutch), *Cornella, Cornelle, Kornelia, Kornela, Kornella.*
Diminutives: Nelia, Neliya.

Corona Latin: a crown.

Corowa Aboriginal: a rocky river, or a pine tree.

Correna *See* Cora.

Correy/Corry *See* Corey.

Corrin/Corrine *See* Cora and Corin.

Corryn/Corynna *See* Cora.

Corsica A Mediterranean island.

Cortina Italian: a curtain.

Corvina Latin: a raven.

Coryn *See* Cora and Corin.

Cosette French: of the victorious army.
Cosetta, Cozette.

Cosima Greek: harmony, perfect order. The feminine form of Cosmo.
Cosma, Kosima, Kosma.

Costantza *See* Constance.

Courtney Old French: probably meaning the short-nosed one. Also a boy's name.
Courtenay, Courtnay, Courtnee, Courtnie, Kourtenay, Kourtnay, Kourtnee, Kourtney, Kourtnie.

Cowra Aboriginal: rocks, or a rocky place. A town in New South Wales.

Cozette *See* Cosette.

Crescentia Latin: to increase. A form of the moon.
Crescencia, Crescent.

Cressida Greek: the golden one. A Shakespearean character.

Cressa.
Cricket A type of insect.
Crickett, Crickette, Criket, Crikett, Crikette.
Crida Irish Gaelic: the name of a saint.
Crisantha/Crisanthe *See* Chrysantha.
Crisiant Welsh: like a crystal.
Crispina Latin: the curly-haired one. The feminine form of Crispin. *Crispine.*
Cristabel *See* Christabel.
Cristal/Cristalle *See* Crystal.
Cristi/Cristie/Cristin/Cristina/ Cristine/Cristíona *See* Christina.
Cristy/Cristyna *See* Christina.
Crocus Latin: a 'plant name'.
Cronia *See* Kronia.
Crystal Greek: as clear as ice. A 'gemstone name'.
Christal, Christalla, Christalle, Christallo, Christel, Christell, Christelle (French), *Chrystal, Cristal, Cristall, Cristalle, Crystell, Crystelle, Kristal, Kristalla, Kristel, Kristell, Kristelle, Krystal, Krystalia* (Greek), *Krystall, Krystalle, Krystallia* (Greek), *Krystel, Krystell, Krystelle, Krystle, Krystol, Krystole, Krystoll, Krystolle.*
Csarina/Csarine *See* Tsarina.
Culley Gaelic: from the forest. Also a boy's name.
Cullee, Culli, Cullie, Cully.
Cullya Aboriginal: an emu.
Culya.
Culmara Aboriginal: a fern.
Culmarah, Culmarra, Culmarrah.
Cumbria The name of an English county.
Cupra/Cuprah/Cupria *See* Copper.
Curra Aboriginal: a spring.
Curtis Old French: one who is courteous. Generally a boy's name.
Curtiss, Curtys, Kurtis, Kurtiss, Kurtys.
Cushla Irish Gaelic: the beat of my heart.
Cushlah, Quishla, Quishlah.
Custodia Spanish: a guardian.
Cvetka Slavic: a blossom.
Cveta, Kveta, Kvetka.
Cyal/Cyall *See* Kyle.
Cyan Greek: a dark-blue colour.
Cyane, Cyanea, Cyann, Cyanne.
Cybele Latin: a Roman nature and mother goddess, whose festival was held from 15–17 March. A suitable name for a Pisces girl.
Cibele, Cybeli, Sibele, Sybele, Sybeli.
Cybil/Cybill/Cybilla *See* Sybil.
Cydney *See* Sidney.
Cygnet Middle English: a young swan.
Cygnett, Cygnette.
Cygni Greek: a swan.
Cygnie.
Cyle *See* Kyle.

Cylla/Cyllah *See* Cilla.
Cynara Greek: an artichoke or thistle.
Cynthia Greek: of the moon. An alternative name for the Greek moon goddess, Artemis.
Cintia (Portuguese), *Cinzia* (Italian), *Cynthie*.
Diminutives: Cindi, Cindie, Cindy, Cyn.
Cyntra Probably derived from Cynthia.
Cintra.
Cypriana Greek: a woman from Cyprus.
Cipriana, Cypra, Cyprienne, Cypris.
Cyra Persian: like the sun.
Cyrella/Cyrelle *See* Cyrilla.
Cyrena Greek: a woman from Cyrene, an ancient Greek colony in North Africa.
Cyrene, Cyrenia, Kyrena, Kyrene, Kyrenia.
Cyreta American: possibly the feminine form of Cyrus.
Cyreeta, Syreeta, Syreta.
Cyria *See* Cyriaca and Cyrilla.
Cyriaca Greek: born on a Sunday.
Cyria, Cyriaka.
Cyrilla Greek: lordly or the proud one. The feminine form of Cyril.
Cerella, Cerilla, Cirilla, Cirille, Cyrella, Cyrelle, Cyria, Cyriella, Cyrielle, Cyrille (French).
Czarina/Czarine *See* Tsarina.

D

Dabria A mythological angel.
Dacey Gaelic: the southerner. Also a boy's name.
Dacie, Dacy, Daycie.
Dacia Greek: a woman from Dacia, an ancient European country.
Dae Korean: greatness.
Dael *See* Dale.
Daeleen/Daelene/Daelyne *See* Dalene.
Daena/Daenah *See* Dana.
Daffodil English from Greek: the asphodel. A 'flower name'.
Dafne *See* Daphne.
Dagmar Old Norse: a maiden of the day, or glorious day.
Dagma.
Dagna Old Norse: a new day.
Dagny.
Dahlas/Dahllas *See* Dallas.
Dahlia English: a flower, named after the Swedish botanist Dahl.
Dahla, Dahlis, Dalia (Arabic), *Dallia, Dallya, Dallyah, Dalya, Dalyah*.
Dai Japanese: great.
Dail/Daile *See* Dale.
Daila Latvian: beautiful.
Daileen/Dailene/Dailine/Dailyne *See* Dalene.
Daina/Dainah *See* Dana.

Dairine Irish Gaelic: one who is fruitful.
Daireen, Dairne.

Daisy Old English: the day's eye; a 'flower name'. Also a diminutive of Margaret.
Daisee, Daisi, Daisian, Daisie, Daizee, Daizi, Daizie, Daizy, Daysee, Daysi, Daysie, Daysy, Deysee, Deysi, Deysie, Deysy.

Daiva/Daivene/Daivine *See* Davina.

Dakota Native American: a friend. Also a boy's name.
Dakoda, Dakodah, Dakotah, Dekota, Dekotah.

Dalas *See* Dallas.

Dale Teutonic/Old English: a valley dweller. Also a boy's name.
Dael, Dail, Daile, Dayle, Daylle.

Dalee *See* Dali.

Dalene A form of Dale.
Daeleen, Daelene, Daeline, Daelyne, Daileen, Dailene, Dailine, Dailyne, Daleen, Daline, Dayleen, Daylene, Dayline, Daylyne.

Daley Irish Gaelic: a counsellor.
Daly.

Dali After the famous Spanish artist (Salvador Dali).
Dalee, Dalie, Dallie, Dalley, Dally.

Dalia *See* Dahlia.

Dalice *See* Dallis.

Dalila Swahili: gentle. *See also* Delilah.

Dalit Hebrew: like flowing water.

Dalla Icelandic: luminous.

Dallas Celtic: skilled, or from the field of water. The name of a city in Texas.
Dahlas, Dahllas, Dalas, Dalice, Dallis, Dallise, Dallys, Dalys, Dellas.

Dallia/Dallya/Dalya *See* Dahlia.

Dalma African: lead or tin.
Dalmah.

Daly *See* Daley.

Dalys *See* Dallas.

Damaris Greek: gentle. A New Testament name.
Damara.

Damayanti Sanskrit: a princess in Hindu mythology.

Damiana Greek: tame, domesticated. The feminine form of Damian or Damon.
Damiane.

Damika A modern, probably made-up, name.
Damikah, Dammika, Dammikah, Dhamika, Dhammika.

Damita Spanish: the little noble lady.

Damola An African name of uncertain meaning.

Damosel Old English: a damsel, or a young unmarried woman.
Damsel, Damzel, Damzelle.

Dana Czech: God is my judge. Old English: from Denmark. Also a diminutive of Bogdana.

Daena, Daenah, Daina, Dainah, Danah, Danuta (Polish), *Dayna*.
Danaë Greek: the mother of Perseus in Greek mythology.
Danee *See* Dani.
Daneika/Daneka *See* Danika.
Danetta/Danette *See* Danielle.
Danielle Hebrew: God is my judge; the feminine form of Daniel. *See also* Danni.
Danell, Danella, Danelle, Danetta, Danette (French), *Dania, Daniela* (Czech, Polish), *Daniele, Daniella, Danila, Danneal, Dannealle, Danniel, Dannielle, Danya, Danyale, Danyella.*
Diminutives: Dani, Dania, Danni, Danny, Dany.
Danika Slavic: the morning star.
Daneika, Daneka, Danica.
Danila *See* Danielle.
Danisha Probably from Dana.
Daneesha.
D'Ann/D'Anna/D'Anne *See* Diana.
Danneal/Dannealle *See* Danielle.
Danni A diminutive of Danielle.
Danee, Dani, Dania, Danie, Danii, Dannee, Dannie, Danny, Dany.
Danniel/Dannielle *See* Danielle.
Dannielyn A combination of Danielle (God is my judge) and Lynn (a waterfall).
Dannie-Lyn, Dannielynn, Dannie-Lynn, Dannilyn.

Danu Gaelic: the goddess of fruitfulness.
Danuta Polish: a little deer. *See also* Dana.
Danutah, Danute.
Dany/Danya/Danyale/Danyella *See* Danielle and Danni.
Daphne Greek: the laurel. In Greek mythology, the name of a nymph who was transformed into a laurel tree.
Dafne, Daphena, Daphene, Daphna, Daphnee, Daphnie, Daphney.
Dara Arabic: a halo. Hebrew: compassion, wisdom.
Darah, Darra, Darrah.
Darby Irish Gaelic: free from envy. Also a boy's name.
Darbee, Darbi, Darbie, Derbie, Derby.
Darcy Old French: a Norman family name.
Darcee, Darcey, Darci, Darcie, Darcia, D'Arcy, Darsey, Darsy.
Dardanelle From the Dardanelles, the strait between Europe and Turkey.
Dardanel, Dardanela, Dardanell, Dardanella.
Darea *See* Daria.
Darel/Darell/Darielle *See* Darrelle.
Daria Greek: wealthy. The feminine form of Darius and the name of a saint.
Darea, Dareah, Dariah, Darian,

Dariann, Darianne, Darice, Darie, Darija (Slavic), **Daris, Darja** (Slavic), **Darria, Darrian, Darrianne, Darya** (Russian), **Djaria, Tarja** (Finnish). *Diminutive:* Darinka (Slavic).
Darija/Darja Slavic forms of Daria.
Darilynn See Darlene.
Darinka Slavic dimutive of Darja (*see* Daria).
Darlene English from Old French: the beloved one. *See also* Darrelle. *Darilynn, Darla, Darleen, Darline, Darralyn, Darralynn, Darralynne, Darrylyn.*
Darra/Darrah See Dara and Darrene.
Darralyn/Darralynne/Darrylyn See Darlene.
Darrelle Old French: the beloved one; a feminine form of Darrell. *See also* Darlene. *Darel, Darell, Darielle, Daryl, Daryll, Darylle.*
Darrene English: the feminine form of Darren. *Daron, Darra, Darrah, Darryn, Darryne, Daryn, Daryne.*
Darri Aboriginal: a track.
Darria/Darrian/Darianne See Daria.
Darsey/Darsy See Darcie.
Darwinia The feminine form of Darwin, meaning a beloved friend. *Darwina.*
Darya See Daria.

Daryl/Daryll/Darylle See Darrelle.
Daryn/Daryne See Darrene.
Daun/Dauna/Daune/Daunia See Dawn.
Dauphina/Dauphine See Dolphina.
Davana/Davena/Davene See Davina.
Davida Hebrew: beloved; a feminine form of David. *See also* Davina. *Davidia, Davita. Diminutive:* Vida.
Davina Hebrew: the beloved one; a feminine form of David. *See also* Davida. *Daiva, Daivene, Daivine, Davana, Davena, Davene, Davine, Davinia, Dayva, Dayvina, Dayvine, Devina.*
Dawa Sherpa/Tibetan: born on a Monday. Also a boy's name.
Dawn English: daybreak, dawn. *Daun, Dauna, Daune, Daunia, Dawna, Dawne, Dawnia.*
Daya Old English: the day. Sanskrit: kindness. *Dayah.*
Dayan See Diana.
Dayanita Sanskrit: tender. *Dayanitha, Dayanthi.*
Daycie See Dacey.
Dayle/Daylle See Dale.
Dayleen/Daylene/Daylyne See Dalene.
Dayna See Dana.
Daysee/Daysie/Daysy See Daisy.
Dayva/Dayvina/Dayvine

D – Girls

See Davina.
Dea/Deah *See* Dia.
Deadra/Deadre *See* Deirdre.
Deahne/Deahnne *See* Diana.
Deana/Deanella/Deanna/Deanne *See* Dena and Diana.
Deandra *See* Dena and Diana.
Deaneen/Deanine/Deanyne *See* Dena.
Dearbháil *See* Dervla.
Dearna/Dearne *See* Diana.
Debbon A modern form of Deborah.
Deban, Debban, Debon.
Deborah Hebrew: the bee, an industrious woman. A biblical name.
Debbora, Debborah, Debor, Debora, Debra, Devora (Jewish), *Devorah* (Jewish), *Devore, Tepora* (Maori), *Tepore* (Maori).
Diminutives: Deb, Debbi, Debbie, Debby, Debs.
Debra *See* Deborah.
Decembra Latin: suitable for a child born in December, covering the zodiac signs Sagittarius and Capricorn.
December, Decembria.
Dechen Sherpa/Tibetan: health and happiness. Originally a Bhutanese name.
Decima Latin: the tenth.
Decia.
Dedra *See* Deirdre.
Dee Diminutive of Audrey, Deirdre, Delia, Diana, etc. Also an independent name.
Dede, Deedee, Dee Dee, Didi.
Deeba An Urdu name of uncertain meaning.
Diba.
Deena *See* Dena and Diana.
Deepika Sanskrit: a little light. A feminine form of Deepak.
Deeta *See* Perdita.
Dehka Greek: ten.
Deka.
Dehlia *See* Delia.
Deirbhile *See* Dervla.
Deirdre Celtic: sorrow. A character in Irish legend.
Deadra, Deadre, Dedra, Deidhre, Deidra, Deidre, Deidrie, Deirdra, Dierdra, Dierdre.
Diminutives: Deedee, Dede, Dee, Didi.
Deka *See* Dehka.
Dekota/Dekotah *See* Dakota.
Dela/Delah *See* Della.
Delaney Gaelic: the challenger's descendant.
Delaina, Delaine, Delainey, Delainy, Delayne.
Diminutives: Del, Delle.
Delcia *See* Delicia.
Delcie/Delcine *See* Dulcie.
Delena/Delene *See* Della.
Delfina/Delfine *See* Delphine.
Delia Greek: a woman from the island of Delos. Another name for Artemis, the Greek moon goddess.

See also Cordelia and Della.
Dehlia, Deliah.
Diminutive: Dee.
Delicia Latin: delight or delightful.
Delcia, Delica, Délice (French), *Delight, Delis, Delise, Deliss, Delissa, Delite.*
Delight/Delite *See* Delicia.
Delilah Hebrew: the beautiful temptress. The lover of Samson in the Bible.
Dalila, Delila, D'Lila, D'Lilah.
Diminutives: Lila, Lilah.
Dell/Delle Diminutives of names such as Delaney and Della.
Della English: probably derived from Delia or Delilah and Ella. Also a diminutive of Adèle and Adelaide.
Dela, Delah, Delena, Delene, Dellah, Dellena, Dellene.
Diminutives: Dell, Delle.
Della-Rose A modern 'combination name'.
Delarose, Dela-Rose, Dela-Roze, Dellarosa, Della-Rosa, Dellarose, Della-Roza, Della-Roze.
Dellas *See* Dallas.
Delloreen/Dellorene/Dellorine *See* Delora.
Dellys/Delys *See* Dilys.
Delma Spanish: of the sea.
Delmah, Delmar, Delmas.
Delora Latin: from the seashore.
Delloreen, Dellorene, Dellorine, Delorah.

Delores/Delorez/Deloris *See* Dolores.
Delphine Latin: a woman from Delphi, or a 'flower name' derived from delphinium.
Delfina (Italian, Spanish), *Delfine, Delpha, Delphia, Delphina, Delphinia, Delphinium, Delvene, Delvine.*
Delta Greek: the fourth, as in fourth child.
Deltah.
Delvene/Delvine *See* Delphine.
Delwyn Welsh: neat and fair.
Delwen, Delwenn, Delwenne, Delwynn, Delwynne.
Delyth Welsh: neat and pretty.
Demelza Cornish: a placename. The heroine of Winston Graham's *Poldark* novels.
Demetria Greek: from Demeter, the goddess of fertility.
Demeter, Demetra, Dimitra, Dimitria.
Diminutive: Demi.
Demi Latin: half. *See also* Demetria.
Demi-Lee A modern 'combination name'.
Demi-Lea, Demi-Leigh.
Dena Old English: from the valley; a feminine form of Dean. Also a diminutive of Adina.
Deana, Deaneen, Deanella, Deanelle, Deanine, Deanna, Deanyne, Deena, Denella, Denelle.

Deni/Denice *See* Denise.
Denise French from Greek: a lover of wine. A feminine form of Dennis.
Denesa, Denese, Denice, Denisa, Denisha, Denisse, Denize, Dennice, Denniscia, Dennise, Dennisse, Denyse, Denysse, Dionysa, Dionyse, Dionyza, Dionyze.
Diminutives: Deni, Dennie, Denny.
Denita A feminine form of Dennis. *See also* Denise.
Dennita, Dennyta, Denyta.
Deniz Turkish: of the sea. Also a boy's name.
Denize.
Denver Old English: from the edge of the valley. A US placename.
Denva, Denvah.
Denyse/Denysse *See* Denise.
Derbie/Derby *See* Darby.
Deren/Derene *See* Derryn.
Derica A feminine form of Derek, ruler of the people.
Dereka, Derika, Derrica, Derrika.
Derin *See* Derryn.
Derora Hebrew: a swallow.
Derrilin Aboriginal: falling stars. Can also be a boy's name.
Derrilyn.
Diminutives: Derri, Derry.
Derry A diminutive of names such as Derryn and Derryth.
Derryn From an old Welsh name.
Deren, Derene, Derin, Derren, Derrene, Derrin, Derryne, Deryn, Deryne.
Diminutive: Derry.
Derryth Welsh: of the oak.
Diminutive: Derry.
Dervla Irish Gaelic: the daughter of the poet.
Dearbháil, Deirbhile, Derval, Dervila.
Derya Hawaiian: the ocean.
Deryn/Deryne *See* Derryn.
Desdemona Greek: ill fated. A Shakespearean character who was murdered by her husband Othello.
Desmona.
Diminutives: Desda, Desi, Desie.
Desi/Desie Diminutives of names such as Desdemona and Desiree.
Desiana A feminine form of Desi (the desired one).
Desianna, Deziana, Dezianna.
Desiree Latin: the desired one.
Deseray, Desiderata, Desideria, Desirata, Desire, Desirée (French), *Desirita* (Spanish), *Desrae, Desray, Desree.*
Diminutives: Desi, Desie.
Desley The meadow of Desdemona or Desiree.
Deslea, Deslee, Desleigh, Desli, Deslie, Desylea, Desylee, Desyleigh, Desylie.
Desma Greek: a pledge.
Despina Greek: a lady or young lady.

Despinah, Despoina, Despoinah.
Desrae/Desray *See* Desiree.
Desta Ethiopian: happiness.
Destiny Old French: fate. A popular name in the USA.
Destina, Destine, Destinee, Destiney, Destinia, Destinie.
Destiny-May A modern 'combination name'.
Destiny-Mae, Destiny-Mai, Destiny-Maie, Destiny-Maye, Destiny-Mei.
Destry The name of a 1950s movie.
Destree, Destrey, Destri, Destrie.
Desylea/Desyleigh *See* Desley.
Deta *See* Edith.
Detta Possibly a diminutive of Odette.
Dettah.
Deva *See* Devi and Diva.
Devaki Sanskrit: black. A Hindu goddess.
Devash Hebrew: like honey.
Devi Sanskrit: godlike, a goddess.
Deva, Devanee, Devee, Devella, Devia, Devina.
Devika Sanskrit: a little goddess.
Devina *See* Davina and Devi.
Devine *See* Divine.
Devisingh Sanskrit: a combination of names meaning a goddess and a lion.
Devona Old English: from the county of Devon.
Devonah, Devonia, Devoniah, Devonee, Devoney, Devonie,
Devony.
Devora/Devorah/Devore *See* Deborah.
Dewi Indonesian/Malay: a goddess.
Dewee.
Dewita Probably the feminine form of De Witt (the blond or fair one).
Dewitta.
Dewynn A modern name, from Wynn.
De-Wynn, Dewynne, De-Wynne.
Dexia Greek: right (the direction).
Dextra Latin: skilful, dextrous. The feminine form of Dexter.
Deysee/Deysi/Deysie/Deysy *See* Daisy.
Deziana/Dezianna *See* Desiana.
Dhamika/Dhammika *See* Damika.
Dhani Hindi/Nepali: rich or prosperous.
Dhanu Sanskrit: a bow. From Dhanus, the Sanskrit name for Sagittarius.
Dhara Hindi: of the earth.
Dharma Hindi: religion, or the religious one. Also a boy's name.
Dhyan/Dyhanne *See* Diana.
Dia Spanish: the day.
Dea, Deah, Diah.
Diahann/Diahnn *See* Diana.
Diamanta French from Latin: adamant, like a diamond.
Diamanda, Diamandra, Diamante, Diamantina, Diamantra, Diamond.
Diana Latin: the divine one. The

D – Girls

goddess of hunting and the moon in Roman mythology.
D'Ann, D'Anna, D'Anne, Dayan, Deahna, Deahne, Deahnne, Deana, Deandra, Deanna, Deanne, Dearna, Dearne, Deena, Dhyan, Dhyann, Dhyanne, Diahann, Diahnn, Dian, Diandra, Diane (French), Dianna, Dianne, Diarna, Diarne, Dijanna, Dijanne, Dyan, Dyana, Dyane, Dyanna, Dyanne, Riana (Maori).
Diminutives: Dee, Di, Didee.

Diandra *See* Diana.
Diane/Dianna/Dianne *See* Diana.
Dianella A genus of flowering plants.
Dianelle.
Diantha Greek: a divine flower.
Dianthe, Dianthia.
Diarna/Diarne *See* Diana.
Diba *See* Deeba.
Didi Nepali: an older sister. *See also* Dee.
Didianne An unusual 'combination name'.
Didiann, Didianna.
Dido Greek: the name of a queen of Carthage.
Didrika Teutonic: the people's ruler.
Diella Latin: one who worships God.
Diellah, Dielle.
Diera Spanish: one who gives.
Dierah.

Dierdra/Dierdre *See* Deirdre.
Dijanna/Dijanne *See* Diana.
Diki Sherpa/Tibetan: healthy and wealthy.
Dilan/Dillon/Dillyn *See* Dylan.
Dilani A Sri Lankan name of uncertain meaning.
Dilara Turkish: a lover.
Dilla African: a python.
Dillah.
Dilys Welsh: true, steadfast.
Dellys, Delys, Dillys.
Dimana Aboriginal: a horse.
Dimanah, Dimanna, Dimannah.
Dimitra/Dimitria *See* Demetria.
Dimity Greek: a thin cotton material.
Dimphina/Dimphna *See* Dymphna.
Dina The angel of wisdom and the law. *See also* Adina and Dinah.
Dinah, Dinara.
Dinah Hebrew: judgment; a biblical name. *See also* Dina.
Dina, Dyna, Dynah.
Dinara The name of a Russian tennis player (Dinara Safina).
Dinarah.
Dinorah Aramaic: the light.
Dinora.
Dion/Diona *See* Dione.
Dione Greek: the daughter of heaven. A goddess in Greek mythology.
Dion, Diona, Dioni, Dionna, Dionne.

Dionyse/Dionyza *See* Denise.
Dior French: the golden one. The name of a famous French fashion and perfume company.
Diora, Diore.
Dirce Greek: a figure from Greek mythology.
Dirke.
Dirkina Possibly the feminine form of Dirk (*see* Derek).
Dirkine.
Disa Greek: double. Old Norse: lively.
Dita *See* Edith and Perdita.
Diva Latin: a goddess.
Deva, Devah, Divah.
Divine Middle English: the heavenly one.
Devine.
Divna A Slavic name of uncertain meaning.
Divonne A modern American name, derived from either Diva or Dione.
Divonn.
Dixie French: the tenth. Also a girl from the American south.
Dixey, Dixy.
Diza Hebrew: joy.
Djaria *See* Daria.
Djava *See* Java.
D'Lila/D'Lilah *See* Delilah.
Doanna Middle English: a doe, a female deer or antelope.
Doana, Doanne.
Dobrila Slavic: kind, good.

Dodie Hebrew: beloved. *See also* Dorothy.
Dodi.
Doff/Doffy Diminutives of Dorothy.
Doina Romanian: a type of folk song.
Dolce/Dolcie *See* Dulcie.
Dolfin/Dolffin *See* Dolphina.
Dolina The name of a river in Romania.
Dolkar Sherpa/Tibetan: the name of a Buddhist goddess.
Doll/Dolla/Dollie/Dolly *See* Dolores and Dorothy.
Dolma Sherpa/Tibetan: a female deity.
Dolores Spanish: sorrow. From the seven sorrows of the Virgin Mary.
Delores, Delorez, Deloris, Dolora, Dolorez, Dolorita, Dolour, Dores (Portuguese).
Diminutives: Dolla, Dollie, Dolly, Lola, Lolita.
Dolphina Latin: like a dolphin. A messenger of Poseidon and Neptune, sea gods in classical mythology.
Dauphina, Dauphine, Dolfin, Dolffin (Welsh), *Dolpha, Dolphine.*
Domenica/Domeniga *See* Dominica.
Dominica Latin: belonging to the lord. The feminine form of Dominic.

D – GIRLS

Domenica (Italian), *Domeniga, Domica, Domina, Dominga* (Spanish), *Domini, Dominicah, Dominika* (Slavic), *Dominique* (French), *Domnica, Domnika, Domoneque.*
Diminutive: Dom.

Dominique French form of Dominica.

Domino Latin: a popular game.
Dominoe.

Domnica/Domnika *See* Dominica.

Domoneque *See* Dominica.

Donalda Scottish Gaelic: the ruler of the world. The feminine form of Donald.
Donna, Donella, Donelle, Donia, Doniella, Donielle.

Donalee *See* Donna.

Donata Latin: given by God, a gift.
Donatella (Italian), *Donetta, Donette, Donica, Donnica.*

Donella/Donelle *See* Donalda.

Donetta/Donette *See* Donata.

Donia *See* Donalda and Donla.

Donica/Donnica *See* Donata.

Doniella/Donielle *See* Donalda.

Donka Slavic: a feminine form of Andon (*see* Anthony).

Donla Irish Gaelic: the brown lady.
Donia, Donlah.

Donna Italian: a lady. A short form of Madonna. *See also* Donalda.
Dona, Donalee, Donnah, Ladonna.

Donna-Kay A 'combination name'.
Donna-Kae, Donna-Kai, Donna-Kaye.

Doone Irish Gaelic: a placename. Also a boy's name.
Doon.

Dora Greek: a gift. Originally a short form of Dorothy, Isadora and Theodora.
Dorah, Doralea, Doreen, Doreene, Dorelia, Dorell, Dorella, Dorelle, Doren, Dorena, Dorene, Doretta, Dorette, Doria, Dorian, Dorin, Dorinda, Dorine, Dorita, Dorra, Dorran, Dorren.
Diminutives: Dorey, Dory.

Dorace *See* Doris.

Dorathea/Dorathee/Dorathy *See* Dorothy.

Dorcas Greek: a gazelle or a doe. *See also* Tabitha.
Dorcia.

Doré French: golden. *See also* Dory.
Dore, Dorée.

Doreen *See* Dora.

Dorelia/Dorell/Dorella/Dorelle *See* Dora.

Dores *See* Dolores.

Dorete/Doretta *See* Dorothy.

Doria The feminine form of Dorian. *See also* Dora and Doris.
Dorian, Doriane, Doriann, Dorianne, Dorien, Dorienne.

Dorian/Doriann *See* Dora and Doria.

Dorice *See* Doris.

Dorien/Dorienne *See* Doria.

Dorigen A character from one of Chaucer's *Canterbury Tales*.
Dorigan, Dorrigan, Dorrigen.

Dorinda Greek: a beautiful gift. Also a variation of Dora.

Doris Greek: a woman from Doria, or from the ocean. A Greek goddess of the sea.
Dorace, Doria, Dorice, Dorisa, Dorise, Dorit (Polynesian), *Dorita, Dorris, Dorryce, Dorrys, Dorryse, Doryce, Dorys, Doryse.*
Diminutives: Dorri, Dorrie, Dory.

Dorit/Dorita *See* Dora, Doris and Dorothy.

Dorothy Greek: the gift of God. *See also* Dora and Theodora.
Dorathee, Dorathy, Dorete (Danish), *Dorethea, Doretta, Dorosia* (Polish), *Dorota* (Czech), *Dorotea* (Italian, Finnish, Spanish), *Dorothea* (Dutch, German, Slavic), *Dorothée* (French), *Dorothie, Dorothya, Dorotka, Dorottya* (Hungarian), *Tarati* (Maori).
Diminutives: Dodie, Doff, Doffy, Doll, Dollie, Dolly, Dorit, Dorrie, Dorrit, Dorritt, Dot, Dottie, Dura (Slavic), Teija (Finnish), Thea.

Dorra/Dorran/Dorren *See* Dora.

Dorrit/Dorritt Diminutives of Dorothy.

Dorryce/Dorrys/Doryce/Dorys *See* Doris.

Dory French: the golden-haired one. *See also* Dora and Doré.
Dori, Dorie.

Dot/Dottie *See* Dorothy.

Douce French: gentle, sweet.

Doutzen Dutch: the feminine form of Douwe, meaning a dove.
Doutzan, Doutze.

Dova Teutonic: peace, a dove.
Dovah, Dove.

Dragana Slavic: the feminine form of Dragan, meaning the dear one.
Draga.

Dragica Slavic: precious.
Dragika.

Dree Possibly Scottish Gaelic; meaning unknown.

Drew A diminutive of Andrew, but occasionally used as a female name.
Dru, Drue.

Drina A diminutive of Alexandrina, the helper of mankind.
Dreena, Dreenah, Drinah.

Drisa Sanskrit: the daughter of the sun.
Drisah.

Drishti Sanskrit: sight.
Dristi.

Dru/Drue *See* Drew.

Druella Teutonic: an elfin vision.

Drupadi A warrior goddess in Javanese mythology.

Drusilla Latin: from an old Roman family name; mentioned in the New Testament.
Drucilla.

Dryandra A species of Australian shrubs and small trees.

Driandra.
Duana Irish Gaelic: a little dark maiden.
Duanna, Dwana, Dwanna.
Duena Spanish: a chaperone.
Duenna.
Duessa Celtic: black.
Dulcie Latin: sweet.
Delcie, Delcine, Dolce, Dolcie, Dulca, Dulce, Dulcea, Dulcia, Dulciana, Dulcine, Dulcinea (Spanish), *Dulcyna* (Polish).
Dulcyna *See* Dulcie.
Duma Swahili: a cheetah.
Dumah.
Dumaka Nigerian: the helper.
Dura Slavic diminutive of Dorothea (*see* Dorothy).
Durga Sanskrit: unattainable; a mythological Hindu goddess. Also a boy's name.
Dusana Czech: a spirit, a soul.
Dusa, Dusanna.
Dusty The feminine form of Dustin.
Dusteen, Dusti, Dustie, Dustine, Dustyn, Dustyne.
Duygu Turkish: emotion. Also a boy's name.
Dwana/Dwanna *See* Duana.
Dyan/Dyana/Dyane *See* Diana.
Dyani Native American: a deer.
Dylan Welsh: from the sea. Generally a boy's name.
Dilan, Dillon, Dilyn, Dyllan, Dyllon.
Dymphna Irish Gaelic: a fawn.
Dimphina, Dimphna, Dympna.
Dyna Greek: powerful. *See also* Dinah.
Dynah.
Dysis Greek: the sunset.
Dyta *See* Edith and Perdita.
Dzenita A Slavic name of uncertain meaning.
Dzidra A Russian name of uncertain meaning.
Dzintra Slavic: amber.
Zintra.

E

Eadie/Eadith/Eadithe *See* Edith.
Eadrea *See* Edrea.
Eadwina/Eadwine/Eadwyne *See* Edwina.
Earla/Earlene/Earline/Earlyne *See* Erline.
Eartha Old English: of the earth. *See also* Erda.
Erta, Ertha, Herta, Hertah, Hertha.
Easter Old English: born at Easter time.
Eastre.
Eastermorn Old English: born on Easter morning.
Eastermorne.
Eba African: a crocodile.
Ebah.
Ebanee/Ebanie/Ebany *See* Ebony.
Ebba Old English: from the rich

fortress.
Ebbani/Ebbony *See* Ebony.
Ebele African: merciful.
Eberta Teutonic: bright, brilliant.
Ebony Greek: a black wood.
Ebanee, Ebanie, Ebany, Ebbani, Ebbanie, Ebboni, Ebbonie, Ebbony, Ebonee, Eboni, Ebonie, Ebonnie.
Ebrel Cornish form of April.
Ebril/Ebrill Welsh forms of April.
Ebru Turkish: a cloud.
Ece Turkish: a queen.
Echo Greek: a repeating sound. The name of a nymph in Greek mythology.
Ecco, Ekko.
Eclipse Middle English: something that obscures, as in an eclipse of the moon.
Eklipse.
Eda Old English: rich, prosperous. Turkish: one who is well mannered.
Edah, Edda, Eddah.
Edain *See* Etain.
Edana Gaelic: fiery. *See also* Aidan.
Eidan, Eidann.
Edda Italian form of Hedda and Hedwig. *See also* Eda.
Edel An Irish Gaelic name of uncertain meaning.
Edeline *See* Adelaide.
Edellion One of the names of British Prime Minister David Cameron's daughter. Meaning unknown.

Eden Hebrew: a place of pleasure; from the Garden of Eden.
Edenn, Edin.
Edena *See* Edwina.
Edery *See* Edrey.
Edeta/Edetta/Edette *See* Edith.
Edeva Old English: a rich gift.
Edin *See* Eden.
Edina *See* Edwina.
Edith Old English: prosperity, or a gift.
Eadith, Eadithe, Edeta, Edetta, Edette, Edit (Hungarian), *Edita* (Italian), *Edite* (Portuguese), *Editha, Edithe, Editta, Ediva, Edyta* (Polish), *Edyth, Edytha, Edythe.*
Diminutives: Deta, Dita, Dyta, Eadie, Edie, Edy, Eydie.
Ediva *See* Edith.
Edjo An Ancient Egyptian cobra goddess.
Edlyn Old English: a noble maiden.
Edelyn.
Edmé Scottish: a variation of Esmé, and a feminine form of Edmund.
Edmée.
Edmonda Old English: a rich protector. A feminine form of Edmund.
Edmondia, Edmunda.
Edna Hebrew: renewal, rejuvenation; a name from the Bible. Also a form of Eithne.
Edrea Old English: prosperous, powerful.

Eadrea, Edra.
Edrey Old English: probably a form of Edrea.
Edery, Edree, Edri, Edrie, Edris, Edry.
Edwardina Old English: a prosperous guardian. A female form of Edward.
Edwarda, Edwardia, Edwardine.
Edwige *See* Hedwig.
Edwina Old English: a prosperous friend. The feminine form of Edwin.
Eadwina, Eadwine, Eadwyne, Edena, Edina, Edweena, Edwine, Edwinna, Edwyna.
Diminutives: Ed, Eddie, Win, Winnie.
Edy/Edyta/Edyth/Edythe *See* Edith.
Eerin Aboriginal: a small grey owl.
Eevarn *See* Yvonne.
Efa Welsh form of Eve.
Effie/Effy *See* Euphemia.
Efia African: born on a Friday.
Efiah, Efua, Epua.
Efstathia Greek: the feminine form of Efstathios, meaning stable or well built.
Egeria Greek: a wise adviser.
Eglantine A flower name, from Old French.
Eglantina, Eglantyne.
Eguzkine Basque: the feminine form of Eguzki, meaning like the sun.

Eguskine.
Ehetera/Ehetere Maori forms of Esther.
Eibhlin Irish Gaelic: beautiful, or pleasant.
Eidan A form of Aidan and Edana.
Eiddwen Welsh: the beloved fair one.
Eiko Japanese: probably meaning a prosperous or splendid child.
Eila A Finnish name of uncertain meaning.
Eileen Irish Gaelic: the light of the sun. The Irish form of Helen.
Aileen (Scottish), *Ailene, Aillee, Aisleen* (Scottish), *Aleen, Alene, Aline, Ayleen, Aylene, Eilen, Eilene, Eiley* (Irish Gaelic), *Eiline, Eillen, Eily* (Irish Gaelic), *Eleen, Elene, Ialeen, Ialene, Ileana, Ileen, Ilena, Ilene, Isleen.*
Diminutives: Aili, Ailie.
Eiley/Eily Irish Gaelic forms of Eileeen.
Eilis Irish Gaelic form of Elizabeth.
Eilish *See* Ailis.
Eir Old Norse: the name of the goddess of healing.
Eira Welsh: snow.
Eirah, Eyra.
Eireen/Eirena/Eirene *See* Irene.
Eirian Welsh: silver.
Eiriol Welsh: a snowdrop.
Eirwen Welsh: as white as snow.
Eister *See* Esther.
Eithne Irish Gaelic: ardent, fiery.

See also Aine and Ena.
Edna, Eithna, Enya, Ethene, Ethna, Ethne, Etna.
Ekala Aboriginal: a lake.
Ekaterina/Ekaterini *See* Catherine.
Ekin Turkish: the harvest.
Ekko *See* Echo.
Eklipse *See* Eclipse.
Ekore Maori: will not.
Ekua *See* Aku.
Ela/Elah *See* Ella.
Elaida A name from *The Wheel of Time* series of fantasy novels.
Elaidah, Elayda, Elaydah.
Elaine English: from the Old French form of Helen.
Alaine, Elaina, Elana, Elane, Elayna, Elayne, Ellaine, Ellayne, Eloaine, Ilayne, Illayne.
Diminutives: Laine, Lainey, Laini, Lainie.
Elan Hebrew: a tree. Native American: the friendly one.
Elana Hebrew: an oak tree. *See also* Elaine and Ilana.
Elani *See* Éliane.
Elanor/Elanore *See* Eleanor.
Elanora Aboriginal: a home by the sea.
Elara Greek: a satellite of the planet Jupiter.
Elata Latin: exalted, of high birth.
Elayda/Elaydah *See* Elaida.
Elayna/Elayne *See* Elaine.
Elba The name of an Italian island.
Elbah, Elbe.

Elberta/Elbertina/Elbertine *See* Alberta.
Elda Italian form of Hilda.
Eldora Spanish: the golden one.
Eleander Probably a feminine form of Leander (the lion man).
Eleandra.
Eleanor Old French: the light of the sun. A form of Helen.
Elanor, Elanore, Eleanora, Eleanore, Elenor, Elenora, Elenore, Eleonora (Italian), *Eleonore* (French, German), *Elinor, Elinora, Elinore, Ellanor, Ellanore, Ellenor, Ellenore, Ellinor, Ellnor, Ellnore, Elnora, Elnore, Heleanor, Heleanore, Helienor, Hellenor, Leanor* (Spanish), *Leanora, Leanorah, Lennore, Lenora, Lenore, Leonora, Leonore.*
Diminutives: Ella, Elli, Ellie, Elly, Ellye, Nell, Nelly, Nora (Scandinavian), Norah, Noreen.
Elecia *See* Alicia.
Electra Greek: brilliant.
Electre, Elektra, Elektre, Elettra (Italian), *Ilectra, Ilektra.*
Eleen/Elene *See* Eileen.
Eleesha *See* Alicia.
Elefteria Greek: one who is free.
Eleftheria, Elephteria.
Eleganza Italian: elegance; the elegant one.
Eleganze.
Eleise *See* Elizabeth and Ellice.

Elen Welsh form of Ellen and Helen.

Elena Italian, Portuguese and Spanish forms of Helen.
Alainya, Elina, Ellena, Ylena, Ylenna.

Eleni Greek form of Helen.
Ellenie.

Elenka *See* Helen.

Elenora/Eleonora/Eleonore *See* Eleanor.

Eleri Welsh: the name of a river.

Eletha/Elethea *See* Alethea.

Eletta/Elette *See* Ella.

Elettra Italian form of Electra.

Eleu Hawaiian: alert and lively. Also a boy's name.

Elf Dutch/German: eleven. Old English: a sprite or a fairy.
Elfe.

Elfreda/Elfreida/Elfrida *See* Alfreda.

Elga *See* Olga.

Éliane Latin: from the Greek word for the sun.
Elani, Elian, Eliana, Eliann, Elianna, Ellian, Elliana, Ellianna, Ellianne, Elyana, Elyann, Elyanne.

Elice/Elicia *See* Alicia and Ellice.

Elida *See* Alida.

Elif Turkish: slender.

Elika An attractive Persian name.
Elikaa, Elikah.

Elin Swedish form of Ellen and Helen.

Elina *See* Elena.

Elinor/Elinora/Elinore *See* Eleanor.

Eliora Hebrew: God is my light.
Eleora.

Elisa/Elise/Elisie *See* Elizabeth and Ellice.

Elisabet/Elisabeth *See* Elizabeth.

Elisandra/Elissandra *See* Alexandra.

Elisebeth/Elizebeth *See* Elizabeth.

Elisha *See* Alicia.

Eliska *See* Elizabeth.

Elissa Greek: a mythological figure. *See also* Elizabeth.

Elita Old French: the chosen one. *See also* Alida.

Elitsa Bulgarian: a little fir tree.
Elitza.

Eliyce/Eliyse *See* Ellice.

Eliza *See* Elizabeth.

Elizabeth Hebrew: consecrated to God. A name from the Bible. *See also* Isabel, Lisa and Lizelle.
Eilis (Irish Gaelic), *Eleise, Elisa* (Italian), *Elisabet* (Scandinavian), *Elisabeth, Elisabetta* (Italian), *Elisavetta* (Russian), *Elise* (French), *Elisebeth, Eliska, Elissa, Eliza, Elizebeth, Elizka, Elizza, Ellise, Ellissa, Elsa, Elsbeth, Else* (Danish, German), *Elspeth, Elysa, Elysabeth, Elyse, Elyssa, Elyzabeth, Elza, Elzira* (Portuguese), *Erihapeti* (Maori), *Erzsebet* (Hungarian), *Ilisapeci*

(Fijian), *Ilsa, Ilse* (German), *Irihapeti* (Maori), *Leis, Leise, Leisel* (German), *Liese* (German), *Liesel, Liesl, Liezel, Lisa, Lisabet, Lisabeth, Lisbet, Lisbeth, Lise* (Scandinavian), *Liza, Yelizaveta* (Russian).
Diminutives: Beith, Bess, Bessie, Bessy, Bet, Beth, Bethan (Welsh), Beti (Welsh), Betina, Betine, Betsan (Welsh), Betsey, Betsi, Betsy, Bette, Bettee, Bettie, Bettina, Bettine, Betty, Bettye, Buffy, Ella, Elsie, Elsje (Dutch), Elske, Erzsi (Hungarian), Libby, Licette, Lili, Lilibet, Lillibet, Lisette (French), Liz, Lizette, Lizzie, Lizzy, Lysette, Lyz, Lyzz, Zizi (Hungarian).

Elizka/Elizza *See* Elizabeth.
Elka Polynesian: black.
Elkah.
Elke Teutonic: noble.
Elkee, Elkie, Elkey.
Ella Old English: elfin, a fairy maiden. Also a diminutive of Eleanor, Elizabeth, Ellen and Helen.
Ela, Elah, Eletta, Elette, Ellah, Ellana, Ellanna.
Diminutives: Elli, Ellie, Elly, Ellye.
Ellaine/Ellayne *See* Elaine.
Ellaleen A combination of Ella and, perhaps, Colleen.
Ellalene, Ellaline.
Ellamay A combination of Ella and May.
Elmai, Elmay, Ellamai.
Ellana/Ellanna *See* Ella.
Ellanor/Ellanore *See* Eleanor.
Elle French: she, a woman.
Ellecia *See* Alicia.
Ellen A form of Helen.
Elen (Wlesh), *Elin* (Swedish), *Ellin, Ellinya, Ellyn, Ellyne, Elyn, Elynn, Eylen, Eylin, Eylyn.*
Diminutives: Ella, Elleigh, Elli, Ellie, Elly, Ellye, Nell.
Ellena/Ellenie *See* Elena and Helen.
Ellenor/Ellinor *See* Eleanor.
Elli/Ellie Diminutives of Alice, Eleanor, Ella, Ellen and Helen.
Elliana/Ellianna *See* Éliane.
Ellice Greek: Jehovah is God. The feminine form of Elias.
Elecia, Eleise, Elice, Elicia, Elise, Elisie, Eliyce, Eliyse, Ellecia, Ellicia, Ellyce, Elyce.
Ellicia *See* Alicia and Ellice.
Elliette A feminine form of Elliott or Ellis.
Eliett, Eliette, Elliett.
Ellin Aboriginal: to move. *See also* Ellen.
Ellis English from Greek: a form of Elias.
Elis.
Ellise/Ellissa *See* Elizabeth.
Ellisha *See* Alicia.
Ellnor/Ellnore *See* Eleanor.
Elloisa/Elloise/Ellouise *See* Eloise.

Ellora From the name of the ancient caves in southern India.
Elora, Ellorah, Ellorian.
Elly/Ellye/Ellyn *See* Alice, Ellen and Elli.
Ellyce/Ellyse *See* Ellice.
Elma Greek: pleasant, amiable.
Ilma.
Elmai/Elmay *See* Ellamay.
Elmas Armenian/Turkish: a diamond.
Elmasa, Elmaz, Elmaza.
Elmira Old English: noble.
Elna A form of Helen.
Eloaine *See* Elaine.
Elodia/Elodie *See* Alodie.
Eloise Teutonic: healthy.
Elloisa, Elloise, Ellouise, Eloisa, Elouise, Heloisa, Heloise.
Elora/Elorian *See* Ellora.
Elouera Aboriginal: from the pleasant place.
Elpis Greek: hope.
Elpida, Elpidia, Elpitha.
Elrica Teutonic: the ruler of all.
Elsa/Else/Elsie *See* Alice and Elizabeth.
Elsje/Elske Diminutives of Elizabeth.
Elspeth *See* Elizabeth.
Elula From Elul, the sixth lunar month of the Hebrew calendar, corresponding to the zodiac sign of Virgo.
Ellula.
Eluned Welsh form of Lynn and Lynette (*see* Linnet).
Elva *See* Alfreda and Elvina.
Elvara *See* Alvara.
Elvina Old English: the friend of the elves.
Alvina, Alvine, Elva, Elvene, Elvey, Elvia, Elvie, Elvin, Elvine, Elvy.
Elvira Latin: the fair one. Teutonic: a true stranger.
Alvera, Alvira, Elvera, Elverey, Elvery, Elvire.
Elwyn Welsh: white- or fair-browed.
Elwin, Elwine, Elwinn, Elwinne, Elwyne, Elwynn, Elwynne.
Elyann/Elyanne *See* Éliane.
Elyce *See* Alice, Elizabeth and Ellice.
Elyn/Elynn *See* Ellen.
Elysa/Elyse/Elyssa/Elyssia *See* Alice and Elizabeth.
Elysabeth/Elyzabeth *See* Elizabeth.
Elysha/Elyshia *See* Alicia.
Elysia Latin: blissful.
Elza *See* Alice and Elizabeth.
Elzira Portuguese form of Elizabeth.
Ema/Emah *See* Emma.
Emajen/Emajin *See* Imogen.
Emalee/Emali/Emalia/Emalie *See* Emily.
Emba Swahili form of Amber. *See also* Ember.
Ember Old English: the glowing remains of a fire. Also a form of Amber.

Emba, Embah, Embar, Embere, Embeur, Embr, Embry, Embur.
Embeth A combination of Emma and Beth (*see* Elizabeth).
Embla Old Norse: the first woman (the equivalent of Eve) in Norse mythology. She was created from an elm tree.
Embr/Embry/Embur *See* Ember.
Emel Turkish: desire.
Emelda *See* Imelda.
Emelia/Emelie/Emelina/Emeline/ Emelye *See* Amelia and Emily.
Emer Irish Gaelic: a traditional name.
Emerald A gemstone name.
Emerant, Emeraude (French), *Emmarald, Emrallt* (Welsh), *Esmeralda* (Spanish), *Esmerelda.*
Diminutives: Meraud, Meraude.
Emere Maori form of Emily.
Emerson The son (or daughter) of Emery, meaning an industrious ruler. Generally a boy's name.
Emmasen, Emmason, Emersen, Emmersen, Emmerson.
Emerson-Rose A modern 'combination name'.
Emmasen-Rose, Emmason-Rose, Emersen-Rose, Emmersen-Rose, Emmerson-Rose.
Emiko Japanese: a smiling child.
Emily Teutonic: industrious. *See also* Amelia.
Emalee, Emali, Emalia, Emalie, Emelia, Emelie, Emelina,
Emeline, Emelye, Emelyn, Emere (Maori), *Emilee, Emiley, Emili, Emilia* (Italian), *Emiliana, Emilida, Émilie* (French), *Emilie, Emilyn, Emmalee.*
Diminutives: Em, Emme, Emmy.
Emina Latin: a noble or lofty maiden.
Emine Turkish: the feminine form of Emin, meaning honest or trustworthy.
Emita/Emity *See* Amity.
Emma Teutonic: the healer of the universe.
Ema, Emah, Emmah, Emmalene, Emmaline, Emmasyn, Emmelene, Emmeline, Emmelyn.
Diminutives: Em, Emme, Emmy.
Emmabelle A combination of Emma and Belle (beautiful).
Emma-Belle.
Emmalee *See* Emily.
Emmamonique An unusual 'combination name'.
Emamonike, Emamonique, Emmahmonike, Emmahmonique, Emmamonike.
Emmanuelle Hebrew: God is with us. The feminine form of Emmanuel.
Emanuela, Emanuelle, Emmanuela, Manuela (Spanish), *Manuella, Manuelle.*
Emmasen/Emmason *See* Emerson.
Emme/Emmy *See* Emily and Emma.
Emmelia *See* Amelia.

Emmylou A combination of Emily and Louise.
Emogen/Emogene/Emojen *See* Imogen.
Emrallt Welsh form of Emerald.
Ena Irish Gaelic: ardent. A variation of Aine and Eithne.
Enaki Hawaiian: the fiery sea.
Encina Spanish: an oak tree.
Enda Irish: a bird.
Endah, Endia, Endiah, Endla.
Endocia Greek: of unquestionable reputation.
Endora Hebrew: a fountain.
Endota Aboriginal: beautiful.
Engelberta Teutonic: a bright angel.
Engracia *See* Grace.
Enid Celtic: a pure soul.
Ened.
Ennea Greek: the ninth.
Enna, Ennia.
Ennis Celtic: from the island. More commonly a boy's name.
Enis, Ennys, Enys.
Ennor Cornish: honour.
Enor.
Enora Greek: light.
Enrica Italian and Spanish forms of Henrietta.
Enya A form of Eithne.
Enyo Greek: a goddess of battle.
Enza Italian: the feminine form of Enzo (*see* Laurence).
Eolanda Greek: the feminine form of Aeolus, the god of the winds in Greek mythology.
Eolande.
Eos Greek: dawn. The mother of the stars and the winged goddess of the dawn; the equivalent of the Roman goddess Aurora.
Ephemia *See* Euphemia.
Epiphany English from Greek: an appearance or revelation. The name of a Christian festival held on 6 January. *See also* Theophania and Tiffany.
Epifanee, Epifhaney, Epifhanie, Epifhany, Epiphanee, Epiphaney, Epiphanie.
Epona A Celtic and Roman goddess of horses.
Eponah, Eponia, Eponina.
Epua *See* Efia.
Eranthe Greek: a flower of spring.
Erato The muse of lyric and erotic poetry in Greek mythology.
Erda The Teutonic earth goddess. *See also* Eartha.
Erdah.
Ereca/Ereka *See* Erica.
Ereena/Erena/Erene *See* Irene.
Erica Old Norse: a powerful ruler. The feminine form of Eric.
Ereca, Ereka, Ericah, Erika (German, Scandinavian), Erikah, Erikka, Eryka, Erykah.
Erihapeti A Maori form of Elizabeth.
Eriko Japanese: a child blessed with logic.
Erin Irish Gaelic: from Ireland.

Aerin, Aerrine, Erina, Erine, Erinee, Erinn, Erinna, Erinne, Erran, Errin, Erryn, Erryne, Eryn.

Eris Greek: the goddess of discord.
Erisa.

Erja *See* Irja.

Erline Old English: a noblewoman. The feminine form of Earl.
Earla, Earlene, Earline, Earlyne, Erlene, Erlyne, Irlene, Irline, Irlyne.

Erma Teutonic: a maiden of the army; the feminine form of Herman. *See also* Armina.
Ermina, Erminia, Erminie, Irma.

Ermine Old French: the name of a fur.
Ermina, Erminia.

Ermione *See* Hermione.

Erna *See* Ernestine.

Ernestine Teutonic: serious, earnest. The feminine form of Ernest.
Erna, Ernesta, Ernestina, Ernestyna, Ernice.

Erran/Errin/Erryn/Erryne *See* Erin.

Ersa Greek: dew. A figure in Greek mythology.
Ersah.

Ersilia Italian: tender or delicate.
Ercilia (Greek).

Erta/Ertha *See* Eartha.

Erwina Teutonic: an honourable friend.
Erwine.

Eryka/Erykah *See* Erica.

Eryn/Erynn/Erynne *See* Erin.

Erzsebet Hungarian form of Elizabeth.
Diminutive: Erzsi.

Esara Hebrew: our treasure.
Esarah.

Esen Turkish: like the wind.

Eser Turkish: achievement. Also a boy's name.

Esha Sanskrit: a wish or desire.

Eshana Sanskrit: a searcher.

Eshtar *See* Ishtar.

Esi Ghanaian: born on a Sunday.
Esie.

Esin Turkish: inspiration.

Esmé Old French: one who is loved. *See also* Edmé.
Esma, Esmae, Esmah, Esmay, Esmey, Ezma, Ezmay.

Esmerelda A form of Emerald.
Esmeralda.

Esperance Latin: hope.
Esperanza (Spanish), *Speranza* (Italian).

Esprit French from Latin: wit, lively intelligence or spirit. Also a boy's name.
Espree, Esprie.

Esra/Esrah *See* Ezra.

Esrela/Esrella *See* Ezrela.

Esta Italian: from the east. Persian: a star. *See also* Estelle and Esther.

Estée *See* Estelle.

Estefania *See* Stephanie.

Estelle French from Latin: a star.
See also Esther and Stella.
Astella, Astelle, Esta (Persian),
Estée (French), *Estell, Estella,*
Estrella (Spanish), *Étoile* (French).
Diminutives: Stella, Stelle, Strella,
Trella.

Esther Hebrew: a star. *See also*
Estelle, Hesper and Stella.
Ehetera (Maori), *Ehetere* (Maori),
Eister (Irish Gaelic), *Esta, Ester,*
Esterita, Esterlita, Esterre
(Italian), *Eszter* (Hungarian),
Hadassa (Jewish), *Hadassah*
(Jewish), *Hester, Hesther.*
Diminutives: Essie, Etty, Hettie,
Hetty.

Estonia A northern European country.
Estonya.

Estrella Spanish form of Estelle, a star.

Esyllt Welsh form of Isolde.

Etain Irish: shining, bright. The name of a mythological figure.
Aideen, Edain, Etaoin.

Etel *See* Ethel.

Eternity Middle English: endless, forever.
Eternal, Eternité.

Ethel Teutonic: a noble maiden.
See also Ethlyn.
Etel, Ethelda, Ethelene,
Ethelinda, Etheline, Ethelyn,
Ethyl.

Ethelbeth A combination of Ethel and Beth (*see* Elizabeth).

Ethelwyn A fair and noble maiden.
Ethelwynn, Ethelwynne.

Ethene *See* Aine and Eithne.

Ethlyn Probably a form of Ethel.
Ethlin, Ethlinn, Ethlinne,
Ethlynn, Ethlynne.

Ethna/Ethne/Etna *See* Eithne.

Étienette French from Greek: a garland or crown; the feminine form of Étienne. *See also* Stephanie.
Diminutive: Ettie.

Étoile *See* Estelle.

Etsu Japanese: delight.

Etsuko Japanese: a joyful or delightful child.

Etta/Ettie *See* Étienette and Henrietta.

Eucharia From Eucharist, the holy sacrament or communion.

Euclea Greek: glory.

Eudocia Greek: wonderful or glorious.
Eudocie (French), *Eudokhia*
(Russian), *Eudokia, Eudoksya*
(Polish), *Eudoxia, Evdokia,*
Evdoxia, Ewdokia.

Eudora Greek: a wonderful gift.

Eufamie/Eufemia/Eufimia
See Euphemia.

Eugenia Greek: noble, well-born. The feminine form of Eugene.
Eugene, Eugénie (French).
Diminutives: Gena, Gene, Genia, Genie.

Eulalia Greek: the well-spoken one.
Eula, Eulalie (French), *Eulaylia, Olalla* (Spanish), *Ulalia*.

Eun Korean: silver.

Euna *See* Úna.

Eunice Greek: victorious. The mother of Timothy in the New Testament.
Eunis, Unice, Unis.

Euphemia Greek: of good reputation.
Ephemia, Eufamie, Eufemia (Italian, Spanish, Portuguese), *Eufimia, Euphémie* (French), *Euphimia*.
Diminutives: Effie, Effy, Phemia, Phimia.

Euphrasia Greek: joy, delight.

Euroka Aboriginal: from a sunny place. A New South Wales placename.

Europa Greek: a princess in mythology, who was abducted by the god Zeus in the form of a white bull. The origin of the name Europe.

Eurwen Welsh: fair.
Eurwyn.

Eurydice Greek: the goddess of the underworld in Greek mythology.
Euridice.

Eusebia Spanish: the feminine form of Eusebios.

Eustacia Greek: fruitful. The feminine form of Eustace.
Eustacie.

Diminutives: Stacey, Stacie, Stacy.

Euterpe Greek: delightful. One of the muses in Greek mythology.

Eva/Evah *See* Eve.

Evadne Greek: fortunate.
Evadna.

Evaleen *See* Evelyn.

Evaleigh *See* Eveleigh.

Evaluna A combination of Eva and Luna (the moon).
Evahluna, Evalunah.

Evana *See* Ivana and Jane.

Evanda The feminine form of Evander, meaning a good man.
Evandah, Evantha, Evanthia.

Evangeline Greek: the bearer of good news.
Evangelia, Evangelie, Evangelina, Ivangela, Ivangelia, Ivangelie, Ivangelina.

Evania Greek: peaceful, tranquil.

Evarn/Evarne *See* Yvonne.

Evdokia/Evdoxia *See* Eudocia.

Eve Hebrew: life-giving. *See also* Evelyn.
Chava (Hebrew), *Efa* (Welsh), *Eva, Evah, Evva* (Russian), *Ewa* (Polish), *Hava* (Jewish), *Havva* (Turkish), *Yeva* (Russian), *Yiva, Yva, Yve*.
Diminutives: Evey, Evie, Evita (Spanish), Evy.

Eveanne A combination of Eve (life-giving) and Anne (grace).
Evann, Evanne, Eveann, Evian, Eviann, Evianne, Evyan,

Evyann, Evyanne.
Eveleigh A combination of Eve and Leigh, or a form of Evelyn.
Evaleigh, Everleigh, Everley, Everly.
Evelisse *See* Ivelisse.
Evelyn English: from an old surname, but also related to Eve.
Aveline, Evaleen (Irish), *Evalyn, Eveleigh, Evelene, Evelina, Eveline, Evelyne, Evelynn, Evelynne, Everlyn, Everlynne, Evley, Evlyn, Evyleen.*
Diminutives: Evey, Evie, Evy.
Everdine Old English: the valley of wild boars.
Everdean, Everdeen, Everdeina, Everdeine, Everdina.
Evgeniya Russian: the feminine form of Evgeniy (Eugene), meaning the noble or well-born one.
Evgenia, Evgenya.
Everil/Everild/Everilda/Everill *See* Averil.
Everleigh/Everley *See* Eveleigh.
Everlyn/Everlynne *See* Evelyn.
Evetta/Evette *See* Yvette.
Evie/Evy/Evyleen *See* Eve and Evelyn.
Evita *See* Eve.
Evley/Evlyn *See* Evelyn.
Evon/Evonn/Evonna/Evonne *See* Yvonne.
Evva *See* Eve.
Evyan/Evyann/Evyanne

See Eveanne.
Ewa *See* Eve.
Ewalani Hawaiian: a heavenly woman.
Ewdokia *See* Eudocia.
Exene American: a modern made-up name.
Exodus Middle English from Greek: to leave or go out. The name of the second book of the Old Testament. Also a boy's name.
Exodos.
Eydie A diminutive of Edith.
Eylen/Eylin/Eylyn *See* Ellen.
Eyota Native American: the greatest.
Eyra *See* Eira.
Eyvette *See* Yvette.
Eyvonn/Eyvonna/Eyvonne *See* Yvonne.
Ezma/Ezmay *See* Esmé.
Ezra Hebrew: the helper, a name from the Bible. More commonly a boy's name.
Esra, Esrah, Ezrah.
Diminutive: Ezzy.
Ezrela Feminine form of Ezra, the helper.
Esrela, Esrella, Ezrella.

F

Fabia Latin: a bean grower. Feminine form of Fabian.
Fabiana, Fabienne (French),

Fabiola (Spanish).
Fabiola Spanish form of Fabia.
Fabrianne Latin: resourceful, or a craftswoman.
Fabriane, Fabrianna, Fabrienne (French).
Fadelma *See* Fidelma.
Fadia Arabic: the feminine form of Fadi, meaning a saviour.
Fadwa.
Fadila Arabic: generous and distinguished.
Fae/Faie *See* Faith and Fay.
Faery/Faerie *See* Fairy.
Faeth/Faethe *See* Faith.
Fahima Arabic: the feminine form of Fahim, meaning a good scholar.
Fahina.
Faine Old English: joyful.
Faina, Fane, Fayna, Fayne.
Fairley Old English: a clearing in the woods. Also a boy's name.
Fairlee, Fairleigh, Fairlie.
Fairuz Arabic: the gemstone, turquoise.
Fairoue, Fayruz, Feruzi (Swahili), *Firuza* (Arabic).
Fairy Middle English: a supernatural being.
Faerie, Faery, Fairee, Fairey, Fairie.
Faith English: trusting in God, having faith. *See also* Fidela.
Faeth, Faethe, Faithe, Faithi (African), *Fayth, Faythe.*
Diminutives: Fai, Faie, Fay, Faye.

Faiza Arabic: victorious.
Faizah, Fayza.
Falda Icelandic: with folded wings.
Fallon Irish: a leader. Also a boy's name.
Fallan, Fallen, Fallyn.
Fanchon *See* Frances
Fane *See* Faine.
Fanna A name from the *Dragonriders of Pern* series of fantasy novels.
Fana, Fanah, Fannah.
Fannie/Fanny *See* Frances.
Farah Arabic: happiness. *See also* Farrah.
Fariha.
Faran/Faren/Farin/Faron *See* Farran.
Farica/Farika *See* Frederica.
Farida Arabic: unique.
Faridah, Faride.
Fariha *See* Farah.
Farina Italian: flour.
Farinah.
Farrah Old English: beautiful.
Fara, Farah, Farra.
Farran Old French: a journey or venture.
Faran, Faren, Farin, Faron, Farren, Farrin, Farron, Farryn.
Farzana Arabic: wise, learned.
Fatima Arabic: a woman who abstains, or who weans a child. A daughter of the prophet Muhammad.
Fatimah, Fatma.
Faun/Fauna/Faunia *See* Fawn.

Fauna An alternative name for Bona Dea, the Roman goddess of chastity and fertility. *See also* Fawn.

Faustine Latin: the fortunate one.
Fausta, Faustina, Faustyna.

Fawn Old French: a young deer.
Faun, Fauna, Faunia, Fawna, Fawnia.

Fay English from Old French: a fairy or magical creature. Also a diminutive of Faith.
Fae, Faie, Faye, Fayeen, Fayene, Fayetta, Fayette, Fayine, Faylena, Faylene, Fey.

Fayme Latin: of high reputation, renowned.
Faym.

Fayna/Fayne *See* Faine.

Fayre Old English: fair.

Fayruz *See* Fairuz.

Fayth/Faythe *See* Faith.

Fayza *See* Faiza.

Fazila Arabic: virtuous or excellent.

Fearna/Fearne *See* Fern.

February Latin: the second month of the year; from februare (purification).
Februar (Danish, German), *Februari* (Swahili), *Februaria, Février* (French), *Fevronia.*

Fedelma *See* Fidelma.

Federica/Federicia *See* Frederica.

Fedha Swahili: silvery; like the metal silver.

Fedora A Russian form of Theodora. Also a type of hat.
Fedorah.

Feebee/Feebie *See* Phoebe.

Feenix *See* Phoenix.

Felda Teutonic: from the field.

Felice/Felicia *See* Felicity.

Felicity Latin: lucky, fortunate. The feminine form of Felix.
Felecity, Felice, Felicia, Felicidad (Spanish), *Felicie* (German), *Felicita* (Italian), *Felicitas, Félicité* (French), *Felicitus, Felis, Felise, Felisha, Felita, Feliza, Felizia, Phelicitie, Phelicity, Phelisitie, Phelisity, Phelissitie, Phelissity.*
Diminutive: Flick.

Feliks *See* Felix.

Felipa *See* Philippa.

Felisha *See* Felicity.

Felita/Feliza/Felizia *See* Felicity.

Felix Latin: fortunate or lucky. More commonly a boy's name.
Feliks, Felixe, Feliz.

Fenella Gaelic: the white- or fair-shouldered one.
Finella, Finola, Fionnuala, Fionola, Fynola, Fynnola.

Fenix *See* Phoenix.

Fennagh An Irish placename.
Fenagh, Fenna, Fennah.

Feodora *See* Theodora.

Feona/Feonah *See* Fiona.

Fera/Ferah *See* Ferra.

Fereniki Greek form of Berenice.

Fergine The feminine form of Fergus, a Gaelic name meaning the chosen man, or a man of vigour.

Fergeen, Fergeena, Fergena, Fergene, Fergina.
Feria Latin: a festival or fair.
Ferida Turkish: unique.
Feridah, Feride.
Fern Old English: fern-like. A 'plant name'.
Fearna, Fearne, Ferna, Ferne.
Fernanda Teutonic: prepared for the journey; a traveller or adventurer. The feminine form of Ferdinand.
Ferdinanda, Fernande (French), *Fernandia, Fernandina.*
Fernleigh A combination of Fern and Leigh (a meadow or clearing).
Fernlea, Fernlee, Fernlei, Fernlie.
Ferola *See* Ferra.
Feronia Latin: a mythological goddess.
Ferra Latin: like iron.
Fera, Ferah, Ferola, Ferrah, Ferria.
Feruzi Swahili form of Fairuz.
Février The French name for February.
Fevronia *See* February.
Fey *See* Fay.
Feyona/Feyonah *See* Fiona.
Ffion Welsh form of Fiona.
Fhebee/Fheebie *See* Phoebe.
Fiala Czech: a violet.
Fidan Turkish: a sapling.
Fidela Latin: faithful. *See also* Faith.
Fidele, Fidelia, Fidelis, Fidelita, Fidelity, Fidella, Fidellia.
Fidelma Irish Gaelic: the name of a saint.
Fadelma, Fedelma.
Fife Scottish: a woman from the region of Fife.
Fyfe, Fyffe.
Fifi *See* Josephine.
Fig Middle English: a 'fruit name'.
Filamena/Filamene *See* Philomena.
Filberta/Filbertha *See* Philberta.
Filippa *See* Philippa.
Filomena/Filomene *See* Philomena.
Fina *See* Fiona.
Finella/Finola/Fionola *See* Fenella.
Finesse French: skill or elegance.
Finess.
Finlay Scottish Gaelic: a fair warrior. More commonly a boy's name.
Findlay, Findley, Finley, Finnlay, Finnley.
Fiona Irish Gaelic: a vine. Scottish Gaelic: the fair one.
Feona, Feonah, Feyona, Feyonah, Ffion (Welsh), *Fina* (Irish), *Fionah, Fione, Fionn, Fionna, Fyona, Fyonah.*
Diminutive: Fee.
Fiora *See* Flora.
Fiore Italian: a flower.
Fioray, Fioreh, Fiorina, Fiorine.
Fiorella Italian: a little flower.
Fiorenza Italian form of Florence.
Fire English from Greek: heat, energy and passion. Also a boy's name.
Fyre.
Firuza *See* Fairuz.

Flair Latin: elegance and style.
Flaire, Flayr, Flayre.
Flame Middle English: something that burns or blazes.
Flaime, Flayme.
Flanna Gaelic: red-haired. The feminine form of Flannan.
Flannery Irish Gaelic: the red one. More commonly a boy's name.
Flanary, Flanery, Flannary, Flanner.
Flavia Latin: the golden-haired one.
Flavie (French).
Flax Middle English: a 'plant name'.
Flaxen.
Flayre *See* Flair.
Fleur Old French: a flower. *See also* Flora.
Fleura, Fleure.
Diminutive: Fleurette.
Flick *See* Felicity.
Flo *See* Flora and Florence.
Flora Latin: a flower. The Roman goddess of flowers and the spring. *See also* Fleur.
Fiora, Floare, Florah, Floralia, Flore (French), *Florea, Floreen, Florella, Florette, Florey, Florez, Floria, Floriana, Florimal, Florinda, Florinka* (Slavic), *Floris, Floura, Flourah.*
Diminutives: Flo, Florrie.
Florence Latin: blossoming, flourishing.
Fiorenza (Italian), *Florance, Florancia, Floreen, Florenca, Florencia, Florinda.*
Diminutives: Flo, Florrie, Flossie.
Florentina A woman from the Italian city of Florence.
Florentia, Florentine, Florentyna, Florentyne.
Florette/Florey/Florez *See* Flora.
Floria/Floriana/Florinda/Floura *See* Flora.
Folole A Samoan name of uncertain meaning.
Fonda Latin: affectionate.
Fontaine French: a spring or fountain.
Fontana (Italian), *Fontayne.*
Formosa The former name of Taiwan.
Fortuna Latin: the fortunate one.
Fortunata, Fortune.
Fosetta French: the dimpled one.
Fosette.
Fotini Greek: light.
Fotene, Fotine, Photene, Photine, Photini.
Fraida *See* Frayda.
Franca Italian form of Frances.
Francee *See* Frances.
Frances Latin: from France, or a free woman. The feminine form of Francis.
Franca (Italian), *Francene, Francesca* (Italian), *Francess, Francesse, Francette, Francheska, Francia, Francielle, Francina* (Dutch), *Francine* (French), *Francisca* (Spanish), *Françoise*

(French), *Franka* (Russian), *Fransia, Frantiska* (Czech), *Franziska* (German).
Diminutives: Fanchon (French), Fannie, Fanny, Fran, France, Francee, Franci, Francie, Frankee, Franki, Frankie, Frannie, Ziska (German).

Francesca/Francisca *See* Frances.
Franci/Francia/Francie/Francina/Francine *See* Frances.
Françoise French form of Frances.
Frangipani French: a scented flower.
Frangipanie, Frangipanni, Frangipannie.
Frankee/Franki/Frankie *See* Frances.
Fransia *See* Frances.
Frantiska Czech form of Frances.
Frasquita The name of a character in the opera *Carmen*.
Frayda Yiddish: joy.
Fraida, Fraydah, Freyde.
Freda Diminutive of names such as Alfreda, Frederica and Winifred.
Fredah, Freeda, Freida, Freide (German), *Frida, Frieda, Friede.*
Frederica Teutonic: a peaceful ruler. The feminine form of Frederick.
Farica, Farika, Federica, Federicia, Fredericka, Frédérique (French), *Fredicia, Frerika, Friederike* (German), *Fryderyka* (Slavic), *Frydryka* (Polish).
Diminutives: Freda, Freddie, Friede (German), Fritzi (German).

Freema The name of a British actress (Freema Agyeman), best known for her role as Martha Jones in the *Doctor Who* TV series.
Frema, Frima.
Freesia A fragrant flower.
Freja *See* Freya.
Frerika *See* Frederica.
Freya Old Norse: a lady. The goddess of love in Scandinavian mythology.
Freja (Swedish), *Freyja.*
Freyde *See* Frayda.
Frida/Frieda/Friede/Friederike *See* Freda, Frederica and Halfrida.
Friday The day of Freya, the Norse equivalent of the Roman god Venus.
Fritzi The feminine form of Fritz, a German diminutive of Frederick. *See also* Frederica.
Fritsee, Fritsi, Fritsie, Fritzee, Fritzie, Fritzy.
Frona A diminutive of Sophronia.
Fronde Latin: a leaf of the fern.
Frond.
Fruma Yiddish: one who is pious.
Frumah.
Fryderyka/Frydryka *See* Frederica.
Fuchsia An unusual 'flower name', after the German botanist Leonhard Fuchs.
Fushia.
Fuki Japanese: joy.
Fukie.
Fukiko Japanese: a joyous child.
Fulla The name of a Norse fertility

goddess.

Fulvia Latin: tawny-haired. The name of the wife of Mark Antony.
Fuyu Japanese: born in winter.
Fuyuko Japanese: a child of the winter.
Fyfe/Fyffe *See* Fife.
Fynola/Fynnola *See* Fenella.
Fyona/Fyonah *See* Fiona.
Fyre *See* Fire.

G

Gabbi/Gabbie/Gabi/Gabie *See* Gabrielle.
Gabbiann A combination of Gabbi (*see* Gabrielle) and Ann.
Gabbianne, Gabiann, Gabianne.
Gabourey African: the unusual name of an American actress (Gabourey Sidibe).
Gabourie, Gaboury.
Gabrielle Hebrew: a woman of God. The feminine form of Gabriel.
Gabrella, Gabrelle, Gabriela (Polish), *Gabriele* (Czech, German), *Gabriella* (Italian), *Gabrilla, Gavrielle, Gavrila.*
Diminutives: Gabbi, Gabbie, Gabe, Gabi, Gabie, Gaby.
Gaby *See* Gabrielle.
Gacinta *See* Jacinta.
Gada Hebrew: lucky.
Gadar Armenian: perfection.

Gae/Gaeda *See* Gay.
Gael/Gaeleen/Gaelle *See* Gail.
Gaelin/Gaelinn/Gaelyn/Gaelynne *See* Gailin.
Gaenor/Gainor *See* Gaynor and Guinevere.
Gaetana Italian: the feminine form of Gaetano.
Gai/Gaida/Gaie *See* Gay.
Gaia Greek: the earth. The earth goddess in Greek mythology.
Gaea, Gaya.
Gail Originally a short form of Abigail.
Gael, Gaeleen, Gaelle, Gaila, Gaile, Gailene, Gailin, Gaille, Gale, Gayl, Gayla, Gayle, Gaylee, Gayleen, Gaylene.
Gailin A combination of Gai (*see* Gay) and Lin.
Gaelin, Gaelinn, Gaelinne, Gaelyn, Gaelynn, Gaelynne, Gailinn, Gailinne, Gailyn, Gailynn, Gailynne, Gaylin, Gaylinn, Gaylinne.
Gaindah Aboriginal: thunder. Also a boy's name.
Gainda, Gaynda, Gayndah.
Gairo Nepali: a dark colour.
Gala Italian: a festival or celebration. Also a diminutive of Galina.
Galatea Greek: milky white. A sea nymph in Greek mythology.
Galaxy Middle English from Greek: a star system.
Galaxi, Galaxia, Galaxie,

Galaxye.
Gale *See* Gail.
Galena Latin: a lead-like metal.
Gali Hebrew: a spring.
Galia Hebrew: a wave.
Galiena Teutonic: a lofty maiden.
Galiana.
Galilee A region of northern Israel.
Galina Russian from Greek: calm.
See also Helen.
Halina (Polish).
Diminutive: Gala.
Galinda Possibly a form of Glenda. The name of a character in the book and musical, *Wicked*. Aboriginal: a girl.
Galindah, Glinda, Glindah.
Galya Hebrew: God has redeemed.
Gamila Possibly derived from Jamila.
Gameela, Gameelah, Gamilah, Gamilla, Gamillah.
Gana Hebrew: a garden.
Ganah, Gania, Ganya.
Garance French: the madder plant.
Garcelle A feminine form of garçon, French for a boy.
Garcel, Garcela, Garcell, Garcella.
Gardenia A 'flower name'.
Gardenya.
Gardner *See* Garner.
Gareema Aboriginal: a camping place.
Gari The feminine form of Gary, a spearman.
Garie, Garyn.

Garland Old French: a crown or wreath of flowers.
Garlande.
Garma Tibetan: a star.
Garner Old French: one who tends a garden. Also a boy's name.
Gardner.
Garnet Old French: dark red, from the colour of pomegranates. Also a 'gemstone name'.
Garnetta, Garnette.
Garriwa Aboriginal: a turtle.
Garriwah.
Garyn *See* Gari.
Gauri *See* Guri.
Gavrielle *See* Gabrielle.
Gavrila Hebrew: a heroine. *See also* Gabrielle.
Gavrilla.
Gay Old French: blithe, cheerful.
Gae, Gaeda, Gai, Gaida, Gaie, Gayda, Gaye.
Gaya *See* Gaia.
Gayanne A combination of Gay and Anne.
Gayan, Gayann.
Gayl/Gayle/Gayleen/Gaylene *See* Gail.
Gaylin/Gaylinne *See* Gailin.
Gaynda/Gayndah *See* Gaindah.
Gaynor Welsh: fair and soft. *See also* Guinevere.
Gaenor (Welsh), *Gainor, Gayna.*
Gazelle French: a small antelope.
Gazella, Gazellah, Ghazal (Arabic), *Ghazala* (Arabic),

G – Girls

Ghazaleh, Ghazella, Ghazelle.
Gean/Geane *See* Jean.
Geanavive *See* Genevieve.
Gedala Aboriginal: the day.
Geena *See* Gina.
Geera/Geerah *See* Gheera.
Geerta/Geertruida *See* Gertrude.
Gelasia Greek: laughing, like a bubbling spring.
Gelasie.
Gelila Hebrew: possibly meaning rolling hills.
Gelilah.
Gella Ladakhi: good.
Gela, Gelah, Gellah.
Gema/Gemah *See* Gemma.
Gemalla Aboriginal: a fish.
Gemallah.
Gemella/Gemelle *See* Gemma.
Gemena *See* Gemina.
Gemiah *See* Gemma.
Gemica Probably from the word gem. *See also* Gemma.
Gemeeca, Gemeecah, Gemeeka, Gemeekah, Gemicah, Gemika, Gemikah, Jemeeca, Jemeecah, Jemeeka, Jemeekah, Jemica, Jemicah, Jemika, Jemikah.
Gemima/Gemimah *See* Jemima.
Gemina Greek: a twin.
Gemini, Geminia, Geminie.
Gemma Italian: a jewel or gem. *See also* Gemica.
Gema, Gemah, Gemella, Gemelle, Gemena, Gemia, Gemiah, Gemmah, Gemmina, Gemminah,
Jema, Jemah, Jemelle, Jemena, Jemiah, Jemina, Jeminia, Jemma, Jemmah, Jemmina.
Gen Japanese: the source.
Gena *See* Eugenia and Gina.
Genaia/Genaya *See* Jenaya.
Gene/Genia *See* Eugenia, Gina and Jean.
Genelle/Gennelle *See* Janelle.
Genesia Latin: the newcomer.
Genesa, Genisia.
Genette *See* Genevieve and Jeannette.
Geneva A city in Switzerland. *See also* Genevieve.
Geneve, Genieve, Jeneva.
Genevieve Old French: a woman of the people. The patron saint of Paris.
Geanavieve, Genavieve, Genavive, Geneva, Genevra, Gennavieve, Genoveva, Genoveve, Ginevra (Italian), *Jeanavive, Jeanevive, Jenavieve, Jenevieve.*
Diminutives: Genette, Ginette, Veva, Vevette (French).
Genia/Genie *See* Eugenia.
Genieve *See* Geneva.
Genista Latin: the broom plant.
Genna/Gennah/Gennifer/Genny *See* Jenna and Jennifer.
Gennavieve *See* Genevieve.
Genoveva/Genoveve *See* Genevieve.
Genowefa A form of Guinevere and

Jennifer.
Geola Hebrew: joy.
Geolah.
Georga *See* Georgia.
Georgeanne/Georgena/Georgene *See* Georgina.
Georgette French form of Georgina.
Georgi/Georgie *See* Georgia and Georgina.
Georgia Originally a diminutive of Georgina. Also an American state and a region of the former USSR. *See also* Jorja.
Georga, Georgah, Georgi, Georgiah, Georgie, Georja, Georjia, Giorga, Giorgia, Giorja, Giorjia.
Georgina Greek: a girl from the farm; the feminine form of George. *See also* Georgia and Jorjina.
Geordene, Geordine, Georgeanne, Georgena, Georgene, Georgeta, Georgette (French), *Georgia, Georgiana, Georgienne* (French), *Georgine* (French), *Georgita, Giorgetta* (Italian), *Giorgia, Giorgina, Jorgelina* (Spanish).
Diminutives: George, Georgi, Georgie, Georgy, Gigi, Gina.
Georja/Georjia *See* Georgia.
Geraldine English from Old French: a noble spear carrier. The feminine form of Gerald. *See also* Gerarda.
Geralda, Geraldeine, Geraldene, Geraldina, Gerelda, Gerraldene,
Gerraldine, Giralda (Italian), *Giraldina, Giraldine, Jeraldene, Jeraldine, Jerraldine.*
Diminutives: Geri, Gerri, Gerry, Gery, Jerri, Jerry.
Geralyn A combination of Geraldine and Lynn (a waterfall). *See also* Jeralyn.
Geralynn, Geralynne, Gerilin, Gerilinn, Gerilinne, Gerilyn, Gerilynn, Gerilynne, Gerralyn, Gerralynn, Gerralynne, Gerrilyn, Gerrilynn, Gerrilynne.
Geranium Greek: a 'flower name'.
Gerarda English from Old French: a brave spear woman. The feminine form of Gerard. *See also* Geraldine.
Geradine, Gerardine, Jeradine, Jerarda, Jerardine.
Gerda Old Norse: the protected one. Also a diminutive of Gertrude.
Gerd (Scandinavian), *Gerde* (German), *Gerdina* (Dutch).
Geri/Gerri/Gerry *See* Geraldine.
Gerlinde Teutonic: of the weak spear.
Gerlina, Gerlinda.
Germaine French: the name of a saint.
Germain, Germana, Germane, Germayne, Jermain, Jermaine, Jermayne.
Gerralyn/Gerrilyn *See* Geralyn.
Gertrude Teutonic: a spear maiden.
Geerta (Dutch), *Geertruida, Geertruide, Gertraud* (German),

Gertrud (German), *Gertruda*.
Diminutives: Gerda, Gert, Gertie, Gesina (Dutch), Gezina (Dutch), Traudl (German), Truda, Truddy, Trudi, Trudie, Trudy.
Gesina/Gezina Dutch diminutives of Gertrude.
Gessica/Gessika *See* Jessica.
Geva Israeli: a hill.
Gevah.
Ghada Arabic: graceful.
Ghazal/Ghazaleh/Ghazelle *See* Gazelle.
Gheera Aboriginal: a wild turkey.
Geera, Geerah.
Ghera Aboriginal: a gum leaf.
Ghisann/Ghisanne *See* Gisanne.
Ghislain/Ghislaine *See* Giselle.
Ghita Italian diminutive of Margaret (a pearl). *See also* Gita.
Ghora Hindi: a horse.
Gora, Gorah.
Gia An Italian diminutive of Gianna and Giovanna (*see* Jane).
Giah, Giya, Giyah.
Giaan/Gian/Gianina/Gianna/Giannetta Italian forms of Jane.
Giacinta Italian form of Hyacinth.
Giacomina The feminine of Giacomo, the Italian form of James.
Giacoma, Giacomia.
Giada Italian form of Jade.
Gicinta *See* Jacinta.
Gigi French: a diminutive of Georgina, Gilberta and Virginia.

Gigliola Italian: a lily.
Gilah Aboriginal: a galah, or type of parrot. *See also* Gilana.
Gilana Hebrew: joy.
Gilah, Gilanah, Gillah.
Gilba Aboriginal: a grassy place.
Gilbah.
Gilberta Teutonic: a bright or famous pledge. The feminine form of Gilbert.
Gilberte, Gilbertha, Gilbertina, Gilbertine.
Diminutives: Berta, Gigi, Gillie, Gilly.
Gilda Old English: coated with gold. Teutonic: a sacrifice.
Gildah, Gylda, Gyldah.
Gillian Latin: from a Roman family name. The feminine form of Julian and a derivative of Julia.
Gilian, Gillane, Gillean, Gillene, Gilliann, Gillianne, Gyllian, Gylliann, Jilane, Jillane, Jillene, Jillian, Jylian, Jyllian.
Diminutives: Gill, Gilla, Gilly, Jill, Jilla, Jilli, Jillie, Jilly.
Gin Japanese: silvery.
Gyn.
Gina A diminutive of names such as Georgina and Regina.
Geena, Gena, Gene, Jeena, Jena.
Ginette/Ginevra *See* Genevieve.
Ginger *See* Virginia. Also the name of a spice.
Ginjer, Jinger, Jinjer.
Diminutives: Gini, Ginnie, Ginny.

Ginia A diminutive of Virginia.
Ginnifer/Ginniffer *See* Jennifer.
Ginta A Latvian name of uncertain meaning.
Gioconda Italian: happy.
Gioia Italian: joy.
Giordana Italian: the feminine form of Giordano (*see* Jordan).
Giorga/Giorja *See* Georgia.
Giorgetta/Giorgia/Giorgina *See* Georgina.
Giota *See* Panagiota.
Giovanna An Italian form of Jane.
Giovanella, Giovanelli.
Gipsie/Gipsy *See* Gypsy.
Gipsy-Lea/Gipsy-Lee *See* Gypsy Lee.
Giralda/Giraldina/Giraldine *See* Geraldine.
Girolama Italian: the feminine form of Girolamo (*see* Jerome).
Girra Aboriginal: a tree, or a creek. Also a boy's name.
Gira, Girrah.
Girraween Aboriginal: a place of wild flowers.
Gisanne A combination of Giselle and Anne.
Ghisann, Ghisanne, Gisann, Gizann, Gizanne.
Giselle Teutonic: a pledge.
Ghislain, Ghislaine (French), *Gisela* (Dutch, German), *Gisele* (French), *Giselia, Gisella, Gisilia, Gissella, Gisselle, Gizela, Gizella, Gizelle, Guisele, Guisella, Guiselle.*
Gita Sanskrit: a song.
Geeta, Ghita.
Gitana Spanish: the gypsy.
Githa *See* Gytha.
Giuditta Italian form of Judith.
Giulia/Giulietta Italian forms of Julia.
Giuseppa/Giuseppina Italian forms of Josephine.
Giya/Giyah *See* Gia.
Gizann/Gizanne *See* Gisanne.
Gizela/Gizelle *See* Giselle.
Gizem Turkish: mystery.
Gladi Hawaiian form of Gladys.
Gladys Welsh: possibly a form of Claudia.
Gladdis, Gladi (Hawaiian), *Gladis, Gladwyn, Gleda, Gwladus* (Welsh), *Gwladys* (Welsh).
Gleda *See* Gladys.
Glen Gaelic/Welsh: from the valley or glen. *See also* Glenda and Glenys.
Glenn, Glenne, Glennette.
Glenda Welsh: pure and good. *See also* Glenys.
Glendah, Glenna.
Diminutives: Glen, Glenn.
Gleness/Glenesse *See* Glenys.
Glenice/Glenis/Glenise/Gleniss *See* Glenys.
Glenna *See* Glenda.
Glenwynne A combination of Glen (from the valley or glen) and

G – Girls

Wynne (fair or blessed).
Glenwin, Glenwinn, Glenwinne, Glenwyn, Glenwynn.

Glenys Welsh: holy, pure. *See also* Glenda.
Gleness, Glenesse, Glenice, Glenis, Glenise, Gleniss, Glennis, Glennisse, Glenyce, Glenyis, Glenyss, Glenysse, Glynis, Glynnis.
Diminutives: Glen, Glenn, Gleny.

Glinda/Glindah *See* Galinda.

Gloria Latin: glorious.
Glori, Gloriana, Gloriane, Glorianna, Glorianne, Glorie, Gloriel, Glorien, Glorina, Glorita, Glory.

Glynis/Glynnis *See* Glenys.

Goda *See* Guda.

Godarra Aboriginal: two.

Godiva Old English: the gift of God.

Golda/Golden *See* Goldie.

Goldie English: the golden one.
Golda (Yiddish), *Golden, Goldi, Goldina, Goldy.*

Goldwin Old English: a golden friend. Also a boy's name.
Goldwinn, Goldwinne, Goldwyn, Golwynn, Goldwynne.

Golnar Persian: a flame, or a red flower.

Golzadeh An Arabic name of uncertain meaning.

Gonca Turkish: the bud of a flower.

Goneril A character in Shakespeare's play *King Lear*.

Gongora Aboriginal: a crocodile.

Goolara/Goolarah/Goolarra *See* Gulara.

Gopi Sanskrit: a cowherd girl in Hindu mythology.
Gopini.

Gora/Gorah *See* Ghora.

Gorana Slavic: a feminine form of Goran (*see* George).
Goranna.

Gordana Slavic: the feminine form of Gordan, meaning dignified.

Gorica Slavic: a feminine form of Goran (*see* George).
Goricah, Gorika, Gorikah.

Gosia Polish diminutive of Agnes.

Gozde Turkish: the favourite.

Grace Latin: graceful.
Engracia (Spanish), *Graça* (Portuguese), *Gracela, Gracele, Gracell, Gracella, Gracelle, Gracia* (Spanish), *Graciela* (Spanish), *Graciell, Graciella, Gracielle, Gracinda, Graice, Gratia* (Dutch, German), *Grayce, Graycin, Graycine, Grazia* (Italian), *Graziella* (Italian), *Grazina.*
Diminutives: Gracee, Gracey, Graci, Gracie.

Grace-Violet An attractive 'combination name'.

Grainne *See* Grania.

Grancis Possibly from Francis.
Grances.

Grania Irish Gaelic: a figure in Irish

legend.
Grainne (Irish Gaelic), *Granya*.
Grayce/Graycin/Graycine
See Grace.
Grayson Old English: the son of the bailiff. A boy's name that is now occasionally used for girls.
Graysan, Graysen, Greysan, Greysen, Greyson.
Grazia/Graziella/Grazina
See Grace.
Grechen A diminutive of Margaret.
Greer/Grier See Gregoria.
Gregoria Greek: watchful, vigilant.
Greer (Scottish), *Grier* (Scottish), *Grigoria*.
Greta/Gretchen/Grete/Gretel/ Gretha/Gretta See Margaret.
Grevillea The feminine form of Greville. Also a genus of Australian plants.
Grevillia.
Greysan/Greysen/Greyson
See Grayson.
Griet Dutch diminutive of Margaret.
Grieta, Grietha, Grietina.
Griselda Teutonic: the grey battle heroine.
Griselde, Grizel (Scottish), *Grizelda*.
Diminutives: Selda, Zelda.
Grit German diminutive of Margaret.
Gro A Norwegian name of uncertain meaning.

Grozda Slavic: the feminine form of Grozdan, meaning grapes.
Gryffyn Cornish/Welsh: little Griffith.
Griffin, Griffyn, Gryffin.
Guadalupe Arabic: the river of the wolf. Generally a Spanish name.
Guan-yin Chinese: the goddess of mercy.
Guba Tibetan: the month of September.
Gubah.
Guda Old English: good.
Goda.
Gudrid Old Norse: divine passion.
Diminutive: Guri.
Gudrun Old Norse: divine lore or wisdom.
Gudrum, Guro (Norwegian).
Guendalen/Guendolen/ Guendolin See Gwendolen.
Guerrina Italian: the feminine form of Guerrino, meaning of the war.
Guida Latin: a guide.
Guin/Guinn/Guinne See Gwyn.
Guinara A Russian name of uncertain meaning.
Guinevere Welsh: fair and soft. The wife of King Arthur. See also Gaynor, Jennifer and Vanora.
Gaenor (Welsh), *Gaynor, Genowefa, Guenevere, Guinever, Gweniver* (Cornish), *Gwenore*.
Guisele/Guisella/Guiselle
See Giselle.
Gulara Aboriginal: moonlight.

Goolara, Goolarah, Goolarra, Goolarrah, Gularah, Gularra, Gularrah.

Gulda Probably from gul, the Arabic word for a flower or rose.
Guldah.

Gulfiya A Russian name of uncertain meaning.

Gulistan Turkish: a rose garden.

Gulla Old Norse: yellow, or from the sea.
Gullah.

Gulzaar Arabic: a rose garden.
Gulzar.

Gumnut A eucalyptus nut.

Gunama/Gunamah *See* Kunama.

Gunda *See* Gunnhild.

Gundega A Latvian name of uncertain meaning.

Gunida Aboriginal: a white stone.
Gunidah.

Gunilla Swedish form of Gunnhild.

Gunnel The upper part of a boat or ship.
Gunnell.

Gunnhild Old Norse: a maiden of battle.
Gunda, Gunhild, Gunhilda, Gunhilde, Gunilla (Swedish).

Guri Hindi: the goddess of abundance. Also yellow or golden in colour. *See also* Gudrid.
Gauri.

Gurit Hebrew: a lion cub.

Gurley Aboriginal: a native willow.

Guro *See* Gudrun.

Guyra Aboriginal: a fishing place, or a white cockatoo. A placename.

Gwandalan Aboriginal: peace or rest.

Gwatan The Japanese moon goddess.

Gwen Welsh: fair, or blessed.
See also Gwendolen, Gwenola, Gwyn and Gwyneth.
Gwynne.

Gwenda *See* Gwendolen.

Gwendolen Welsh: a white ring or brow.
Guendalen, Guendolen, Guendolene, Guendolin, Guendoline, Gwenda, Gwendalyn, Gwendalynn, Gwendalynne, Gwendell, Gwendolene, Gwendolin, Gwendolina, Gwendoline, Gwendolyn, Gwendolyne, Gwendolynne.
Diminutives: Gwen, Gweni, Gwenie, Gwennie.

Gwener Welsh: the name for Friday and the planet Venus.

Gweneth/Gwenith *See* Gwyneth.

Gwenfra/Gwenfrewi Welsh forms of Winifred.

Gwenfrynne Welsh: a white hill.
Gwenfryn, Gwenfrynn, Gwynfryn, Gwynfrynn, Gwynfrynne.

Gweniver Cornish form of Guinevere.

Gwenllian Welsh: fair or blessed, and flaxen.

Gwenilian, Gwenillian, Gwenlian.
Gwenllyn A combination of two Welsh names, Gwen (fair or blessed) and Llyn (a lake). *Gwenllynn, Gwenlyn, Gwenlynn, Gwenlynne.*
Diminutive: Gwen.
Gwennap Cornish: the name of a saint and a placename.
Gwenneth *See* Gwyneth.
Gwenola A form of Gwen. *Gwenolia.*
Gwenor *See* Guinevere.
Gwinau Welsh: brown. *Gwynau.*
Gwladys *See* Gladys.
Gwyn Welsh: white. Also a diminutive of Gwyneth. *Guin, Guinn, Guinne, Gwen, Gwinn, Gwynn, Gwynne.*
Gwyneth Welsh: from a region of north Wales. *Gweneth, Gwenith, Gwenneth, Gwenwyth, Gwenwythe, Gwenyth, Gwynedd, Gwynith, Gwynneth.*
Diminutives: Gwen, Gwyn.
Gwynfor Welsh: from a fair place. More commonly a boy's name. *Gwynnfor, Gwynnefor.*
Gwynfryn *See* Gwenfrynne.
Gwynne *See* Gwen.
Gylda/Gyldah *See* Gilda.
Gyllian/Gylliann *See* Gillian.
Gymea Aboriginal: a small bird, or a lily.
Gyn *See* Gin.
Gypsy Old English: a wanderer. *Gipsie, Gipsy, Gypsie.*
Gypsy-Lee A 'combination name', meaning a wanderer from the meadow or clearing. *Gipsy-Lea, Gipsy-Lee, Gipsy-Leigh, Gypsy-Lea, Gypsy-Leigh.*
Gytha Old English: warlike. *Githa, Gytta.*

H

Haala *See* Hala.
Habiba Arabic: the beloved, the dear one. *Habibah, Haviva.*
Hadan/Hadein/Haden/Hadin *See* Hayden.
Hadara Arabic: splendour or beauty. *Hadarah.*
Hadassa/Hadassah Jewish forms of Esther.
Hadil Arabic: cooing like a dove.
Hadiya Arabic/Swahili: a gift. *Hadia, Hadija, Hadiyah.*
Hadria *See* Adriana.
Hadya Arabic: a leader or guide. *Huda.*
Hafwen Welsh: as beautiful as summer.
Hagar Hebrew: forsaken, or taking flight.

Hagir (Arabic), *Hajar* (Arabic), *Hajira*.
Haidee Greek: modest.
Haifa Arabic: slender. The name of an Israeli city.
Haifaa, Hayfa.
Haile/Hailee/Haileigh/Hailey *See* Hayley.
Haimi Hawaiian: the seeker.
Haize *See* Haze.
Hajar/Hajira *See* Hagar.
Haki Maori form of Jackie. *See* Jacqueline.
Hakima Arabic: the feminine form of Hakim, meaning wise and judicious.
Hakeema.
Hala Arabic: a halo around the moon.
Haala.
Halaina/Halainah *See* Helen.
Halcyone Greek: the kingfisher.
Alcyon, Alycone, Halcyon.
Haldana Old Norse: half Danish.
Haldis Teutonic: a spirit of the stones.
Haleigh/Haley *See* Hayley.
Halena *See* Halina.
Halfrida Teutonic: a peaceful heroine.
Halia Hawaiian: fond remembrance.
Halea, Haleia.
Halima Arabic: kind, gentle.
Halimah, Halma.
Halimeda Greek: thinking of the sea.

Halina Polish: a variation of Helen and Galina.
Halena, Halinka, Halyna (Ukrainian).
Halle/Hallie *See* Hayley.
Halo Latin: a circle of light.
Haloe, Halow.
Haloke Native American: a salmon.
Halona Native American: fortunate.
Halyna Ukrainian form of Halina.
Hama Japanese: a child of the shore.
Hamida Arabic: praised.
Hamidah.
Hana Arabic: bliss, happiness. Japanese: a blossom. Maori: to glow. Also the Czech form of Joanne.
Hanai Hawaiian: lucky.
Hanako Japanese: a child of the flowers or blossom.
Hanan Arabic: the tender affectionate one.
Hande Turkish: the smiling one.
Hania Polish form of Hannah.
Hanka Japanese: grace or favour.
Hannah Hebrew: favoured by God, or graceful. *See also* Anne.
Hania (Polish), *Hanisa, Hanisah, Hanna*.
Hanne German form of Joanne.
Hanneke, Hannelore, Hanni (Swiss), *Hanny*.
Hannelore *See* Hanne.
Hannora A combination of Hannah (graceful) and Nora (the light of the sun).

Hannorah, Hanora, Hanorah.
Hansine German from Hebrew: God is gracious. A feminine form of Hans.
Hansi, Hansie, Hansina.
Hanya Aboriginal: a stone.
Hapai Polynesian: a legendary figure.
Happy English: bright and cheerful.
Happi, Happie, Happye.
Hara Aboriginal: the sky. *See also* Hariyo.
Variation: Harah.
Haralda Old English: the ruler of the army. The feminine form of Harold.
Haraldina, Harelda, Hareldina, Harolda, Haroldina.
Harata Maori form of Charlotte.
Hariata Maori form of Charlotte. Polynesian form of Harriet.
Harika Turkish: beautiful.
Hariklia Greek: glorious grace.
Hariklea.
Harikoa Maori: the happy one.
Hariyo Nepali: green.
Hara (Hindi).
Harleen The feminine form of Harlan, meaning from the rocky land.
Harlena, Harlana, Harlene, Harlina, Harline.
Harley Old English: from the meadow of the hares, or from the grey wood. *See also* Hartley.
Arlie, Harlee, Harleigh, Harlene,
Harlie, Harly.
Harlow Old English: a meeting place. The surname of a legendary 1920s–1930s actress (Jean Harlow).
Harlo, Harloe, Harlowe.
Harmony Greek: concordant, in harmony.
Armonia (Italian), *Harmonee, Harmoney, Harmoni, Harmonia, Harmonie.*
Harolda/Haroldina *See* Haralda.
Haroula A Greek name of uncertain meaning.
Harper Old English: a harp maker or player.
Harpreet Sikh: one who loves God.
Harriet Teutonic: the ruler of the home. A feminine form of Harry and Henry. *See also* Henrietta.
Hariata (Polynesian), *Hariet, Hariett, Hariette, Harried* (Breton), *Harriett, Harrietta, Harriette, Harriot.*
Diminutives: Hattie, Hettie, Hetty.
Harris The son of Harry (Henry). More commonly a boy's name.
Harries.
Harshita Sanskrit: one who brings happiness.
Hartley Old English: from the meadow of the hare or stag. *See also* Harley.
Hartlea, Hartlee, Hartleigh, Hartlie, Hartly.
Haru Japanese: born in the

springtime.
Haruka Japanese: a spring flower.
Haruko Japanese: child of the spring.
Haryana Sanskrit: a state in northwest India.
Hasana African: a firstborn female twin.
Hassana.
Hasika Sanskrit: laughter.
Hasina Swahili: good.
Hasuko Japanese: the child of the lotus.
Hathor Ancient Egyptian: the goddess of love and joy.
Athor.
Hati Nepali: an elephant.
Hathi (Hindi).
Hatsu Japanese: the firstborn child.
Hatsuko.
Hattie *See* Harriet and Henrietta.
Hausu Native American: a bear.
Hava Jewish form of Eve.
Havana Spanish: the capital of Cuba.
Havanah, Havanna, Havannah.
Haviva *See* Habiba.
Havva Turkish form of Eve.
Hawa Sanskrit: like the air or the wind.
Haya Hebrew: life.
Hayat (Arabic).
Hayden A boy's name, now used occasionally for girls and meaning from the heathery hill.
Hadan, Hadein, Haden, Hadin,
Hadon, Haydan, Haydn, Haydon, Haydyn, Heydan, Heyden, Heydon, Heydyn.
Hayette Possibly derived from Hayley.
Hayetta.
Hayfa *See* Haifa.
Hayley Old English: a high clearing or meadow.
Haile, Hailea, Hailee, Haileigh, Hailey, Halea, Halee, Haleigh, Haley, Halle, Hallie, Haylea, Haylee, Hayleigh, Haylie, Hayly, Heylea, Heylee, Heyleigh, Heyley, Heylie.
Hazan Turkish: autumn.
Haze A type of mist.
Haize, Hayze.
Hazel Old English: from the hazel tree.
Hayzel, Hayzell, Hayzelle, Hazell, Hazelle, Hazle.
Heartsease Middle English: another name for the pansy.
Heartease.
Heather Old English: a 'flower name'.
Heatherann An unusual 'combination name'.
Heather-Ann, Heatheranne, Heather-Anne.
Heavenly Middle English: blissful, resembling heaven.
Heaven, Heavenlee, Heavenlie, Hevenly.
Hebe Greek: youthful. A goddess of

youth in mythology.
Hebron Hebrew: an Israeli city, mentioned in the Bible.
Hedda *See* Hedwig.
Hedea Greek: pleasing.
Hedia, Hedya.
Hedwig Teutonic: the contentious one; a fighter. The name of a saint.
Edda (Italian), *Edwige* (French), *Hedvig* (Scandinavian), *Hedviga* (Hungarian), *Jadwiga* (Polish), *Jadzia* (Polish).
Diminutives: Hedda (Scandinavian), Hedy (Scandinavian), Iga (Polish).
Hedy *See* Hedwig.
Hedya *See* Hedea.
Heera *See* Hira.
Heidi Swiss diminutive of Adelheid (*see* Adelaide). Best known from Johanna Spyri's classic children's book.
Heide, Heidee, Heidie.
Heidrun A character from Norse mythology.
Heike German and Scandinavian diminutives of Henrike (*see* Henrietta).
Hela The Norse goddess of the underworld.
Heleanor/Heleanore *See* Eleanor.
Heledd Welsh: a traditional name of uncertain meaning.
Hyledd.
Helen Greek: the light of the sun. *See also* Eileen, Elaine, Eleanor and Ellen.
Alena (Lithuanian), *Alina* (Russian), *Elen* (Welsh), *Elena* (Italian, Portuguese, Spanish), *Eleni* (Greek), *Elenka, Elin* (Swedish), *Ellena, Ellenie, Elna, Elyn, Elynn, Galina* (Russian), *Halaina, Halainah, Halina* (Polish), *Helaine, Helayne, Helena, Helene* (German), *Hélène* (French), *Helenka* (Polish), *Hellen, Ileana* (Romanian), *Illona* (Irish), *Ilona* (Hungarian), *Jelena* (Slavic), *Léan* (Irish Gaelic), *Olena* (Ukrainian), *Yelena* (Russian).
Diminutives: Alyona (Russian), Ella, Elli, Ellie, Elly, Ellye, Hels, Ilka (Hungarian), Lana, Lena, Lene (Dutch, German), Nell, Nellie, Nelly.
Helena/Helene *See* Helen.
Helga Old Norse: successful, prosperous. *See also* Olga.
Hella, Helle (Danish).
Helia Greek: the sun.
Helianthe Greek: a sunflower.
Heliantha.
Helice Greek: a spiral.
Helica.
Helienor/Hellenor *See* Eleanor.
Hella/Helle *See* Helga.
Helma/Helmine German diminutives of Wilhelmina.
Helmi/Helmie Scandinavian diminutives of Vilhelmina.
Heloisa/Heloise *See* Eloise.

H – Girls

Helvetia Latin: a woman from Switzerland.
Hema Sanskrit: possibly meaning gold or golden.
Hemanta The Sanskrit name for winter and the feminine form of Hemant.
Hemanti.
Hemera The Greek goddess of the day.
Henderika/Hendrietta/Hendrika/Hendrina See Henrietta.
Hengameh An Iranian name of uncertain meaning.
Heni Maori form of Jane.
Henrietta Teutonic: the ruler of the home. A feminine form of Henry. See also Harriet.
Enrica (Italian, Spanish), *Henderika, Hendrietta, Hendrika* (Dutch), *Hendrina, Henrica, Henrieta, Henriette* (French), *Henrika* (Swedish), *Henrike* (German, Scandinavian), *Henryka* (Polish), *Henzina.*
Diminutives: Etta, Ettie, Hattie, Heike (German, Scandinavian), Hettie, Hetty, Netta, Nette, Nettie, Netty, Yetta.
Henrika/Henrike/Henryka See Henrietta.
Henzina See Henrietta.
Hepzibah Hebrew: a name from the Bible.
Hera Greek: a queen. The wife of Zeus, ruler of the heavens, in Greek mythology. Also a Maori form of Sarah.
Herma/Hermia/Hermina/Hermine See Hermione.
Hermila A Spanish name of uncertain meaning.
Hermilia, Hermilla.
Hermione Greek: the feminine form of Hermes, the messenger of the gods.
Ermione, Herma, Hermene, Hermia, Hermina, Hermine (German), *Herminia.*
Hermosa Spanish: beautiful.
Hero A priestess of Aphrodite, the goddess of love in Greek mythology.
Herta/Hertah/Hertha See Eartha.
Heshu Chinese: a star in the constellation of Canis Minor.
Hesper Greek: the evening star. See also Esther.
Hesba, Hespa, Hespera, Hesperia.
Hester/Hesther See Esther.
Hestia Greek: the goddess of the hearth.
Hettie/Hetty Diminutives of Harriet, Henrietta and Esther.
Heulwen Welsh: sunshine.
Heulwyn, Heulyn.
Hevenly See Heavenly.
Heydan/Heyden/Heydyn See Hayden.
Heylea/Heyleigh/Heyley/Heylie See Hayley.
Hibernia Latin: a woman from

Ireland.
Hiberna.
Hibiscus Greek: a 'flower name'.
Hidé Japanese: excellent, fruitful.
Hideyo Japanese: superior.
Hihiria A Maori form of Cecilia.
Hika Polynesian: a daughter.
Hikaru Japanese: one who shines.
Hikitia Maori: to lift by the arms.
Hikurangi Maori: the name of a sacred New Zealand mountain.
Hilaire *See* Hilary.
Hilary Latin: the cheerful one. Originally a boy's name.
Hilaire (French), *Hilaria* (Spanish), *Hilarie, Hilery, Hilla, Hillary, Hillery, Ilaria, Ildiko* (Hungarian), *Illaria.*
Hilda Teutonic: a battle maiden.
Elda (Italian), *Hildah, Hilde* (German), *Hillda, Hyla, Hylah, Hylda.*
Hildegard Teutonic: a battle stronghold.
Hildegarde, Hildergard, Hildergarde.
Hildemar Teutonic: battle celebrated.
Hilkka Finnish: a scarf.
Himalia Greek: of the mountains, relating to the Himalaya. Also a satellite of the planet Jupiter.
Himala, Himalaya, Himalla, Himallia, Himalya.
Himanshi A Hindi name of uncertain meaning.

Hina Japanese: like the sun. Polynesian: the wife of Maui, a legendary hero. Tongan: a spider.
Hina-Uri Polynesian: the mythological goddess of the moon.
Hinda Jewish: a female deer.
Hindah, Hinde.
Hine Polynesian: a maiden.
Hinemoa Polynesian: a girl from legend.
Hinengaro Maori: conscience.
Hippolyta Greek: she who frees the horses.
Hippolita, Ippolita (Italian).
Hira Hindi: a diamond. Also the Maori form of Jean.
Heera.
Hiraani The unusual name of the daughter of Michael Hutchence and Paula Yates.
Hiraanie, Hirani, Hiranie.
Hiria A Maori form of Cecilia.
Hiriwa Polynesian: silver.
Hiroko Japanese: generous.
Hisako Japanese: probably meaning an auspicious child.
Hiwa Hawaiian: jet-black, or choice. Also a boy's name.
Hiwakea Hawaiian: black and white. Also a boy's name.
Hjördis Old Norse: a sword goddess.
Hoala Hawaiian: to agitate.
Hoda Arabic: generally an Egyptian name.
Hodah.
Hoki Maori: also, because.

Hoku Polynesian: a star.
Holda Teutonic: concealed. *See also* Hulda.
Holde, Holle.
Holee/Holeigh/Holie *See* Holly.
Holiday Old English: a holy or religious day. Also a boy's name.
Holliday.
Holland Old English: from the enclosed or sacred ground. A 'country name'.
Holand, Hollan.
Holle *See* Holda.
Holly Old English: a type of tree. Suitable for a child born around Christmas.
Holee, Holeigh, Holi, Holie, Hollea, Hollee, Holleigh, Holley, Holli, Hollie, Holy.
Honey Old English: the sweet one.
Honee, Honie.
Honeyblossom The unusual name of one of Bob Geldof's daughters.
Honeysuckle Middle English: a fragrant flower.
Honiesuckle.
Honour Latin: honourable.
Honor, Honora, Honorah, Honorata (Italian), *Honore* (French), *Honoria, Honoriah, Honorine* (French), *Onóra* (Irish Gaelic), *Onorah.*
Diminutive: Nano (Irish).
Hoong Chinese: pink.
Hong.
Hope Old English: hopeful, optimistic.
Horatia Latin: from a Roman family name. The feminine form of Horace.
Horacia.
Horia/Horiya/Horiyya *See* Houria.
Hortense Latin: the garden lover.
Hortencia, Hortensia, Hortensze, Hortenze, Ortense (Italian), *Ortensia* (Italian).
Hosanna Latin: in praise of God.
Hosana, Osana, Osanna.
Hoshi Japanese: a star.
Hotoke Maori: winter.
Houria Arabic: a beautiful woman.
Horia, Horiya, Horiyya, Houriya, Houriyya.
Hua Chinese: a flower.
Huberta Teutonic: a brilliant mind. The feminine form of Hubert.
Hubertha, Huberthe, Hubertina.
Huda *See* Hadya.
Hughette French from Teutonic: heart and mind. The feminine form of Hugh.
Huetta, Huette, Hughetta, Hughette, Hughina (Scottish), *Hughine, Hughla, Huguette* (French).
Huhana Maori form of Susannah.
Huia Maori: the name of an extinct native New Zealand bird.
Hula Polynesian: a Hawaiian dance.
Hulda Hebrew: a prophetess, a name from the Old Testament. Old Norse: lovable.

Holda, Huldah.
Huma Sanskrit: an eagle.
Humah.
Humarie Maori: a peaceful or lovely person.
Humayra Arabic: of a red colour
Humaira, Humayraa.
Hune Maori form of June.
Hunna A 7th-century French saint. The name is probably related to Una.
Hunnah.
Hunter Old English: one who hunts. Also a boy's name.
Hunt, Huntah, Hunte.
Hura Maori form of Jude. See Judith.
Huria/Huriana Maori forms of Julia.
Hurihia Maori: the changeable one.
Hushniya Arabic: goodness.
Husna, Hushnara.
Hussana Arabic: a beautiful woman.
Huwaida An Arabic name of uncertain meaning.
Hweiling Chinese: infinite wisdom.
Hyacinth Greek: young and beautiful; a 'flower name'. *See also* Jacinta and Jacinth.
Giacinta (Italian), *Hyacintha, Hyacinthe* (French), *Hyacinthia.*
Hyla/Hylah/Hylda *See* Hilda.
Hyledd *See* Heledd.
Hypatia Greek: the highest.

I

Ialeen/Ialene *See* Eileen.
Ianthe Greek: a violet-coloured flower. *See also* Iolanthe.
Iantha, Ianthea, Ianthia, Ianthina, Janthina, Janthine.
Iben A popular Danish name.
Ichiko Japanese: the first child.
Ida Old Norse: diligent. Teutonic: happy, or youthful.
Idah, Idalina, Idaline, Idella, Idelle, Idette (German).
Idalia Spanish: the sun.
Idaliah.
Idelia Teutonic: noble.
Idella/Idelle/Idette *See* Ida.
Idina *See* Adina.
Idona Old Norse: a Norse goddess who was in charge of the apples of eternal youth.
Idonea, Idonia, Idonie, Idony, Idun, Iduna, Idunn.
Idra Aramaic: a fig tree.
Idylla Greek: perfect.
Idyll, Idylle, Idyllia.
Ierne Latin: from Ireland.
Ieshia Swahili: life, or lively.
Iesha, Ieysha.
Iga Polish: a diminutive of Jadwiga. *See* Hedwig.
Ignatia Latin: ardent, fiery. The feminine form of Ignatius.
Ignacia, Ignazia (Italian), *Ineika, Ineka, Ineke, Iniga.*

Igrayne The mother of King Arthur.
Igraine, Ygraine, Ygrayne.
Ihipera Maori form of Isabel.
Ijumaa Swahili: Friday.
Ijuma, Ijumah.
Iku Japanese: nourishing.
Ikuko.
Ila Old French: from the island.
Ilana Hebrew: a tree.
Elana.
Ilaria/Illaria *See* Hilary.
Ilayne/Illayne *See* Elaine.
Ildiko Hungarian form of Hilda.
Ileana Greek: from the city of Ilion (Troy). Also a form of Helen and Eileen.
Ilia, Ilija (Slavic), *Iliana, Illyana, Illyanna.*
Ilectra/Ilektra *See* Electra.
Ileen/Ilena/Ilene *See* Eileen.
Ilia/Iliana/Ilija *See* Ileana.
Ilisapeci Fijian form of Elizabeth.
Ilisha *See* Alicia.
Ilka *See* Ilona.
Illona Irish form of Helen.
Illusion Middle English: something that is not quite real.
Illyana/Illyanna *See* Ilena.
Ilma Finnish: like the air. *See also* Elma.
Ilona Hungarian form of Helen.
Diminutives: Ilka, Ilonka.
Iloura Aboriginal: calm water.
Ilsa *See* Alice and Elizabeth.
Ilse German diminutive of Elizabeth.
Iluka Aboriginal: near the sea.
Ima Japanese: now, the present.
Imah, Yma, Ymah.
Imagin/Imajin *See* Imogen.
Iman Arabic: one who believes in God.
Imber Polish/Yiddish: ginger.
Imelda Italian/Spanish: a fighter.
Emelda, Imalda.
Diminutive: Melda.
Imijin *See* Imogen.
Imke German diminutive of Irma.
Immacolata Italian: after the Immaculate Conception.
Immaculada (Spanish), *Immaculata.*
Imogen Celtic: a girl or maiden. Latin: the image of her mother.
Emajen, Emajin, Emogen, Emogene, Emojen, Emojin, Imagin, Imajin, Imijin, Imogene, Imogine, Imojin.
Imperia Latin: imperious, the imperial one.
Imperio (Spanish).
Ina Polynesian: a moon goddess in mythology. *See also* Agnes.
Inanna The Sumerian goddess of heaven, love and fertility. The equivalent of the Greek goddess Aphrodite and the Roman goddess Diana.
Inara A goddess in Hittite mythology, similar to Artemis, the Greek goddess of the moon.
Inarah, Innara, Innarah.

Inari Finnish: a lake. Japanese: the rice goddess.
Inas Polynesian: the wife of the moon.
Inbar Hebrew: amber.
Inca Spanish: a Peruvian tribe.
Inka.
Indara The earth goddess in the mythology of the Indonesian island of Sulawesi.
Indea/Indeah *See* India.
Indeana/Indeanna *See* Indiana.
Indi A diminutive of Indiana and similar names, but also used independently.
Indee, Indie, Indy.
India A 'country name'. Also a character in the novel and film, *Gone with the Wind*.
Indea, Indeah, Indiah, Indiella, Indya, Indyah.
Indiana The name of a US state. Also a boy's name.
Indeana, Indeanna, Indianna, Indi-Anna, Indie-Anna, Indyana, Indyanna, Indy-Anna.
India-Rose An attractive 'combination name'.
Indica Possibly a modern form of India.
Indicah, Indika, Indikah.
Indie A genre of alternative rock music. *See also* Indi.
Indigo Latin: a deep blue-violet colour.
Indira Sanskrit: an alternative name for Lakshmi, wife of the god Vishnu.
Indrani Sanskrit: a Hindu goddess, the wife of Indra.
Indranee, Indriani.
Indred Sanskrit: the feminine form of Indra, god of thunder, lightning and the sky in Hindu mythology.
Indri.
Indya/Indyah *See* India.
Indyana/Indyanna *See* Indiana.
Ineika/Ineka/Ineke *See* Ignatia.
Ines/Inese/Inessa/Inez *See* Agnes.
Inga/Ingaberg *See* Ingrid.
Ingah Aboriginal: a crayfish.
Ingar.
Inge/Ingeborg/Inger *See* Ingrid.
Ingrid Old Norse: a hero's daughter.
Inga, Ingaberg, Inge, Ingeborg, Ingeborga, Ingeborge, Inger, Inkeri (Finnish).
Diminutive: Ingse.
Iniga *See* Ignatia.
Iniki Hawaiian: the name of a famous hurricane.
Inka *See* Inca.
Inkeri Finnish form of Ingrid.
Inna A Russian name of uncertain meaning.
Innes Celtic/Gaelic: an island in the river, or from the island.
Iniss, Inness, Innis.
Innocentia Latin: innocent.
Inocencia (Spanish), *Inocenta* (Polish).
Inoki Hawaiian: devoted.

I – GIRLS

Io A maiden in Greek mythology. A satellite of the planet Jupiter.
Ioana Slavic form of Joanne.
Iokina Hawaiian: God will develop.
Iola Greek: violet-coloured.
Iolanda, Iole.
Iolana Hawaiian: to soar like a hawk.
Iolanthe Greek: a violet flower. The title of a Gilbert and Sullivan opera. *See also* Ianthe, Violet and Yolanda.
Iona Aboriginal: a tree. Hawaiian: a dove. Scottish: a Hebridean island.
Ione Greek: a violet-coloured stone.
Ipek Turkish: like silk.
Iphigenia Greek: the daughter of Agamemnon in Greek mythology.
Iphigénie (French).
Ipo Hawaiian: a sweetheart.
Ippolita Italian form of Hippolyta.
Ira Aboriginal: a camp. Polynesian: a sky goddess.
Iraine *See* Irene.
Ireen *See* Irene.
Ireland Old English: the land of the Irish.
Irene Greek: peace.
Aireen, Airene, Arina (Romanian, Russian), *Eireen, Eirena, Eirene, Ereena, Erena, Erene, Iraine, Ireen, Ireena, Iren* (Hungarian), *Irena* (Slavic), *Irène* (French), *Irina* (Russian), *Irine, Iryna, Iryne.*
Ireta Latin: angry, enraged.

Iriaka Maori: a hanging vine.
Irihapeti Maori form of Elizabeth.
Irina/Irine *See* Irene.
Irinka Aboriginal: a dog.
Iris Greek: a rainbow. A 'flower name'.
Irisa (Russian), *Irissa, Irris.*
Irit Hebrew: an asphodel.
Irja Finnish: probably a diminutive of Irina.
Arja, Erja.
Irlene/Irline/Irlyne *See* Erline.
Irma Latin: noble. Teutonic: whole, strong. *See also* Erma.
Erma, Irmina, Irmine.
Diminutive: Imke (German).
Irmak Turkish: a river.
Irmgard Teutonic: a war goddess.
Irmigard.
Irmtraud Teutonic: universal strength.
Irmentrud, Irmtraut.
Iroda An unusual Russian name.
Irralee A character in the *Elfquest* fantasy comic book series.
Irva *See* Irvette.
Irvette Old English: a friend from the sea.
Irva, Irvetta.
Iryna/Iryne *See* Irene.
Isa Teutonic: strong-willed.
Iza.
Isabel Spanish: a form of Elizabeth, meaning consecrated to God. *See also* Isabella.
Ihipera (Maori), *Isabeau* (French),

IsaBel, Isabele, Isabelita (Spanish), *Isabell, IsaBell, Isabella* (Italian, Spanish), *Isabelle* (French), *IsaBelle, Isabellita, Isbel* (Scottish), *Iseabail* (Scottish Gaelic), *Iseabel, Ishbel, Isobel, Isobell, Isobelle, Izabel, Izabele, Izabella, Izabellah, Izabelle, Ysabel* (Spanish), *Ysobel.*
Diminutives: Bebel, Bel, Bella, Belle, Issie, Izzie, Izzy, Sabella, Sabelle.

Isabella A very popular name; the Italian and Spanish forms of Isabel. *Isabellah, Isobella, Isobellah, Issabella, Issabellah, Izabella, Izabellah.*

Isadora Greek: the gift of Isis. The feminine of Isidore.
Isadore, Isidora, Isidore, Izadora, Izadore.
Diminutives: Dora, Dory.

Isako Japanese: a child of the sand.

Isaura Portuguese/Spanish: a woman from Isauria, a region of Asia Minor.
Isaure (French), *Isauria.*

Isbel/Ishbel *See* Isabel.

Isel/Isell *See* Izel.

Iseult *See* Isolde.

Ishana Sanskrit: desirable.
Ishanna, Ishara.

Ishi Japanese: a stone.

Ishtar The Babylonian goddess of love and fertility; the equivalent of the Greek goddess Aphrodite and the Roman goddess Venus.
Eshtar.

Isi Native American: a deer.

Isidora/Isidore *See* Isadora.

Isis Ancient Egyptian: the goddess of fertility; the supreme goddess.
Iside (Italian).

Iskra Slavic: like a spark.

Isla The name of a Scottish island. Spanish: an island.
Islah, Islay.

Isla-Jae A combination of Isla and Jay (a bird).
Isla-Jai, Isla-Jaie, Isla-Jay, Isla-Jaye.

Isleen *See* Eileen.

Ismena Greek: learned.
Ismenia.

Isobel/Isobella/Isobelle *See* Isabel and Isabella.

Isola Latin: isolated, a loner.
Isolene.

Isolde Welsh: the fair one.
Esyllt (Welsh), *Iseult, Isoda, Isolda, Yseult, Yseulte, Ysolda, Ysolde.*

Isra Arabic: journeying by night. Thai: freedom.

Issabella/Issabellah *See* Isabel.

Ita Aboriginal: scrub. Irish Gaelic: thirsty; the name of a 6th-century saint.
Ite, Itta, Yootha, Ytha.

Italia Latin: from Italy.
Itala.

Ithaca The name of a Greek island.

Ithaka.
Ithneen Arabic: Monday.
Ithnayn.
Iva Old French: a yew tree. *See also* Ivana.
Ivalo Greenlandic: possibly meaning a sinew or tendon. Also a Lapland placename.
Ivalu.
Ivana Slavic form of Jane and a feminine form of Ivan.
Evana, Ivanka (Czech), *Ivanna, Ivanovna, Iveta* (Slavic), *Yvana, Yvanna.*
Diminutives: Iva, Ivka.
Ivangela/Ivangelina *See* Evangeline.
Ivelisse An unusual Spanish name.
Evelisse.
Iveta Czech and Slovak forms of Yvette.
Ivete/Ivetha/Ivetta/Ivette *See* Yvette.
Ivis A Spanish name of uncertain meaning.
Ivka Slavic diminutive of Iva, a short form of Ivana.
Ivon/Ivonn/Ivonne *See* Yvonne.
Ivory Latin: from the tusks of an elephant.
Ivoree, Ivorey, Ivori, Ivorie.
Ivy Old English: a plant name.
Ivey, Ivie, Ivye.
Iwi Maori: a tribe.
Iza *See* Isa.
Izabel/Izabella/Izabelle *See* Isabel and Isabella.

Izadora/Izadore *See* Isadora.
Izanami Japanese: she who invites you to enter.
Izel A Turkish name of uncertain meaning.
Isel, Isell, Izell.
Izett A modern name; a combination of Isabel and the feminine 'ette'.
Izet, Izette.

J

Jaaia *See* Jaya.
Jaala/Jaalah *See* Jala.
Jaali A modern name, probably made-up.
Jaalee, Jaalie, Jalee, Jali, Jalie.
Jabali Swahili: a cliff.
Jacalin/Jacalyn *See* Jacqueline.
Jaçana Portuguese: a type of wading bird.
Jacaranda A tropical tree with lavender-coloured flowers.
Jacarandah.
Jacenta *See* Jacinta.
Jacey Native American: the moon.
Jacee, Jacie, Jacy, Jasee, Jasey, Jasie, Jaycee, Jayci, Jaycie.
Jacilyn *See* Jacqueline.
Jacinta Spanish from Greek: beautiful. Also a form of Hyacinth.
Gacinta, Gicinta, Jacenta, Jacinda

GIRLS – J

(Greek), *Jacinna, Jacinte, Jacinth, Jacintha, Jacinthe* (French), *Jacinthia, Jacynth, Jasinta, Jecinta, Jesinta, Jycinda, Jycinta.*

Jacinth Greek: a purple-coloured gemstone. *See also* Jacinta. *Jacintha, Jacinthe* (French), *Jacinthia, Jacynth, Jacynthe.*

Jack/Jackee/Jackie/Jacklin
 See Jacqueline.

Jacklyn/Jacky/Jaclyn
 See Jacqueline.

Jacksee/Jacksey/Jacksie *See* Jaxi.

Jacoba Hebrew: the supplanter. A feminine form of Jacob. *Jacobella* (Italian), *Jacobina, Jacobine, Jakoba, Jakuba* (Polish).

Jacqueline French from Hebrew: the supplanter. A feminine form of Jacob and James. *Jacalin, Jacalyn, Jacilyn, Jackeline, Jackelyn, Jacklin, Jackline, Jacklyn, Jackolin, Jackqui, Jaclyn, Jacqualyn Jacquelien, Jacquelina, Jacquelyn, Jacquetta* (French), *Jacquette, Jacquilyn, Jacquilynn, Jacquilynne, Jakica, Jaklin, Jaklinn, Jaklyn, Jaklynn, Jaqel, Jaqlin, Jaqueline, Jaquenetta, Jaquenette, Jaquiline.*
 Diminutives: Haki (Maori), Jack, Jackee, Jacki, Jackie, Jacky, Jacqui, Jacquie.

Jacy *See* Jacey.

Jacynth *See* Jacinta and Jacinth.

Jada Hebrew: the wise one. *See also* Jade. *Jadah, Jahda, Jaida, Jaidah, Jayda, Jaydah.*

Jade Spanish: the jade stone. *Giada* (Italian), *Jaed, Jaedd, Jaedde, Jaede, Jaid, Jaide, Jayd, Jayde, Jaydie.*

Jadida Arabic: new or novel. *Jahida.*

Jadranka Slavic: the feminine form of Adrian.

Jadwiga/Jadzia *See* Hedwig.

Jae *See* Jay.

Jaed/Jaede/Jaedde *See* Jade.

Jaedeen/Jaedene/Jaedyne
 See Jaydine.

Jael *See* Yael.

Jaelah *See* Jaylah.

Jaelea/Jaelee/Jaeleigh/Jaelie
 See Jaylee.

Jaen *See* Jane.

Jaffa Hebrew: beautiful. *Jaffe, Jafit, Yaffa, Yaffah.*

Jahda *See* Jada.

Jahmilla *See* Jamila.

Jahmima *See* Jemima.

Jahnaya/Jahneya *See* Janaya.

Jahnel/Jahnella/Jahnelle
 See Janelle.

Jai/Jaie *See* Jay.

Jaia *See* Jaya.

Jaid/Jaida/Jaide *See* Jada and Jade.

Jaideen/Jaidene/Jaidyne
 See Jaydine.

Jaikea/Jaikeah *See* Jakeah.

Jailah *See* Jaylah.

Jailea/Jailee/Jaileigh *See* Jaylee.

Jaime English: a modern feminine form of James. Also from j'aime, French for I love you. *See also* Jamelie and Jamesina.
Jaimee, Jaimey, Jaimi, Jaimie, Jaimielle, Jamai, Jamais, Jamea, Jameah, Jamey, Jamie, Ja'mie, Jamiee, Jamielle, Jamii, Jamiie, Jayme, Jaymee, Jaymi, Jaymie, Jeamai, Jeamais.

Jaime-Lee A combination of Jaime and Lee (a meadow or clearing).
Jaimee-Lee.

Jain/Jaina/Jaine *See* Jane.

Jakeah A feminine form of Jake, meaning the supplanter (*see* Jacob).
Jaikea, Jaikeah, Jakea.

Jakica A variation of Jacqueline or Jessica.

Jaklin/Jaklyn/Jaklynn *See* Jacqueline.

Jakoba/Jakuba *See* Jacoba.

Jaksee/Jaksey/Jaksie *See* Jaxi.

Jala African: a fish. Arabic: clarity; shining.
Jaala, Jaalah, Jalah.

Jalal Glory. One of the Baha'i months, encompassing 9–24 April so suitable for an Aries or Taurus girl.

Jalee/Jali/Jalie *See* Jaali.

Jalila Arabic: grand or noble.
Jaleela, Jaleelah, Jalilah, Jaliya, Jaliyah.

Jalissa/Jalissah/Jalyssa *See* Jelissa.

Jaliya/Jaliyah *See* Jalila.

Jamai/Jamais *See* Jaime.

Jamaica A Carribbean island.
Jamaika, Jamayca, Jamayka.

Jamal Arabic: beautiful, comely. The name of the Baha'i month that encompasses late April–16 May, so a suitable name for a Taurus baby.
Jamala, Jamalah.

Jamea/Jameah *See* Jaime.

Jameela/Jamelia/Jamella *See* Jamila.

Jamelie A feminine form of James, meaning the supplanter. *See also* Jaime and Jamesina.
Jamelee, Jameli, Jamelia.

Jamesina Hebrew: the supplanter. A feminine form of James. *See also* Jaime and Jamelie.
Jamesetta, Jamesette, Jamesine.

Jamey/Jamiee/Jamielle *See* Jaime.

Jamieson Old English: the son (or daughter) of James. Traditionally a boy's name, but now also used for girls.
Jameson, Jamison.

Jamii/Jamiie *See* Jaime.

Jamila Arabic/Swahili: beautiful.
Jahmila, Jahmilla, Jameela, Jameelah, Jamelia, Jamella, Jamellah, Jamilah, Jamile, Jamilia, Jemilla, Jemillah, Yamila (Spanish), *Yamile, Yamillah.*

Jamima *See* Jemima.

Jamuna The name of a river in Banglashesh.

Jamuni Hindi: purple.
Jamunie.
Jamyma/Jamymah *See* Jemima.
Jan/Jana *See* Jane, Janet and Joanne.
Janata/Jannatta *See* Janet.
Janaya A modern name, derived from Jan or Janet.
Jahnaya, Jahneya, Janayah, Jhanaya, Jhanya, Jhanayah.
Jancis A modern name, probably from Jane and Frances.
Jances, Jancess, Jancesse, Janciss, Jancisse.
Jandy Probably from Jan or Janet.
Jandee, Jandi, Jandie.
Jane Hebrew: God is gracious. A feminine form of John, and one of the most popular female names for centuries. *See also* Janelle, Janet, Janice, Janine, Jean, Joan, Joanne, Shane and Sian.
Evana (Slavic), *Giaan, Gianina* (Italian), *Gianna* (Italian), *Giovanna* (Italian), *Heni* (Maori), *Ivana* (Czech), *Ivanna* (Russian), *Jain, Jaina, Jaine, Jana* (Czech, Polish), *Janna, Janneke* (Dutch), *Jannike* (Dutch, Scandinavian), *Jantje* (Dutch), *Jayn, Jayne, Jeanne* (French), *Jehanne* (French), *Juana* (Spanish), *Juanita* (Spanish), *Shane* (Irish Gaelic), *Shaun, Shauna, Shawn, Shawna, Sheena, Sheenah, Shena, Shevaun* (Irish), *Shivaun* (Irish), *Sian* (Welsh), *Siobhán* (Irish Gaelic).
Diminutives: Gia (Italian), Gian (Italian), Gianetta (Italian), Ivanka (Czech), Jan, Janey, Janie, Jantine (Dutch), Jaynee, Jayni, Jaynie.

Janeane/Janeanne/Janeen *See* Janine.

Janelle English: a modern name, from Jane and the feminine suffix 'elle'.
Genelle, Gennelle, Jahnel, Jahnell, Jahnella, Jahnelle, Janeille, Janel, Janell, Janella, Jannel, Jannelle, Jeanelle, Jenel, Jenella, Jenelle.

Janenne *See* Janine.

Janet *See also* Jane, Jeannette and Sinéad.
Janatta, Janeth, Janett, Janetta, Janette, Janita, Jannah, Jannatta, Janne, Jeanette, Jeannette, Jenette, Sinéad (Irish Gaelic), *Sioned* (Welsh).
Diminutives: Jan, Jann.

Janeve A combination of Jan (God is gracious) and Eve (life-giving).
Janneve.

Jangal Nepali: a forest.

Janice A form of Jane.
Janace, Janeace, Janessa, Janis, Jannice, Janyce, Janyse, Jenice, Jennice, Junnice.

Janine A form of Jane.
Janeane, Janeanne, Janeen, Janenne, Janiene, Janina (Polish), *Janita, Janyne, Jeaneane, Jeaneen, Jeanine, Jeannine* (French), *Jeanyne, Jenean, Jeneane, Jeneen,*

J – Girls

Jenine, Jennean, Jenneane, Jenneen, Jennene, Jennine.
Janisha Sanskrit: one who dispels ignorance.
Janita *See* Janet and Janine.
Jann/Janne *See* Janet and Joan.
Janna Hebrew: flourishing. *See also* Jane.
Jannah.
Jannali Aboriginal: the moon. A Sydney placename.
Janneke/Jannike *See* Jane and Jantje.
Jannel/Jannelle *See* Janelle.
Janthina/Janthine *See* Ianthe.
Janti A modern name, derived from Jan, Jane or Janet.
Jantee, Janti, Jantie, Jantina, Jantine, Jantti, Janty.
Jantina/Jantine *See* Jane, Janti and Jantje.
Jantje Dutch form of Jane.
Janneke, Jannike.
Diminutive: Jantine.
January English from Latin: born in the first month of the year. After Janus, the Roman god of beginnings and endings.
Januar (German), *Januarea, Januari* (Swahili), *Januaria, Januarie, Janvier* (French).
Janyne *See* Janine.
Japonica Latin: a shrub with pink, red or white flowers.
Japonika.
Jaqlin/Jaquiline *See* Jacqueline.

Jaquenetta/Jaquenette
See Jacqueline.
Jarah Hebrew: honey.
Jarra.
Jarilyn A modern made-up name, possibly from Marilyn.
Jarilin, Jarilinn, Jarilinne, Jarilynn, Jarilynne.
Jarita Sanskrit: a legendary bird.
Jarka Slavic: spring-like.
Jarmila Slavic: the grace of spring.
Jarmilla.
Jaroslava Slavic: the feminine form of Jaroslav, meaning the glory of spring.
Jaroslawa, Yaroslava.
Jarrah Aboriginal: a type of eucalypt.
Jarra.
Jarvia Teutonic: as sharp or keen as a spear.
Jarvinia.
Jasee/Jasey/Jasie *See* Jacey.
Jasenka Slavic: an ash tree.
Jasinta *See* Jacinta.
Jaslyn A modern name, possibly a combination of Jasmine and Lyn (a waterfall).
Jasleen, Jaslene, Jaslin, Jaslyne, Jaslynn, Jaslynne, Jazlyn, Jazlyne, Jazlynn, Jazlynne.
Diminutives: Jas, Jassie, Jaz, Jazz, Jazzie, Jazzy.
Jasmine Persian: a fragrant flower.
Jasmin, Jasmina, Jasminka, Jasmyn, Jasmyne, Jazmin, Jazmina, Jazmine, Jazmyn,

Jazmyne, Jazzmin, Jazzmine, Jazzmyn, Jazzmyne, Jessame, Jessamin, Jessamina, Jessamine, Jessamy, Jessamyn, Yasemin, Yashmin, Yasmeen (Arabic), **Yasmin** (Arabic), *Yasmina, Yasmine, Yassmin, Yassmine.*
Diminutives: Jas, Jassie, Jaz, Jazz, Jazzie, Jazzy, Jess.
Jasna Slavic: clear or sharp.
Jasvinder Sikh: the glory of the Lord.
Jasvinda, Jasvindah.
Jati An unusual name from Cyprus.
Java An Indonesian island. Also a boy's name.
Djava, Javah.
Javiera *See* Xaviera.
Jaxi A modern made-up name, possibly from Jack.
Jacksee, Jacksey, Jacksi, Jacksie, Jacksy, Jaksee, Jaksey, Jaksi, Jaksie, Jaksy, Jaxee, Jaxey, Jaxie, Jaxy.
Jay Old English: a bird. Also a boy's name.
Jae, Jai, Jaie, Jaye, Jhae, Jhai, Jhaie, Jhaye.
Jaya Sanskrit: victory. The name of a Buddhist goddess.
Jaaia, Jaia, Jayah.
Jaycee/Jayci/Jaycie *See* Jacey.
Jayd/Jayda/Jayde *See* Jada and Jade.
Jaydine A 'combination name' meaning a little jaybird.
Jaedeen, Jaedene, Jaedine, Jaedyne, Jaideen, Jaidene, Jaidine, Jaidyne,
Jaydeen, Jaydene, Jaydyne, Jayedeen, Jayedene, Jayedine, Jayedyne.
Jaylah Another Jay 'combination name'.
Variations: Jaelah, Jailah.
Jaylee A 'combination name' meaning a bird from the meadow or clearing.
Jaelea, Jaelee, Jaelei, Jaeleigh, Jaeilie, Jailea, Jailee, Jailei, Jaileigh, Jailie, Jayelea, Jayelei, Jayeleigh, Jaylea, Jaylei, Jayleigh, Jaylie.
Jayme/Jaymee/Jaymi/Jaymie *See* Jaime.
Jayn/Jayne/Jayni *See* Jane.
Jazlyn *See* Jaslyn.
Jazmin/Jazmyn *See* Jasmine.
Jazz A musical genre. Also a diminutive of Jaslyn and Jasmine.
Jaz, Jazann, Jazra, Jazza, Jazzah, Jazze, Jazzi, Jazzie, Jazzra, Jazzy.
Jazzmin/Jazzmyn *See* Jasmine.
Jeamai/Jeamais *See* Jaime.
Jean A form of Jane.
Gean, Geane, Gene, Genia, Hira (Maori), *Jeana, Jeane, Jeanella, Jeanna, Jeanne, Jeen, Jeene, Jenella.*
Diminutives: Jeanie, Jeanni, Jeannie.
Jeanais A French-sounding form of Jean.
Jeanavive/Jeanevive *See* Genevieve.

Jeanelle *See* Janelle.
Jeanene/Jeanine/Jeanyne *See* Janine.
Jeannette A form of Janet.
Genette, Jeanetta, Jeanette, Jenetta, Jenette, Jennet, Jennett, Jennette.
Diminutives: Jeanie, Jeannie.
Jeannine *See* Janine.
Jearl Modern American: perhaps based on Pearl.
Jearle.
Jecinta *See* Jacinta.
Jedda Aboriginal: a beautiful girl.
Jeda, Jedah, Jeddah.
Jedna *See* Jenna and Jennifer.
Jeen/Jeene *See* Jean.
Jeera Nepali: the spice, cummin.
Jeerah, Jira, Jirah.
Jehan Arabic: a beautiful flower.
Jehanne *See* Jane.
Jehmima *See* Jemima.
Jelena *See* Helen.
Jelissa Possibly derived from Melissa.
Jalissa, Jalissah, Jalyssa, Jalyssah, Jelissah, Jelyssa, Jelyssah.
Jeliza A character in the 2005 film *Tideland*.
Jelisa.
Jema/Jemah *See* Gemma.
Jemeeka/Jemica/Jemika *See* Gemica.
Jemena/Jemina/Jeminia/Jemmina *See* Gemina.
Jemiah *See* Gemma and Jemima.

Jemilla/Jemillah *See* Jamila.
Jemima Hebrew: a dove. A biblical name.
Gemima, Gemimah, Jahmima, Jamima, Jamyma, Jamymah, Jehmima, Jemiah, Jemimah, Jemmima, Jemyma, Jemymah, Jimima, Jimimah, Jimyma, Jimymah, Yemima, Yemimah.
Jemma/Jemmah/Jemelle *See* Gemma.
Jemyma/Jemymah *See* Jemima.
Jen/Jenafer/Jeni *See* Jennifer.
Jena Sanskrit: patience. *See also* Gina.
Jeena.
Jenalin/Jenalyn *See* Jennalyn.
Jenavieve/Jenevieve *See* Genevieve.
Jenaya Probably a form of Jennifer.
Genaia, Genaya, Jenaia, Jeneya, Jenya.
Jendaya African: the thankful one.
Jendayah.
Jeneane/Jeneen/Jenine *See* Janine.
Jenel/Jenella/Jenelle *See* Janelle.
Jenepher *See* Jennifer.
Jenetta/Jenette *See* Jeannette.
Jeneva *See* Geneva.
Jenica/Jenicah/Jenika *See* Jennica.
Jenifa/Jenifer/Jeniffa *See* Jennifer.
Jenilin/Jenilyn *See* Jennalyn.
Jenith/Jenithe *See* Jenyth.
Jenna A form of Jennifer.
Genna, Gennah, Jedna, Jennah.
Jennalyn From Jennifer (the fair one) and Lynn (a waterfall).

Jenalin, Jenalyn, Jenilin, Jenilyn, Jennalin, Jenna-Lin, Jenna-Lyn, Jenna-Lynn, Jenna-Lynne, Jennlyn.
Jenna-Alyssa An attractive 'combination name'.
Jenna-Alissa.
Jennean/Jenneen/Jennene/ Jennine See Janine.
Jennet/Jennett/Jennette See Jeannette.
Jennianne A combination of Jenny (fair and soft) and Anne (grace).
Jeniann, Jeni-Ann, Jenniann, Jenni-Ann, Jennyann, Jenny-Ann, Jennyanne, Jenny-Anne, Jenyann, Jeny-Ann, Jenyanne, Jeny-Anne.
Jennica A modern form of Jenna or Jennifer.
Jenica, Jenicah, Jenika, Jenikah, Jennicah, Jennika, Jennikah.
Jennie/Jenny Diminutives of Jennifer.
Jennifer Cornish/Welsh: fair and soft. A form of Guinevere. See also Jenna.
Genna, Gennah, Gennifer, Genowefa, Giniffer, Ginnifer, Jedna, Jenafer, Jenepher, Jenifa, Jenifer, Jeniffa, Jenna, Jennah, Jennefer, Jenniffer, Jenniva.
Diminutives: Genny, Jen, Jeni, Jenni, Jennie, Jenny.
Jennlyn See Jennalyn.
Jenya See Jenaya.

Jenyann/Jeny-Ann/Jenyanne See Jennianne.
Jenyth Probably a form of Jennifer.
Jenith, Jenithe, Jenythe.
Jeorgena/Jeorgina See Jorjina.
Jeorgia/Jeorgiah See Jorja.
Jeraldine See Geraldine.
Jeralyn A combination of Jeraldine (*see* Geraldine) and Lynne (a waterfall). See also Geralyn.
Jeralynn, Jeralynne, Jerilin, Jerilinn, Jerilinne, Jerilyn, Jerilynn, Jerilynne, Jerralyn, Jerralynn, Jerralynne, Jerrilyn, Jerrilynn, Jerrilynne.
Jerarda/Jerardine See Gerarda.
Jerelle A feminine form of Jerry (*see* Gerald).
Jerelda, Jerella.
Jeremia Hebrew: appointed by God. The feminine form of Jeremiah and Jeremy.
Jeremiah, Jeremie, Jeremya, Jeremyah, Jeroma, Jeromah, Jeromia, Jeromiah.
Jermain/Jermaine/Jermayne See Germaine.
Jerralyn/Jerrilyn See Jeralyn.
Jerri/Jerry See Geraldine.
Jerula Aboriginal: a spear made from reeds.
Jerulah.
Jerusha Hebrew: the married one.
Jesa/Jesah/Jesay See Jessa.
Jesana/Jesanna/Jesanne See Jessanna.

Jesenia/Jesenya *See* Jessenia.
Jesika/Jesikah *See* Jessica.
Jesinta *See* Jacinta.
Jeska *See* Jessica.
Jesmond A suburb of Newcastle upon Tyne, England. The name possibly means the hill of Jesus.
Jesmonde, Jezmond, Jezmonde.
Jess *See* Jasmine and Jessica.
Jessa A form of Jess or Jessica.
Jesa, Jesah, Jesay, Jessah, Jessay.
Jessalin/Jessalynn *See* Jessica.
Jessamine/Jessamy/Jessamyn *See* Jasmine.
Jessanna A combination of Jess and Anna or Anne (grace).
Jesana, Jesanna, Jesanne, Jessana, Jessanne.
Jesse/Jessie Diminutives of Jessica. Also independent names, particularly in Scotland.
Jessenia Spanish: a type of South American tree.
Jesenia, Jesenya, Jessenya, Jezenia, Jezenya, Yesenia, Yessenia.
Jessica Hebrew: wealthy. A character in Shakespeare's *The Merchant of Venice. See also* Jessa.
Gessica, Gessicah, Gessika, Gessikah, Jakica, Jesika, Jesikah, Jeska, Jessa, Jessaca, Jessalin, Jessalynn, Jessicah, Jessika, Jessikah, Jesska, Jesslyn.
Diminutives: Jess, Jesse, Jessi, Jessie, Jessye.
Jessina A form of Jess.

Jessin, Jessinah, Jessine, Jessyn, Jessyna, Jessynah, Jessyne.
Jesska *See* Jessica.
Jesslyn *See* Jessica.
Jessyna/Jessynah *See* Jessina.
Jesúsa Spanish from Hebrew: the feminine of Jesus, meaning the saviour or God is salvation.
Jesualda.
Jet Latin: black, a material used for making jewellery.
Jett, Jetta, Jette, Jhet, Jhett, Jhetta, Jhette.
Jetta Sanskrit: the Hindu month of May/June, corresponding to the zodiac sign of Gemini.
Jeta, Jettha.
Jetty Middle English: a wharf or pier.
Jetee, Jetey, Jeti, Jetie, Jettee, Jettey, Jetti, Jettie.
Jeudi French: Thursday.
Jeune French: young.
Jeunesse.
Jewel Old French: a gemstone; or the precious one.
Jewell, Jewelle, Jewels.
Jezenia/Jezenya *See* Jessenia.
Jezmond *See* Jesmond.
Jhae/Jhai/Jhaie/Jhaye *See* Jay.
Jhanaya/Jhanya *See* Janaya.
Jhet/Jhett/Jhetta *See* Jet.
Jiba Aboriginal: the moon.
Jie Chinese: pure.
Jilane/Jillane/Jillene *See* Gillian.
Jili Aboriginal: a spring.

Jilli, Jilliby.
Jill/Jilla/Jillian/Jillie/Jilly
See Gillian.
Jillette A diminutive of Jill.
Jilette, Jiletta, Jilletta.
Jillith A form of Jill.
Jilith, Jilithe, Jillithe.
Jimalyn A feminine form of Jim (*see* James), meaning the supplanter.
Jimalin, Jimalynn, Jimalynne, Jimmalin, Jimmalyn, Jimmalynn, Jimmalynne.
Jimaya A feminine form of Jim.
Jimelle Another feminine form of Jim.
Jimel, Jimela, Jimell, Jimella.
Jimena Spanish form of Ximena.
Jimima/Jimyma *See* Jemima.
Jin Chinese: golden. Korean: a jewel.
Jing.
Jinger/Jinjer *See* Ginger.
Jira/Jirah *See* Jeera.
Jirina The feminine of Jiri, the Czech form of George.
Jirra Aboriginal: a kangaroo.
Jirrah.
Jiruna Aboriginal: a pelican.
Jiselle Possibly a modern form of Giselle.
Jisell, Jisella, Jissell, Jissella, Jisselle.
Jitka Czech diminutive of Judita. *See* Judith.
Joadi/Joadie/Joady *See* Jody.
Joan *See* Jane and Joanne.
Jo-Ann/Joanna/Jo-Anne *See* Joanne.
Joanne A form of Jane.
Hanne (German), *Ioana* (Slavic), *Ioanna, Ioannah, Janne* (Scandinavian), *Joan, Joana, Joann, Jo-Ann, Joanna, Joannah, Joanette, Jo-Anne, Joannie, Joeanna, Joeanne, Johana* (Czech), *Johane, Johanna* (Dutch, German, Scandinavian), *Johannah, Johanne, Joina, Jone, Jonella, Jonna* (Danish), *Seònaid* (Scottish), *Shona* (Scottish), *Siôna* (Welsh), *Yoana* (Bulgarian).
Diminutives: Hana (Czech), Jana, Jo, Joanie, Joe, Joni, Jonie, Oana (Bulgarian).
Jobina Hebrew: the persecuted one. The female form of Job.
Jobie, Joby, Jobyna.
Jocasta Greek: the shining moon. The mother of Oedipus in Greek mythology.
Jocelyn Latin: the merry one.
See also Joss.
Jocelin, Joceline, Jocelyne, Jocelynne, Joscelin, Josceline, Joscelyn, Joselyn, Joselynn, Joselynne, Joslin, Josline, Joslyn, Joslynn, Joslynne, Josselin, Josselina, Josseline, Josselyn, Josslyn, Joycelin, Joyceline, Joycelyn, Joycelyne.
Diminutive: Joss.
Jocosa Latin: humorous, playful.
*Jocco*a.

Jocunda Latin: cheerful, merry.

Jodie A diminutive of Judith.
Joadi, Joadie, Joady, Jodana, Jodanna, Jodee, Jodelle, Jodene, Jodette, Jodey, Jodhi, Jodi, Jodia, Jodiea, Jody, Johdee, Johdi, Johdie, Johdy.

Joe/Joeanna/Joeanne *See* Joanne.

Joelan *See* Jolanka and Yolanda.

Joeleen *See* Jolene.

Joelle French from Hebrew: the Lord is God. The feminine form of Joel.
Joeli, Joell, Joella, Jo-Elle, Joellen, Joellyn, Joely, Jouella, Jouelle, Jowell, Jowelle.

Joette *See* Josephine.

Joffrette The feminine form of Joffre or Joffrey (*see* Geoffrey).
Joffret, Joffrett.

Johana/Johane/Johanna/Johanne *See* Joanne.

Johdee/Johdie/Johdy *See* Jodie.

Johnna A feminine form of John, meaning God is gracious. *See also* Joneen and Jonica.
Johna, Johnetta, Johnette, Johnnetta, Johnnette, Jonetta, Jonette, Jonna, Jonnah.

Johnnie Normally a boy's name, but occasionally given to girls.
Johnny, Jonnie, Jony.

Joi/Joie *See* Joy.

Joi-Ann/Joi-Anne *See* Joyanne.

Joi-Bella/Joi-Belle *See* Joybelle.

Joice *See* Joyce.

Joina *See* Joanne.

Jolan/Jolanda/Jolanta *See* Jolanka and Yolanda.

Jolanka Hungarian: one who is good.
Jola, Jolah, Joelan, Jolan.

Jolene American: a modern combination, perhaps of Jo and Marlene.
Joeleen, Joeleene, Joleen, Joleene, Jolijne, Joline.

Jolie French: pretty.
Jolee, Joley, Joli, Joliette, Joly.

Jolijne *See* Jolene.

Jona/Jonah *See* Jonina.

Jone/Jonella *See* Joanne.

Joneen A feminine form of John. *See also* Johnna and Jonica.
Johneen, Johnine, Jonine.

Jonetta/Jonette *See* Johnna.

Joni/Jonie *See* Joanne.

Jonica A feminine form of John. *See also* Joneen and Johnna.
Jonicah, Jonika, Jonikah, Jonnica, Jonnicah, Jonnika, Jonnikah.

Jonina Hebrew: a dove; a feminine form of Jonah. *See also* Yona.
Jona, Jonah, Jonia, Joniah, Joninah.

Jonna/Jonnah *See* Joanne and Johnna.

Jonnie/Jonny *See* Johnnie.

Jonquil A 'flower name', from the Latin word for a reed.
Jonquill, Jonquille.

Jools A diminutive of Julia.

Jora Hebrew: autumn rain.
Jorah.

Jord An earth goddess in Norse mythology.
Yord.

Jordan Hebrew: flowing down, as in the River Jordan. Also a boy's name.
Jordaine, Jordana, Jordane, Jordann, Jordanna, Jordanne, Jordayne, Jordena, Jordin, Jordinn, Jordinne, Jordyn, Jordynn, Jordynne.
Diminutives: Jordi, Jordie, Jordy, Jori, Jory.

Jorgelina Spanish form of Georgina.

Jori/Jory *See* Jordan.

Jorja A modern form of Georgia.
Jeorgia, Jeorgiah, Jorgia, Jorgiah, Jorjah, Jorjia, Jorjiah.
Diminutives: Jorji, Jorjie.

Jorjina A modern form of Georgina.
Jeorgena, Jeorgenah, Jeorgina, Jeorginah, Jorjena, Jorjenah, Jorjinah.
Diminutives: Jorji, Jorjie.

Josana/Josanna *See* Josephine.

Joscelin *See* Jocelyn.

Josée French form of Josephine.

Joselyn/Joselynn/Joselynne *See* Jocelyn.

Josephine Hebrew: God shall add. The feminine form of Joseph. *See also* Posy.
Giuseppa (Italian), *Giuseppina* (Italian), *Joette, Josanna, Josée* (French), *Josefina* (Spanish), *Josefine, Josepha, Josèphe* (French), *Josephina, Josetta, Josette, Josezinha, Josian, Josiane* (French), *Josine, Jozefa* (Slavic), *Jozefina, Jozefine, Jozetta, Jozette.*
Diminutives: Fifi, Jo, Joe, José, Josee, Josey, Josie, Jozsi, Jozsie, Pepa (Spanish), Pepita (Spanish), Posy.

Josetta/Josette *See* Josephine.

Josezinha *See* Josephine.

Josiane/Josine *See* Josephine.

Joslin/Joslyn/Josselin/Josslyn *See* Jocelyn.

Joss Originally a diminutive of Jocelyn.
Josonia, Josse, Jossonia.

Jouella/Jouelle *See* Joelle.

Joumana/Joumanah *See* Jumana.

Jovana Slavic: a feminine form of John.
Jovanah, Jovanna, Jovannah.

Jovanka Slavic: a mythological nymph.

Jovita Latin: the joyful one.

Jowell/Jowelle *See* Joelle.

Joy Latin: joyful.
Joi, Joie, Joya, Joyah, Joye, Joyita, Joyitah.

Joya Spanish: a jewel. *See also* Joy.
Joyah.

Joyanne A combination of Joy and Anne.
Joiann, Joi-Ann, Joianne, Joi-Anne, Joyan, Joyann, Joy-Ann, Joy-Anne.

Joybelle An unusual 'combination name'.
Joibell, Joibella, Joi-Bella, Joibelle, Joi-Belle, Joybell, Joybella, Joy-Bella, Joy-Belle.

Joyce Middle English from Breton: a lord. Originally a male name.
Joice, Joyous.
Diminutive: Joycie.

Joycelin/Joycelyn *See* Jocelyn.

Joyita *See* Joy.

Jozefa/Jozefine/Jozette *See* Josephine.

Jozsi/Jozsie Diminutives of Josephine.

Juanita A Spanish form of Jane.
Juana, Wanita, Wonita.
Diminutive: Nita.

Juba Tibetan: October.
Jubaa, Jubah.

Jubilee Middle English: a celebration.
Jubilie.

Judah Hebrew: the praised one; a son of Jacob in the Bible. More commonly a boy's name.
Juda, Jude.

Jude/Judee/Judeen/Judetta *See* Judah and Judith.

Judi Native American: an antelope. *See also* Judith.

Judianne A combination of Judy (Judith, the praised one) and Anne (gracious).
Judiann, Judi-Ann, Judi-Anne, Judieann, Judie-Ann, Judieanne, Judie-Anne, Judyann, Judy-Ann, Judyanne, Judy-Anne.

Judie/Judina *See* Judith.

Judith Hebrew: a woman from Judea, or the praised one. A name from the Bible. *See also* Jodie.
Giuditta (Italian), *Judeen, Judetta, Judina, Judit* (Spanish), *Judita* (Czech, Spanish), *Judite* (Portuguese), *Juditha, Judithe* (French), *Judyth, Judythe, Jytte* (Danish), *Siobhán* (Irish), *Siubhan* (Scottish), *Turuhira* (Maori), *Yehudit* (Hebrew).
Diminutives: Hura (Maori), Jitka (Czech), Jodie, Jude, Judee, Judi, Judie, Judy, Juta, Jutta (German), Jutte (Dutch).

Judy/Judy-Ann/Judy-Anne *See* Judith and Judianne.

Juen *See* June.

Jueva Spanish: from Jueves, meaning Thursday.

Juilia/Juilie *See* Julia.

Juillet French: the month of July.

Juin The French name for the month of June.

Juiris/Juirisa *See* Jurisa.

Jular Aboriginal: a koala.

Julea/Juleena/Julene/Jules *See* Julia.

Juleen *See* Julia.

Juli *See* Julia and July.

Julia Latin: from a Roman family name, possibly meaning youthful. *See also* Gillian.

Giulia (Italian), *Giulietta* (Italian), *Huria* (Maori), *Huriana* (Maori), *Juilia, Juilie, Julea, Juleen, Juleena, Julene, Juli* (Hungarian), *Juliana, Juliane, Juliann, Julianna* (German), *Julianne, Julie* (French), *Julieanne, Julienne, Juliet, Julietta* (Spanish), *Juliette* (French), *Julijana* (Slavic), *Julina, Juline, Julisa, Julissa, Julita* (Filipino, Spanish), *Julitta, Julya* (Russian), *Youlia, Yulia, Yuliana, Yuliya* (Russian).
Diminutives: Jill, Jools, Jules, Julz, Julze, Yula.

Julie/Juliet/Juliette *See* Julia.

Julina/Juline *See* Julia.

Julisa/Julissa *See* Julia.

Julitta The name of a 4th-century saint. *See also* Julia.
Julita, Julitha.

July A 'month name'.
Juillet (French), *Julai* (Swahili), *Juli* (Dutch, Swedish).

Julya *See* Julia.

Julz/Julze Diminutives of Julia.

Jumah Arabic: Friday.
Juma, Jumaa (Swahili).

Jumana Arabic: a pearl.
Joumana, Joumanah, Jumanah.

Jumoke Nigerian: the beloved one.

Jun Chinese: the truth. Nepali: moonlight.

June English: a 'month name'. *See also* Junia.
Hune (Maori), *Juen, Juin* (French), *Juna, Junaidi, Junella, Junelle, Junetta, Junette, Juni* (Danish, Swahili), *Junina, Junine, Junio* (Spanish), *Junita*.
Diminutives: Juney, Junie, Juny.

Junee Aboriginal: speaking, or a frog. A town in New South Wales.
Juni, Junie.

Juneffer A combination of June and Jennifer (fair and soft).
Juniffer.

Juni/Junie/Junina/Junita *See* June and Junee.

Junia The feminine form of Junius (born in June); a name from the New Testament.

Juniper Latin: a 'plant name'.

Junko Japanese: an obedient child.

Junna Arabic: shelter.

Juno Latin: the heavenly one; the wife of Jupiter in Roman mythology. Also a form of Úna.

Juny *See* June.

Jupitra Latin: from Jupiter, a planet and the Roman god of the heavens.
Jupita, Jupitia, Jupitria.

Jura A mountain range in France.
Jurah.

Jurisa Slavic: a storm.
Juiris, Juirisa, Juirisah, Juris, Jurisah.

Jurnee A modern name, probably derived from the word journey.
Jurney, Jurni, Jurnie.

Justice Middle English: rightness. *See also* Justine.

Justica, Justicia, Justisa, Justise, Justyce, Justyse.
Justine Latin: fair, just; the feminine form of Justin. See also Justice. *Justa, Justicia, Justina, Justyna, Justyne.*
Juta/Jutta/Jutte See Judith.
Jycinda/Jycinta See Jacinta.
Jylian/Jyllian See Gillian.
Jyoti Sanskrit: light.
Jytte Danish form of Judith.

K

Kaa Swahili: a crab.
Kaala/Kaalah See Kalaa.
Kaami See Kami.
Kaaren/Kaarena/Kaarin/Kaarina See Karen.
Kaari/Kaarie See Carrie.
Kaarla/Kaarle See Carla.
Kaasha See Keisha.
Kabira Arabic: powerful.
Kacee/Kacie See Casey.
Kade Indonesian: a popular girl's name.
Kadee Aboriginal: a mother. *KaDee, Kaydee.*
Kadence See Cadence.
Kadia/Kadija See Khadija.
Kadina Aboriginal: the plain of lizards. A town in South Australia.
Kadira See Qadira.
Kadla Aboriginal: sweet. *Kadlah, Kadlunga.*
Kadli Aboriginal: a dog. *Kadlee.*
Kae/Kaede See Kay.
Kael See Cale.
Kaela/Kaelah/Kaelia See Kaila and Kayley.
Kaelan/Kaelin/Kaelyn See Kalan.
Kaer Breton form of Katherine.
Kaera See Kiera.
Kagami Japanese: a mirror.
Kahili Hawaiian: a feather.
Kahla See Kala.
Kahlan/Kahlen/Kahlyn See Kalan.
Kahli/Kahlie See Kayley.
Kahlina See Kalina.
Kahlo See Kalo.
Kahu Maori: a cloak.
Kai Native American: a willow. See also Kay. *Kaie, Khi, Ki, Kie, Ky, Kye.*
Kaia/Kaiah See Caja and Kaya.
Kaidance/Kaidence See Cadence.
Kaie See Kai and Kay.
Kaikala Hawaiian: sea and sun.
Kaiko Japanese: forgiveness.
Kail See Cale.
Kaila Hebrew: crowned with laurel. *Kaelah, Kailah, Kayla, Kaylah.*
Kailana Hawaiian: the adored one.
Kailani Hawaiian: sea and sky.
Kailee/Kaileigh/Kailey See Kayley.
Kailin/Kailli/Kailyn See Kaylynn.
Kailmana Hawaiian: a diamond.
Kaimana Hawaiian: the power of the sea.

Kairo Nepali: brown. Also a form of Cairo.
Kaisa Finnish: pure.
Kaisee/Kaisey/Kaisie *See* Casey.
Kait/Kaite/Kaity Diminutives of Katherine.
Kaitlin/Kaitlinn/Kaitlyn *See* Caitlin.
Kaiya Aboriginal: a type of spear. *See also* Caja and Kaya.
Kaja *See* Caja and Kaya.
Kaki A nickname, probably a form of Katherine.
Kakra Ghanaian: a second-born twin.
Kaku Maori: a hawk.
Kala Hawaiian: the sun. *See also* Kali.
Kahla.
Kalaa Finnish: a fish.
Kaala, Kaalah, Kala, Kalaah, Kalah.
Kalai Hindi: the metal, tin.
Kalais *See* Calais.
Kalama Hawaiian: a flaming torch.
Kalamah.
Kalan A popular modern name, more commonly given to boys.
Caelan, Caelen, Caelyn, Calan, Calen, Calyn, Kaelan, Kaelen, Kaelin, Kaelyn, Kahlan, Kahlen, Kahlin, Kahlyn, Kalen, Kalin, Kalyn, Kaylan, Kaylen, Kaylin, Khalan, Khalen, Khalin, Khalyn.
Kalandra *See* Calandra.
Kalang *See* Kallang.
Kalani Hawaiian: the sky.
Kaliani.
Kalantha *See* Calantha.
Kalari Aboriginal: a lizard.
Kale *See* Cale.
Kalea Hawaiian: bright.
Kalece/Kalecia/Kaleesha *See* Kalisha.
Kaleen A Canberra suburb; the name is probably Aboriginal. *See also* Kayleen.
Kaleena/Kaleenah *See* Kalina.
Kalei Hawaiian: a flower wreath, or the beloved one.
Kalena Hawaiian form of Karen. *See also* Kalina.
Kalenah.
Kaleria An unusual name of Russian origin.
Kaley *See* Kayley.
Kali Aboriginal: water. Sanskrit: black.
Kala, Kalli, Kallie, Kally, Khali.
Kalia *See* Kaliya.
Kaliani *See* Kalani.
Kalico/Kallico *See* Calico.
Kalika Greek: a rosebud.
Kalila Arabic: beloved.
Kalimera Greek: morning (literally 'good morning').
Kalimerah.
Kalina Aboriginal: love.
Kahlina, Kaleena, Kaleenah, Kalena, Kalenah, Kalinah, Khalina.
Kalinda Aboriginal: a lookout.

K – Girls

Sanskrit: the sun.
Kalinn Scandinavian: a river.
Kalin, Kalyn, Kalynn.
Kalipso *See* Calypso.
Kalisha A modern, generally American, name.
Kalece, Kalecia, Kaleesha, Kalesha, Kalyce, Kalycia, Kalysha, Kalyshia.
Kalista/Kallista *See* Calista.
Kaliya Aboriginal: a lizard.
Kalia, Kaliyah.
Kalla Aboriginal: fire.
Kallah.
Kallang Aboriginal: heat.
Kalang.
Kalli Greek: a lark. *See also* Calandra and Kali.
Kallie, Kally.
Kalliope/Kalliopi *See* Calliope.
Kallisto *See* Callisto.
Kalo Nepali: black.
Kahlo.
Kaloni Hawaiian: the sky, or a chieftain.
Kalowna/Kalownah *See* Kelowna.
Kalpana Sanskrit: a fantasy.
Kalpara Aboriginal: a dry riverbed.
Kalparra.
Kalpurnia *See* Calpurnia.
Kalyan Aboriginal: to stop or remain.
Kalyana, Kalyanah, Kalyann.
Kalyani Sanskrit: auspicious or beautiful.
Kalyce/Kalycia/Kalysha *See* Kalisha.
Kalyn/Kalynn *See* Kalinn.
Kalypso *See* Calypso.
Kama Aboriginal: a spear. Sanskrit: love.
Kamal Perfection. The name of the Baha'i month that encompasses 1–19 August, so a suitable name for a Leo child. *See also* Kamala.
Kamala Sanskrit: a lotus.
Kamal (Nepali), *Kamalika.*
Kamarah Aboriginal: to sleep.
Kamara.
Kamaria African: of the moon.
Kamballa Aboriginal: a young woman.
Kambar Aboriginal: a crocodile.
Kambarah, Kambarra, Kambarrah.
Kambiri An African name of uncertain meaning.
Kame Japanese: a tortoise, implying longevity.
Kamea Hawaiian: the one and only.
Kameko Japanese: the child of the tortoise, implying longevity.
Kameo *See* Cameo.
Kameron *See* Cameron.
Kami Aboriginal: a prickly lizard. Japanese: a goddess.
Kaami.
Kamila Czech and Polish forms of Camilla.
Kamilah Arabic: the perfect one.
Kamla Sanskrit: a lotus flower. An alternative name for the Hindu

goddess Lakshmi.
Kamlah.
Kamra/Kamrah *See* Qamra.
Kamryn *See* Cameron.
Kana Japanese: beautiful.
Kanace *See* Canace.
Kanan Sanskrit: a garden or a jungle.
Kanaan.
Kanandah Aboriginal: sunset.
Kananda.
Kanani Hawaiian: beauty.
Kanapa Maori: radiant.
Kandace/Kandice *See* Candace.
Kandelka Aboriginal: good.
Kandi/Kandie/Kandy/Kandyce *See* Candace and Candy.
Kandiah A form of Kandi.
Kandia.
Kané Japanese: bronze.
Kanella/Kanelle *See* Kenella.
Kani Hawaiian: sound.
Kanika African: a black cloth.
Kanitha Sanskrit: an iris, as in the eye.
Kaneetha.
Kaniva Polynesian: the Milky Way.
Kanivah.
Kanoa Polynesian: free.
Kansa Hindi: bronze.
Kansah.
Kanti Sanskrit: lovely.
Kanuha Hawaiian: the sulky one. Also a boy's name.
Kanya Sanskrit: pure; the Hindu name for the zodiac sign of Virgo.

Thai: a young lady.
Kanyana, Kauni.
Kaoru Japanese: the fragrant one.
Kaprice *See* Caprice.
Kapua Hawaiian: a flower.
Kara Aboriginal: golden. *See also* Cara.
Karalee/Karalie *See* Cara.
Karalta Aboriginal: blue or green.
Kararaina Maori form of Caroline.
Karee/Karey *See* Carey.
Kareela Aboriginal: the south wind.
Kareelah, Karela, Karila.
Kareen/Kareena *See* Karen.
Karel *See* Carol.
Karen Danish form of Katherine.
Caran, Caren, Carin, Caryn, Kaaran, Kaaren, Kaarena, Kaarin, Kaarina, Kalena (Hawaiian), *Kareen, Kareena, Karena, Karenna, Karenne, Karin* (Swedish), *Karina, Karine, Karinne, Karon, Karran, Karren, Karrena, Karyn, Karryn, Karryne.*
Karensa/Karenza *See* Kerensa.
Karewa Maori: a buoy.
Kareyann/Kareyann *See* Karyanne.
Kari *See* Carrie.
Kariann/Karianne *See* Karyanne.
Karida Arabic: virginal.
Karidah.
Karie *See* Carey.
Karila *See* Kareela.
Karima Arabic: noble, generous.
Karin/Karina/Karinne *See* Karen.

K – Girls

Karis/Karisa/Karise/Karissa *See* Carissa.
Karisma *See* Charisma.
Karita Scandinavian form of Charity.
Karkata Sanskrit: a crab. The Hindu name for the zodiac sign of Cancer. *Kartaka, Kataka.*
Karla Aboriginal: fire. *See also* Carla. *Karlah.*
Karlee/Karleigh/Karley *See* Carla and Karli.
Karleen/Karleena/Karlena/Karlene *See* Carleen and Caroline.
Karli Turkish: the girl of the snow. *Karlee, Karleigh, Karlie, Karly, Karlye.*
Karlotte *See* Charlotte.
Karly/Karlye *See* Carla and Karli.
Karma Sanskrit: fate or destiny. Sherpa/Tibetan: a star. Also a boy's name. *Carma, Karmah.*
Karmé *See* Carmé.
Karmel/Karmen *See* Carmel.
Karmene/Karmina/Karmine *See* Carmine.
Karol/Karola *See* Carol.
Karolin/Karoline/Karolyn *See* Caroline.
Karon/Karran/Karren/Karrena *See* Karen.
Karra/Karrah *See* Cara.
Karri Aboriginal: a type of eucalypt. *See also* Carrie.
Karrie *See* Carrie.
Karsha *See* Kasha.
Kartaka *See* Karkata.
Kartika Sanskrit: the Hindu month of October/November, corresponding to Scorpio. *Karthika, Kattika.*
Karuah Aboriginal: a native plum tree.
Karyanne A modern name, probably a combination of Karey (*see* Carey) and Anne. *Kareyann, Kareyanne, Kariann, Karianne, Karyann.*
Karyl/Karyle *See* Carol.
Karyn/Karyne *See* Karen.
Kasa Native American: a lizard. Swahili: a turtle. *Kasah.*
Kasandra *See* Cassandra.
Kasey/Kasie *See* Casey.
Kasha Native American: a type of lizard. *Karsha, Karshah, Kasa, Kashah, Kashaya, Kashia.*
Kashmira From Kashmir, an Indian state. *Cashmira, Kashmirah, Kashmyra.*
Kasia *See* Kezia.
Kasimera/Kasimiera *See* Kazimiera.
Kass/Kassandra/Kassie *See* Cassandra.
Kassidy *See* Cassidy.
Kaster *See* Caster.
Kata Aboriginal: a little mother, or a mountain.

GIRLS – K

Kataka *See* Karkata.
Katalin A Basque form of Katherine.
Kataraina/Katarina/Katarzyna *See* Katherine.
Kate A diminutive of Catherine or Katherine.
Cait (Irish), *Caite, Cate, Kait, Kaite, Kayt, Kayte.*
Katelin/Katelinn/Katelinne *See* Caitlin.
Katelyn/Kate-Lynn/Katelynne *See* Caitlin and Catherine.
Katena/Katenah *See* Katina.
Katenka Russian diminutive of Yekaterina (*see* Katherine). *Katinka.*
Kateri Native American: the name of America's first native saint.
Katerina/Katerine *See* Katherine.
Katherine Greek: pure. A 4th-century saint who was martyred on a wheel. *See also* Catherine, Karen, Kate and Kathleen.
Kaer (Breton), *Karen* (Danish), *Katalin* (Basque), *Kataraina* (Maori), *Katarina* (Maori, Swedish), *Katarzina, Katarzyna, Katerina* (Czech, Russian), *Katerine* (Czech, Russian), *Kateryna* (Slavic), *Katharin, Katharina, Katharine, Katherin, Katherina* (German), *Katheryn, Kathleen* (Irish), *Kathri* (Swiss), *Kathrin, Kathrina* (Danish), *Kathrine, Kathryn, Katina, Katja* (German), *Katra* (Slavic), *Katren, Katrian, Katrien* (Dutch, German), *Katrin, Katrina* (German, Scandinavian), *Katrine* (Dutch, German), *Katriona, Katryn, Kattalin* (Basque), *Katya* (Russian), *Yekaterina* (Russian). *Diminutives:* Kait, Kaite, Kaity, Kass, Kate, Katee, Katenka (Russian), Kath, Kathe, Kathee, Kathie, Kathy, Katica (Slavic), Katie, Katika (Slavic), Katina (Slavic), Katinka (Russian), Katusha (Russian), Katy, Kay, Kaye, Kerry, Kit, Kitty, Treena, Trina.
Kathleen Irish form of Katherine. *See also* Catherine and Caitlin. *Caitlin, Cathleen, Cathlene, Kateleen, Kathlene, Kathlyn, Kathlynn, Kathlynne, Katyleen. Diminutives:* Kath, Kathy, Katie, Katy.
Kathrin/Kathrine/Kathryn *See* Katherine.
Katia/Katiah Variations of Katya.
Katica/Katika Slavic diminutives of Katherine.
Katina Aboriginal: first, or the firstborn child. Also a diminutive of Katerina (*see* Katherine). *Katena, Katenah, Katinah.*
Katinka *See* Katenka.
Katiya *See* Katya.
Katja/Katra *See* Katherine.
Kato *See* Cato.
Katrece/Katrice *See* Catrice.

Katren/Katrian/Katrina/Katrine *See* Katherine and Katya.
Katriel An unusual name from Israel.
Katriela.
Katsuko A Japanese name of uncertain meaning.
Kattalin A Basque form of Katherine.
Kattika *See* Kartika.
Katusha Russian: a diminutive of Yekaterina (*see* Katherine).
Katoucha, Katousha, Katyusha.
Katya A Russian form of Katherine.
Katia, Katiah, Katiya, Katja (German), *Katyah, Khatia, Khatija.*
Katyin Aboriginal: water.
Kauni *See* Kanya.
Kavita Sanskrit: a poem.
Kavitha.
Kawana Aboriginal: a wildflower.
Kawanah, Kawanna, Kawannah.
Kawena Hawaiian: glowing like a fire or the sunset.
Kay Originally a diminutive of Katherine.
Kae, Kaede, Kai, Kaie, Kailah, Kaye, Kayla, Kaylah, Kaysa, Khay, Khaye.
Kaya Japanese: a place of rest. Also a form of Caja.
Kaia, Kaiah, Kaiya, Kayaa, Khya, Khyah, Kya, Kyah, Kyha.
Kaycee/Kayci/Kaycie *See* Casey.
Kaydance/Kaydence *See* Cadence.
Kaydee *See* Kadee.
Kayla/Kaylah *See* Kaila, Kay and Kayley.
Kaylan/Kaylen/Kaylin *See* Kalan.
Kayleen A form of Kay (from Katherine, meaning pure).
Kaileen, Kailene, Kaleen, Kayelene, Kaylee, Kaylene, Kayline.
Kayley Irish Gaelic: slender. *See also* Caley.
Kaela, Kaelia, Kahli, Kahlie, Kailee, Kaileigh, Kailey, Kaley, Kayla, Kaylee, Kayleigh, Kayli, Kaylie, Khyla.
Kaylynn A combination of Kay and Lynn.
Kailin, Kaillin, Kailyn, Kailynne, Kaillyn, Kaillyne, Kaillynne, Kaylin, Kaylinn, Kaylyn, Kaylynne.
Kayna Cornish: a saint's name.
Kayoko Japanese: the child of a good generation.
Kaysa *See* Kay.
Kayscha/Kaysha *See* Keisha.
Kayt/Kayte Diminutives of Catherine.
Kazia *See* Kezia.
Kazimiera Polish: the feminine form of Kazimierz (*see* Casimir).
Kasimera, Kasimiera, Kazimera.
Kazu Japanese: obedient.
Kazuko Japanese: an obedient child.
Kazumi Japanese: beautiful

harmony.
Kea Maori: the name of a mountain parrot.
Keah.
Keala Hawaiian: a pathway.
Kealee/Kealeigh/Kealey See Keeley.
Keana/Keanna See Kiana.
Keara See Kiera.
Kearna See Kiana.
Kearoa Polynesian: a legendary figure.
Keatyn Old English: from the place of the kites or hawks.
Keatin, Keating, Keaton, Keetyn, Keyton.
Kedra A modern American name.
Kedrah, Khedra, Khedrah.
Kedsarin A Thai name of uncertain meaning.
Keeahn/Keeahna See Kiana.
Keeley Irish Gaelic: beautiful.
Kealee, Kealeigh, Kealey, Keali, Kealie, Kealy, Keelah, Keelee, Keeleigh, Keeli, Keelie, Keely, Keilee, Keilie, Kely, Kieley, Kiely.
Keena See Kena.
Keesha/Keesja See Keisha.
Keeva/Keevah See Keiva.
Kefira Hebrew: a lioness.
Kefirah.
Kei Hawaiian: dignified or glorious. Also a boy's name.
Keiarna See Kiana.
Keiko Japanese: the beloved or adored one.
Keilani Hawaiian: a glorious chief.
Keilee/Keilie See Keeley.
Keina Aboriginal: the moon. See also Keyna.
Keinah, Keyna, Keynah.
Keira Aboriginal: a big lagoon, or a mountain. See also Kiera.
Keera.
Keiralea/Keiralee/Keirle See Kirilee.
Keiri/Keirrie See Kerry.
Keiri-Beth See Kerri-Beth.
Keisha Contemporary American: possibly from Keshia (the favourite). See also Lakeisha and Rekeisha.
Kaasha, Kaisha, Karsha, Kayscha, Kaysha, Keesha, Keesja, Kesha, Keysha, Keyshia, Kiesha.
Keitha Celtic: from the forest; a feminine form of Keith. See also Keiva.
Keithia, Ketha.
Keiva Probably a feminine form of Keith. See also Keitha.
Keeva, Keevah, Keivah, Keva, Kevah, Kieva, Kievah.
Kekipi Hawaiian: a rebel. Also a boy's name.
Kekra Hindi: a crab.
Kelda Old Norse: a fountain or mountain spring.
Kelebek Turkish: a butterfly.
Keli/Kely See Keeley and Kelly.
Kelila Hebrew: a crown of laurel.
Kellina See Kelly.

K – Girls

Kelly Irish Gaelic: a warrior maid.
Keli, Kelle, Kellee, Kelley, Kelli, Kellie, Kellina, Kellye, Kely.

Kelowna A city in British Columbia, Canada.
Kalowna, Kalownah, Kelownah.

Kelsey Old Norse: the dweller on the island, or by the water. Generally a Norwegian name.
Kelsea, Kelsee, Kelsi, Kelsie, Kelsley, Kelsy.

Keltie From Latin: a Celtic person. Also a boy's name.
Celtee, Celtey, Celti, Celtie, Celty, Keltee, Keltey, Kelti, Kelty.

Kembla Aboriginal: plenty of game or wild fowl.

Kena Aboriginal: a freshwater crocodile.
Keena.

Kenda African: a child of the water. Also a feminine form of Kenneth, meaning handsome and fair.
Kendah.

Kendall English: from the bright valley. A placename.
Kendal, Kendalle, Kendel, Kendell, Kendelle, Kendle, Kendyl, Kendyll, Kendylle.

Kendra Celtic: a hill. Old English: royal power. The feminine form of Kendrick.

Kenecia/Kenesha/Kenicia *See* Kenisha.

Kenella A feminine form of Ken, meaning handsome and fair.
Kanella, Kanelle, Kenelle.

Keneve Another feminine form of Ken.
Kenneve.

Kenisha American: the beautiful one.
Kenecia, Keneesha, Kenesha, Kenicia, Kenishah.

Kenlynn A combination of Ken and Lynn (a waterfall).
Kenlin, Kenlinn, Kenlinne, Kenlyn, Kenlynne.

Kenna Celtic: love.
Kennah, Kenia, Kennia.

Kennedy Irish Gaelic: an ugly head, or a helmeted chief. More commonly a boy's name.
Kenedee, Kenedy, Kennedee.
Diminutives: Kenni, Kenny.

Kensa/Kensah *See* Kenzie.

Kensee/Kensey/Kensie *See* Kenzie.

Kenwyn Cornish/Welsh: the name of a saint. Also a boy's name.
Kenwyne, Kenwynne.

Kenya An African country.
Kenyah.

Kenzie A modern name; a diminutive of the popular Mackenzie.
Kensa, Kensah, Kensee, Kensey, Kensi, Kensie, Kensy, Kenza, Kenzah, Kenzee, Kenzey, Kenzi, Kenzy.

Keona Hawaiian: God's precious gift.

Kerala A state in southern India.
Keralah, Keralla, Kerallah.

Kerani Sanskrit: sacred bells.
Keren Hebrew: a ray, or a horn. A biblical name.
Kerena, Kerin.
Keren-Lee A combination of Keren and Lee (a meadow or clearing).
Keren-Lea, Keren-Leigh, Kerin-Lea, Kerin-Lee, Kerin-Leigh, Kerren-Lea, Kerren-Lee, Kerren-Leigh, Kerrin-Lea, Kerrin-Lee, Kerrin-Leigh.
Kerensa Cornish: love.
Carensa, Carenza, Karensa, Karenza, Kerenza.
Kereru Maori: a wood pigeon.
Kerewin Maori: the heroine of New Zealand author Keri Hulme's novel *The Bone People*.
Keri Maori: skin. *See also* Kerry.
Kerie.
Keriaki *See* Kyriaki.
Kerin *See* Keren.
Kerin-Lea/Kerin-Lee *See* Keren-Lee.
Kerith Hebrew: the name of a stream mentioned in the Bible.
Kereeth.
Kerralynn A combination of Kerry and Lynn (a waterfall).
Keralin, Kerlin, Kerralin, Kerralinn, Kerralinne, Kerralyn, Kerralynne, Kerrylin, Kerrylinn, Kerrylinne, Kerrylyn, Kerrylynne.
Kerreli/Kerrelie *See* Kirilee.
Kerren/Kerrin/Kerron *See* Kerryn.
Kerren-Lea/Kerren-Leigh *See* Keren-Lee.
Kerrera Scottish Gaelic: an island in the Inner Hebrides.
Kerri/Kerrie *See* Kerry.
Kerri-Beth A modern 'combination name'.
Keiri-Beth, Kerie-Beth, Kerry-Beth.
Kerrielea/Kerrieleagh/Kerrielee *See* Kirilee.
Kerrin-Lea/Kerrin-Lee *See* Keren-Lee.
Kerry Irish Gaelic: dark; the name of an Irish county. Also a diminutive of Catherine and Katherine.
Keiri, Keirie, Keirri, Keirrie, Keri, Kerie, Kerre, Kerrey, Kerri, Kerrie, Kerryn, Kery, Kierre, Kierry.
Kerry-Ann A 'combination name'.
Kerri-Ann, Kerri-Anne, Kerry-Anne.
Kerryn A form of Kerry.
Kerren, Kerrin, Kerron, Keryn, Kyrren, Kyrrin.
Kersti/Kerstie/Kersty *See* Kirstie.
Kerstin Swedish form of Christina.
Kerstyn.
Kesang Sherpa/Tibetan: of the golden age.
Keshia African: the favourite. *See also* Keisha.
Kesha.
Keshvar A Persian name of uncertain meaning.

Kesia/Kesiah *See* Kezia.
Kestrel A 'bird name'.
  Kestrell, Kestrelle.
Ketha *See* Keitha.
Keti Nepali: a young woman.
Keto *See* Ceto.
Keturah Hebrew: fragrant incense.
  Ketura.
Ketzia *See* Kezia.
Keva/Kevah *See* Keiva.
Kevaleen *See* Kevine.
Keverne Irish Gaelic: beloved, lovable; a feminine form of Kevin, an Irish Gaelic name meaning beloved. *See also* Kevine.
Kevine A female form of Kevin. *See also* Keverne.
  Kevaleen, Kevalene, Kevaline, Keveen, Keveena, Kevina, Kevinah.
Keyana/Keyanna *See* Kiana.
Keyna Welsh: a jewel. *See also* Keina.
  Keina, Keinah, Keynah.
Keysha/Keyshia *See* Keisha.
Keyt/Keyte *See* Kite.
Keyton *See* Keatyn.
Kezia Hebrew: the cassia tree. A daughter of Job in the Old Testament. *See also* Cassia.
  Kasia, Kazia, Kesia, Kesiah, Ketzia, Keziah.
  Diminutives: Kezzie, Kezzy.
Khadija Arabic: the first wife of the prophet Muhammad.
  Kadia, Kadija, Khadia.
Khalan/Khalen/Khalyn *See* Kalan.
Khali *See* Kali.
Khalida Arabic: eternal.
Khalina *See* Kalina.
Khandi/Khandy *See* Candace and Candy.
Kharis/Kharisma *See* Charisma.
Kharla *See* Carla.
Khatia/Khatija *See* Katya.
Khay/Khaye *See* Kay.
Khi *See* Kai.
Khia *See* Kah.
Khin Burmese: lovable.
Khloe *See* Chloe.
Khloris *See* Cloris.
Khola Nepali: a river.
  Kola, Kolah.
Khrista A diminutive of Christina.
Khusi Nepali: happy.
Khya/Khyah *See* Kaya.
Khyla *See* Kayley.
Khym *See* Kim and Kimberley.
Ki *See* Kai.
Kiah Aboriginal: from the beautiful place.
  Kia, Khia.
Kiama An Aboriginal word of uncertain meaning. A seaside town in NSW.
  Kiamah.
Kiana Irish Gaelic: ancient.
  Ciana, Cianna, Cianne, Ciarna, Ciarne, Ciarni, Keana, Keanna, Kearna, Keeahn, Keeahna, Keirna, Keyana, Keyanna, Kiahna, Kianna, Kiannah,

Kiarna, Kiarney, Kiarni, Kijana, Kijanna, Kinna, Kinnah, Kyan, Kyana, Kyanah, Kyanna, Kyannah.
Kiani A character in the *Fathom* comic book series.
Kiara Aboriginal: a white cockatoo. Also the name of an Irish saint. *See also* Chiara.
Kiarah, Kiarra.
Kiarna/Kiarni *See* Kiana.
Kiata Aboriginal: summer.
Kichi Japanese: fortunate.
Kidani Swahili: a bracelet.
Kie *See* Kai.
Kiele Hawaiian: a gardenia.
Kieley/Kiely *See* Keeley.
Kiera Irish Gaelic: dark, black. The feminine form of Kieran.
Ciara (Irish), *Kaera, Keara, Keera, Keira, Kierah, Kierra, Kira.*
Kieralee/Kierlee *See* Kirilee.
Kierre/Kierry *See* Kerry.
Kiersten/Kierstin/Kierstyn *See* Kirsten.
Kiesha *See* Keisha.
Kieva/Kievah *See* Keiva.
Kijana/Kijanna *See* Kiana.
Kiji Japanese: a pheasant.
Kiki Aboriginal: a waterhole. Egyptian: a castor plant.
Kiku Japanese: a chrysanthemum.
Kilda The name of a group of Scottish islands and a Melbourne suburb (St Kilda).
Kildah.
Kilee/Kileigh/Kiley *See* Kylie.
Kilia Hawaiian: heaven.
Killara Aboriginal: permanent; always there. Also a boy's name.
Kilpanie Aboriginal: winter.
Kilpani.
Kim Originally a male name, as in the hero in Rudyard Kipling's novel. Vietnamese: the golden one. Also a diminutive of Kimberley.
Khym, Kimm, Kimya, Kyhm, Kym, Kymm.
Diminutives: Kimmi, Kimmie, Kimmy.
Kima Swahili: a blue monkey.
Kimah.
Kimana African: a butterfly.
Kimama, Kimanna.
Kimba Aboriginal: a bushfire. Also a boy's name.
Kimbah, Kymba, Kymbah.
Kimberley Old English: from the meadow.
Kimber, Kimberlea, Kimberlee, Kimberleigh, Kimberlie, Kimberlin, Kimberly, Kimbra, Kymberlea, Kymberlee, Kymberley, Kymberlie, Kymberly, Kymberlyn.
Diminutives: Khym, Kim, Kimm, Kimmi, Kyhm, Kym, Kymm.
Kimbra *See* Kimberley.
Kimi Japanese: supreme, the best.
Kimiko Japanese: heavenly.
Kimina A variation of Kim.
Kiminah, Kimmina, Kimminah,

K – Girls

Kymina, Kyminah, Kymmina, Kymminah.
Kimora A modern name, probably from Kim.
Kimmora, Kimmorah, Kimorah.
Kimya *See* Kim.
Kin Japanese: golden.
Kina The Hawaiian name for China.
Kinay An African name of uncertain meaning.
Kindilan Aboriginal: joyful.
Kineta Greek: active.
Kini Polynesian: God is gracious.
Kinka Aboriginal: laughter, or a night owl.
Kinna/Kinnah *See* Kiana.
Kinta Native American: a beaver.
Kintah.
Kinu Japanese: like silk.
Kioko *See* Kyoko.
Kiona Native American: from the brown hills.
Kionah.
Kira Japanese: dark. Persian: the sun. *See also* Kiera.
Kiran, Kirra, Kyra, Kyrah.
Kiraa Nepali: an insect.
Kiran Sanskrit: a ray of light.
Kirran.
Kirby Old Norse/Teutonic: from the church town.
Kirbea, Kirbee, Kirbeigh, Kirbi, Kirbie, Kirbina, Kirbyna.
Kiri Polynesian: the bark of a tree.
Kirri, Kirry.
Kiriaki *See* Kyriaki.

Kiriana Probably from Kiri.
Kiria, Kirianna, Kirria, Kirriana, Kirrianna.
Kirilee A modern 'combination name', from Kiri and Lee.
Keiralea, Keiralee, Keirle, Kerreli, Kerrelie, Kerrilea, Kerrieleagh, Kerrielee, Kerrilea, Kieralee, Kierlee, Kirally, Kirilly, Kirralea, Kirrilly.
Kirimei A Maori name of uncertain meaning.
Kirra Aboriginal: a leaf. *See also* Kira.
Kirralea/Kirrilly *See* Kirilee.
Kirran *See* Kiran.
Kirri/Kirry *See* Kiri.
Kirria/Kirriana/Kirrianna *See* Kiriana.
Kirsten Scandinavian form of Christina.
Kiersten, Kierstin, Kierstyn, Kirstin, Kirstyn, Kjersti.
Kirstie Scottish form of Christina.
Chirsty, Kersti, Kerstie, Kersty, Kirsti, Kirsty.
Kisa Russian/Slavic: a kitten.
Kisah.
Kismet Persian: destiny.
Kit/Kitty *See* Katherine.
Kita Japanese: from the north.
Kite Middle English: a type of hawk. Also a boy's name.
Keyt, Keyte, Kyte.
Kiwa Aboriginal: daylight. Polynesian: the mother of all

shellfish in mythology. *Kiwah*.
Kiya Ancient Egyptian: a wife of one of the pharaohs. *Kiyah*.
Kiyo Japanese: purity.
Kiyoko Japanese: clear.
Kiyomi Japanese: pure beauty.
Kjersti Norwegian form of Christina.
Klara German, Scandinavian and Slavic forms of Clare.
Klarice/Klarise/Klarissa/Klarisse *See* Clarice.
Klaudia *See* Claudia.
Kleantha/Kleanthe/Kleanthy *See* Cleantha.
Klemence/Klemencia/Klementine/Klementyna *See* Clemence.
Kleo/Kleopatra *See* Cleopatra.
Klimentina Slavic form of Clementine. *See* Clemence.
Klio/Kliopatra *See* Cleopatra.
Kloee/Klohe *See* Chloe.
Kloris *See* Cloris.
Koanga Maori: spring, or happiness.
Kobla Ghanaian: Tuesday.
Koda/Kodah *See* Coda.
Kodee/Kodi/Kodie/Kody *See* Cody.
Kofi Ghanaian: born on a Friday.
Kohana Japanese: a little flower.
Kohdee/Kohdi/Kohdy *See* Cody.
Kohia Polynesian: a passionflower.
Koko Aboriginal: rain. Japanese: a stork. Native American: of the night. *See also* Coco.
Kokora Aboriginal: the rain.
Kola/Kolah *See* Cola and Khola.
Kolina Greek: pure. Swedish: a maiden.
Kolohe Hawaiian: a rascal.
Kolora Aboriginal: a freshwater lagoon.
Kolya Aboriginal: winter.
Komala Sanskrit: delicate or tender. *Komal*.
Kona Hawaiian: a lady. Sanskrit: a name for the planet Saturn. *Konah*.
Kono Polynesian: a basket.
Konstandina/Konstantina/Konstanze *See* Constance.
Koolyn Aboriginal: a black swan.
Koora Aboriginal: plenty, abundant. *Koorah*.
Koorine Aboriginal: a daughter.
Koosi *See* Kuusi.
Kooya Aboriginal: a fish. *Kuya*.
Kopu The Maori name for Venus.
Kora Aboriginal: a companion. *See also* Cora.
Korana Aboriginal: the moon.
Kordelia/Kordelya *See* Cordelia.
Koree/Korey *See* Corey.
Koren Greek: a maiden.
Kori Maori: exercise. *See also* Corey. *Korie*.
Korin *See* Corin.
Korina/Korinne *See* Cora.

Kornelia/Kornella *See* Cornelia.
Korra Aboriginal: grass.
Korrin/Koryn *See* Corin.
Korryn/Korryne *See* Cora.
Kosima/Kosma *See* Cosima.
Koula Tongan: golden.
Kourtenay/Kourtney *See* Courtney.
Kowhai Maori: yellow.
Kresimira Slavic: the feminine form of Kresimir, meaning light and peace.
Kris *See* Christina.
Krisane A combination of Kris (follower of Christ) and Anne (grace).
Krisanne.
Krishna Sanskrit: black or dark. More commonly a boy's name.
Chrishna.
Kriss/Krissie/Krisstene/Kristee *See* Christina.
Krista/Kristie Diminutives of Christina.
Kristabel *See* Christabel.
Kristain/Kristan *See* Christina.
Kristal/Kristalla *See* Crystal.
Kristeen/Kristen/Kristern *See* Christina.
Kristel/Kristell/Kristelle *See* Crystal.
Kristiani/Kristiann/Kristianna *See* Christina.
Kristien *See* Christina.
Kristina/Kristine/Kristy/Kristyn *See* Christina.
Krita Sanskrit: perfection.
Kritisha.
Kronia After Kronos (or Chronos), the Greek god of fertility and agriculture, and the equivalent of the Roman god Saturn.
Cronia.
Krysia/Krystena/Krystene/Krystyna *See* Christina.
Krystal/Krystel/Krystle *See* Crystal.
Krystalia/Krystallia Greek forms of Crystal.
Krystol/Krystole/Krystoll *See* Crystal.
Krythia An unusual classical-sounding name.
Ksenia Polish form of Xenia.
Kuan-Yin Chinese: the goddess of love and mercy.
Kuine Maori form of Queenie.
See Queena.
Kuini Samoan form of Queenie.
See Queena.
Kuja Sanskrit: a name for the planet Mars.
Kuku Maori: a dove.
Kulka Aboriginal: a star.
Kuma Japanese: a bear.
Kumari Sanskrit: a girl or daughter.
Kumbelin Aboriginal: sweet.
Kumberlin.
Kumi Japanese: a braid.
Kumiko Japanese: a beautiful child.
Kumuda Sanskrit: a lotus.
Kumud, Kumudah, Kumudini.
Kuna Aboriginal: grey.

Kunama Aboriginal: the snow.
Gunama, Gunamah, Kunamah.
Kunara Aboriginal: a tiger shark.
Kunika Aboriginal: a fire.
Kupala Aboriginal: white.
Kura Maori: treasure. Polynesian: red.
Kuri Japanese: a chestnut.
Kurria Aboriginal: a crocodile.
Kurtis/Kurtiss/Kurtys *See* Curtis.
Kurumi A Japanese name of uncertain meaning.
Kuusi Finnish: six.
Koosi, Kusi.
Kuya *See* Kooya.
Kveta/Kvetka *See* Cvetka.
Kwabena Ghanaian: Monday.
Kwame Ghanaian: Saturday.
Kwayde/Kwayden/Kweyde *See* Quade.
Kwinana Aboriginal: a young woman.
Ky/Kye *See* Kai.
Kya/Kyah *See* Caja and Kaya.
Kyan/Kyanna/Kyannah *See* Kiana.
Kyeema Aboriginal: of the dawn, or a kangaroo.
Kyeemagh, Kyeemah.
Kyha *See* Caja and Kaya.
Kyhm *See* Kim and Kimberley.
Kyla Scottish Gaelic: from the narrow strait. The feminine form of Kyle.
Kylah.
Kylara A name from the *Dragonriders of Pern* series of fantasy novels.
Kylarah, Kylarra, Kylarrah.
Kyle Scottish Gaelic: from the narrow strait. More commonly a boy's name.
Cyal, Cyall, Cyle, Kyal, Kyall.
Kylie Aboriginal: a boomerang.
Kilea, Kilee, Kileigh, Kiley, Kylea, Kylee, Kyleigh, Kyli, Kyliee, Kyly.
Diminutives: Kiles, Kyles, Kylz, Kylze.
Kylli Finnish: a name from a legend.
Kym/Kymm *See* Kim and Kimberley.
Kymba/Kymbah *See* Kimba.
Kymberley/Kymberlie/Kymberlyn *See* Kimberley.
Kymina/Kymmina *See* Kimina.
Kyna Irish Gaelic: wise.
Kyoko Japanese: a mirror.
Kioko.
Kyon Korean: brightness.
Kyra/Kyrah *See* Kira.
Kyrann The feminine of Kyran, a form of Kieran (meaning dark or black).
Kyranne, Kyrran, Kyrranne.
Kyrena/Kyrene/Kyrenia *See* Cyrena.
Kyria Greek: ladylike.
Kyriaki Greek: the feminine form of Kyriakos, meaning of the Lord.
Keriaki, Kiriaki, Kyriake.
Kyriakoula Greek: probably a form of Kyria.
Kyriacoula.

Kyrren/Kyrrin *See* Kerryn.
Kyte *See* Kite.

L

Lacena A modern American name of uncertain meaning.
Lacerta Latin: a lizard. The name of a northern constellation.
Lacey Old French: lace.
Lacee, Lacie, Lacy, Laycee, Laycie.
Lada Russian/Slavic: the goddess of beauty.
Ladasha/LaDasha *See* Latasha.
Ladene American: possibly a feminine form of Dean, meaning a religious official, or from the valley.
Ladeen, Ladine.
Ladonna Modern American: a lady.
La Donna.
Ladybird A colourful beetle, or the bird of our Lady (the Virgin Mary).
Ladibird, Ladibyrd, Ladybyrd.
Lael Hebrew: belonging to God. More commonly a boy's name.
Lale.
Laelia Latin: a type of orchid.
Lelia.
Laetitia Latin: happiness.
Latesha, Latisha, Letesha, Leticia (Spanish), *Letisha, Letitia, Lettice, Lettitia, Letizia* (Italian). *Diminutives:* Lettie, Letty.

Laguna Italian: a lake or lagoon.
Lagoona, Lagoonah, Lagunah.
Lahela Hawaiian form of Rachel.
Lahetta A modern 'La name'.
See also Lakeisha.
Lehetta.
Lahni/Lahnie *See* Lani.
Laiba A Pakistani name of uncertain meaning.
Laik/Laike *See* Lake.
Laila/Lailah *See* Layla and Leila.
Lailani *See* Leilani.
Laima A goddess in Baltic mythology.
Laina/Laine/Lainey/Lainie *See* Elaine and Lane.
Laione *See* Leona.
Laiten/Laiton/Laityn *See* Leighton.
Laka Hawaiian: gentle.
Lakah.
Lakari Aboriginal: a honeysuckle tree.
Lakkari.
Lake Old English: the original meaning was a stream rather than a pool or pond. Also a boy's name.
Laik, Laike, Layke.
Lakeisha Contemporary American: possibly from Keshia (the favourite) or Aisha (life), along with la – the French feminine form of 'the'. *See also* Keisha.
Lakaisha, Lakeshia, Lekaisha, Lekeisha, Lekeshia.
Lakena Another modern American 'La name'. *See also* Ladonna, Lakeisha, Lalena and Laneka.

Lakeena, Lakeenah, Lakenah, Lakenia, Lakenna, Lakennah, Lakenya, Lakhena, Lakhenah.
Lakshmi Sanskrit: a lucky omen. The Hindu goddess of beauty and wealth. *See also* Indira.
Lakmé, Laxmi.
Lakya Hindi: born on a Thursday.
Lala Slavic: a tulip.
Lahla, Lalah, Lalla.
Lalage Greek: chatter, babble.
Lalena A modern 'La name', probably from Lena.
Laleena, Laleenah, Lalenah, Lalina, Lalinah.
Lali Hindi: red. Polynesian: the highest point of the heavens.
Lalli, Lally.
Lalina/Lalinah *See* Lalena.
Lalirra Aboriginal: the sun.
Lalita Sanskrit: playful, charming.
Lalitha.
Lamberta The feminine form of Lambert, from the bright land.
Lambertha, Lambertia.
Lamesha From Mesha, the Sanskrit name for the zodiac sign of Aries.
Lameesha.
Lamilla Aboriginal: a stone.
Lamorna Cornish: a placename.
Lan Vietnamese: an orchid.
Lana Spanish: wool. Also a diminutive of Alana, Helena and Svetlana.
Lanah, Lanelle, Lanina, Lanna, Lannah, Llana.
Diminutives: Lanni, Lannie, Lanny.
Lanai Hawaiian: a verandah.
Lancey The feminine form of Lance, a lance-bearer.
Lancee, Lanci, Lancie, Lancy.
Lane English: from the narrow road. *See also* Alana.
Laina, Laine, Lainey, Laini, Lainie, Laney, Layna, Layne.
Laneka A modern American 'La name'. *See also* Lakeisha, Lakena, Lalena and LaRhonda.
Laneeka, Laneekah, Lanekah, Laneke, Lanneka, Lannekah, Lanneke, Lannekeh, Leneka, Lenekah, Leneke, Lenekeh.
Lanelle *See* Lana.
Lani Polynesian: the sky. *See also* Larni.
Lahni, Lahnie, Lanee, Lania, Laniah, Lanie, Lanyi.
Lanikais Hawaiian: the heavenly sea.
Lanina *See* Lana.
Lanna/Lannah *See* Alana and Lana.
Lanyi *See* Lani.
Lapis Latin: from lapis lazuli, a deep-blue gemstone.
Lara Russian: a diminutive of Larissa. A name that became popular through the 1960s film *Dr Zhivago*.
Larah, Laragh.
Laraine/Larayne/Lareine/Lareyne *See* Lorraine.

Larella/Larelle *See* Lorelle.
LaRhonda American: a variation of Rhonda, meaning a valley.
Larhonda, Larhondda, LaRhondda, Laronda, LaRonda, Larondda, Larondah, LaRondah.
Larida/Laridah *See* Lerida.
Lariel Hebrew: God's lioness. A form of Ariel.
Larina Either a form of Laura/Lauren, or a modern 'La name'.
Larinah, Laryna, Larynah.
Larissa Russian from Greek: cheerful, lighthearted.
Larisa, Larisah, Larissah, Larisse, Laryssa, Larysse, Lorissa, Lorissah, Loryssa, Loryssah.
Diminutives: Lara, Larah, Laragh.
Lark Aboriginal: a cloud. English: a songbird.
Larke.
Larna A name from the *Dragonriders of Pern* series of fantasy novels.
Larnah.
Larni Possibly a variation of Lani, a Polynesian name meaning the sky.
Larne, Larnee, Larney, Larnie, Larny.
Larrain/Larraine *See* Lorraine.
Laryn/Larynn *See* Lauren.
Laryna/Larynah *See* Larina.
Lasca Latin: weary.
Laschelle A modern 'La name', probably from Michelle.
Laschell, LaSchell, LaSchelle.
Lashinda A modern name of uncertain meaning.
LaShinda, Lashindah, LaShindah.
Lassie English/Scottish: a little girl.
Lastri Indonesian: a common girl's name.
Lata Sanskrit: a vine.
Latah.
Latai The name of a figure in Polynesian mythology.
Latasha A modern American name, a combination of la and Tasha (*see* Natasha).
Ladasha, LaDasha, La Dasha, LaTasha, La Tasha.
Latifa Arabic: kind and gentle.
Lateefa, Lateefah, Latifah.
Latisha *See* Laetitia.
Latonia Latin: The mother of Diana in Roman mythology.
Latona, Latonya.
Latoya Spanish: victorious. A popular name in the USA.
LaToya, La Toya, Latoyah, LaToyah, La Toyah.
Diminutives: Toya, Toyah.
Latrelle Another modern 'La name'.
Latrell, Letrell, Letrelle.
Lauma A figure in Baltic mythology.
Launa/Launah *See* Lorna.
Laura Latin: a laurel wreath or a tree. *See also* Lauren.
Laurana, Laure (French), *Laureen, Laurel, Laurell, Laurene, Lauretta* (Italian), *Laurette, Lauria, Laurian,*

Lauriane, Laurice, Laurina, Laurine, Laurinda, Lauris, Laurisa, Lora (German), *Loras, Lore* (German), *Lorena, Lorenza* (Italian), *Lores, Loretta, Lorinda, Loris, Lorita, Lowri* (Welsh). *Diminutives:* Lauri, Laurie, Lori, Lorri, Lorrie, Lory, Retta.

Lauraine *See* Lorraine.

Lauralee A combination of Laura (a laurel tree) and Lee (a meadow or clearing).
Lauralea, Laura-Lea, Laura-Lee, Lauraleigh, Laura-Leigh.

Laure/Laurel/Laurella/Laurelle *See* Laura and Lorelle.

Lauren English: a feminine form of Laurence. Originally made popular by the actress Lauren Bacall. *See also* Laura.
Laryn, Larynn, Lauran, Laurann, Lauranne, Laureen, Laureena, Laurena, Laurence, Laurencina, Laurencine, Laurene, Laurenn, Laurenne, Laurentia (Italian), *Laurentina* (Italian), *Laurien, Laurienn, Laurienne, Laurine, Lauryn, Lauryne, Lawren, Lawrencina, Lawrencine, Lawrenn, Lawrenne, Loreen, Loreena, Loren, Lorena, Lorene, Lorenn, Lorien, Lorienn, Lorienne, Lorin, Lorine, Lorren, Lorrin, L'Wren, L'Wrenn, L'Wrenne.*
Diminutives: Lauri, Laurie, Lori, Lorri, Lorrie, Lory.

Laurene *See* Laura and Lauren.

Laurenza *See* Lorenza.

Lauretta *See* Laura.

Lauria/Laurina/Laurinda *See* Laura.

Laurice *See* Laura.

Laurien/Laurienne *See* Lauren.

Laurine *See* Lauren.

Lauris/Laurisa *See* Laura.

Laurraine *See* Lorraine.

Lauryn/Lauryne *See* Lauren.

Laveda Latin: one who is purified or innocent.
Lavedah.

Lavelle A modern American name.
Lavell, LaVell, LaVelle.

Lavena/Lavenia *See* Lavinia.

Lavender English from Latin: a 'plant name'.
Lavenda, Lavinda, Lavindah.

Laverne French: spring-like, or from the alder tree. Popular in the USA.
Lavern, LaVern, Laverna, LaVerne.
Diminutives: Vern, Verna, Verne.

Lavinda *See* Lavender.

Lavinia Latin: a lady, or a mother of Rome.
Lavena, Lavenia, Lavina, Lavine, Laviniah, Levina, Levinia, Livenia, Livinia, Lovenia, Lovinia.
Diminutives: Vina, Vinia, Vinny.

Lavonne American: a form of Yvonne, the archer.

Lavonna, Lavonnah, Levonne.
Lawan Thai: pretty.
Lawanda A combination of la and Wanda.
LaWanda, Lawandah, LaWandah.
Lawella *See* Llawella.
Lawren/Lawrencina *See* Laura.
Laxmi *See* Lakshmi.
Layaleta Aboriginal: the ocean.
Layaleeta.
Laycie *See* Lacey.
Layke *See* Lake.
Layla Arabic: as intoxicating as wine.
Laila, Lailah, Laylah, Leyla, Leylah.
Layne *See* Lane.
Layten/Layton *See* Leighton.
Lazette A feminine form of Laz (*see* Laurence and Lazarus).
Lazel, Lazell, Lazelle, Lazetta.
Le Vietnamese: a pearl.
Lea Hawaiian: the mythological goddess of canoe builders. *See also* Leah, Leandra and Lee.
Leah Hebrew: languid, weary. The wife of Jacob in the Bible. *See also* Leandra.
Lea, Leaha, Leata, Leatah, Leea (Finnish), *Leia, Leigha, Leyah, Lia* (Italian), *Liah, Lija, Lijia.*
Leahtrice A combination of Leah (languid or weary) and Beatrice (the blessed one).
Leatrice, Leeatrice, Leighatrice, Liahtrice, Liatrice.
Leala French: the loyal one.

Lealeen/Lealine *See* Leeleen.
Léan Irish Gaelic form of Helen.
Leana/Leanna *See* Leanne and Liana.
Leandra Latin: like a lioness; the female version of Leander. *See also* Leona and Lionelle.
Leanda, Leandah, Leandrah.
Diminutives: Lea, Leah.
Leani/Leanni *See* Leanne.
Leanne A modern invention, formed from Lee and Anne and generally an Australian name.
Leana, Leane, Leani, LeAnn, Leanna, Leannah, LeAnne, Leeanna, Lee-Anne, Lee-Arne, Leanni, Learne, Le-Arne, Leearne, Leiahan, Leiahann, Leiahanne, Leigh-Ann, Leigh-Anne, Leighanne, Leigharne, Leyann, Leyanne, Lian, Liann, Li-Ann, Lianne, Li-Anne, Liarne, Lliann, Llianne, Lyan, Lyann, Lyanne.
Leanor/Leanora *See* Eleanor.
Learne/Leearne *See* Leanne.
Leata/Leatah *See* Leah.
Leath *See* Leith.
Lecia *See* Licia.
Leda Greek: a mythological queen and the mother of Helen of Troy. *See also* Alida.
Ledah, Leida, Leidah, Lieda, Liedah.
Lee Old English: a meadow or a clearing. Also a Chinese family

name.
Lea, Leigh, Leigha.
Leea Finnish form of Leah.
Leela Sanskrit: playful.
Lila, Lilah.
Leeleen Little Lee.
Lealeen, Lealine, Leeline.
Leena Aboriginal: a possum. *See also* Lena.
Leene A character in the Japanese *Vampire Game* series.
Leeroi/Leeroy *See* Leroy.
Leesa/Leeza *See* Lisa.
Leesha *See* Licia.
Leeston A modern name, derived from Lee. Also a boy's name.
Leesten, Leestyn, Leisten, Leiston, Leistyn.
Leeta *See* Leta.
Leeth *See* Leith.
Leewana Aboriginal: the wind.
Leewan, Leewanah.
Lefki Greek: white.
Lei Hawaiian: a flower garland.
Leia *See* Leah.
Leiahnn/Leihanne *See* Leanne.
Leida/Leidah *See* Leda.
Leigh/Leigha *See* Leah and Lee.
Leighanne/Leigharne *See* Leanne.
Leighton Old English: from the farm by the meadow. More commonly a boy's name.
Laiten, Laiton, Laityn, Layten, Layton, Leyten, Leyton, Lleyton.
Leila Arabic: dark as the night.
Laila, Lela, Lelah, Lelila, Lelilah,
Lila, Lilah, Lyla, Lylah.
Leila-Mae A combination of Leila and Mae (*see* May).
Leila-May.
Leilani Hawaiian: a heavenly flower.
Lailani.
Leira A goddess in the role-playing game *Dungeons & Dragons*.
Leisa/Leisha *See* Licia and Lisa.
Leisel German form of Elizabeth.
Leis, Leise.
Leiselotte *See* Liselotte.
Leisten/Leiston/Leistyn *See* Leeston.
Leita Aboriginal: the little one.
Leith Scottish Gaelic: a broad river; a Scottish placename. More commonly a boy's name.
Leath, Leathe, Leeth, Leethe, Leithe.
Lekaisha/Lekeisha/Lekeshia *See* Lakeisha.
Leksi A diminutive of Alexandra.
Lela/Lelah *See* Leila.
Lelia *See* Laelia.
Lelila/Lelilah *See* Leila.
Lella A modern name, possibly from Bella.
Lellah.
Lema/Lemah *See* Lima.
Lemana Aboriginal: the she-oak tree.
Lemonia From lemon, a fruit or a light-yellow colour.
Lemoniah, Lemonya, Lemonyah.
Lemuela Hebrew: devoted to God.

The feminine form of Lemuel.
Lena A diminutive of Caroline, Helen and other names.
Leena, Leenah, Lenah, Lene (Danish, German), *Leni* (German), *Lenita, Liina, Lina, Linah.*
Lencey A modern name, possibly a form of Lena or Len.
Lencee, Lenci, Lencie, Lency.
Lene German/Scandinavian: a diminutive of Helen and Magdalene (*see* Madeline). See also Lena.
Leneka/Lenekah/Leneke See Laneka.
Leneve/LeNeve See Lynneve.
Leni/Lenita See Lena.
Lenis Latin: gentle and smooth.
Leneta, Lenita.
Lenka A diminutive of Malenka, a Czech form of Madeline.
Lenkah, Lenkhia, Lenkia, Lenkiah.
Lenna Possibly a form of Lena.
Lennah.
Lennora/Lennorah See Leonora.
Lenora/Lenore See Eleanor and Leonora.
Leocadia Spanish: the name of a 3rd-century saint.
Leokadia (Slavic).
Leoda Teutonic: a woman of the people.
Leodah, Leota, Leotah.
Leoene A feminine form of Leo.
Leoeen, Leoeene, Leoine.
Leola Another feminine form of Leo.
Liola, Lyola.
Leoma Old English: light, bright.
Leona Latin: a lioness. A feminine form of Leo or Leon. See also Leandra, Leonarda, Leoene, Leontine and Lionelle.
Laione (Polynesian), *Leonarda, Leone, Leonelle, Leoni, Leonia, Leonice, Leonie, Léonie, Léonne* (French), *Leonnie, Leontia, Liona, Lione.*
Diminutive: Loni.
Leonarda Old French: a brave lioness. The feminine form of Leonard. See also Leona and Lionelle.
Leonia/Leonice/Leonie See Leona.
Leonora A form of Eleanor.
Leanora, Leanorah, Lennora, Lennorah, Lennore, Lenora, Lenore, Leonor, Leonorah, Leonore, Lynora, Lynore.
Leontine Latin: like a lion. See also Leona and Lionelle.
Leontina, Leontyne.
Leora Greek: light.
Leor, Leorah, Lior, Liora, Liorah.
Leposava A Slavic name of uncertain meaning.
Lerida From Rida, an Arabic name meaning the favoured one.
Larida, Laridah, Leridah.
Leroy French: the king. More commonly a boy's name.
Leeroi, Leeroy, Leroi.

Lerra Aboriginal: a river.
Lesa/Lesah *See* Lisa.
Lesha/Leshia *See* Licia.
Leshae A form of Shae (*see* Shay).
Leshai, Leshaie, Leshay, Leshaye, Leshea.
Lesia *See* Alesia and Licia.
Lesley Scottish Gaelic: from an ancient surname. Also a boy's name.
Leslea, Leslee, Lesleigh, Leslie, Lesly, Leslye, Lezli, Lezlie, Lezly.
Diminutive: Les.
Leta Swahili: to bring.
Leeta.
Letesha *See* Laetitia.
Letha Greek: from Lethe, the river of forgetfulness.
Leithia, Lethia.
Leticia/Letisha/Letitia/Letizia *See* Laetitia.
Leto The mother of Artemis and Apollo in Greek mythology.
Letrell/Letrelle *See* Latrelle.
Letta A diminutive of names such as Violetta.
Lettah.
Letteria Italian: a name associated with St Maria of the Letter, the patron saint of Messina, Sicily.
Lettice *See* Laetitia.
Leura Aboriginal: lava.
Levana Hebrew: the moon. Latin: the rising sun.
Levanah, Levania, Levanna, Levona.
Levia Feminine form of Levi, meaning united.
Leviah.
Levina Old English: a bright flash. *See also* Lavinia.
Levinia.
Levona *See* Levana.
Levonne *See* Lavonne.
Lewa Possibly a feminine form of Lew.
Lewah.
Lewanna Hebrew: the moon.
Lewella *See* Llawella.
Lewenna *See* Lowenna.
Lex/Lexa/Lexi/Lexie/Lexine/Lexy *See* Alexandra.
Leyah *See* Leah.
Leyann/Leyanne *See* Leanne.
Leyla/Leylah *See* Layla.
Leyscha/Leysha/Leyshia *See* Licia.
Leyten/Leyton *See* Leighton.
Leza/Lezah *See* Lisa.
Lezli/Lezlie/Lezly *See* Lesley.
Lhakpa Sherpa/Tibetan: born on a Wednesday. Also a boy's name.
Lhamu Sherpa/Tibetan: a goddess.
Li Chinese: plum blossom.
Lia/Liah *See* Leah.
Liahtrice/Liatrice *See* Leahtrice.
Lial/Liall *See* Lyle.
Lian Chinese: a graceful willow. *See also* Leanne.
Liana French: to bind like a vine.
Leana, Leanna, Liane, Lianna, Lianne, Lliane.
Li-Ann/Li-Anne *See* Leanne.

Liarne *See* Leanne.
Libby A diminutive of Elizabeth and Sybil.
Liberty Latin: freedom.
Liberta, Libertey, Libertia, Libertie, Libertina, Libertine.
Libra Latin: a pair of scales. A zodiac sign.
Librah, Librea, Librena, Libria, Librina.
Libuse Czech: the loved one.
Licette A diminutive of Elizabeth.
Licia A diminutive of Alicia.
Lecia, Leesha, Leisha, Lesha, Leshia, Lesia, Leyscha, Leysha, Leyshia, Lisha, Lishia, Lisia, Lissha, Lycia, Lysia.
Lida Slavic: loved by the people; a form of Ludmila. *See also* Alida and Lydia.
Lieda, Liedah, Lidah.
Lidia/Lidya *See* Lydia.
Lieda/Leidah *See* Leda and Lida.
Liel/Liell *See* Lyle.
Lien Chinese: a lotus.
Liesa/Liessa *See* Lisa.
Lieselotte *See* Liselotte.
Liesl A German form of Elizabeth.
Liese, Liesel, Liezel.
Lieve *See* Liv.
Liga Latvian: a midsummer child.
Lihnida *See* Linida.
Liina *See* Lena.
Lija/Lijia *See* Leah.
Lil A diminutive of Lillian and Lily.
Lila German: mauve. Spanish: a lilac flower. *See also* Delilah, Leela and Leila.
Lilah, Lyla, Lylah.
Lilac Persian: a mauve flower.
Lilea/Lilee *See* Lily.
Lili *See* Elizabeth, Lillian and Lily.
Li-Li Chinese: a beautiful plum blossom.
Lilia/Lilian/Lilias *See* Lillian and Lily.
Lilibet/Lillibet Diminutives of Elizabeth.
Lilie/Lilli *See* Lily.
Lilija/Lilijanna *See* Lillian and Lily.
Lilith Arabic/Hebrew: dark, a woman of the night.
Lillith.
Lill/Lilla/Lillea *See* Lillian and Lily.
Lillian A diminutive of Elizabeth. *See also* Lily.
Lilian, Liliana, Liliane (French), *Liliann, Lilianti, Lilias* (Scottish), *Lilijanna, Lilla, Lilliane, Lilliann, Lillianne, Lillianti, Lillias, Lillice, Lillijannah, Lillise, Lillyn, Lilyan, Lilyann, Lilyanne, Lylian, Lyliann, Lyliann, Lyllian, Lylliann, Lyllianne.*
Diminutives: Lil, Lili, Lill, Lilli, Lily, Lyli, Lylie.
Lillice/Lillise *See* Lillian.
Lilo Hawaiian: the generous one.
Liloh, Lylo, Lyloh.
Lily Latin: a 'flower name', a symbol of purity. *See also* Lillian.

Lilea, Lilee, Lili, Lilia (Hawaiian), *Lilias, Lilie* (German), *Lilija* (Icelandic), *Lillea, Lillee, Lilley, Lilli, Lillia, Lillie, Lillis, Lilly, Lyli, Lylie, Lys* (French).
Diminutives: Lil, Lill.
Lilyan/Lilyann/Lilyanne *See* Lillian.
Lily-Rose A delightful 'combination flower name'.
Lima Spanish: a lime tree. The name of the capital of Peru.
Lema, Lemah, Limah.
Lin Chinese: a jade stone. Also a diminutive of Linda and similar names.
Lina/Linah *See* Lena.
Linda Spanish: pretty. Also a diminutive of names such as Belinda and Melinda.
Lindah, Lindee, Lindey, Lindie, Lindy, Llynda, Lynda, Lyndah, Lyndee, Lyndey, Lyndie.
Diminutives: Lin, Lindie, Linn, Lyn.
Lindal/Lindall/Lindel/Lindell *See* Lyndal.
Lindamarie/Lindeymarie *See* Lyndamarie.
Lindee/Lindie *See* Linda.
Linden Old English: a 'tree name'.
Lindan, Lindon, Llyndan, Llynden, Llyndon, Lyndan, Lynden, Lyndon.
Lindis/Linndis *See* Lynndis.

Lindsey Originally a Scottish surname.
Lindesay, Lindesey, Lindsay, Lindsy, Linzee, Linzi, Linzie, Linzy, Lyndsey, Lyndsie, Lynsey.
Lindy *See* Linda.
Linell/Linelle *See* Lynelle.
Linetta/Linette *See* Linnet.
Lineve/Linneve *See* Lynneve.
Ling Chinese: delicate.
Linida A modern form of Lin or Linda.
Lihnida, Linidah.
Linley Old English: from the field of flax. Also a boy's name.
Linleigh, Linnley, Lynleigh, Lynley, Lynnley.
Linnea Old Norse: a lime tree or lime blossom.
Linea, Lynea, Lynnea.
Linnet Old French: a small bird.
Eluned (Welsh), *Linett, Linetta, Linette, Linnette, Lynett, Lynetta, Lynette, Lynnetta, Lynnette.*
Linzee/Linzi *See* Lindsey.
Liola *See* Leola.
Liona/Lione *See* Leona.
Lionelle Old French: a young lion. The feminine form of Lionel.
See also Leandra, Leona, Leonarda and Leontine.
Lionel, Lionella, Lyonell, Lyonella, Lyonelle.
Lior/Liora/Liorah *See* Leora.
Lirene A name from *The Wheel of*

Time series of fantasy novels.
Lirean, Lireen, Lirine, Lyrean, Lyreen, Lyrene, Lyrine.
Lirio Spanish: a lily.
Lirra Aboriginal: a wren.
Lira, Lirah, Lirrah, Lirrina.
Lisa A diminutive of Elizabeth.
Leesa, Leesah, Leeza, Leezah, Leisa, Leisha, Lesa, Lesah, Leza, Lezah, Liesa, Liesah, Liessa, Lisah, Liselle, Lisi, Liza.
Lisabel/Lisabell *See* Lizabelle.
Lisabet/Lisabeth/Lisbet/Lisbeth *See* Elizabeth.
Lisann/Lisanna/Lisanne *See* Lizanne.
Lise/Lisette *See* Elizabeth.
Lisella/Liselle *See* Lizelle.
Liselotte Teutonic: a combination of Elizabeth and Charlotte.
Leiselotte, Lieselotte.
Lisha/Lishia/Lisia *See* Licia.
Lisi *See* Lisa.
Lisle *See* Lyle.
Lissa *See* Melissa.
Lissann/Lissanna/Lissanne *See* Lizanne.
Lissha *See* Licia.
Lita *See* Alida.
Liv Old Norse: defence, protection.
Lieve.
Livana Hebrew: of the moon.
Livenia/Livinia *See* Lavinia.
Livia A diminutive of Olivia. Also an ancient Roman family name.
Liviah, Liviana, Livija.

Liviya Hebrew: a lioness.
Livia, Liviah, Liviyah.
Liya Aboriginal: the west.
Liz/Lizette *See* Elizabeth.
Liza *See* Elizabeth and Lisa.
Lizabelle A combination of Liza and Belle (beautiful).
Lisabel, Lisabell, Lisabelle, Lizabel, Lizabell.
Lizanne A modern combination of Liz and Anne.
Lisann, Lisanna, Lisanne, Lissann, Lissanna, Lissanne, Lizana, Lizann, Lizanna.
Lizelle A combination of Liz and Elle (a woman).
Lisella, Liselle, Lizella.
Lizzie/Lizzy *See* Elizabeth.
Ljerka Slavic: a lily.
Ljubica Slavic: the little loved one.
Lubica, Lyubica.
Llana *See* Lana.
Llawella Welsh: a lion-like leader. The feminine form of Llewellyn.
Lawella, Lewella, Llawela, Llewellyn.
Llewenna *See* Lowenna.
Lleyton *See* Leighton.
Lliane/Llianne *See* Leanne.
Llyn Welsh: a lake.
Llynn.
Llynda *See* Linda.
Llyndan/Llynden/Llyndon *See* Linden.
Lobelia Latin: a 'flower name'.
Lobeliah, Lobellia, Lobelliah.

Lobsang Sherpa/Tibetan: the kindhearted one. Also a boy's name.
Lodema Old English: a guide or leader.
Loella/Loelle *See* Louella.
Loene Probably a form of Lois.
Loeen, Loeene, Loeena, Loena.
Loes/Loess *See* Lois.
Logain A name from *The Wheel of Time* series of fantasy novels.
Logaine, Logayn, Logayne.
Loha Hindi: the metal, iron.
Loida Spanish form of Lois.
Loidah, Loyda, Loydah.
Lois Greek: agreeable. A name from the New Testament. *See also* Loida.
Loida (Spanish), *Loes, Loess, Loesse, Loise, Loiss, Loisse.*
Lokelani Hawaiian: a heavenly rose.
Lola Spanish: a diminutive of Dolores.
Lolah.
Diminutive: Lolita.
Lolita *See* Lola.
Lolo Probably a variation of Lola or Lulu.
Loloma A form of Lola or Lolo.
Loma/Lomah Diminutives of Paloma.
Lona English/Spanish: solitary. Polynesian: a moon goddess.
Lone Danish: a diminutive of names such as Magdalone (*see* Madeline).
Loni Hawaiian: the sky, or heaven.

See also Leona.
Lonneke A femine form of Lon or Lonny, diminutives of Laurence (meaning from the laurel tree, or crowned with laurels).
Loneka, Loneke, Lonneka.
Lonzina An Italian name of uncertain meaning.
Loorea Aboriginal: the moon.
Lora/Loras *See* Laura.
Loraine/Lorane/Lorayne *See* Lorraine.
Loralee/Loralei *See* Lorelei.
Lore/Lores *See* Laura.
Lorean/Loreana/Loreanna *See* Lorian.
Loreen/Loreena *See* Lauren.
Lorelei German: alluring. A mythical river goddess who lured sailors to their death.
Loralee, Loralei, Lorelai, Lorelaie, Lorelia, Lorelie, Lorilee, Lurleen, Lurlene, Lurline, Lyrleen, Lyrline.
Lorelle A modern name, probably a combination of Laura (a laurel tree) and Elle (a woman).
Larella, Larelle, Laurella, Laurelle, Lorella, Lurella, Lurelle.
Loren/Lorena/Lorene/Loretta *See* Laura and Lauren.
Lorenza Italian: from the laurel tree. The feminine form of Lorenzo.
Laurenza.
Loreto The name of a town in Italy.
Loretto.
Lori *See* Laura and Lauren.

Lorian A combination of Lori and Ann.
Lorean, Loreana, Loreann, Loreanna, Loriana, Loriann, Lorianna, Lorianne.

Lorica Probably a form of Lori.
Loricah, Lorika, Lorikah.

Lorien/Lorienne/Lorin/Lorine See Lauren.

Lorima A form of Lori.
Lorimah.

Lorinda A combindation of Lori and Linda.
Lorindah.

Loris See Laura and Lauren.

Lorissa/Loryssa See Larissa.

Lorna Invented by R D Blackmore for the heroine of his 1860s novel *Lorna Doone*, and possibly derived from a Scottish placename.
Lornah, Launa, Launah.

Lorne A Scottish placename. Also a boy's name.
Lorn.

Lorrae Australian: a combination of Lorraine and Rae.

Lorraine Old German: a province on the border of France and Germany.
Larain, Laraine, Larayne, Lareine, Lareyne, Larrain, Larraine, Laurain, Lauraine, Laurraine, Lorain, Loraine, Lorane, Lorayne, Lorrain, Lorrayne.
Diminutives: Raine, Reine, Rayne.

Lorren/Lorrin See Lauren.

Lorri/Lorrie/Lory See Laura and Lauren.

Losa Polynesian: a rose.

Lotta/Lottie/Lotty See Charlotte.

Lotus Greek: a 'flower name'.

Louanna/Louanne See Luana.

Loueen See Louise.

Louella English: a modern name derived from Louise and Ella.
Loella, Loelle, Louelle, Luella, Luelle.
Diminutives: Lou, Lu, Lulu (German).

Louida See Louise.

Louisa See Louise.

Louise Teutonic: a famous warrior maiden. The feminine form of Louis.
Aloisa, Aloysia, Aloyza, Loise, Loueen, Louida, Louisa, Louisea, Louisetta, Louisette, Louisiana, Louiza (Greek), *Louyce, Louyse, Lovisa* (Swedish), *Loyce, Luice, Luicia, Luisa* (Italian, Spanish), *Luisana* (Spanish), *Luise* (German), *Luisel, Luiselle, Ruiha* (Maori), *Ruihia* (Maori).
Diminutives: Lou, Loui, Louie, Louita, Lova (Swedish), Lu, Luita, Lulu (German).

Louisiana The name of a US state. Also a form of Louise.
Louisanna, Louisianna, Luisiana, Luisianna.

Loula A form of either Lou or Louella.

Loulah, Loulia, Loulla.
Louna/Lounah *See* Luna.
Lourdes French/Spanish: a pilgrimage town in southern France.
Lourdas, Lurdas, Lurdes.
Louvain The name of a Belgian city.
Louvaine, Lovain, Lovaine.
Louyce/Louyse *See* Louise.
Lova *See* Louise.
Love *See* Lovella.
Loveday Old English: dear day.
Lovella A modern name, derived from the word love.
Love, Lovell, Lovelle, Lovetta, Lovette.
Lovenia/Lovinia *See* Lavinia.
Lovisa *See* Louise.
Lowanna Aboriginal: a girl.
Lowana, Lowani, Lowanni.
Lowenna Cornish: joyful.
Lewenna, Llewenna, Lowena, Lowenek.
Diminutive: Wenna.
Lowitja After Lowitja O'Donoghue, a prominent Aboriginal figure.
Lowri Welsh form of Laura.
Loyal Old French: true and faithful.
Loyale, Loyla, Loylah, Loyola, Loyolah.
Loyce *See* Louise.
Loyda/Loydah *See* Loida.
Lua A goddess in Roman mythology.
Luah.
Luana Hawaiian: happy. Old German: a graceful warrior maiden.
Louana, Louanna, Louanne, Luane, Luanna, Luwana, Luwanna.
Luba Russian/Slavic: a lover.
Lubica (Slavic), *Luby.*
Lubica *See* Ljubica and Luba.
Lubov Slavic: a name derived from the word love.
Lyubov.
Luby *See* Luba.
Luca A feminine form of Luke, one of Christ's apostles. More commonly a boy's name.
Lucah, Luka, Lukah.
Luca-May A modern 'combination name'.
Lucah-Mai, Lucah-May, Luca-Mai, Luka-Mai, Luka-May, Lukah-Mai, Lukah-May.
Lucci/Luccie *See* Lucy.
Luce *See* Lucy.
Lucee/Lucetta/Lucette *See* Lucy.
Lucerne French: light. A city in Switzerland.
Lucern, Luzern, Luzerne.
Lucia/Luciana/Lucie *See* Lucy and Lucienne.
Lucienne French: the feminine form of Lucien.
Lucian, Luciana (Italian), *Luciann, Lucianna, Lucianne, Lucien, Lucienn, Lucienna.*
Lucija Slavic form of Lucy.
Lucilla/Lucille *See* Lucy.
Lucina Latin: the Roman goddess of childbirth and the moon. *See also*

Lucy.
Lucyna.
Lucinda/Lucinde *See* Lucy.
Lucine Armenian form of Lucy.
Lucita *See* Lucy.
Lucretia Latin: reward, riches.
Lucrece, Lucrecia (Spanish), *Lucrezia* (Italian).
Lucsandra *See* Lusandra.
Lucy Latin: light. The feminine form of Lucius and Luke.
Lucci, Luccie, Luce (French, Italian), *Lucee, Lucetta, Lucette, Lucey, Lucia* (Italian, Spanish), *Lucida, Lucie, Lucija* (Slavic), *Lucile, Lucilla, Lucille, Lucina, Lucinda, Lucinde* (French), *Lucine* (Armenian), *Lucita, Lucya* (Polish), *Lucyl, Lucylle, Lucyna, Lucyne, Luiseach* (Irish Gaelic), *Lusi, Lusia, Lusie, Luzia* (Italian), *Luzie* (German), *Ruhia* (Maori), *Ruia* (Maori).
Diminutives: Cindi, Cindie, Cindy, Lou, Lu, Luciella (Italian).
Lucyna *See* Lucina and Lucy.
Luda *See* Ludmila.
Ludella Old English: an elf or pixie maiden.
Ludivine An unusual French name.
Ludevine.
Ludmila Slavic: loved by the people. *See also* Lida and Mila.
Ludmilla, Lyudmila (Russian), *Lyudmilla, Lyudmyla, Lyudmylla.*
Diminutives: Luda, Mila.

Ludo A popular board game.
Ludoe, Ludow.
Ludovica The feminine form of Ludovic (*see* Louis).
Ludovicka, Ludowicka (Slavic), *Ludwika* (Slavic).
Luella/Luelle *See* Louella.
Luice/Luicia *See* Louise.
Luigina Italian: the feminine of Luigi, a form of Louis and meaning a famous warrior.
Luigia.
Luisa/Luise/Luisel *See* Louise.
Luiseach Irish Gaelic form of Lucy.
Luisiana/Luisianna *See* Louisiana.
Luita A diminutive of Louise.
Louita.
Luka/Lukah *See* Luca.
Luka-May *See* Luca-May.
Lula Eritrean: a little sister.
Lulu Arabic/Swahili: a pearl. Also a diminutive of Louella and Louise.
Luletta, Lulette, Lulua (Arabic).
Luna Latin: the moon.
Louna, Lounah, Lunah, Lunella, Lunelle, Luneta, Lunetta, Lunette.
Lundi French: Monday.
Lundy, Lunedi (Italian).
Lupe Spanish: a she-wolf. *See also* Lupina.
Lupetu Native American: a climbing bear.
Lupi Tongan: a ruby.
Lupia, Lupiah.
Lupina Latin: like a wolf. *See also*

Lupe.
Lupa, Lupinah, Lupine, Lupita.
Lurdas/Lurdes *See* Lourdes.
Lurella/Lurelle *See* Lorelle.
Lurena Probably a form of Lorena.
Lurene.
Lurleen/Lurlene/Lurline
See Lorelei.
Lurnea Aboriginal: a resting place.
Lusandra Probably a form of Lysandra.
Lucsandra.
Lusela Native American: a bear.
Lusi/Lusia/Lusie *See* Lucy.
Luspida An Indonesian name of uncertain meaning.
Luvena Latin: the little beloved one.
Luz Hebrew: an almond or almond tree.
Luzanne Spanish: a lady of light.
Luzan, Luzann.
Luzern/Luzerne *See* Lucerne.
Luzia/Luzie *See* Lucy.
L'Wren/L'Wrenne *See* Lauren.
Lyan/Lyann/Lyanne *See* Leanne.
Lycia *See* Lecia.
Lycoris Greek: twilight.
Lychorida, Lycorise.
Lydia Greek: a woman from Lydia, an ancient kingdom in Asia Minor. The name has come to imply a cultured woman.
Lida (Czech), *Lidia* (Italian, Polish), *Lidya, Lyddie, Lydie* (French).
Lykke Danish: the fortunate one.

Lyla/Lylah *See* Leila and Lila.
Lyle Old French: from the island. Originally a boy's name.
Lial, Liall, Liel, Liell, Lisle (French), *Lyall, Lyell.*
Lyli/Lylie/Lylian/Lyllian
See Lillian and Lily.
Lylo/Lyloh *See* Lilo.
Lynda/Lyndee/Lyndey *See* Linda.
Lyndal Australian/English: a modern name, probably from Lynn and Dale.
Lindal, Lindall, Lindel, Lindell, Lindle, Lyndall, Lyndel, Lyndell, Lyndle.
Lyndamarie A 'combination name' meaning pretty (from Linda) and bitter, or star of the sea (from Mary/Marie).
Lindamarie, Lindeymarie, Lindymarie, Lyndeymarie, Lyndymarie.
Lyndan/Lynden/Lyndon
See Linden.
Lyndsey/Lyndsie *See* Lindsey.
Lynece A modern form of Lynn.
Lynese, Lynnece, Lynnese.
Lynelle A combination of Lynne and Elle.
Linell, Linelle, Lynell.
Lynetta/Lynette/Lynnette
See Linnet.
Lynleigh/Lynley/Lynnley
See Linley.
Lynn Old English: a waterfall. Also a diminutive of Carolyn and other

names.
Eluned (Welsh), *Lin, Linn, Linne, Lyn, Lynelle, Lynne.*
Lynndis A modern form of Lynn.
Lindis, Linndis, Lyndis, Lynnedis.
Lynnea *See* Linnea.
Lynneve A combination of Lynn (a waterfall) and Eve (life-giving).
Leneve, LeNeve, Lineve, Linneve, Lyneve.
Lynora/Lynore *See* Leonora.
Lynsey *See* Lindsey.
Lynwen A combination of Lynn and, perhaps, Bronwen.
Lynnwen, Lynnwenn, Lynnwenne, Lynwenn, Lynwenne.
Lynx English from Greek: a North American wild cat.
Lyola *See* Leola.
Lyonella/Lyonelle *See* Lionelle.
Lyra A northern constellation. *See also* Lyris.
Lyre *See* Lyris.
Lyrean/Lyrene/Lyrine *See* Lirene.
Lyris Greek: she who plays the harp or lyre.
Lyra, Lyrah, Lyre, Lyrian, Lyrias, Lyric, Lyrique.
Lyrleen/Lyrline *See* Lorelei.
Lys *See* Lily.
Lysandra Greek: the liberator.
Lysette *See* Elizabeth.
Lysia *See* Lecia.
Lysithea Greek: a satellite of the planet Jupiter.
Lystra Greek: free.
Lyubica *See* Ljubica.
Lyubov *See* Lubov.
Lyudmila/Lyudmylla *See* Ludmila.
Lyz/Lyzz Diminutives of Elizabeth.

M

Maaike Dutch diminutive of Margaret and Maria (*see* Mary).
Maani *See* Mani.
Maarit Finnish form of Margaret.
Marit.
Maarna *See* Marna.
Maata A Maori form of Martha.
Mab *See* Maeve.
Mabel Old French: amiable, lovable. *See also* Amabel.
Mabe, Mabele, Mabelee, Mabelie, Mabell, Ma-Bell, Mabella, Mabelle, Ma-Belle, Mable, Mabli (Welsh), *Maibel, Maibell, Maibelle, Maybel, Maybell, Maybelle.*
Mabyn Welsh/Cornish: the name of a saint and a placename.
Maben, Mabin, Mabon.
Macalla Aboriginal: the full moon.
Maccalla.
Macarena Spanish: the name of a dance.
Makarena.
Macaria Greek: a mythological figure.

Makaria, Micaria, Mikaria.
Macey Old English: little Matthew.
Macee, Maci, Macie, Macy.
Machi Swahili: the month of March.
Machiko Japanese: the fortunate one.
Maci/Macie *See* Macey.
McKenna Irish Gaelic: the son or daughter of Ken or Kennedy.
Mackenna, MacKenna, Makenna.
Mackenzie Scottish Gaelic: son or daughter of the handsome one. *See also* Kenzie.
Mackensie, MacKenzie, Makenzee, Makenzie, Makenzy, McKenzie, Mekenzee, Mekenzie, Mekenzy.
Mackinley Scottish Gaelic: the son of Finlay.
Mackinlay, Mackinlee, Mackinleigh, McKinlay, McKinley.
Maclean Scottish Gaelic: son of the follower of St John.
Maclaine, Maclayne, McLaine, McLane, McLean.
Madalen/Madalene *See* Madeline.
Maddeson/Maddison *See* Madison.
Maddi/Maddie/Maddy *See* Madeline and Madison.
Madeira Portuguese: an island off the African coast and the name of a fortified wine.
Madira.
Madel/Madelia/Madelle *See* Madeline.
Madeline Hebrew: from Magdalene, meaning a woman from the village of Magdala. *See also* Marlene.
Madalen, Madalena (Spanish), *Madalene, Madaline, Madalyn, Maddalena* (Italian), *Madel, Madelain, Madelaine, Madeleina, Madeleine* (French), *Madelia, Madeliene, Madelienn, Madelienne, Madelin, Madelina, Madella, Madelle, Madelon* (French), *Madelyn, Madelyne, Madilyn, Madlen, Madlena* (German), *Madlin, Madlon, Madlyn, Madolen, Madolene, Madoline, Magdala, Magdalen, Magdalena, Magdalene, Magdalina* (Russian), *Magdaline, Magdalini, Magdalone* (Danish), *Magdelin, Magdelina, Magdeline, Magdolen, Magdolene, Magdolin, Magdoline, Magdolna* (Hungarian), *Makarena* (Maori), *Malena, Malene* (Danish), *Malenka* (Czech), *Malina, Medelin, Medeline, Modlen* (Welsh).
Diminutives: Alena (Czech, German), Alenka (Slavic), Lena, Lene (German), Lenka (Czech), Lone (Danish), Maddi, Maddie, Maddy, Magda (German), Mala, Malin (Swedish).
Madge *See* Margaret and Marjorie.
Madhuri Sanskrit: sweet.
Madhu, Madhur.
Madiha/Madiya *See* Mahdiya.

Madini Swahili: pewter.
Madison Old English: the son of Maud or Matthew. Also a boy's name.
Maddeson, Maddison, Madisen, Madisyn, Madysen, Madyson. Diminutives: Maddi, Maddie, Maddy.
Madlen/Madlin/Madlon/Madlyn *See* Madeline.
Madoka Japanese: tranquil.
Madolen/Madolene *See* Madeline.
Madonna Italian: my lady. A title of the Virgin Mary.
MaDonna.
Madrona Latin: a lady or noblewoman. A Jewish name.
Madra (Spanish), *Madrun, Matrona* (Russian), *Matryona* (Russian).
Madura An Indonesian island.
Madysen *See* Madison.
Mae *See* May.
Maebritt *See* Maybritt.
Maeda *See* Maida.
Maegan/Maegen *See* Megan.
Maeko Japanese: truthful, or joyous.
Maella A combination of May and Ella (a fairy maiden).
Maelle, Maiella, Maielle, Mayel, Mayell, Mayella, Mayelle.
Maeve Irish Gaelic: the intoxicating one. A queen in Irish legend.
Mab, Maeva, Maevie, Maiva, Maive, Maivie, Mave, Meave.
Maeya/Maeyah *See* Mia.

Maeya-Jane/Maeya-Jayne *See* Mia-Jane.
Maeya-Jo *See* Mia-Jo.
Mafalda Italian and Portuguese forms of Matilda.
Mafata An African name of uncertain meaning.
Maga *See* Magha.
Magali A popular Turkish name.
Magda/Magdala/Magdalen *See* Madeline.
Magdalene/Magdelina *See* Madeline.
Magdalone Danish form of Madeline.
Magdolen/Magdolene/Magdolin/Magdoline *See* Madeline.
Magella *See* Majella.
Magena Native American: the coming moon.
Magina, Migena, Migena.
Magenta Italian: a town in Italy and a 'colour name'.
Maggi/Maggie *See* Margaret.
Magha Sanskrit: the Hindu month of January/February, corresponding to Aquarius.
Maga.
Magna Latin: great. Norwegian: strength.
Magnolia French: a 'flower name', after the French botanist Pierre Magnol.
Magnollia, Magnollya, Magnolya.
Magryta Lithuanian form of

Margaret.
Magura Aboriginal: a fish.
Magurah.
Maha Arabic: beauty.
Mahal Sanskrit: a palace.
Mahalia Hebrew: tenderness.
Mahailia, Mahala, Mahalah, Mahali, Mahila, Mehalia.
Mahdiya Arabic: one who is rightly guided.
Madiha, Madiya, Mahdiyya.
Mahesa Sanskrit: the feminine form of Mahesh, a great ruler.
Mahesha.
Mahia Maori: a deed or act.
Mahima Hindi: great or glorious.
Mahina Polynesian: the moon.
Mahindi Swahili: sweet corn.
Mahira Hebrew: energetic.
Mahli/Mahlie *See* Mali.
Mahogany A 'tree name'.
Mahrie *See* Mary.
Mahsa Persian: like the moon.
Mahuika Polynesian: the goddess of fire.
Mahuru Polynesian: the goddess of spring.
Mahura.
Mai Swedish diminutive of Margaret and Mary. *See also* May.
Maia The most beautiful of the mythological nymphs, the Pleiades. The name of a fertility goddess. *See also* Mary and Maya.
Maya.
Maibel/Maibelle *See* Mabel.

Maiberrie/Maiberry *See* Mayberry.
Maibritt/Maiebritt *See* Maybritt.
Maida Old English: a maiden.
Maeda, Maide, Maidel, Maidie (Irish, Scottish), *Mayda.*
Maiella/Maielle *See* Maella.
Maiette *See* May.
Maigan/Maigen *See* Megan.
Maija *See* Maya.
Maiko Japanese: a dancing child.
Maili Polynesian: a summer breeze.
Mailkah *See* Malika.
Maimie *See* Mame.
Maimu Estonian/Finnish: the little one.
Maine The name of a US state.
Main, Mayn, Mayne.
Mair Welsh form of Mary.
Maire/Mairi/Mairie Irish Gaelic forms of Mary.
Mairead Irish and Scottish forms of Margaret.
Mairianne *See* Marion.
Mairin Irish Gaelic form of Maureen.
Mairwen Welsh: a combination of Mair and Gwen (fair or blessed).
Mairwenn, Mairwenne, Mairwyn, Mairwynn, Mairwynne.
Maisie Scottish diminutive of Margaret.
Maisee, Maisey, Maizee, Maizey, Maizi, Maizie, Maysee, Maysi, Maysie, Mazi, Mazie.
Maite Spanish: probably a combination of Maria and Teresa.

M – GIRLS

Mayte.
Maiva/Maive/Maivie *See* Maeve.
Maiya Aboriginal: a vegetable.
Maja *See* Maya.
Majani Swahili: green.
Majella Italian: the name of a saint.
  Magella, Marjella.
Majesta Latin: the majestic one.
Maji Swahili: water.
Majida Arabic: the illustrious one.
  Majeda, Majedah, Majidah.
Majivu Swahili: grey.
Majoli Possibly from majolica, a type of Italian pottery.
  Majolee, Majolie, Majoly.
Majorana Spanish form of Marjorie.
Maka Native American: the earth.
Makaela *See* Michaela.
Makala Polynesian: the myrtle tree.
Makalee *See* Michaela.
Makali Sanskrit: the moon.
Makana Polynesian: a gift.
Makani Polynesian: the wind.
Makara Sanskrit: a crocodile. The Hindu name for the zodiac sign of Capricorn.
  Makarah.
Makarena Maori form of Madeline. *See also* Macarena.
Makareta Maori form of Margaret.
Makari Sanskrit: a spider.
  Makura (Nepali).
Makaria *See* Macaria.
Makayla *See* Michaela.
Makeely Probably a combination of Mackenzie and Keeley (beautiful).
  Makeelee, Makeeli, Makeeley.
Makenna *See* MacKenna.
Makenzee/Makenzie/Makenzy *See* Mackenzie.
Maki Japanese: a true record.
Makoto Japanese: sincere or sincerity.
Maksimilia/Maksymilia *See* Maximilia.
Maku Maori: wet.
Makura *See* Makari.
Mala Sanskrit: a necklace. *See also* Madeline.
  Malah.
Malaika *See* Malika.
Malak Arabic: an angel.
Malana Hawaiian: light or buoyant.
  Malanah, Malanna, Malannah.
Malara The morning star (Venus) in New Guinea legend.
Malati Sanskrit: a jasmine flower.
Malawi Native American: flaming. Also the name of an African country.
Malaya Spanish: free. A country name.
Malena/Malene *See* Madeline.
Malerie Either a form of Valerie, or from Mallory.
  Maleree, Malleree, Mallerie.
Mali Hindi: A gardener. Thai: a flower. *See also* Molley.
  Mahli, Mahlie, Malie.
Malia Hawaiian form of Mary.
Malika Arabic: the feminine form of Malik, the master. Sanskrit: an

empress.
Mailkah, Malaika, Mallika, Mallikah, Melika, Melikah.
Malila Native American: a swimming salmon.
Malilah.
Malin Swedish diminutive of Magdalene (*see* Madeline).
Malina Hawaiian: calming or soothing. See also Madeline.
Malinda/Malinta *See* Melinda.
Malise Gaelic: the servant of God.
Malisa, Maliza, Malize.
Malissa *See* Melissa.
Malkah Hebrew: a queen.
Malka, Malkeh.
Malla Aboriginal: a swamp plant.
Mallah.
Mallana Aboriginal: a canoe.
Mallee Aboriginal: scrubland. Also a boy's name.
Malley, Mallie.
Mallory Old French: unlucky. Also a boy's name.
Malloree, Mallorey, Mallorie, Maloree, Malorey, Malorie, Malory.
Malva Greek: soft and tender.
Malvah, Malvy, Melva, Melvah.
Malvina Gaelic: the smooth-browed one.
Malvena, Melvena, Melvina, Milvena, Milvina.
Malya Aboriginal: a python.
Malynda/Malyndah *See* Melinda.
Mamba Swahili: a crocodile.

Mame A diminutive of Margaret and Mary.
Maimie, Mamie.
Mami Japanese: beautiful and truthful.
Mana Hawaiian: heavenly. Maori: power.
Manal Arabic: achievement.
Manaal.
Manar/Manara *See* Munira.
Manawa Maori: the heart.
Manawaroa Maori: a big heart.
Manda/Mandi/Mandie *See* Amanda.
Mandala Sanskrit: a circle. A mystic symbol of the universe in the Hindu religion.
Mandara Sanskrit: the name of a tree.
Mandarah.
Mandela An attractive name, in honour of the legendary South African activist and politician, Nelson Mandela.
Mandella.
Mandisa African: sweet.
Mandolin A stringed musical instrument.
Mandolina, Mandoline, Mandolinn, Mandolinne, Mandolyn, Mandolynn, Mandolynne.
Mandy *See* Amanda.
Mangala Sanskrit: born on a Tuesday.
Mangalah.

M – Girls

Mangu Maori: a big heart.
Mani Aboriginal: equal. Sanskrit: a jewel.
Manie.
Manilla Aboriginal: a winding river.
Manjano Swahili: yellow.
Manju Sanskrit: pleasant.
Manjula Sanskrit: lovely or charming.
Mankara Aboriginal: a girl.
Mankarah, Munkara, Munkarah.
Manmaya A Nepalese name of uncertain meaning.
Manon French diminutive of Marie. See Mary.
Manoora Aboriginal: a spring.
Manoorah, Manora, Manorah.
Mantra Sanskrit: a prayer or incantation. Also a boy's name.
Mantrah.
Manuela/Manuella/Manuelle See Emmanuelle.
Manya Aboriginal: small.
Minya.
Manyana Spanish: the morning, tomorrow.
Manyanah, Manyanna, Manyannah.
Manyura Indonesian: a peacock.
Manzana Spanish: an apple.
Mara Aboriginal: a black duck. Hebrew: bitter, the original form of Mary. Also a diminutive of Tamara.
Marah.
Marabel A combination of Mary and Belle.
Marabell, Marabelle.
Marakata Sanskrit: green, like an emerald.
Marala Sanskrit: a swan.
Maralin/Maralyn See Marilyn and Mary.
Marama Aboriginal: a white duck. Maori: the moon. Polynesian: radiant.
Marambra A Spanish name of uncertain meaning.
Maran See Maren.
Maranda/Marandah See Miranda.
Marbeth See Marybeth.
Marcasite Latin: an iron-based mineral, used to make jewellery and ornaments.
Marcasita.
Marcea See Marcia.
Marcella Latin: belonging to Mars; the feminine form of Marcus or Mark. See also Marcia, Marta and Martina.
Marcela (Czech), *Marcelia, Marcell, Marcelle* (French, Spanish), *Marcellia, Marcellina, Marcelline, Marcheline, Marchelle, Marsell, Marsella, Marselle.*
Diminutives: Marci, Marcie, Marcy.
Marchesa/Marchessa See Marquise.
Marcia Latin: belonging to Mars. See also Marcella, Marta and Martina.
Marcea, Marsha, Marsia,

210

Girls – M

Martia, Marzia.
Diminutives: Marci, Marcie, Marcy, Marsi, Marsie.
Marda Aboriginal: a stone.
Mardah.
Mardi French: Tuesday.
Mardee, Mardey, Mardie, Mardy.
Mardrea An unusual name from the West Indies.
Mardra, Mardria.
Marea/Maree/Mareea *See* Mary.
Mareeba The name of a Queensland town.
Mareebah.
Mareena *See* Marina.
Mareikura Maori: a supernatural being.
Marelda Teutonic: a famous battle maiden.
Marelsa.
Marelle A combination of Mary and Elle.
Marel, Marell, Marella.
Maren Basque: from the sea.
Maran, Marin, Maron.
Marene *See* Maureen.
Maresa *See* Maris.
Maret/Mareta *See* Margaret.
Maretta/Marette *See* Marietta and Mary.
Marfa *See* Martha.
Marganit Hebrew: a lovely flower.
Margaret Latin: a pearl. *See also* Margot, Marguerite, Marion and Megan.
Maarit (Finnish), *Magryta* (Lithuanian), *Mairead* (Irish, Scottish), *Makareta* (Maori), *Maret, Mareta, Marga, Marganita* (Jewish), *Margareta, Margarete, Margaretha* (German), *Margaretta, Margarette, Margarida* (Portuguese), *Margarita* (Spanish), *Margarite, Marged* (Welsh), *Margene, Marget, Margette, Margherita* (Italian), *Marghita, Margit* (Hungarian, Swedish), *Margitta, Margred* (Welsh), *Margret* (German), *Margreta, Margrethe* (Danish), *Margriet* (Dutch), *Margrit, Margrith, Margrithe, Marguerita, Marguerite* (French), *Marguret, Margurette, Mari* (Bohemian), *Marit* (Finnish), *Marjeta* (Czech), *Marketa, Marketta* (Finnish), *Megan* (Welsh), *Mererid* (Welsh).
Diminutives: Daisy, Ghita (Italian), Grechen, Greta (German, Swedish), Gretchen (German), Grete (German), Gretel (Swiss), Gretha, Grethe, Gretta, Griet (Dutch), Grieta (Dutch) Grieth, Grietina, Grit (German), Maaike (Dutch), Madge, Maggi, Maggie, Mags, Mai (Swedish), Maisie (Scottish), Mame, Mamie, Marge, Margie, Margot (French), May, Meg, Meggie, Mette (Norwegian), Peg, Peggie, Peggy, Rita.
Margaux *See* Margot.
Marged/Marget/Margette

See Margaret.
Margerie/Margery/Margory
See Marjorie.
Margherita/Marghita
See Margaret.
Margit/Margitta *See* Margaret.
Margot Originally a diminutive of Margaret.
Margo, Margoe, Margaux.
Margriet/Margrit *See* Margaret.
Marguerite *See* Margaret. Also a 'flower name'.
Marguerita.
Marguret/Margurette
See Margaret.
Mari *See* Margaret and Mary.
Maria/Mariah *See* Mary.
Mariaan *See* Marion.
Mariam/Mariama/Mariamne
See Miriam.
Marian/Marianina/Marianne/ Marianthe *See* Marion.
Maribel Spanish: a combination of Maria and Belle or Isabel.
Maribell, Maribella, Maribelle, Marybell, Marybella, Marybelle.
Marica Hungarian and Slavic diminutives of Mary.
Marie French form of Mary. Maori: peaceful.
Mariea/Mariee *See* Mary.
Marie-Claire An attractive 'combination name'.
Marie-Clare.
Marieke *See* Mary.
Mariel *See* Marielle, Mary and Muriel.
Marielle French: a form of Marie.
See Mary.
Mariel, Mariella (Italian),
Marriel, Marrielle, Maryella, Maryelle.
Marielyn/Marielynne *See* Marilyn.
Marien/Marienne *See* Marion.
Marietta Italian form of Maria.
See Mary.
Maretta, Marette, Mariet (Dutch),
Marieta (Spanish), *Mariette, Marita* (Spanish), *Marite, Merita, Merrita.*
Mariezer *See* Maris.
Marigold Old English: a golden flower.
Marigo, Marygold.
Marija Slavic form of Mary.
Marijan/Marijana *See* Marion.
Marijka/Marijke *See* Marika.
Marijosé A Spanish 'combination name'; from Mary and José (*see* Josephine).
Marika Maori: quiet and careful. Slavic: a form of Mary.
Marijka, Marijke, Marikka.
Mariko A popular Japanese name, possibly meaning the child of the village.
Marilia Portuguese: a form of Maria.
Marilha, Marilla, Marillia.
Marilou *See* Marylou.
Marilyn A combination of Mary and Lynn.
Maralin, Maralyn, Marielyn,

Marielynn, Marielynne, Marilene, Marilin, Marilynn, Marilynne, Marylene, Marylin, Maryline, Maryllyn, Marylyn, Meralin, Meralyn, Meralynn, Meralynne.

Marin *See* Maren.

Marina Latin: of the sea. *See also* Maris and Mary.
Mareena, Mareenah, Marinah, Marine (French), *Marinela, Marinella, Marna* (Swedish), *Maryna, Marynah, Merina, Merinah.*
Diminutives: Marne, Marnie.

Marinela/Marinella *See* Marina.

Marini Swahili: pretty.

Marinna Aboriginal: a song.

Marion Originally a French diminutive of Marie. *See also* Mary.
Mairianne, Mariaan, Marian, Mariana, Mariane (German), *Marianina, Mariann, Marianna, Marianne* (French), *Mariannina, Marianthe, Marianthi* (Greek), *Marien, Marienn, Marienne, Marijan, Marijana, Marionne, Marrion, Marrionn, Marrionne, Maryon, Mereana, Mereanna* (Maori), *Mereanne, Merianna, Meriannne, Merriann, Merrianne, Mirijana* (Slavic).

Mariposa Spanish: a butterfly.

Mariquita Spanish form of Mary.

Maris Latin: of the sea. *See also* Marina and Mary.
Maresa, Marice, Mariezer, Marisa, Marise, Marissa, Marisse, Marlis, Marris, Meris, Merisa, Merissa.

Marisol Spanish: a combination of Maria and sol, the sun.

Marison Possibly from Maris, meaning of the sea.
Marisson, Marrison, Marryson, Maryson.

Marissa/Marisse *See* Maris.

Maristella A combination of Mary and Stella.
Maristela, Marystela, Marystella.

Marit *See* Maarit.

Marita/Marite *See* Marietta and Mary.

Maritza/Mariza *See* Mary.

Mariya/Marja *See* Mary.

Marjani Swahili: coral.
Marajani, Marjan.

Marjella *See* Majella.

Marjeta Czech form of Margaret.

Marjo/Marjolaine *See* Marjolyn and Marjorie.

Marjolein Dutch form of Marjorie.

Marjolynn A combination of Marjorie and Lynn (a waterfall).
Marjolin, Marjolinn, Marjolinne, Marjolyn, Marjolynne.
Diminutive: Marjo.

Marjorie English: from the herb name, marjoram.
Majorana (Spanish), *Margeri, Margerie, Margery, Margori, Margorie, Margory, Marjery,*

Marjolain, Marjolaine (French), *Marjolein* (Dutch), *Marjori, Marjory.*
Diminutives: Madge, Marge, Margie, Marj, Marji, Marjie, Marjo.

Marketa/Marketta *See* Margaret.

Markisa/Markise *See* Marquise.

Marla *See* Marlene and Mary.

Marlaina/Marlane *See* Marlene.

Marlay *See* Marley.

Marlayna *See* Marlene.

Marlee Aboriginal: an elder tree. *See also* Marlene and Marley.

Marlene German: a combination of Maria (*see* Mary) and Magdalene, popularised by actress Marlene Dietrich.
Marla, Marlaina, Marlane, Marlayna, Marlee, Marleen, Marlena, Marlina, Marlita, Marlyne.

Marley Old English: from the pleasant meadow.
Marlay, Marlee, Marleigh, Marli, Marlie, Marly.

Marlies Dutch: a combination of Maria and Elisabeth.
Marleis, Marleisha, Marliesha.

Marlika Dutch diminutive of Maria (*see* Mary).

Marlis *See* Maris.

Marlita *See* Marlene.

Marloes Dutch: a combination of Maria and Louise.

Marlon Old French: a little hawk.
Marlen.

Marlow Old English: from the lake or pond. Also a boy's name.
Marlowe.

Marlyne *See* Marlene.

Marmara Greek: radiant.

Marna Aboriginal: a shark. Also a form of Marina.
Maarna.

Marne/Marni/Marnie Diminutives of Marina and other names.

Maron *See* Maren and Marron.

Maroulla An unusual Greek name.
Maroula.

Marquise The feminine form of Marquis, French for a nobleman.
Marchesa (Italian), *Marchessa, Markisa, Markise, Marquess, Marquessa, Marquesse, Marquisa.*

Marree Aboriginal: the place of possums; a South Australian placename.
Marri, Marrie.

Marriel *See* Marielle, Mary and Muriel.

Marrion/Marionne *See* Marion.

Marron Aboriginal: a leaf. French: brown or a chestnut. Spanish: brown.
Maron.

Marryson *See* Marison.

Marsala Italian: a town, and a sweet fortified wine.

Marsell/Marsella *See* Marcella.

Marsena Persian: worthy, or dignified. Also a boy's name.

Marsha *See* Marcia.

Marshevet A modern American name of uncertain meaning.
Marsi/Marsia/Marsie *See* Marcia.
Marta A form of March, from Mars, the Roman god of war. Similar to Marcia, and also a variation of Martha.
Marte, Martia, Marz (German), *Marza, Marzia.*
Martelle A feminine form of Martin, meaning of Mars. *See also* Marta and Martina.
Martel, Martela, Martell, Martella.
Martha Aramaic: a lady. A name from the Bible.
Maata (Maori), *Marfa, Marta* (Italian, Spanish), *Marte* (Scandinavian), *Martella, Marthe* (French, German), *Marthesa, Marthese, Mata* (Maori). *Diminutives:* Marti, Martie, Martita (Spanish), Marty.
Marti/Martie/Marty *See* Martha and Martina.
Martia *See* Marcia and Marta.
Martina Latin: of Mars, the Roman god of war; a feminine form of Martin. *See also* Marcella, Marcia and Marta.
Martine (French), *Martineau, Martyna* (Polish), *Martyne. Diminutives:* Marti, Martie, Marty.
Martiza Arabic: the blessed one.
Martyr An unusual modern name, implying someone with strong convictions.
Marter.
Maru Polynesian: gentle.
Maruja A Filipino name of uncertain meaning.
Marula African: a southern African shrub with spiky flowers.
Marusa A Slavic name of uncertain meaning.
Maruska A Slavic diminutive of Marie.
Marusca.
Marva/Marvah *See* Marvel.
Marvel Latin: a wonderful thing.
Marva, Marvah, Marvela, Marvell, Marvella, Marvelle, Marvi, Marvie.
Marwah Arabic: a flinty stone.
Marwa.
Mary Hebrew: bitter, as in a bitterly wanted child. Latin: the star of the sea. From the same root as Miriam, and one of the most enduringly popular female names. *See also* Mara, Maralyn, Marilyn, Marina, Marion, Marlene, Mia, Mimi, Miriam, Moira, Maureen and Ria.
Mahrie, Mair (Welsh), *Maire* (Irish Gaelic), *Mairee, Mairie* (Irish Gaelic), *Mairi, Malia* (Hawaiian), *Mara* (Hebrew), *Marah, Marea, Maree, Mareea, Mareeya, Maretta, Marette, Mari, Maria, Mariah, Marie* (French), *Mariea, Mariee,*

Marieke (Dutch), *Mariel*, *Mariella* (Italian), *Marielle* (French), *Marieta* (Spanish), *Marietta* (Italian), *Mariette*, *Marija* (Slavic), *Marika* (Slavic), *Marilia* (Portuguese), *Mariquita* (Spanish), *Marisa*, *Marita* (Spanish), *Maritza*, *Mariya* (Russian), *Mariyah*, *Mariza*, *Marja* (Dutch, Finnish), *Marla* (Bavarian), *Marya* (Cornish, Russian), *Marye*, *Maryla*, *Maryse* (French), *Marysia*, *Maureen* (Irish), *Mere* (Polynesian), *Meri* (Polynesian), *Meria*, *Meriah*, *Mhairi*, *Moira* (Irish Gaelic). *Diminutives:* Maaike (Dutch), Mai (Swedish), Maia, Maja, Mali (Welsh), Mame, Mamie, Manon (French), Marica (Hungarian, Slavic), Marlika (Dutch), Masa (Slavic), Masha (Russian), May, Maya, Meike (Dutch, German), Mia (Danish, Swedish), Mieke (Dutch), Miep (Dutch), Mies (Dutch), Miesje (Dutch), Mimi (Italian), Mitsi, Mitzi (Swiss), Molley, Molli, Mollie, Molly, Polly, Ria (Spanish).

Marya Arabic: white and pure. Cornish: a form of Mary.

Maryam *See* Miriam.

Maryann A combination of Mary and Anne.
Maryan, Maryane, Maryanna, Mary-Anna, Maryanne, Mary-Anne, Miriama (Maori).

Marybella/Marybelle *See* Maribel.

Marybeth One of many 'Mary combination' names.
Marbeth, MaryBeth, Mary-Beth.

Mary-Cate *See* Marykate.

Marydai A variation of Mary.
Marydae.

Marye *See* Mary.

Maryella/Maryelle *See* Marielle.

Mary-Ellen From Mary and Ellen.

Mary-Jane A combination of Mary and Jane.

Marykate Another 'Mary combination' name.
Marycate, MaryCate, Mary-Cate, MaryKate, Mary-Kate.

Maryla *See* Mary.

Marylene/Maryline *See* Marilyn.

Marylin/Maryline/Marylyn *See* Marilyn.

Marylou From Mary and Louise.
Marielou, Marie-Lou, Marilou, Mary-Lou.

Marylouise A combination of Mary and Louise (a warrior maiden).
MaryLouise, Mary-Louise.

Maryna/Marynah *See* Marina.

Maryon *See* Marion.

Maryrose A combination of Mary and Rose.
MaryRose, Mary-Rose.

Maryse/Marysia *See* Mary.

Maryson *See* Marison.

Marystela/Marystella *See* Maristella.

Maryvonne French: from Marie and

Yvonne.

Marz/Marza *See* Marta.

Marzia Arabic: one who is pleasing. Also a form of Marcia and Marta. *Marziah.*

Masa Japanese: straightforward. Slavic: a diminutive of Mary.

Masada Hebrew: an ancient site of palaces and fortifications in Israel. The name means a fortress, *Masadah, Metzada, Metzadah.*

Masako Japanese: justice.

Masala Sanskrit: spicy. *Masalah.*

Masara Sanskrit: an emerald.

Mascot Something that brings good luck. *Mascott, Mascotte.*

Mashara Possibly a form of Shara (a variation of Sharon), meaning a flat plain. *Masharra.*

Mashona From Shona, the name of a people from southern Africa.

Masika Swahili: the rainy season. *Masikah.*

Masina Samoan: the moon.

Masuma Arabic: one who is innocent or protected. *Masouma, Masoumah, Masoumeh, Masumah, Masumeh.*

Mata A Maori form of Martha.

Matea/Mateah/Mateja *See* Mattea.

Matessa/Matesse *See* Mattea.

Mathea/Mathia/Matthea *See* Mattea.

Mathoura Aboriginal: of the wind.

Matilda Teutonic: the mighty battle maiden. *Mafalda* (Italian, Portuguese), *Matelda, Mathilda, Mathilde* (French), *Matila, Matilde* (Italian), *Matylda* (Czech, Polish), *Maud, Maude, Maudie, Mechteld* (Dutch), *Mechtilda* (Dutch). *Diminutives:* Mattie, Tilda, Tilla, Tillie, Tilly.

Matina Of the morning. Also a feminine form of Matt (Matthew), meaning a gift of God. *See also* Mattea. *Matinah, Mattina, Mattinah, Mattyna, Mattynah, Matyna, Matynah.*

Matisse An unusual name; after Henri Matisse, a famous French painter and sculptor. *Matysse, Metisse, Metysse.*

Matrika Hindi: a mother.

Matrona/Matryona *See* Madrona.

Matsu Japanese: a pine tree.

Matsuko Japanese: the child of the pine tree.

Mattea Hebrew: the gift of God; a feminine form of Matthew. *See also* Matina. *Matea, Mateah, Mateja* (Slavic), *Matessa, Matesse, Mathea, Mathia, Matthea, Matthia, Mattia.*

Mattina/Mattyna *See* Matina.

Matuta A goddess of the dawn in

Roman mythology.
Matylda *See* Matilda.
Matyna/Matynah *See* Matina.
Maud/Maude/Maudie *See* Matilda.
Maura Celtic: a 5th-century saint.
Maure, Mora.
Maureen Irish form of Mary.
See also Moira.
Mairin (Irish Gaelic), *Marene, Maureene, Maurena, Maurene, Mauretta, Maurette, Maurina, Maurine, Maurn, Maurren, Moirean, Moireen, Moreen, Morena, Morene, Morine, Morreen, Morrine, Morryne, Moryne.*
Diminutives: Maurie, Mo.
Mauretta/Maurette *See* Maureen.
Maurilia A feminine form of Maurice, the dark-skinned one.
Maurella, Maurelle, Mauricia, Mauriza, Maurizia (Italian).
Mauve French from Greek: violet-coloured.
Mauv, Mauva, Mauvia, Mauviel, Mauviell, Mauvielle.
Mave *See* Maeve and Mavis.
Maven Yiddish: an expert in a particular field.
Mavin.
Mavis French: a songbird.
Diminutive: Mave.
Mavourneen Irish Gaelic: possibly meaning my darling.
Mavoura, Mavourna.
Mavra A Russian name of uncertain meaning.
Maweke Polynesian: a sea breeze.
Maxelle A feminine form of Max, meaning the greatest.
Maxcel, Maxcell, Maxcella, Maxcelle, Maxel, Maxell, Maxella.
Maximilia The feminine form of Maximilian (the greatest).
Maksimilia, Maksimillia, Maksymilia, Maksymillia, Maxime, Maximilienne, Maximillia, Maxymilia, Maxymillia.
Maxine Latin: the greatest. Another feminine form of Max.
Maxeen, Maxene, Maxyne.
Diminutives: Max, Maxi, Maxie, Maxy.
May A diminutive of Margaret and Mary. Also a 'month name'.
Mae, Mai, Maie, Maiette, Maye, Mayet, Mayett, Mayetta, Mayette, Mei (Maori).
Maya Latin: the great one. The name of a Roman goddess and a Hindu goddess, and a diminutive of Maria. *See also* Maia and Mary.
Maia, Maija, Maja, Mayaa, Mayah, Mya, Myah.
Mayaluna A combination of Maya and Luna (the moon).
Mayalunah.
Maybell/Maybelle *See* Mabel.
Mayberry A combination of May and Berry.

Maiberri, Maiberrie, Maiberry, Mayberri, Mayberrie.
Maybritt A Scandinavian 'combination name' (*see* Britt).
Maebritt, Maibritt, Maiebritt.
Mayda *See* Maida.
Mayella/Mayelle *See* Maella.
Mayet/Mayette *See* May.
Mayjoy A 'combination name'.
Mayla *See* Mela.
Maylee May combined with Lee (a meadow).
Maylea, May-Lea, May-Lee, Mayleigh, May-Leigh, Mayli, May-Li.
Mayleen A combination of May and, perhaps, Eileen.
Maylean, Maylene, Mayline.
May-Ling *See* Mei-Ling.
Maymay A form of May.
Maymae, Maymai, Maymaie, Maymaye, Maymei.
Mayn/Mayne *See* Maine.
Mayoree Thai: beautiful.
Mayrah Aboriginal: spring, or the wind.
Mayra.
Maysa Arabic: she who walks gracefully.
Maysee/Maysie *See* Maisie.
Mayte *See* Maite.
Mayu Japanese: gentle.
Mazi/Mazie *See* Maisie.
Mc names – *See* Mac.
Mea/Meah *See* Mia.
Meadow Middle English: a small grassy field.
Meadowe, Meddow, Meddowe.
Meagan/Meagen/Meaghan *See* Megan.
Meara/Mearah *See* Meera.
Mearl/Mearle *See* Merle.
Meave *See* Maeve.
Mechan *See* Megan.
Mechel/Mechelle *See* Michelle.
Mechteld/Mechtilda Dutch forms of Matilda.
Meda Latin: the healer, or the middle one.
Medah.
Medea Greek: a princess in classical mythology.
Medelin/Medeline *See* Madeline.
Medina Arabic: a city in Saudi Arabia.
Medinah.
Medley Middle English: a mixture.
Medlee, Medlie, Medly.
Medusa Greek: a character from mythology.
Mee Chinese: beautiful.
Meegan *See* Megan.
Meeka *See* Mika.
Meeme *See* Mimi.
Meena Sanskrit: a precious gem, or a fish. The name represents the zodiac sign Pisces.
Mina.
Meera Aboriginal: a string bag. Sanskrit: a devotee of the god Krishna.
Meara, Mearah, Meerah.

Meesha *See* Misha.
Meetah Hindi: sweet.
Meeta, Mita, Mitha.
Meg/Meggie Diminutives of Margaret and Megan.
Mega Aboriginal: the moon.
Megan Welsh form of Margaret.
Maegan, Maegann, Maegen, Maegenn, Maigan, Maigen, Meagan, Meagen, Meaghan, Mechan, Meegan, Megane, Megann, Megen, Meggan, Meggen, Meghan, Meghann, Meigan, Meighan, Meigun.
Diminutives: Meg, Meggie.
Megara Greek: a mythological figure.
Megumi Japanese: a blessing.
Mehadi Sanskrit: a flower.
Mehalia *See* Mahalia.
Mehitabel Hebrew: God is our joy. An Old Testament name.
Mei Chinese: beautiful. *See also* May.
Meichell/Meichelle *See* Michelle.
Meigan/Meighan/Meigun *See* Megan.
Meika *See* Mika.
Meike Dutch and German diminutives of Maria.
Meiko Japanese: a bud.
Meila/Meilah *See* Mela.
Mei-Lin Chinese: a beautiful lotus.
Mei-Ling Chinese: the name of a princess.
May-Ling, Meiling.
Meinwen Welsh: fair and slender.
Meisha *See* Misha.
Meissa Arabic: a star.
Mei-Yu Chinese: beautiful jade.
Meizhen Chinese: possibly meaning a precious plum.
Meka *See* Mika.
Mekenzee/Mekenzie/Mekenzy *See* Mackenzie.
Mel *See* Amelia, Carmel, Melanie, Melinda and Melissa.
Mela Italian: an apple. Sanskrit: a fair, or a religious festival or ceremony. *See also* Melanie.
Mayla, Meila, Meilah, Melah.
Melaleuca A type of Australian tree.
Melaleuka.
Melanie Greek: the dark or black one.
Mela, Melaina, Melaine, Melanee, Melania, Melannie, Melany, Melenie, Melennie, Melka (Polish), *Mellaney, Mellanie, Mellany, Melloney* (Cornish), *Mellony, Melonie, Melony.*
Diminutives: Mel, Melli, Mellie, Melly.
Melantha Greek: a dark flower.
Melanthe.
Melati Indonesian: a jasmine flower.
Melba After the famous opera singer Dame Nellie Melba.
Melbah, Milba, Milbah.
Melda *See* Imelda.
Melek Arabic: an angel.

Melenie/Melennie *See* Melanie.
Melesa *See* Melissa.
Melesand/Melesande *See* Millicent.
Meli Hawaiian: honey.
Melia Greek: a mythological nymph.
Meliah, Melijah, Meliya, Meliyah.
Melicent *See* Millicent.
Melika/Melikah *See* Malika.
Melina Greek: gentle. *See also* Carmel.
Melinda A combination of Melanie or Melissa and Linda.
Malinda, Malindah, Malinta, Malintha, Malynda, Melindah, Melinta, Melintha, Melynda.
Diminutives: Linda, Mel, Melli, Mellie, Melly.
Melinga Aboriginal: plenty.
Melisa *See* Melissa.
Melisanda/Mélisande/Melisende *See* Millicent.
Melissa Greek: the honeybee.
Malissa, Malissah, Melesa, Melisa, Melisah, Melissah, Melisse, Melita, Melitta, Mellissa, Mellissah, Melysha, Melyssa, Melyssah, Milissa, Milissah, Millissa, Mylissa, Mylissah, Mylisse.
Diminutives: Lissa, Mel, Melle, Melli, Mellie, Melly.
Melita/Melitta *See* Melissa.
Melka *See* Melanie.
Mellaney/Mellanie *See* Melanie.
Melle/Melli *See* Melissa.

Mellie/Melly *See* Amelia, Carmel, Melanie, Melinda and Melissa.
Mellin/Mellyn *See* Melyn.
Melloney/Mellony/Melony *See* Melanie.
Melody Greek: like a song.
Melodee, Melodi, Melodia, Melodie, Melodye.
Melora Celtic: a daughter of King Arthur in Celtic mythology.
Mellora, Mellorah, Melorah.
Melva Welsh: a sweet place. *See also* Malva.
Melvah, Melveta, Melvia, Melviah, Melvita.
Melvena/Melvina *See* Malvina.
Melwyn Cornish: as fair as honey.
Melwyn, Melwynne.
Melyn Welsh: yellow.
Mellin, Mellyn, Melynn, Melynne.
Melys Welsh: sweet.
Mellys, Mellyss, Melyss.
Melysha/Melyssa *See* Melissa.
Memee *See* Mimi.
Memphis The Ancient Egyptian capital and a city in Tennessee, USA. Also a boy's name.
Memphys.
Mena A goddess in Roman mythology. Also a diminutive of Philomena.
Menah.
Menaka The Hindu goddess of snow.
Menakah.
Mengtao A Chinese name of

uncertain meaning.
Menorah Hebrew: the seven-branched candelabra of the Jewish religion.
Menora.
Menta *See* Minta.
Menuha Hebrew: tranquillity.
Merab Hebrew: increase or abundance. A daughter of Saul in the Old Testament.
Meralin/Meralina/Meralyn *See* Marilyn and Merilyn.
Meran *See* Merryn.
Meraude A diminutive of Emeraude. *See* Emerald.
Meraud.
Mercedes Spanish: merciful. From a title of the Virgin Mary.
Mercadies, Mercede (Italian), *Mercedita, Merci, Mercia, Mercie, Mercy.*
Diminutive: Merche (Spanish).
Mercredi French: Wednesday (Mercury's day).
Mercoledi (Italian).
Mercuria Latin: the feminine form of Mercury, the messenger of the gods in Roman mythology.
Mercurina, Mercurine.
Mercy *See* Mercedes.
Mere Polynesian form of Mary.
Mereanna Maori form of Marianne. *See* Marion.
Merean, Mereana, Mereann, Mereanne.
Meredith Old Welsh: lordly. Also a boy's name.
Meredeth, Meredyth, Merideth, Meridith, Meridyth.
Diminutives: Merrie, Merry.
Mereeka/Mereekah *See* Merika.
Mereki Aboriginal: a peacemaker.
Merelyn/Merelynn *See* Merilyn.
Meren *See* Merryn.
Merenda/Merendah *See* Miranda.
Mererid Welsh form of Margaret.
Merette From French words meaning a little sea.
Meretta.
Meri Finnish: the sea. Polynesian: a form of Mary.
Meria/Meriah Forms of Mary.
Merianna/Merianne *See* Marion.
Meridee/Merideen/Meridie/ Meridy *See* Merridee.
Meriel/Meriell/Merielle *See* Muriel.
Merika A name from the *Dragonriders of Pern* series of fantasy novels.
Mereeka, Mereekah, Merikah.
Merilee/Merily *See* Merry.
Merilyn From Merry and Lynn.
Meralin, Meralyn, Merelina, Merelyn, Merelynn, Merralin, Merralyn, Merrelynn, Merrelynne, Merrilyn, Merylyn, Merelynn.
Merina/Merinah *See* Marina.
Merinda Aboriginal: a beautiful woman.
Meris/Merisa/Merissa *See* Maris.

GIRLS – M

Merita *See* Marietta.
Meritabel From merit, meaning excellence or worth. *Meritabell, Meritabelle, Meritable.*
Merivale Old English: a pleasant valley. Also a boy's name. *Merrivale, Merryvale, Meryvale.*
Merja A Finnish name of uncertain meaning.
Merkabah Hebrew: a chariot. *Merkaba.*
Merle Old French: a blackbird. Also a diminutive of Muriel. *Mearl, Mearle, Merl, Merla, Merleen, Merlene, Merlie, Merline, Merlyle, Merril, Merrill, Merryl, Merryle, Meryl, Meryle, Murl, Murle, Myrla, Myrle, Myrleen, Myrlene, Myrline.*
Merlwynne A combination of Merle and Wynne (fair or blessed). *Merlwinn, Merlwinne, Merlwyn, Merlwynn.*
Merlyle *See* Merle.
Merlyn Old Welsh: from the fort by the sea, or the falcon. Also a boy's name (Merlin). *Merlin, Merlina, Merlinda, Merline, Merlinn, Merlinne, Merlynda, Merlynn, Merlynne, Myrlin, Myrlyn.*
Merna *See* Myrna.
Merola Latin: a thrush.
Meron *See* Merryn.
Meropi A Greek name of uncertain meaning.
Merpati Indonesian: a dove.
Merralea/Merralee *See* Merry.
Merralin/Merralyn/Merrelynn *See* Merilyn.
Merran/Merren/Merrian *See* Merryn.
Merri Aboriginal: a stone, or a dingo.
Merriann/Merianne *See* Marion.
Merrice *See* Mertice.
Merridee A combination of Merry and Dee. *See also* Merry. *Meridee, Merideen, Meridie, Meridy, Merrideen, Merridie, Merridy, Miradee, Miradie, Mirady, Mirradee, Mirradie, Mirrady.*
Merriel/Merrill *See* Muriel.
Merrigal Aboriginal: plenty of dingoes.
Merril/Merrill/Merryl *See* Merle.
Merrilie/Merrily *See* Merry.
Merrilyn *See* Merilyn.
Merrin *See* Merryn.
Merrita *See* Marietta.
Merriwa Aboriginal: a beautiful place.
Merry Old English: joyful, happy. *See also* Meredith and Merridee. *Merilee, Merily, Merralea, Merralee, Merralie, Merrey, Merri, Merrie, Merrilee, Merrilie, Merrily, Merylea, Merylee, Merylie.*
Merryce *See* Mertice.

Merryn Cornish: a saint's name and a placename.
Meran, Meren, Meron, Merran, Merren, Merrian, Merrien, Merrin, Meryn, Myrran, Myrren.
Merryvale *See* Merivale.
Mertice Old English: pleasant and famous.
Merrice, Merryce, Mertyce.
Mertle *See* Myrtle.
Merva A feminine form of Mervyn, meaning a famous friend.
Mervah, Mervorna, Mervyn, Mervynn, Mervynne.
Merwenna *See* Morwenna.
Meryem Turkish form of Miriam.
Meryl/Merlyle/Meryle *See* Merle.
Merylea/Merylee *See* Merry.
Merylyn/Merylynn *See* Merilyn.
Meryn *See* Merryn.
Meryvale *See* Merivale.
Mesha Sanskrit: the zodiac sign of Aries. *See also* Lamesha.
Meshel/Meshelle *See* Michelle.
Messina Latin: the middle child.
Meta Aboriginal: the land. Latin: the ambitious one.
Metah, Mita, Mitah.
Metaxia A Greek name of uncertain meaning.
Metis Greek: the wise one.
Metys.
Metisse/Metysse *See* Matisse.
Mette Norwegian diminutive of Margaret.
Metzada/Metzadah *See* Masada.
Mhairi *See* Mary.
Mia Scandinavian diminutive of Mary.
Maeya, Maeyah, Mea, Meah, Miah, Miya, Miyah, Mya, Myah.
Miah Aboriginal: the moon. *See also* Mia.
Mia-Jane A modern 'combination name'.
Maeya-Jane, Maeya-Jayne, Mia-Jayne, Miah-Jane, Miah-Jayne, Miya-Jane, Miya-Jayne, Mya-Jane, Mya-Jayne, Myah-Jane, Myah-Jayne.
Mia-Jo Another Mia combination.
Maeya-Jo, Miah-Jo, Miya-Jo, Mya-Jo, Myah-Jo.
Mial/Miall *See* Myall.
Miandetta Aboriginal: a bend in the river.
Miarlee Possibly from Mia.
Miarli, Miarlie, Miarleigh.
Mica Latin: a mineral.
Micah, Mikah, Myca, Mycah, Myka, Mykah.
Micaria *See* Macaria.
Michaela Hebrew: like the Lord; a feminine form of Michael. *See also* Michelle and Mikaedy.
Makaela, Makaelah, Makalee, Makayla, Makaylah, Micaela, Micayla, Michaele, Michaelene, Michaeli, Michaelie, Michaelina, Michaeline, Michaella, Michala, Michalina, Michela, Michella,

*Mikaela, Mikaeli, Mikaella,
Mikaila, Mikala, Mikalei,
Mikarla, Mikayla, Mikaylah,
Mikaylee, Mikeeli, Mikele,
Mikelina, Mikhaila, Mikhayla,
Mikyla, Mikylah, Mycaela,
Mychaela, Mykaela.*
Diminutives: Micki, Mickie,
Micky, Mikki.

Michal Hebrew: a brook. A biblical name.

Michelle French from Hebrew: like the Lord; a feminine form of Michael. *See also* Michaela and Misha.
*Mechel, Mechele, Mechell,
Mechelle, Meichell, Meichelle,
Meshel, Meshele, Meshell,
Meshelle, Michaelle, Michel,
Michele, Michelina, Micheline*
(French), *Michell, Michella,
Michiel, Michiell, Michielle,
Mishell, Mishella, Mishelle,
Mishshell.*
Diminutives: Chelle, Misha, Shell, Shelley, Shelli, Shellie, Shelly.

Michiko Japanese: the righteous way.
Michi.

Micki/Mickie/Micky Diminutives of Michaela.

Midori Japanese: green.

Midwinter The middle of winter. Also a boy's name.
Midwynter.

Mieke Dutch diminutive of Mary.
Mieka, Miekah.

Miep Dutch diminutive of Mary.

Mies A Dutch diminutive of Maria. *See* Mary.
Miesje.

Mietta French: a sweet little thing.
Miettte.

Mif/Mifanwy/Miffany
See Myfanwy.

Mifina *See* Myfina.

Migena/Migina *See* Magena.

Mignon French: sweet and dainty. *See also* Minette.
Mignone, Mignonette.

Mijonique *See* Monica.

Mika Japanese: the new moon.
Meeka, Meika, Meka.

Mikaedy A modern version of Michaela.
*Mikadee, Mikadi, Mikadie,
Mikayde, Mikaydi, Mikaydie.*

Mikaela/Mikaeli/Mikaila
See Michaela.

Mikah *See* Mica.

Mikaria *See* Macaria.

Mikarla/Mikayla/Mikaylee
See Michaela.

Mikayde/Mikaydie *See* Mikaedy.

Mikeeli/Mikele/Mikelina
See Michaela.

Mikhaila/Mikhayla *See* Michaela.

Miki Hawaiian: quick or nimble.
Japanese: a stem.
Mikiyo.

Mikki *See* Michaela.

Miko Japanese: virginal.

Mila A short form of Ludmila (loved by the people) and Milena (the favoured one). *See also* Milana and Miley.
Milada (Slavic), *Milana, Milanda, Milani, Milia, Miliah, Miliana, Milla, Millani, Myla, Mylah, Mylla, Myllah.*

Milagros Spanish: the miraculous one.
Milagro.

Milah *See* Miley.

Milana From Milan, an Italian city. *See also* Mila and Milena.
Milan, Milanah, Milann, Milanna, Milannah, Miliana, Milianah, Miljana, Miljanah.

Milba/Milbah *See* Melba.

Milda The Lithuanian goddess of love.
Mildah.

Mildred Old English: strong yet gentle.
Milda, Mildrid.
Diminutives: Milli, Millie, Milly.

Milena Czech: the favoured one.
Mila, Milana, Milenna, Millena, Millenna, Mileva.

Miley A modern name, made popular by the singer and actress Miley Cyrus.
Mila, Milah, Milea, Milee, Milei, Mileigh, Milie, Myalea, Myalee, Myalie, Myaleigh, Myla, Mylah, Mylea, Mylee, Mylei, Myleigh, Mylie.

Milia *See* Mila.

Miliana/Miljana *See* Milana.

Miliani Hawaiian: a gentle caress.

Milica Slavic: the dear one.
Milicah, Milika, Milikah, Militza, Milka, Milkah.

Milina Aboriginal: a paperbark tree.

Milissa/Milissah *See* Melissa.

Milka/Milkah *See* Milica.

Milla/Millani *See* Mila.

Millena/Millenna *See* Milena.

Milli/Millie/Milly Diminutives of Amelia, Camilla, Mildred and Millicent.

Millicent Teutonic: strong and industrious.
Melesand, Melesande, Melicent, Melisanda, Mélisande (French), *Meliscent, Melisende* (French), *Mellicent, Mellisent, Milicent, Milissent.*
Diminutives: Milli, Millie, Milly, Millye.

Milojka A Slavic name of uncertain meaning.

Miloslava Slavic: the feminine form of Miloslav, meaning one who is favoured by glory.
Miloslawa (Polish).

Milvena/Milvina *See* Malvina.

Mima Burmese: a woman.

Mimi Italian diminutive of Maria. *See also* Mary.
Meeme, Meemee, Mimee, Mimie.

Mimosa Latin: a 'plant name'.

Mina A diminutive of several names.

See also Meena.
Minal Sanskrit: a precious stone.
Minami Japanese: from the south.
Mincarlie Aboriginal: rain.
Mindi/Mindie *See* Myndie.
Mineko Japanese: a child of the mountains.
Minerva Latin: the mythological goddess of wisdom.
Minette A diminutive of Mignonette. *See* Mignon.
Minet, Minett, Minetta, Mynett, Mynetta, Mynette.
Ming Chinese: light, or enlightenment.
Mingara Aboriginal: a good spirit who controls the clouds.
Mink A weasel-like animal, famous for its highly prized fur.
Minke, Mynk, Mynke.
Minka Teutonic: the resolute one.
Minke.
Minkie Aboriginal: daylight.
Minki.
Minks/Minkse *See* Minx.
Minna Teutonic: love. Also a diminutive of Wilhelmina.
Minne.
Minne/Minney/Minnie *See* Wilhelmina.
Minore Aboriginal: a white flower.
Minoru Japanese: the truth.
Minta Aboriginal: a shadow. Greek: of the mint plant.
Menta, Mentah, Minnta, Minntah, Mintah, Mintha.

Minti Possibly a diminutive of Araminta.
Mintie, Minty.
Minx A flirtatious girl.
Minks, Minkse, Minxe, Mynx, Mynxe.
Minya *See* Manya.
Mira Latin: wonderful. Slavic: the famous one. *See also* Myra.
Mirah, Mirra, Mirrah.
Mirabelle Latin: lovely.
Mirabel, Mirabell, Mirabella, Mireia (Catalan), *Mireille* (French), *Mirella* (Italian).
Mirabooka/Mirabrooka
See Mirrabooka.
Miraca From miracle, meaning a marvel or a wonderful thing.
Miracca, Miraka, Mirakka.
Miradee/Miradie/Mirady
See Merridee.
Mirage French: an illusion; something unreal.
Mirag, Miraj, Miraje.
Mirai Japanese: the future.
Mirana Slavic: the feminine form of Miran (peaceful).
Miranda Latin: the admired one. Probably invented by Shakespeare for the heroine of *The Tempest*.
Maranda, Marandah, Meranda, Merandah, Merenda, Merendah, Mirandah, Mirenda, Mirendah, Myranda, Myrandah.
Diminutives: Randa, Randi, Randie, Randy.

Mirdza A Latvian name of uncertain meaning.
Mireia/Mireille/Mirella *See* Mirabelle.
Miretta Probably a form of Mira. *Mireta, Mirett, Mirette.*
Miri A mythological angel.
Miria *See* Mirria.
Miriam Hebrew: a biblical name meaning bitter. *See also* Mary. *Mariam, Mariama, Mariamne* (Hebrew), *Maryam* (Arabic), *Meryem* (Turkish), *Miriama* (Maori), *Miriamu* (African), *Miriana* (Slavic), *Miriyana, Mirjam* (Slavic), *Mirjana* (Slavic), *Mirriam, Myriam.*
Miriama Maori form of Maryann and Miriam.
Miriana Slavic form of Miriam.
Mirijana Slavic form of Marion.
Miriyan Aboriginal: a star.
Miriyana *See* Miriam.
Mirjam/Mirjana Slavic forms of Miriam.
Mirka Czech: tranquil.
Mirna *See* Myrna.
Miromiro Maori: a tomtit (bird).
Miron *See* Myron.
Miroslava Slavic: glorious peace.
Mirra/Mirrah *See* Mira.
Mirrabooka An Aboriginal name for the Southern Cross. *Mirabooka, Mirabrooka, Mirrabook, Mirrabrook, Mirrabrooka.*
Mirradee/Mirradie/Mirrady *See* Merridee.
Mirren The surname of famous British actress Dame Helen Mirren.
Mirria Aboriginal: a shrub. *Miria, Mirrya, Mirya.*
Mirrin Aboriginal: a cloud.
Misaki Japanese: like a beautiful blossom.
Misayo Japanese: loyal; a helper.
Misha A diminutive of Michelle or Michael, meaning like the Lord. *Meesha, Meisha, Mischa* (Russian).
Mishell/Mishella/Mishelle *See* Michelle.
Missy A young lady. *Missie.*
Mistic/Mistique *See* Mystic.
Misty Old English: of the mist.
Mita/Mitah *See* Meta.
Mithuna Sanskrit: a name for the zodiac sign of Gemini.
Mitsuko Japanese: a child of the light.
Mitza Possibly a form of Mitzi. *Mitsa.*
Mitzi Swiss diminutive of Maria. *See* Mary. *Mitsi.*
Miwako A Japanese name of uncertain meaning.
Miya Japanese: a temple. *See also* Mia. *Miyah.*
Miya-Jane *See* Mia-Jane.
Miya-Jo *See* Mia-Jo.

Miyu Japanese: beautiful, truthful or gentle.
Miyuki Japanese: deep snow.
Mladenka Slavic: the feminine form of Mladen (the young one).
Moana Maori/Polynesian: the sea or ocean. Also a boy's name.
Moanah.
Moata Maori: early.
Mochi Japanese: the full moon.
Modesty Latin: the moderate or modest one.
Modest (Russian), *Modesta, Modeste, Modestia, Modestine, Modesto* (Italian).
Modlen *See* Madeline.
Moe Maori: sleep.
Moeka A Japanese name of uncertain meaning.
Moerangi Maori: the sleepy sky.
Moetuma Polynesian: a legendary figure.
Mohana Sanskrit: bewitching; the enchantress.
Mohini.
Moina *See* Mona.
Moira Aboriginal: a possum. Greek: a goddess of fate. Irish Gaelic: a form of Mary. *See also* Maureen.
Maura, Maurya, Moirah, Moiraine, Moirayne, Mora, Morane, Moyra, Moyrah.
Moirean/Moireen *See* Maureen.
Mokai Maori: a pet.
Moko Maori: a personal mark.
Molley A diminutive of Mary.

Mali (Welsh), *Molli, Mollie, Molly, Polly.*
Momi Hawaiian: a pearl.
Momo Japanese: a peach.
Momoko Japanese: child of the peach.
Mona Irish Gaelic: the noble one. Also a diminutive of Monica.
Moina, Monah, Moya, Moyna.
Monday Middle English: the day of the moon.
Mondae, Mondai, Mondaye.
Monet After the famous French Impressionist artist, Claude Monet.
Monay, Monée.
Moneta Latin: the admonisher, or one who reminds. One of the titles of Juno, the Roman queen of the heavens. The word money comes from this name.
Monita.
Monica Latin: an adviser or counsellor. The name of a saint.
Mijonique, Monika (German, Slavic), *Monike, Moniqua, Mo'niqua, Monique* (French), *Mo'Nique, Mo'nique.*
Diminutive: Mona.
Monique French form of Monica.
Monita *See* Moneta.
Montana Latin: from the mountains. The name of an American state.
Montagna, Montanah, Montanna, Montannah.
Montserrat The name of a Spanish

mountain.
Monserrat.

Monyetta A modern American name.
Monyette.

Moon Middle English: a heavenly body. Suitable for a Cancerian child as Cancer is ruled by the moon.
Moone.

Moona Aboriginal: plenty.
Moonah.

Mo'onia The unusual name of Australian netball star Mo'onia Gerrard. Possibly Polynesian.

Mopsa A shepherdess in Shakespeare's *The Winter's Tale*. Of uncertain meaning.

Mora *See* Maura and Moira.

Morae/Morai *See* Moray.

Morag Scottish Gaelic: the great one.
Moreen.

Morana Slavic: A goddess of winter and death.

Morang Aboriginal: the sky, or clouds.
Moorang.

Moravia A district of the Czech Republic.

Moray A region of Scotland.
Morae, Morai.

Moraya *See* Moriah.

Moreau French: probably after the actress Jeanne Moreau.
Moreaux.

Moree Aboriginal: water or a spring.

Moreen *See* Maureen and Morag.

Morela Slavic: apricot.
Morelah, Morella, Morellah.

Morena/Morene *See* Maureen.

Morenwyn Cornish: a fair maiden.

Morewen/Morewenna
See Morwenna.

Morgan Welsh: bright sea. Also a boy's name.
Morgain, Morgaine, Morgana, Morgane, Morgann, Morganna, Morganne, Morgayne, Morgen, Morgenn, Morgenne, Morgwn (Welsh).

Moriah Hebrew: God is my teacher. An Old Testament placename.
Moraya, Moria, Moryah.

Moriko Japanese: a child of the forest.

Morilla Aboriginal: from the stony ridge.

Morine *See* Maureen.

Morinn/Morinne *See* Moryn.

Morna/Mornah *See* Myrna.

Morreen/Morrine/Morryne
See Maureen.

Morva Cornish: from a placename.
Morvah.

Morven Gaelic: a region of Scotland.
Morvenn, Morvenne.

Morwenna Cornish/Welsh: a maiden. The name of a saint.
Merwenna, Morewen, Morewenn, Morewenna,

Morwen, Morwenn, Morwenne, Morwyn (Welsh), *Morwynn, Morwynna, Morwynne.*
Moryah *See* Moriah.
Moryn Welsh: the sea.
Morinn, Morinne, Moryne, Morynne.
Moryne *See* Maureen and Moryn.
Moselle French from Egyptian: probably meaning delivered or saved. The feminine form of Moses. *Mosella, Mozella, Mozelle.*
Mosi Swahili: the firstborn child. Also a boy's name.
Moti Hindi: a pearl.
Mouna *See* Muna.
Mounira *See* Munira.
Moxie A modern name, of uncertain meaning.
Moxey, Moxi, Moxy.
Moya/Moyna *See* Mona.
Moyra *See* Moira.
Mozella/Mozelle *See* Moselle.
Mridula Sanskrit: the soft one.
Muffy A nickname, probably from the word muffin.
Muffee, Muffey, Muffi, Muffie.
Muge Turkish: a lily.
Muirenn Irish Gaelic: the fair or white one from the sea.
Muireann.
Muiriol Irish Gaelic form of Muriel.
Muirne *See* Myrna.
Muka Maori: flax fibre.
Mukaddes A Turkish name of uncertain meaning.
Muna Aboriginal: a green snake. Arabic: a hope, or a wish.
Mouna.
Munda Aboriginal: the earth.
Mundah.
Mundara Aboriginal: thunder. Also a boy's name.
Mundarra.
Muniamma A Hindi name of uncertain meaning.
Muniyamma.
Munira Arabic: the luminous one.
Manar, Manara, Mounira, Mounirah, Munirah.
Munkara *See* Mankara.
Mura Japanese: from the village.
Murasaki Japanese: lavender or purple.
Muriel Gaelic: of the bright sea.
Mariel, Marriel, Marrielle, Meriel, Meriell, Merielle, Merriel, Merrill, Muireall (Scottish Gaelic), *Murial, Muriele, Murielle, Muiriol* (Irish Gaelic).
Diminutive: Merle.
Murl/Murle *See* Merle.
Murna Aboriginal: the great one.
Murphy Irish Gaelic: a warrior of the sea. More commonly a boy's name.
Murphey.
Murrami Aboriginal: a crayfish.
Musetta Greek: a little muse.
Musette.
Mya Burmese: an emerald. *See also* Maya and Mia.

Myah.
Mya-Jane/Mya-Jayne *See* Mia-Jane.
Mya-Jo/Myah-Jo *See* Mia-Jo.
Myalea/Myalee/Myalie/Myaleigh *See* Miley.
Myall Aboriginal: wild, and an acacia tree.
Mial, Miall, Myal.
Myca/Myka *See* Mica.
Mycaela/Mykaela *See* Michaela.
Myee Aboriginal: native-born.
Myfanwy Welsh: the beloved one.
Mifanwy, Miffanwy, Miffany, Myffanwy, Myvanwy.
Diminutives: Mif, Miff, Myf, Myff.
Myfina Possibly a form of Myfanwy.
Mifina.
Myika Swahili: the moorland.
Myla/Mylah *See* Mila and Miley.
Mylee/Myleigh/Mylie *See* Miley.
Myleen/Mylene/Myline *See* Myolene.
Mylissa/Mylisse *See* Melissa.
Mylla *See* Mila.
Myndee Aboriginal: a sycamore.
Myndie Aboriginal: a snake.
Mindi, Mindie, Myndi.
Mynetta/Mynette *See* Minette.
Mynk/Mynke *See* Mink.
Mynx/Mynxe *See* Minx.
Myo-Jo Japanese: bright love.
Myolene A contemporary, and probably made-up, name.
Myleen, Myleene, Mylene, Myline, Myola, Myoleen,
Myoline.
Myra Greek: fragrant; from myrrh, an aromatic shrub. A biblical placename. *See also* Myron.
Mira, Mirah, Myrah, Myria, Myriah.
Myranda/Myrandah *See* Miranda.
Myri Possibly a form of Myra.
Myree, Myreen, Myrene, Myreth, Myrie, Myrine, Myrith.
Myria/Myriah *See* Myra.
Myriad Greek: many, innumerable.
Myriam *See* Miriam.
Myrla/Myrle *See* Merle.
Myrlene/Myrline *See* Merle.
Myrlin/Myrlyn *See* Merlyn.
Myrna Irish Gaelic: beloved.
Merna, Mernah, Mirna, Mirnah, Morna, Mornah, Muirne (Gaelic), *Myrnah.*
Myron Greek: fragrant. From myrrh, an aromatic shrub. *See also* Myra.
Miron.
Myrran/Myrren *See* Merryn.
Myrthene Possibly from Myrtle.
Myrthine.
Myrtle Greek: a 'plant name'.
Mertle, Myrta, Myrtell, Myrtis.
Mysti/Mystie *See* Misty.
Mystic From a Latin word meaning secret.
Mistic, Mistique, Mystik, Mystique (French).
Myuna Aboriginal: clear water.

N

Naazma/Naazmi *See* Nazima.
Nabila Arabic: noble.
Nabeel, Nabeela, Nabil.
Nabitha Possibly from Tabitha (a doe or gazelle).
Nabetha.
Nada Arabic: the generous one. Also a form of Nadia.
Nadya.
Nadda Aboriginal: a camp.
Nadeema *See* Nadima.
Nadeja/Nadelle *See* Nadia.
Naderja/Naderjda *See* Nadia.
Nadi Hindi/Nepali: a river.
Nadia Slavic: hope.
Nada, Nadeen, Nadeene, Nadeja, Nadejda (Russian), *Nadelle, Nadene, Naderja, Naderjda, Nadezda, Nadezhda* (Russian), *Nadina, Nadine* (French), *Nadiya, Nadya* (Russian), *Nadyne, Nadzeya.*
Nadima Arabic: the feminine form of Nadim, meaning a friend.
Nadeema, Nadhima.
Nadine French form of Nadia.
Nadira Arabic: precious. Sanskrit: the pinnacle.
Nadya/Nadyne *See* Nada and Nadia.
Nadzeya *See* Nadia.
Nafisa Arabic: excellent or valuable.
Nafeesa, Nafeesah, Nafisah.
Nagina Urdu: a snake.
Nageena.
Nago Tibetan: black.
Nahid Persian: the goddess of love, the equivalent of Venus.
Nahla/Nahlani *See* Nalani.
Nahn *See* Nancy.
Naia Polynesian: a dolphin.
Naya.
Naiara An unusual Basque name.
Nayara.
Naida Greek: a water nymph.
Naiad, Nayad, Nayda, Nyad.
Naiki/Naikie *See* Nike.
Naikita *See* Nikita.
Naina A Hindi name of uncertain meaning.
Nairne Scottish Gaelic: from the river.
Najam Arabic: a star.
Naja, Najma.
Najiba Arabic: the feminine form of Najib, the noble one.
Najeeba.
Najila Arabic: wide-eyed.
Najeela, Najla.
Nakeita/Nakita *See* Nikita.
Nalani Hawaiian: the calm of the skies.
Nahla, Nahlani, Nala, Nalah.
Nalda/Nallda *See* Nelda.
Naleya An African-American name of uncertain meaning.
Naliandrah Aboriginal: a butterfly.
Naliandra.

N – Girls

Diminutive: Nali.
Nalika Sanskrit: a lotus.
Nalikah.
Nalini Sanskrit: a lotus.
Nahlini.
Nama Aboriginal: a tea-tree.
Namaga Aboriginal: a pearl shell.
Nami Japanese: a wave.
Namiko.
Namoi Aboriginal: an acacia tree.
Nan A diminutive of Anne, Nancy and Nanette.
Nana Aboriginal: a small lizard. *See also* Nancy and Nanna.
Nanaia Maori: a biblical name.
Nanala Polynesian: a sunflower.
Nancy Originally a diminutive of Anne.
Nancee, Nancey, Nanci, Nancie, Nancye, Nanette.
Diminutives: Nahn, Nan, Nana, Nance, Nhan.
Nandalie Aboriginal: fire.
Nanda.
Nanette *See* Nancy. Also a French diminutive of Anne.
Nanett, Nynett, Nynette.
Diminutive: Nan.
Nani Polynesian: beautiful.
Nanine *See* Anne.
Nanna The wife of Balder, the god of the sun in Norse mythology.
Nana.
Nano *See* Honour.
Nanon French diminutive of Anne.
Nanook Eskimo: a bear god, representing noble strength and purpose.
Nanuk, Nanuq.
Naoki Japanese: a straight tree.
Naoko Japanese: an honest child.
Naomi Hebrew: pleasant. A biblical name, the feminine form of Noam.
Naoma, Naomee, Naomie, Nayomi, Neomi, Neomie, Niomi, Niomie, Noami, Noamie, Noemi, Noémi, Noemia (Portuguese), *Noemie, Nohemi* (Spanish), *Nohemie, Nohemy, Nyomi, Nyomie.*
Napea Latin: a girl of the valley, or a wood nymph.
Nara Aboriginal: a companion. Japanese: an oak tree. Old English: the nearest and dearest one.
Narada Japanese: the mythological messenger of the gods, the equivalent of the Roman god Mercury.
Naradah.
Narang Aboriginal: the little one, or a small creek.
Naranja Spanish: the colour orange.
Narangi (Hindi).
Narara Aboriginal: a black snake.
Narcisse French from Latin: the narcissus or daffodil flower.
Narcisa, Narciss, Narcissa.
Narda Latin: a fragrant ointment or perfume.
Nardah, Nardia, Nardiah.
Narelle Australian: from Nara and

Elle.
Narell, Narella, Narellan, Nerell, Nerella, Nerelle.
Naresha Sanskrit: a queen. The feminine form of Naresh.
Naretha Aboriginal: a saltbush.
Nari Japanese: a thunderbolt.
Narice Probably a form of Narelle. *Nareece, Nareese, Narise.*
Nariel The angel of the midday winds. *Nariell, Narielle.*
Nariko Japanese: humble.
Narisa/Narissa *See* Nerissa.
Narise *See* Narice.
Narooma Aboriginal: a magical stone. A New South Wales placename.
Nascha Native American: an owl.
Naseeba *See* Nasiba.
Naseem Arabic: a gentle wind. *Nasim.*
Nashira A star in the constellation of Capricornus.
Nashota Native American: a twin.
Nasia Hebrew: God's miracle. *Nasya.*
Nasiba Arabic: the feminine form of Nasib, meaning noble. *Naseeba, Naseebah, Nasibah.*
Nasrin Persian: a wild rose. *Nasreen, Nasri, Nesrin* (Turkish).
Nastasia/Nastia/Nastya *See* Anastasia.
Nata Sanskrit: a dancer.
Natacha *See* Natasha.

Natalie Latin: born at Christmas. *Natala, Natale, Natalee, Natali, Natalia, Natalina* (Italian), *Natalya* (Russian), *Nathalia, Nathalie* (French), *Nattalia, Nattalie, Nattalina.* *Diminutives:* Natasha (Russian), Nattie, Nettie, Talia (Russian), Talya (Russian).
Natania/Natanya *See* Nathania.
Natasha Russian diminutive of Natalie. *Natacha, Natarsha, Natasa, Natascha, Natashia, Natashya, Natassa, Natassha, Natasza* (Polish), *Natisha, Natishia, Nattasha, Nattassha.* *Diminutives:* Taasha, Tacha, Tasha, Tasa.
Nathalia/Nathalie *See* Natalie.
Nathania Hebrew: the gift of God; the feminine form of Nathan. *Natania, Nataniya, Natanya, Nathana, Nathena, Nathene.*
Natiqa Arabic: eloquent. *Natika.*
Natisha *See* Natasha.
Natividad Spanish: of the nativity.
Natsu Japanese: summer.
Natsuki Japanese: summer hope.
Natsumi Japanese: summer beauty.
Nattalia/Nattalie/Nattalina *See* Natalie.
Nattasha/Nattassha *See* Natasha.
Naura/Naureen/Naurine *See* Nora.
Nava Hebrew: beautiful.

N – Girls

Navana A modern American name.
Navanah, Navanna, Navannah, Navianah, Navianna, Naviannah.

Navy Either a 'colour name' or referring to a fleet of ships.
Navee, Navey, Navie.

Navya Sanskrit: one who is worth praising.
Navia.

Nawal Arabic: a gift.

Naya Aboriginal: thunder. Hindi: new. *See also* Naia.

Nayad/Nayda *See* Naida.

Nayara *See* Naiara.

Nayomi *See* Naomi.

Nazarena The feminine form of Nazarene, a person from Nazareth.
Nazaret (Spanish), *Nazareth, Nazarina, Nazzarena, Nazzarina.*

Nazima Arabic: the feminine form of Nazim, the organiser.
Naazma, Naazmi, Nazeema, Nazma, Nazmi.

Nea *See* Neala and Nova.

Neala Irish Gaelic: the champion; the feminine form of Neal or Neil. *See also* Nola.
Neale, Nealima, Nealina, Neela, Neelah, Neelima, Neelina, Neila, Neilina (Scottish).
Diminutives: Nea, Nia.

Neasha *See* Nisha.

Neave Old English: a nephew. Generally a boy's name.
Neavah, Neaves, Neiv, Neive, Neve, Neveah, Niev, Nieve.

Nebbia Italian: mist or fog.

Nebula Latin: a cluster of stars in astronomy. Also cloud or mist.

Nechola/Nechole/Necola/Necole *See* Nicola.

Necia *See* Nisha.

Neco *See* Nico.

Nectaria From nectar, the sweet juice of a plant.
Nectarina, Nectarine, Nektaria, Nektarina, Nektarine.

Neda Slavic: born on Sunday.
Nedda, Nedela, Nedele (Czech), *Nedelka, Nedena, Nedene.*

Nedra/Needra *See* Nidra.

Neeka *See* Neka.

Neela African: a cicada. *See also* Neala and Nila.
Neelah.

Neelima/Neelina *See* Neala.

Neena/Neenah *See* Nina.

Neesha *See* Nisha.

Neila/Neilina *See* Neala.

Neith The Ancient Egyptian creator goddess, represented with a shield and arrows.

Neiv/Neive *See* Neave.

Neka Native American: a wild goose.
Neeka, Neekah, Nekah.

Neko *See* Nico.

Nektaria/Nektarina/Nektarine *See* Nectaria.

Nelda Old English: of the elder tree.
Nalda, Naldah, Nallda, Nalldah,

GIRLS – N

Neldah, Nellda, Nelldah.
Nelia/Neliya Diminutives of Cornelia.
Nell A diminutive of Eleanor, Ellen and Helen.
Nella, Nellah, Nelli, Nellie, Nelle, Nelly.
Nellma A form of Nell.
Nellmah, Nelma, Nelmah.
Nellori A combination of Nell and Lori.
Nelloree, Nellorey, Nellorie, Nellory.
Nellwyn Old English: a bright companion.
Nellwynn, Nellwynne.
Nena/Nenah See Nina.
Nenga A genus of flowering plants.
Nengah.
Neola Greek: the new or young one.
Neoma Greek: the new moon.
Neomi/Neomie See Naomi.
Nepa Native American: a name for the constellation of Scorpius.
Nepah.
Nepelle Aboriginal: the mythological ruler of the heavens.
Neptunia Latin: from Neptune, the Roman god of the sea and a planet.
Neptuna.
Nerada/Neradine See Nerida.
Nerali/Nerelie See Neroli.
Neree See Ngaire.
Nereid/Nereida/Nereidah See Neridah and Nerina.
Nerell/Nerella/Nerelle See Narelle.
Nergis Turkish: a daffodil.

Neria An angel of the moon; the name means lamp of God. Also a maiden in Roman mythology who was loved by Mars, the god of war.
Neriel.
Nerida Aboriginal: a flower.
Nerada, Neradah, Neradine, Nereda, Neredah, Neredine, Nereida, Nereidah, Neridah, Neridine, Neryda, Nerydah.
Nerili/Nerilie See Neroli.
Nerina Greek: a sea nymph. *See also* Nerissa.
Nereid, Nereida, Nerice, Nerine, Nerita.
Nerissa Possibly a form of Nerina.
Narisa, Narissa, Nerisa.
Neroli The name of an Italian princess.
Nerali, Neralie, Nereli, Nerelie, Nerili, Nerilie, Nerolia, Nerolie.
Neryda/Nerydah See Nerida.
Neryl From either Narelle or Meryl.
Neryle.
Nerys Welsh: a lady.
Nesrin See Nasrin.
Nessa Cornish: the nearest one. Also a diminutive of Agnes and Vanessa.
Nessi, Nessie.
Nesta Welsh form of Agnes.
Nestor Greek: wisdom. More commonly a boy's name.
Nestora, Nestore, Nestoria.
Neta/Netah See Nita.
Netta/Nette/Nettie/Netty Diminutives of Antonia, Henrietta

N – Girls

and other names ending with etta or ette.

Neva/Nevah *See* Nevada.

Nevada Spanish: snow, or as white as snow. An American state.
Neva, Nevadah, Nevah.

Nevan Irish: holy, or a little saint.
Neven, Nevin, Nevyn.

Neve/Neveah *See* Neave.

Nevena Slavic: a marigold.
Nevenah, Nevenka, Nevina, Nevinah.

Neysa/Neza *See* Agnes.

Nga Maori: a witch.

Ngahere Maori: a forest.

Ngahiwi Maori: many hills.

Ngahuia Maori: prized feathers.

Ngahuru Maori: autumn.

Ngaio Maori: the name of a native New Zealand tree.

Ngaire Maori: flaxen.
Neree, Niree, Nyra, Nyrah, Nyree, Nyria.

Ngoikore Maori: the weak one.

Nhan *See* Nancy.

Nia *See* Neala and Nova.

Niabi Native American: a fawn.

Niamh Irish Gaelic: beautiful, bright. The daughter of a sea god in Irish mythology.
Niam.

Niangala Aboriginal: an eclipse of the moon.

Nicalah/Nicalie *See* Nicola.

Nicetta Italian form of Berenice.

Nicharla *See* Nicola.

Nichelle Probably a variation of Michelle.
Nichel, Nichell.

Nichohla/Nichole/Nicholette *See* Nicola.

Nicholina/Nicholla *See* Nicola.

Nicia *See* Nisha.

Nick/Nicky Diminutives of Nicola.

Nickarla/Nicla *See* Nicola.

Nickeisha A combination of Nicola and Keisha.
Nickeesha, Nickesha, Nickiesha, Nikeesha, Nikeisha, Nikesha, Nikiesha.

Nickola/Nickole/Nickoletta *See* Nicole.

Nico A diminutive of Nicola.
Neco, Neko, Niko.

Nicola Latin: the people's victory. The feminine form of Nicholas.
Nechola, Nechole, Necola, Necole, Nicalah, Nicalie, Niccola, Niccole, Nicharla, Nichohla, Nichohle, Nichola, Nichole, Nicholette, Nicholina, Nicholla, Nicholle, Nickarla, Nickola, Nickole, Nickoletta, Nickolette, Nicla (Italian), *Nicohle, Nicole* (French), *Nicoletta, Nicolette* (French), *Nicolien, Nicolina, Nicoline, Nicolla, Nicollette, Nikeyla, Niki* (Greek), *Nikila, Nikola, Nikole, Nikolina, Nikolinka* (Slavic).
Diminutives: Coleta, Colette (French), Colletta, Collette, Nick, Nicky, Nico, Nika (Russian, Slavic),

Nik, Nikki.
Nicole/Nicolette/Nicollette See Nicola.
Nida Arabic: to call out.
Nidia See Nydia.
Nidra Sanskrit: the sleeping one.
Nedra, Nedrah, Needra, Needrah, Nidrah.
Niev/Nieve See Neave.
Nieves Spanish: of the snows.
Nieva, Nievah, Nives (Italian).
Nigella The feminine form of Nigel.
Nigellah, Nijella, Nijellah, Nygella, Nygellah.
Nihla See Nila.
Nijella/Nijellah See Nigella.
Nijole Possibly a form of Nicole.
Nijola.
Nika Russian/Slavic: a diminutive of Nikola and names such as Veronika.
Nikau Maori: a palm tree.
Nike Greek: a winged maiden who was the goddess of victory in mythology (the equivalent of the Roman goddess Victoria).
Naiki, Naikie, Nikey.
Nikeisha/Nikesha/Nikiesha See Nickeisha.
Nikeyla See Nicola.
Niki/Nikki Diminutives of Nicola.
Nikita Russian: unconquerable. Traditionally a boy's name, but now used for girls.
Naikita, Naikitah, Nakeita, Nakeitah, Nakita, Nakitah, Niketa, Niketah, Nikitah.
Nikoda A modern name, possibly derived from Nikita.
Nikodah.
Nikola/Nikole/Nikolina/Nikolinka See Nicola.
Nila Hindi: blue, or a sapphire.
Neela, Neelah, Nihla, Nilah, Nilo (Nepali), *Nyla, Nylah.*
Niley Aboriginal: a shell.
Nilee, Nileigh, Nilie, Nylee, Nyeleigh, Nyley, Nylie.
Nili Hebrew: indigo or deep-blue.
Nilufer Persian/Turkish: a waterlily.
Nilofer, Niloofar, Nilufar (Arabic).
Niluh An Indonesian name of uncertain meaning.
Nima Sherpa/Tibetan: born on a Sunday. Also a boy's name.
Nimfa/Nimfea See Nymphea.
Nimue A character from Welsh mythology.
Nina Spanish: a girl. *See also* Anne and Antonia.
Neena, Neenah, Nena, Nenah, Ninah, Ninetta, Ninette.
Ninfa Italian: a spouse.
Ninive The Latin name for the ancient Assyrian city of Nineveh.
Nineve, Nineves, Ninives.
Ninja A Japanese fighter or warrior.
Ninjah.
Ninon French diminutive of Anne.
Niobe The personification of maternal sorrow in Greek mythology.
Nioka See Nyoka.

Niomi/Niomie *See* Naomi.
Nira Modern Hebrew: of the loom.
Niree *See* Ngaire.
Nirma Sanskrit: the feminine form of Nirmal, meaning pure or clear.
Nirmala.
Nirvana Sanskrit: happy, or a heavenly state.
Nirvanah, Nirvanna, Nirvannah.
Nisana From Nisan, the first lunar month (March/April) of the Hebrew calendar, associated with the zodiac sign Aries and the spring.
Nisanna.
Nisha Sanskrit: the night.
Neasha, Necia, Neesha, Nicia.
Nishi Japanese: from the west.
Nissa Scandinavian: a friendly elf. *See also* Nyssa.
Nisa, Nissah, Nissareen, Nyssa, Nyssah.
Nita Native American: a bear. Also a Spanish form of Anne, and a diminutive of Anita, Bonita, Juanita and other names.
Neta, Netah, Nitah.
Nitika The angel of precious stones.
Nitikah.
Nitza Hebrew: a flower bud.
Nitsa.
Nives *See* Nieves.
Nixie German: a water sprite.
Nixee, Nixey, Nixi, Nixy.
Nizana Hebrew: a flower bud.
Nizanna.

Diminutives: Zana, Zanna.
Noa A feminine form of Noah, a Hebrew name meaning rest or comfort.
Noah, Noha.
Noami/Noamie *See* Naomi.
Noa-Rose A modern 'combination name'.
Noah-Rose, Noha-Rose.
Nobuko Japanese: trustworthy.
Noe Hawaiian: misty rain.
Noela/Noelie/Noeline *See* Noelle.
Noelani Hawaiian: a beautiful girl from heaven.
Noelle Old French: Christmas, or born at Christmas. The feminine form of Noel.
Noel, Noela, Noele, Noeli, Noelie, Noeline, Noell, Noella, Noëlle, Noellen, Noellyn, Noelyne, Noleen, Nolene, Noline, Nolyne.
Noemi/Noemia/Noemie *See* Naomi.
Noha/Noha-Rose *See* Noa and Noa-Rose.
Nohea Hawaiian: lovely.
Nohemi/Nohemy *See* Naomi.
Noilani A popular Thai name.
Nokomis Native American: the daughter of the moon.
Nola Irish Gaelic: the champion, or the fair-shouldered one. *See also* Neala and Nuala.
Nolah.
Noleen/Nolene/Noline *See* Noelle.
Noleta Latin: unwilling.

Nolita.
Nolwenn Breton: the name of a saint.
Nolwen, Nolwenne.
Nolyne *See* Noelle.
Nona Latin: the ninth, as in the ninth child.
Diminutives: Noni, Nonie.
Noni/Nonie Diminutives of Nona and Nora.
Nonna Russian: the name of a saint.
Nonziata *See* Annunziata.
Noola *See* Nuala.
Noomi An unusual Scandinavian name.
Noomie.
Noor Arabic: light or fire. The name of the Baha'i month that encompasses 5–23 June, so a suitable name for a Gemini baby. *Nooria, Nour, Noura, Nur, Nura, Nuri, Nuria* (Hebrew, Spanish).
Noora Aboriginal: a camp.
Noorah.
Noorjahan Arabic/Sanskrit: the light or fire of the world.
Nurjahan.
Noppawan A Thai name of uncertain meaning.
Nora A diminutive of Eleanor. Also a Scottish feminine form of Norman.
Naura, Naurah, Naureen, Naurine, Norah, Noreen, Noreena, Norelle, Norene, Noretta, Norette, Norina, Norine, Norita, Norlene, Norreen, Norrene, Norrine.
Diminutives: Noni, Nonie.
Nordica Teutonic: from the north.
Norda, Nordia, Nordika.
Noreen/Norelle/Norette *See* Nora.
Nori Japanese: a doctrine.
Diminutive: Noriko.
Norine/Norlene *See* Nora.
Noris *See* Norris.
Norita *See* Nora.
Norlie Probably a feminine form of Norman.
Norlee, Norleigh, Norley.
Norma Latin: a rule or standard; the perfect girl or woman. Also a Scottish feminine form of Norman.
Normah.
Normandy A French province.
Normandea, Normandee, Normandey, Normandie.
Norna Old Norse: the goddess of fate.
Norreen/Norrene/Norrine *See* Nora.
Norris An English surname, derived from Norman. More commonly a boy's name.
Noris.
Noumea The capital of New Caledonia.
Noumeah.
Nour/Noura *See* Noor.
Nouvelle French: the new one, or the newcomer. *See also* Nova.
Nouveau (French), *Nouveaux, Nouvel, Nouvella, Novella,*

Novellah, Novelle.
Nova Greek: new, the newcomer. *See also* Nouvelle.
Nea, Nia, Novah, Novalee, Novara, Novelene, Noveta, Novia, Novleen, Novlene.
November From novem, the Latin word for nine (November was originally the ninth month). *Novemba* (Swahili), *Novembra*, *Novembre* (French, Italian), *Novembro* (Portuguese).
Novleen/Novlene *See* Nova.
Nu Burmese: tender. Vietnamese: a woman.
Nuala Irish Gaelic: the fair-shouldered one. *See also* Nola. *Noola, Nula.*
Numira Aboriginal: a place where reeds grow. *Numirah.*
Nuna Native American: the land.
Nunda Aboriginal: a mulberry tree. *Nundah.*
Nunkerie Aboriginal: beautiful. *Nunkeri.*
Nunziata *See* Annunziata.
Nur/Nura/Nuria *See* Noor.
Nuray Turkish: a bright moon. *Nureil.*
Nurcan Turkish: joyful. *Nurjan.*
Nurit Hebrew: a yellow flower. *Nurita.*
Nurjahan *See* Noorjahan.
Nuta Aboriginal: the night.

Nutah.
Nya Thai: from the north. *Nyah.*
Nyad *See* Naida.
Nyala African: an antelope. *Nyalla, Nyela, Nyella.*
Nyani Swahili: a monkey.
Nyati Swahili: a buffalo.
Nydia Latin: a refuge or nest. *Nidia.*
Nyela/Nyella *See* Nyala.
Nygella/Nygellah *See* Nigella.
Nyika Swahili: the savannah grasslands.
Nyla/Nylah *See* Nila.
Nyleigh/Nyley/Nylie *See* Niley.
Nymphea Greek: a maiden. *Nimfa* (Polish, Spanish), *Nimfea, Nimfia, Nymfa, Nymfea, Nymfia, Nymph, Nympha, Nymphia.*
Nynett/Nynette *See* Nanette.
Nyoka Swahili: a snake. *Nioka, Niokah, Nyokah.*
Nyoko Japanese: a gem or treasure.
Nyomi *See* Naomi.
Nyra/Nyree/Nyria *See* Ngaire.
Nyrang Aboriginal: small; the little one.
Nyssa Greek: the beginning. *See also* Nissa. *Nissa, Nissah, Nissareen, Nysa, Nyssah, Nyssareen.*
Nyx Latin: white-haired. *Nyxie.*

O

Oana Bulgarian: a diminutive of Yoana (*see* Joanne).
Oba Aboriginal: water. Nigerian: an ancient river goddess.
Obelia Greek: a pillar or needle.
Oceana Greek: of the sea.
Ocea, Oceanea, Oceania, Oceanna, Ocia, Ociana, Ocianna.
Octavia Latin: the eighth. Suitable for an eighth child.
Octava, Octavie (French), *Ottavia* (Italian).
Diminutive: Tavia.
October/Octobra *See* Ottobra.
Oda Teutonic: rich.
Odela/Odele/Odella *See* Odile.
Odelia Hebrew: I will praise God.
See also Odile.
Odena *See* Odina.
Odessa Greek: a long journey.
Odessah.
Odette French: a home-lover.
Odett, Odetta.
Odile French: riches, prosperity. From a medieval German name, and a feminine version of Otto. *See also* Otilia.
Odela, Odele, Odelia, Odelie, Odelinda, Odella, Odilia, Odilla.
Odina Native American: a mountain.
Odena.
Odrey Probably a modern form of Audrey.
Odree, Odri, Odrie, Odry.
Ofelia/Ofilia *See* Ophelia.
Ofira Hebrew: golden.
Ofir, Ophir, Ophira.
Ofra/Ofrah *See* Ophrah.
Ohara Japanese: a field.
Ohma *See* Oma.
Ohorere Maori: suddenly.
Ojdana A Slavic name of uncertain meaning.
Okalani Hawaiian: from heaven.
Okelani.
Okeroa Maori: a long search.
Oki Japanese: from the ocean.
Oksana An exotic Russian name, possibly meaning a treasure.
Oksanna, Oxana, Oxanna, Oxzana, Oxzanna.
Oktoba/Oktober *See* Ottobra.
Ola Scandinavian: a descendant. The feminine form of Olaf.
Olalla Spanish form of Eulalia.
Olathe Native American: beautiful.
Olba Aboriginal: red ochre.
Oldree/Oldrie/Oldrey *See* Aldrey.
Oleander Greek: an evergreen tree.
Olea, Oleanda, Oleandah, Oliana (Polynesian).
Olena Hawaiian: turmeric. Also the Ukrainian form of Helen.
Olina.
Olenka *See* Olga.
Olesia An unusual Ukrainian name.
Olessia.

Olethea Latin: truthful
Oleta, Oletah, Olita, Olitah.
Olga Russian: the holy one, the feminine form of Oleg. The name of a 10th-century saint.
Elga, Helga (Scandinavian), *Olenka, Olgah, Olia, Olienka, Olva, Olya.*
Oli/Olie Diminutives of Olivia.
Olia A form of Olga.
Oliana Polynesian form of Oleander.
Olien Russian: like a deer.
Olimpia/Olimpiade/Olimpie *See* Olympia.
Olina *See* Olena.
Olinda Latin: fragrant. A Victorian placename.
Olynda.
Olita/Olitah *See* Olethea.
Oliva *See* Olivia and Olivine.
Olive *See* Olivia.
Olivia Latin: an olive tree or branch, a symbol of peace and the feminine version of Oliver. The name was used by Shakespeare for a character in *Twelfth Night*.
Alivia, Alivya, Alivyah, Allivia, Oliva, Olive, Olivette, Oliviah, Olivya, Olivyah, Ollivia, Ollivya, Olyve, Olyvia, Olyviah, Olyvya.
Diminutives: Livia, Livvie, Livvy, Oli, Olie, Ollie.
Olivine Latin: a green- or olive-coloured gemstone.
Oliva, Olivena, Olivene, Olivina.
Olono Aboriginal: a hill.

Olva/Olya *See* Olga.
Olwen Welsh: white or fair footprints. The name of a character in Welsh legend.
Olwenn, Olwenne, Olwyn, Olwynn, Olwynne.
Olympia Latin: the heavenly one; from the home of the gods.
Olimpia (Italian), *Olimpiad, Olimpiada, Olimpiade, Olimpias, Olimpie, Olympe* (French), *Olympiad, Olympiada, Olympiade, Olympias, Olympya, Olympyade.*
Olynda *See* Olinda.
Olyve/Olyvia *See* Olivia.
Oma Arabic: long-lived. The feminine form of Omar.
Ohma, Omah.
Omaira Arabic: the red one.
Omara, Omarah.
Omaka Maori: the place where the stream flows.
Ombra Italian: shade or a shadow.
Ombrah.
Omega Greek: the last.
Ona Lithuanian form of Anne. *See also* Úna.
Onaedo Nigerian: gold or golden.
Onata Native American: a daughter of the earth.
Onatah.
Onawa Native American: one who is wide awake.
Ondine Latin: a water sprite.
Ondina, Undina, Undine.

Onida Native American: the expected or awaited one.
Oneida.
Onike/Ónix *See* Onyx.
Onil The name of a Spanish town.
Ono Hawiian: sweet, or delicious.
Onóra Irish Gaelic version of Honour.
Onórah.
Ons A Tunisian name of uncertain meaning.
Onyx Greek: a semi-precious stone.
Onike (Tongan), *Ónix* (Spanish), *Onixe, Onyxe.*
Oola Aboriginal: a red lizard.
Oona/Oonagh/Oonha *See* Úna.
Opa Native American: an owl.
Opal Sanskrit: a jewel or precious stone.
Opale, Opalina, Opaline (French).
Ophelia Greek: to help, a helper. A character in Shakespeare's *Hamlet*.
Ofelia (Spanish), *Ofilia, Ophélie* (French).
Diminutive: Phelia.
Ophir/Ophira *See* Ofira.
Ophrah Hebrew: a fawn, or a lively maiden.
Ofra, Ofrah, Ophra, Opra, Oprah, Orpah.
Ora Latin: light, golden.
Orabella, Orabellah, Orabelle, Orah.
Oralee/Oralia/Oralie *See* Aurelia.
Orana Aboriginal: the moon, or to welcome.
Orani.
Orange A 'colour name'.
Orancia (Italian), *Oranje, Orena* (Welsh).
Orazia Italian: the feminine form of Orazio (*see* Horace).
Orchid Latin: a 'flower name'.
Orcid, Orkid.
Ordelia Teutonic: the spear of the elf.
Ordella.
Orea Greek: the maid of the mountains.
Oread, Oreah.
Orelia *See* Aurelia.
Orella Latin: she who listens.
Orel, Orela, Orell, Orelle.
Orena *See* Orange.
Oriana Latin: to rise. An Italian name.
Oriane (French), *Oriann, Orianna, Orianne, Oriantha, Orianthe, Orianthi, Oryana, Oryann, Oryanna, Oryanne.*
Oriel The angel of destiny. *See also* Aurelia.
Orinda Hebrew: a pine tree.
Orinthia The name of a character in *The Apple Cart*, a play by George Bernard Shaw.
Oriole Latin: a golden bird.
Oriol.
Orissa A state in eastern India.
Orla Irish Gaelic form of Aurelia.
Orlagh, Orlah, Orlena, Orlene, Orlia, Orliah, Orliya, Orliyah.

Orlanda The feminine form of Orlando, meaning from the famed land.
Orlandia, Orlandie.
Orlena/Orlene *See* Orla.
Orlenda Russian/Slavic: an eagle.
Orlinda, Orlitza, Orlynda.
Orli Hebrew: of the light.
Orlee, Orlie, Orley, Orly.
Orlia/Orliya *See* Orla.
Orlitza *See* Orlenda.
Orna Hebrew: light. Irish Gaelic: pale.
Ornah.
Ornella Italian: a flowering ash tree.
Ornelle, Ornetta, Ornette (French).
Ornice Hebrew: a fir or cedar tree.
Orpah *See* Ophrah.
Orsa/Orseline/Orsola *See* Ursula.
Orsina The feminine form of Orson, a little bear.
Orsinah, Orsine, Orsinia.
Ortense/Ortensia *See* Hortense.
Orvokki Finnish form of Violet.
Oryana/Oryanna/Oryanne *See* Oriana.
Orysia An unusual Ukrainian name.
Orycia.
Osana/Osanna *See* Hosanna.
Ossia Irish Gaelic: a fawn. The feminine form of Ossian.
Ostara The Anglo-Saxon goddess of the moon and dawn.
Otilia A form of Odile, meaning riches or prosperity.
Otilie, Ottilia, Ottilie, Ottoline, Otylia (Slavic), *Otylie.*
Otira Maori: but; however.
Ottavia *See* Octavia.
Ottilia/Ottilie/Ottoline *See* Otilia.
Ottobra The Italian word for October, so suitable for a Libra or Scorpio child.
October, Octobra, Octobre (French), *Octobria, Oktoba* (Swahili), *Oktober* (Dutch, German, Norwegian).
Otylia/Otylie *See* Otilia.
Ouida The pseudonym of English novelist Marie Louise Ramé.
Oura Aboriginal: wood.
Ourania *See* Urania.
Owena Welsh: well-born; the feminine form of Owen.
Awena, Awenia, Owenia.
Oxana/Oxzana/Oxzanna *See* Oksana.
Ozge Turkish: one who is different.
Ozgur Turkish: free. Also a boy's name.
Ozger.
Ozlem Turkish: yearning.
Ozora Hebrew: the strength of the Lord.

P

Paciencia *See* Patience.
Pacifica Latin: calm, as in the Pacific Ocean.
Pacita *See* Paz.

Paddy A diminutive of Patrick, meaning noble or well-born.
Paddee, Paddey, Paddi, Paddie.

Padma Sanskrit: a lotus.
Padme.

Padulla Aboriginal: a stone.
Padullah.

Paget A little page. *See also* Paige.
Padget, Padgett, Padgette, Pagett, Pagette.

Pahala Hindi: the first; suitable for a firstborn child.
Pahal.

Pahelo Nepali: yellow.

Paige Old English: a young child.
Page, Paig, Paij, Paije, Payg, Payge.

Painter Middle English: one who paints pictures.
Paynter, Peinter, Peynter.

Paisley A Scottish town, after which the well-known paisley pattern was named.
Paislea, Paislee, Paisleigh, Paisly.

Paiton/Paityn *See* Payton.

Paka Swahili: a cat or kitten.

Pakuna Native American: a bounding deer.

Palam Tibetan: a diamond.

Palila Hawaiian: a bird.

Pallano Aboriginal: the new moon.

Pallas Greek: knowledge and wisdom.

Palma Latin: a palm tree. The name of a town in Majorca.
Palmah, Palmira, Palmire, Palmyra, Palmyre.

Paloma Spanish from Latin: a dove.
Palomah, Palometa, Palomita.
Diminutives: Loma, Lomah.

Pamala/Pamallia *See* Pamela.

Pambula Aboriginal: two waters. A NSW placename.

Pameela Sanskrit form of Pamela.

Pamela English: a name invented by the 16th-century poet Sir Philip Sidney, possibly based on the Greek word for sweetness or honey.
Pamala, Pamalla, Pamallia, Pameela (Sanskrit), *Pamelia, Pamelina, Pamella, Pamellia, Pamina, Pamine, Pamla.*
Diminutives: Pam, Pammi, Pammie, Pammy, Pani (Maori).

Pamina/Pamla *See* Pamela.

Pana A Native American name of uncertain meaning.

Panagiota Greek: all holy. The feminine form of Panagiotis.
Panagia, Panayiota, Panayota, Pangiota, Panyiota.
Diminutive: Giota.

Pandia Greek: divine. A figure in Greek mythology.
Panda, Pandah, Pandiah.

Pandita Sanskrit: a wise woman or scholar.
Pandeeta.

Pandonia Latin: the name of a 10th-century saint.

Pandora Greek: all-gifted, talented. A figure from Greek mythology.

Paneeta *See* Panita.
Pangari Aboriginal: a shadow, or of the soul.
Pangiota *See* Panagiota.
Pani Maori form of Pam (*see* Pamela). Nepali: water.
Pania Maori: a mythological sea maiden.
Panina Hebrew: a pearl, or coral.
Paninah, Penina, Peninah.
Panita Sanskrit: one who is admired.
Paneeta.
Panna Hindi: an emerald. Also the Hungarian form of Anne.
Pansy Old French: thoughts. A 'flower name'.
Pansee, Pansey, Pansi, Pansie.
Panthea Greek: all of the gods.
Panyiota *See* Panagiota.
Paola/Paolina *See* Paula.
Paquita Spanish: one who is free.
Pequita.
Para Hindi: the metal, mercury.
Parah.
Paradis French for paradise.
Paradee, Paradi, Paradie.
Paramita *See* Parmita.
Paraskeve Greek: the name of a 2nd-century saint.
Paraska (Russian), *Paraskeva.*
Pare Maori form of Polly.
Pari Persian: an eagle.
Paringa Aboriginal: a whirlpool.
Parirau Maori: the wing of a bird.
Paris Greek: a character in mythology, and the name of the French capital. Also a boy's name.
Parris, Parrys, Parys.
Parisa Persian: fairy-like.
Parysa.
Parker Old English: the park-keeper.
Parmelia The name of a ship that brought settlers to Western Australia in 1829.
Parmita Sanskrit: wisdom.
Parmida, Paramita.
Parnella Old French: a little rock.
See also Perella, Peta and Petronel.
Parnela, Parnele, Parnell, Parnelle.
Parris/Parrys *See* Paris.
Parthenia Greek: maidenly, virginal.
Parthena, Parthene, Parthenie.
Parvati Sanskrit: the daughter of the mountain. The name of a Hindu goddess.
Parvin The Persian name for the Pleiades, a group of stars in the constellation of Taurus.
Parveen, Parween, Perween.
Parysa *See* Parisa.
Pasang Sherpa/Tibetan: born on a Friday. Also a boy's name.
Pascale French from Latin: Easter, or born at Easter.
Pascal, Pascaline, Pascall, Pascalle, Paschale, Pascoe (Cornish), *Pascuala* (Spanish), *Pasena* (Spanish), *Paskal, Paskale, Pasqua* (Italian), *Pasqualina, Pasqualine, Pasquelina* (Italian), *Pasqueline, Pasquette* (French).

Diminutives: Pasca, Pascha, Paska, Pasqua.
Pascoe Cornish form of Pascale.
Pasena *See* Pascale.
Pashmina Persian: woollen.
Pashmeena, Pasmeena, Pasmeenah, Pasmina, Pasminah.
Pasiphae A mythological woman who was in love with a bull. A satellite of the planet Jupiter.
Paska/Paskal/Paskale *See* Pascale.
Pasqua/Pasqualina/Pasquelina/ Pasquette *See* Pascale.
Pateka Czech: born on a Friday.
Patia *See* Patya.
Patience English: one of the seven virtues.
Paciencia (Spanish), *Pazienza* (Italian).
Patra/Patrea *See* Patricia.
Patrice French form of Patricia.
Patricia Latin: noble, well-born. The feminine form of Patrick.
Patra, Patrea, Patria, Patrice (French), *Patricka, Patrina, Patrine, Patrisha, Patrizia* (Italian), *Pratisha, Pratricia, Preticia, Pretisha.*
Diminutives: Pat, Patsi, Patsie, Patsy, Patti, Pattie, Patty, Patzi, Patzie, Patzy, Tricia, Trish, Trisha, Tritia, Tritian.
Patsy/Patti/Pattie/Patty Diminutives of Patricia.
Pattina A form of Pat or Patricia. *Pattine.*

Patya Aboriginal: a flower. *Patia.*
Patzi/Patzie/Patzy Diminutives of Patricia.
Paula Latin: small. Feminine form of Paul.
Paulla, Paulline, Paola (Italian), *Paolina, Paule, Pauleen, Paulene, Pauletta, Paulette* (French), *Paulina* (Spanish), *Pauline* (French), *Paulini, Paulita, Paullene, Paulline, Pavelle, Pavla* (Czech), *Polina, Poline, Poulena, Poulene, Pouline.*
Pauletta/Paulette *See* Paula.
Pauline French form of Paula.
Pausa Sanskrit: the Hindu month of December/January, corresponding to Capricorn.
Pausha.
Pavelle/Pavla *See* Paula.
Pavlovna Russian: the feminine form of Pavlov (*see* Paul).
Pavlova.
Pax Latin: peace. *See also* Paz and Peace.
Payge *See* Paige.
Paynter *See* Painter.
Payton Old English: from the warrior's farm.
Paiten, Paiton, Paityn, Paton, Payten, Peyton.
Paz Spanish from Latin: peace. *See also* Pax and Peace.
Pacita, Pazia, Pazice, Pazita.
Pazia Hebrew: golden.

Paziah, Pazice, Pazya.
Peace Middle English: the peaceful one. *See also* Pax and Paz.
Peaches Middle English: a 'fruit name'.
Peach, Pêche (French).
Pearl Old French: a little sphere. Also a precious gem.
Pearla, Pearle, Pearli, Pearlie, Pearline, Pearly, Perl (Welsh), *Perla* (Italian, Spanish), *Perle, Perlette* (French), *Perlina, Perlita* (Italian), *Purl, Purla, Purle.*
Peata Maori form of Beatrice.
Peeta/Peetah *See* Peta.
Peg/Peggie/Peggy Diminutives of Margaret.
Pega The name of an 8th-century saint.
Peinter *See* Painter.
Peita/Peitra *See* Peta.
Pelagia Greek: from the sea.
Pele Hawaiian: a mythological goddess of fire.
Pelipa *See* Philippa.
Pema Sherpa/Tibetan: a lotus.
Pembe Swahili: ivory. Turkish: pink.
Pember Old English: the pasture with an enclosure.
Pembah.
Penaluna Cornish: the end or head of the pools.
Pennaluna.
Pencast Cornish form of Pentecost.
Penelope Greek: the weaver. A character in Greek mythology.
Diminutives: Pen, Penni, Pennie, Penny.
Pengana Aboriginal: a hawk.
Penina/Peninah *See* Panina.
Penni/Pennie/Penny *See* Penelope.
Pensiri A Thai name of uncertain meaning.
Pentecosta Greek: born at Pentecost, the fiftieth day (or seventh Sunday) after Easter, generally falling mid-May to mid-June, so appropriate for Taurus and Gemini babies.
Pencast (Cornish), *Pentecost, Pentecoste.*
Penthea Greek: the fifth.
Penta, Pente, Pentea, Penthia, Pentia.
Peony Latin: healing. A 'flower name'.
Peonee, Peoney, Peoni, Peonie.
Pepa/Pepita Spanish diminutives of Josephine.
Pepe Tongan: a butterfly.
Pepper Middle English: from the spice.
Pepa, Pepah, Peppa, Peppah.
Pequita *See* Paquita.
Pera Italian/Spanish: a pear.
Perdita Latin: the lost one. A name invented by Shakespeare for a character in *The Winter's Tale*.
Perdeeta, Perditah, Perdyta, Perdytah.
Diminutives: Dita, Deeta, Dyta.
Perella A feminine form of Per, the Scandinavian version of Peter.

See also Peta and Petronel.
Perelle, Peretta, Perette (French).
Perez Hebrew: to blossom. Spanish: a surname, meaning the son of Pedro (Peter).
Peretz.
Peri Greek: from the mountains. *See also* Perry.
Perie, Perri, Perrie, Perry.
Peridot Arabic: a green gemstone.
Perin *See* Perry.
Perizada Persian: an elf or fairy.
Perizade.
Perkanna Aboriginal: white.
Perl/Perla/Perle/Perlina *See* Pearl.
Pernille *See* Petronel.
Peronel/Peronella *See* Petronel.
Perouze Armenian: turquoise.
Perpetua Latin: continuing, enduring. The name of a saint.
Perry French: the dweller by the pear tree. *See also* Peri.
Peri, Perie, Perin, Perri, Perrie, Perrin, Perrye, Perryn, Pery.
Persephone Greek: the goddess of the underworld. *See also* Proserpina.
Persia A 'country name'.
Persis Latin: a woman from Persia. A New Testament name.
Perween *See* Parvin.
Peta Aboriginal: a tree. Greek: a rock or stone; a feminine form of Peter. *See also* Parnella, Perella and Petronel.
Peeta, Peetah, Peita, Peitra, Petah,

Petenka (Russian), *Petra, Petrea, Petrina, Petrine* (Danish), *Petrova* (Russian), *Petrovna* (Russian), *Petya* (Russian), *Piedra* (Spanish), *Pier, Pierette, Pierina, Pieta, Pietah, Pietra* (Italian).
Petal English from Latin: part of a flower.
Petall.
Petenka A Russian form of Peta.
Peternella/Peternelle *See* Petronel.
Petoula/Petoulia *See* Petula.
Petra/Petrea *See* Peta.
Petrina/Petrine *See* Peta.
Petronel Latin: the name of an early saint, and related to the boy's name Peter. *See also* Parnella, Perella and Peta.
Peronel, Peronella, Peternella, Peternelle, Petronella, Petronelle, Petronilla (Scandinavian), *Pieternella, Pieternelle.*
Diminutive: Pernille (Scandinavian).
Petrova/Petrovna *See* Peta.
Pettina Probably derived from Bettina, a form of Elizabeth.
Petina.
Petula Possibly from the Latin word for to ask or to *Seek*.
Petoula, Petoulia, Petulia.
Diminutive: Pet.
Petunia A 'flower name'.
Petuniah, Petunya, Petunyah.
Petya A Russian form of Peta.
Pevara A name from *The Wheel of*

Time series of fantasy novels.
Pevarah, Pevarra, Pevarrah.
Peynter *See* Painter.
Peyton *See* Payton.
Phaedra Greek: the bright one. The wife of Theseus in Greek mythology.
Phaidra, Phedra.
Phailin Thai: a sapphire.
Phebe/Phebee/Phebie *See* Phoebe.
Phelia *See* Ophelia.
Phelicitie/Phelicity/Phelissitie/ Phelissity *See* Felicity.
Phemia/Phemie Diminutives of Euphemia.
Pheonix *See* Phoenix.
Pherenike Greek form of Berenice.
Philadelphia Greek: brotherly love. A city in the USA.
Philadelfa, Philadelfia, Philadelpha.
Philana Greek: a friend of mankind.
Philantha Greek: a lover of flowers.
Philanthe.
Philberta Old English: very brilliant.
Filberta, Filbertha, Philbertha.
Philida/Phillida *See* Phyllis.
Philippa Greek: a lover of horses. The feminine form of Philip.
Felipa (Spanish), *Filippa* (Italian), *Pelipa* (Native American), *Philipa, Philippina, Phillipa, Philippine* (French, German), *Phillippa.*
Diminutives: Phil, Philly, Pip, Pippa, Pippi.
Philomela Greek: a lover of song.
Philomel.
Philomena Greek: a lover of the moon.
Filamena, Filamene, Filomena, Filomene, Philamena, Philamene, Philomene.
Diminutive: Mena.
Philyra Greek: a lime tree.
Phiper *See* Piper.
Phoebe Greek: radiant, bright. The name of a Greek deity and mentioned in the New Testament.
Feebee, Feebi, Feebie, Fhebee, Fheebi, Fheebie, Phebe (Italian), *Phebee, Phebie, Phoebee, Phoebie.*
Phoenix Greek: the legendary bird that rose again from its own ashes.
Feenix, Fenix, Pheonix.
Photene/Photine/Photini *See* Fotini.
Phrona A diminutive of Sophronia.
Phyllia From phyllon, the Greek word for a leaf.
Phylia.
Phyllis Greek: a green bough or branch. A character from mythology.
Philida, Philis, Phillida, Phillis, Phylis, Phyllida, Phyllys.
Phyper *See* Piper.
Pia Latin: pious, devout. An Italian and Spanish name.
Piaf French: the surname of a legendary singer (Édith Piaf). The name is believed to mean a sparrow or little bird in French slang.
Piaff.

Picea/Picia *See* Pisces.
Piedra/Pier/Pierette/Pierina *See* Peta.
Pier *See* Pierre.
Pierah Aboriginal: the moon.
Pirra.
Pierre The French version of Peter. More commonly a boy's name, but sometimes used for girls.
Pier, Piera, Pierina, Pierine, Pierr, Pierra.
Pieta Latin: piety or pity. *See also* Peta.
Pietah, Pietta, Piettah.
Pieternella/Pieternelle *See* Petronel.
Pietra Italian form of Peta.
Pievitza A Russian name of uncertain meaning.
Piki Maori: a fig.
Pila Hindi: yellow.
Pilah.
Pilar Aboriginal: a spear. Spanish: supportive, a pillar.
Piltti An unusual Finnish name.
Pimienta Spanish: pepper.
Pina Spanish: a pine tree.
Pinah, Pine, Pineta, Pinetah.
Pinar Turkish: like the spring.
Pine *See* Pina.
Pinga Sanskrit: bronze.
Pingah.
Pink A 'colour name'.
Pinke, Pynk, Pynke.
Pinterry Aboriginal: a star. Also suitable for boys.

Pinyali Aboriginal: an emu.
Pip A diminutive of Philippa.
Piper English: a pipe player.
Phiper, Phyper, Pipa, Pipah, Pyper.
Pipi Maori: a shellfish.
Pipiana A combination of Pip or Pippi and Anna.
Pippianna.
Pippa A diminutive of Philippa.
Pippi.
Pippi *See* Philippa and Pippa.
Pirenee/Pirrenee *See* Pyrenee.
Piri *See* Piroska.
Piritta Estonian and Finnish forms of Birgitta (*see* Bridget).
Diminutive: Pirjo.
Pirkko Finnish: a form of Birgitta (*see* Bridget).
Piroska A popular Hungarian name.
Diminutive: Piri.
Pirra *See* Pierah.
Pisces Latin: fishes. The last sign of the zodiac.
Picea, Picia, Piscea, Piscia.
Pita African: fourth, or the fourth child.
Pitah.
Pitta Aboriginal: a goose.
Pixie Celtic/English: a fairy or sprite.
Pixee, Pixey, Pixy.
Placida Latin: peaceful, serene. Feminine form of Placido.
Placidia, Placidina.
Platona Greek: wise, or broad-shouldered. The feminine form of

Plato.
Pleasance One who is pleasant.
Plaisance (French).
Pluto Latin: the mythological god of the underworld, and the planet that rules the zodiac sign of Scorpio.
Pluta, Plutia.
Poet Middle English: one who writes poetry.
Poete, Poett, Poette.
Polina/Poline *See* Paula.
Polly A form of Molly (*see* Mary).
Pare (Maori).
Pollyanna A combination of Polly and Anna.
Pollyana, Pollyann, Polly-Ann, Polly-Anna, Pollyanne, Polly-Anne.
Poloma Native American: a bow (a weapon).
Polona Aboriginal: a hawk. Also a boy's name.
Polonia Latin: a woman from Poland.
Polydora From Polydorus, the name of a 1st-century BC sculptor.
Pomona Latin: fertile, fruitful. The Roman goddess of fruit trees.
Pondela Czech: born on a Monday.
Poni African: the second, or second-born child.
Pooja *See* Puja.
Poonam Sanskrit: merit, or the full moon.
Punam, Punamban.
Poppy Old English: a 'flower name'.
Poppee, Poppey, Poppi, Poppie, Popy.
Portia Latin: an offering. The heroine of Shakespeare's *The Merchant of Venice.*
Porcha, Porchia, Porsha, Porshia.
Posy English: a bunch of flowers. Also a diminutive of Josephine.
Posee, Posey, Posi, Posie.
Potenza Italian: the powerful one.
Potenzia.
Poulene/Pouline *See* Paula.
Pounamu Maori: greenstone.
See also Waipounamu.
Prabhawati A Sanskrit name of uncertain meaning.
Pradeepa Sanskrit: the feminine form of Pradeep, meaning a light or lantern.
Pradipa.
Praise Midde English: one who deserves approval or admiration.
Praiz, Praize, Pryse, Prayze.
Prakriti Sanskrit: nature, or beautiful.
Pramsiri An unusual Thai name.
Pranita Sanskrit: one who is promoted.
Praneeta, Praneetha, Pranitha.
Prasana Sanskrit: bright and tranquil, or rising.
Prasanna.
Prasheila Sanskrit: from an ancient time.
Prashila, Prasila.
Prasidha Nepali: the famous one.

Prasida.
Praskovya Russian: from Paraskeve, a 2nd-century saint.
Praskoviya, Praskowia.
Pratibha Sanskrit: splendour or brightness.
Praticia/Pratisha *See* Patricia.
Pratika Sanskrit: symbolic.
Prayse/Prayze *See* Praise.
Precious Middle English: something of great value.
Precios, Preshus.
Preeti Sanskrit: love.
Preedika, Preet, Preethi, Preetika.
Prema Sanskrit: love, affection.
Premah, Premala, Premalla, Premila, Premilla, Premillah.
Premrudee An unusual Thai name.
Prescila/Prescilla/Presilla *See* Priscilla.
Presley Old English: from the priest's meadow. More often a boy's name.
Presleigh, Presly.
Pretella Aboriginal: the moon.
Pretoria The name of a city in South Africa.
Pretricia/Pretrisha *See* Patricia.
Prima Latin: the firstborn.
Primah, Primalia.
Primavera Spanish: springtime, or a child of the spring.
Primrose Latin: the first rose; a 'flower name'. *See also* Primula.
Primula An alternative name for a primrose.
Prioska Hungarian: the blushing one.

Priscilla Latin: from a Roman family name. *See also* Cilla.
Prescila, Prescilla, Prescillah, Presila, Presilla, Presillah, Prisca (Spanish), *Priscella, Priscillah, Prisella, Prisellah, Prisilla, Prisillah.*
Diminutives: Cilla, Cillah, Pris, Prissie, Silla.
Priya Sanskrit: beloved.
Priyah, Priyanka.
Prize Middle English: a reward.
Pryse, Pryze.
Proserpina The Roman equivalent of Persephone, the Greek goddess of the underworld.
Proserpine.
Prospera Latin: favourable.
Provence A region of France.
Providence Middle English: foresight, or divine protection or care.
Providenca, Providenza, Provvidenza, Provydence.
Prudence Latin: one who shows careful foresight.
Prudencia, Prudentia.
Diminutives: Pru, Prue.
Prunella Latin: a little plum.
Prunelle.
Diminutives: Pru, Prue.
Pryse/Pryze *See* Prize.
Psyche Greek: the immortal, or the soul. A mythological butterfly-winged maiden who was adored by Eros, the god of love.
Pualani Hawaiian: a heavenly flower.

Pualena Hawaiian: yellow.
Puanani Hawaiian: a beautiful flower.
Puatara Polynesian: a legendary figure.
Puja Sanskrit: to worship.
Pooja.
Puma Spanish: an American wild cat.
Pumah.
Puna Finnish: red. Hawaiian: a child of the moon. Maori: a spring.
Puntira: an unusual name from Thailand.
Pupuhi Maori: the wind.
Pura Latin: the pure one.
Purl/Purla/Purle *See* Pearl.
Purnima Sanskrit: the night of the full moon.
Diminutive: Purni.
Pushpa Sanskrit: like a flower.
Putali Nepali: a butterfly.
Putiputi Maori: a flower.
Pynk/Pynke *See* Pink.
Pyper *See* Piper.
Pyrena Greek: the fiery one.
Pirena, Pirenia, Pyra, Pyrenia.
Pyrenee From the Pyrenees, a European mountain range.
Pirenee, Pirrenee, Pyrrenee.
Pythia Greek: from the word python and meaning a prophet.
Pythea.

Q

Qadira Arabic: powerful.
Kadira.
Qamra Arabic: the moon.
Kamra, Kamrah, Qamrah.
Qing Chinese: greenish-blue.
Ching.
Qona *See* Quona.
Quade A modern name, possibly of Gaelic origin. More commonly a boy's name.
Quaden, Quaid, Quaide, Quaiden, Quayd, Quayde, Quayden, Qwade, Qwaden, Qwaid, Qwaide, Qwaiden, Kwayd, Kwayde, Kwayden, Kweyd, Kweyde, Kweyden.
Quadra Latin: four, or the fourth.
Quadria.
Quaide/Quaiden *See* Quade.
Quaile Manx Gaelic: the son of Paul. Also a boy's name.
Quail, Quale, Quayl, Quayle.
Quarallia Aboriginal: a star.
Quarta Latin: the fourth, or fourth child.
Quartana, Quartilla.
Quashi African: born on a Sunday. Also a boy's name.
Quattro Italian: four.
Quayde/Quayden *See* Quade.
Quayle *See* Quaile.
Queen Middle English: A female sovereign.
Queane, Queene, Quene.

Queena Middle English: a woman.
Kuine (Maori), *Kuini* (Samoan),
Queenee, Queeney, Queenie.
Queenan An Irish Gaelic surname.
Quenan.
Queenida Aboriginal: fire.
Quella English: to pacify.
Quela, Quelah, Quellah.
Quenby Scandinavian: womanly.
Quenbee, Quenbey, Quenbi, Quenbie.
Quendryth An unusual Welsh name.
Quendreth, Quendrethe, Quendrith, Quendrithe, Quendrythe.
Quentin Latin: fifth. Generally a male name, but sometimes used for girls. *See also* Quinta.
Quenten, Quenton, Quentyn, Quinten, Quinton, Quintyn.
Querida Spanish: the beloved one.
Questa French: the searcher.
Quiana A modern name, derived from either Queenie or Quinn.
Quianah, Quianna, Quiannah, Quinna, Quinnah.
Quilla The moon goddess of the Incas.
Quincey/Quincy *See* Quinta.
Quinette *See* Quinta.
Quinn Irish Gaelic: wise and intelligent. Also a boy's name.
Quin, Quinne, Quinnie, Quyn, Quynn, Quynne.
Quinta Latin: the fifth, as in fifth child. *See also* Quentin.
Quincey, Quincy, Quinette, Quintana, Quintella, Quintilla, Quintina.
Quintessa Latin: the essence.
Quentessa.
Quinton/Quintyn *See* Quentin.
Quiric Greek: born on a Sunday. Also a boy's name.
Quirina Italian/Spanish: the feminine form of Quirino (*see* Corin).
Quirita Latin: a good citizen.
Quishla/Quishlah *See* Cushla.
Quoba Aboriginal: good.
Quona The name of a medieval noble Italian family.
Qona.
Quynn/Quynne *See* Quinn.
Qwade/Qwaden/Qwaide *See* Quade.

R

Ra Maori/Polynesian: the sun.
Raadhika/Raadika *See* Radhika.
Raani *See* Rani.
Rabia Arabic: the harvest, or the spring.
Rabea, Rabeah, Rabi, Rabi'a, Rabiah, Rabie, Rabiya, Rabiyah, Raby, Rabye.
Rachana Sanskrit: creation.
Racha, Rachna.
Rachel Hebrew: an ewe. The wife of

Jacob and mother of Joseph in the Bible. *See also* Rae.
Lahela (Hawaiian), *Rachael, Rachal, Racheal, Rachela* (Polish), *Rachele* (Italian), *Rachell, Rachella, Rachelle, Rachial, Rachieal, Raechel, Raechell, Raechelle, Raghnailt* (Irish Gaelic), *Rahel* (Hebrew), *Rahela, Rahera* (Maori), *Rakel* (Scandinavian), *Rakella, Rakelle, Raqueal, Raquel* (Spanish), *Raquelle, Rashell, Rashelle, Raychel, Raychelle, Reachell, Reachelle, Rechelle, Reichel, Reichell, Reichelle, Rokel, Rokell, Rokella, Rokelle.*
Diminutives: Rae, Ray, Shelley.

Rachida *See* Rashida.

Rada Slavic: glad.
Rahda, Rhada.

Radella Old English: an elfin adviser.
Radell, Radellah, Radelle.

Radha Sanskrit: success. The name of a Hindu goddess.
Radhia (Arabic).

Radhika Sanskrit: prosperity.
Raadhika, Raadika, Radika.

Radinka Slavic: joyful, active.

Radka Czech: the feminine form of Radko, meaning joyful.
Ratka.

Radmilla Slavic: a worker for the people.
Radmila.

Rae English: a doe. *See also* Rachel and Raelene.
Rai, Raie, Ray, Raye, Rea, Rei, Rey, Rhae, Rhai, Rhay.

Raechel/Raechelle *See* Rachel.

Raedyn Probably derived from Rae.
Raydyn, Rhaedyn.

Raelene Australian: a modern invented name. *See also* Rae.
Raelea, Raelean, Raelee, Rae-lee, Raelein, Raeleine, Raeli, Raelie, Raeline, Raelyne, Raelynne, Raylean, Raylee, Rayleen, Raylene, Raylie, Rayline, Reylean, Reylene, Reylie, Reyline.
Diminutives: Rae, Rael, Raele, Ray.

Raema/Raemonda *See* Ramona.

Rafaela/Rafaella/Raffaela *See* Raphaella.

Rafiqa Arabic: the feminine form of Rafiq, a companion or friend.
Rafika.

Raga Sanskrit: a musical passage or movement.

Raghnailt Irish Gaelic form of Rachel.
Raghnaid (Scottish Gaelic).

Ragini Sanskrit: a melody.

Rahda *See* Rada.

Rahel/Rahela *See* Rachel.

Rahera Maori form of Rachel.

Rahna *See* Rana.

Rahnee/Rahni *See* Rani.

Rai/Raie *See* Rae.

Raihan/Raihana *See* Rayhan.

Raija/Raijah *See* Raya.

Raimona/Raimonda/Raimonde See Ramona.
Rain Middle English: water that falls from the sky. See also Raine.
Raina Polish and Czech forms of Regina.
Rainbow Old English: an array of bright colours.
Rainebow, Raynbow, Raynbowe.
Raine Old German: advice, decision. Also a diminutive of Lorraine.
Rain, Rainn, Rainne, Rayn, Rayne, Raynne, Reine, Rhain, Rhaine, Rhane, Rhayne, Rhaynne.
Raisa Russian from Greek: adaptable.
Raissa Old French: the believer. *Raisse.*
Raiven/Raivenne See Raven.
Raiyan See Rayhan.
Raiza Hebrew: a rose.
Raizal, Raizel, Raizza, Rayza, Rayzil.
Raja Aboriginal: the stars. Arabic: the hopeful one.
Rajah, Rajia, Rajiah, Rajina, Rajini, Rajya.
Rajani Sanskrit: dark, of the night.
Rajiva Sanskrit: the feminine form of Rajiv, meaning a lotus flower.
Rajkumari Sanskrit: a princess.
Rakel/Rakella/Rakelle See Rachel.
Raluca An unusual Romanian name. *Raluka.*
Ramla Swahili: one who predicts the future.
Ramona Spanish: a wise protector. The feminine form of Ramon and Raymond.
Raema, Raemonda, Raimona, Raimonda, Raimonde, Ramonah, Ramonda, Ramondah, Ramonde, Rayma, Raymona, Raymonah, Raymonda, Raymondah, Raymonde, Remona, Remonda, Rimona, Rimonda.
Rampali A Sri Lankan name of uncertain meaning.
Ran Japanese: a waterlily. Old Norse: a mythological goddess of the sea.
Rana Arabic: beautiful to gaze upon. See also Rani.
Rahna, Ranah, Ranessa, Ranya, Ranyah.
Randa/Randi/Randy See Miranda.
Ranea See Raniya.
Ranelle A modern 'elle name'. *Ranella.*
Rangi Maori/Polynesian: the sky.
Rangimarie Maori: the peaceful one.
Rani Sanskrit: a queen.
Raani, Rahnee, Rahni, Rana, Ranee, Rannee, Ranni, Rhani.
Raniya Arabic: one who gazes.
Ranea, Rania, Raniyah, Rhania.
Ranjani A Sanskrit name, possibly a form of Rani.
Ranya/Ranyah See Rana.
Raoula See Raula.
Raphaela Hebrew: the divine healer,

or healed by God. The feminine form of Raphael.
Rafaela, Rafaella, Rafaelle, Raffaela, Raffaele, Raphael, Raphaella, Raphaelle.

Raqueal/Raquel/Raquelle *See* Rachel.

Rasha Arabic: a young gazelle.

Rashell/Rashelle *See* Rachel.

Rashida Arabic: righteous.
Rachida, Rashda, Rasheda.

Rata Aboriginal: a plant. Maori: a tree with large red flowers.

Ratana Thai: crystal, or a jewel.
Ratania, Ratanna, Ratanya.

Rati Sanskrit: love. The name of the Balinese goddess of love and fertility.

Ratka *See* Radka.

Ratna Sanskrit: a jewel.

Rato Nepali: red.

Ratri Sanskrit: the Hindu goddess of the night.

Raukura Maori: a plume of feathers.

Raula Italian: a fearless wolf. The feminine form of Raul.
Raoula.

Ravel French: the name of a famous composer.
Ravell, Ravella, Ravelle, Ravello.

Raven Middle English: a bird name.
Raiven, Raivenn, Raivenne, Ravenn, Ravenne, Rayven, Rayvenn, Rayvenne.

Ravenna The name of a city in Italy.
Ravennah.

Ravia Hebrew: four, or the fourth. Sanskrit: the feminine form of Ravi, meaning the sun.
Raviah, Ravya.

Ray *See* Rae, Rachel and Raelene.

Raya Arabic: fragrant.
Raija, Raijah, Rayah, Rayya, Rayyah.

Rayaan/Rayan *See* Rayhan.

Raychel/Raychelle *See* Rachel.

Raydyn *See* Raedyn.

Rayette A feminine form of Ray, a king (*see also* Raymond).
Rayetta, Rayonetta, Rayonette.

Rayhan Arabic: a fragrant plant
Raihan, Raihana, Raiyan, Raiyana, Rayaan, Rayan, Rayann, Rayhana, Rayhanna.

Raylean/Raylee/Raylene *See* Raelene.

Rayma/Raymona/Raymonda/Raymonde *See* Ramona.

Rayn/Rayne *See* Raine.

Rayna Polish and Czech forms of Regina.

Raynbow/Raynbowe *See* Rainbow.

Rayonette *See* Rayette.

Rayven *See* Raven.

Rayya *See* Raya.

Rayza/Rayzil *See* Raiza.

Rea *See* Rae and Rhea.

Reachell/Reachelle *See* Rachel.

Reagain *See* Regan.

Reanan/Reanna/Reanyn *See* **Rhiannon**.

Reave/Reaves *See* Reeves.

Reba *See* Rebecca.
Rebecca Hebrew: possibly meaning a heifer or a knotted cord. The wife of Isaac in the Bible.
Rebbeca, Rebbecca, Rebeca (Spanish), *Rebecka, Rebeckah, Rebeka, Rebekah, Rebekka* (German), *Rebekkah, Reveka* (Greek), *Revekka* (Russian), *Rifka* (Yiddish), *Ripeka* (Maori), *Rivka* (Hebrew), *Robeca, Robecah, Robecca, Robeccah, Robecka, Robeckah, Robeka, Robekka*.
Diminutives: Bec, Becca, Beck, Becki, Beckie, Becky, Bek, Bekki, Bekkie, Bekky, Reba, Riba.
Rebeka/Rebekah/Rebekka *See* Rebecca.
Rebel Latin: the rebellious one. *Rebele, Rebell, Rebelle*.
Rechelle *See* Rachel.
Reda Lithuanian: red-haired. *Redah*.
Reece English from Welsh: ardent. Formerly a boy's name, but now popular for girls.
Rees, Reese, Rhys (Welsh), *Rhyse*.
Reema *See* Rima.
Reena *See* Rena.
Reeta/Reetta *See* Rita.
Reeves Old English: a steward. More commonly a boy's name. *Reave, Reaves, Reeve, Reve, Reves*.
Regan A character in Shakespeare's *King Lear*. *See also* Regina.
Reagain, Reagan, Reegan, Regann, Reganne, Regen, Regenn, Regenne, Rehgan, Rehgen, Rhegan, Rhegan, Reigan, Reigen.
Regina Latin: a queen.
Raina, Rayna, Reagan, Regan, Regena, Regenia, Regia, Régine (French), *Reginia, Reina, Reine* (French), *Réjeanne* (French), *Renia* (Polish), *Renya* (Greek), *Rigena, Rigina*.
Diminutives: Gina, Reg, Reggie, Rina.
Rehgan/Rehgen *See* Regan.
Rehua The Polynesian goddess of the stars.
Rei *See* Rae.
Reiarnah *See* Rhiannon.
Reichel/Reichell/Reichelle *See* Rachel.
Reigan/Reigen *See* Regan.
Reiko Japanese: a grateful child.
Reiley/Reilley/Reilly *See* Riley.
Reima/Reimah *See* Rima.
Reina/Reine *See* Raine and Regina.
Reita/Reitah *See* Rita.
Réjeanne French form of Regina.
Reka Maori: sweet.
Rekha Hindi: fine.
Rekeisha Probably a form of Keisha. *Rekeesha, Rekesha, Rekeysha, Rekeyshia, Rekiesha*.
Remona/Remonda *See* Ramona.
Rémy French from Latin: an oarsman, one who rows. Generally

a boy's name.
Remee, Remey, Remi, Remia, Remie, Remola, Remy, Remya.

Ren Japanese: a waterlily. *See also* Wren.
Renn.

Rena Hebrew: a joyous song.
Reena, Rina.

Renata Latin: one who is reborn. Originally an Italian name.
Renae, Renatah, Renate (German), *Renay, Renaye, Rene, Renea, Renée* (French), *Renella, Renelle, Renetta, Renette, Renez, Rennae, Rennay, Rennaye.*
Diminutives: Renni, Rennie.

Renay/Renaye *See* Renata.

Rene/Renea/Renée *See* Renata.

Reneisha Probably a form of Keisha.

Renella/Renelle *See* Renata.

Renetta/Renette/Renez *See* Renata.

Reni/Renie *See* Renny.

Renia Polish form of Regina.

Renita Latin: a rebel.

Rennae/Rennay/Rennaye *See* Renata.

Renny Irish Gaelic: small but powerful.
Reni, Renie, Renna, Renney, Renni, Rennie, Reny.

Renske Dutch: the feminine form of Rens.

Renuka Sanskrit: the name of a Hindu goddess.

Renya Greek form of Regina.

Reonie Possibly from Leonie (*see* Leona).
Reone, Reonee, Reoney, Reony.

Rere Maori: a waterfall.

Reseda Latin: a mignonette flower.

Reshae Probably derived from Shae.
Reshai, Reshaie, Reshay, Reshaye, Reshea.

Reshma A Sanskrit name of uncertain meaning.

Resmin A Turkish name of uncertain meaning.

Reta/Retah *See* Rheta and Rita.

Retta A diminutive of Loretta. *See* Laura.

Reva Latin: renewed strength. *See also* Riva.
Revah.

Reve/Reves *See* Reeves.

Reveka/Revekka *See* Rebecca.

Revel Old French: a rebel, or one who makes merry. Also a boy's name.
Revell, Revelle, Revil, Revill, Reville.

Rewa Polynesian: slender.

Rex Latin: a king. More commonly a boy's name, but now occasionally used for girls.
Reks, Rexx.

Rexana Latin: regally graceful.
Rexanna, Rexanne, Rexeen, Rexeena, Rexena, Rexene, Rezana, Rezanna, Rezanne.

Rey *See* Rae.

Reyhan *See* Rhiannon.

Reylean/Reylene/Reylie/Reyline *See* Raelene.
Rez Hungarian: red- or copper-coloured.
Reza Slavic: a diminutive of Teresa, the reaper or harvester.
Rezah, Rezia (Hungarian), *Riza, Rizah.*
Rezana/Rezanna/Rezanne *See* Rexana.
Rhada *See* Rada.
Rhae/Rhaedyn/Rhai/Rhay *See* Rae and Raedyn.
Rhaine/Rhane *See* Raine.
Rhani *See* Rani.
Rhania *See* Raniya.
Rhea Greek: a stream, or a mother. A Greek earth goddess.
Rea, Rhia.
Rhegan/Rhegen *See* Regan.
Rheta Greek: an orator. *See also* Rita.
Reta, Rhita.
Rhia *See* Rhea and Ria.
Rhiain/Rhian *See* Ryan.
Rhiannon Welsh: a nymph, or a queen. A Celtic goddess associated with the moon.
Reanan, Reanna, Reannan, Reanyn, Reiarnah, Reyhan, Rheanna, Rheannon, Rheanon, Rhianna, Rhianon, Rhiannan, Riahna, Riahne, Riana, Riann, Rianna, Rianne, Riannon.
Rhianwen Welsh: a blessed or pure maiden.
Rhianwyn, Rhianwynne.
Rhiarne *See* Ryan.
Rhly/Rhlye *See* Riley.
Rhoanna/Rhoanne *See* Roanna.
Rhoda Greek: a rose, the colour pink, or a woman from the island of Rhodes. A New Testament name.
Rhodah, Rhodeia, Rhodelia, Rhodia, Rhodina, Rhodine, Roda, Rodah.
Rhodanthe Greek: like a rose.
Rhodanthy.
Rhoinda *See* Rhonda.
Rhoma/Rhomah *See* Roma.
Rhona *See* Rona.
Rhonda Welsh: the name of a valley.
Rhoinda, Rhoindah, Rhondda, Ronda, Rondah.
Rhondalynn A 'combination name' meaning a valley with a waterfall.
Rhondahlynn, Rhondalin, Rhondalinn, Rhonda-Lynn, Rhonddalin, Rhonddalinn, Rhonddalynn, Rhondalynne, Rondahlin, Rondahlinn, Rondahlynne, Rondalin, Rondalinn, Rondalynne.
Rhonwen Welsh: a white lance, or white hair.
Rhosyn Welsh form of Rose.
Rhubee/Rhubie/Rhuby *See* Ruby.
Rhyan/Rhyann *See* Ryan.
Rhyana/Rhyanna *See* Rihana.
Rhylea/Rhylee/Rhyley *See* Riley.
Rhyll The name of a Welsh town.

Also a boy's name.
Rhyl, Rhyllis, Ryl, Ryll.
Rhys/Rhyse *See* Reece.
Ria Spanish: of the river. Also a short form of Maria (*see* Mary).
Riaa, Riah, Rhia, Riha, Riia.
Riahn/Rian/Rianne *See* Ryan.
Riana/Rianna *See* Diana and Rhiannon.
Riba *See* Rebecca.
Rica Spanish: prosperous.
Ricah, Ricca, Riccah, Rika, Rikah, Rikka, Rikkah.
Ricarda A feminine form of Richard. *See also* Richella and Richenda.
Richarda, Richarde, Richardene, Richardine, Richetta, Richette, Ryszarda (Slavic).
Richella A feminine form of Richard. *See also* Ricarda and Richenda.
Richelle.
Richenda A feminine form of Richard. *See also* Ricarda and Richella.
Richende.
Richmal After Richmal Crompton, the English authoress of the *Just William* books.
Richmall, Richmalle.
Rickee/Ricki/Rickie/Ricky Diminutives of several names.
Ricki-Lee/Rickie-Lee *See* Rikki-Lee.
Rida Arabic: the favoured one.
Rider Old English: a horseman or knight.
Ridah, Rydah, Ryder.
Rielle A modern American name, possibly a diminutive of Gabrielle.
Riella.
Rielly/Riely *See* Riley.
Rien *See* Ryan.
Rifka Yiddish form of Rebecca.
Rigena/Rigina *See* Regina.
Rigmor Scandinavian: a ruler.
Riha/Riia/Riia *See* Ria.
Rihab Arabic: spaciousness.
Rihaab.
Rihana Arabic: sweet basil.
Rhyana, Rhyanna, Rihanah, Rihanna, Rihannah.
Rika/Rikah *See* Rica.
Riki/Rikki/Rikky Diminutives of several names.
Rikka Finnish: the feminine form of Rikkard. *See also* Rica.
Riika, Rikkah.
Rikkara Aboriginal: from the south.
Rikara.
Rikki-Lee A modern 'combination name'.
Ricki-Lee, Rickie-Lee, Riki-Lee, Rikky-Lee.
Riko Japanese: possibly meaning a child of the jasmine.
Riley Irish Gaelic: valiant. Old English: a rye meadow. Generally a boy's name, but now also used for girls.
Reiley, Reilley, Reilly, Rhly, Rhlye, Rhylea, Rhylee, Rhyleigh, Rhyley,

Rielly, Riely, Rilea, Rilee, Rileigh, Rily, Rilye, Rylea, Rylee, Ryleigh, Rylie, Ryly, Rylye, Rylyee.
Rilla Teutonic: a stream.
Rily/Rilye *See* Riley.
Rim Arabic: a white antelope.
Rima.
Rima Maori: five.
Reema, Reemah, Reima, Reimah, Rimah.
Rimona/Rimonda *See* Ramona.
Rimu Polynesian: a tree. Also a boy's name.
Rina *See* Regina and Rena.
Rinat Hebrew: joy or happiness.
Rinda A wife of Odin, the supreme god in Norse mythology.
Rindill Icelandic: a wren.
Rindil.
Rinzen Sherpa/Tibetan: the holder of intellect. Also a boy's name.
Rion *See* Ryan.
Riona Irish Gaelic: a queen, or queenly.
Rionah.
Ripeka Maori form of Rebecca.
Ripley Old English: from the meadow of the shouter or loud one.
Riplea, Riplee, Ripleigh, Riply. Diminutive: *Rip.*
Risa Latin: laughter.
Rita Originally a short form of Margarita (*see* Margaret). *See also* Rheta.
Reeta, Reetah, Reetta, Reettah, Reita, Reitah, Reta, Retah, Rheta,
Rhita, Ritah.
Riva French from Latin: the shore or a riverbank.
Reva, Revah, Rivah, River, Rivera, Riverina, Riverine, Rivier, Riviera, Rivière (French), *Ryva, Ryvah.*
River/Rivier/Riviera/Rivière *See* Riva.
Rivka A Hebrew form of Rebecca.
Riyala Aboriginal: a river.
Riyalla.
Riza *See* Reza.
Roan/Roanne *See* Roanna and Rowan.
Roanna Latin: gracious. Also derived from names such as Rose and Anna. *See also* Rosanna.
Rhoanna, Rhoannah, Rhoanne, Roana, Roanah, Roane, Ro-Ann, Ro-Anna, Roannah, Roanne, Ro-Anne.
Robalyn A combination of Robin and Lynn.
Robalin, Robalinn, Robalinne, Robalynn, Robalynne, Robbalin, Robbalinn, Robbalinne, Robbalyn, Robbalynn, Robbalynne.
Robbi/Robbie/Robby Diminutives of Roberta and similar names.
Robbin/Robbyn/Robbyne *See* Robin.
Robecca/Robeckah/Robekka *See* **Rebecca.**
Robena *See* Robin.
Roberta Old English/Teutonic:

bright fame, famous; a feminine form of Robert. *See also* Robin.
Roberte, Robertha, Roberthe, Robertia, Ruperta (German), *Rupertia.*
Diminutives: Berta, Bertha, Bobbi, Bobbie, Bobby, Robbi, Robbie, Robby.

Robin English: originally a diminutive of Roberta. Also a 'bird name'.
Robbin, Robbine, Robbyn, Robbyne, Robena, Robina, Robine (French), *Robinette, Robinia, Robinn, Robinne, Robyn, Robyna, Robyne, Robynn, Robynne.*

Robyn/Robyna/Robynne *See* Robin.

Roca Spanish: a rock.
Rocah, Roka, Rokah.

Rochelle French: a small rock. Also from La Rochelle, a French fishing port. *See also* Rockelle.
Rocheen, Rochell, Rochella, Rochetta, Rochette, Rochine, Roshell, Roshella, Roshelle.

Rockelle A little rock. *See also* Rochelle.
Rockella, Rocketta, Rockette.

Roda/Rodah *See* Rhoda.

Roderica Teutonic: a famous ruler. The feminine form of Roderick.
Roderika, Roderyca, Roderyka, Rodrica, Rodrika.

Rodica Romanian: one who is fertile.
Rodika.

Rodolfa/Rodolpha *See* Rudolpha.

Roelene Probably a variation of Raelene.
Roelean, Roeleane, Roeleen, Roelie, Roeline.

Roena/Roenah *See* Rowena.

Roese *See* Rose.

Rohan Sanskrit: ascending. More commonly a boy's name. *See also* Rowan.
Rohen.

Rohana Sanskrit: sandalwood.
Rohanna.

Rohen *See* Rohan and Rowan.

Rohese/Rohesia *See* Rose.

Rohna *See* Rona.

Roimata Maori: tears.

Róis/Róisín Irish Gaelic forms of Rose.

Rojana/Rojanna *See* Roxana.

Roka Aboriginal: the number one. *See also* Roca.
Rokah.

Rokell/Rokella/Rokelle Modern forms of Raquel (*see* Rachel).

Rokeya/Rokia *See* Roqia.

Roksana *See* Roxana.

Rokuko Japanese: the sixth, or the sixth child.

Rolanda Teutonic: from the famed land. The feminine form of Roland.
Rola, Rolah, Rolande, Rolma.

Roma Latin: from Rome.
Rhoma, Rhomah, Romah, Romaine, Romana, Romane, Romella, Romelle, Romina

(Italian), *Rominah, Romine, Romola.*
Romain/Romaine *See* Romany.
Romany A gypsy.
Romain, Romaine, Romanee, Romani, Romanie, Romayn, Romayne, Rommanee, Rommanie, Rommany.
Romay *See* Romilda and Romy.
Romayn/Romayne *See* Romany.
Romee/Romi/Romie *See* Romilda and Romy.
Romella/Romelle *See* Roma.
Romilda Teutonic: a glorious warrior maiden.
Romelda, Romilde.
Diminutives: Romay, Romee, Romi, Romie, Romy.
Romina/Romine *See* Roma.
Rommanie/Rommany
See Romany.
Romola *See* Roma.
Romy German diminutive of Rosemary. *See also* Romilda.
Romay, Romee, Romi, Romie.
Rona Maori: the female moon. Scottish: the name of an island.
Rhona, Rohna, Ronah.
Ronalda Old Norse: powerful. Also a feminine form of Ronald.
Ronan Irish Gaelic: a little seal (the animal).
Ronin.
Ronda/Rondah *See* Rhonda.
Rondahlin/Rondalynne
See Rhondalynn.

Ronelle A feminine form of Ron or Ronald.
Ronaele, Ronel, Ronela, Ronell, Ronella, Ronnel, Ronnela, Ronnele, Ronnella, Ronnelle.
Ronette Another feminisation of Ron, meaning little Ron.
Ronet, Roneta, Ronett, Ronetta.
Rongo Maori: to obey.
Rongopai Maori: the gospel.
Ronja Swedish: a character in a children's book by famous Swedish author Astrid Lindgren.
Ronia.
Ronni/Ronnie/Ronny Diminutives of Veronica.
Roopa Sanskrit: blessed with beauty.
Roopah.
Roqia Persian: the dawn.
Rokeya, Rokeyah, Rokia, Rokiah, Roquia.
Rory Irish Gaelic: the red king. Generally a boy's name.
Roree, Rorey, Rori, Rorie.
Ros *See* Rosalind and Rosamond.
Rosa Italian and Spanish forms of Rose.
Rosetta (Italian), *Rosita* (Spanish), *Roza.*
Diminutive: Zita.
Rosa-Angela An attractive 'combination name'.
Rosabelle Latin: a beautiful rose.
Rosabel, Rosabell, Rosabella.
Rosalba Italian: a white rose.
Rosalean/Rosaleen/Rosalein

See Rosalind.

Rosalia Latin: a form of Rosa. The name of a 12th-century saint.
Rosalea, Rosalee, Rosa-Lee, Rosalie, Rosealea, Rosealee, Rosealia, Rosealie, Rose-Lee, Roslea, Roslee, Roslie, Rozalee, Rozalia, Rozalie, Rozlea, Rozlee, Rozlie.

Rosalie *See* Rosalia.

Rosalind Latin: a beautiful rose. Old German: from the word for a horse. Shakespeare's heroine in *As You Like It*. *See also* Rosamond.
Rosalean, Rosaleen (Irish), *Rosalein, Rosalin, Rosalina, Rosalinda, Rosalinde, Rosaline, Rosalyn, Rosalynd, Rosalynne, Roseleen, Roseleenda, Roselind, Roselinda, Roselinde, Roseline, Roselyn, Roselyne, Roslaini, Rosleen, Rosleenda, Roslyn, Rozalin, Rozalind, Rozalinda, Rozaline, Rozlin, Rozlind, Rozlinde.*
Diminutives: Ros, Roz.

Rosamond Latin: a pure rose, or the rose of the world. Old German: from the word for a horse. *See also* Rosalind.
Rosamund, Rosamunda, Rosamunde, Rosemonda, Rosemonde (French), *Rosemund, Rosmunda* (Italian), *Rozamond, Rozamonde.*
Diminutives: Ros, Roz.

Rosanna A combination of Rose and Anna.
Roanna, Roanne, Rosanda, Rosa-Anna, Rosanne, Roseann, Rose-Ann, Roseanna, Rose-Anna, Roseanne, Rose-Anne, Rosena, Rosezan, Rosezann, Rosezanna, Rosezanne, Rossana, Rossanna (Spanish), *Rozanda, Rozanna, Rozanne.*

Rosario Spanish: from the word for a rosary.
Rosaria, Rosarie, Rosary, Rozaria, Rozarie, Rozario, Rozary.
Diminutives: Charina (Spanish), Charo (Spanish).

Rose Latin: a 'flower name' (from rosa). *See also* Raiza, Rhoda, Rosa, Rosabelle, Rosalia, Rosamond and Rosemary.
Raiza (Hebrew), *Rhosyn* (Welsh), *Roese, Rohesia, Rohese, Róis* (Irish Gaelic), *Rosa* (Italian, Spanish), *Rosea, Rosel, Rosen* (Cornish), *Rosena, Roseta* (Portuguese), *Rosetta* (Italian), *Rosette* (French), *Rosia, Rosina* (Italian), *Rosita* (Spanish), *Roskia* (Hungarian), *Roza* (Polish), *Roze, Rozea, Rozen* (Cornish), *Rozena, Rozene, Rozia, Rozina* (Slavic), *Rozita.*
Diminutives: Róisín (Irish Gaelic), Rosheen (Irish), Rosie, Rosine (French), Rosy, Rozie, Rozy, Ruzena (Czech), Zita (Italian, Spanish).

Rosealea/Rosealia *See* Rosalia.

Rose-Anna/Roseanne *See* Rosanna.
Roseland From the land of roses.
Rozeland.
Roselani Hawaiian: a heavenly rose.
Roseleen/Roselind/Roseline
See Rosalind.
Roselle A combination of Rose and Elle.
Rosella, Rossella (Italian), *Rosselle, Rozella, Rozelle.*
Roselyne *See* Rosalind.
Rosemary Latin: dew of the sea; the name of a fragrant herb
Rosamaria, Rosamarie, Rosemaree, Rose-Maree, Rosemaria, Rosemarie, Rose-Marie, Rose-Mary, Rosemarye, Rosmaree, Rosmari, Rosmira, Rozemarie, Rozemary.
Diminutives: Romy (German), Rosie, Rosy, Rozie, Rozey, Rozy.
Rosemi A modern name, probably from Rose.
Rosemee, Rosemey, Rosemie.
Rosemund *See* Rosamond.
Rosen A Cornish form of Rose.
Rosena *See* Rosanna and Rose.
Rosenwyn Cornish: a fair rose.
Rosenwynn, Rosenwynne.
Roseta/Rosetta *See* Rosa and Rose.
Rosevear Cornish: from the moorland.
Rosezanna/Rosezanne *See* Rosanna.
Roshan Persian: splendid. Also a boy's name.
Roshana, Roshann, Roshanna,
Roshini.
Rosheen An Irish Gaelic form of Rose.
Roshella/Roshelle *See* Rochelle.
Rosia/Rosina/Rosine *See* Rose.
Rosie *See* Rose and Rosemary.
Rosita *See* Rosa and Rose.
Roskear A Cornish placename, probably meaning a moor or heath.
Roskia Hungarian form of Rose.
Roslaini *See* Rosalind.
Roslea/Roslee/Roslie *See* Rosalia.
Rosleen/Rosleenda/Roslyn *See* Rosalind.
Rosmarie/Rosmira *See* Rosemary.
Rossana/Rossanna *See* Rosanna.
Rossella Italian form of Roselle.
Roswitha Teutonic: famous strength. The name of a 10th-century German nun.
Rosy *See* Rose and Rosemary.
Rouba/Roubee/Roubey *See* Ruby.
Rouge French: red.
Rougia.
Roula Greek: the rebellious one.
Roumiana An unusual Bulgarian name.
Rousa/Rousalka *See* Rusalka.
Rouslana/Rouslanah *See* Ruslana.
Rowan Irish Gaelic: the little red-haired one. More commonly a boy's name.
Roan, Roann, Roanne, Rohan, Rohen, Rowana, Rowann, Rowanna, Rowanne, Rowen.
Rowena Celtic: the white-haired

one. Old English: a well-known friend.
Roena, Roenah, Rowenah, Rowenna, Rowennah, Rowina, Rowinah.

Roya Arabic: a sweet dream or vision.
Royah, Ruya, Ruyah.

Roxana Persian: dawn. The name of the wife of Alexander the Great.
Rojana, Rojanna, Roksana (Russian), *Roxane, Roxanna, Roxanne, Roxeen, Roxene, Roxetta, Roxette, Roxine, Rukhsana, Ruksana.*
Diminutives: Roxee, Roxey, Roxi, Roxie, Roxy.

Roxene/Roxine *See* Roxana.

Royale Old French: the regal one. A feminine form of Roy.
Royal, Royall, Royalle.

Roz *See* Rosalind and Rosamond.

Roza/Rozia/Rozina *See* Rosa and Rose.

Rozalee/Rozalia/Rozalie *See* Rosalia.

Rozalin/Rozaline *See* Rosalind.

Rozamond *See* Rosamond.

Rozanda/Rozanna/Rozanne *See* Rosanna.

Rozaria/Rozario/Rozary *See* Rosario.

Roze/Rozea *See* Rose.

Rozeland *See* Roseland.

Rozella/Rozelle *See* Roselle.

Rozemary *See* Rosemary.

Rozen A Cornish form of Rose.

Rozena/Rozene *See* Rose.

Rozia/Rozina/Rozita *See* Rose.

Rozie/Rozy See Rose and Rosemary.

Rozlea/Rozlee/Rozlie *See* Rosalia.

Rozlin/Rozlind/Rozlinde *See* Rosalind.

Ruange Polynesian: a legendary figure.

Rubea/Rubette *See* Ruby.

Rubi/Rubia/Rubie/Rubina/Rubinia *See* Ruby.

Ruby Latin: a precious stone.
Rhubee, Rhubi, Rhubie, Rhuby, Rouba, Roubee, Roubey, Roubi, Roubia, Roubie, Rouby, Roubye, Ruba, Rubea, Rubeah, Rubetta, Rubette, Rubey, Rubi (Spanish), *Rubia, Rubie, Rubina, Rubinia, Rubye.*

Rudea/Rudee/Rudie *See* Rudolpha.

Rudelle Teutonic: the famous one.
Rudella.

Rudolpha Teutonic: the famous wolf. A feminine form of Rudolph.
Rodolfa, Rodolpha, Rudea, Rudee, Rudi, Rudia, Rudie, Rudolfa, Rudy.

Rue Old English from Greek: an aromatic medicinal plant. *See also* Ruth.
Rua, Rueina, Ruena.

Ruella A combination of Ruth and Ella.

Rufina Latin: red-haired. The

feminine form of Rufus.
Ruhia/Ruia Maori forms of Lucy.
Ruiha/Ruihia Maori forms of Louise.
Rukhsana/Ruksana *See* Roxana.
Rukmini Sanskrit: the wife of Lord Krishna. Often used in Indonesia.
Diminutives: Ruki, Ruksha, Ruky.
Rula Latin: a ruler. A popular Polish name.
Ruma A Sanskrit name of uncertain meaning.
Rumer English: a gypsy.
Ruma, Rumah.
Rumi Japanese: possibly meaning lapis lazuli.
Runa Old Norse: secret lore.
Rupa Sanskrit: like silver or like a statue.
Rupah, Rupal.
Rupali Sanskrit: beautiful.
Rupashi.
Ruperta/Rupertia *See* Roberta.
Ruri Japanese: an emerald.
Rusa/Rusah *See* Rusalka and Ruslana.
Rusalka Czech: a wood nymph. Russian/Slavic: a fairy or mermaid.
Rousalka, Rousalkah, Rusalkah, Ruzalka, Ruzalkah.
Diminutives: Rousa, Rousah, Rusa, Rusah, Ruza, Ruzah.
Ruslana An unusual Russian name.
Rouslana, Rouslanah, Ruslanah, Ruzlana, Ruzlanah.
Diminutives: Rousa, Rousah, Rusa, Rusah, Ruza, Ruzah.
Rut/Ruta *See* Ruth.
Ruth Hebrew: beautiful and compassionate. A biblical name.
Rut (German, Scandinavian), *Ruta, Rutha, Ruthe, Ruther, Rutu* (Maori).
Diminutives: Rue, Ruthie, Ruthy.
Ruth-Anne An unusual combination of Ruth and Anne (graceful).
Ruthann, Ruth-Ann, Ruthanne.
Ruya/Ruyah *See* Roya.
Ruza/Ruzah *See* Rusalka and Ruslana.
Ruzalka/Ruzalkah *See* Rusalka.
Ruzena *See* Rose.
Ruzlana/Ruzlanah *See* Ruslana.
Ryan Irish Gaelic: a little king. More commonly a boy's name.
Rhiain, Rhian, Rhiann, Rhianne, Rhiarne, Rhyan, Rhyann, Riahn, Riahnn, Rian, Riann, Rianne, Riany, Rien, Rion, Ryann, Ryanne, Ryen, Ryenne, Ryhan, Ryhann, Rhyanne, Ryon, Ryonn, Ryonne.
Ryba Slavic: a fish.
Rybah.
Rydah/Ryder *See* Rider.
Ryhan/Ryhann *See* Ryan.
Ryl/Ryll *See* Rhyll.
Rylee/Ryleigh/Rylie/Ryly *See* Riley.
Ryoko Japanese: a dragon.
Ryon/Ryonne *See* Ryan.
Ryszarda Slavic form of Ricarda.

Ryva/Ryvah *See* Riva.

S

Saacha/Saachi/Saasha *See* Sasha.
Saba *See* Sabah and Sabina.
Sabada/Sabas *See* Sabbathe.
Sabah Arabic: the morning.
Saba, Sabha.
Sabbathe Hebrew: born on the Sabbath.
Sabada, Sabas (Hebrew), *Sabata, Sabath, Sabbata, Sabbath, Sabbatha, Shabbat* (Hebrew).
Sabbia Italian: of the sand.
Sabella/Sabelle *See* Isabel.
Sabena/Sabene *See* Sabina.
Sabia Irish: the sweet one.
Sabih Arabic: pretty or graceful.
Sabeeh.
Sabiha *See* Sabiya.
Sabina Latin: a Sabine woman (from central Italy). The name of a saint.
Sabena, Sabene, Sabienne, Sabine (French), *Sabinella, Sabyna, Sabyne, Savina* (Russian).
Diminutives: Bina, Saba (Slavic).
Sabira Arabic: the patient one.
Sabirah.
Sabiya Arabic: of the morning.
Sabiha, Sabiyah.
Sable Middle English: black, or very dark.
Sabel, Sabelle.
Sabra Hebrew: a thorny cactus, or to rest.
Sabrah.
Sabrina Celtic: a legendary character, after whom the River Severn in Britain is named.
Sabreena, Sabrine, Sabrinna, Sabryna, Zabrina.
Sabyna/Sabyne *See* Sabina.
Sacha *See* Sasha.
Sachi Japanese: joy.
Sachiko Japanese: a joyful child.
Sada Japanese: the pure one.
Sadie Originally a diminutive of Sarah.
Sadye, Saidee, Saidy, Saidye, Zadee, Zadie, Zaidee.
Sadira Persian: a lotus.
Sadirah.
Sadwyn Welsh: the name for both Saturday and the planet Saturn.
Sadwynn, Sadwynne.
Safari Swahili: an adventurous expedition. Also a boy's name.
Safarri, Saffari, Saffarri.
Safed Hindi: white.
Safeda, Safedia.
Saffi Danish form of Sophie.
See also Saffron.
Saffir/Safira *See* Sapphira.
Saffron Arabic: the name of a spice.
Safron.
Diminutives: Saffi, Saffy.
Safia Arabic: the confidante, or the pure one.
Safina, Safiyya.
Safura Arabic: the wife of a Muslim

prophet.
Safuraa.
Saga Swedish: a Norse goddess.
Sagah.
Sagan After Françoise Sagan, the famous French novelist.
Sagann, Saganne.
Sagara Hindi: the ocean.
Sage Old French: wise. Also a 'herb name'.
Saige, Sayge.
Sagitta Latin: an arrow. Suitable for a girl born under the zodiac sign of Sagittarius, the archer.
Sagita, Sagitaria, Sagittaria.
Sahar Arabic: dawn.
Sahara Arabic: the name of a desert.
Sahira Sanskrit: a mountain.
Sahryn Possibly a form of Sarah.
Sahrin, Sahrinn, Sahrynn, Sarin, Sarrin, Sarryn, Saryn.
Saidee/Saidy *See* Sadie.
Sailor Middle English: one who sails. Also a boy's name.
Sailer, Sayla, Saylah, Sayler, Saylor.
Saima Arabic: a woman who fasts.
Saira/Sairah *See* Sarah.
Sakana Japanese: a little fish.
Sakara Native American: sweet.
Sakinah Arabic: God-inspired peace of mind.
Sakeena, Sakeenah, Sakina, Sakineh, Sikina, Sikinah.
Sakti *See* Shakti.
Sakuko A Japanese name of uncertain meaning.
Sakura Japanese: cherry blossom.
Salacia The wife of Neptune, god of the sea, in Roman mythology.
Diminutive: Sala.
Salama *See* Salima.
Salamina The name of a town in Greece.
Salena *See* Salina.
Salima Arabic: safe, secure. The feminine form of Salim.
Salama, Saleema, Salema, Salma, Salme, Selima, Selma, Selmah, Zelma, Zelmah.
Salina Latin: solemn.
Salena, Salini.
Sally Originally a diminutive of Sarah.
Sallee, Salli, Sallie, Sallye, Sali, Saly.
Diminutives: Sal, Sall.
Salma *See* Salima.
Salome Hebrew: peace. A biblical name.
Saloma, Salomea (Polish)*, Salomeh.*
Salote Polynesian: a lady.
Saloteh.
Salus The Roman goddess of health and wellbeing.
Salvadora Spanish: a feminine form of Salvador, meaning a saviour.
Salvadore, Salvatora, Salvatore, Salvatrea, Salvatria, Salvatrice, Salvatrise.
Salvia Latin: a 'plant name'.

Salvina.
Saly *See* Sally.
Sam A diminutive of Samantha and Samuela.
Samah Arabic: generosity or forgiveness.
Samaah.
Samaki Swahili: a fish.
Samakhi.
Samala *See* Samuela.
Samantha Aramaic: she who listens.
Semantha, Symantha.
Diminutives: Sam, Sammi, Sammie, Sammy.
Samara Hebrew: guarded by God.
Samar, Samaire.
Samaria Hebrew: a biblical placename.
Samedi French: Saturday.
Samella *See* Samuela.
Samina Arabic: happy, or happiness. Also a feminine form of Sam, meaning asked of God.
Sameena, Sameenah, Saminah, Samyna, Samynah.
Samira Arabic: one who entertains.
Sameera (Sanskrit), *Sameerah, Samirah, Zameera, Zameerah, Zamira, Zamirah.*
Samiya Sanskrit: incomparabale.
Samiyah.
Sammi/Sammie/Sammy Diminutives of Samantha and Samuela.
Samoa The name of a group of South Pacific islands.
Samuela Hebrew: asked of God. The feminine form of Samuel.
Samala, Samella, Samelle, Samuele, Samuella, Samuelle.
Diminutives: Sam, Sammi, Sammie, Sammy.
Samunda/Samundah
See Zamunda.
Samundra Nepali: the ocean or sea.
Sana Arabic: the radiant one.
Hebrew: a lily.
Sanaa, Sanah.
Sanam Arabic: a sweetheart.
Sancia Latin: sacred.
Sancha, Sanchia, Sancya.
Sandhya Sanskrit: dusk, or perfection.
Sandya, Sandyah.
Sandi/Sandie/Sandy Diminutives of Alexandra and Sandra.
Sandra A diminutive of Alexandra.
Sandrah, Sandria, Sandrine, Saundra, Sondra, Zandra.
Diminutives: Sandi, Sandie, Sandy.
Sangita Sanskrit: like music.
Sangeeta, Sangeetha, Sangitha, Sangitta.
Sangmu Sherpa/Tibetan: the kind-hearted one.
Sania Sanskrit: born on a Saturday.
Sanya.
Sanivara Sanskrit: Saturday.
Sanibar (Nepali), *Sanichar* (Urdu), *Saniva, Sanivar.*
Sanja Slavic: a dream.
Sanskrity An Indian name, from Sanskrit – the ancient classical language of India.

Santa Italian: the feminine form of Santo (of the saints).

Santina Italian/Spanish: saint-like. *Santinah, Santine, Santyna, Santyne.*

Sanura Swahili: cat-like. *Sanora, Sanurah.*

Saoirse Irish Gaelic: freedom.

Saori A Japanese name of uncertain meaning.

Sapata Native American: a dancing bear.

Sapna Sanskrit: a dream.

Sapphira Greek: deep blue. A 'gemstone name'. *See also* Zafira. *Saffir* (Welsh), *Saffira, Saffirah, Safira, Safirah, Saphira, Saphyra, Saphyre, Sapphire, Sephira, Sephirah.*

Sara *See* Sarah.

Sarafina/Saraphina *See* Seraphina.

Sarah Hebrew: a princess. The wife of Abraham and mother of Isaac in the Bible. *See also* Sarina. *Hera* (Maori), *Saira, Sairah, Sara* (Arabic, French, German), *Sarai, Saraid* (Irish Gaelic), *Sarena, Sarene, Saretta, Sarette, Sari, Saria, Sariah, Sarina, Sarine, Sarita, Saritia, Sarka* (Czech), *Sarra, Sarrah, Sharee, Shari, Sharie, Zara, Zarah, Zaria.* *Diminutives:* Sadie, Saidee, Saidy, Sal, Sallee, Sallie, Sally, Zadee, Zadie, Zaidee.

Sarahanna A combination of Sarah and Hannah (graceful). *Sarahana, Sarahannah, Saranna.*

Sarah-May A 'combination name'. *Sara Mae, Sara-Mae, Sara May, Sara-May, Sarah Mae, Sarah-Mae, Sarah May.*

Sarai/Saraid *See* Sarah.

Sarala Sanskrit: honest.

Sarasvati A Hindu water goddess. *Sarasvathi, Saraswati.*

Sarea A mythological angel.

Sarena/Sarene *See* Sarah and Sarina.

Saretta/Sarette *See* Sarah.

Sari Hindi: After the dress of Indian women. *See also* Sarah. *Sarie, Sary, Sarye.*

Saria/Sariah *See* Sarah.

Sarica/Sarika *See* Serica.

Saril Turkish: water that flows. *Sarila.*

Sarin *See* Sahryn.

Sarina Hebrew: a princess; a variation of Sara. Also the name of a town in north Queensland. *Sarena, Sarenah, Sarene, Sarinah, Sarine, Zarina, Zarinah, Zarine.*

Sarine/Sarita/Saritia *See* Sarah and Sarina.

Saringa *See* Sarnga.

Sarisha Sanskrit: charming.

Sarka Czech form of Sarah.

Sarmila/Sarmilla *See* Sharmila.

Sarna Sanskrit: religion. *Sarnah.*

Sarnga Hindi: an archer. *Saringa.*

Saroja Sanskrit: born in a lake.
Sarpa Nepali: a snake.
Sarra/Sarrah *See* Sarah.
Sarrin/Sarryn *See* Sahryn.
Sarwat An Arabic name of uncertain meaning.
Sary/Sarye *See* Sari.
Saryn *See* Sahryn.
Sasa/Sasi *See* Sasha.
Sasha A Russian diminutive of Alexandra.
Saacha, Saachi, Saasha, Saashi, Sacha (French), *Sasa, Sascha* (German), *Sashika, Sashka, Sasi.*
Saskia Dutch: a Saxon.
Sasona Hebrew: happy, or happiness.
Satarah Hebrew: a princess. Persian: a star.
Satara, Sataria.
Satine Middle English: a smooth silky fabric.
Satin, Satina, Satinah, Satinea.
Sato Japanese: sweet.
Satomi Japanese: wise and beautiful.
Satu Japanese: sugar, or a fairytale. Also a Finnish name of uncertain meaning.
Saturday Middle English: a 'day name'. After Saturn, the Roman god of agriculture and fertility.
Samedi (French), *Satordi* (Basque), *Satordie.*
Saturnia Latin: of Saturn, a Roman god.
Saturna, Saturne, Saturnia, Saturnina.

Satya Sanskrit: truth.
Satyana.
Saule The Baltic sun goddess.
Saul.
Saundra *See* Sandra.
Saura Hindi: one who worships the sun.
Saurah, Sora, Sorah.
Sauren/Saurenne *See* Soren.
Sausan An Arabic form of Susan and Susannah.
Savana Sanskrit: the Hindu month of July/August, corresponding to Leo. *See also* Savanna.
Savan, Savanah, Sawan, Sawana, Shravana, Sravana.
Savanna Spanish: from the grasslands or open plains.
Savaana, Savaanah, Savana, Savanah, Savannah, Zavanna.
Saviera *See* Xaviera.
Savina *See* Sabina.
Savitri Sanskrit: of the sun.
Diminutive: Savi.
Savoie A region of France.
Savoi, Savoy, Savoye.
Sawan/Sawana *See* Savanna.
Sawsan An Arabic form of Susan and Susannah.
Saxona Teutonic: a Saxon.
Saxonah, Saxonia.
Sayge *See* Sage.
Sayla/Saylor *See* Sailor.
Sayo Japanese: born during the night.
Sayoko.

Scarlett Old French: a 'colour name'. Made popular by the heroine of Margaret Mitchell's *Gone with the Wind*.
Scarlet, Scarlette.
Schaine/Schayne/Scheine
See Shane.
Schanee/Schaney/Schanie
See Sharney.
Schapelle A modern made-up name, utilising the feminine elle suffix. Alternatively from Shappa, a Native American name meaning red thunder.
Shapelle.
Schazia/Schaziah *See* Shazia.
Scheryl *See* Cheryl.
Scholastica Latin: the name of a 6th-century saint.
Schuyla/Schuyler/Schylar
See Skylar.
Scorpia Greek: from Scorpio, meaning a scorpion. A zodiac sign and a constellation (Scorpius).
Scorpio, Skorpia, Skorpio.
Scout Middle English: one who observes and reports.
Scoutt, Scoutte, Scowte.
Scylla A sea monster in Greek mythology.
Scyllah.
Sean *See* Shaun.
Seana/Seanna *See* Siana.
Season Latin: the time of sowing.
Sebastiana Latin: a woman from Sebasta. The feminine form of Sebastian.
Sebasta, Sebastia, Sebastianna, Sebastianne, Sebastienne (French).
Sebila *See* Sybil.
Seble African: born in autumn.
Sebnem Turkish: dew.
Secilia *See* Cecilia.
Secunda Latin: the second child.
Seconda.
Seda Spanish: silky.
Sedah.
Sedna Eskimo: the sea mother, the goddess of sea animals.
Seela/Seelah *See* Sela.
Seeta *See* Sita.
Segolene The French form of Sieglinde.
Segovia Spanish: the name of a town, and after the famous classical guitarist.
Seirian Welsh: sparkling.
Seiriol Welsh: the bright one.
Sekhmet The Ancient Egyptian lion-headed goddess of fire.
Seki Japanese: wonderful.
Sela Hebrew: a rock. An Old Testament placename.
Seela, Seelah, Selah.
Selby Old Norse: from the willow tree. Also a boy's name.
Selbee, Selbeigh, Selbey, Selbie.
Selda *See* Griselda.
Selena Greek: the goddess of the moon.
Celena, Celene, Celina, Celine, Celyn, Celyna, Celyne, Selene,

Selenia, Selina, Selinda, Selyna, Selyne, Zelena, Zelene.
Seleste *See* Celeste.
Selia *See* Cecilia.
Selina *See* Selena.
Selma A diminutive of Anselma. *See also* Salima.
Selmah, Zelma, Zelmah.
Sema Turkish: the sky.
Semah.
Semantha *See* Samantha.
Semele Greek: a figure from Greek mythology.
Semelia.
Semira Hebrew: the uppermost part of the heavens.
Semirah.
Sen Japanese: a fairy of the woods.
Senga Scottish Gaelic: the slender one.
Senja Finnish form of Xenia.
Senka Slavic: A shadow.
Seònaid Scottish Gaelic form of Joanne.
Seona, Shona.
Sephira/Sephirah *See* Sapphira.
September A 'month name'.
From the Latin word for seven (September was originally the seventh month).
Septembra (Swahili), *Setembra, Settembra.*
Septima Latin: the seventh-born.
Seqinek Eskimo: the sun goddess, representing summer and the light.
Sequoia Native American: a large coniferous tree. Also a boy's name.
Sequoya.
Sera Italian: the evening. Tibetan: hailstones. *See also* Seraphina.
Serah, Serale.
Serafima/Serafina/Serafine *See* Seraphina.
Serai Hindi: a place of rest and accommodation for travellers.
Serale Italian: of the evening.
Seraphina Hebrew: the ardent burning one. The Seraphim are an order of angels in the Bible.
Sarafina, Saraphina, Serafima (Russian), *Serafina* (Italian, Spanish), *Serafine, Seraphine* (French).
Diminutive: Sera.
Serbia A 'country name'.
Serbiah, Serbya, Serbyah.
Serena Latin: calm, serene. Welsh: a star. *See also* Serenity.
Cerena, Cerene, Cerenna, Cerina, Cerine, Sarene, Sarine, Serene, Serenna, Serina.
Serenity One who is serene. *See also* Serena.
Cerenitee, Cerenitie, Cerenity, Serenitee, Serenitie.
Sergeya The feminine form of Sergei (*see* Sergius).
Sergeia, Sergia, Sergeja.
Serica Latin: the silken one.
Sarica, Sarika, Serika.
Serilda Teutonic: the armoured battle maiden.

Serilde.
Serina *See* Serena.
Sesil An unusual Bulgarian name.
Seta Italian from Latin: silky.
Setah.
Setembra/Settembra *See* September.
Seto Nepali: white.
Setsuko Japanese: the child of melody.
Seven Middle English: an unusual 'number name'.
Severina Latin: the stern or severe one.
Séverine (French).
Sevil Turkish: the loved one.
Sevilla Spanish: the name of a city.
Seville.
Shaan *See* Sian.
Shabana Arabic: a queen.
Shabanna.
Shabbat *See* Sabbathe.
Shada Native American: a pelican.
Shade Middle English: comparative darkness. Also a boy's name.
Shady, Shadye, Shaida, Shaide, Shayda, Shayde.
Shae *See* Shay.
Shaelee/Shaeleigh/Shaelie *See* Shaylie.
Shaelen/Shaelinn/Shaelynne *See* Shaylen and Shay-Lynn.
Shafiqa Arabic: the feminine form of Shafiq, meaning compassionate.
Shahana Arabic: royal or magnificent.
Shahanara, Shahanna.
Shahar Arabic: born on a moonlit night.
Shahina Arabic: a falcon.
Shahira Arabic: famous.
Shahnaz Persian: the pride of the emperor.
Shahnaaz, Shahinaz, Shenaaz, Shenaz.
Shai/Shaie *See* Shay.
Shaiann/Shaianne *See* Cheyenne.
Shaida/Shaide *See* Shade.
Shaila Arabic: a burning candle.
Shailee/Shaileigh/Shailie *See* Shaylie.
Shailen *See* Shaylen.
Shain/Shaine *See* Shane.
Shaina Hebrew: beautiful.
Shainna, Shaney, Shayni, Shaynie, Shayna, Shaynna, Sheina, Sheinna.
Shaiza/Shaizia *See* Shazia.
Shaka Zulu: the founder. Also a boy's name.
Chaka, Chakka, Shakka.
Shakira Arabic: thankful.
Shakti Sanskrit: the powerful one.
Sakthi, Sakti.
Shakuntala Sanskrit: a bird.
Shalaila A modern, probably made-up name.
Shalailah.
Shaldan/Shaldon *See* Sheldon.
Shalee/Shalei/Shaleigh *See* Shaylie.
Shalini Sanskrit: modest.
Shamal Iraqi: the constant one.
Shamaila, Shamala, Shamalah, Shamali, Shamayla.

Shamarnie A modern made-up name, of uncertain meaning but possibly a variation of Sharney.
Shamarnee, Shamarney, Shamarni, Shamarny.

Shamarra Arabic: one who is ready for battle.
Shamara, Shamarah, Shamarrah, Shamra, Shamrah, Shanara, Shanarah, Shanarra, Shanarrah, Shanra, Shanrah.

Shamayla *See* Shamal.

Shameeka Arabic: high or lofty.
Shamika, Shamikh, Shamikha.

Shameena Sanskrit: beautiful.
Shameen, Shamin, Shamina.

Shamonee/Shamonie *See* Chamonix.

Shamra/Shamrah *See* Shamarra.

Shan/Shani *See* Sian.

Shana *See* Shannah.

Shanara/Shanarah *See* Shamarra.

Shanaya/Shanayah *See* Shania.

Shandelle A modern name, possibly a feminine form of Shane.
Shandel, Shandell.

Shane From Irish Gaelic: a variation of Sean (John), and so a form of Jane. *See also* Shaun and Shay.
Schain, Schaine, Schayn, Schayne, Schein, Scheine, Scheyn, Scheyn, Shain, Shaine, Shayn, Shayne, Sheyne.

Shaneen/Shanese/Shanessa *See* Shanice.

Shanel/Shanelle *See* Chanel.

Shanette Another 'Shane name'.
Shanett, Shanetta, Shannett, Shannetta, Shannette.

Shaney *See* Shaina.

Shani Hebrew: red. Swahili: wonderful. Also a form of Sian.
Shanee, Shanie, Sharney, Sharni, Sharnie.

Shania A name made popular by the Canadian country singer Shania Twain.
Shanaya, Shanayah, Shaniah.

Shanice Probably a form of Shane.
Shaneen, Shanese, Shanessa, Shanika, Shanike, Shanina, Shanine, Shaniqua, Shanique, Shanyce, Shanyna, Shanyne, Shanyse.

Shannae/Shannay *See* Shenay.

Shannah Irish Gaelic: from an old surname.
Shana, Shanna, Shannagh.

Shannele/Shannelle *See* Chanel.

Shannon Irish: the name of a river in Ireland. Also a boy's name.
Shannan, Shannen, Shannyn, Shanon, Shanyn.

Shanoa/Shanoah *See* Shonoa.

Shanra *See* Shamarra.

Shanta *See* Shanti.

Shantal/Shantel/Shantelle *See* **Chantal.**

Shantala Sanskrit: another name for the goddess Parvati.
Shantarla.

Shanti Sanskrit: the tranquil one.

Shanta, Shantha, Shanthi.
Shanyce/Shanyne/Shanyse
  See Shanice.
Shappa Native American: red thunder.
  Shappah.
Shara Aboriginal: salty water. *See also* Sharon.
  Sharra.
Sharan *See* Sharon.
Sharatan A star in the constellation of Aries.
  Sheratan.
Sharee/Shari/Sharie *See* Sarah.
Shareen/Shareena/Sharene *See* Cher.
Sharelle Probably derived from Cheryl.
  Sharel, Sharell.
Sharen/Sharenne *See* Sharon.
Sharifa Arabic: the honourable one. The feminine form of Sharif.
  Sharifah.
Sharina/Sharine/Sharini *See* Cher.
Sharis *See* Charis.
Sharland A modern name, probably from Charlotte.
  Sharlan.
Sharleen/Sharleine/Sharlene *See* Caroline.
Sharlie A variation of Charlie, a diminutive of Charlotte.
  Sharla, Sharlah, Sharlaine, Sharlee, Sharleigh, Sharley, Sharli, Sharly.
Sharlot/Sharlott/Sharlotte *See* Charlotte.
Sharmaine/Sharman/Sharmayne *See* Charmaine.
Sharmila Sanskrit: the protected one.
  Sarmila, Sarmilla, Sharmilla.
Sharnelle/Sharnielle *See* Sharney.
Sharney A modern name, probably from Shani or Sharon.
  Charnee, Charney, Charni, Charnie, Schanee, Schaney, Schani, Schanie, Sharna, Sharnae, Sharnah, Sharne, Sharnee, Sharnelle, Sharni, Sharnie, Sharnielle, Sharnye, Shiarna, Shiarne, Shiarney, Xarnee, Xarney, Xarni, Xarnie, Xarny, Zarnee, Zarney, Zarni, Zarnie, Zarny.
Sharon Hebrew: a flat plain; a biblical placename. *See also* Sharona.
  Charon, Charonn, Charonne, Charron, Shara, Sharan, Sharen, Sharenne, Sharona, Sharonda, Sharonne, Sharra, Sharran, Sharron, Sharryn, Sharryne, Sheron, Sherron.
  Diminutives: Sharna, Sharney, Sharni, Sharnie, Shaz, Shazza.
Sharona A form of Sharon.
  Charona, Cherona, Cheronne, Sharonah, Sharonna, Sharonne, Sherona, Sheronah, Sherone, Sherowna, Sherowne.
Sharra *See* Shara and Sharon.

Sharris *See* Charis.
Sharryn/Sharryne *See* Sharon.
Sharwynn a combination of Sharon and Wynn (fair or blessed).
Sharwin, Sharwinn, Sharwinne, Sharwyn, Sharwynne.
Shashi Hindi: a moonbeam.
Shaula Arabic: a tail. A star in the constellation of Scorpius, the scorpion.
Shaun A form of Sean. *See also* Jane and Shane.
Sean, Shauna, Shaunagh, Shaune, Shaunella, Shaunelle, Shaunya, Shawn, Shawna, Shawndella, Shawndelle, Shawnella, Shawnelle.
Shavaun/Shavon/Shavonne *See* Siobhán.
Shawn/Shawna/Shawnella *See* Shaun.
Shay Tibetan: crystal. Also a form of Shane. *See also* Shaylie.
Chae, Chay, Chaye, Shae, Shai, Shaie, Shaye, Shea.
Shayahn/Shayenne *See* Cheyenne.
Shayda/Shayde *See* Shade.
Shaylen A modern form of Shay.
Chaelen, Chayelen, Chaylen, Cheylen, Shaelen, Shailen, Shayelen, Sheylen.
Shaylie A form of Shay.
Shaelee, Shaeleigh, Shaeli, Shaelie, Shailee, Shailei, Shaileigh, Shaili, Shailie, Shalee, Shalei, Shaleigh, Shayla, Shaylah, Shaylee, Shaylei, Shayleigh, Shayli, Shaylie, Shealee, Shealei, Shealeigh, Sheali, Shealie.
Shay-Lynn A modern 'combination name'.
Shaelen, Shaelin, Shaelinn, Shaelynne, Shaylin, Shaylinn, Shaylynn, Shaylynne, Shayelin, Shayelinn, Shayelynn, Shayelynne, Shealin, Shealinn, Shealynn, Shealynne.
Shayn/Shayne *See* Shane.
Shayna/Shaynna *See* Shaina.
Shaynae *See* Shenay.
Shayni/Shaynie *See* Shaina.
Shazia Arabic: the precious or unique one.
Shaiza, Shaizia, Schazia, Schaziah, Shazi, Shaziah.
Shea *See* Shay.
Shealee/Shealeigh/Sheali *See* Shaylie.
Shealinn/Shealynn/Shealynne *See* Shay-Lynn.
Sheana *See* Sheena.
Sheba Greek: a woman of Sheba, an ancient Arabian country.
Sheehan Irish Gaelic: peaceful. Also a boy's name.
Sheeyan.
Sheela Sanskrit: of good character. *See also* Sheila.
Sheelah, Shila, Shilah.
Sheelagh/Sheelah *See* Sheela and Sheila.
Sheena Scottish Gaelic form of Jane.
Sheana, Sheenah, Shena, Shenah.
Sheenae/Sheenaye *See* Shenay.

Sheera *See* Shira.
Sheerin *See* Shirin.
Shefali A Sanskrit name of uncertain meaning.
Sheila Irish form of Cecilia.
Sheela, Sheelagh, Sheelah, Sheilah, Shela, Shelagh (Irish), *Shiela, Shielah, Síle* (Irish Gaelic), *Sìleas* (Scottish Gaelic).
Sheina/Sheinna *See* Shaina.
Sheirdan/Sheirden *See* Sheridan.
Shelby Old English: the dweller of the estate on the ledge. More commonly a boy's name.
Shelbee, Shelbeigh, Shelbey, Shelbi, Shelbie.
Sheldon Old English: from the steep valley.
Shaldan, Shaldon, Sheldan.
Shelley Old English: from the wood, or the meadow's edge. Also a diminutive of Michelle and Rachel.
Shell, Shellay, Shellee, Shelli, Shellie, Shelly.
Shenaaz/Shenaz *See* Shahnaz.
Shenaide/Shenayde *See* Sinéad.
Shenay A contemporary American name, of uncertain meaning.
Shannae, Shannay, Shaynae, Sheenae, Sheenaye, Shenae, Shenaye, Shennay, Shennaye, Shinae, Shynae.
Sheni Hebrew: Monday.
Shentel/Shentelle *See* Chantal.
Sher/Sheree *See* Cheryl.
Shera Aramaic: light. Sanskrit: a lion.
Sherae/Sheray *See* Cheray.
Sheralyn *See* Cherilyn.
Sheratan *See* Sharatan.
Sheraton An English surname, and the name of a famous chain of hotels.
Sheraz *See* Shiraz.
Shereen *See* Sherine.
Sheresa A combination of Sher and Teresa.
Shereesa, Shereeza, Shereza.
Sherica/Sherika *See* Cher.
Sheridan Irish Gaelic: the wild one.
Sheirdan, Sheirden, Sherida, Sheriden, Sheridyn.
Sherilyn *See* Cherilyn.
Sherin/Sheryn *See* Shirin.
Sherine A form of either Sher or Shirin.
Shereen, Shereene, Sheryne, Shireen, Shireene, Shirine, Shiryne.
Sherlee/Sherleen *See* Shirley.
Shermine A form of Sher.
Shermeen, Shermene.
Sheron/Sherron *See* Sharon.
Sherona/Sherone/Sherowna *See* Sharona.
Sherree *See* Cheryl.
Sherri/Sherrie/Sherry *See* Cher.
Sherril/Sheryl *See* Cheryl.
Sherrin/Sherryn *See* Shirin.
Sheryne *See* Sherine.
Shevat The eleventh lunar month of the Hebrew calendar, corresponding

to Aquarius.
Shevata.
Shevaun *See* Siobhán.
Sheyana/Sheyanna/Sheyanne
See Cheyenne.
Sheylen *See* Shaylen.
Sheyne *See* Shane.
Shiarna/Shiarne/Shiarney
See Sharney.
Shiba Tibetan: the month of April.
Shiela/Shielah *See* Sheila.
Shifra Hebrew: beauty and grace. A biblical name.
Shifrah, Shiphrah.
Shiho Japanese: to maintain the original intention.
Shika Japanese: a deer.
Shila *See* Sheela.
Shiloh Hebrew: a place of rest. A biblical name.
Shila, Shilah, Shilo, Shyla, Shylah, Shylo, Shyloh.
Shilpa Sanskrit: one who is perfectly created.
Shima Japanese: an island.
Shimona Hebrew: a little princess.
Shimrit A Hebrew name of uncertain meaning.
Shina Japanese: virtuous.
Shinae *See* Shenay.
Shine Middle English: a glow, or to excel.
Shyne.
Shiori Japanese: a bookmark.
Shira Hebrew: my song.
Sheera, Shirah, Shiri.

Shiralee Australian: a colloquial name for a bundle or burden.
Shirilee.
Shiraz A city in Iran, and a type of red wine.
Sheraz.
Shireen/Shirine/Shiryne
See Sherine.
Shiri *See* Shira.
Shirin Persian: charming.
Sheerin, Sherin, Sherrin, Sherryn, Sheryn, Shirrin.
Shirley Old English: from the bright meadow. Originally a boy's name.
Sherlee, Sherleen, Sherley, Shirlee, Shirleen, Shirlene, Shirlie, Shirly.
Diminutives: Sherl, Shirl.
Shirley-Anne A 'combination name'.
Shirley-Ann.
Shivali Sanskrit: beloved of Shiva, a Hindu god.
Shivani Sanskrit: another name for the goddess Parvati.
Shivaun *See* Siobhán.
Shizu Japanese: calm and peaceful.
Shobhana Sanskrit: the beautiful one.
Shoba, Shoban.
Shoko Japanese: an auspicious child.
Shouko.
Shona The name of a Southern African people. *See also* Joanne, Seònaid and Siôna.
Shondelle A modern name, possibly a form of Chantal.
Shondal, Shondall, Shondalle,

Shondel, Shondell, Shontal, Shontalia, Shontall, Shontalle, Shontel, Shontell, Shontelle.
Shonoa Probably a form of Shona.
Shanoa, Shanoah, Shonoah.
Shoshana Hebrew: a lily, or a rose. *See also* Susannah.
Shravana *See* Savana.
Shreya Sanskrit: beautiful.
Shri *See* Sri.
Shrishti Sanskrit: creation or evolution.
Shuang Chinese: bright and clear.
Shui Chinese: water.
Shukra Sanskrit: Friday. Also the Hindu name for the planet Venus. *Shukravara, Sukra, Sukravara.*
Shukriya Arabic: one who is grateful.
Shukria, Shukriyya.
Shula Arabic: a flame. Also a variation of Shulamit.
Shulamit Hebrew: peacefulness. An Old Testament name.
Shula, Shulamite, Shulamith, Shulammit.
Shumana Native American: possibly meaning the rattlesnake girl.
Shumanna.
Shusan/Shusann *See* Susan.
Shyamala Sanskrit: another name for the goddess Durga.
Shyama.
Shyla/Shylo *See* Shiloh.
Shynae *See* Shenay.
Shyne *See* Shine.

Sian Welsh form of Jane.
Shaan, Shan, Shani, Siân, Siani, Sjani, Sjanie.
Siana A modern name, possibly a variation of Siena.
Seana, Seanna, Sianna, Sianne, Sieanna.
Sibel/Sibella/Sibil *See* Sybil.
Sibele *See* Cybele.
Sibyl/Sibylla/Sibylle *See* Sybil.
Sidney Old English: from the riverside meadow. Old French: from St Denis.
Cidney, Cydney, Sidnee, Sidnei, Sidni, Sidnie, Sidny, Sydnee, Sydnei, Sydney, Sydnie, Sydny.
Sidonie Latin: a woman from Sidon, in modern-day Lebanon.
Cidonie, Sidonia, Sidony, Sydonia, Sydonie.
Sidra Latin: of the stars.
Sedra, Sedrah, Sidrah, Sidria.
Sieanna *See* Siana.
Sieglinde Old Norse: a name that is related to Signy.
Segolene (French), *Sieglind, Siglind, Siglinde, Sigolene* (French).
Sien Dutch: a diminutive of names such as Francina.
Sieneke.
Siena Italian: a city in Tuscany. *See also* Siana.
Sienah, Sienna, Siennah.
Sierra Latin: from the mountains.
Siera, Sierah, Sierrah.
Sieuwke/Sieuwki *See* Suki.

Sif A wife of Thor in Norse mythology who was famous for her long golden hair.

Siglind/Siglinde *See* Sieglinde.

Signy Old Norse: a new victory.
Signe, Signey, Signi.

Sigolene *See* Sieglinde.

Sigourney Old Norse: the conqueror.
Zigourney.

Sigrid Old Norse: a beautiful victory.
Sigrida, Sigrud, Zigrid, Zigrida.
Diminutives: Siiri, Siri.

Sigrun Old Norse: a secret victory.
Sigryn.

Siiri *See* Sigrid.

Sikina/Sikinah *See* Sakina.

Síle/Sileas *See* Cecilia and Sheila.

Silje Norwegian diminutive of Cecilia.

Silk Middle English: a fine fabric.
Silke, Silkey, Silkie, Silky, Sylk, Sylke, Sylkey, Sylkie, Sylky.

Silke German form of Cecilia. *See also* Silk.

Silla/Sillah *See* Cilla and Priscilla.

Silva/Silvana *See* Sylvia.

Silver Old English: the fair or silvery one.
Silvah.

Silvestra Latin: of the woods; the feminine form of Silvester. *See also* Sylvia.
Sylvestra.

Silvia/Silvianna/Silvie/Silvija *See* Sylvia.

Sima Aramaic: a little treasure.

Simba Swahili: a lion.

Simcha Hebrew: joy or happiness.

Simge Turkish: a symbol.

Simin Persian: silvery.

Simone Hebrew: the listener. The feminine form of Simon.
Samone, Simmone, Simona, Simonetta (Italian), *Simonette* (French), *Simonne, Symona, Symone, Symonne.*

Sina A moon goddess in Samoan mythology.

Sindhuja A Hindi name of uncertain meaning.

Sindy *See* Cindy.

Sinéad Irish Gaelic form of Janet.
Chenaid, Chenaide, Chenayd, Chenayde, Shenaid, Shenaide, Shenayd, Shenayde.

Sinope Greek: a satellite of the planet Jupiter.

Siobhán Irish Gaelic form of Jane and Judith.
Chavaun, Chavaune, Chevonne, Chivon, Chivonn, Chivonne, Shavaun, Shavaune, Shavon, Shavonne, Shevaun, Shivaun, Siubhan (Scottish Gaelic).

Sion *See* Zion.

Siôna Welsh: the feminine form of Siôn (John). Also a form of Joanne.

Sioned Welsh form of Janet.

Siran Armenian: alluring.
Siranouche.

Sirena Greek: a sea nymph. In mythology, the Sirens lured

mariners to their death through seductive singing.
Siren, Sirène (French), *Sirine, Syren, Syrena.*
Siri *See* Sigrid.
Siriani Possibly a form of Siri.
Syriani.
Sirikit Thai: the name of a queen.
Sirios Greek: a glowing star.
Sirkka Finnish: she who makes music.
Sirka.
Sisilia Fijian form of Cecilia.
Sisira Sanskrit: the Indian rainy season, lasting from mid-December to mid-February.
Sissey/Sissie/Sissy Diminutives of Cecilia.
Sistine The name of the Pope's chapel in the Vatican.
Sita Sanskrit: a furrow. The Hindu goddess of the harvest.
Seeta.
Sitara Sanskrit: a star.
Siùsan *See* Susannah.
Sivanah Hebrew: the ninth lunar month of the Jewish year, corresponding to the zodiac sign of Gemini.
Sivan, Sivana.
Sjani/Sjanie *See* Sian.
Sjonelina/Sjonia *See* Sonia.
Skade The wife of the sea god Njord in Norse mythology.
Skorpia/Skorpio *See* Scorpia.
Sky Middle English: the heavens.

See also Skye.
Skye Scottish: an island in the Inner Hebrides.
Sky, Zky, Zkye.
Skylar From a Dutch word for a scholar or schoolmaster. Also a boy's name.
Schuyla, Schuyler (Dutch), *Schylar, Schyler, Skuyla, Skuylar, Skyla, Skylah, Skyler, Skylor, Skyyla, Skyylah.*
Slaney Irish Gaelic: a placename, meaning a river.
Slany.
Slavena Slavic: glory.
Slavica Slavic: the feminine form of Slava.
Slava, Slavicaa, Slavika, Slavitza.
Sloan Irish Gaelic: a warrior. More often a boy's name.
Sloane.
Slobodanka Slavic: the feminine form of Slobodan, meaning freedom.
Smaragda Greek: probably from a word meaning a green gem.
Smaragdia.
Smiljana Slavic: a 'plant name'.
Snezana Croatian: a woman of the snow.
Snjezana.
Sobena Slavic: herself.
Sobota Czech/Polish: Saturday.
Soelae/Soelai/Soelay *See* Soleil.
Sofala An old mining town in New South Wales.

Sofalla.
Soffia/Sofia/Sofie/Sofya *See* Sophia.
Sofronia/Sofronie *See* Sophronia.
Soheila An Arabic/Persian name of uncertain meaning.
Sohaila, Sohayla, Soheyla.
Soila Finnish: a flame or a light.
Soile, Soili.
Solada Thai: one who listens.
Solana.
Solae/Solai/Solay *See* Soleil.
Solana Latin: the sun; generally a Spanish name. *See also* Solada.
Sol, Solina, Solita, Soluna.
Solange Latin: the solemn one. A French name.
Solangia.
Soledad Spanish: good health.
Soleil French: the sun.
Soelae, Soelai, Soelay, Solae, Solai, Solay.
Solema/Solemah *See* Solomona.
Solest Latin: of the sun.
Soleste.
Solidea An Italian name of uncertain meaning.
Solina/Solita *See* Solana.
Solomona A feminine form of Solomon, meaning wise and peaceful.
Solema, Solemah, Solomea, Solomeah, Solomia, Solomiah, Solomonah, Solomonia.
Solrun A Norwegian name derived from sol, meaning the sun.
Soluna *See* Solana.

Solveig Old Norse: from the strong house; generally a Norwegian name. The heroine of Henrik Ibsen's *Peer Gynt.*
Solvig (Swedish).
Soma Sanskrit: intoxicating. The Hindi name for the moon.
Somalia A 'country name'.
Somali, Somaliah, Somalie, Somaly, Somalya, Somalyah.
Somavara The Hindi name for Monday.
Soma, Somavar.
Somer/Sommer *See* Summer.
Sona Hindi: golden. *See also* Sonora.
Sonah, Sonal.
Sonali A contemporary name of uncertain meaning.
Sonalia.
Sonam Sherpa/Tibetan: the fortunate one. Also a boy's name.
Sonata Italian: a musical composition.
Sonnata.
Sonday/Sondi *See* Sunday.
Sondra *See* Sandra.
Song Old English: a musical composition. Also a Korean name.
Songe.
Sonia A form of Sophia.
Sjonelina, Sjonia, Sonia, Sonicka, Sonika, Soniya, Sonja (Scandinavian), *Sonje* (Scandinavian), *Sonnya, Sonya* (Russian).
Sonja/Sonje/Sonya *See* Sonia.

Sonnet English from French: a type of poem.
Sonet, Sonnett, Sonnette.
Sonnie/Sonny *See* Sunny.
Sonora English from Latin: a loud or resonant sound.
Sona, Sonah, Sonorah, Sonore, Sonoria.
Sonyla Probably a form of Sonya.
Sonylah.
Soo Korean: a long life.
Sophalia A modern form of Sophia.
Sophalie, Sophallia, Sophallie, Sophally, Sophaly.
Sophia Greek: wisdom. *See also* Sonia.
Saffi (Danish), *Sofea, Soffea, Soffia, Sofi* (Greek), *Sofia* (Norwegian, Swedish), *Sofie* (Danish, Dutch), *Sofina, Sofine, Sofya* (Russian), *Sophea, Sophee, Sophie, Sophina, Sophine, Sophy, Sopia, Te Paea* (Maori), *Zofia* (Polish), *Zofie* (Czech), *Zofja* (Slavic), *Zosia* (Polish).
Sophronia Greek: sensible.
Sofronia, Sofronie, Sophronie. Diminutives: Frona, Phrona.
Sora Native American: a songbird.
See also Saura.
Soraya Persian: seven stars.
Soraia, Soraja, Sorayah.
Sorcha Gaelic: brightness.
Sorka.
Sorella Italian: a sister.
Sorelle.

Soren Danish from Latin: the stern one. More commonly a boy's name.
Sauren, Saurenn, Saurenne, Sorin, Sorren, Sorrin.
Sorina Romanian: of the sun.
Sorana.
Sorkunde A Basque name of uncertain meaning.
Sorrel Old French: bitter. A 'plant name'.
Sorel, Sorell, Sorelle, Sorrell, Sorrelle.
Sosi/Sosie *See* Susan.
Sosina An African name of uncertain meaning.
Sotiria Greek: salvation.
Sotiriana.
Souad *See* Suad.
Soultana *See* Sultana.
Sousan/Sousanna/Sousanne *See* Susan and Susannah.
Souzana Persian: fire.
Souzan, Souzanah, Souzanna, Souzannah.
Speranza Italian form of Esperance.
Spring A 'season name'.
Sravana *See* Savana.
Sri Sanskrit: the Hindu goddess of prosperity.
Shri.
Stacey A diminutive of Anastasia and Eustacia. Also a boy's name.
Stacee, Staci, Stacia, Stacie, Stacy.
Staci/Stacia/Stacie *See* Stacey.
Stamatina Greek: one who stops.
Stamatia.

Stancie Probably a form of Stacey.
Stancee, Stancey, Stanci, Stancy.

Stanislava Slavic: the feminine form of Stanislaus, meaning the glorious government.
Stanislawa.
Diminutives: Stani, Stanka.

Star English: a star. *See also* Stella.
Starla, Starlia, Starlie, Starr, Starre.

Stavroula Greek: the feminine form of Stavros, the Greek version of Stephen (a crown or garland).

Stefanie/Stefenie/Steffany *See* Stephanie.

Steffi/Steffie/Steffy *See* Stephanie.

Stefka Slavic form of Stephanie.

Stella Latin: a star. *See also* Estelle, Esther and Star.
Steliana, Stellah, Stelle, Stelliana.

Stephanie Greek: a garland or crown. The feminine form of Stephen.
Estefani, Estefania (Spanish), *Estefanie, Estefany, Étienette* (French), *Stefanee, Stefani, Stefania* (Italian, Greek, Polish), *Stefanie, Stefenie, Steffanie, Steffany, Steffenie, Stefka* (Slavic), *Stepania, Stephana, Stephane, Stephani, Stephania, Stéphanie* (French), *Stephanine* (German), *Stephannie, Stephena, Stephenie, Stephne, Stephnee, Stephnie, Stevana, Stevania, Steveana, Steveanna, Stevena, Tapania* (Finnish).
Diminutives: Stef, Steffi (German), Steffie, Steffy, Steph, Stevi, Stevie.

Stevana/Steveana/Stevena *See* Stephanie.

Stevi/Stevie Diminutives of Stephanie.

Stina A diminutive of Christina.

Stockard An English surname. Also a boy's name.

Storey Old Norse: the large one. Also a boy's name.
Storee, Stori, Storie, Story.

Storm Old English: a tempest. Also a boy's name.
Storme.

Streda Czech: Wednesday.

Strella *See* Estelle.

Styliani Greek: the feminine form of Stylianos, meaning a pillar.
Styliana.

Su Turkish: water. Also a diminutive of Susan.

Suad Arabic: happiness.
Souad.

Suadela The Greek goddess of persuasion.

Suchin Thai: a wonderful thought.

Sue A diminutive of Susan and Susannah.

Suela *See* Consuela.

Suellen American: from Susan and Ellen.
Suelain, Suelaine, Su-Ellen, Sue-Ellen.

Suelly A modern form of Susan.

Suelley, Suelli, Suellie.
Suesan/Suesanna/Suesanne
  See Susan and Susannah.
Sugi Japanese: a cedar tree.
Suisana/Suisanna *See* Susannah.
Sujata Sanskrit: of noble birth.
Sujatmi Indonesian: a popular girl's name.
Suka Swahili: a woman with braided hair.
Sukari Swahili: as sweet as sugar.
  Sukarie, Zukari, Zukarie.
Suki Japanese: beloved. *See also* Susan.
  Sieuwke, Sieuwki, Sieuwkie, Sukey, Sukie.
Sukra/Sukravara *See* Shukra.
Sula Icelandic: the sun. Welsh: Sunday.
Sulakshana Sanskrit: one who is well brought up.
Sulema *See* Zulema.
Sulia Possibly a form of Julia.
  Sulea, Suleah, Suliah, Sulya, Sulyah.
Sultana Arabic: a queen or empress.
  Soultana.
Sumalee Thai: a beautiful flower.
Sumi Japanese: the refined one.
  Sumiko.
Summer Old English: a 'season name'.
  Somer, Sommer, Suma, Sumah, Sumer, Sumher, Summa, Summah, Summar, Zommer (German).
Sun Korean: goodness. Nepali: golden.
Suna Turkish: a cypress tree.
Sundar Hindi: beautiful.
Sunday Old English: a 'day name', literally meaning the day of the sun.
  Sonday, Sondi, Sundai, Sundaye, Sundi.
Sunee Thai: good.
Sunflower A yellow flower of the sun.
Sunita Sanskrit: of good conduct.
Sunna The Norse sun goddess, who rode a chariot drawn by two horses.
Sunniva Old English: the gift of the sun. The name of a saint.
  Suniva.
Sunny English: bright, cheerful.
  Sonnie, Sonny, Sunni, Sunnie.
Sunshine The brightness and radiance of the sun.
  Sunshyne.
Suntala Nepali: a tangerine.
Supriya Sanskrit: well loved.
Suraiya/Suraya *See* Surya.
Surata Sanskrit: bliss.
Suri Japanese: a princess. Persian: a red rose.
  Sury, Surye, Surie.
Suriani Possibly a form of Suri.
  Suryiani.
Surya Nepali: the sun. Sanskrit: a sun god.
  Suraya, Suria, Suriaya.
Susan Hebrew: a lily. *See also* Susannah.

Sausan (Arabic), *Sawsan* (Arabic), *Shusan, Shusann, Sousan, Suesan, Suse, Suska* (Slavic), *Sussan, Suzan, Suzen, Suzian, Suzien, Suzin*. *Diminutives:* Sosi, Sosie, Su, Sue, Sukey, Suki, Sukie, Suse, Susi, Susie, Susy, Suz, Suze, Suzie, Suzzie, Suzzy.

Susannah Hebrew: a lily. The original, biblical, form of Susan. *See also* Susan.
Huhana (Maori), *Sausan* (Arabic), *Sawsan* (Arabic), *Shoshana* (Hebrew), *Siùsan* (Scottish Gaelic), *Sousanna, Sousanne, Suesanna, Suesanne, Suisana, Suisanna, Susana* (Spanish), *Susanna, Susanne* (German), *Susette, Sussana, Suzana, Suzanna, Suzannah, Suzanne* (French), *Suzetta, Suzette* (French), *Suzsi, Zsusanna, Zsuzsanna, Zuzana* (Czech), *Zuzanna* (Latvian, Polish). *Diminutives:* Sanna, Su, Sue, Suse, Susi, Susie, Susy, Suzie, Suzzie, Suzzy, Xuxa (Brazilian), Zanna, Zsa Zsa (Hungarian), Zula (Polish), Zulya, Zuzu (Slavic).

Susette *See* Susannah.
Susheela Sanskrit: a woman of good character.
Sushila.
Susi/Susie/Susy Diminutives of Susan and Susannah.
Suska Slavic form of Susan.
Susmita Hindi: a pleasant smile.
Sushmita.
Sussan/Sussanna *See* Susan and Susannah.
Sutra Sanskrit: a Buddhist or Hindu teaching.
Suvla Turkish: a bay on the Gallipoli peninsula.
Suyin Chinese: the surname of well-known author Han Suyin.
Suz/Suzan/Suzen *See* Susan.
Suzanna/Suzannah/Suzanne *See* Susannah.
Suzetta/Suzette/Suzsi *See* Susannah.
Suzian/Suzie/Suzien *See* Susan and Susannah.
Suzu Japanese: a little bell.
Suzuki.
Suzuko Japanese: born in autumn.
Suzzie/Suzzy Diminutives of Susan.
Svana/Svanhild *See* Swanhild.
Svea Swedish: a woman of Sweden.
Svetlana Slavic: of the light. Generally a Russian name.
Sveta (Slavic), *Svetla* (Czech), *Tsvetana, Tsvetlana*.
Diminutive: Lana.
Sveva An Italian name of uncertain meaning.
Swan Old English: a 'bird name'.
Swann, Swanne.
Swanhild Teutonic: a swan of battle.
Svana (Icelandic), *Svanhild, Swanhilda, Swanhilde*.
Swati Sanskrit: a star.
Sweeney Irish Gaelic: the little hero.

Sweeny.
Sybele/Sybeli *See* Cybele.
Sybil Greek: the prophetess. A name from Greek mythology.
Cybil, Cybill, Cybilla, Cybille, Sebila, Sibel, Sibele, Sibella, Sibelle, Sibil, Sibilla, Sibille, Sibyl, Sibylla, Sibylle (German), *Sybel, Sybeli, Sybella, Sybelle, Sybelli, Sybilla, Sybille* (French), *Syble.*
Diminutives: Libby, Sib, Syb.
Syda An African name of uncertain meaning.
Sydnee/Sydney/Sydnie/Sydny *See* Sidney.
Sydonia/Sydonie *See* Sidonie.
Sylke/Sylkey/Sylkie *See* Silk.
Sylla/Syllah *See* Cilla.
Sylph Greek: a spirit of the air and the protector of young maidens, sometimes appearing as a butterfly.
Sylvestra *See* Silvestra.
Sylvette/Sylvie *See* Sylvia.
Sylvia Latin: from the forest. *See also* Silvestra.
Silva, Silvana (Italian), *Silvi, Silvia, Silviana, Silviane, Silvianna, Silvie, Silvija, Silvy, Sylva, Sylvana, Sylvania, Sylvanna, Sylve, Sylvette, Sylvian, Sylviana, Sylviane, Sylvianna, Sylvie* (French).
Symantha *See* Samantha.
Symona/Symone/Symonne *See* Simone.

Syna Greek: together.
Syntyche Greek: a name from the New Testament.
Syon *See* Zion.
Syreeta/Syreta *See* Cyreta.
Syren/Syrena *See* Sirena.
Syria Aramaic: a Middle Eastern country.
Syriani *See* Siriani.
Syrinx A mythological Greek nymph.

T

Taal Nepali: a lake.
Tal.
Tabea German form of Tabitha.
Tabeta *See* Tabitha and Teveta.
Tabitha Aramaic: a doe or gazelle. A biblical name. *See also* Dorcas.
Tabatha, Tabea (German), *Tabeta, Tabetha.*
Tabla Sanskrit: a small drum.
Tacey/Tacye *See* Tacita.
Tacha A diminutive of Natasha.
Tacita Latin: silent or peaceful.
Tacey, Tacitah, Tacye.
Tadja/Tadji *See* Taja.
Taesha/Taeshea/Taeshia *See* Taysha.
Tahanee/Tahani *See* Tahni.
Taheisha A variation of Takeisha.
Taheesha, Tahesha, Tahiesha, Tahisha.

Tahila *See* Talia.
Tahira Arabic: pure and virtuous.
Tahiti Polynesian: sunrise. A 'country name'.
Tahj/Tahja/Tahjee *See* Taja.
Tahlea/Tahli/Tahlia *See* Talia.
Tahni A modern name, probably derived from Tanya.
Tahanee, Tahani, Tahanie, Tahnee, Tahnie.
Tahnia/Tahnya *See* Tanya and Tatyana.
Tahshi *See* Tashi.
Tahuri Maori: to start.
Tai Polynesian: the ocean.
Ty, Tye.
Taia *See* Tia.
Tailah/Tailer/Tailor *See* Taylor.
Tailee/Tailei/Tailie *See* Taylee.
Tailin/Tailyn/Tailynne *See* Taylin.
Taimana Maori: a diamond.
Tain Native American: the new moon.
Taine, Tayn, Tayne.
Tais *See* Thais.
Taisiya A Russian name of uncertain meaning.
Tait/Taite *See* Tate.
Taiwo Nigerian: the firstborn twin.
Taja Hindi: a crown, or the crowned one.
Tadja, Tadji, Tahj, Tahja, Tahjee, Tahji, Taj, Tajah, Tajee, Taji.
Taka Japanese: tall, or honourable. Polynesian: a name from legend.
Takala *See* Takia.
Takara Japanese: a treasure.

Takeisha A modern American 'Ta name', a variation of Keisha.
Takeesha, Takesha, Takiesha, Takisha.
Takenya Native American: a falcon.
Takenia.
Taki Japanese: a waterfall.
Takia Arabic: possibly meaning a worshipper.
Takala, Takalia, Takaliah, Takeiah, Takeya, Takeyah, Takiah, T'Keyah.
Tal *See* Taal.
Tala German: from the valley. Native American: a wolf. Persian: golden.
Talah, Talla, Tallah.
Talaine A 'Ta name', possibly from Elaine.
Talaina, Talayna, Talayne, Telaina, Telaine, Telayna, Telayne, Tilaina, Tilaine, Tilayna, Tilayne.
Talara *See* Tallara.
Talata Arabic: born on a Tuesday. Also a boy's name.
Talatah.
Taldra Aboriginal: a kangaroo.
Taldrah.
Tale African: green.
Taleisha Contemporary American: possibly from Aisha (life).
Taleesha, Taleeshia, Talisa, Talisha, Talishia, Talissa.
Talena Another modern 'Ta name', possibly from Lena.
Taleena, Taleenah, Taleene,

Talenah, Talene, Talina, Talinah, Taline.
Talia Aboriginal: near water. Greek: flourishing. Hebrew: dew. Russian: a diminutive of Natalya (*see also* Talya).
Tahila, Tahlea, Tahleah, Tahlee, Tahli, Tahlia, Taleah, Talei, Taleigha, Taleya, Tali, Taliah, Talli, Tallie, Tarlia, Thalia.
Talika Sanskrit: a bird.
Talikah.
Talina/Talinah/Taline *See* Talena.
Talitha Aramaic: a little girl or maiden. A biblical name.
Taletha, Talhetha, Talhitha, Talita.
Talla *See* Tala.
Tallara Aboriginal: rain.
Talara.
Talli/Tallie *See* Talia.
Tallulah Native American: running water.
Talloulah, Talula, Tollula, Tollulah, Tolula, Tolulah.
Talma Hebrew: a small hill.
Talmah.
Talor *See* Taylor.
Talulla Irish Gaelic: a prosperous lady.
Taluta Native American: red.
Talutah.
Talwyn Cornish: a fair brow.
Talwynn, Talwynne.
Talya Hebrew: a lamb. Russian: a diminutive of Natalya.
Talia, Taliah, Taliana, Talyah,
Talyana.
Tam Vietnamese: of the heart.
See also Tamara and Tamsin.
Tama Japanese: a jewel.
Tamae *See* Tamara.
Tamahine Maori: a girl or a daughter.
Tamala/Tamalla *See* Tamela.
Tamami Japanese: a beautiful jewel.
Tamantha Possibly a variation of Samantha, meaning she who listens.
Tymantha.
Tamar Jewish form of Tamara.
Tamara Hebrew: a palm tree. A popular name in Germany and Russia.
Tamae, Tamar (Jewish), *Tamarah, Tamarra, Tamarrah, Tamaya, Tamayah, Tameea, Tameeah, Tamina, Taminah, Tamira, Tamirah, Tamora, Tamorah, Tamra, Tamrah, Tamryn.*
Diminutives: Mara, Tam, Tammi, Tammie, Tammy.
Tamarine An unusual name from Thailand.
Tamarin, Tammarin, Tammarine.
Tamasin/Tamasina/Tamasine *See* Tamsin and Thomasina.
Tamaya/Tamayah *See* Tamara.
Tamba Aboriginal: an ibis.
Tamee/Tami *See* Tammy.
Tameea/Tamina *See* Tamara.
Tameka Hebrew: a twin. A feminine form of Thomas. *See also* Tamsin.

Tameika, Tameikah, Tamekah, Tamika, Tamikah, Tomeika, Tomeikah.
Tamela Probably a combination of Tamara and Pamela.
Tamala, Tamalla, Tameela, Tameila, Tamelia, Tamella.
Tamiko Japanese: a child of the people.
Tamima Arabic: the femimine form of Tamim, meaning solid or well formed.
Tameema, Tameemah, Tamimah.
Tamira/Tamirah *See* Tamara.
Tammiku Finnish: January.
Tamiku.
Tammin/Tammyn *See* Tamsin.
Tammuza From Tammuz, the fourth lunar month of the Hebrew calendar, which corresponds to Cancer.
Tammy A diminutive of names such as Tamara and Tamsin.
Tamee, Tami, Tammee, Tammi, Tammie.
Tamora *See* Tamara.
Tamra/Tamrah/Tamryn *See* Tamara.
Tamsin Cornish: a feminine form of Thomas. *See also* Tameka and Thomasina.
Tamasin, Tammin, Tammyn, Tamsen, Tamsene, Tamsine, Tamsyn, Tamsyne, Tamzen, Tamzin, Tamzine.
Diminutives: Tam, Tammi, Tammie, Tammy.
Tamzen/Tamzin/Tamzine *See* Tamsin.
Tan *See* Thanh.
Tana/Tanah *See* Tanna.
Tanaka An unusual name from Zimbabwe, possibly meaning blessed.
Tandy A modern name, possibly a diminutive of Andrew (strong and manly).
Tandee, Tandey, Tandi, Tandie.
Taneal/Tanealle *See* Tennille.
Tanedra A modern 'Tan name', probably from Tanya. Tanedra Howard is an American actress.
Tanedrah, Tanidra, Tanidrah.
Taneisha/Tanesha *See* Tanisha.
Taneka Another modern American 'Tan name'.
Taneeka, Tanika, Tanike, Teneeka, Teneka, Teneke, Tineeka, Tineka, Tineke, Tinika, Tinike.
Tangelo An orange-coloured fruit.
Tangello.
Tangerine English: an orange-coloured fruit, or a woman from Tangier (Morocco).
Tangeryne, Tanjerine, Tanjeryne.
Tangiwai Maori: a type of green-stone.
Tango Spanish: a dance. Tibetan: the first; the name for January.
Tangoe.
Tani Japanese: from the valley.
Taniko.

Tania *See* Tanya, Tatyana and Titania.

Tanidra/Tanidrah *See* Tanedra.

Taniel A form of Tania or perhaps a variation of Danielle, meaning God is my judge.
Taniele, Tanielle.

Tanisha African: born on a Monday.
Taneisha, Tanesha, Tanissa, Tanisse, Tannissa, Tannisse, Tanissha, Teneisha, Tenisha, Tynisha.

Tanith The Phoenician goddess of love, the equivalent of the Roman goddess Venus.
Tanitha, Tanithe.

Tanja *See* Tanya and Tatyana.

Tanjerine *See* Tangerine.

Tanna Aramaic: a teacher.
Tana, Tanah, Tannah.

Tansy Greek: immortal. A 'flower name'.
Tansee, Tansey, Tansi, Tansie, Tansin, Tansyn, Tanzey, Tanzie, Tanzin, Tanzy.

Tanya Russian: a diminutive of Tatyana. *See also* Titania.
Tahnia, Tahnya, Tania, Tanja (German), Tarnia, Tarnya.

Tanzey/Tanzie/Tanzin/Tanzy *See* Tansy.

Tao Chinese: long life.

Tapairo Polynesian: a legendary figure.

Tapania Finnish form of Stephanie.

Tapora Maori: a New Zealand placename.

Tara Irish Gaelic: a rocky hill, from the ancient home of Ireland's kings. Polynesian: a sea goddess. Sanskrit: a star; the name of a Buddhist goddess. *See also* Tarin.
Tarah, Tarra, Tarrah.

Tarah Hebrew: an Old Testament placename. *See also* Tara.

Taraka A figure in Hindu mythology.

Tarama An unusual name that may be derived from Tara.

Taran *See* Tarin.

Tarana Aboriginal: a large waterhole. Arabic: a melody or song.

Taranga Polynesian: a figure from legend.

Taranna Aboriginal: a wallaby.
Tarana.

Tarati Maori form of Dorothy.

Tarcisia Italian: the feminine form of Tarcisio.
Tarchisia, Tarchizia, Tarcizia.

Tarcoola Aboriginal: a bend in the river.

Taren *See* Tarin.

Tarika Hindi: a star
Tareka.

Tarin A modern name, probably a form of Tara.
Taran, Taren, Tarran, Tarren, Tarrin, Tarryn, Tarrynn, Taryn, Taryna, Tarynn.

Tarita A Polynesian name of uncertain meaning.

Tarja Finnish form of Daria.

Tarna A name from *The Wheel of Time* series of fantasy novels.
Tarnah.

Tarni Aboriginal: the surf.
Tarnee, Tarnie.

Tarnia/Tarnya *See* Tanya.

Tarniqa A modern name, possibly a form of Tarna or Tarni.
Tarneka, Tarneke, Tarneqa, Tarnequa, Tarneque, Tarnika, Tarnike, Tarniqua, Tarnique.

Taronga Aboriginal: a beautiful view.

Tarra Aboriginal: a creek. *See also* Tara.
Tarrah.

Tarran/Tarrin/Tarrynn/Taryn *See* Tarin.

Tarsha *See* Tasha.

Tasanee Thai: wonderful.

Tasaria Gypsy: born in the morning.
Tasara, Tasarla, Tassaria.

Tasha A diminutive of Natasha. *See also* Tashana and Taysha.
Taasha, Tarsha, Tasa, Tashia, Taska, Taysha.

Tashana Probably a form of Tasha.
Tashanah, Tashanna, Tashannah, Tasharna.

Tashi Sherpa/Tibetan: prosperity. Also a boy's name.
Tahshi.

Tasia *See* Taysha.

Tasida Native American: one who rides horses.
Tasidah.

Taska *See* Tasha.

Tasma The feminine version of Tasman, a name derived from Tasmania and the explorer Abel Tasman.
Tasmah, Tasman, Tasmin, Tasmyn, Tazma, Tazmah, Tazman, Tazmin, Tazmyn.

Tasnim Arabic: a spring in paradise.
Tasneem.

Tasoula Greek diminutive of Anastasia.

Tassaria *See* Tasaria.

Tatania *See* Tatyana.

Tate Old Norse: cheerful. Also a diminutive of Tatum.
Tait, Taite, Tayt, Tayte.

Tathiana/Tatia/Tatiana *See* Tatyana.

Tathra Aboriginal: beautiful country.

Tatienne/Tatjana *See* Tatyana.

Tatum Old English: from Tate's homestead. Also a boy's name.
Tatom.
Diminutive: Tate.

Tatya Aboriginal: a goanna.

Tatyana Latin: silver-haired. A popular Russian name. *See also* Tanya.
Tatania, Tathiana (Italian), *Tatia, Tatiana, Tatianna, Tatienne* (French), *Tatjana, Tatjanna, Tatyanna, Tetiana* (Russian), *Tetianna.*
Diminutives: Tahnia, Tahnya, Tania, Tanja (German), Tanya.

Taura Greek: a bull. A suitable name for a girl born under the zodiac sign of Taurus.
Taurah, Taurea, Tauria, Tauriah, Taurine, Taurua.

Tautiti Polynesian: a graceful dancer.

Tavake Polynesian: a daughter in legend.

Tavia *See* Octavia.

Tawny Old French: with yellowish-brown hair.
Tawna, Tawnee, Tawney, Tawni, Tawnie.

Taya/Tayah *See* Tia.

Tayanita Native American: a young beaver.
Tayana, Tayanah.

Taylee A modern name, probably from Taylor.
Tailee, Tailei, Taileigh, Tailie, Taylei, Tayleigh, Taylie.

Taylin A combination of Taylor and Lin.
Tailin, Tailinn, Tailyn, Tailynn, Tailynne, Taylinn, Taylyn, Taylynn, Tailynne.

Taylor Old French: a tailor.
Tailah, Tailer, Tailor, Talor, Tayla, Taylah, Tayleh, Tayler.

Tayn/Tayne *See* Tain.

Taysha Possibly a form of Tasha.
Taesha, Taeshea, Taeshia, Tasia, Tayisha, Tayissa, Taysha, Tayshea, Tayshia.

Tayte *See* Tate.

Tazma/Tazman/Tazmyn *See* Tasma.

Tazu Japanese: a stork; implying one who is long-lived.

Tcharli/Tcharlie *See* Charlie.

Tea *See* Tia.

Teagan/Teaghan *See* Tegan and Tegen.

Teague Irish Gaelic: a philosopher or poet. Generally a boy's name.
Teag, Teage, Teigue.

Téah *See* Tia.

Teal English: a waterbird.
Teale.

Tean Cornish: one of the Isles of Scilly, off the coast of Cornwall.
Variation: Tehan.

Teanna/Teannah *See* Tianna.

Tearra *See* Tiara.

Te Atawhai Maori: to look after.

Te Awatea Maori: the dawning.

Teena/Teenah *See* Tina.

Teesha *See* Ticia.

Tega Probably a form of Tegan.
Tegah.

Tegan Welsh: of doe-like beauty.
Teagan, Teaghan, Teigan, Teigen, Teighan, Tigan.

Tegen Cornish: a pretty little thing.
Teagan.

Tegwen Welsh: beautiful and blessed.

Tehya *See* Tia.

Teigra *See* Tigra.

Teija Finnish diminutive of Dorothy.

Teina Maori: the youngest.

Teisha *See* Ticia.

Tekiya A modern name, popular in the USA
Tekeya, Tekeyah, Tekiyah, T'Keya, T'Keyah, T'Kiya, T'Kiyah.

Tekla *See* Thecla.

Telaina/Telaine/Telayne
See Talaine.

Tellus The Roman equivalent of Gaia, the Greek earth goddess. *See also* Terra.

Telma *See* Thelma.

Telopea A genus of Australian plants, better known as waratahs.
Telopia.

Temepara A Maori name of uncertain meaning.

Temima Arabic: honest.

Te Mira Polynesian: a flour miller.

Temora The name of a New South Wales town.
Temorah.

Temperance Latin: one who is moderate.

Tempest Old French: stormy.
Tempesta, Tempeste, Tempestt, Tempestte.

Tenaya Native American: the name of a chief.
Tenai, Tenaia, Tenayah, Teniya, Teniyah.

Tenee Possibly a form of Tennille.
Tenie, Tennee, Tennie, Tenny, Teny.

Teneeka/Teneka/Teneke
See Taneka.

Teneisha/Tenisha *See* Tanisha.

Tenley A modern name, probably from an English surname.
Tenlea, Tenlee, Tenleigh, Tenli, Tenlie, Tenly.

Tennessee The name of a US state. Also a boy's name.
Tenessee, Tennesee.

Tennille A city in Georgia, the USA. Can also by a boy's name.
Taneal, Taneale, Tanealle, Teneal, Teneale, Teneel, Teneele, Tenielle, Tenille, Tenneal, Tennealle, Tenneel, Tenneele, Tenniel, Tennielle.

Tenny/Teny *See* Tenee.

Teodora *See* Theodora.

Teofilia *See* Theophilia.

Te Paea Maori form of Sophia.

Tepora/Tepore Maori forms of Deborah.

Te Puna Maori: the spring.

Tera Japanese: a temple.

Tereasa/Terease *See* Teresa.

Tereca *See* Terencia.

Terehia Maori form of Teresa.

Terencia Latin: smooth and polished. A feminine form of Terence.
Tereca, Terecia, Terentia, Terenzia, Terica, Terina, Terreca, Terrencia, Terrentia, Terrenzia, Terrina, Terryna, Teryna.

Teresa Greek: the harvester or reaper.
Tereasa, Terease, Terehia (Maori), *Terese, Teresia, Teresina* (Italian), *Teresinha* (Portuguese), *Teresita*

(Spanish), *Teressa, Teressae, Teressah, Tereza* (Breton), *Terezia* (Hungarian), *Terezinha* (Portuguese), *Terezon* (French), *Tersina, Theresa, Therese, Theresia* (German), *Treasa* (Irish Gaelic), *Tresiana, Tressa, Treza.*
Diminutives: Reza (Slavic), Rezia (Hungarian), Teresita (Spanish), Teri, Terri, Terry, Teschia, Teshia, Tess, Tessa, Tessie, Tree.

Tereza/Terezia/Terezinha/ Terezon *See* Teresa.

Teri A diminutive of Teresa.

Terica/Terina *See* Terencia.

Teril/Terill *See* Terryl.

Terra Latin: of the earth. The Roman equivalent of Gaia, the Greek earth goddess.
Terrah, Terre, Terria, Terryn, Teryn, Tierra (Spanish).

Terreca/Terrencia/Terrentia/ Terrenzia *See* Terencia.

Terri/Terry Diminutives of Teresa.

Terrie-Marie A combination of Teresa and Marie (star of the sea).
Teri-Marie, Terri-Marie, Terry-Marie.

Terrina *See* Terencia.

Terryl A modern name, probably from Terri or Terry.
Teril, Terill, Terille, Terril, Terrill, Terrille, Terryle, Teryl, Teryle, Tyrel, Tyrell, Tyrelle.

Terryna/Teryna *See* Terencia.

Tersina *See* Teresa.

Tertia Latin: the third child.
Tersha, Tertiah, Terza, Terzah, Terzia.

Teryl/Teryle *See* Terryl.

Teryn *See* Terra.

Terza *See* Tertia and Thirza.

Teschia/Teshia Diminutives of Teresa.

Tesha *See* Ticia.

Teslyn A name from *The Wheel of Time* series of fantasy novels.
Teslin, Teslinn, Teslinne, Teslynn, Teslynne.

Tess/Tessa/Tessie Diminutives of Teresa.

Tessabelle A modern combination of Tessa and Belle (beautiful).
Tessabel, Tessabell.

Tethys Greek: a figure in mythology and a satellite of the planet Saturn.

Tetiana A Russia form of Tatyana.

Tetsu Japanese: like iron.

Teveta From Tevet, the tenth lunar month of the Hebrew calendar, corresponding to the zodiac sign of Capricorn.
Tabeta (Babylonian).

Tewesday/Tewsday *See* Tuesday.

Teya/Teyah *See* Tia.

Teyana/Teyanna *See* Tianna.

Tezzhan An unusual Bulgarian name.
Tezan, Tezann, Tezhan, Tezhann, Tezzhann.

Thaddea Greek: courageous.
Thada, Thadda, Thadine.

Thais Greek: one who is bound.
Tais.

Thaisa A character in Shakespeare's *Pericles*. Of uncertain meaning.

Thala Aboriginal: a bee.

Thalassa Greek: from the sea.

Thalia *See* Talia.

Thalma *See* Thelma.

Thana Arabic: gratitude.

Thandi Zimbabwean: the beloved one.
Thandie, Thandiwe.

Thanh Vietnamese: brilliant.
Tan.

Thao Vietnamese: one who respects her parents.

Tharah Aboriginal: the wind, or thunder.
Thara.

Thea Greek: a goddess. Also a diminutive of Alethea, Althea, Anthea, Dorothy, Theodora and Timothea.
Thia.

Theano Greek: a divine name.
Theana.

Thecla Greek: the glory of God.
Tecla, Tekla (Scandinavian), *Thekla*.

Theda Teutonic: of the people. *See also* Theodora.

Theftera Greek: Monday, or born on a Monday.

Thella A character from the *Dragonriders of Pern* fantasy novels by Anne McCaffrey.

Thelma Greek: a wish, or will.
Telma, Thalma, Thelmae.

Themis Greek: the goddess of justice and order in mythology.
Themys.

Theodelinda/Theodelynda *See* Theolinda.

Theodora Greek: the gift of God; the feminine form of Theodore. *See also* Dora and Dorothy. *Fedora* (Russian), *Feodora* (Russian), *Teodora* (Italian, Polish, Spanish), *Theadora, Theodor, Theodore, Theodra* (Greek). *Diminutives:* Dora, Thea, Theda, Theo.

Theodosia Greek: God-given.

Theolinda A combination of Theo (*see* Theodora) and Linda.
Theodelinda, Theodelynda, Theolynda.

Theonie From Theo; *see* Theodora.
Theona, Theone, Theonee, Theoni.

Theophania Greek: a manifestation of God. A suitable name for a girl born on 6 January, the Epiphany. *See also* Epiphany and Tiffany. *Théophanie* (French), *Tifaine* (French), *Tiffany, Tiphaine, Tiphanee, Tiphani, Tiphanie*. *Diminutives:* Tiff, Tiffi, Tiffy.

Theophilia Greek: divinely loved.
Teofilia, Theofila, Theophila.

Theora Greek: a thinker or watcher.

Thera Greek: wild. From the name of an island.

Theresa/Therese/Theresia
See Teresa.
Theta Greek: eight, or the eighth.
Thetis Greek: positive or determined. A sea nymph in mythology.
Thetys.
Thia *See* Thea.
Thilani An unusual name from Sri Lanka.
Thira *See* Thyra.
Thirza Hebrew: pleasant.
Terza, Thirzah, Thirtza, Thyrza, Tirtza, Tirza, Tirzah.
Thistle Middle English: a 'plant name'.
Thystle.
Thomasina Greek: a twin. The feminine form of Thomas. *See also* Tamsin.
Tamasina, Tamasine, Thomasa, Thomasena, Thomasin, Thomasine, Tomasa, Tomase, Tomasena, Tomasina, Tomasine, Tomisina, Tommasina.
Diminutives: Tommi, Tommie, Tommy.
Thora Old Norse: thunder. A feminine form of Thor.
Thoria, Tora.
Thorberta Old Norse: the brilliance of Thor.
Thordis Old Norse: the spirit of Thor.
Thordia, Thordys.
Thula *See* Tula.
Thursday Middle English: literally the day of Thor. A 'day name'.
Thyra Greek: a shield-bearer.
Thira.
Tia A popular contemporary name; probably a diminutive of Tianna and Tiara. Maori: the abdomen.
Taia, Taya, Tayah, Téa, Téah, Teea, Teeah, Tehya, Teya, Teyah, Tiah, Tiala, Tialah.
Tiahanna/Tiahna *See* Tianna.
Tiaki Maori: to look after.
Tiala/Tialah *See* Tia.
Tianna A popular modern name, of uncertain meaning. Possibly a short form of Christiana or Tatyana, or just a variation of Anna. *See also* Tiarne.
Teanna, Teannah, Teyana, Teyanna, Teyannah, Tiaana, Tiahn, Tiahna, Tiahnna, Tiana, Ti'ana, Tianah, Tianne, Tijana, Tijanah, Tijanna, Tijannah, Tyana, Tyanah, Tyanna, Tyannah.
Tiara Latin: a crown or coronet.
Tearra, Tiar, Tiarah, Tiare, Tiarra, Tjara, Tjarah, Tjarra, Tjarrah.
Diminutives: Tea, Tia.
Tiarne Probably from Tianna.
Tiarn, Tiarna, Tiarnan, Tyarn, Tyarna, Tyarne.
Tiba Native American: grey.
Tibah.
Tiberia Latin: after the River Tiber.
Ticia A modern name, possibly from

Leticia.
Teesha, Teisha, Tesha, Tishia, Titia.

Tida Thai: a daughter.

Tien Chinese: heavenly. Vietnamese: the first. Also a boy's name.

Tierney Irish Gaelic: the descendant of a lord.
Tiarney.

Tierra *See* Terra.

Tieson *See* Tyson.

Tifaine *See* Theophania.

Tiffany Old English form of Theophania. *See also* Epiphany.
Tiffanee, Tiffani, Tiffanie, Tiffiny, Tiphanee, Tiphani, Tiphanie, Tyfany, Tyffany, Typhanee, Typhani, Typhanie.
Diminutives: Tiff, Tiffi, Tiffy.

Tigan *See* Tegan.

Tigerlily A 'flower name'.
Tigerlilly.

Tigra Latin: a tiger.
Teigra (Welsh), *Tigrea, Tigria, Tigris.*

Tihi Maori: the summit.

Tijana/Tijanna *See* Tianna.

Tika A character from the *Dragonlance* series of fantasy novels.
Tikah.

Tilah/Tilar/Tiler *See* Tyler.

Tilaina/Tilaine/Tilayne *See* Talaine.

Tilda/Tilla/Tillie/Tilly Diminutives of Matilda.

Timandra A name used by William Shakespeare in one of his plays.

Timea/Timeah *See* Timothea.

Timna Arabic: an ancient city in Yemen.

Timora Hebrew: tall.

Timothea Greek: honouring God, or honoured by God. The female form of Timothy.
Timathea, Timea, Timeah.
Diminutives: Thea, Tim, Timmie, Timmy.

Timpanee/Timpani/Timpanie *See* Tympani.

Tina A diminutive of names such as Bettina, Christina and Valentina.
Teena, Teenah, Tinah.

Tinan *See* Tynan.

Tinar Aboriginal: a woman.
Tinara.

Tindarra Aboriginal: shallow water.
Tindara.

Tineka/Tineeka/Tinika/Tineke *See* Taneka.

Tingira Aboriginal: the sea.

Tinka Aboriginal: the day.

Tinsley Old English: a hill or mound.
Tinslea, Tinslee, Tinsleigh, Tinsli, Tinslie, Tinsly.

Tionetta/Tionette *See* Tonette.

Tiphaine/Tiphanie *See* Theophania and Tiffany.

Tira/Tirah *See* Tyra.

Tirion Welsh: gentle.

Tiro/Tiroh *See* Tyro.

Tirranna Aboriginal: running water.

Tiranna.
Tirtza/Tirza/Tirzah *See* Thirza.
Tisa Swahili: the ninth or ninth-born.
Tishia *See* Ticia.
Tishra Hebrew: from Tishri, the seventh lunar month of the Hebrew calendar. This period corresponds to the zodiac sign of Libra.
Tison *See* Tyson.
Titali Hindi: a butterfly.
Titania Greek: the great one. The name of the fairy queen in Shakespeare's *A Midsummer Night's Dream*.
Diminutives: Tania, Tanya.
Titia *See* Ticia.
Tivoli An Italian town.
Tivolie.
Tivona Hebrew: a lover of nature.
Tiwa Aboriginal: honey.
Tizane Hungarian: a gypsy.
Tjara/Tjarra *See* Tiara.
T'Keya/T'Kiyah *See* Tekiya.
Tobie Hebrew: God is good; a feminine form of Tobias. *See also* Tuvia.
Toba, Tobah, Tobee, Tobey, Tobi, Tobia, Tobiah, Toby.
Tofa *See* Tove.
Toinette *See* Antonia.
Toku Japanese: virtuous.
Tola Greek: priceless.
Tolah, Tolita, Tolla, Tollah, Tollita.

Tollula/Tolula *See* Tallulah.
Tomasa/Tomasina *See* Thomasina.
Tomeika/Tomeikah *See* Tameka.
Tomi Japanese: wealthy.
Tomiko Japanese: happy.
Tomisina *See* Thomasina.
Tomoko Japanese: a wise child.
Tonette A feminine form of Tony, meaning praiseworthy. *See also* Tontine.
Tionetta, Tionette, Toneta, Tonetta, Tonita.
Tonga Hindi: a horsedrawn carriage. Also a country name.
Tongatea Polynesian: a woman from Tonga.
Toni/Tonia/Tonie *See* Antonia.
Toni-Ann A 'combination name'.
Toni-Anna, Toni-Anne.
Tonique A modern American name.
Tonike.
Tonita *See* Tonette.
Tontine A feminine form of Tony (praiseworthy). *See also* Tonette.
Tonteen, Tontene, Tontyne.
Tonya *See* Antonia.
Toora Aboriginal: a woman, or a mallee bird.
Topaz Greek: the name of a gemstone.
Topaza, Topaze, Topazia, Topazz, Topazza, Topazze.
Topsy Probably a nickname; rarely used.
Topsee, Topsey, Topsi, Topsie.
Tora Japanese: a tiger. *See also* Thora.
Torah Hebrew: teaching. The basis

of the Jewish doctrine and religion.
Tora.
Tori/Torie/Torigh *See* Victoria.
Torin Gaelic: a chief.
Torinn, Toryn, Torynn.
Torri/Tory *See* Victoria.
Torsta Finnish: born on a Thursday.
Tosca The name of an opera by the Italian composer Puccini.
Toscah, Toska, Toskah.
Toshi Japanese: an arrowhead.
Toshia A Japanese name of uncertain meaning.
Tottie/Totty *See* Charlotte.
Toula Greek: light, or brightness.
Toulah.
Tourmaline Singhalese: a 'gemstone name'.
Tourmalina.
Tova The name of a saint.
Tove Scandinavian: beautiful thunder.
Tofa, Tova.
Toveine A name from *The Wheel of Time* series of fantasy novels.
Tovaine, Tovayne, Toveyne.
Toya/Toyah Diminutives of Latoya.
Toyin A Nigerian name of uncertain meaning. Also a boy's name.
Tracey Old French: from a placename.
Tracee, Traci, Tracie, Tracy, Tracye, Traecey, Traecy, Traisee, Traisi, Traisie, Traisy, Treaci, Treacie, Treacy.
Traisee/Traisie *See* Tracey.

Trajanka Slavic: the feminine form of Trajan.
Tranquilla Italian: one who is calm and tranquil.
Tranquila, Tranquilina, Tranquillina.
Traudl German: a diminutive of names such as Gertraud (*see* Gertrude) and Waltraud.
Trava Czech: fresh, like the springtime.
Traviata Italian: one who wanders.
Traylor Old French: a hunter or tracker. Also a boy's name.
Trayler.
Treaci/Treacy *See* Tracey.
Treasa *See* Teresa.
Treea Greek: three.
Tregenna Cornish: the homestead on the downs.
Tregennah, Tregunna, Tregunnah.
Tregenza Cornish: from the first homestead.
Tregensa, Tregensah, Tregenzah.
Trelise Cornish: the homestead by the court or hall.
Trelease, Treleaze, Trelize, Trelys, Trelyse, Trelyze.
Trella *See* Estelle.
Tresiana *See* Teresa.
Treska Probably a form of Teresa.
Tresna A Polish placename.
Tressa Cornish: the third. *See also* Teresa.
Trevena Cornish/Welsh: a homestead on the hill. Also a boy's name.

Treveena, Treveenah, Trevenah, Trevenna, Trevennah, Trevina, Trevinah.
Treza *See* Teresa.
Tricia *See* Patricia.
Trieste The name of an Italian seaport.
Trilby Italian: one who sings with trills.
Trilbee, Trilbey, Trilbi, Trilbie.
Trina Greek: pure. Also a diminutive of Catherine, Katherine and Katrina.
Treena.
Trinella/Trinetta/Trinette *See* Trinity.
Trinidad Spanish: a Caribbean island. Also a boy's name.
Trinity Latin: a trio or triad, as in the Holy Trinity.
Trinella, Trinelle, Trinetta, Trinette, Trinety, Trini, Trinitey, Triniti, Trinita (Italian), *Trinitie, Trynity.*
Triona A diminutive of Catriona.
Triphena *See* Tryphena.
Trisette French form of Trista.
Trish/Trisha Diminutives of Patricia.
Trishna Sanskrit: desire.
Trista Latin: the melancholy one.
Trisette (French), *Tristel, Tristell, Tristella, Tristelle, Tristia, Trystel, Trystell, Trystelle.*
Tristanne A feminine form of Tristan or Tristram, a Celtic name meaning the noisy one.
Tristaine, Tristan, Tristane, Tristann, Tristanna, Tristian, Tristiann, Tristianna, Tristianne, Trystaine, Trystan, Trystane, Trystann, Trystanne.
Triti Greek: Tuesday.
Tritia/Tritian Diminutives of Patricia.
Trix/Trixi/Trixie/Trixy *See* Beatrice.
Trixibelle A combination of Trixi (the blessed one) and Belle (beautiful).
Trixiebelle, Trixybelle.
Troylene A feminine form of Troy.
Troyene, Troyetta, Troyette, Troylena.
Truda/Truddy/Trudie/Trudy *See* Gertrude.
True Old English: genuine or real.
Truea, Truett, Truetta, Truette.
Tryna Greek: the third.
Trynah.
Tryphena An unusual biblical name of Greek origin.
Triphena, Tryphaina.
Trystaine/Trystan/Trystane/Trystann *See* Tristanne.
Trystel/Trystelle *See* Trista.
Tsarina The feminine form of tsar, a Russian emperor.
Csarina, Csarine, Czarina, Czarine, Tsara, Tsarah, Tsarine, Tzara, Tzarah, Tzarina, Tzarine.
Tseten Sherpa/Tibetan: the

defender of religion. Also a boy's name.
Tshering Sherpa/Tibetan: long life. Also a boy's name.
Tsvetana/Tsvetlana *See* Svetlana.
Tu Chinese: jade.
Tuesday Old English: a 'day name'. *See also* Mardi.
Tewesday, Tewsday.
Tui Maori: a native New Zealand bird.
Tuki Aboriginal: a bullfrog. Japanese: the moon.
Tula Sanskrit: the Hindu name for the zodiac sign of Libra.
Thula, Tulah.
Tulay Turkish: the new moon.
Tulip Turkish: a 'flower name'.
Tulipan (Spanish), *Tulipe, Tulipp, Tulippe.*
Tullarah A modern name of uncertain origin, possibly from Tullia or Tully.
Tullara.
Tullia Irish Gaelic: peaceful.
Tully An Irish surname. A town in Queensland.
Tullee, Tulley, Tulli, Tullie.
Tulsa A city in Oklahoma, the USA. Also a boy's name.
Tulsah.
Tumanako Maori: hope.
Tupelo A city in the state of Mississippi, the USA.
Turella Aboriginal: a waterlily.
Turilwa.

Turquoise Old French: a precious stone. Also a 'colour name'.
Turua Polynesian: beautiful.
Turuhira Maori form of Judith.
Tuti Indonesian: an unusual girl's name.
Tuvia Hebrew: God is good; a female form of Tobias. *See also* Tobie.
Tuwa Native American: of the earth.
Twiga Swahili: a giraffe.
Twiggy The name of a famous 1960s model.
Twiggey, Twiggi, Twiggie.
Twyla Old English: woven with double thread.
Twila.
Twynette A little twin.
Twinett, Twinette, Tywnett.
Ty/Tye *See* Tai.
Tya Aboriginal: the earth.
Tyah.
Tyah *See* Tia and Tya.
Tyana/Tyanna *See* Tianna.
Tyarn/Tyarna/Tyarne *See* Tiarne.
Tyeson *See* Tyson.
Tyfany/Tyffany *See* Tiffany.
Tyler Old English: a tiler or tilemaker.
Tila, Tilah, Tilar, Tiler, Tyla, Tylah, Tylar.
Tymantha *See* Tamantha.
Tympani Latin: a set of drums.
Timpanee, Timpani, Timpanie, Tympanee, Tympanie.
Tynan Gaelic: the dark one.

Tinan.
Tyne The name of an English river. Also a boy's name.
Tynisha *See* Tanisha.
Typhani/Typhanie *See* Tiffany.
Tyra From Tyr, the Norse god of war and victory.
Tira, Tirah, Tyrah, Tyria, Tyriah, Tyrian.
Tyrel/Tyrell/Tyrelle *See* Terryl.
Tyro A nymph in Greek mythology.
Tiro, Tiroh, Tyroh.
Tyson Old French: a firebrand. More commonly a boy's name.
Tieson, Tison, Tyeson.
Tzara/Tzarina *See* Tsara.
Tzipora/Tzippora *See* Zippora.

U

Uaina Maori: to rain.
Uda Teutonic: prosperous, rich. *See also* Ute.
Udah, Udele, Udella, Udelle.
Ude *See* Ute.
Udele/Udella/Udelle *See* Uda.
Udiya Hebrew: God's fire.
Udia.
Uilani Hawaiian: heavenly beauty.
Uka Aboriginal: a white snake.
Ula Arabic: of high rank. Celtic: a jewel of the sea. Cornish: an owl.
Ulalia *See* Eulalia.
Uland/Ulanda/Ulande *See* Yolanda.

Ulani Polynesian: cheerful, lighthearted.
Ularit Aboriginal: a star.
Uli/Ulli Diminutives of Ulrike.
Ulima Arabic: wise, learned.
Uleema, Ulema, Ulimah.
Ulla Aboriginal: a well. Old Norse: will. *See also* Ulrike.
Ullu Hindi: an owl.
Ulma Latin: of the elm tree.
Ulrike Scandinavian/Teutonic: the ruler of all. The feminine form of Ulrich.
Ulrica, Ulrika (Russian), *Ulryka* (Polish).
Diminutives: Rica, Ricki, Ricky, Rikki, Rikky, Uli (German), Ulla (Scandinavian), Ulli.
Ultima Latin: the greatest, the most distant.
Ultimah.
Ultra Latin: something that is beyond or excessive.
Ultrah.
Ulu Nigerian: the second, or second-born child.
Ululani Hawaiian: heavenly inspiration.
Ulva Teutonic: a she-wolf, brave.
Ulyana An unusual name of Russian origin.
Ulyannah.
Uma Hebrew: the nation. Sanskrit: light, peace; the name of a goddess in Hindu mythology.
Umei Polynesian: a mythological

figure.

Umeko Japanese: the child of the plum blossom.
Umeyo.

Umiko Japanese: a child of the sea.

Umina Aboriginal: sleep.

Úna Irish Gaelic: a traditional name, possibly meaning a lamb. Latin: one. *See also* Juno.
Euna (Scottish), *Ona, Oona* (Irish), *Oonagh* (Irish), *Oonah, Oonha, Una, Unah.*

Unda A Basque name of uncertain meaning.

Undina/Undine *See* Ondine.

Undurra Aboriginal: a silver wattle tree.

Unice *See* Eunice.

Unity Oneness. From the Latin word unus, meaning one.
Uneta, Unetta, Unety, Unita.

Unna Icelandic/Teutonic: a woman.

Uno Latin: one, or the first child.

Uralla Aboriginal: a large hill.

Urania Greek: heavenly. The muse of astronomy in Greek mythology.
Ourania.

Urbana Latin: courteous, belonging to the city.

Urmila Sanskrit: wave-like.
Urmi, Urmilla.

Ursa Latin: a bear. The name of two northern constellations: Ursa Major and Ursa Minor, the Great Bear and Little Bear respectively. *See also* Ursula.
Ursah, Ursina.

Ursel/Ursela/Urseline *See* Ursula.

Ursell Cornish: from the bottom of the hill.

Ursella *See* Ursula.

Ursola *See* Ursula.

Ursula Latin: a female bear. The name of a 4th-century saint. *See also* Ursa.
Orsa, Orseline, Orsola, Ursa, Ursel, Ursela, Urseline, Ursella, Urshula, Ursola, Ursule, Ursulette, Ursuline, Urszula (Polish).
Diminutives: Ursie, Uschi (German), Ushi.

Ursuline *See* Ursula.

Uschi/Ushi *See* Ursula.

Usha Sanskrit: the Hindu goddess of the dawn.
Ushas.

Ushi Chinese: an ox. *See also* Ursula.

Utah The name of an American state.
Yutah.

Ute Teutonic: prosperity; fortunate, rich. *See also* Uda.
Ude, Uta.

Utina Native American: a woman of my country.

Uuna Aboriginal: the sun.

Uzume Japanese: the goddess of dance, happiness and good health.

Vaila Old Norse: the name of one of the Shetland Islands, off the coast of Scotland.
Vailah.

Vaire From J R R Tolkein's book *The Silmarillion.*
Vair.

Vaisakha *See* Vesaka.

Val A diminutive of names such as Valda, Valentina and Valerie.

Vala Teutonic: the chosen one.

Valaree/Valarie *See* Valerie.

Valda Teutonic: a ruler, a battle heroine.
Valdah, Valma, Velda, Veldah, Walda.
Diminutive: Val.

Valdis Icelandic: a goddess.

Valdore A character from the *Star Trek* TV series.
Valdor, Valldor, Valldore.

Valea/Valeah *See* Valina.

Valeda *See* Valentina.

Valeena/Valeene/Valena/Valene *See* Valina.

Valella Probably derived from Valerie.
Valelle, Velella, Velelle.

Valencia/Valencianna/Valensia *See* Valentina.

Valentina Latin: strong and healthy. A popular name in Eastern Europe.
Valeda, Valencia, Valencianna, Valencienne, Valensia, Valentia, Valentine, Valentyna, Valentyne,
Vallentina, Vallentine.
Diminutives: Tina, Val.

Valerie French: strong.
Valaree, Valarie, Valeare, Valeree, Valeri, Valeria (Italian), *Valeriana* (Spanish), *Valérie* (French), *Valery, Valeryi, Valeska* (Polish), *Valiere, Vallaree, Vallarie, Vallery, Valliere, Valorie, Valrene, Valrine, Valyrie, Velarie, Vellarie, Velree, Velrie.*
Diminutive: Val.

Valeska Polish form of Valerie.

Valiere *See* Valerie.

Valina Probably a form of Valerie.
Valea, Valeah, Valeen, Valeena, Valeenah, Valeene, Valena, Valenah, Valene, Valia, Valiah, Valija, Valinah, Valine.

Valldor/Valldore *See* Valdore.

Vallentina/Vallentine *See* Valentina.

Vallery *See* Valerie.

Valletta The capital of Malta.
Valetta.

Valma *See* Valda.

Valmai Welsh: a mayflower.
Valmae, Valmali, Valmay, Valmie.

Valonia Latin: from the valley.
Valloniah, Valona.

Valora Latin: brave.
Valorah, Valore, Valoria, Valoura, Valourah, Valouria.

Valorie/Valyrie *See* Valerie.

Valrene/Valrine *See* Valerie.

Van/Vana Diminutives of Vanessa.

Vana Polynesian: a sea urchin.

Vanda *See* Wanda.
Vandana Sanskrit: worship.
Vanessa A name invented by the 18th-century poet and author Jonathan Swift.
Vanesa, Vanessah, Vanetta, Vanita, Venessa, Venessah.
Diminutives: Nessa, Nessi, Nessie, Van, Vana, Vanna, Vanni.
Vanetta *See* Vanessa.
Vania *See* Vanja.
Vanida Thai: a young lady.
Vanita *See* Vanessa.
Vanja Scandinavian: the feminine form of Vanya, a Russian diminutive of Ivan.
Vania, Vanina, Vanya.
Vanka Russian form of Anne.
Vanna A diminutive of Vanessa.
Vanni Italian form of Anne. *See also* Vanessa.
Vanora Celtic: a white wave. A form of Guinevere.
Vanorah, Vannora, Vannorah, Vanore.
Vanya *See* Vanja.
Varana Hindi: a river.
Varanah, Varanna, Varannah.
Varda Hebrew: a rose.
Vardah, Vardia, Vardice, Vardis.
Vardice/Vardis *See* Varda.
Varina *See* Varvara.
Varley An English surname, possibly a variation of Farley (from the fern clearing).
Varlee, Varlei, Varleigh, Varli,
Varlie, Varlli, Varllie, Varlly, Varly.
Varsa Sanskrit: the Indian rainy season, lasting from mid June to mid August, so suitable for Gemini, Cancer and Leo babies.
Varsha, Varshini.
Varuna Sanskrit: the god of the night sky. In Balinese mythology, Varuna is the wind god, associated with sunsets and the colour yellow.
Varunah, Varuni.
Varvara Russian form of Barbara.
Diminutive: Varina.
Vasanti Sanskrit: spring.
Varsanta, Vasanta, Vasanthi.
Vashti Persian: the beautiful one. An Old Testament name.
Vasilisa Russian: the feminine form of Vasily, meaning royal or king-like.
Vasiliki (Greek), *Vasilisia, Vassilea, Vassiliki, Vassoula.*
Veda Sanskrit: wisdom and knowledge.
Vedah.
Vedette Italian/Old French: a sentinel.
Vedetta.
Veena Sanskrit: a musical instrument.
Vena, Vina.
Vega Arabic: a falling star.
Veira/Veirah *See* Vera.
Veita/Veitah *See* Vita.
Vela Latin: a sail. A constellation in the Milky Way.
Velah.

Velda/Veldah *See* Valda.
Veleda Teutonic: inspired wisdom.
Veleta, Velida, Velita.
Velella/Velelle *See* Valella.
Velia Italian: from an old Roman family name.
Vellia, Vellya, Velya.
Velika Slavic: the great one.
Velinda Possibly a variation of Belinda, meaning beautiful.
Velindah, Vellinda, Vellindah, Vellynda, Vellyndah, Velynda, Velyndah, Vilinda, Vilindah, Villinda, Villindah.
Vellarie/Velree/Velrie *See* Valerie.
Velma A modern name that has been popular in the USA. Also a diminutive of Wilhelmina.
Velmah, Vilma, Vilmah.
Velta A Latvian name of uncertain meaning.
Velvet English: a soft fabric.
Velvett, Velvette, Velvey, Velvi, Velvie, Velvy.
Velya *See* Velia.
Vena *See* Veena.
Venda *See* Venus.
Vendela/Vendelah *See* Venla.
Venece/Venese *See* Venice.
Venera Italian: one who is respectful
Venerah, Veneranda, Veneria, Veneriah.
Venessa/Venessah *See* Vanessa.
Venetia Latin: a lady of Venice. *See also* Venice.
Veneda, Veneita, Veneitta, Venesia,
Veneta, Venezia.
Venezia *See* Venetia and Venice.
Venica *See* Venus.
Venice Anglicised form of Venezia, an Italian city. *See also* Venetia.
Venece, Venese, Venezia, Venise, Veniss, Venisse.
Venisa/Venisha/Venita *See* Venus.
Venla Finnish: a feminine form of Wendell, meaning a wanderer.
Vendela (Swedish), *Vendelah, Venlah.*
Ventura Spanish: good luck, happiness.
Ventoura, Ventourina, Venturia, Venturina (Italian), *Venturino.*
Venuka Sanskrit: a flute.
Venus Latin: beautiful. The Roman goddess of beauty and love.
Venda, Venica, Venisa, Venisha, Venita, Venusa.
Vera Latin: true. Russian: faith. A common name in Russia that became used in the English-speaking world in the early 20th century.
Veira, Veirah, Verah, Vere, Verelle, Verla, Verle, Verlene, Verlie, Verra (Slavic), *Viera* (Czech), *Vierah. Diminutive:* Verushka (Czech).
Veracruz Spanish: the true cross. A Mexican state.
Verbena Latin: a sacred bough or plant.
Vervain.
Verda Latin: fresh. *See also* Verna.

Verdi Latin: green. *See also* Virida.
Verdey, Verdia, Verdie, Verdy.
Vere/Verelle *See* Vera.
Verena Swiss: the name of a 3rd-century saint.
Verene, Verina, Verine.
Diminutive: Vreni.
Verginia/Verginie *See* Virginia.
Verity Old French from Latin: truth.
Verita.
Verla/Verle/Verlene/Verlie *See* Vera.
Verna Latin: spring-like, fresh. The feminine form of Vernon. *See also* Laverne and Verda.
Verda, Vernah, Verne, Verneta, Vernetta, Vernette, Vernice, Vernise, Vernita, Vernola.
Diminutives: Vern, Verne.
Verona Latin: an Italian city. Also a variation of Veronica.
Veronica Latin: a true likeness or image. Also a variation of Berenice.
Verona, Veronicah, Veronika (Hungarian, Scandinavian), *Veronikah, Veronike* (German), *Véronique* (French).
Diminutives: Nika (Russian, Slavic), Ronni, Ronnie, Ronny, Vonni, Vonnie, Vonny.
Véronique French form of Veronica.
Verra *See* Vera.
Verran Cornish: the short or little one.
Verren, Verrin.
Verushka *See* Vera.

Vervain *See* Verbena.
Vesaka Sanskrit: the Hindu month of April/May, corresponding to the zodiac sign of Taurus.
Vesakha, Vaisakha.
Vesela Slavic: cheerful.
Veselina, Veselinka, Vesella, Vessela, Vesselina, Vesselinka.
Vesna Slavic: spring.
Vespera Latin: an evening star.
Vespa, Vesper, Vesperia.
Vesta Latin: a guardian of the sacred fire. The Roman goddess of the hearth.
Veta *See* Vita.
Vetta A diminutive of Yvette.
Veva *See* Genevieve.
Vevette French form of Genevieve.
Vevila Irish Gaelic: the melodious one.
Vevina.
Viann/Vianne *See* Vivien.
Vica/Vicah *See* Vika.
Vicki/Vickii/Vicky *See* Victoria.
Victoria Latin: victory, the victorious one. *See also* Vika.
Victoire (French), *Victorie, Victorija* (Slavic), *Victorina, Victorine* (French), *Victory, Viktoria* (German, Scandinavian), *Viktoriya* (Russian), *Vitoria* (Spanish), *Vittoria* (Italian), *Wikitoria* (Maori).
Diminutives: Tori, Torie, Torigh, Torri, Torrie, Tory, Vic, Vick, Vicki, Vickii, Vicky, Vika, Vikki.

Vida Hebrew: the beloved one. A short form of Davida, the feminine version of David.
Vidah, Videtta, Vidette.
Videtta/Vidette *See* Vida.
Vidonia Portuguese: a vine branch.
Vidya Sanskrit: knowledge.
Vienna Anglicised form of Wien, an Austrian city.
Viennah.
Viera/Vierah *See* Vera.
Vigilia Latin: alert, vigilant.
Vigila.
Vija A Latvian name of uncertain meaning.
Vijoleta A Slavic form of Violet.
Vika A Norwegian placename and also a diminutive of Victoria.
Vica, Vicah, Vikah.
Vikki/Viktoria/Viktoriya *See* Victoria.
Vilhelmina *See* Wilhelmina.
Vilia The name of a character in Slavic mythology.
Vilya.
Vilinda/Villinda *See* Velinda.
Vilma *See* Velma.
Vimala Sanskrit: pure.
Vina Spanish: from the vineyard. Also a diminutive of Lavinia and a form of Veena.
Vineta, Vinetta, Vinette, Vinia, Vinita, Vinna, Vinnia.
Vincentia Latin: the conqueror. The feminine form of Vincent.
Vincencia, Vincenta, Vincenza (Italian), *Vincenzina* (Italian).
Diminutives: Vincey, Vincie, Vincy.
Vine Middle English: a 'plant name'.
Vyne.
Vineta/Vinetta/Vinette *See* Vina.
Vinia/Vinita/Vinna/Vinnia *See* Vina.
Vinita Sanskrit: modest.
Binita, Vineeta.
Viola A name from the Shakespearean play *Twelfth Night*. *See also* Violet.
Violah, Violanta, Violenta.
Violet A 'flower name'. *See also* Iolanthe and Yolanda.
Orvokki (Finnish), *Vijoleta* (Slavic), *Viola* (Italian), *Violah, Violante* (Spanish), *Violeta* (Spanish), *Violetta* (Italian), *Violette* (French), *Vyoletta, Vyolette, Wioletta* (Slavic).
Diminutives: Letta, Lettah, Vi, Vye.
Viorica Romanian: a bluebell.
Viorika.
Vipasha Sanskrit: a river.
Bipasha, Vipasa.
Virdis *See* Virida.
Virgilia Latin: a staff bearer.
Virgila, Virgilie.
Virginia Latin: maidenly, pure.
Verginia, Verginie, Virginie (French), *Virginnia, Wirginia* (Slavic).
Diminutives: Gigi (French), Ginger, Gini, Ginia, Ginnie,

Ginny, Vergie.
Virgo Latin: a virgin. A zodiac sign and the Roman goddess of justice. *See also* Virginia.
Virgoe, Virgonia.
Virida Latin: green. *See also* Verdi.
Viridiana, Viridienne (French), *Virdis, Viridis, Vrida.*
Virna A popular Italian name.
Vita Latin: life.
Veita, Veitah, Veta, Vetah, Vitah, Vitia, Vitina, Vitta.
Vitalia Italian: the feminine form of Vitale, meaning lively.
Vitoria/Vittoria *See* Victoria.
Vitta *See* Vita.
Viva/Vivanta *See* Vivien.
Vivaldi After the Italian composer, Antonio Vivaldi.
Viveka Scandinavian: lively.
Viveca, Vivica, Vivika.
Vivenne *See* Vivien.
Vivette Little Viv (*see* Vivien).
Vivett.
Vivica/Vivika *See* Viveka.
Vivien Latin: full of life, vital. *See also* Vivette and Vyvyan.
Viann, Vianne, Viva, Vivanta, Vivenne, Vivia, Vivian, Viviana (Italian), *Viviann, Vivianna, Vivianne, Vivianta, Vivienn, Vivienne* (French), *Vivijana* (Slavic), *Vivvien, Vivvienn, Vivvienne, Vivyan, Vyvian, Vyvien, Vyvienne.*
Diminutives: Viv, Vivi, Vivie.

Vivonne French: a placename from Kangaroo Island, South Australia.
Vivonn.
Vladimira Slavic: the feminine form of Vladimir, a powerful ruler.
Vladislava Slavic: the femine form of Vladislav, a glorious ruler.
Wladyslawa.
Vlasta Slavic: the feminine form of Vlastislav (the glorious homeland).
Vogue French: a fashion or style.
Voile French: a fine fabric.
Voila, Voyle, Voyla.
Volante Latin: the flying one.
Volah, Volah, Volanta, Volantah.
Voletta Greek/Old French: veiled.
Voleta.
Volcana/Volcania/Volkana/Volkania *See* Vulcania.
Volga The name of a Russian river.
Volgah.
Volumnia A character in Shakespeare's *Coriolanus*.
Volva A wise woman or prophetess in Norse mythology.
Vonda From Von, a diminutive of Yvonne (an archer).
Vondah.
Vonetta A diminutive of Von or Yvonne.
Vonette.
Vonni/Vonnie/Vonny Diminutives of Veronica and Yvonne.
Voyle/Voyla *See* Voile.
Vreni *See* Verena.
Vrida *See* Virida.

Vrinda Sanskrit: a figure in Hindu mythology.
Vrischika Sanskrit: the Hindu name for the zodiac sign of Scorpio. *Vriksha.*
Vulcania From Vulcan, the Roman god of fire and metalworking. *Volcana, Volcania, Volkana, Volkania, Vulcana, Vulkana, Vulkania.*
Vyne *See* Vine.
Vyoletta/Vyolette *See* Violet.
Vyoma Sanskrit: the sky.
Vyvian/Vyvien/Vyvienne *See* Vivien.
Vyvyan Cornish: an old surname. Could also be used as a variation of Vivien.

W

Wafa Arabic: one who is faithful. *Wafah, Waffa, Waffah.*
Wafiqa Arabic: the feminine form of Wafiq, a friend or companion. *Wafeeqa, Wafica, Waficah, Wafiqah.*
Wahiba Arabic: the generous one.
Wahida Arabic: unique.
Wailana Hawaiian: calm waters.
Waimarama Maori: clear waters.
Waipounamu Maori: a type of greenstone. *See also* Pounamu.
Waipuna Maori: a spring (water).
Wajiha Arabic: one who is honoured or illustrious.
Wala Aboriginal: a blue-tongued lizard.
Walda *See* Valda.
Walida Arabic: the newborn girl.
Wallis Old French: a foreigner, particularly a woman from Wales. *Wallace, Wallice.*
Waltraud Teutonic: a strong ruler. A feminine form of Walter. *Diminutive:* Traudl.
Wanda Aboriginal: a sandhill. Teutonic: a Slavic woman, or a wanderer. *Vanda, Wandah, Wandis.*
Wandis *See* Wanda.
Waneta Native American: a horse of battle. *Wanetah, Wanita, Wanitah.*
Wanetta Old English: pale. *Waneta, Wanette.*
Wangari An African name of uncertain meaning.
Wanika Hawaiian: God's gracious gift.
Wanita *See* Juanita and Waneta.
Wanya Aboriginal: a boomerang.
Waratah Aboriginal: a red flower.
Warrah Aboriginal: honeysuckle.
Warrina Aboriginal: to give.
Wasima Arabic: graceful, pretty. The feminine form of Wasim. *Waseema, Wasimah.*
Wayamba Aboriginal: a turtle.
Waynette A feminine form of Wayne (a cart- or wagon-maker).

Waynella, Waynelle, Waynetta.
Wednesday Middle English: the day of Odin, also known as Woden or Wotan.
Wednesdai, Wensdai, Wensday.
Weema Aboriginal: small.
Weka Maori: a woodhen.
Welma *See* Wilhelmina.
Welya Aboriginal: summer.
Wenda/Wendeline *See* Wendy.
Wendy A name invented by J M Barrie in the early 1900s for his play *Peter Pan*.
Wenda, Wendee, Wendeline, Wendey, Wendi, Wendie, Wyndee, Wyndey, Wyndi, Wyndie, Wyndy.
Wenfreda *See* Winifred.
Wenna Diminutive of Lowenna.
Wenona/Wenonah *See* Winona.
Wensdai/Wensday *See* Wednesday.
Werna Possibly the feminine form of Werner, the German version of Warner.
Wernah, Wernia.
Wesselina German: the feminine form of Wessel.
Whetu Maori: a star.
Whetuaroha Maori: the shining moon.
Whetumarama Maori: shining love.
Whilma/Whilmina *See* Wilhelmina and Wilma.
Whina Maori: the helper.
Whitney Old English: from the white island. Also a boy's name.
Whitnee, Whitnie, Whitny,
Witnee, Witney, Witnie, Witny.
Wielhelmina *See* Wilhelmina.
Wikitoria Maori form of Victoria.
Wilda Teutonic: the untamed one.
Wylda.
Wiley *See* Wylie.
Wilfreda Teutonic: desiring peace. The feminine form of Wilfred.
Wildrida, Wilfrieda.
Wilga Aboriginal: a small tree.
Wilhelmina Teutonic: the resolute protector. A feminine form of William. *See also* Wilma.
Vilhelmina, Welma, Whilmina, Wielhelmina, Wilhelma, Wilhelmine (German)*, Willamena, Willamina, Willetta, Willette, Williamena, Williamina, Wilmena.*
Diminutives: Billie, Billy, Helma (German), Helmi, Helmie, Helmine (German), Mina, Minna (German), Minne, Minney, Minnie, Velma, Vilma, Willa, Willeke (Dutch), Willie, Willye, Wilma.
Willa Aboriginal: a woman or wife. Also a diminutive of Wilhelmina.
Willeke Dutch diminutive of Wilhelmina.
Willetta/Willette *See* Wilhelmina.
Williamena/Williamina *See* Wilhelmina.
Willow Old English: a 'tree name'.
Willowe, Wyllow, Wyllowe.
Willva Old English: determined,

strong-willed.
Willvah, Wilva, Wilvah, Wyllva, Wyllvah, Wylva, Wylvah.

Wilma A diminutive of Wilhelmina.
Whilma, Wilmah, Wilmetta, Wilmette, Wylma, Wylmah.

Wilmena *See* Wilhelmina.

Wilona Old English: desired.

Win *See* Edwina, Winifred and Wynne.

Wincey Aboriginal: the east wind.
Wincie, Wincy.

Winda Swahili: a hunter.

Winema Native American: a female chief.

Wini Maori: a window. *See also* Winifred.

Winifred Teutonic: a peaceful friend. Welsh: joyful peace.
Gwenfra (Welsh), *Gwenfrewi* (Welsh), *Wenfreda, Winefred, Winfred, Winifreda, Winifrida, Winnefred, Winnifred, Wynefred, Wynifred.*
Diminutives: Freda, Win, Wini, Winn, Winne, Winnie, Wynn, Wynne.

Winn/Winne/Winnie *See* Edwina, Winifred and Wynne.

Winona Native American: the firstborn daughter. The name of a town in Minnesota.
Wenona, Wenonah, Winonah, Wynona.

Winsome English: pleasant and attractive.
Winsom, Wynsom, Wynsome.

Winta Aboriginal: an owl. *See also* Winter.

Winter Old English: born in the winter months.
Winta, Wintah, Winters, Wynter, Wynters.

Wioletta Slavic form of Violet.

Virginia Slavic form of Virginia.

Wirrah Aboriginal: a fish.

Wirruna Aboriginal: the sunset.

Wisteria A 'plant name'.
Wistaria, Wistariah, Wisteriah.

Witney/Witnie *See* Whitney.

Wladyslawa *See* Vladislava.

Wonita *See* Juanita.

Woora Aboriginal: a kangaroo.

Wraith A spirit.
Wraithe, Wrayth, Wraythe.

Wren Old English: a tiny bird.
Ren, Renn, Renne, Wrenn, Wrenna, Wrenne.

Wyanet Native American: beautiful.

Wylda *See* Wilda.

Wylie Old English: wily or beguiling.
Wiley.

Wyllow *See* Willow.

Wyllva/Wylva *See* Willva.

Wylma *See* Wilma.

Wyndee/Wyndie/Wyndy *See* Wendy.

Wynefred/Wynifred *See* Winifred.

Wynne Cornish/Welsh: fair, or blessed. Also a diminutive of Winifred.

W – Girls

Win, Winn, Winne, Wyn, Wynette, Wynn.
Wynona *See* Winona.
Wynsome *See* Winsome.
Wynter/Wynters *See* Winter.
Wyomia From Wyoming, the name of a US state.
Wyomea, Wyomeah, Wyomiah.
Wyuna Aboriginal: clear water.

Xalapa A Mexican placename.
Xamia A type of butterfly.
Xamiah, Zamia, Zamiah.
Xana *See* Xanthe.
Xandra A diminutive of Alexandra.
Xanthe Greek: yellow, bright or golden-haired.
Xana, Xanthea, Xanthi, Xanthia, Xanthie, Xanthine, Xanthis, Xanthy, Xanya, Xanyia, Zanthe, Zanthea, Zanthi, Zanthia, Zanthie, Zanthy.
Xara *See* Zara.
Xarnee/Xarney/Xarnie *See* Sharney.
Xaviera Arabic: brilliant, bright. Spanish: of the new house; the feminine form of Xavier.
Javiera, Xaverie, Xavia, Xavier, Xavière (French), *Zavia, Zavier, Zaviera, Zaviere.*
Xelia *See* Zelia.
Xena/Xene *See* Xenia.
Xenia Greek: hospitable, welcoming.
Ksenia (Polish), *Senja* (Finnish), *Xena, Xene, Xenya, Xina, Zena, Zenia, Zenya.*
Xiang Chinese: the fragrant one.
Ziang.
Xiaoli Chinese: morning jasmine.
Ximena Basque: the feminine form of Ximeno (*see* Simon).
Chimena, Chimene (French), *Jimena* (Spanish), *Ximene.*
Xina *See* Xenia.
Xingxing Chinese: twin stars.
Xiomara Portuguese/Spanish: famous in war.
Xochi Mexican: a flower.
Xsara *See* Zara.
Xuan Vietnamese: springtime.
Zuan.
Xuela *See* Zuela.
Xuxa Brazilian: a form of Susan, meaning a lily.
Xuxah, Zuza, Zuzah.
Xylia Greek: from the woods.
Xylina, Xylona.
Xylina/Xylona *See* Xylia.

Y

Ya Ghanaian: born on a Thursday.
Yaa.
Yachi Japanese: eight thousand. A 'number name'.
Yachiko.
Yael Hebrew: a wild goat; an Old Testament name. Also a boy's name.
Jael, Yaelle.
Yaffa/Yaffah *See* Jaffa.
Yagmur Turkish: the rain.
Yagoona Aboriginal: today, or now.
Yahriel An angel of the moon.
Yaisha *See* Aisha.
Yakira Hebrew: precious.
Yakirah.
Yalanda *See* Yolanda.
Yalda Persian: the name of ancient festival.
Yaldah.
Yamba Aboriginal: a headland. A NSW placename.
Yamila/Yamile *See* Jamila.
Yamini Hindi: night.
Yamuna Hindi: a sacred river.
Yan *See* Yannah.
Yana Native American: a bear. *See also* Yannah.
Yanah, Yanna, Yannah.
Yandina Aboriginal: a path or road.
Yandeena, Yandinah.
Yang Chinese: the sun.
Yangchen Sherpa/Tibetan: the sacred one.
Yangzom Sherpa/Tibetan: an accomplished woman.
Yani Aboriginal: peace.
Yanisa An attractive Thai name.
Yannah The feminine form of Yann, the Breton version of John.
Yan, Yana, Yanah, Yanina, Yannina.
Yantra Sanskrit: an instrument.
Yantrah.
Yara Aboriginal: a seagull, or a crab.
Yaralla Aboriginal: a camp.
Yardley Old English: from the enclosed meadow.
Yardlee, Yardlie, Yardly, Yeardlee, Yeardley, Yeardlie, Yeardly.
Yarelis An unusual name from Cuba.
Yargeris, Yarisley.
Yarkona Hebrew: green.
Yarkonah.
Yarni An unusual name from Indonesia.
Yaroslava *See* Jaroslava.
Yarrah Aboriginal: a river red gum.
Yarra.
Yasemin/Yashmin/Yasmin/Yassmine *See* Jasmine.
Yasu Japanese: tranquil.
Yeardley/Yeardlie *See* Yardley.
Yedda Old English: a singer, one with a melodious voice.
Yehudit A Jewish form of Judith.

Y – Girls

Yekaterina Russian form of Katherine.
Diminutives: Katenka, Katinka.
Yelena Russian form of Helen.
Yelizaveta A Russian form of Elizabeth.
Yelka Aboriginal: a dog.
Yelga.
Yemima/Yemimah *See* Jemima.
Yenisel An unusual Cuban name.
Yenysel.
Diminutives: Yeni, Yeny.
Yeran Aboriginal: a girl.
Yeranda Aboriginal: a black cockatoo.
Yerandah.
Yesenia/Yessenia *See* Jessenia.
Yesim Turkish: beautiful.
Yeter Turkish: enough, sufficient.
Yetta Old English/German: to give. Also a diminutive of Henrietta.
Yetunde A contemporary American name.
Yeva Russian form of Eve.
Yiva.
Yevgenia The feminine form of Yevgeni, the Russian version of Eugene (the noble one).
Yevgenija, Yevgenya.
Ygraine/Ygrayne *See* Igrayne.
Yi Chinese: happy.
Yildiz Turkish: a star.
Yileen Aboriginal: a dream.
Yilla Aboriginal: a cicada.
Yin Chinese: the moon, or silvery. Yin is the feminine, passive, principle in Chinese philosophy; the opposite of Yang.
Yindi Aboriginal: the sun.
Yipsi The name of a Cuban athlete.
Ylena/Ylenna *See* Elena.
Yma/Ymah *See* Ima.
Ynes/Ynez Spanish forms of Agnes.
Yoana Bulgarian form of Joanne.
Ioana (Slavic).
Diminutive: Oana.
Yogita Sanskrit: one who can concentrate.
Yogeeta.
Yoi Japanese: born during the evening.
Yoko Japanese: good.
Yola African: a firefly.
Yolah.
Yolana/Yolane *See* Yolanda.
Yolanda Greek/Old French: a violet flower. *See also* Violet and Iolanthe.
Joelan, Jolan (Hungarian), *Jolana, Jolanda* (Italian), *Jolande, Jolani, Jolania, Jolanta* (Polish), *Uland, Ulanda, Ulande, Yalanda, Yolana, Yoland, Yolandah, Yolande* (French), *Yolandita* (Spanish), *Yolane, Yolanta, Yolanthe, Yollanda, Yollandah.*
Yon Burmese: a little rabbit. Korean: a lotus blossom.
Yona Hebrew: a dove; a feminine form of Jonah. *See also* Jonina.
Yonah, Yonina, Yonita.
Yonca Turkish: clover.
Yonga Aboriginal: the sun.

Yonica Possibly a form of Yona.
Yonicah, Yonnica, Yonnicah, Yonika, Yonikah, Yonnika, Yonnikah.

Yonina/Yonita *See* Yona.

Yooralla Aboriginal: love.

Yoorana Aboriginal: the beloved one.

Yootha/Ytha *See* Ita.

Yord *See* Jord.

Yori Japanese: trustworthy.

Yosana Sanskrit: a girl.

Yoshi Japanese: good. Also a boy's name.
Yoshiko.

Youlia *See* Yulia.

Yovela Hebrew: rejoicing.

Ysabel/Ysobel *See* Isabel.

Ysanne A combination of Anne and, possibly, Yseult.
Ysan, Ysann.

Yseult Medieval French form of Isolde.
Yseulte.

Ysolda/Ysolde *See* Isolde.

Yu Chinese: jade. Tibetan: turquoise.

Yue Chinese: the moon.

Yukari Japanese: affinity.

Yuki Aboriginal: a dingo. Japanese: lucky, or from the snow.

Yukiko Japanese: a child of the snow.

Yuku Aboriginal: daylight.

Yula/Yulia/Yuliana/Yuliya *See* Julia.

Yumi Japanese: like an arrow.

Yumiko Japanese: a child of the arrow.

Yuna Japanese: powerful.

Yunaika The name of a Cuban athlete.

Yungara Aboriginal: a wife.

Yunta Aboriginal: a woman.
Yuntah.

Yuri Aboriginal: to hear. Japanese: a lily.
Yuriko.

Yurrah Aboriginal: plenty of trees.
Yurra.

Yusra Arabic: the prosperous one.

Yutah *See* Utah.

Yva/Yve *See* Eve.

Yvana/Yvanna *See* Ivana.

Yvette French diminutive of Yvonne.
Evetta, Evette, Eyvette, Iveta (Czech, Slovak), *Ivete, Iveth, Ivetha, Ivett, Ivetta, Ivette, Yvett, Yvetta.*
Diminutive: Vetta.

Yvona *See* Yvonne.

Yvonne French: an archer. Greek: the wood of the yew tree. *See also* Lavonne and Yvette.
Eevarn, Evarn, Evarne, Evon, Evonn, Evonna, Evonne, Eyvon, Eyvonn, Eyvonna, Eyvonne, Ivon, Ivonn, Ivonne, Yvon, Yvona, Yvonna.
Diminutives: Von, Vonetta, Vonette, Vonni, Vonnie, Vonny, Yvetta, Yvette.

Z

Zaanee/Zaani *See* Zani.
Zabrina *See* Sabrina.
Zada Arabic: the lucky one.
Zadah, Zadee, Zaida, Zaide, Zaidee, Zayda.
Zadee/Zadie *See* Sarah and Zada.
Zadora The name of a Polish coat of arms.
Zadorah, Zedora, Zedorah.
Zaelea/Zaelee *See* Zali.
Zafira Spanish: a sapphire. *See also* Sapphira.
Zafera (Greek), *Zaffira, Zaffirah, Zafirah.*
Zagir Armenian: a flower.
Zahara/Zahira *See* Zara.
Zahava Hebrew: golden.
Zehava.
Zahia Arabic: one who is beautiful or brilliant. The feminine form of Zahi.
Zahli/Zahlia/Zahlie *See* Zali.
Zahnee/Zahni/Zahnie *See* Zani.
Zahra *See* Zara.
Zaida *See* Zada.
Zaide/Zaidee *See* Sarah and Zada.
Zaina Arabic: beautiful.
Zainem.
Zainab/Zaineb/Zainep
See Zaynab.
Zaira *See* Zara.
Zali A modern name, possibly made-up.
Zaelea, Zaelee, Zahli, Zahlia, Zahlie, Zalea, Zalee, Zalia, Zaliah, Zalie, Zalih, Zaylia, Zayliah.
Zalika Arabic/Swahili: well-born.
Zaleeka, Zaleekah, Zaleika, Zaleikah, Zalikah.
Zameera/Zameerah *See* Samira.
Zamia/Zamiah *See* Xamia.
Zamika Possibly a variation of Zalika.
Zameeka, Zameekah, Zameika, Zameikah, Zamikah.
Zamira *See* Samira.
Zamunda A fictitious African country, featured in the Eddie Murphy movie *Coming to America*.
Samunda, Samundah, Zamundah.
Zana *See* Nizana.
Zandra *See* Alexandra and Sandra.
Zaneta Hebrew: the grace of God.
Zanetka, Zanetta.
Zani A modern name, possibly the feminine form of Zane.
Zaanee, Zaani, Zaanie, Zahnee, Zahni, Zahnie, Zanee, Zanie, Zanni, Zannie.
Zanna English: a modern short form of Suzanna. *See also* Nizana.
Zanthe/Zanthie/Zanthy
See Xanthe.
Zara Arabic: a blossom or flower. Hebrew: the bright dawn.

See also Sarah.
Xara, Xsara, Zahara, Zahira, Zahirah, Zahra, Zaira, Zarah, Zareena, Zarina, Zarra, Zarrah, Zhara, Zhra.
Zareena *See* Zara.
Zaria *See* Azaria and Sarah.
Zarifa Arabic: graceful.
Zarina *See* Sarina and Zara.
Zarnee/Zarney/Zarni *See* Sharney.
Zarra/Zarrah *See* Zara.
Zavanna *See* Savanna.
Zavia/Zavier/Zaviera *See* Xaviera.
Zawadi Swahili: olive; a 'colour name'.
Zawati.
Zayda *See* Zada.
Zayita Hebrew: an olive.
Zayit, Zayitah.
Zaylia/Zayliah *See* Zali.
Zaynab Arabic: a perfumed flower.
Zainab, Zaineb, Zainep, Zaynep, Zeineb (Slavic), *Zeynab, Zeynep* (Turkish), *Zeynib.*
Zazel The angel of love invocations.
Zazu Hebrew: movement.
Zea Latin: ripened grain.
Zeah, Zeya, Zeyah, Zia, Ziah, Ziya, Ziyah.
Zedora/Zedorah *See* Zadora.
Zeela/Zeelah *See* Zelah.
Zeena/Zeenah *See* Zena.
Zeenat Sanskrit: beauty.
Zeeta/Zeetah *See* Zeta.
Zeffa Portuguese: a rose.
Zeffah.

Zehava *See* Zahava.
Zehra/Zehria/Zehriah *See* Zerah.
Zeina/Zeinah *See* Zena.
Zeineb *See* Zaynab.
Zel/Zell Diminutives of names such as Zelma.
Zela/Zella/Zellah *See* Zelah and Zillah.
Zelah Hebrew: a side. A Cornish placename.
Zeela, Zeelah, Zela.
Zelda Diminutive of Griselda. The name of the wife of American writer F Scott Fitzgerald.
Zeldah.
Zele *See* Zelia.
Zelena/Zelene *See* Selena.
Zelenka Czech: the little green one, implying youth and freshness
Zelia Greek: zealous, devoted to one's duty.
Zele, Zélie (French), *Zelina.*
Zelina *See* Zelia.
Zelma *See* Anselma, Salima and Selma.
Zellma, Zellmah, Zelmah, Zhelma.
Diminutives: Zel, Zell.
Zen Japanese: the name of a Buddhist sect. Also a boy's name.
Zenn, Zenne.
Zena Scottish: short form of Alexina (*see* Alexandra). *See also* Xenia and Zenobia.
Zeena, Zeenah, Zeina, Zeinah, Zenah.

Z – Girls

Zenaida *See* Zenobia.
Zenani African: the name of one of Nelson Mandela's daughters.
Zennani.
Diminutives: Zeni, Zeny.
Zenda Persian: a sacred woman.
Zendah, Zenta, Zentah, Zinda, Zindah, Zinta, Zintah.
Zeni *See* Zenani and Zenobia.
Zenia *See* Xenia and Zenobia.
Zenib *See* Zenobia.
Zenith Middle English from Arabic: the highest point; the culmination.
Zenithe, Zenyth, Zenythe.
Zenna/Zennetta *See* Zenobia.
Zennor Cornish: the name of a village.
Zenobia Greek: given life by Zeus.
Zena, Zenaida, Zenia, Zenib, Zenna, Zennetta, Zenobie (French), *Zenovia* (Russian), *Zinaida* (Russian).
Diminutives: Zeni, Zeny.
Zenta A Latvian name of uncertain meaning.
Zentah.
Zeny/Zenya *See* Xenia, Zenani and Zenobia.
Zephir/Zephira *See* Zephyr.
Zephyr Greek: a breeze. The feminine form of Zephyrus, the god of the west wind in mythology.
Zephir, Zephira, Zephra, Zephrina, Zephrine, Zephyra, Zephyrina, Zephyrine.
Zeporah *See* Zippora.

Zerah Hebrew: bright morning.
Zehra, Zehria, Zehriah, Zera, Zeria, Zeriah.
Zerdali Turkish: a wild apricot.
Zeresh Hebrew: golden.
Zerla *See* Zerlina.
Zerlina Teutonic: serene beauty.
Zerla, Zerlena, Zerlene, Zerlinda, Zerline.
Zerrin Turkish: the golden one.
Zeta Greek: the sixth letter of the Greek alphabet.
Zeeta, Zeetah, Zetah, Zetta, Zettah, Zita, Zitah.
Zethu An African name of uncertain meaning.
Zeva Greek: a sword. Hebrew: a wolf.
Zeya/Zeyah *See* Zea.
Zeynab/Zeynep/Zeynib *See* Zaynab.
Zezia A modern name of uncertain origin.
Zhara/Zhra *See* Zara.
Zhelma *See* Zelma.
Zhivka *See* Zivka.
Zia Italian: an aunt. *See also* Zea.
Ziah.
Ziang *See* Xiang.
Zigana Hungarian: a gypsy.
Zigourney *See* Sigourney.
Zigrid/Zigrida *See* Sigrid.
Zillah Hebrew: shade or a shadow. A biblical name.
Zela, Zella, Zellah, Zila, Zilah, Zilla.

Zilpah A biblical name.
Zilpa, Zylpa, Zylpah, Zylpha.
Zimba The name of a town in Zambia.
Zimbah.
Zina A diminutive of Alexina. *See* Alexandra.
Zinaida Russian form of Zenobia.
Zinda/Zinta *See* Zenda.
Zindzi African: the name of one of Nelson Mandela's daughters.
Zinzi.
Zingara Italian: a gypsy.
Zinka A Slavic name of uncertain meaning.
Zinnia Latin: a 'flower name'.
Zinia, Zinta, Zintia, Zyna, Zynia, Zynnia.
Zintra *See* Dzintra.
Zinzi *See* Zindzi.
Zion A hill in Jerusalem, the site of a holy temple. Also a name for the Jewish people.
Sion, Syon, Zyon.
Ziona Hebrew: belonging to Zion.
Zionah, Zyona, Zyonah.
Zippora Hebrew: a little bird, a sparrow. A biblical name.
Tzipora, Tziporra, Zeporah, Zipporah.
Ziska German diminutive of Franziska (*see* Frances).
Zizka.
Zita Italian: a diminutive of Rosita (*see* Rosa) and the name of a 13th-century Tuscan saint. *See also* Zeta.

Ziva Hebrew: brightness.
Zivah, Zivana, Zivanna.
Zivka Slavic: life, or lively.
Zhivka.
Ziwa Swahili: a lake.
Ziya/Ziyah *See* Zea.
Zizi Hungarian diminutive of Elizabeth.
Zky/Zkye *See* Skye.
Zlata Slavic: the feminine form of Zlatan, meaning golden.
Diminutive: Zlatica.
Zoa *See* Zoë.
Zocha Greek: the wise one.
Zoka, Zokah.
Zodiac Greek: the circle of the astrological signs.
Zodiak.
Zoë Greek: life.
Zoa, Zoee, Zoelle, Zoey, Zoi, Zoia (Russian), *Zoie, Zooey, Zoya.*
Zofeya Hebrew: God sees.
Zofeyah.
Zofia/Zofie/Zofja *See* Sophia.
Zohra Arabic: blooming.
Zohri, Zohrie, Zohry.
Zoi/Zoia/Zoie *See* Zoë.
Zoka/Zokah *See* Zocha.
Zola A modern name, probably derived from Zoë. Also after Emile Zola, a 19th-century French author.
Zolah.
Zollie A diminutive of Solomon and more commonly a boy's name.
Zollee, Zolley, Zolli, Zolly.

Z – Girls

Zommer *See* Summer.
Zona After Zona Gale, an American author and playwright.
Zonah.
Zonda Spanish: the name of a type of wind in Argentina.
Zondah.
Zooey *See* Zoë.
Zora Slavic: dawn.
Zorah, Zorana, Zoria, Zorica, Zorika, Zorina, Zorine, Zorita.
Zorina/Zorita *See* Zora.
Zorka Slavic: a 19th-century princess.
Zorkah.
Zosia Polish form of Sophia.
Zoya *See* Zoë.
Zsa Zsa Hungarian diminutive of Susannah.
Zsusanna/Zsuzsanna *See* Susannah.
Zuan *See* Xuan.
Zuela Spanish: possibly a variation of Suela, a diminutive of Consuela.
Xuela.
Zukari/Zukarie *See* Sukari.
Zula/Zulya *See* Susannah.
Zuleika Persian: brilliant beauty.
Zulema Arabic/Hebrew: peace.
Sulema, Zulima.
Zumaradi Swahili: an emerald.
Zuni Native American: the name of a tribe.
Zunee, Zunie.
Zuri Swahili: beautiful.
Zuza/Zuzah *See* Xuxa.
Zuzana/Zuzanna *See* Susannah.
Zuzu A Slavic diminutive of Susannah.
Zylpa/Zylpah/Zylpha *See* Zilpah.
Zyna/Zynia/Zynnia *See* Zinnia.

Boys' names

A

Aaden/Aadyn *See* Aden.
Aadil *See* Adil.
Aage Scandinavian: an ancestor.
Aago Nepali: fire.
Ago.
Aamadou A French form of Ahmed.
Aandi Nepali: thunder.
Andi.
Aaras *See* Arras.
Aaron Hebrew: exalted. Aaron was the brother of Moses in the Bible.
Aaran, Aarron, Aaryn, Aharon (Hebrew), *Aron, Arone, Aronne* (German, Italian), *Arran, Arron, Eron, Erron, Haroon, Haroun* (Arabic), *Harun* (Arabic).
Diminutives: Ari, Arie.
Aart/Aarti Diminutives of Arthur.
Abad *See* Abbott.
Abaddon Hebrew: destruction. A biblical name.
Aban Persian: the angel of the month of October.
Abasi *See* Abbas.
Abba Hebrew: a father.
Abban Latin: white.
Abbas Arabic: stern.
Abasi (Swahili).

Abbott Old English: the father of the abbey.
Abad (Spanish), *Abbe* (French), *Abboid* (Gaelic), *Abbot* (French).
Abboud Arabic: a devoted worshipper.
Abbood, Abood, Aboud.
Abdal/Abdallah/Abdulah
See Abdul and Abdullah.
Abdalmajeed/Abdelmajeed
See Abdulmajid.
Abdiel Hebrew: the servant of God, a faithful servant.
Abdon.
Abdul Arabic: the son of, or servant of.
Abdal, Abdel.
Abdullah Arabic: the servant of Allah.
Abdallah, Abdulah.
Abdulmajid Arabic: a combination of Abdul and Majid, meaning the son of the illustrious one.
Abdalmajeed, Abdalmajid, Abdelmajeed, Abdelmajid, Abdulmajeed.
Abe/Abie *See* Abel and Abraham.
Abel Hebrew: breath, or the son. A son of Adam and Eve in the Bible.
Diminutives: Abe, Abie.
Abelard Teutonic: nobly resolute.
Adelard.
Abernethy Scottish Gaelic: the

mouth of the Nethy River.
Abhijit Sanskrit: victorious.
Abi Turkish: an elder brother.
Abiel Hebrew: God is the father.
Abijah Hebrew: the Lord is my father.
Abir Hebrew: strong.
Abisha Hebrew: God's gift.
Abner Hebrew: the father of light. A biblical name.
Avner.
Abood/Aboud *See* Abboud.
Abraham Hebrew: the father of many; a biblical figure.
Abram, Abramo (Italian), *Abran* (Spanish), *Aperahama* (Maori), *Avram* (Greek), *Avrom* (Hebrew), *Avron* (Hebrew), *Ebrahim* (Arabic), *Ibrahim* (Arabic), *Ibrahima.*
Diminutives: Abe, Abie, Braham, Brahim, Bram.
Abram/Abran *See* Abraham.
Abraxas Greek: a mystical word.
Abril *See* Aprilo.
Absalom Hebrew: the father of peace. A son of David in the Bible. *See also* Axel.
Absolom, Absolon.
Abu The fifth lunar month of the Babylonian calendar, beginning in July/August.
Acastus One of the Argonauts, heroic soldier-sailors in Greek mythology.
Akastus.

Ace Latin: unity.
Acelin French: noble.
Achelous A Greek river god.
Achelus.
Achilles Greek: a handsome figure in Greek mythology.
Achille (French), *Achilleo* (Italian), *Akille, Akilles.*
Achim *See* Joachim.
Achraf *See* Ashraf.
Ackbar *See* Akbar.
Ackerley Old English: a dweller in the meadow.
Ackley Old English: a dweller in the oak tree meadow.
Actaeon A great hunter in Greek mythology who was turned into a stag by the goddess Artemis.
Acteon.
Acton Old English: from the settlement with oak trees.
Adair Scottish Gaelic: from the oak tree near the ford. Also a girl's name.
Adalbert *See* Albert.
Adam Hebrew: a man of the red earth. According to the Bible, the first man. *See also* Atkin.
Adama, Adamah, Adamo (Italian), *Adan* (Italian, Spanish), *Adao* (Portuguese), *Adda* (Welsh), *Adem* (Turkish), *Adhamh* (Irish, Scottish), *Arama* (Maori).
Adamson The son of Adam.
Adamsen.
Adan *See* Adam and Aidan.
Adao *See* Adam.

A – Boys

Adar Hebrew: the twelfth month of the Hebrew calendar, corresponding to the zodiac sign of Pisces.
Adaru, Addaru (Babylonian).
Adda Welsh form of Adam.
Addison Old English: a son of Adam.
Addis, Addyson, Adison, Adyson.
Ade African: royal, or a crown.
Adel Teutonic: noble.
Adelard *See* Abelard.
Adelbert *See* Albert.
Adelpho Greek: a brother.
Adem *See* Adam.
Aden Arabic: the Red Sea gulf and port. *See also* Aidan.
Aaden, Aadyn, Adyn, Aedan, Aeden, Aedyn, Aydan, Aydein, Ayden, Aydin.
Adhamh *See* Adam.
Adil Sanskrit: just and sincere.
Aadil.
Adin Hebrew: sensual.
Adir Hebrew: noble, majestic.
Adita Native American: a priest.
Adlai Hebrew: my witness. A biblical name.
Adlard *See* Allard.
Adler Teutonic: an eagle. A man of keen perception.
Adnan Arabic: the settler.
Adney Old English: a dweller on the island.
Adolph Teutonic: a noble wolf.
Adolf (German), *Adolfo* (Italian), *Adolphe* (French), *Adolphus* (Swedish).
Diminutives: Dolf, Dolph.
Adon Hebrew: the Lord.
Adoni Aboriginal: the sunset.
Adonis Greek: in mythology, the handsome youth loved by Aphrodite.
Adrastos Greek: he who does not flee.
Adrian Latin: the dark one, or a man from the sea, as in the Adriatic.
Adriaan, Adriannos, Adriano (Italian, Spanish), *Adrianus* (Dutch), *Adrie, Adrien* (French), *Arje* (Dutch), *Arjen* (Dutch), *Hadrian, Harian.*
Adric/Adrick *See* Edric.
Adriel Hebrew: from God's congregation.
Adrial.
Adrien French form of Adrian.
Advent Latin: the arrival. Suitable for a child born during Advent, starting on the last Sunday in November and leading up to Christmas.
Advento, Avent (French), *Aventin, Aventio, Avento.*
Adyn *See* Aden.
Aedan/Aeddon/Aeden/Aedyn *See* Aden and Aidan.
Aegir A Norse god of the sea.
Aemon *See* Amon.
Aeneas Greek: the praised one.
Eneas.

Aengus *See* Angus.
Aeolus Greek: in mythology, the ruler of the winds.
Aeon *See* Eon.
Aeron Welsh: an unusual boy's name.
Aesh *See* Ash.
Aesop Greek: the name of an ancient Greek author of fables.
Afanasiy/Afanasy Russian forms of Athanasius.
Afon Welsh: a river. *See also* Avon.
Afro From the word African. The name of a hairstyle.
Agai Russian: the name of a 16th-century prince.
Agamemnon Greek: one who is resolute. The name of a king in Greek legend.
Agapito Italian/Spanish: the beloved one.
Agapetos, Agapetus, Agapitos (Greek), *Agapitus*.
Agate French: a precious stone.
Agilard Teutonic: bright.
Agkarajit A Thai name of uncertain meaning.
Agnello An Italian form of Angelo.
Agnew Old French: a lamb.
Agni The Hindu god of fire and lightning.
Ago *See* Aago.
Agosto/Agostino/Aguistin/Agustin *See* Augustus.
Agrippa Latin: the name of a Roman statesman and general.
Agryppa.

Agu Nigerian: a leopard.
Ahab Hebrew: an uncle. A king of Israel in the Bible.
Ahad Arabic: Sunday. Also an alternative name for Allah.
Aharon *See* Aaron.
Ahearn Irish Gaelic: a horse lord. *See also* Hearn.
Aherin, Ahern, Aherne.
Ahi Maori: fire.
Ahil A Sri Lankan name of uncertain meaning.
Ahmed Arabic: most highly praised.
Aamadou (French), *Ahmad, Ahmet, Amadou* (French).
Ahmik Native American: a beaver, implying skill.
Amik.
Ahren Teutonic: an eagle.
Ahrens.
Ahti The god of the sea in Finnish mythology.
Ahto.
Aidan Irish Gaelic: the little fiery one. The name of a saint.
Adan, Aden, Aedan, Aeddon, Aiden, Aydan, Ayden, Aydin, Edan, Eden.
Aikane Polynesian: friendly.
Aiken Old English: little Adam.
Aickin, Aikin.
Ailani Hawaiian: a high chief. Also a girl's name.
Ailbert Scottish form of Albert.
Ailean/Ailin *See* Alan.
Aillen A figure from Irish

mythology.

Aimé French: the masculine form of Amy, meaning beloved.

Aimon French from Teutonic: a house.

Aindréas Scottish Gaelic form of Andrew.

Ainsley Old English: a meadow or clearing. Also a girl's name.
Ainslea, Ainslee, Ainsleigh, Ainslie, Aynsley.

Aion *See* Eon.

Airamis *See* Aramis.

Airlie After the Earl of Airlie, a Scottish lord.
Airlee, Airley, Airli, Airly.

Aithan/Aithen *See* Ethan.

Aitken/Aitkin *See* Atkin.

Aitor Basque: a name from legend.

Ajala West African: a potter.

Ajani Nigerian: the victor.

Ajax Greek: the legendary hero of the Trojan War.

Ajay Sanskrit: invincible.

Ajmal Arabic: handsome.

Aka Hawaiian: a shadow. Also a girl's name.

Akama Aboriginal: a whale.

Akamu Hawaiian: red earth.

Akar Turkish: flowing water.

Akash Hindi: the sky.
Akasha.

Akastus *See* Acastus.

Akbar Arabic: great.
Ackbar, Aqbar.

Akelin Russian: an eagle.
Akelina, Akeline.

Akemi Japanese: the dawn.

Akeno Japanese: the morning.

Aker The Ancient Egyptian god of the earth.

Akihiro A well-known Japanese name.

Akil Arabic: intelligent.
Akeel.

Akille/Akilles *See* Achilles.

Akim Russian form of Joachim.

Akin Nigerian: a hero.

Akira Japanese: intelligent.

Akiva Hebrew: the supplanter.

Akiyama Japanese: the autumn, or a mountain.

Akmal Arabic: perfection.

Akos Hungarian: a white falcon.

Akram Arabic: generous, noble.
Akrem, Ekram, Ekrem.

Aksel *See* Axel.

Akuhata Maori: August.

Akuila *See* Aquila.

Al Diminutive of names such as Alan, Albert and Alfred.

Aladin Arabic: the servant of Allah.
Aladdin, Aladino.

Alain *See* Alan.

Alako The Romany Gypsy moon god.

Alamein From El Alamein, a city in Egypt.
Alamain, Alamaine, Alamayn, Alamayne, Alameine.

Alamisi *See* Alhamisi.

Alamo The name of a place in Texas, USA.

Alamoe, Alamoh.
Alan Irish and Scottish Gaelic: harmony, or the cheerful handsome one.
Ailean (Scottish), *Ailin* (Irish), *Alain* (French), *Aland, Alen, Allan, Alleine, Allen, Alleyne, Allon, Allyn, Alun* (Welsh), *Alyn, Arana* (Maori, Polynesian).
Diminutives: Al, Alsey, Alsy.
Aland Celtic: as bright as the sun.
Alland.
Alard Teutonic: a noble ruler.
Alart, Ellard.
Alaric Teutonic: the ruler of all.
Alasdair/Alasdhair/Alastair Scottish forms of Alexander.
Alawn Welsh: harmony. Can also be used as a form of Alan.
Alban Latin: fair-complexioned. A saint's name.
Alben, Albin, Albino (Italian, Spanish), *Aubin* (French).
Albany A poetic name for England.
Alber Teutonic: a quick mind.
Alberich Teutonic: the king of the dwarfs in German legend.
Alberico Italian: the king of the mountains.
Albern Old English: a noble warrior.
Albero Italian: a tree.
Albert Teutonic: noble and illustrious. The name became popular after the marriage of Queen Victoria to Prince Albert.
Adalbert, Adelbert, Ailbert (Scottish), *Albertje, Alberto* (Italian), *Albizo* (Spanish), *Albrecht* (German), *Arapata* (Maori), *Arapeta* (Maori), *Aubert* (French), *Elbert.*
Diminutives: Al, Albie, Bert, Bertie.
Albin/Albino *See* Alban.
Albion Latin: white. Also an archaic name for England.
Albizo Spanish form of Albert.
Albrecht German form of Albert.
Albury Old English: the old fort. A NSW placename.
Aldbury.
Alcides An archaic form of Heracles – *see* Hercules.
Alcide (Italian), *Alcyde, Alcydes.*
Alcott Old English: from the stone cottage.
Alcyde/Alcydes *See* Alcides.
Alcyon *See* Halcyon.
Alden Old English: an old, wise friend.
Aldin, Aldon, Aldwin, Aldwyn, Elden, Eldin, Eldon.
Alder Old English: the alder tree.
Alderney English: one of the Channel Isles.
Aldis *See* Aldous.
Aldo *See* Aldous.
Aldous Teutonic: old, wise or great.
Aldis, Aldo (Italian), *Aldus.*
Aldred Old English: a great counsellor.
Eldred.
Aldrey Old English: from the alder tree. Also a girl's name.
Aldree, Aldrie, Aldry, Oldree,

Oldrie, Oldrey, Oldry.
Aldrich Old English: an old, wise ruler.
Aldric, Audric (French), *Eldric, Eldrich, Oldric, Oldrich.*
Aldridge *See* Eldridge.
Aldus *See* Aldous.
Aldwin/Aldwyn *See* Alden and Alvin.
Alec/Aleck *See* Alexander.
Aleczander *See* Alexander.
Aled Welsh: offspring, a son.
Alejandro/Alejo *See* Alexander.
Alek/Alekos/Aleks/Aleksandr *See* Alexander.
Alem Arabic: a wise man.
Alemana Hawaiian: a warrior.
Alen *See* Alan.
Aleph Hebrew: the first letter of the alphabet, similar to the Greek alpha. *Alef.*
Aleron Latin: an eagle.
Alessandro/Alessio Italian forms of Alexander.
Alex *See* Alexander.
Alexander Greek: the protector and helper of mankind. *See also* Sanders and Sasha.
Alasdair (Scottish), *Alasdhair* (Scottish), *Alastair* (Scottish), *Aleczander, Alejandro* (Spanish), *Alejo* (Spanish), *Alekos* (Greek), *Aleksandr* (Russian), *Alessandro* (Italian), *Alessio* (Italian), *Alexanda, Alexandr* (Russian), *Alexandre* (French), *Alexandros* (Greek), *Alexandru* (Romanian), *Alexas, Alexei* (Russian), *Alexi, Alexio* (Portuguese), *Alexios* (Greek), *Alexis* (Greek), *Alexius, Alexsandar, Alexsander, Alistair* (Scottish), *Alister, Allister* (Scottish), *Alsandair* (Irish Gaelic), *Alyxander, Alyxsander, Araketenara* (Maori), *Iskandar* (Arabic), *Iskander* (Turkish), *Iskender* (Turkish), *Oleksander* (Polish), *Oleksandr* (Ukrainian).
Diminutives: Alec, Aleck, Alek, Aleks, Alex, Alic, Alik, Alix, Alleck, Alyk, Alyks, Alyxs, Leks, Lex, Olek (Polish), Sacha (French), Sandi, Sandie, Sandor (Hungarian), Sandy, Sascha (German), Sasha (Russian), Santo (Cornish), Xander, Zahn, Zan, Zander.
Alexas *See* Alexander.
Alexavier A combination of Alex and Xavier (bright).
Alexi/Alexio/Alexis/Alexius *See* Alexander.
Alf/Alfie *See* Alfred.
Alfa Greek: the first, or firstborn. *Alpha.*
Alfons/Alfonsas/Alfonso *See* Alphonso.
Alford Old English: from the old ford.
Alfred Old English: a wise counsellor. King Alfred the Great ruled England from AD 871–899.
Ailfrid (Irish), *Alfio* (Italian),

Alfredo (Italian, Spanish), *Alfreds*, *Arapeti* (Maori).
Diminutives: Al, Alf, Alfi, Alfie, Fred, Freddie, Freddy.
Alger Old English: a noble spearman.
Algernon French: with whiskers, bearded.
Diminutives: Al, Algie, Algis, Algy.
Algirdas A Lithuanian name of uncertain meaning.
Algot A figure from Norse legend; the name probably means a great elf.
Algaut, Algodt.
Alhamisi Swahili: Thursday.
Alamisi.
Ali Arabic: exalted, or noble.
Alia.
Alic/Alik/Alix Diminutives of Alexander.
Alika Polynesian: the defender of mankind.
Alipate Polynesian: bright.
Alison Old English: the son of a nobleman. More commonly a girl's name.
Allison.
Alistair/Alister *See* Alexander.
Allambee Aboriginal: a quiet resting place.
Allambie.
Allan *See* Alan.
Alland *See* Aland.
Allard Old English: noble and hard.
Adlard, Allart.
Alleck *See* Alexander.

Allegro Italian: merry or happy.
Alleine/Allen/Alleyne *See* Alan.
Allenby Old Norse: Alan's farm.
Allanby, Allenbeigh, Allenbey, Allenbie, Allonby.
Allighiero Italian: a noble spear.
Allegri.
Allison *See* Alison.
Allister *See* Alexander.
Allon/Allyn *See* Alan and Alon.
Allunga Aboriginal: the sun.
Almo Old English: noble and famous. Greek: a river god.
Almon Hebrew: forsaken.
Alojz Slavic form of Aloysius.
Alujz.
Alok Sanskrit: divine light.
Alon Hebrew: an oak tree.
Allon.
Alonso/Alonzo *See* Alphonso.
Aloysius *See* Louis.
Alois, Aloisia (Italian), *Alojz* (Slavic), *Aloys, Aloysha, Alujz* (Slavic).
Diminutives: Lewey, Lewie.
Alp Turkish: brave
Alpha *See* Alfa.
Alphonso Teutonic: noble and ready.
Alfons (German), *Alfonsas, Alfonso* (Italian, Spanish, Swedish), *Alonso* (Spanish), *Alonzo, Alphonse* (French), *Alphonsus* (Irish), *Elonso, Elonzo.*
Diminutives: Fonz, Fonzie, Lon, Lonnie.
Alric *See* Ulrich.

Alroy Irish Gaelic: a red-headed boy.
Alsandair Irish Gaelic form of Alexander.
Alsey/Alsy *See* Alan.
Alston Old English: from the old place.
Alton.
Altair Arabic: a bird.
Altan Turkish: golden, or the dawn.
Altun.
Altman Teutonic: an old wise man.
Alto Italian: the tall one.
Alton Old English: the source of the stream.
Altun *See* Altan.
Alujz *See* Alojz.
Alun Welsh form of Alan.
Alun-Wynn Welsh: the fair and harmonious one.
Alun-Wyn.
Alvah Hebrew: the exalted one.
Alva.
Alvar Swedish: the elf warrior.
Alvars.
Alvarez A Spanish surname.
Alvern Latin: of the springtime.
Alverne.
Alvin Teutonic: a noble friend.
Aldwin, Aldwyn, Alvan, Alven, Alwan, Alwin, Alwyn, Alwynn, Alwynne, Aylwin, Elvin, Elvyn.
Alvis Old Norse: all wise.
Alvise, Elvis.
Alwan/Alwin/Alwyn/Alwynn *See* Alvin.
Alyk/Alyxander/Alyxs *See* Alexander.
Alyn *See* Alan.
Alyosha *See* Aloysius.
Amadeus Latin: a lover of God.
Amadeo (Italian), *Amado* (Spanish), *Amedeo, Amedeus.*
Amadou A French form of Ahmed.
Amaethon Welsh: the Celtic god of agriculture.
Amal Arabic: hope. Hebrew: work or labour.
Amahl.
Amama Polynesian: open-mouthed.
Aman Indonesian: secure and safe.
Amana Hawaiian: a warrior.
Amar Hindi: the immortal one.
Amarillo Spanish: yellow.
Amarildo (Portuguese).
Amaro Portuguese: dark, like a Moor.
Amaroo Aboriginal: a beautiful place.
Amat Indonesian: the observer.
Ambar Sanskrit: the sky.
Ambert Teutonic: a bright, shining light.
Ambler Old English: a stable-keeper.
Ambr Welsh: amber.
Ambrose Greek: an immortal one. The name of a saint.
Ambrogio (Italian), *Ambroise* (French), *Ambros* (Irish), *Ambrosi* (Italian), *Emrys* (Welsh).
Amedeo/Amedeus *See* Amadeus.
Ameer *See* Amir.
Ameki An African name of uncertain meaning.

Amer Arabic: plentiful.
Amerigo Italian: the original name of America, after the Italian explorer Amerigo Vespucci.
America.
Amery *See* Amory.
Amida Japanese: the name of the Buddha of pure light.
Amiel Hebrew: the Lord of my people.
Amigo Spanish: a friend.
Amico (Italian).
Amik *See* Ahmik.
Amin Arabic/Hebrew: honest and trustworthy.
Amine.
Amir Arabic: princely.
Ameer, Amr.
Amiri Maori: the east wind.
Amirov Hebrew: my people are great.
Amit Sanskrit: boundless.
Ammon Ancient Egyptian: hidden. The name of a god.
Ammun, Amon, Amun.
Amoho Maori form of Amos and Moses.
Amoka Hawaiian form of Amos.
Amokura Maori: a red-tailed bird.
Amon Hebrew: trustworthy. *See also* Ammon.
Aemon, Amun.
Amor Spanish: love.
Amores (Italian).
Amory Teutonic: divine, or a famous ruler.
Amery.
Amos Hebrew: the bearer of burdens. The name of an Old Testament prophet.
Amoho (Maori), *Amoka* (Hawaiian).
Amparo Spanish: shelter or protection.
Ampelio Italian: a vine. From Ampelius, the name of a 7th-century saint.
Ampelios (Greek), *Ampelius.*
Amphion The son of Zeus and twin brother of Zethus in Greek mythology, known for his love of poetry and music.
Amr *See* Amir.
Amrit Sanskrit: the immortal one.
Amsden Old English: from the valley of Ambrose.
Amun *See* Ammon and Amon.
Amund Scandinavian: divine protection.
An *See* Anh.
Anakin A character in the *Star Wars* movie series, also known as Darth Vader.
Annakin.
Anakoni Hawaiian: valuable.
Analu Hawaiian: manly.
Anand Sanskrit: joyful.
Ananda.
Anaru Maori and Polynesian forms of Andrew.
Anas Arabic: friendly.
Anass.

Anastasius Greek: resurrection, one who shall rise again.
Anastase (French), *Anastasios* (Greek).

Anatole Greek: from the east.
Anatol, Anatoli, Anatolie, Anatolij (Slavic), *Anatolio* (Italian, Spanish), *Anatolios* (Greek), *Anatoly* (Russian).

Ancel Teutonic: godlike. *See also* Ansel.
Ancelin, Ancelot.

Anders Scandinavian form of Andrew.

Anderson The son of Andrew, the strong and manly one.
Andersen.

Andi *See* Aandi.

Andian An Indonesian name of uncertain meaning.

Andis Greek: of strong desire.

Andon Slavic form of Anthony.

Andrae/Andras/Andraz
See Andrew.

André/Andreas *See* Andrew.

Andrew Greek: strong and manly. St Andrew is the patron saint of Scotland and Russia.
Aindréas (Scottish), *Anaru* (Maori, Polynesian), *Anders* (Scandinavian), *Andrae, Andras* (Hungarian), *Andraz* (Slavic), *André* (French), *Andrea* (Italian), *Andreas* (Dutch, German, Welsh), *Andrei, Andrej* (Slavic), *Andrejs* (Slavic), *Andres* (Spanish), *Andretti, Andreus, Andrey, Andric, Andries, Andris* (Latvian), *Andrius, Andriya, Andro, Andrus, Andrzej* (Polish), *Ani* (Maori), *Antero* (Finnish), *Antti* (Finnish), *Indri* (Maltese), *Ondray, Ondré, Ondrej* (Slavic).
Diminutives: Andie, Andy, Drew (Scottish), Drue, Tero (Finnish).

Andrews The son of Andrew.
Andrewes.

Andris/Andrius/Andriya
See Andrew.

Andro/Andrus *See* Andrew.

Androcles Greek: a man, and glory. A figure from Roman legend.

Andronicus Greek: a conqueror of men.
Andronica, Andronicos, Androniki (Greek), *Andronikos* (Greek), *Andronikus.*

Aneurin Welsh: truly golden.
Diminutive: Nye.

Angat African: a mythological prince of the sea.

Angelo Italian: an angel or saintly messenger.
Agnello (Italian), *Ange* (French), *Angel, Angelico, Angelino* (Spanish), *Angell, Angelos* (Greek), *Angelus, Aniello* (Italian).

Angus Scottish Gaelic: unique strength, outstanding. The name of a former Scottish county.
Aengus, Angas, Aonghas, Enos (Irish Gaelic).
Diminutives: Gus, Gussy.

Angwyn Welsh: very handsome.
Anh Vietnamese: peace.
An.
Ani Maori form of Andrew.
Anibal/Anibale *See* Annibale.
Aniello An Italian form of Angelo.
Anil Sanskrit: of the wind.
Aningan Eskimo: the moon god.
Anis Arabic: friendly and sociable.
Anish Sanskrit: supreme.
Anker A Scandinavian name of uncertain meaning.
Ankit Sanskrit: possibly meaning one who is marked.
Ankur Sanskrit: a shoot or sapling.
Ankush Hindi: one who is in control.
Anlon Celtic: a great champion.
Annakin *See* Anakin.
Annan Celtic: from the stream.
Annibale Italian form of Hannibal.
Anibal, Anibale, Annibal.
Anno Hebrew: grace. The masculine form of Anne.
Anntoin Irish form of Anthony.
Anoke Native American: the actor.
Anoki.
Ansari Arabic: a helper.
Anscom Old English: a dweller in the secret valley.
Anscomb.
Ansel Old French: a nobleman's follower. Also a diminutive of Anselm.
Ancel, Ansell, Anshel, Anshell.
Anselm Teutonic: a divine helmet. The name of a saint.
Anselme (French), *Anselmo* (Spanish).
Diminutive: Ansel.
Anshel/Anshell *See* Ansel.
Ansley Old English: from the hermitage clearing.
Anson Old English: the son of Anne or Agnes.
Anstice Greek: the resurrected one. *Anstiss*.
Antal Hungarian form of Anthony.
Antares Greek: like Mars, or the rival of Mars. A red-coloured star in the constellation of Scorpius.
Antero Finnish form of Andrew.
Anteros The son of the goddess Aphrodite in Greek mythology, representing mutual love.
Anthony Latin: praiseworthy, of inestimable worth.
Andon (Slavic), *Anntoin* (Irish), *Antal* (Hungarian), *Anthan, Anthani, Anthanie, Anthany, Anthon, Anthoni, Anthonie, Antin, Antoine* (French), *Anton* (German), *Antoni* (Polish), *Antonio* (Italian, Spanish), *Antonios, Antonius, Antony, Antoun, Antun* (Croatian), *Atonio* (Maori, Samoan).
Diminutives: Ant, Anto, Toney, Toni, Tonie, Tony.
Antin *See* Anthony.
Antoine *See* Anthony.
Anton/Antoni/Antonio/

Antonios *See* Anthony.
Antti A Finnish form of Andrew.
Antun Croatian form of Anthony.
Anu The king of the gods in Babylonian mythology.
Anubis The Ancient Egyptian jackal-headed god of the dead. Similar to the Roman god Pluto.
Anup Sanskrit: without comparison. *Anoop.*
Anwar Arabic: the bright one. *Anwer.*
Anwell Celtic: the beloved, dear one. *Anwyl, Anwyll.*
Anyon Celtic: an anvil.
Anzac A patriotic Australian or New Zealand name! From the World War I Australian and New Zealand Army Corps. *Anzak.*
Aonghas *See* Angus.
Apache The name of a Native American tribe.
Apari Aboriginal: a father.
Aperahama Maori form of Abraham.
Api Malaysian: fire.
Apis A sacred bull in Ancient Egyptian mythology.
Apollo Greek: a beautiful youth. The god of light, music, poetry and healing in Greek mythology. *Apolinar, Apollon, Apollos.*
Apostolos Greek: an apostle.
Aprilo Latin: the month of April. *Abril* (Portuguese, Spanish), *Aprili* (Swahili), *Aprilio, Avril* (French), *Avrilo.*
Apus Latin: a bird of paradise. The name of a constellation.
Aqbar *See* Akbar.
Aquarius Latin: from aqua, meaning water. The name of a zodiac sign and a constellation. *Aquarian, Aquarien, Aquario, Aquarios.*
Aquila Greek: like an eagle. The name of a constellation. *Akuila, Aquilino* (Italian).
Ara Armenian: kingly. Latin: an altar. The name of a constellation.
Aragon A region of Spain. *Arragon.*
Arailt *See* Harold.
Araketenara Maori form of Alexander.
Araluen Aboriginal: the place of waterlilies.
Aram Jewish: from the heights.
Arama Maori form of Adam.
Aramis One of Alexandre Dumas' three musketeers. *Airamis, Aramits, Aramitz.*
Aran Hebrew: active, nimble. Thai: a forest. *See also* Arran.
Arana Maori and Polynesian forms of Alan.
Arapata/Arapeta Maori forms of Albert.
Arapeti Maori form of Alfred.
Aras *See* Arras.
Aravind *See* Arvind.

Arawa Maori: a shark.
Arcadio Greek: a man from Arcadia, a region of Greece.
Arcadios, Arcady, Arkadi, Arkadios, Arkady.
Arcas A figure in Greek mythology who became the constellation of Ursa Minor, the little bear.
Archard Teutonic: sacred and powerful.
Archdale From the dale of the archer.
Archdall.
Archer Old English: a bowman.
Archibald Teutonic: noble and bold.
Diminutives: Arch, Archi, Archie, Archy.
Archimedes Greek: the name of a 3rd-century mathematician and astronomer.
Arcturus Greek: a bear keeper. The name of a star in a Northern Hemisphere constellation.
Ardal Irish Gaelic: a brave warrior.
Arda, Ardall, Ardel, Ardell, Ardghal, Ardil, Ardill.
Ardan Celtic: a name from the Arthurian legends.
Ardel/Ardell *See* Ardal.
Arden Old English: a dwelling place. Latin: ardent and sincere.
Ardin.
Ardghal/Ardil *See* Ardal.
Ardley Old English: from the meadow of the home-lover.
Ardsley.
Ardolph Old English: the wolf (a wanderer) who longs for home.
Ardon Hebrew: bronze.
Ardun.
Arduino Italian: a strong friend.
Ardwick Old English: from the homestead or dairy farm.
Ardwicke, Ardwyck, Ardwycke.
Arel *See* Ariel.
Aren Danish: the ruler of the eagles.
Arend Dutch form of Arnold.
Ares Greek: the god of war. Latin: a ram (originally the golden ram whose fleece was sought by Jason and the Argonauts). Also a constellation and the root of the name Aries, a zodiac sign.
Arian, Arien, Aries, Arius.
Argento Italian: silver. *See also* Argyro.
Argent, Argental, Argentine, Argentino, Argentum.
Argos Greek: watchful. The name of the hound of Odysseus (also known as Ulysses) in mythology.
Argus.
Argyll Scottish Gaelic: from the land of the Gaels. The name of a Scottish county.
Argyle.
Argyro Greek: silvery. *See also* Argento.
Argirio, Argirios, Argiro, Argiros, Argyros.
Ari Hebrew: a lion. Also a diminutive of names such as Aaron and

Aristotle.
Arie.
Arian Welsh: silver. *See also* Ares.
Aryan.
Aric Old English: a sacred ruler.
Ariel Hebrew: a lion of God.
Arel.
Arien/Aries *See* Ares.
Arietis A star in the constellation of Aries.
Ariki Polynesian: a chief.
Arion A figure from Greek mythology.
Arioso Italian: airy, of the air.
Ariosto Italian: one who is quick to fight.
Aristedes Greek: descended from the best; the aristocracy.
Aristede (Italian), *Aristeo, Aristo, Ariston.*
Aristomenes Greek: one of great power or strength.
Aristotle Greek: a thinker. The name of a famous Greek philosopher.
Diminutives: Ari, Arie.
Aritz Basque: an oak tree.
Ariz.
Arius *See* Ares.
Arizona The name of a state in the USA.
Arje/Arjen Dutch forms of Adrian.
Arjun Sanskrit: the white one. A warrior in Hindu mythology.
Arjuna.
Diminutive: Arj.
Arkadi/Arkadios/Arkady *See* Arcadio.
Arkwright Old English: a carpenter.
Arlen Irish Gaelic: a pledge.
Arlan, Arlin.
Arley Old English: from the hare or stag meadow.
Arlee, Arleigh, Arlie, Harleigh, Harley, Harly, Hartlee, Hartleigh, Hartley.
Arlin *See* Arlyn.
Arlo Old English: from the protected town or hill.
Arloe, Arlow, Arlowe.
Arlyn Teutonic: a waterfall.
Arlin.
Armand French form of Herman.
Arman, Armando, Armond, Armondo.
Armature English from Latin: a protective covering, like armour.
Armatura.
Armen Armenian: a man from Armenia.
Armenio Portuguese form of Herman.
Armeur *See* Armour.
Armin/Armindo *See* Herman.
Armistead Old French: the place of the hermit.
Armisted, Armitstead, Armitsted.
Armitage Old French: from the hermitage.
Armytage.
Armon Hebrew: a castle.
Armond/Armondo *See* Armand and Herman.

Armour Old French: protective covering.
Armeur, Armor, Armore, Armoure, Armure.

Armstrong Old English: a strong-armed warrior.

Armytage *See* Armitage.

Arnall Teutonic: a gracious eagle.

Arnaud *See* Arnold.

Arne Dutch form of Arnold.

Arnel *See* Arnold.

Arnett French: a little eagle.
Arnatt, Arnott.

Arnhem From Arnhem Land, a region of the Northern Territory that was named after a Dutch ship, the *Arnhem*.

Arnold Teutonic: strong as an eagle. A name introduced to England by the Normans.
Arend (Dutch), *Arnaldo* (Spanish), *Arnau* (Catalan), *Arnaud* (French), *Arne* (Dutch), *Arnel, Arno* (Teutonic), *Arnoldo* (Italian), *Arnoldus* (Dutch).
Diminutives: Arn, Arne (German, Scandinavian), Arni (Icelandic), Arnie.

Aroha Maori: love.

Aron/Arone/Aronne *See* Aaron.

Aroon Thai: of the dawn.

Aroona Aboriginal: running water. Also a girl's name.
Aroonah.

Arpad Hungarian form of Arvad.

Arragon *See* Aragon.

Arran The name of a Scottish island. *See also* Aaron.
Aran.

Arras French: a tapestry or wall-hanging.
Aaras, Aras.

Arrol/Arroll Forms of Errol.

Arron A modern form of Aaron.

Arsalan/Arslan *See* Aslan.

Arsen Greek: virile.
Arsène (French), *Arseni* (Greek), *Arsenio* (Italian), *Arsenios, Arsenius.*

Art/Artie *See* Arthur.

Artair *See* Arthur.

Artan Turkish: a lion.

Artek Polish form of Arthur.

Artemas Greek: perfect. The masculine form of Artemis, Greek goddess of the moon and hunting.
Artemi, Artemio (Italian), *Artemios, Artemisios* (Greek), *Artemiso, Artemus, Artimas, Artimus, Artyom* (Russian).

Arthea/Arthes/Artis *See* Arthur.

Arthur Celtic: strong as a bear, or strong as a rock. The name of a legendary king of Britain.
Artair (Scottish), *Artek* (Polish), *Arthea, Arthes* (Welsh), *Artis, Arttu* (Finnish), *Artu* (Finnish), *Artur* (Irish), *Arturo* (Italian, Spanish), *Artus* (French).
Diminutives: Aart, Aarti, Art, Artie.

Artyom Russian form of Artemas.

Aru Babylonian: a lion.
Arun Sanskrit: the dawn.
Arundel Old English: he who dwells with the eagles. Also a modern girl's name.
Arundale, Arundell.
Arunta Aboriginal: a white cockatoo.
Arva Latin: from the coast.
Arvad Hebrew: the wanderer.
Arpad (Hungarian).
Arval Latin: from the cultivated land.
Arvan Sanskrit: a horse in Hindu mythology.
Arve Scandinavian: an heir.
Arvin Teutonic: a friend of the people.
Arvid.
Arvind Sanskrit: a lotus.
Aravind, Arvinda.
Arvo Finnish: one who is valued.
Aryan *See* Arian.
Asa Hebrew: the healer, a physician; a biblical name. Japanese: born in the morning.
Asad Arabic: like a lion.
Assad.
Asamoah An African name of uncertain meaning.
Asbel A Kenyan name of uncertain meaning.
Ascam/Ascham *See* Askham.
Asch/Asche *See* Ash.
Ascher *See* Asher.
Ascot Old English: one who lives in the east cottage.
Ascott.
Aseel Arabic: the noble one.
Asil (Turkish).
Asef *See* Asif.
Asera Hawaiian: lucky.
Asgard Old Norse: a divine stronghold. The city of the gods in Norse mythology.
Ash Middle English: a type of tree. Also a dimutive of names such as Asher and Ashley.
Aesh, Asch, Asche, Ashe, Ashen.
Ashad Sanskrit: from Ashada, the Hindu month of June/July.
Ashburn Old English: from the brook by the ash tree.
Ashby Old English: a farm by the ash tree.
Ashbeigh, Ashbey.
Ashcroft Old English: the croft among the ash trees.
Ashcrofte.
Diminutive: Ash.
Ashden Old English: from the hill of the ash trees.
Ashenden.
Diminutive: Ash.
Asher Hebrew: happy, a fortunate one. A biblical name.
Ascher.
Diminutives: Ash, Ashe.
Ashfaq Arabic: compassionate.
Ashford Old English: one who lives at the ford by the ash tree.
Ashforde, Ayshford, Ayshforde.
Ashish Sanskrit: one who is blessed.

Asheesh.
Ashley Old English: from the ash tree meadow.
Ashleigh, Ashlie.
Diminutives: Ash, Ashe.
Ashlin Old English: a dweller by the ash tree pool.
Ashlen.
Ashmore Old English: from the lake among the ash trees.
Ashmoor.
Ashok Sanskrit: without sadness.
Ashoka, Asoka.
Ashon Swahili: the seventh, or seventh child.
Ashraf Arabic: honourable.
Achraf.
Ashton Old English: one who lives at the ash tree farm.
Ashten, Ashtin, Ashtyn.
Ashur Hebrew: black.
Ashoor.
Ashwell Old English: the stream among the ash trees.
Diminutive: Ash.
Ashwin Old English: a spear comrade or protector. Hindi: a star. Also the Hindi name for the month of October.
Ashvin, Ashwyn, Asvin, Aswin.
Asiah *See* Isaiah.
Asif Arabic: one who is forgiven.
Asef, Assef, Assif.
Asil *See* Aseel.
Asim Arabic: the protector.
Aseem.

Ask The first man (the equivalent of Adam) in Norse mythology, created from an ash tree.
Askel Norse: a divine cauldron.
Asker Turkish: a warrior.
Askham Old English: the homestead in the ash trees.
Ascam, Ascham, Askam.
Askwith/Askwythe *See* Asquith.
Aslak Norse: divine sport.
Aslan Turkish: a lion.
Arsalan (Arabic), *Arslan.*
Aspen Old English: the aspen tree, a type of poplar.
Aspin, Aspyn.
Asquith Old Norse: the ash-tree wood.
Askwith, Askwyth, Askwythe, Asquithe.
Assad *See* Asad.
Assef/Assif *See* Asif.
Assisi The name of a town in Italy.
Aston Old English: from the eastern place.
Asten, Astin.
Astron A modern name, derived from the Greek word astro, meaning a star.
Astro.
Asvin/Aswin *See* Ashwin.
Aswad Arabic: black.
Ata Turkish: an ancestor.
Atalik Hungarian: like his father.
Atanasio/Atanasius *See* Athanasius.
Atar The Zoroastrian (Persian) god of fire and the sun.
Attar.

Atarah Hebrew: a crown. Also a girl's name.
Atara.
Atea A god of the sky in Polynesian mythology.
Ateesh See Atish.
Athan Welsh: the name of a saint.
Athen, Athyn.
Athanasius Greek: noble, or the immortal one.
Afanasiy (Russian), *Afanasy* (Russian), *Atanas* (Bulgarian), *Atanasij* (Slavic), *Atanasije* (Slavic), *Atanasio, Atanasius, Athanasio, Athanasios.*
Athelstan Old English: a noble stone. The name of an early English king.
Athen See Athan.
Atherton Old English: one who lives at the spring farm.
Atherden, Atherdon, Atherten.
Athlone The name of an Irish town.
Athol Scottish Gaelic: new Ireland. A placename.
Athole, Atholl, Atthol, Atthole.
Athos Greek: an alternative name for Zeus, the ruler of the heavens.
Athyn See Athan.
Atilo/Atilius See Attilio.
Atish Hindi/Sanskrit: dynamic.
Ateesh.
Atiu Polynesian: the eldest.
Atkin The son of Adam.
Aitken, Aitkens, Aitkin, Aitkins, Atkins, Atkinson.
Atlantis Greek: of the Atlantic.
Atlantys.
Atlas Greek: a mythological demi-god who supported the sky on his shoulders.
Atley Old English: from the meadow.
Atlee, Attlee, Attley.
Atom An Armenian name of uncertain meaning.
Atonio Maori and Samoan forms of Anthony.
Attar See Atar.
Atticus Greek: a man of Athens.
Attila The warlike king of the Huns.
Atli.
Attilio Italian: from an old Roman family name.
Atilio, Atilius, Attilius.
Attlee/Attley See Atley.
Atum The Ancient Egyptian creator god, whose symbol was the scarab, or sacred beetle.
Atwater Old English: one who lives by the water.
Atwell Old English: a dweller by the spring.
Atworth Old English: from the farm.
Auberon Teutonic: noble.
Oberon.
Aubert See Albert.
Aubin See Alban.
Aubrey Teutonic: the golden-haired ruler of the elves.
Aubrie, Aubry.
Auburn Middle English: golden-

brown or reddish-brown.

Auden An English surname, best known through the poet W H Auden.

Audley Old English: the name of village in Staffordshire, England. *Audlee, Audleigh, Audly.*

Audric *See* Aldrich.

August *See* Augustus.

Augustine Latin: belonging to Augustus. *See also* Austin. *Augusten, Augustijn* (Dutch), *Augustin, Augustino* (Spanish), *Austin, Awstin* (Welsh). *Diminutive:* Stijn (Dutch).

Augustus Latin: venerable, the exalted one. The name of the first great Roman emperor. *Agostino* (Italian), *Agosto* (Italian), *Aguistin* (Irish), *Agustin* (Spanish), *August* (German), *Augustas, Auguste* (French). *Diminutives:* Augie, Gus, Gussy.

Aurek Polish form of Aurelius.

Aurelius Latin: the golden one. *Aurek* (Polish), *Aurel, Aurele* (French), *Aurelian, Aureliano* (Spanish), *Aurélien* (French), *Aurelio* (Italian), *Aurian, Auric, Aurien, Auryn* (Welsh), *Orel* (Swiss).

Auric/Aurien *See* Aurelius.

Auryn Welsh form of Aurelius.

Auska/Auskah/Auskar Modern forms of Oscar.

Austell The name of a Cornish saint and a placename.

Auster The south wind in Roman mythology.

Austin A modern form of Augustine. *Austen, Austyn, Awstin* (Welsh), *Osten, Ostin, Ostyn.*

Austral From a Latin word meaning southern, or of the south. *Australe.*

Avalon The name of a legendary island, believed to be the place where King Arthur is buried. Also a girl's name. *Avilion, Avilon.*

Avan Hebrew: proud.

Avatar Sanskrit: an incarnation. *Avitar.*

Avel Greek/Russian: breath.

Aven *See* Avon.

Avenall Old French: a dweller in the oat field. *Avenal, Avenel, Avenell.*

Avent/Aventin/Aventio/Avento *See* Advent.

Averell Old English: the slayer of the boar. *Averel, Averil, Averill, Everild.*

Avery Old English: a ruler of the elves. Also a girl's name. *Averey, Averi, Averie.*

Avi Hebrew: from Av, the fifth lunar month of the Hebrew calendar, corresponding to the zodiac sign of Leo. *Avie.*

Avidan Hebrew: God is just.

Aviel Hebrew: God is my father.
Avilion/Avilon *See* Avalon.
Avitar *See* Avatar.
Aviv Hebrew: of the springtime.
Avner *See* Abner.
Avon The name of an English county, and rivers in England and New Zealand. *See also* Afon.
Afon, Aven, Avonn.
Avram/Avrom/Avron *See* Abraham.
Avril/Avrilo *See* Aprilo.
Awad Arabic: a reward.
Awst Welsh: August.
Awstin Welsh form of Augustine and Austin.
Axel Teutonic from Hebrew: the father of peace. A form of Absalom.
Aksel (Norwegian), *Axell, Axl, Axle.*
Axion A scientific term.
Axton Old English: the stone of the sword-wielder.
Ayani Native American: a buffalo.
Ayaru *See* Iyar.
Aydan/Aydein/Ayden *See* Aden and Aidan.
Aydin Turkish: the enlightened one. Also a form of Aden.
Ayer Old French: an heir.
Ayers, Ayre, Ayres, Ayrten, Ayrton.
Aylmer Old English: noble and famous.
Aylward Old English: an awe-inspiring guardian.
Aylwin *See* Alvin.
Aynsley *See* Ainsley.
Ayre/Ayres *See* Ayer.
Ayrten/Ayrton Forms of Ayer.
Ayshford *See* Ashford.
Ayton Middle English: the town on the Eye Water, a Scottish river.
Ayten.
Azad Hindi: free.
Azadeh Arabic/Persian: one who is free.
Azafrán Spanish: saffron.
Azamat Grandeur. The Baha'i month that encompasses 17 May–4 June, so a suitable name for a Taurus or Gemini baby.
Azmat.
Azar The angel of November.
Azariah Hebrew: he whom the Lord helps.
Azarias.
Azi Nigerian: a youth.
Azim Arabic: grand or glorious.
Azeem.
Aziz Arabic: the powerful one.
Azize.
Azizah Malaysian: powerful.
Azriel Hebrew: an angel of the Lord.
Azrael.
Azul Spanish: blue.
Azzan Hebrew: very strong.
Azzurro Italian: blue.

B

Baadar *See* Bandar.
Baalu *See* Balu.
Baaru *See* Baru.
Babak A Persian name of uncertain meaning.
Babar Turkish: a lion.
Bacchus Greek: the Roman god of wine.
Bach German: a stream.
Badar Arabic: the full moon.
Badr.
Baden A popular modern name, of uncertain meaning.
Badin, Badon, Badyn, Bayden, Baydin, Baydon, Baydyn.
Badge Middle English: an emblem or token.
Badg, Badj, Badje.
Badon *See* Baden and Bhadon.
Bae Korean: inspiration.
Bael/Baele *See* Bail.
Baez Welsh: a boar.
Baghatur Turkish: a warrior.
Bagatur, Baghadur.
Bahadur A popular Malaysian name.
Bahari Swahili: the sea.
Bahloo Aboriginal: the god of the moon.
Bahram Persian: victorious.
Behram (Iranian).
Bail Old French: the outer wall of a castle.
Bael, Baele, Baile, Bale, Bayl, Bayle.
Bailey Old French: a bailiff or administrative official. Also a modern girl's name.
Baileigh, Bailiegh, Bailley, Baillie, Bailly, Baily, Bayley, Bayly.
Bailly The name of a crater on the moon. *See also* Bailey.
Bailley.
Bain Old Norse: the hospitable one.
Baine, Bane, Bayn, Bayne.
Baird Scottish Gaelic: a bard or minstrel.
Bairde, Bard, Barde.
Bakari Swahili: promising.
Bakri Hindi: a goat.
Bala Tibetan: a father.
Balan One of the knights of King Arthur's legendary Round Table.
Balantine *See* Ballantyne.
Baldassare Italian form of Balthasar.
Balder A Norse god, known for his radiance, wisdom and bravery.
Baldur, Baulder.
Baldric Teutonic: a bold or princely ruler.
Baldrick, Baldrik.
Baldwin Teutonic: a brave friend or protector.
Baldwinn, Baldwyn, Baldwynn, Baudouin (French).
Bale *See* Bail.
Balentine *See* Ballantyne.
Balfour Scottish Gaelic: from the village by the pasture.

Balin Sanskrit: a mighty warrior.
Ballantyne Scottish Gaelic: possibly meaning a god of fire.
Balantine, Balentine, Ballantine, Ballentine, Ballentyne.
Ballard Teutonic: strong, bold.
Ballas Hungarian form of Blaise.
Balonne Aboriginal: a pelican.
Balthasar Greek: the Lord protects the king. One of the three wise men in the Bible.
Baldassare (Italian), *Baltasar, Balthazar, Belshazzar* (Hebrew). *Diminutives:* Balthus, Baltus.
Balu Nepali: a bear.
Baalu.
Balun Aboriginal: a river.
Balunn.
Bamboo A subtropical plant.
Bambu.
Bancroft Old English: from the bean field.
Bandar Hindi: a monkey.
Baadar (Nepali).
Bandit A robber or outlaw.
Bandito (Italian).
Bane Hawaiian: a long-awaited child. Also a form of Bain.
Banen Celtic: white.
Banan, Banin.
Banji The name of a genus of dinosaur.
Banjee, Banjey, Banjie, Banjy.
Banjo A musical instrument. Also the nickname of one of Australia's most famous poets, Andrew Barton Paterson.
Banjoe, Banjow, Banjowe.
Banjora Aboriginal: a koala.
Banquo Celtic: the white or pale one.
Baptist/Baptiste *See* Batiste.
Bara/Barah *See* Barra.
Baradine Aboriginal: a red wallaby.
Barak Hebrew: a flash of lightning.
Barack, Barrack, Barrak.
Baran Russian: a ram.
Barran.
Barat *See* Barrett.
Baratunde An African-American name of uncertain meaning.
Barchiel The angel of February.
Barclay Old English: from the birch tree wood or meadow.
Berkeley, Berkly.
Bard/Barde *See* Baird.
Barden Old English: from the valley of barley.
Bardon.
Bardo Aboriginal: water.
Bardolf Teutonic: a fierce wolf.
Bardolph.
Baree Aboriginal: a mountain.
Barega Aboriginal: the wind.
Bareki Aboriginal: water.
Barend Dutch: a strong bear.
Berend.
Baret/Barett *See* Barrett.
Barian *See* Barrian.
Baringa Aboriginal: a light.
Baris Turkish: peace.
Barley Middle English: a grain.

Barlee, Barleigh, Barli, Barlie, Barly.
Barlow Old English: from the barley hill.
Barnabas Hebrew: a son of consolation. A name from the Bible.
Barnaba, Barnabé (French), *Barnaby, Barnebas, Bernabe* (Spanish).
Diminutives: Barney, Barnie, Barny.
Barnaby *See* Barnabas.
Barnard/Barnerd *See* Bernard.
Barnet Old English: from the place cleared by burning.
Barnett, Barnot, Barnott.
Barney/Barnie/Barny Diminutives of Barnabas.
Barnsley Old English: from the barn meadow.
Barnslee, Barnsleigh, Barnsly.
Barnum Old English: a stone house.
Baron Old French: a nobleman.
Barron.
Barr Teutonic: a bear.
Barra Hindi: big or great.
Bara, Barah, Barrah.
Barrack/Barrak *See* Barak.
Barran *See* Baran.
Barrence A form of Barry.
Barence.
Barrett Old French: possibly meaning a bonnet-maker.
Barat, Baret, Barett, Barrat, Barret.
Barri *See* Barrington and Barry.

Barrian Probably a form of Barry.
Barian, Barryan, Baryan.
Barrimor/Barrimoore *See* Barrymore.
Barrington Old English: the place of the warrior, or the warrior's followers.
Barington.
Diminutives: Barri, Barry.
Barry Irish Gaelic: like a spear.
See also Barrian and Barrence.
Barrey, Barri, Barrie.
Diminutives: Baz, Bazza.
Barrymore The moor of Barry.
Barrimor, Barrimore, Barrimoore, Barrymoore, Barrymor.
Bart Diminutive of Bartholomew and Barton.
Bartek/Bartel *See* Bartholomew.
Bartholomew Hebrew: a son of the furrows; a farmer. A biblical name.
Bartek (Polish), *Bartholomeus* (Dutch, Welsh), *Bartolo* (Italian), *Bartolomeo* (Italian), *Bertalan* (Hungarian), *Jernej* (Slovene).
Diminutives: Bart, Bartel, Barth, Bartle (Irish).
Barti Aboriginal: an insect.
Barton Old English: from the barley fields.
Barten, Bartyn.
Diminutive: Bart.
Bartram/Bartrand *See* Bertram.
Baru Aboriginal: a crocodile.
Baaru.
Baruch Hebrew: blessed. A biblical name.

Barwick *See* Berwick.
Barwon Aboriginal: a wide river.
Baryan *See* Barrian.
Bashir Arabic: a good omen.
Basil Greek: royal, kingly. Also the name of a herb. *See also* Vasily.
Basile (French), *Basileos* (Greek), *Basilio* (Spanish), *Basill, Basille, Bazel* (Dutch), *Bazil, Bazill, Bazille, Bazyl, Bazyll, Bazylle, Vasily* (Russian).
Diminutives: Bas, Baz.
Basim Arabic: the smiling one.
Basam, Bassam, Bassim.
Bass Old English: the short or lowly one.
Basse.
Bassett A diminutive of Bass.
Basset.
Bastian/Bastien *See* Sebastian.
Bates Old English: possibly the son of Bate, a boatman.
Bateson.
Bathurst The name of a New South Wales town.
Batiste French from Greek: the baptiser.
Baptist, Baptiste (French), *Battista* (Italian), *Battisto, Bautista* (Spanish).
Baudilio Spanish: after St Baudilus, an early Christian martyr.
Baudelio, Baudile (French).
Baudouin *See* Baldwin.
Baue A Dutch name of uncertain meaning.

Diminutive: Bauke.
Bauer German: a farmer.
Baulder *See* Balder.
Bautista Spanish form of Batiste.
Bavol Gypsy: the air, or the wind.
Beval.
Baxter Old English: a baker.
Bay Vietnamese: born on a Saturday. Also a herb and a reddish-brown colour.
Baye.
Bayanda An African name of uncertain meaning.
Bayard Old French: with reddish-brown hair.
Baynard.
Bayden/Baydin/Baydon *See* Baden.
Bayl/Bayle *See* Bail.
Bayley/Bayly *See* Bailey.
Bayn/Bayne *See* Bain.
Baynon *See* Beynon.
Baz *See* Barry and Basil.
Bazel/Bazil/Bazyl *See* Basil.
Beacham *See* Beauchamp.
Beagan Irish Gaelic: the little one.
Beale Old French: the beautiful one.
Beal.
Bear Middle English: an 'animal name'.
Beare, Bere.
Bearnard Gaelic form of Bernard.
Beathan Scottish Gaelic form of Benjamin.
Beattie Irish Gaelic: the provider.
Beau French: handsome. *See also* Beaumont and Beauregard.

Beauh, Bo, Boh, Bow, Bowe.
Beauchamp Old French: a beautiful field.
Beacham, Beauchamps, Beecham.
Beaudel A modern form of Beau.
Beaudell, Beaudelle.
Beaumont Old French: a beautiful hill or mountain.
Diminutives: Beau, Bo.
Beauregard Old French: a beautiful view or expression.
Diminutives: Beau, Bo.
Beavan/Beaven *See* Bevan.
Beaver Middle English: an 'animal name'.
Bever.
Beavis *See* Bevis.
Becán Irish Gaelic: a little one.
Beck Old English: a brook or stream.
Becke, Bek, Bekk, Bekke.
Becket Old English: from the small stream.
Beckett.
Beckham Old Norse: the stream by the meadow. The surname of a famous English soccer player.
Beckenham, Bekham.
Bede Old English: a prayer.
Beda (Welsh).
Bedford Old English: from Bede's ford.
Bedforde.
Bedir Turkish: the full moon.
Bedeer.
Bedivere One of the Arthurian Knights of the Round Table.
Bedevere, Bedwyr (Welsh).
Bedrich/Bedros *See* Frederick.
Bedward Welsh: from ap Edward, meaning the son of Edward. (Ap is the Welsh equivalent of the Scottish Mac or Mc, and the English suffix 'son'.)
Bedwyr Welsh form of Bedivere.
Beecham *See* Beauchamp.
Behram *See* Bahram.
Bek/Bekk *See* Beck.
Bekham *See* Beckham.
Bela Hungarian: the white one.
Belal *See* Bilal.
Belar Aboriginal: a forest of oak trees.
Belém The Portuguese name for Bethlehem.
Belen Greek: an arrow.
Belenus Celtic: a sun god.
Belford Old English: the ford by the bell.
Belforde, Bellford, Bellforde.
Belgium A 'country name'.
Belgrave Old French: a lovely grove.
Bellgrave.
Bellamy Old French: a handsome friend.
Bellford/Bellforde *See* Belford.
Belo Portuguese: beautiful or handsome.
Belshazzar *See* Balthasar.
Beltane Celtic: the name of an ancient festival held on 1 May, which celebrated the beginning

of summer. Suitable for a Taurus child.

Beltran Spanish: the name of a saint (St Luis Beltran).

Ben Hebrew: the son of. Also a diminutive of names such as Benedict and Benjamin.

Benalla Aboriginal: a musk duck. The name of a town in Victoria.

Benat Basque form of Bernard.

Benaud English from French: after the legendary Australian cricketer, Richie Benaud.

Bendek/Bendick/Bendix See Benedict.

Benedict Latin: blessed. *Bendek* (Hungarian), *Bendick, Bendix, Bendt, Benedetto* (Italian), *Benedick, Benedickt, Benedikt* (Dutch, German), *Benedykt* (Slavic), *Benen* (Irish), *Benet, Bengt* (Scandinavian), *Benito* (Spanish), *Bennet, Benneit* (Scottish Gaelic), *Bennett, Benoit* (French).
Diminutives: Ben, Bendix, Bene, Benn, Bennie, Benny.

Benes Probably a form of Benedict. *Benesh.*

Bengt Scandinavian form of Benedict.

Beniamino Italian form of Benjamin.

Benigno Spanish: the kind or benevolent one.
Benicio, Benignus.

Benito See Benedict.

Benjamin Hebrew: a son of the south, or the son of the right hand. The brother of Joseph in the Bible. *Beathan* (Scottish Gaelic), *Beniamino* (Italian), *Benjamen, Benjan, Benjen, Benjimen, Benjo, Binjamen, Binjamin, Binyamin* (Jewish).
Diminutives: Ben, Benji, Benjie, Benjy, Benn, Bennie, Benny.

Benmont An English surname of uncertain meaning.
Benmonte.

Benn/Bennie/Benny Diminutive of names such as Benedict and Benjamin.

Bennet/Benneit/Bennett See Benedict.

Benoit French form of Benedict.

Benson Old English: the son of Benedict or Benjamin.

Benstead Old English: from the place where beans grow.
Bensted.

Bentley Old English: from the bent-grass clearing or meadow.
Bentleigh, Bentlie, Bently.

Benton Old English: from the bent-grass farm.

Benvindo A Brazilian name of uncertain meaning.

Benvolio Italian: of good will. A character in Shakespeare's *Romeo and Juliet*.

Benwell Old English: inside the

wall.
Benwall.
Beppe Italian diminutive of Giuseppe (*see* Joseph).
Berend *See* Barend.
Beresford An English surname, probably meaning the ford of the beaver.
Beresforde.
Berg Teutonic: a mountain.
Bergen The name of a Norwegian port.
Berger Teutonic: from the mountains.
Beringar *See* Berringar.
Berk Turkish: strong.
Berkant Turkish: a solid oath.
Berkeley/Berkly *See* Barclay.
Berker Turkish: a solid man.
Berlin Teutonic: from the waterfall of the bear. The name of a German city.
Berlyn.
Bernabe Spanish form of Barnaby.
Bernard Teutonic: as brave as a bear. *See also* Barend and Björn.
Barnard, Barnerd, Bearnard (Gaelic), *Benat* (Basque), *Bernadus, Bernardo* (Italian, Spanish), *Bernd, Bernhard* (German), *Burnard.*
Diminutives: Bern, Berney, Berni, Bernie, Berny.
Bernstein Teutonic: amber, a semi-precious stone.
Berrick *See* Berwick.
Berridge The Scottish version of a name meaning a beverage.
Burridge.
Berrigan Aboriginal: wattle.
Berrima Aboriginal: from the south. The name of a NSW town.
Berrimah.
Berringar Aboriginal: sunset.
Beringar.
Bersh Gypsy: the young one, or one year.
Bershen, Besch, Beschen, Besh, Beshen.
Bershawn Modern American: a form of Shawn.
Bershaun, Bershaune, Bershawne.
Bert/Bertie Diminutives of Albert, Bertram, Herbert, Robert and other names. *See also* Burt.
Bertalan Hungarian form of Bartholomew.
Berthold Teutonic: a bright ruler.
Bertram Teutonic: a bright raven.
Bartram, Bartrand, Bertran, Bertrand.
Diminutives: Bert, Bertie.
Berwick Old English: from the barley farm.
Barwick, Berrick.
Berwyn Welsh: fair-haired, or a bright friend. Also a girl's name.
Berwin, Berwinn, Berwynn.
Besak/Besakh *See* Vesak.
Besch/Beschen *See* Bersh.
Bethune The name of a French city.
Beval *See* Bavol.
Bevan Welsh: from ap Evan,

meaning the son of Evan (*see also* Bedward). *See* John.
Beavan, Beaven, Beven, Bevin.
Bever *See* Beaver.
Beverly Old English: from the stream of the beaver. More commonly a female name.
Bevin *See* Bevan.
Bevis French: after the city of Beauvais, meaning a beautiful outlook or view.
Beavis, Bevys.
Bexley Old English: from the box-tree wood or clearing.
Bexlee, Bexleigh, Bexly.
Beynon Welsh: the son of Ennion.
Baynon.
Bhadon Sanskrit: the month of September.
Badon.
Bharat Sanskrit: being maintained. The Hindu god of fire.
Bhavin Sanskrit: the expressive one.
Bheki An African name of uncertain meaning.
Bhima Sanskrit: the mighty one.
Biaggio/Biagio Italian forms of Blaise.
Bianco *See* Blanco.
Bilal Arabic: a convert
Belal.
Bilawal Sanskrit: a term from Indian classical music.
Bilaval.
Bill/Bille/Billy Diminutives of William.

Billiejo A combination of Billie and Joe (*see* Joseph).
Billeejo, Billee-Jo, Billeejoe, Billee-Joe, Billie-Jo, Billijo, Billi-Jo, Billijoe, Billi-Joe, Billyjo, Billy-Jo, Billyjoe, Billy-Joe.
Billyoscar An unusual 'combination name'.
Billy-Oscar.
Biloela Aboriginal: a cockatoo.
Bilyana Aboriginal: a wedge-tailed eagle.
Bilyarra Aboriginal: an eagle.
Bilyara.
Bin *See* Binh.
Bindar Aboriginal: a kangaroo.
Bing Old English: from the hollow.
Byng.
Bingley Old English: a clearing with a hollow.
Binglee, Bingleigh.
Binh Vietnamese: the peaceful one.
Bin.
Binjamen/Binjamin *See* Benjamin.
Binyamin *See* Benjamin.
Biralo Nepali: a cat.
Birch Old English: at the birch tree.
Birchall/Birchell/Birchill *See* Burchill.
Birjis The Arabic name for the planet Jupiter.
Birjees.
Bismarck German: the surname of a 19th-century German statesman (Otto von Bismarck).
Bismark.

Bizu An African name of uncertain meaning.
Björn Old Norse: brave, like a bear. *See also* Bernard.
Bjarne (Norwegian).
Blackmore Old English: the black moor or forest.
Blackmoor, Blackmor, Blakemoor, Blakemore.
Blackwood Old English: from the black or dark wood.
Blade Old English: glory, prosperity. *Blaid, Blaide, Blayd, Blayde.*
Blaike *See* Blake.
Blaine Gaelic: thin. Also a girl's name.
Blain, Blane, Blayne.
Blainee/Blainey *See* Blaney.
Blair Scottish Gaelic: from the plain or field.
Blaire, Blayr, Blayre.
Blaise Latin: one who lisps or stammers. The name of a saint. *See also* Blaze.
Ballas (Hungarian), *Biaggio* (Italian), *Biagio* (Italian), *Blaisot* (French), *Blaize, Blassius* (German), *Blaz* (Slavic), *Blaze, Blazej* (Polish), *Blazo.*
Blaize *See* Blaise and Blaze.
Blake Old English: very pale.
Blaike, Blayke.
Blakeley Old English: from the black meadow.
Blakeleigh, Blakely.
Blakemoor/Blakemore *See* Blackmore.
Blanco Spanish: the white one. *Bianco* (Italian), *Blanko.*
Blane *See* Blaine.
Blaney Irish Gaelic: the place of the creeks.
Blainee, Blainey, Blainie, Blanee, Blaynee, Blayney, Blaynie.
Blassius German form of Blaise.
Blaxland Old English: from the black land.
Blaxton Old English: a black stone.
Blayd/Blayde *See* Blade.
Blayke *See* Blake.
Blayne *See* Blaine.
Blaynee/Blayney/Blaynie *See* Blaney.
Blayr/Blayre *See* Blair.
Blaz/Blazej/Blazo *See* Blaise.
Blaze Old English: a bright fire or flame. Also a form of Blaise.
Blaize, Blayz, Blayze, Blazey.
Bledig Welsh: like a wolf.
Bledri.
Bleu French form of Blue.
Bligh *See* Blythe.
Blue Middle English from Old French: a modern 'colour name'.
Bleu (French), *Blu.*
Blythe Old English: cheerful, gentle.
Bligh, Blyth.
Bo Chinese: precious. Old Norse: a householder. *See also* Beau.
Boadey/Boadi/Boadie/Boady *See* Bodie.
Boaz Hebrew: swift and strong. The

husband of Ruth in the Bible.
Boas.
Bob/Bobbie/Bobby *See* Robert.
Bobo Ghanaian: born on a Tuesday.
Bodeen/Bodene *See* Bodie.
Bodey *See* Bodi and Bodie.
Bodhi *See* Bodi and Bodie.
Bodi Hungarian: God protects the king. *See also* Bodie.
Bodey, Bodhi.
Bodie A modern name, also sometimes given to girls.
Boadey, Boadi, Boadie, Boady, Bode, Bodeen, Bodene, Bodey, Bodhi, Bodi, Bodine, Bowdey, Bowdi, Bowdie.
Bodil Scandinavian: the commander.
Boel (Swedish).
Bodo Teutonic: a leader.
Boel Swedish form of Bodil.
Bogart Old French/Teutonic: a strong bow.
Bogdan Slavic: a gift from God.
Bohdan.
Boguslaw Slavic: the glory of God.
Bogoslaw.
Boh *See* Beau.
Bohumil Czech/Slovak: favoured by God.
Bogumil (Polish).
Bojan Slavic: a warrior.
Bokah Nepali: a male goat.
Boka, Bokaa, Bokaah.
Boleslav Slavic: great glory.
Boleslaw.
Bolton Old English: of the manor farm.
Bombala Aboriginal: a place where the waters meet. Can also be a girl's name.
Bon French: good. Also a diminutive of names beginning with Bon.
Bonamy French: a good friend.
Bonamey, Bonami, Bonamie.
Bonar Old French: kind and gentle.
Bonart.
Bond Old English/Old Norse: a peasant farmer.
Boniface The name of an 8th-century saint.
Bonifacio.
Bonner Old French: gracious, gentle.
Bonnar.
Booral Aboriginal: large or big.
Booran Aboriginal: a pelican, or the south wind.
Boorea/Booreah *See* Boree.
Booth Old Norse: a hut or shelter.
Boothe.
Bora Turkish: like a hurricane.
Borak Arabic: like lightning.
Borden Old English: from the valley of the boar.
Boreas The north wind in Greek mythology.
Boree Aboriginal: fire.
Boorea, Booreah.
Borg Scandinavian: from the castle.
Boris Slavic/Russian: a warrior.
Borlslav Slavic: a famous warrior
Borislav, Borislaw.

Borun Aboriginal: night-time.
Boseda Nigerian: born on a Sunday.
Bosley Old English: a grove of trees.
Bosleigh.
Boston Old English: possibly meaning the stone of Botulf. The name of a US city.
Bosten, Bostyn.
Bosworth Old English: from the boar enclosure.
Botan Japanese: a peony, the flower of June.
Bourke *See* Burke.
Bow/Bowe *See* Beau.
Bowden Old English: the curved hill, or above the hill.
Bowen Welsh: the son of Owen.
Bowie Scottish Gaelic: golden-haired.
Bowral Aboriginal: large or high. The name of a NSW town.
Boyce Old French: from the wood or forest.
Boyd Scottish Gaelic: yellow-haired.
Bozek Slavic: a warrior.
Bozidar Slavic: a divine gift.
Bracken Middle English: a type of fern.
Brackin, Brackyn, Braken, Brakin, Brakyn.
Brad A diminutive of Bradley and other names beginning with Brad.
Bradbury Old English: the fort made of boards.
Bradbree, Bradbrie, Bradburey, Bradburie.
Bradee/Bradie *See* Brady.
Braden Old English: from the wide valley.
Bradan, Braedan, Braeden, Braedyn, Braiden, Braidyn, Braydan, Brayden, Braydon, Breaten, Breaton, Breyton.
Bradfield Old English: from the broad open land.
Bradford Old English: from the broad ford.
Bradley Old English: from the broad meadow.
Bradlee, Bradleigh, Bradly.
Diminutive: Brad.
Bradwell Old English: from the broad stream.
Brady Irish Gaelic: from an old surname. Also a modern girl's name.
Bradee, Bradie, Braydee, Braydie.
Brae Cornish/Gaelic: a hill.
Bray, Braye, Brea.
Braedan/Breaden/Braedyn *See* Braden.
Bragi The Norse god of poetry, music and eloquence.
Brage.
Braham/Brahim Diminutives of Abraham.
Brahma Sanskrit: the Hindu creator god.
Braiden/Braidyn *See* Braden.
Braith Middle English: the broad one.
Braithe, Brayth, Braythe.
Braken/Brakin/Brakyn

See Bracken.
Braksten/Brakstyn *See* Braxton.
Bram *See* Abraham.
Bramley Old English: from the field overgrown with broom.
Bramlee, Bramleigh, Bramlie, Bramly.
Bramwell Old English: from the well by the broom bushes.
Branwell.
Bran Celtic: a raven.
Brann.
Branagh Irish Gaelic: a Welshman.
Brana, Branah, Branna, Brannah, Brannagh.
Branco Portuguese: white. *See also* Bronislav.
Brandan *See* Brandon.
Brander Old Norse: a fiery sword.
Brando After the legendary actor, Marlon Brando.
Brandoe, Brandow.
Brandon Old English: from the gorse-covered hill.
Brandan, Brandyn, Branton.
Brandt/Brant *See* Brent.
Branduff Irish Gaelic: a black raven.
Branduf.
Branford English from Celtic: from the ford of the raven.
Brandford.
Branislav *See* Bronislav.
Branko *See* Bronislav.
Branna/Brannagh *See* Branagh.
Branwell *See* Bramwell.
Brasil/Brasiliano *See* Brazil.

Bratislav Slavic: brother or fighter of glory.
Bretislav.
Braun German form of Bruno.
Brawley From the sloping meadow.
Brawlee, Brawleigh.
Braxton A modern name, of uncertain meaning.
Braksten, Brakston, Brakstyn, Braxten, Braxtyn.
Bray/Braye *See* Brae.
Braydan/Brayden/Braydon *See* Braden.
Braydee/Braydie *See* Brady.
Brayth/Braythe *See* Braith.
Brazil The name of a South American country.
Brasil, Brasiliano, Braziliano.
Brea *See* Brae.
Breandan *See* Brendan.
Breaten/Breaton *See* Braden.
Breck Manx Gaelic: dappled or speckled.
Brek.
Brecon Welsh: the name of a group of mountains.
Breckon, Brekon.
Brede Old English: a broad open space.
Breeze English from Spanish: a light wind; someone who is carefree.
Breese, Breez.
Breighton *See* Brighton.
Brek *See* Breck.
Brekon *See* Brecon.
Brendall *See* Brendle.

Brendan Irish Gaelic: a prince.
Breandan (Irish), *Brenden, Brendhan, Brendin, Brendon, Brennan, Brentan, Brindan, Brinden.*
Brendle A modern form of Brent.
Brendall, Brendel, Brendell.
Brenin Welsh: a king.
Brennin, Brenon.
Brenleigh/Brenley/Brenly *See* Brinley.
Brennan *See* Brendan.
Brennin *See* Brenin.
Brent Old English/Celtic: from the steep hill.
Brandt, Brant, Brentan, Brenton.
Brentan *See* Brendan.
Breok Cornish/Welsh: the name of an early saint.
Bryok.
Bretislav *See* Bratislav.
Breton Old English: the place of the Briton. Also a native of Brittany, a region of France.
Bretton.
Brett Old English: a Breton, or native of Brittany.
Bret.
Brewster Middle English: a brewer.
Breyton *See* Braden.
Brian Celtic: noble and virtuous. The name of a famous 10th-century Irish king.
Briain, Briand, Briant, Brien, Bryan, Bryant, Bryon.
Brice Celtic: the speckled, or freckled, one.
Bryce, Brychan (Welsh), *Bryz, Bryze.*
Briceland *See* Bryceland.
Bridan/Briden/Bridon/Bridyn *See* Bryden.
Brien *See* Brian.
Brigham Old English: from the homestead by the bridge.
Brighton Old English: a farm by the bridge.
Bryton.
Briley Possibly a form of Riley.
Brilee, Brileigh, Brylee, Bryleigh, Bryley.
Brin/Brinn *See* Bryn.
Brinley Old Norse: burning wood.
Brenleigh, Brenley, Brenly, Brindley, Brinleigh, Brinlie, Brinly, Brynleigh, Brynley, Brynlie.
Brinsley The name of a village in Nottinghamshire, England.
Brinslea, Brinslee, Brinslie, Brinsly, Brinzlea, Brinzlee, Brinzley, Brinzlie, Brinzly.
Brisen/Brison/Brisyn *See* Bryson.
Bristol Old English: the site of a fort. The name of a British city.
Bristole, Bristoll.
Britannicus English from Latin: a man of Britain.
Briton An inhabitant of Britain.
Britain, Brittan, Britten, Britton.
Brock Old English: a badger.
Broc, Brok.

Brockwell Old English: the well of the badger.
Broderick Welsh: son of Roderick.
Broderic.
Brodie Irish Gaelic: a ditch. Also a girl's name.
Broden, Brodey, Brodin, Brody, Brodyn.
Brogan Irish Gaelic: an Irish surname of uncertain meaning
Brogain, Brogann.
Broid/Broide *See* Broyd.
Brolga Aboriginal: a large crane (a bird).
Bromfield Old English: a clearing where broom grows.
Broomfield.
Bromley Old English: from the place where broom grows.
Bromleigh, Bromly.
Brone Celtic: one who is sorrowful.
Bronislav Polish: glorious protection.
Branislav, Bronislaw.
Diminutives: Branco, Branko.
Bronson Old English: son of the brown-haired one.
Bronsen, Bronsyn.
Bronx A region of New York City.
Bronks.
Bronzo Italian: like bronze.
Bronze, Bronzio.
Brook Old English: at the brook or stream. Also a girl's name.
Brooke, Brooks.
Brooklyn A New York suburb; the name of one of David Beckham's sons.
Brooklin.
Brosnan Possibly Irish Gaelic. The surname of well-known actor Pierce Brosnan.
Brosnahan, Brosnen.
Brougham Old English: the homestead by the fort.
Broughton Old English: from the town on a hill.
Brown Old English: a 'colour name'.
Browne.
Broyd Probably a form of Boyd, meaning yellow-haired.
Broid, Broide, Broyde.
Bruce Old French: from a surname and possibly a French placename.
Diminutives: Brucie, Brucey.
Bruin Dutch form of Bruno.
Bruno Teutonic: brown.
Braun (German), *Bruin* (Dutch), *Brun, Brunet* (French), *Brunon* (Polish).
Brunton Old English: from the place by the stream.
Brunten.
Bruton Old English: from a place in Somerset.
Brutus Latin: one who is heavy.
Bryan/Bryant *See* Brian.
Bryce/Brychan *See* Brice.
Bryceland From the land of Bryce.
Briceland.
Bryden A popular modern name, possibly from an English placename.
Bridan, Briden, Bridon, Bridyn,

Brydan, Brydon, Brydyn, Bryten, Bryton.
Brylee/Bryleigh/Bryley *See* Briley.
Bryn Welsh: a hill. Also a modern girl's name.
Brin, Brinn, Brynn.
Brynleigh/Brynley/Brynlie *See* Brinley.
Brynmor Welsh: a large hill.
Bryok *See* Breok.
Bryon *See* Brian.
Bryson Middle English: the son of Brice or Bryce.
Brisen, Brison, Brisyn, Bryscen, Bryscon, Brysen.
Bryten/Bryton *See* Brighton and Bryden.
Bryz/Bryze *See* Brice.
Buchan Scottish Gaelic: a placename.
Buchanan Scottish Gaelic: possibly meaning the canon's house.
Buck Old English: a male deer.
Bucke.
Buckley Old English: from the meadow of the buck deer.
Buckleigh, Buckly.
Bud American: originally a short form of buddy (friend), but now used as an independent name, particularly in the USA.
Budd, Buddy.
Buddha Sanskrit: one who is wise or enlightened.
Buddhika.
Budhvar The Sanskrit name for Wednesday and the planet/god Mercury.
Budhvara, Budhwar.
Budi Indonesian: the wise one.
Budimir Slavic: possibly meaning to awaken peace.
Budock Cornish: a placename and the name of a saint.
Budoc.
Bulut Turkish: a cloud.
Bundok Tagalog (a Philippine language): a mountain.
Burchard Teutonic: a strong protector.
Burgrard, Burkhard (German), *Burkhart.*
Burchill Middle English: from the birch hill.
Birchall, Birchell, Birchill, Burchall, Burchel, Burchell, Burchil.
Burdett Old English: the small fort.
Burdet.
Burdon Old English: a dweller at the hill fort.
Burden.
Burgess Old French from Teutonic: the citizen of a town.
Burge.
Burke Old English: from the fort or hill.
Bourke.
Burkhard/Burkhart *See* Burchard.
Burl Old English: a cup bearer or wine server.
Burley Old English: from the fort or castle meadow.

Burleigh.
Burnaby Old Norse: the warrior's estate.
Burnard *See* Bernard.
Burnell Old French: the little brown-haired one.
Burnel.
Burnet Old French: the brown one. Also the name of a plant.
Burnett.
Burnu Aboriginal: a tree.
Burnum Aboriginal: a great warrior.
Burra Aboriginal: a large stone. The name of a town in South Australia.
Burridge *See* Berridge.
Burrill Aboriginal: a wallaby.
Burt English: a short form of the name Burton. Also a variation of Bert.
Burton Old English: from the fortified farm or town.
Burtan, Burten.
Diminutive: Burt.
Burwood Old English: the wood by the fort.
Busby Old Norse: from the farm in the thicket.
Buzby.
Buster English: generally a nickname.
Butler Old French: the head servant.
Button Old French: a button-maker.
Butten.
Buzz Generally an American nickname, but suitable for a first name.
Buz.
Byford Old English: a dweller by the ford.
Byng *See* Bing.
Byrne Irish: a descendant of the bear or raven.
Byrn.
Byron Old English: from the byres or cattle sheds. Originally a surname.
Byram, Byran, Byrom.

C

Caballo *See* Cavallo.
Caban Mayan: an earthquake.
Cadby Old Norse: the warrior's settlement.
Cade A modern name – possibly from Cadell, meaning the battle spirit.
Caed, Caede, Caid, Caide, Cayd, Cayde, Kade, Kaede, Kaid, Kaide, Kayd, Kayde.
Cadell Welsh: the battle spirit.
Cadel, Kadel, Kadell.
Caden A popular modern name, of uncertain origin.
Caeden, Caiden, Caidyn, Cayden, Caydn, Kaden, Kaeden, Kaiden, Kaidyn, Kayden, Kaydn.
Cadenz Probably a form of Caden.
Caydenz, Caydnz, Kadenz, Kaydenz, Kaydnz.
Cadman Celtic: a man of battle.
Cadmus Greek: a man from the east. A mythological figure.

Cadog Welsh: warlike. A saint's name.
Cadoc.

Cadogan Old Welsh: honour in battle.

Caed/Caede *See* Cade.

Caeden *See* Caden.

Caedmon Celtic: a wise warrior. The first English poet.

Cael *See* Cale.

Caelan/Caelen/Caelyn *See* Kalan.

Caeleb *See* Caleb.

Caelum Latin: a chisel; the name of a southern constellation. *See also* Calum.
Caellum.

Caerwyn Welsh: a blessed or holy fort.

Caesar Latin: the name of a famous Roman emperor.
Césaire (French), *Cesar* (Welsh), *César* (French), *Cesare* (Italian), *Cezair, Cezar, Cezary, Kazar, Kesar* (Russian), *Keysar.*

Caethan *See* Cathan.

Cagatay A popular Turkish name.

Cahil Turkish: young and inexperienced.

Cahill *See* Cale.

Cahm A diminutive of names such as Cameron and Campbell.

Cahn *See* Khan.

Cahvan *See* Cavan.

Cai/Caie *See* Kay and Ky.

Caid/Caide *See* Cade.

Caiden/Caidyn *See* Caden.

Cail/Caile *See* Cale.

Cailean *See* Colin.

Cailey *See* Caley.

Cain Hebrew: possessed. In the Bible, the son of Adam and Eve who murdered his brother Abel. Old French: a battlefield. *See also* Cane.

Cainaan/Cainan *See* Canaan.

Cairns The name of a city in northern Queensland.
Cairnes.

Cairo From Arabic: the capital of Egypt. *See also* Kairo.

Caitanya *See* Chaitanya.

Caius *See* Gaius.

Cal *See* Calvert and Calvin.

Calais A port in northern France.

Calan/Calen *See* Callan and Kalan.

Calca Aboriginal: a star. Also a girl's name.

Calder Old English: from the rocky river.

Cale Probably derived from Caley, an Irish Gaelic name meaning slender. Also a modern girl's name.
Cael, Cahill, Cail, Caile, Kael, Kail, Kaile, Kale.

Caleb Hebrew: the devoted one. A biblical name.
Caeleb, Calaeb, Caled, Cayleb, Kaleb, Kayleb.

Calem *See* Calum.

Caley Irish Gaelic: slender. Also a girl's name. *See also* Calum.
Cailey, Calie, Kailey, Kaley,

Kalie.
Caliban A character in Shakespeare's play *The Tempest.*
California The name of an American state.
Callaghan Irish Gaelic: the warlike one. *See also* Callan.
Callahan, Kallaghan, Kallahan.
Callan A popular modern name, probably from Callaghan. Also an Aboriginal word for a sparrow hawk.
Calan, Callen, Callin, Callun, Callyn, Kallan, Kallen, Kallin, Kallun, Kallyn.
Calogero Italian: a 5th-century saint.
Calum Scottish Gaelic form of Columba. *See also* Coleman.
Caelem, Caelum, Caellum, Calem, Callum, Kaelem, Kaelum, Kailem, Kalem, Kallem, Kallum, Kalum.
Diminutives: Caley, Cally.
Calvert Old English: a calf herder.
Calverd.
Diminutive: Cal.
Calvin Latin: the little bald one.
Calven, Calvino (Italian, Spanish), *Calvyn, Kalven, Kalvin, Kalvyn.*
Diminutives: Cal, Kal.
Calyn *See* Kalan.
Cam/Camm Diminutives of Cameron, Campbell and similar names.
Camden Gaelic: from the winding valley.
Cameron Scottish Gaelic: a crooked nose. From an old Scottish surname. Also a modern girl's name.
Cameren, Camren, Camron.
Diminutives: Cahm, Cam, Camm.
Camille Latin: from a Roman family name. The French masculine form of Camilla.
Camillo (Italian), *Camillus, Camilo, Kamil* (Czech), *Kamilo.*
Campbell Scottish Gaelic: a crooked mouth. The name of one of the great Scottish Highland clans.
Cambell.
Diminutives: Cahm, Cam, Camm.
Campion Old English: a champion.
Campo Italian: from the field.
Camren/Camron *See* Cameron.
Can Turkish: life, or the beloved one.
Canaan Hebrew: the name of a biblical region.
Cainaan, Cainan, Canan, Canen, Kainaan, Kainan, Kanaan, Kanan, Kanen.
Candelario Italian: from Candlemas, an important Christian festival.
Candide Latin: pure, or glowing white.
Candido (Italian).
Cane Manx Gaelic: an old surname.
Cain, Caine.
Canice Irish Gaelic: the handsome one. The name of several early saints.
Canley Old English: the pot- or

bucket-maker's meadow.
Canlee, Canleigh, Canlie, Cannlee, Cannleigh, Cannlie, Canly, Cannly.
Cannon English from French: a large gun.
Canon.
Canute *See* Knut.
Cappi English Gypsy: good luck.
Kappi.
Capricorn Latin: goat-horned. The name of a zodiac sign and a constellation (Capricornus).
Capri.
Caradoc Celtic/Welsh: beloved or amiable.
Caradog.
Carden Irish Gaelic: from the black fortress.
Cardin.
Cardew Cornish/Welsh: the black fort.
Carew.
Carel *See* Charles.
Carey Irish: the name of a castle. Celtic: from the river. Cornish: the loved one.
Carie, Cary, Karey, Karie, Kary.
Cariño Spanish: affection, or the affectionate one.
Carinio, Carinyo.
Carl *See* Charles.
Carleon *See* Carlyon.
Carlin Cornish: from the fort by the pool. Irish Gaelic: the little champion. Also a girl's name.
Carling, Carlyn.
Carlisle Old English: the place of the fort. Also a town in north-west England.
Carlile, Carlyle.
Carlo/Carlos *See* Charles.
Carlton Old English: from the settlement of the free peasants.
Carleton, Charlton, Charleton, Karleton, Karlton.
Carlyle *See* Carlisle.
Carlyn *See* Carlin.
Carlyon Cornish: from the slate earthworks. Also a girl's name.
Carleon.
Carmelo Hebrew: from the garden. After Mount Carmel in the Holy Land.
Carmello, Carmine (Italian).
Carmesi *See* Carmine.
Carmichael From the fort of Michael.
Karmichael.
Carmine Spanish: crimson. *See also* Carmelo.
Carmesi (Spanish), *Carmino, Karmine, Karmino.*
Carnaby An English placename.
Carnabee, Carnabie, Karnabee, Karnabie, Karnaby.
Carnarvon English from Celtic: the name of towns in Wales and Western Australia.
Caernarfon (Welsh), *Caernarvon* (Welsh).
Carne Cornish: a pile of rocks.

Carn.
Carnelian The name of a gemstone.
Cornelian.
Carney Celtic: a warrior.
Carnie, Carny.
Caro Italian: the dear or beloved one.
Carr Old Norse: from the marshland. *See also* Carson.
Carrick Irish Gaelic: from the rocky cliff or cape.
Carrington Old French: the town on the marsh.
Carington.
Carroll Irish Gaelic: a fierce warrior.
Caryl.
Carson Old English: the son of the marsh dweller. *See also* Carr.
Carsen, Carrsen, Carrson.
Carsten *See* Christian.
Carter Old English: a cart driver or maker.
Carvell Old French: the marshy estate, or the estate of the spearman.
Carvel (Manx Gaelic).
Carver Old English: a carver or sculptor.
Carwyn Welsh: blessed love.
Carwynn.
Cary *See* Carey.
Caryl *See* Carroll.
Case An English surname, sometimes used as a first name.
Cayce, Cayse, Kase, Kayce, Kayse.
Casey Irish Gaelic: the vigilant one.
Casee, Casie, Kacey, Kacie, Kaisey,
Kasey, Kasie, Kaycee, Kaycie.
Cash A predominantly Irish surname.
Cashe, Cassh, Casshe, Kash, Kashe.
Cashel Irish: a bulwark; also a placename.
Cashell.
Cashmir *See* Kashmir.
Casimir Old Slavic: the great destroyer. The name of several Polish kings and a saint.
Casimiro (Spanish), *Kasimier, Kasimierz, Kasimir* (German), *Kazimierz* (Polish), *Kazimir* (Czech).
Caspar Persian: the treasurer. One of the three wise men in the New Testament. *See also* Caspian, Gaspar and Jasper.
Caspah, Casper, Kaspah, Kaspar (German), *Kasper* (Polish).
Diminutive: Cass.
Caspian From the name of a vast lake, the Caspian Sea. Also a form of Caspar.
Caspien, Kaspian, Kaspien.
Cass *See* Caspar.
Cassh/Casshe *See* Cash.
Cassidy Irish Gaelic: the clever or ingenious one. Also a modern girl's name.
Kassidy.
Cassius Latin: hollow, empty.
Cassian, Cassio, Kassian, Kassius.
Castor Greek: a beaver. The star

Castor, along with its twin Pollux, forms part of the constellation of Gemini.
Kastor.
Cathal Irish Gaelic: a battle ruler.
Catheld, Kathel.
Cathan Irish Gaelic: of the battle. *See also* Kane.
Caethan.
Cathmor Irish Gaelic: a great warrior.
Cato Latin: the wise one.
Caton (French).
Cavallo Italian: a horse.
Caballo (Spanish).
Cavan Irish Gaelic: the handsome one. The name of an Irish county.
Cahvan, Caven, Cavian, Cavien, Kahvan, Kavan, Kaven, Kavian, Kavien.
Diminutives: Cav, Kav.
Cavanagh Irish Gaelic: a follower or descendant of St Caomhan.
Cavanna, Cavannah, Kavanagh, Kavanna, Kavannah.
Cavell Old French: the bald one.
Caval, Cavall, Cavel.
Caven/Cavian *See* Cavan.
Cavill Old English: the field of the jackdaw.
Cavil, Caville.
Cawley Middle English: probably meaning a calf meadow.
Cawlee, Cawleigh.
Caxton After William Caxton, the 15th-century writer and printer.
Caxten, Caxtin, Caxtyn.
Cayd/Cayde *See* Cade.
Cayden/Caydn *See* Caden.
Caydenz/Caydnz *See* Cadenz.
Cayleb *See* Caleb.
Cazaly After the legendary Australian Rules Football player, Roy Cazaly.
Cazalee, Cazaleigh, Cazaley.
Cecil Latin: the blind one, or the sixth.
Cecilio, Cecilius, Cecyl, Cesil, Secil, Sesil.
Diminutives: Cec, Cece.
Cedar Middle English: a coniferous tree.
Ceder.
Cedomir Slavic: a child of peace.
Cedric English: invented in the early 1800s by Sir Walter Scott for a character in *Ivanhoe*.
Cedrick, Cedrik.
Cedro Spanish: a cedar tree.
Cedron (Spanish).
Ceduna Aboriginal: a waterhole. A town in South Australia.
Celestine Latin: heavenly. The masculine form of Celeste.
Celestin, Celestino (Italian), *Celesto, Celestyn, Celestyne.*
Diminutive: Tino (Italian).
Celsus Latin: high and lofty.
Celso (Italian).
Celt *See* Kelt.
Celtee/Celtey/Celtie *See* Keltie.
Cemal *See* Kamal.

Cengiz Turkish form of Genghis.
Census English from Latin: an official count and survey of citizens or inhabitants.
Censuss.
Centauri Greek: a centaur, a creature that is half-man, half-horse. The centaur is the symbol of the zodiac sign of Sagittarius.
Centaur, Centaurus.
Cephas Aramaic: a stone.
Kephas.
Cesaire/César/Cesare *See* Caesar.
Cesil *See* Cecil.
Ceslaus/Ceslav/Ceslovas *See* Czeslaw.
Cetus Latin: a whale. The name of a constellation.
Cezair/Cezar/Cezary *See* Caesar.
Chace *See* Chase.
Chad Old English: from the name of a 7th-century saint. Also a diminutive of Chadwick, and the name of an African country.
Chadd, Chaddi, Chadi.
Chadwick Old English: the town of the warrior.
Chadwicke, Chadwyck, Chadwycke.
Diminutives: Chad, Chadd.
Chahaya Indonesian: light.
Chaim *See* Hyam.
Chaise *See* Chase.
Chait Sanskrit: the Hindu month of March/April, corresponding to the zodiac sign of Aries.
Chaitanya A 16th-century Hindu saint.
Caitanya.
Challis Old French: a ladder or stairs.
Chalis, Challys, Chalys.
Chalmers The Scottish form of Chambers, meaning of the chamber.
Chaloner Old French: a blanket-maker.
Chalener, Challener, Challoner.
Chaman Sanskrit: a garden.
Chamba Sherpa/Tibetan: the loved one.
Chaminda A Sri Lankan name of uncertain meaning.
Chaminder.
Champika Sri Lankan: probably meaning a flower.
Chan A Chinese clan name.
Chance/Chancey *See* Chauncey.
Chand Sanskrit: the moon.
Chandak.
Chandan Sanskrit: of the sandalwood tree.
Chander *See* Chandra.
Chandi Sanskrit: silver.
Chandler Old French: the candle-maker.
Chandos An English surname, of uncertain meaning.
Chandra Sanskrit: a shining moon.
Chander, Chandran.
Chaney Old French: from the oak grove.
Chane, Cheney, Cheyney.
Chang Chinese: free.

Channing Old French: a canon.
Chaplin Middle English: a priest or chaplain.
Chaplain, Chapling.
Chapman Old English: a merchant or trader.
Charif *See* Sharif.
Chariton The name of an ancient Greek author.
Charriton.
Charles Teutonic: a free man. A popular name since the time of the Holy Roman Emperor Charlemagne (AD 742–814), and the name of many kings.
Carel (Dutch), *Carl* (German), *Carlo* (Italian), *Carlos* (Portuguese, Spanish), *Carolus, Charleston, Hare* (Maori), *Karel* (Czech, Dutch), *Karl* (German, Scandinavian), *Karlis* (Latvian), *Karlo* (Croatian), *Karol* (Polish), *Károly* (Hungarian), *Siarl* (Welsh), *Tiare* (Maori).
Diminutives: Charley, Charli, Charlie, Chas, Chaz, Chico, Chuck, Chuckie.
Charleston *See* Charles.
Charleton/Charlton *See* Carlton.
Charli/Charlie Diminutives of Charles.
Charon Greek: in mythology, the ferryman of the River Styx in the Underworld. Also a satellite of the planet Pluto.
Kharon.

Chas A diminutive of Charles.
Chase Old French: the hunter.
Chace, Chaise, Chayce, Chayse.
Chaseley A modern name, probably derived from Chase.
Chaselee, Chaseleigh.
Chaska Native American: the first, or firstborn son.
Chau Vietnamese: a pearl. Also a girl's name.
Chaucer Old French: a bootmaker.
Chauncey Old French: a church official or chancellor.
Chance, Chancey, Chauncy.
Chay *See* Che.
Chayce/Chayse *See* Chase.
Chayla A name from the *Dragon Prince* and *Dragon Star* fantasy novels.
Chaylah.
Chayn/Chayne *See* Shane.
Chaz A diminutive of Charles.
Che Spanish: diminutive of Joseph.
Chay.
Cheiron *See* Chiron.
Chembo Tibetan: big.
Chen Chinese: great or vast.
Cheney *See* Chaney.
Cherokee Native American: the name of a tribe.
Chesley Old English: the camp on the meadow.
Cheslee, Chesleigh, Cheslie, Chesly.
Chesney Old French: the oak grove.
Chesnay.
Chester Latin: a Roman site or

camp. The name of an English city.
Cheston.
Diminutive: Chet.
Cheston *See* Chester.
Chet Thai: a brother. Also a diminutive of Chester and Chetwin.
Chetan Sanskrit: possibly meaning of the soul.
Chetwin Old English: from the cottage on the winding path.
Chetwyn.
Diminutive: Chet.
Cheung Chinese: good luck.
Chevy French: from chevalier, meaning a knight.
Chevey, Chevi, Chevie.
Chewang Sherpa/Tibetan: life and power.
Cheyenne Native American: a tribe and the name of a city in the USA.
Cheyn/Cheyne *See* Shane.
Cheyney *See* Chaney.
Chico *See* Charles and Francis.
Chidozie An unusual African name.
Chidozi.
Chifley After Ben Chifley, an Australian Prime Minister.
Chiffleigh, Chiffley, Chifleigh, Chifly.
Chiko Japanese: like an arrow.
Chilli From a Native American word, meaning spicy.
Chili, Chillie.
Chilton Old English: from the children's farm.
Chin Korean: the precious one.

China A 'country name'.
Chyna.
Chino Spanish: the name of a fabric.
Chiron Greek: a wise teacher. A centaur in mythology and a symbol of the zodiac sign Sagittarius.
Cheiron, Kiron, Kyron.
Chisholm An English surname occasionally used as a first name.
Chisholme.
Chitta Sanskrit: knowledge.
Chivan A Cambodian name of uncertain meaning.
Chivas Scottish Gaelic: a narrow place. The name of a famous whisky.
Schivas.
Chola Tibetan: an elder brother.
Chord Latin: a musical term.
Chorde.
Chrétien *See* Christian.
Chris A diminutive of Christian, Christopher, etc.
Chrishna *See* Krishna.
Christian Latin: a follower of Christ; a Christian. *See also* Christopher.
Carsten (German), *Chrétien* (French), *Christen, Christer* (Danish, Swedish), *Christiaan, Christien, Cristan, Cristen, Cristian, Cristiano* (Italian), *Cristien, Criston, Karsten* (German), *Khristian, Kiritowha* (Maori), *Kristen* (Danish),

Kristian (Swedish), *Kristijan* (Slavic), *Kristinn* (Icelandic), *Kristjan, Krisztian* (Hungarian). *Diminutives:* Chris, Christie, Christy, Kit, Kris.
Christie/Christy Irish and Scottish diminutives of Christian and Christopher.
Christien *See* Christian.
Christmas Old English: born at Christmas.
Christopher Greek: bearing Christ. The patron saint of travellers. *See also* Christian.
Christof, Christoff, Christoffe, Christoffel, Christoph (German), *Christophe* (French), *Christos* (Greek), *Cristóbal* (Spanish), *Cristof, Cristoff, Cristoffe, Cristoforo* (Italian), *Cristopher, Kester* (Scottish), *Kristof* (Slavic), *Kristoff, Kristoffer* (Scandinavian), *Krystof* (Czech), *Krystoff*. *Diminutives:* Chris, Christie, Christy, Cristo (Spanish), Kit, Kitto (Cornish), Kittow (Cornish), Kris, Kristo (Finnish), Krys, Risto (Finnish), Topher.
Christos *See* Christopher.
Chronos *See* Kronos.
Chrysander Greek: a golden man.
Chrysostomos Greek: the golden-mouthed one.
Chrysostom.
Chubie Aboriginal: a crab.
Chuck/Chuckie *See* Charles.

Chuen Mayan: a monkey.
Chui Swahili: a leopard.
Chula Native American: a fox.
Chung Chinese: the wise one.
Chungda Sherpa/Tibetan: the youngest.
Churchill Old English: from the church on the hill.
Chyna *See* China.
Cian/Cianan/Ciian *See* Kean.
Ciarán *See* Kieran.
Cicero Latin: a famous Roman statesman and orator.
Ciceron.
Cigfran Welsh: a raven.
Cillian Irish Gaelic: a warrior.
Cillan.
Cimon Greek: the name of an ancient Greek statesman.
Kimon.
Cipress/Cipresso *See* Cypress.
Ciprian/Cipriano/Ciprien *See* Cyprian.
Ciriaco Italian and Spanish forms of Kyriakos.
Ciril/Cirille *See* Cyril.
Cirino/Ciro *See* Cyrus.
Cisco A diminutive of Francisco, the Spanish form of Francis.
Cisko.
Clae/Claeten/Claeton *See* Clay and Clayton.
Clairey/Clarey *See* Clary.
Clancy Irish Gaelic: a red or ruddy warrior. Also a modern girl's name.
Clancee, Clancey, Clanci, Clancie.

Claremont English from French: from the bright hill.
Clairemont, Clairmont.

Clarence Latin: the illustrious one.
Diminutive: Clarrie.

Clark Old French: a cleric or scholar. *See also* Cleary.
Clarke.

Claro Spanish: light-coloured.
Klaro.

Clarrie *See* Clarence.

Clary An English surname, probably derived from clarus, Latin for bright.
Clairey, Clairy, Clarey.

Claten/Claton *See* Clayton.

Claude Latin: the lame one.
Claud, Claudio (Italian, Spanish), *Claudius* (German), *Klaud, Klaude.*

Claus *See* Nicholas.

Clay Old English: from the clay. Also a diminutive of Clayton.
Clae, Klae, Klay.

Clayton Old English: from the settlement in the clay.
Claeten, Claeton, Claten, Claton, Clayten, Klaeten, Klaeton, Klaten, Klaton, Klayten, Klayten.
Diminutives: Clae, Clay, Klae, Klay.

Cleary Irish Gaelic: a clerk or scholar. *See also* Clark.
Clery.

Cleat/Cleate *See* Clete.

Cleave Middle English: to cut or split apart.
Cleaver, Cleve, Clieve, Kleave, Kleaver, Kleve.

Cleavon American: a contemporary name.
Clevon, Kleavon, Klevon.

Cledwyn Welsh: rough but blessed.

Clegg Old Norse: from the haystack-shaped hill.

Clein *See* Klein.

Clement Latin: merciful, mild.
Clemence, Clemens, Clément (French), *Clements, Clemon, Klemens* (German), *Kliment* (Russian).
Diminutives: Clem, Clemmie.

Clent/Clenton *See* Clinton.

Cleon Greek: the famous one.
Kleon.

Clery *See* Cleary.

Clete Middle English: a wedge.
Cleat, Cleate, Kleat, Kleate, Klete.

Cleto Italian/Spanish: a form of Anacletus, the name of a pope.
Clito, Kleto, Klito.

Cleve *See* Cleave, Cleveland and Clive.

Cleveland Old English: from the hilly place, or the place of cliffs. An English and US placename.
Diminutive: Cleve.

Clide *See* Clyde.

Clieve *See* Cleave and Clive.

Cliff A diminutive of Clifford and Clifton.
Cliffe, Clift.

Clifford Old English: from the ford

by the cliff or slope.
Diminutives: Cliff, Cliff.
Clifton Old English: from the settlement on the cliff.
Diminutives: Cliff, Cliffe.
Cline *See* Klein.
Clinton Old English: from the place on the headland.
Clenton, Klenton, Klinton.
Diminutives: Clent, Clint, Klent, Klint.
Clive Old English: from the cliff.
Cleve, Clieve, Clyve.
Clooney/Cloony *See* Cluny.
Clorian Welsh: a set of scales.
Clovelly A town in Devon, England, and a Sydney suburb.
Clovelley, Clovellie.
Clovis Teutonic: a famous warrior.
Clunes Scottish Gaelic: a resting place, or a meadow.
Clunies.
Cluny Irish Gaelic: from the meadow.
Clooney, Cloony, Cluney.
Clyde Scottish: the name of a river.
Clide, Clyte.
Clyve *See* Clive.
Coan/Coen *See* Cohen.
Cobar Aboriginal: burnt earth. A New South Wales placename.
Cobden Old English: from the hill with a knob.
Cobe/Cobi/Coby *See* Kobe.
Cobefox/Cobyfox *See* Kobyfox.
Cobe-Lee/Coby-Lee *See* Kobe-Lee.
Cobre *See* Copper.

Cochrane Welsh: from the red brook or stream.
Cochran.
Coda Italian: a musical passage. Also a girl's name.
Codah, Koda, Kodah.
Cody Old English: a pillow or cushion.
Codee, Codey, Codi, Codie, Cohdee, Cohdi, Cohdie, Cohdy, Kodee, Kodey, Kodi, Kodie, Kody, Kohdee, Kohdi, Kohdie, Kohdy.
Cohdi/Cohdie/Cohdy *See* Cody.
Cohen Hebrew: a priest.
Coan, Coen, Cohan, Koen, Kohan, Kohen, Kowan, Kowen.
Col Diminutive of names such as Colin, Collingwood and Colville.
Cola African: a type of nut.
Colah, Kola, Kolah.
Colan *See* Colin.
Colane Aboriginal: a tree.
Colain.
Colbert Teutonic: a bright seafarer.
Colby Old Norse: from the dark country.
Coleby, Kolbey, Kolby.
Cole Old English/Teutonic: dark and swarthy. Also a diminutive of Nicholas.
Kole.
Colefax Old English: literally a coal fox, probably referring to a fox with black markings.
Colfax.
Coleman Teutonic: dark. Latin: like a

dove. *See also* Calum and Columba.
Collman, Colman, Colomen (Welsh).

Coli A diminutive of Colin.
Colli, Collie.

Colin Greek: the victory of the people. Originally a diminutive of Nicholas.
Cailean (Scottish Gaelic), *Colan, Collin.*
Diminutives: Col, Coll.

Coll Diminutive of names such as Colin, Collingwood and Colville.

Collen Welsh: a hazel tree.

Collier Old English: a charcoal burner or seller.
Collyer, Colyer.
Diminutives: Col, Coll.

Collin Aboriginal: fire. *See also* Colin.

Collingwood Old English: a wood whose ownership is disputed.
Diminutives: Col, Coll.

Collis The son of Coll or Cole.
Diminutives: Col, Coll.

Collman/Colman *See* Coleman and Columba.

Colm *See* Columba.

Coloman *See* Columba.

Colomen Welsh form of Coleman and Columba.

Colorado Spanish: ruddy, or red. The name of a US river and state.

Colt Old English: a young horse.
Colte, Kolt, Kolte.

Colton Old English: from the dark town.
Colsten, Colston, Colten.

Columba Latin: dove-like. The name of a 6th-century Irish saint, and also a southern constellation. *See also* Calum and Coleman.
Colm (Irish Gaelic), *Colman, Coloman, Colomen* (Welsh), *Colum* (Irish Gaelic), *Columb, Koloman* (Turkish).

Colville French/Old English: from the cool or cold place.
Colvil, Colvill.
Diminutives: Col, Coll.

Colvin An English surname of uncertain meaning.
Colvinn, Colvinne, Colvyn, Colvynn, Colvynne.
Diminutives: Col, Coll.

Coman Arabic: noble.

Compton Old English: from the farm in the valley.
Compten.

Con A diminutive of Conrad, Constantine, etc.

Conall Celtic: as strong as a wolf.
Conal, Connall, Connell.

Conan Irish Gaelic: wise and intelligent. The name of a saint.
Conant, Connan, Conyn (Welsh), *Konan, Kyenan, Kynan.*

Concetto Italian: the masculine form of Concetta, meaning the beginning.

Concord Middle English: agreement or peace.

Conchord, Conchorde, Concorde.
Condor Spanish: a bird of the Americas.
Conlan Irish Gaelic: the hero.
Conlin, Conlon.
Conn Irish Gaelic: a chief. Also a diminutive of Connor.
Connah/Connaugh *See* Connor.
Connall/Connell *See* Conall.
Connan *See* Conan.
Connaught Irish Gaelic: brave and wise.
Connacht.
Connery Irish Gaelic: a surname of uncertain meaning.
Connolly Irish Gaelic: brave or wise.
Conolly.
Connor Irish Gaelic: with a strong will.
Connah, Connaugh, Conner, Conor.
Diminutive: Con.
Conrad Teutonic: a bold counsellor.
Conrade (French), *Corrado* (Italian), *Konrad* (German, Polish), *Konrade.*
Diminutives: Con, Curt, Kort, Kurt (German).
Conroy Irish Gaelic: wise.
Consolato Italian: consolation.
Constantine Latin: steadfast.
Constant, Constantijn (Dutch), *Constantin, Constantino* (Spanish), *Costante, Costantino* (Italian), *Costanzo* (Italian), *Cystennin* (Welsh), *Konstadena, Konstadene, Konstadine, Konstantin* (German, Russian, Scandinavian), *Konstantyn* (Polish), *Kosta, Kostadin, Kostandin* (Albanian), *Kostas* (Greek).
Diminutives: Con, Costain, Costin (Romanian), Kostya (Russian), Stijn (Dutch).
Conway Welsh: holy water. Irish: a yellow hound.
Conwy.
Conwil Welsh: after St Cynwyl.
Conwill, Conwyl, Conwyll.
Conyn Welsh form of Conan.
Coombah Aboriginal: a baby boy.
Coomba.
Cooper Middle English: a barrel or tub maker.
Coopa, Coopah, Kooper, Kupah.
Coorain Aboriginal: the wind. A NSW placename.
Cooran Aboriginal: an ash tree.
Coran.
Coorong Aboriginal: a narrow lagoon.
Cooyong Aboriginal: a bandicoot.
Cope Old English: a cape wearer or maker.
Copeland Old English: from the bought land.
Copland, Coupland.
Copper Old English: a reddish-brown metal.
Cobre (Spanish), *Copor* (Welsh), *Cupri, Cupro.*
Coran *See* Corin.
Corbett Old French: a raven.

Corban, Corbet, Corbin, Corbyn, Corvin, Korbin, Korbyn, Korvin.
Corbin/Corbyn *See* Corbett.
Cord Middle English: a string or small rope.
Corde.
Cordell Old French: a rope-maker.
Cordel.
Cordero Spanish: a lamb.
Corey Celtic/Gaelic: dweller in the hollow. Also a modern girl's name.
Coree, Cori, Corie, Correy, Corry, Cory, Koree, Korey, Kori, Korie.
Corigan/Corigen *See* Corrigan.
Corin Cornish: from the corner. Latin: the name of a Roman deity, possibly meaning a spear.
Coran, Coren, Corrin, Coryn, Korin, Korrin, Koryn, Quirino (Italian).
Corlett Manx Gaelic: the son of Thor's people.
Corlet.
Corley Old English: from the wood of the herons.
Corleigh, Korleigh, Korley.
Cormac Irish Gaelic: the lad of the chariot.
Cormack, Cormag (Scottish Gaelic), *Cormick.*
Cormick *See* Cormac.
Cornelian *See* Carnelian.
Cornelius Latin: a horn.
Corneille (French), *Cornel, Cornelio, Cornelis* (Dutch), *Cornell, Kornel* (Czech, Polish).

Diminutives: Kees (Dutch), Niels.
Corowra Aboriginal: a rocky river, or a pine tree.
Corrado *See* Conrad.
Correy/Corry *See* Corey.
Corrigan Irish Gaelic: a little spear, or a spear-carrier.
Corigan, Corigen, Corrigen.
Corrin *See* Corin.
Cortez Spanish: the name of the conqueror of Mexico.
Cortes.
Corvin *See* Corbett.
Corvus Greek: a crow, a bird that is associated with the sun god Apollo. The name of a southern constellation.
Corwin Old French: a friend of the heart.
Corwen, Corwyn.
Cory *See* Corey.
Corydon Greek: a lark.
Coryn *See* Corin.
Cosimo Italian form of Cosmo.
Coskun Turkish: the enthusiastic one.
Cosmo Greek: perfect order, harmony.
Cosimo (Italian), *Cosmas, Cosmino, Cosmos, Kosmo.*
Costain/Costin *See* Constantine.
Costantino/Costanzo Italian forms of Constantine.
Costello An Irish surname with Norman (French) origins.
Costelloe.
Coulson The son of Cole or Nicholas.

Coulsan, Coulstan, Coulston.
Coupland *See* Copeland.
Courtis *See* Curtis.
Courtland Old English: from the court land.
Courtney Old French: the short-nosed one, or from a placename. Also a modern girl's name.
Courtenay, Courtnay.
Coventry The name of an English city, possibly meaning the place where the waters meet.
Coventree, Coventrey, Coventrie, Koventree, Koventrey, Koventrie, Koventry.
Cowan Aboriginal: from the big water.
Craig Scottish Gaelic: a rock or crag.
Craige, Craigh, Craigie, Kraig, Kraige, Kraigh.
Crandon Old English: from the hill of the cranes.
Cranden.
Cranley Old English: from the meadow of the cranes.
Cranleigh, Cranly.
Cranog Welsh: a heron.
Crantock Cornish: a placename and the name of a saint.
Carantoc, Crantoc.
Crawford Old English: from the ford with the crows.
Crawforde, Crawfurd, Crawfurde.
Creagh Irish Gaelic: a branch.
Creed Middle English from Latin: one who believes.

Crede, Creedan, Creeden.
Cregan Irish Gaelic: an Irish surname.
Creegan.
Creighton Old English/Welsh: a rocky place.
Creighten, Crichton, Cryten, Cryton.
Creon Greek: a prince, or princely ruler, a King of Thebes in Greek legend.
Kreon.
Crepin/Crespin *See* Crispin.
Crevan Irish Gaelic: a fox.
Crewe Old English: stepping-stones or a ford. An English placename.
Crisiant Welsh: a crystal.
Crispin Latin: the curly-haired one. St Crispin was a 3rd-century martyr.
Crepin, Crespin, Crispen, Crispian, Crispus, Krispen, Krispin.
Cristan/Cristen *See* Christian.
Cristian/Cristiano/Cristien *See* Christian.
Cristo Diminutive of Christopher, but also used as an independent name.
Cristóbal Spanish form of Christopher.
Cristof/Cristoffe/Cristoforo *See* Christopher.
Criston *See* Christopher.
Cromwell Old English: from the winding stream.
Cronan Irish Gaelic: the swarthy one.
Cronos *See* Kronos.

Crosby Old Norse: from the village with the cross.
Crosbey, Crosbie.

Cruise A modern name, probably after the actor Tom Cruise.
Cruis, Cruiz, Cruize, Cruz, Cruze, Kruis, Kruise, Kruiz, Kruize, Kruze.

Cruz Spanish: a cross (as in the crucifixion). *See also* Cruise.

Cryten/Cryton *See* Creighton.

Cuan Irish Gaelic: a little hound or wolf.

Cuba The name of a Caribbean country.

Cubert Cornish: a Celtic saint and a placename.

Cuin Irish Gaelic: wise.
Cuen.

Cullen Old French: from the colony.
Cullan, Cullin.

Culley Gaelic: from the forest.
Cullee, Culli, Cullie, Cully.

Cullya Aboriginal: an emu.

Cumal Irish Gaelic: the sky. The name of a figure in Gaelic mythology.
Cumall, Cumhall.

Cunningham A Scottish placename.

Cupid Latin: desire, passion. The ancient Roman god of love, the son of Venus.

Cupri/Cupro *See* Copper.

Curan A character in Shakespeare's play *King Lear*.

Curio Something that is of a rare or curious nature.

Curnow *See* Kernow.

Curran Irish Gaelic: an old family name.
Curren.

Currumbin Aboriginal: a pine tree.

Curt A diminutive of Conrad and Curtis.

Curtis Old French: the courteous one.
Courtis, Courtiss, Curtiss, Kertis, Kertiss, Kurtis, Kurtiss.
Diminutives: Curt, Kert, Kort, Kurt.

Curtleigh A combination of Curt and Leigh (a meadow or clearing).
Curtlee, Curtlie, Curtly, Kurtlee, Kurtleigh, Kurtlie, Kurtly.

Custodio Spanish: a guardian.

Cuthbert Old English: famous and bright.

Cy A diminutive of names such as Cyprian and Cyrus.
Cye.

Cyal/Cyall/Cyell *See* Kyle.

Cygnus Greek: a swan. A bird associated with the sun god Apollo, and the name of a northern constellation.
Cygni.

Cyle *See* Kyle.

Cymbeline Celtic: a sun lord. The title of one of Shakespeare's plays.
Diminutive: Cymby.

Cynfor Welsh: a great chief.

Cynric Old English: of kingly lineage.

Cypress English from Latin: an evergreen tree.
Cipress, Cipresso (Italian), *Cypresso*.

Cyprian Latin: a man from the island of Cyprus.
Ciprian, Cipriano, Cyprien (French), *Sibran* (Breton). *Diminutives:* Cy, Cye.

Cyr/Cyriac/Cyriacus See Kyriakos.

Cyrano Greek: a man from Cyrene, an ancient Greek colony in North Africa.

Cyril Greek: lordly. The name of several early saints.
Ciril, Cirill, Cirille, Cyrill, Cyrille (French), *Cyrillus, Cyryl, Cyryll, Cyrylle, Kirill* (Russian), *Sirroul*.

Cyro See Cyrus.

Cyrus Persian: the name of the founder of the Persian empire. *See also* Kourosh.
Ciro (Italian), *Cyro, Kourosh* (Persian), *Syrus*. *Diminutives:* Cirino (Italian), Cy, Cye.

Cystennin Welsh form of Constantine.

Czeslaw Polish: honour and glory.
Ceslaus, Ceslav, Ceslovas.

D

Daan/Daaniel *See* Daniel.

Dabert French: bright action.

Dabir Arabic: a teacher or secretary. *Dabeer*.

Dacey Gaelic: the southerner. Also a girl's name.
Dacie, Dacy.

Dack Old Norse: the daytime. *Dak*.

Dade A modern, probably invented, name.
Daed, Daede, Daid, Daide, Dayd, Dayde.

Dae Korean: greatness.

Daed *See* Dade.

Daedalus A figure in Greek mythology who, with his son Icarus, flew with wings coated in wax.

Daemon *See* Damon.

Daen/Daene *See* Dane.

Dafad Welsh: a sheep or ram.

Dafydd Welsh form of David. *See also* Dewi.

Dag Old Norse: the day.

Dagan Hebrew: grain, or the earth.

Dagfinn Scandinavian: a combination of day (dag) and a person from Finland.
Dagfin.

Dagon The fish god of the Philistines.

Dahr/Dahre *See* Darius.

Dai Japanese: the large one. Welsh:

a diminutive of David and Dewi. *See also* Dhai.

Daibhidh Irish and Scottish forms of David.

Daid/Daide *See* Dade.

Daido Japanese: large.

Dail/Daile *See* Dale.

Daimon *See* Damon.

Dain A stag in Norse mythology. Also a form of Dane.
Daine.

Daisuke Japanese: the helper.

Daividh *See* David.

Dak *See* Dack.

Dakota Native American: a friend. The name of two US states.
Dakoda, Dakodah, Dakotah, Dekota, Dekotah.

Daku Aboriginal: sand.

Dalajit Sanskrit: one who can win people over.
Daljait, Daljit.

Dalbert Old English: from the shining valley.

Dale Old English/Teutonic: a valley dweller. Also a girl's name.
Dail, Daile, Dayl, Dayle, Daylle.

Daley Irish Gaelic: a counsellor.
Daly.

Dalgleish Gaelic: the field with a brook.
Dalglish.

Dallas Celtic: skilled, or from the field of water. A city in Texas and also a girl's name.
Dalas, Dallis.

Dallen A modern name, possibly a variation of Allen (*see* Alan).
Dallan, Dallin, Dallyn.

Dalley Middle English: from the dale.
Dallea, Dallee, Dalli, Dallie, Dally.

Dalo Aboriginal: fire.
Dallo.

Dalton Old English: from the farm in the valley.

Dalyo Aboriginal: light.

Dalziel Scottish Gaelic: from the little field.

Daman/Damen *See* Damon.

Damarcus/Damarkus *See* DeMarcus.

Damian/Damien/Damion *See* Damon.

Damir Slavic: one who provides peace.

Damodar Sanskrit: tied with a rope around the belly.

Damon Greek: tame, domesticated. Also meaning a true friend.
Daemon, Daimon, Daman, Damen, Damian, Damiano (Italian), *Damien, Damion, Damyon, Dayman, Daymon, Demian, Demyan* (Russian), *Dyfan* (Welsh).

Damu The god of vegetation in Sumerian mythology.

Dan *See* Daniel.

Dana Old English: from Denmark. *See also* Dane.

Danai An unusual Thai name.
Danail Bulgarian form of Daniel.
Danbey/Danby *See* Denby.
Dane A man from Denmark.
Daen, Daene, Dain, Daine, Dayn, Dayne.
Daneel Dutch form of Daniel.
Danek *See* Daniel.
Danesh Arabic: knowledge.
D'Angelo Italian: of (belonging to) Angelo.
Danger Middle English: risk or peril.
Dani Israeli form of Daniel.
Daniel Hebrew: God is my judge. An Old Testament prophet.
Daaniel, Danail (Bulgarian), *Daneel* (Dutch), *Dani* (Israeli), *Danial, Daniale, Daniall, Danialle, Daniele* (Italian), *Daniell, Danijel* (Slavic), *Danil* (Russian), *Danilo, Dannel* (Swiss), *Danniel, Danya* (Russian), *Danyal, Danyall, Danyel, Danyell, Deiniol, Raniera* (Maori), *Taniel* (Armenian). *Diminutives:* Daan, Dan, Danek (Czech), Danko (Slavic), Dannie, Danny.
Danko Slavic: a diminutive of names such as Gordan and Danijel.
Danladi African: born on a Sunday.
Dannie/Danny *See* Daniel.
Dante Italian: enduring, steadfast. *See also* Durant.
Danton French: after Georges Danton, an 18th-century revolutionary.
Danu *See* Dhanu.
Danya/Danyal/Danyel *See* Daniel.
Danyon A name made popular by the New Zealand swimmer, Danyon Loader.
Danyan, Danyen.
Daoud An Arabic form of David.
Dar Hebrew: a pearl.
Darr.
Dara Cambodian: a star. Irish Gaelic: a son of oak.
Daran *See* Darren.
Darby Irish Gaelic: free from envy (*see also* Dermot). Middle English: the deer settlement.
Derby.
Darcy Old French: a placename and a Norman family name.
Darcey, D'Arcy, Darsey, Darsy.
Dare *See* Darius.
Darel Aboriginal: blue sky. *See also* Darrell.
Darell *See* Darrell.
Daren Nigerian: born at night. *See also* Darren.
Dargan English/Irish: the red one.
Dargen, Dargon.
Darien Greek: wealthy. Spanish: a placename.
Darian, Darrian, Darrien.
Darin *See* Darren.
Darius Greek: wealthy. The name of several ancient Persian kings.
Dahr, Dahre, Dare, Dario, Dhare.

Darko Slavic: a gift.
Darley Old English: from the deer wood or clearing.
Darlee, Darleigh, Darnlee, Darnleigh, Darnley.
Darnell French: from the hidden place.
Darnall, Darnel.
Darragh Irish Gaelic: wealthy.
Darra, Darrah, Darrach.
Darrell Old French: the dear one, the beloved.
Darel, Darell, Darrel, Darryl, Darryle, Daryl, Derel, Derrell, Derryl, Deryl.
Darren English: a modern name, possibly a form of Dorian.
Daran, Daren, Darin, Darran, Darrant, Darrent, Darrin, Darryen, Darryn.
Darrick *See* Derek.
Darryen/Darryn *See* Darren.
Darryl/Daryl *See* Darrell.
Darsey/Darsy *See* Darcy.
Darshan Sanskrit: an audience with a sage or guru. The name implies a seeker of knowledge.
Darth From Darth Vader, a character in the *Star Wars* movie series.
Darton Old English: from the deer forest or estate.
Daru Hindi: a pine tree.
Darwin Old English: a beloved friend.
Darwyn, Derwin, Derwyn.

Dashiell After Dashiell Hammett, US novelist and author of *The Maltese Falcon*. Made popular by actor Cate Blanchett's son.
Dashiel.
Diminutives: Dash, Dashe.
Dathan Hebrew: possibly meaning a fountain. A biblical name.
Daud An Arabic form of David.
Dauphin French from Latin: like a dolphin.
Dolffin (Welsh), *Dolphin.*
Davee/Dave/Davey Diminutives of David.
Daved/Daveth *See* David.
Daven Old Norse: two rivers.
Davin, Davyn.
Davenport Old English: from the town on the River Dane; a UK placename.
David Hebrew: the beloved, the adored one. The famous Israelite king in the Bible, and also the patron saint of Wales. *See also* Davidson.
Dafydd (Welsh), *Daibhidh* (Irish, Scottish), *Daividh, Daoud* (Arabic), *Daud* (Arabic), *Daved, Daveth* (Cornish), *Davi* (Portuguese), *Davide* (French), *Davyd, Davyyd, Dawood* (Arabic), *Dawud* (Arabic), *Devi* (Breton), *Dewi* (Welsh), *Dowd* (Middle English), *Rawiri* (Maori), *Taavi* (Finnish).
Diminutives: Dai (Welsh), Dave, Davee, Davey, Davie, Davy, Rewi

(Maori), Taffy (Welsh), Tavi (Jewish).

Davidson English: the son of David. *Davis, Davison.*

Davie A diminutive of David.

Davin Scandinavian: the bright one from Finland. *See also* Daven.

Davis *See* Davidson.

Davor A Slavic name of uncertain meaning.

Davy/Davyd/Davyyd *See* David.

Dawa Sherpa/Tibetan: born on a Monday. Also a girl's name.

Dawes Old English: the son of Dawe or David. *Dawsey, Dawson.*

Dawood/Dawud Arabic forms of David.

Dax An English surname; the meaning is unknown.

Dayd/Dayde *See* Dade.

Dayl/Dayle/Daylle *See* Dale.

Dayman/Daymon *See* Damon.

Dayn/Dayne *See* Dane.

Dayron A modern name of uncertain meaning.

Dayten/Dayton *See* Deighton.

Deacon Middle English: an officer of the church. *Deakin, Dekan, Dekon. Diminutives:* Deak, Deke.

Dean Latin: a religious official. Old English: from the valley. *See also* Din. *Deahn, Deahne, Deane, Dein, Dene, Dinho, Dino* (Italian).

December Latin: the last month of the year – from decem, the Latin word for ten. (December was originally the tenth month.) *Desemba* (Swahili), *Desember* (Norwegian), *Dezem, Dezember* (German), *Dezembro* (Portuguese), *Dicembre* (Italian).

Decius Latin: the tenth. *Decimus.*

Declan Irish Gaelic: the name of a 5th-century bishop. *Decklan, Declyn, Deklan, Deklyn.*

Dedric/Dedrick *See* Derek.

Deegan An unusual modern name. *Deagan, Degan.*

Deen *See* Din.

Deepak Sanskrit: like a lamp or light. *Dipak.*

Degan *See* Deegan.

Deighton Old English: a place surrounded by a ditch. *Dayten, Dayton, Deighten, Deyten, Deyton.*

Deimos Greek: a moon of the planet Mars.

Dein *See* Dean.

Deiniol *See* Daniel.

Deion *See* Dennis.

Dejan Slavic: one who acts or achieves.

Dekan/Deke/Dekon *See* Deacon.

Dekel Arabic: a palm tree.

Deklan/Deklyn *See* Declan.

Dekota/Dekotah *See* Dakota.

Del A diminutive of Derek and

names beginning with Del.

Delahaye Old French: of the fence or enclosure.
Delahay, De La Hay, De La Haye.

Delan See Dylan.

Delaney Gaelic: the challenger's descendant. Also a modern girl's name.
Delainey, Delainy, Delanoy, Delany, Delenoy.
Diminutive: Del.

Delano Old French: from the forest of nut trees.

Delbert Old English: bright as day.

Delfino Italian/Spanish: a masculine form of Delfina (*see* Delphine), a woman from Delphi.
Delphino.

Delius Greek: a man from the island of Delos. The feminine form of Delia.
Delios.

Dell English: from the dell or hollow. Also a diminutive of names such as Wendell.
Delle.

Delling Old Norse: the shining one.

Dellwin/Dellwyn See Delwyn.

Delmar Latin: from the sea.
Delmer, Delmor, Delmore.

Delon a French surname.

Delphino See Delfino.

Delroy Old French: the son or servant of the king.
Delray.

Delwyn Old English: a friend from the valley.
Delvin, Delvyn, Dellwin, Dellwyn, Delwin, Delwinn, Delwynn.

DeMarcus American: a modern name, meaning of Marcus (*see* Mark).
Damarcus, DaMarcus, Damarkus, DaMarkus, Demarcus, Demarkus, DeMarkus.

Demas Greek: popular.

Demeryst An unusual modern name.
Demerist.

Demetrius Greek: belonging to Demeter, the Earth Mother and goddess of fertility.
Demetre (Portuguese), *Demetri, Demetrio* (Italian, Spanish), *Demetrios* (Greek), *Dimitar* (Bulgarian), *Dimitri, Dimitrios* (Greek), *Dimitrious, Dmitri* (Russian), *Dmitriy* (Russian), *Dmitry* (Russian), *Dumitru* (Romanian).
Diminutives: Mitja (Russian), Mitya (Russian).

Demian/Demyan See Damon.

Demos Greek: of the people.
Dimos.

Dempsey Irish Gaelic: the proud one.

Dempster Old English: the judge.

Denby Old Norse: from the Dane's settlement.
Danbey, Danby, Denbeigh,

Denbey, Denbigh.
Dene *See* Dean.
Denes/Deness *See* Dennis.
Denesh *See* Dinesh.
Denham Old English: a homestead in the valley.
Denholm.
Denholm *See* Denham.
Denim The name of a fabric: from de Nîmes, meaning 'of Nîmes' (the French town from which the material originated).
Denym.
Denis/Deniss *See* Dennis.
Deniz Turkish: of the sea. *See also* Dennis.
Denize.
Denley Old English: from the meadow in the valley.
Denmark A 'country name'.
Dennis Greek: a lover of wine. A modern form of Dionysus, the mythological god of wine and drama. *See also* Dennison and Tennyson.
Deion, Denes, Deness, Denis, Deniss, Deniz, Denize, Denys, Deon, Dinis, Dinnis, Dion, Dione, Dionisio (Italian), *Dionysos, Dionysus* (German), *Zdenek* (Slavic).
Diminutives: Den, Dennie, Denny.
Dennison Old English: the son of Dennis. *See also* Tennyson.
Denison.

Densil *See* Denzil.
Denton Old English: from the farm or town in the valley.
Denver Old English: from the edge of the valley. A USA placename.
Denym *See* Denim.
Denys *See* Dennis.
Denzil Cornish: from a placename meaning a high stronghold.
Densil, Denzel, Denzell, Denzill.
Denzo Japanese: the discreet one.
Deo *See* Dev.
Deon *See* Dennis.
Derain Aboriginal: of the mountains.
Derby *See* Darby.
Dereb An Ethiopian name of uncertain meaning.
DeReese American: a modern name, meaning 'of Reese' (*see* Rhys).
DeReece, DeRees, DeReis, DeRheece, DeRhyce, DeRhys, DeRhyse.
Derek Teutonic: a ruler of the people. *See also* Theodoric.
Darrick, Dedric, Dedrick (German), *Derick, Derik, Derk, Derrek, Derrick, Derryck, Deryck, Diederik* (Danish), *Dierk, Dietrich* (German), *Dirk* (Dutch, Flemish), *Dirke, Dyrke.*
Diminutives: Del, Derry.
Deren/Derin *See* Derren.
DeRheece/DeRhys *See* DeReese.
Derk/Derrek *See* Derek.
Dermot Irish Gaelic: without envy. *See also* Darby.

Dermid, Dermott, Diarmad (Scottish Gaelic), *Diarmid, Diarmit, Diarmuid.*
Derrell *See* Darrell.
Derren From an old Welsh name. Also a girl's name.
Deren, Derin, Derrin, Derryn, Deryn.
Derrick Cornish: from the oak grove. *See also* Derek.
Derrilin Aboriginal: falling stars. Can also be a girl's name.
Derrilyn.
Diminutives: Derri, Derry.
Derry Cornish: of the oak trees. Irish Gaelic: red-headed; the name of an Irish county. *See also* Derek and Derrilin.
Derrey, Derri, Derrie.
Derryck/Deryck *See* Derek.
Derryl/Deryl *See* Darrell.
Derryn *See* Derren.
Derward Old English: the deer-keeper.
Derwen Welsh: an oak tree.
Derwenn, Derwin, Derwinn, Derwyn, Derwynn.
Derwent Welsh: the name of rivers in England and Tasmania.
Derwin/Derwyn *See* Darwin and Derwen.
Derwood *See* Durward.
Derya Turkish: the ocean.
Deryn *See* Derren.
Des A diminutive of Desmond.
Desemba/Desember *See* December.

DeShawn American: a variation of Shawn (*see* Sean).
De Shaun, DeShaun, Deshaun, Deshaune, Deshawn, De Shawne, Deshawne.
Desi Diminutive of Desiderius.
Desea, Desee, Desie, Dezi, Dezie.
Desiderius Latin: the desired one.
Desiderio (Italian, Spanish), *Dezso* (Hungarian), *Didier* (French).
Diminutive: Desi.
Desmond Irish Gaelic: a man from South Munster, an Irish province.
Desmonde, Desmund, Desmunde.
Diminutives: Des, Desy.
Detlef German: the heritage of the people.
Deuce Old French: two (as in a duo).
Dev Sanskrit: godlike.
Deo, Devan, Deven.
Devan/Deven *See* Dev and Devon.
Devdan Sanskrit: the gift of the gods.
Devendra Sanskrit: the king of the gods.
Deveraux English/Old French: an English placename.
Devereux, Deveroux.
Deverell Celtic: from the riverbank.
Devi *See* David.
Devin Celtic: a poet.
Devyn.
Devino *See* Divino.
Devkumar Sanskrit: a son of the gods.
Dev Kumar.

Devlin Irish Gaelic: fierce bravery.
Devlen, Devlyn.
Devon English: the name of a south-western English county.
Devan, Deven.
Devonte African-American: possibly a form of Devon.
Devron A modern name, possibly a form of Devon.
Devran, Devren.
Devyn *See* Devin.
Dewar A pilgrim.
Dewer.
Dewayne *See* Duane.
Dewi Welsh form of David. *See also* Dafydd.
Dewey, Dewie, Dewy.
Diminutive: Dai.
De Witt Flemish: the blond or fair one. *See also* Dwight.
Dewitt.
Dewy *See* Dewi.
Dexter Latin: right-handed, dextrous.
Diminutive: Dex.
Deyten/Deyton *See* Deighton.
Dezem/Dezembro *See* December.
Dezi/Dezie *See* Desi.
Dezso Hungarian form of Desiderius.
Dhai Nepali: an older brother.
Dai.
Dhani Hindi/Nepali: wealthy.
Dhanu Sanskrit: a bow, one of the symbols of the zodiac sign of Sagittarius.
Dhanus, Danu.
Dhare *See* Darius.
Dharma Sanskrit: religion, or the religious one. Also a girl's name.
Dheran Aboriginal: a gully.
Dhilan/Dhillan/Dhilon *See* Dylan.
Dhiren A Sanskrit name of uncertain meaning.
Dhon *See* Donald.
Dhondup Sherpa/Tibetan: one who accomplishes.
Dhu Cornish/Welsh: black.
Dhugald *See* Dougal.
Dhylan/Dhylon *See* Dylan.
Dia Spanish: the day.
Dias.
Diablo Spanish: a devil.
Diaghilev Russian: the name of the founder of the Ballets Russes.
Diaghileff.
Diamond Old English: a shining protector.
Dymond, Dymonde.
Dian Indonesian: a candle.
Dyan.
Diarmad/Diarmid/Diarmuid *See* Dermot.
Dicembre The Italian word for December.
Dick/Dickie/Dicky *See* Richard.
Dickson Old English: the son of Richard (Dick).
Dixon.
Didier *See* Desiderius.
Diederik Danish form of Derek.
Diego Spanish form of James.

See also Santiago.
Dierk See Derek.
Diesel After Rudolf Diesel, the German engineer who invented the diesel engine.
Diezel.
Dieter Old German: of a warrior race.
Dietrich See Derek.
Diez Spanish: ten.
Digby Old Norse: from the settlement by the dyke.
Diggory Cornish from Old French: lost or strayed.
Digory.
Dilan/Dillan/Dillon See Dylan.
Diles Possibly a form of Miles.
Dyles.
Dilhara A Sri Lankan name of uncertain meaning.
Dili Aboriginal: a flame.
Dilli.
Dilip Sanskrit: an ancestor of the god Rama.
Dimas Portuguese/Spanish: from a Greek word meaning the sunset.
Dimaz.
Dime The name of a US silver coin.
Dyme.
Dimitar/Dimitri/Dimitrios See Demetrius.
Dimos See Demos.
Din Sanskrit: the day.
Dean, Deen.
Dinesh Sanskrit: the lord of the day; the sun.
Denesh, Dineish.
Dinh Vietnamese: the summit of the mountain.
Dinho/Dino See Dean.
Dinis/Dinnis See Dennis.
Dinko Slavic: born on a Sunday
Dynko.
Dinsdale Welsh: born on a Sunday.
Diomedes Greek: a legendary warrior.
Dion/Dione/Dionysus See Dennis.
Dipak See Deepak.
Direnc Turkish: resistance.
Dirk/Dirke See Derek.
Diron See Dyron.
Divino Italian: the divine one.
Devino, Divo.
Dix Latin: ten, or the tenth.
Dixie.
Dixon See Dickson.
Dizzy After Dizzy Gillespie, a legendary jazz musician.
Dizzey, Dizzie.
Django An unusual name, after the jazz musician Django Reinhardt.
Djanko.
Djava See Java.
Djimon A West African name.
Jimon.
Djuan/Djuann See Juan.
Djuka Slavic: a diminutive of Juraj (*see* George).
Djuke See Duke.
Djuro Slavic: a diminutive of Juraj (*see* George).
Dmitri/Dmitriy/Dmitry Russian

forms of Demetrius.
Doane Celtic: from the sand dunes.
Dobry Polish: good.
Dobri, Dobrie.
Dodd Teutonic: of the people.
Dolan Irish Gaelic: black-haired.
Dolf/Dolph *See* Adolf and Rudolph.
Dolffin/Dolphin *See* Dauphin.
Dom A diminutive of Dominic.
Domani Italian: tomorrow.
Domenic/Domenico *See* Dominic.
Domhnall Irish Gaelic form of Donald.
Domingo/Dominique *See* Dominic.
Dominic Latin: belonging to the Lord. St Dominic founded an important order of monks.
Domenic, Domenico (Italian), *Domingo* (Portuguese, Spanish), *Dominick, Dominik* (Czech, Polish), *Dominique* (French).
Diminutives: Dom, Nic, Nick, Nickie, Nicky.
Don Diminutive of Donald and other Don names.
Donagh Irish Gaelic: a brown or dark warrior.
Donnacha, Donnagh, Donncha, Donnchadh.
Donahue Irish Gaelic: a warrior dressed in brown.
Donaghue, Donoghue, Donohue.
Donal/Donall Irish forms of Donald.
Donalbain Scottish Gaelic: a character in Shakespeare's *Macbeth*; the name probably means Donald the fair.
Donald Scottish Gaelic: the ruler of the world.
Domhnall (Irish Gaelic) *Donal* (Irish), *Donall* (Irish), *Donalt, Donell, Donnell.*
Diminutives: Dhon, Don, Donnie, Donny.
Donato Latin: a gift, given by God.
Donat (Polish), *Donatello* (Italian), *Donatien* (French), *Donatus.*
Donavan/Donavon *See* Donovan.
Donegal Irish Gaelic: the name of a county.
Donell/Donnell *See* Donald.
Donn Irish Gaelic: the dark one.
Donne.
Donnacha/Donnagh/Donncha *See* Donagh.
Donnelly Gaelic: the dark brave one.
Donnel, Donnell.
Donnie/Donny Diminutives of Donald and other Don names.
Donoghue/Donohue *See* Donahue.
Donovan Irish Gaelic: dark brown. A name made popular by the 1960s folk singer Donovan.
Donavan, Donaven, Donavon, Donoven, Donovon.
Diminutives: Don, Donnie, Donny.
Dontaye A modern made-up name.
Dontae, Dontay.
Dooley Irish Gaelic: a dark hero.

Doone Irish Gaelic: a placename.
Doon.

Doongara Aboriginal: lightning.
Doongarra.

Dorado Spanish: the golden one. The name of a southern constellation.

Dorak Aboriginal: lively.

Doran Irish Gaelic: a wanderer or stranger. *See also* Doron.
Dorran.

Dorey *See* Dory.

Dorf German: from the village.

Dorian Greek: a man belonging to the Dorian tribe (one of the ancient Greek tribes). The name was probably invented by Oscar Wilde for the main character of his 1890s novel *The Portrait of Dorian Gray*.
Doriann, Dorien, Dorienn.

Doric A region of ancient Greece, and also a form of Greek architecture.
Dorik.

Dorjee Sherpa/Tibetan: a thunderbolt.
Dorjé.

Doron Greek: a gift. A modern Jewish name, and also the male form of Dora.
Doran, Dorran, Dorron.

Dorran *See* Doran and Doron.

Dorsey Irish Gaelic: the place of the gateways.
Dorsee, Dorsie, Dorsy.

Dory French: golden-haired.
Dorey.

Doug/Dougie *See* Douglas.

Dougal Gaelic: a dark stranger.
Dhugald, Dougall, Doyle, Dugal, Dugald.

Dougan Aboriginal: a large mountain.
Dugan.

Douglas Scottish Gaelic: from the dark stream.
Douglass, Duglas, Duglass.
Diminutives: Doug, Dougie, Duggie.

Dougray An unusual 'combination name'.
Dougrae, Dougrai, Dougraye.

Douwe Dutch: a dove.

Dov Hebrew: a bear.

Dover Old English: of the waters. A coastal town in Kent, England.

Dow Irish Gaelic: black-haired.
Dowe.

Dowd Middle English form of David.

Dowden Middle English: the valley of Dowd or David.
Dowdan, Dowdon.

Dowling From Gaelic: of the Dow family.

Downing Old English: of the Down or Dunn family.
Downey, Downie.

Doyle *See* Dougal.

Draco Greek: a dragon. The name of a constellation in the northern sky.
Dracoe, Draconis, Drako, Drakoe.

Drae/Drai *See* Dre.

Dragan Slavic: the dear one.
Dragisha Slavic: one who is precious or beloved.
Dragomir Slavic: precious and peaceful.
Dragos (Romanian).
Dragutin Slavic: precious.
Drago.
Draig Welsh: a dragon.
Drake Old English: the dragon.
Drako/Drakoe *See* Draco.
Draven A modern name of uncertain meaning.
Drayven, Drayvyn, Dreaven, Dreayven, Dreayvyn.
Drax Old English: possibly from the word 'drag'.
Draxx.
Drayton Old English: the farm by the steep hill.
Drayten.
Drazen Slavic: the precious one.
Drazan.
Dre Probably a short form of André.
Drae, Drai, Drey.
Dreaven/Dreayven *See* Draven.
Drew Scottish diminutive of Andrew. *See also* Druce.
Dru, Drue.
Drey *See* Dre.
Dreyden/Dreydon *See* Dryden.
Driscoll Irish: the interpreter.
Driscol, Driscolle, Driskol, Driskoll, Driskolle.
Dristan/Dristin *See* Tristram.
Driver Old English: one who drives.

Drona Sanskrit: a warrior in Hindu mythology.
Dror Israeli: freedom.
Drostan *See* Tristram.
Dru Tibetan: a snake. *See also* Drew and Druce.
Drue.
Druce Celtic: the son of Drew.
Diminutives: Dru, Drue.
Druid A priest in ancient Celtic religions.
Druide.
Drury Old French: the dear one, a sweetheart.
Dryden Old English: from the dry valley.
Dreyden, Dreydon, Drydon.
Drysdale An English surname of uncertain meaning.
Drystan *See* Tristram.
Duane Irish Gaelic: a little dark one. A popular name in the USA.
Dewayne, Duaine, Du'aine, Duayne, Dwain, Dwaine, Dwane, Dwayne.
Duarte Portuguese form of Edward.
Dubois Old French: of the wood.
DuBois, Du Bois.
Duc Vietnamese: the virtuous one.
Duca Italian: a duke or nobleman.
Duka.
Dudi An Israeli name of uncertain meaning.
Dudley English: a town in the UK, and the name of an aristocratic family.

D – Boys

Dudlea, Dudleigh, Dudlie, Dudly.
Diminutives: Dud, Duddy.
Duff Scottish Gaelic: dark-haired, or of a dark complexion.
Duffy Gaelic: a dark man of peace.
Duffey, Duffie.
Dugal/Dugald *See* Dougal.
Dugan Gaelic: dark-skinned.
See also Dougan.
Duggie/Duglass *See* Douglas.
Duka *See* Duca.
Dukale An African name of uncertain meaning.
Duke Old French: a leader. Also a diminutive of Marmaduke.
Djuke.
Duma Swahili: a cheetah
Dumah.
Duman Turkish: smoke, or mist.
Dumen.
Dumitru Romanian form of Demetrius.
Dunbar Gaelic: a dark branch.
Duncan Scottish Gaelic: a dark warrior.
Diminutive: Dunc.
Dundas A Scottish surname.
Dundee The name of a Scottish city.
Dunedin A town in New Zealand's south island.
Dunham Celtic: a dark man.
Dunley Old English: from the meadow on the hill.
Dunlea, Dunleigh, Dunlie, Dunly.
Dunmore Scottish Gaelic: from the fortress on the hill.
Dunmoor.
Dunstan Old English: from the dark stone or hill. The name of a saint.
Dupree Old French: of the price or prize (du prix).
Durack Irish: the surname of a famous Australian pioneering family.
Durak.
Dural Aboriginal: a hollow tree that is on fire.
Duran/Durand *See* Durant.
Durant Latin: enduring, steadfast.
See also Dante.
Duran, Durand, Durante.
Durban A city in South Africa.
Durbin, Durbyn.
Durga Sanskrit: unattainable. The name of a Hindu goddess, and also a girl's name.
Durham Old English: a hilly peninsula. An English city and county.
Durward Old English: a gatekeeper.
Derwood, Durwood.
Durwin Old English: a dear friend.
Durwyn.
Durwood *See* Durward.
Dusan Czech: the soul, the spirit.
Dustin Old Norse: Thor's stone, or valiant.
Dustan, Dusten, Dustyn.
Diminutives: Dustie, Dusty.
Dutch A Dutchman.
Duval French: from the valley.

Duvall, Duvalle.
Duygu Turkish: emotion. Also a girl's name.
Dwaine/Dwane/Dwayne *See* Duane.
Dweezil A name made up by musician Frank Zappa for his son.
Dwight Teutonic: fair or blond. *See also* De Witt.
Dyami Native American: an eagle.
Dyan *See* Dian.
Dyfan Welsh form of Damon.
Dylan Welsh: a man from the sea. Can also be a girl's name.
Delan, Dhilan, Dhillan, Dhillon, Dhilon, Dhylan, Dhylon, Dilan, Dillan, Dillon, Dyllan, Dyllon, Dylon.
Dyles *See* Diles.
Dyme *See* Dime.
Dymond/Dymonde *See* Diamond.
Dynko *See* Dinko.
Dyre Scandinavian: a dear or precious one.
Dyrke *See* Derek.
Dyron A modern name, possibly from Myron.
Diron.
Dyson Old English: the son of Dye (from Dionysus).
Dysen.
Dzong Tibetan: a fortress.

E

Eachan Scottish Gaelic: a brown horse.
Eachann.
Eadgar *See* Edgar.
Eamonn Irish Gaelic form of Edmund.
Eammon, Eamon, Emon, Emonn.
Ean *See* Ian.
Eanraig Scottish Gaelic form of Henry.
Eardley Old English: a dwelling-place clearing.
Eardleigh, Erdleigh, Erdley.
Earl Old English: a nobleman.
Earle, Erle, Errol, Erroll.
Earnest *See* Ernest.
Earvin *See* Irving.
Easter Old English: born at Easter time.
Eastre.
Easton Old English: a place that faces east.
Easten, Eastyn.
Eathan/Eathen *See* Ethan.
Eaton Old English: from the estate by the river.
Eton.
Ebenezer Hebrew: the rock of help. A placename mentioned in the Bible.
Ebanezer.
Diminutives: Eban, Eben.

Eberhard Teutonic: as brave as a wild boar. *See also* Everard.
Eberhart.

Ebisu The Japanese god of good fortune.

Ebo African: born on a Tuesday.
Eboh.

Ebrahim Arabic form of Abraham.

Ed/Eddie/Eddy Diminutives of Edgar, Edmund, Edward, Edwin and other names.

Edan *See* Aidan.

Edbert Old English: prosperous and bright.

Edega Hawaiian: wealthy.

Eden Hebrew: the place of pleasure (as in the Garden of Eden). Irish Gaelic: fiery (*see also* Aidan). Old English: a bear cub.
Edenn.

Edgar Old English: a prosperous spearman.
Eadgar, Edgard (French), *Edgardo* (Italian, Spanish). *Diminutives:* Ed, Eddie, Eddy.

Edgeley Old English: the clearing in the park or pasture.
Edgley.

Edgerton Old English: the place of the army, or the brave one.
Egerton.

Edison Old English: the son of Edgar, Edmund or Edward.
Edinson, Edson.

Ediz Turkish: high.

Edlin Old English: a prosperous friend.

Edmands/Edmandson *See* Edmunds.

Edmund Old English: a prosperous protector. *See also* Eamonn.
Eamonn (Irish Gaelic), *Edmond* (Dutch, French), *Edmondo* (Italian), *Edmundo* (Spanish), *Eumann* (Scottish Gaelic). *Diminutives:* Ed, Eddie, Eddy.

Edmunds The son of Edmund.
Edmands, Edmandsen, Edmandson, Edmonds, Edmondsen, Edmondson, Edmundsen, Edmundson.

Edoardo/Édouard *See* Edward.

Edolf Old English: a prosperous wolf.

Edom Hebrew: red.

Edric Old English: a prosperous ruler.
Adric, Adrick, Edrick, Edris.

Edryd Welsh: a storyteller.
Edred, Edrydd.

Edsel *See* Etzel.

Edson *See* Edison.

Edu African: the name of a region in Nigeria. *See also* Edward.

Eduard/Eduward *See* Edward.

Edur Basque: white, like the snow.

Edwada Hawaiian form of Edward.

Edward Old English: a rich guardian.
Duarte (Portuguese), *Edoardo* (Italian), *Édouard* (French), *Edu, Eduard* (Czech, German),

Eduardo (Spanish), *Eduward, Edvard* (Russian, Scandinavian), *Edwada* (Hawaiian), *Edwar, Edwer, Edwerd, Eetu* (Finnish), *Eideard* (Scottish Gaelic), *Eruera* (Maori).
Diminutives: Ed, Eddie, Eddy, Ned, Neddie, Neddy, Ted, Teddie, Teddy.
Edwin Old English: a prosperous friend.
Edwinn, Edwyn, Edwynn.
Diminutives: Ed, Eddie, Eddy.
Eerik/Eero Finnish forms of Eric.
Eetu Finnish form of Edward.
Efim Russian form of Euphemios.
Efrain/Efram/Efrem *See* Ephraim.
Efstathios Greek: stable, or well built.
Eustathios.
Efstratios *See* Eustratios.
Efthimios Greek: to think hopefully.
Efthimio.
Efydd Welsh: bronze or brass.
Efyd.
Egan Irish Gaelic: the little fiery one.
Iagan (Scottish).
Egbert Old English: a bright sword.
Egerton *See* Edgerton.
Egidio Italian: a young goat.
Egil Scandinavian: a character from Norse mythology.
Egill.
Egon Teutonic: the point of a sword.
Egor Russian form of George.
Eguzki Basque: like the sun.

Egypt An unusual 'country name'.
Ehran *See* Eran.
Ehren Teutonic: honourable.
Ehud Hebrew: the sympathetic one. An Old Testament name.
Eian *See* Ian.
Eideard *See* Edward.
Eimar Irish Gaelic: one who is swift.
Einar Old Norse: a lone warrior.
Inar.
Einstein After Albert Einstein, the famous German physicist.
Eiran *See* Eran.
Eirik *See* Eric.
Eitan *See* Ethan.
Eivind Norwegian: a happy warrior.
Eyvind, Eyvindur (Icelandic).
Ekram/Ekrem *See* Akram.
Eladio Latin: a man from Greece.
Elam Hebrew: eternity.
Elan Hebrew: a tree. Native American: the friendly one.
Eland Afrikaans: a large antelope. Old English: from the island.
Elbert *See* Albert.
Eldad Hebrew: God has loved.
Elden/Eldin *See* Alden.
Eldene A modern American name.
Eldeen, Eldeene, Eldine.
Eldon Old English: from the hill.
See also Alden.
Elden, Eldyn.
Eldred *See* Aldred.
Eldric/Eldrich *See* Aldrich.
Eldridge Old English: from the alder-tree ridge.

Aldridge, Eldredge.
Eldur Icelandic: like fire.
Eldar.
Eldyn *See* Eldon.
Eleazar/Elezar *See* Lazarus.
Eleias Welsh form of Elijah.
Eleu Hawaiian: alert and lively. Also a girl's name.
Elfed Welsh: autumn.
Elfedd.
Elfynian Welsh: possibly derived from Elfed.
Elfynnian.
Elgar Old English: a noble spear.
Elgin A Scottish placename.
Elginn, Elgyn, Elgynn.
Eli Hebrew: the highest; a biblical name. Also a diminutive of names such as Elias, Elijah and Elisha.
Elie, Eligh, Elih, Ely.
Elia/Eliah/Elias *See* Elijah.
Elian Latin: the bright one.
Eliel Finnish form of Elisha.
Elijah Hebrew: the Lord is God. The name of an Israelite prophet in the Bible. *See also* Elliott, Ellis and Ellison.
Eleias (Welsh), *Elia, Eliah, Elias, Elihu, Eliyahu* (Jewish), *Ellia, Elliah, Eriha* (Maori), *Ilie* (Romanian), *Ilya* (Russian).
Diminutives: Eli, Ely.
Eliot/Eliott *See* Elliott.
Elis/Eliss *See* Ellis.
Eliseo *See* Elisha.
Elisha Hebrew: God is my salvation. The successor of Elijah in the Bible.
Eliel (Finnish), *Eliseo* (Italian, Spanish).
Diminutives: Eli, Ely.
Elison *See* Ellison.
Eliston *See* Elston.
Elkan Hebrew: possessed by God.
Elkanah.
Ellar Scottish Gaelic: a butler or steward.
Ellard *See* Alard.
Ellery Cornish: a swan. Teutonic: from the elder tree. Also a form of Hilary.
Eller, Ellerie.
Ellia/Elliah *See* Elijah.
Elliott English from Old French: a form of Elias. *See also* Elijah.
Eliot, Eliott, Eliotte, Elliot, Elliotte.
Ellis English from Greek: a form of Elias. *See* Elijah.
Elis, Eliss, Elliss.
Ellison English from Greek: the son of Ellis or Elias. *See also* Elijah.
Elison.
Elliston/Ellston/Ellyston *See* Elston.
Ellul *See* Elul.
Elmer Old English: noble and famous.
Elmar.
Elmo Italian from Teutonic: a protector. The name of a saint.
Elmore Old English: from the riverbank with elm trees.

Elmor.
Elner Teutonic: famous.
Elokuu Finnish: the month of August.
Eloku.
Elonso/Elonzo *See* Alphonso.
Eloy Latin: to choose. A Spanish name.
Elroy English from French: the king. *See also* Leroy.
Elsdon Old English: from the noble one's valley.
Elsden.
Elston Old English: from the noble one's farm.
Eliston, Elliston, Ellston, Ellyston, Elyston.
Elsu Native American: a falcon.
Elton Old English: from the old settlement or estate.
Elul The sixth Hebrew lunar month, beginning in late August and corresponding to the zodiac sign of Virgo.
Ellul.
Elvig Scandinavian form of Elvy.
Elvin/Elvyn *See* Alvin.
Elvis *See* Alvis.
Elvy Old English: an elfin warrior.
Elvey, Elvig (Scandinavian).
Elward Old English: a noble guardian.
Elwell Old English: to wish one well.
Elwel.
Elwin Old English: a friend of the elves. Also a girl's name.
Elwyn.
Elwood Old English: the ruler of the elves.
Elwyn *See* Elwin.
Ely *See* Eli, Elijah and Elisha.
Elyston *See* Elston.
Eman A Filipino name of uncertain meaning.
Emanuel/Emanuele *See* Emmanuel.
Emek Hebrew: a valley.
Emerson The son of Emery.
Emmerson.
Emery Teutonic: an industrious ruler.
Emeran, Emeric, Emmeric, Emmerich, Emmery, Emory, Emrey, Emric, Imre (Hungarian).
Emidio Italian: a demigod.
Emil Teutonic: industrious. The masculine form of Emily.
Emiel, Emiele, Émile (French), *Emiliano, Émilien* (French), *Emilio* (Italian, Spanish), *Emlen, Emlyn* (Welsh).
Emilio *See* Emil.
Emin Turkish: honest or trustworthy.
Emlen/Emlyn *See* Emil.
Emmanuel Hebrew: God is with us.
Emanual, Emanuel (Scandinavian), *Emanuele* (Italian), *Emmanouil, Emmanual, Emminouel, Immanuel* (German), *Manel* (Catalan), *Manoel* (Portuguese), *Manuel* (Spanish), *Manuell, Manuelle.*
Diminutives: Mannie, Manny.

Emmerich *See* Emery.
Emmery *See* Emery.
Emmet Old English: little Emma.
Emmett, Emmit.
Emmons The son of Emma.
Emmonson.
Emon/Emonn *See* Eamonn.
Emory *See* Emery.
Emre Turkish form of Henry.
Emrey/Emric *See* Emery.
Emrys Welsh form of Ambrose.
Emyr Welsh: honour.
Enda Irish Gaelic: bird-like.
Endymion Greek: a beautiful youth from mythology.
Endimion.
Eneas *See* Aeneas.
Eneki Hawaiian: eager.
Enero Spanish: the month of January.
Engelbert Teutonic: a bright Angle (a Germanic people).
Englebert, Inglebert.
Engin Turkish: vast.
Enki A Sumerian messenger god, the equivalent of Hermes and Mercury.
Ennio Italian: favoured by God.
Enio.
Ennion Welsh: from a Latin family name. *See also* Beynon.
Eynon.
Ennis Celtic: from the island.
See also Innes.
Enis, Ennys, Enys.
Ennor Cornish: from the boundary.

Enoch Hebrew: experienced, or consecrated. A biblical name.
Enock.
Enos Hebrew: mankind; a character in the Bible. Also an Irish form of Angus.
Enrico/Enrique/Enriquez *See* Henry.
Ensio Finnish: the first.
Enys *See* Ennis.
Enzio Italian: the ruler of the home.
Enzo Italian diminutive of Lorenzo and other names.
Eoghan Irish Gaelic: from the yew tree.
Eoin Gaelic form of John and Owen.
Eon Greek: an age or lifetime.
Aeon, Aion.
Epeha Maori: of the Ephesians.
Ephraim Hebrew: fruitful. One of the sons of Joseph in the Bible.
Efrain (Spanish), *Efram, Efrem, Ephrem, Yefrem* (Russian).
Diminutives: Effie, Effy.
Equinox Middle English: the time of equality between day and night.
Erad Aboriginal: one, or the first.
Eran Hebrew: watchful. *See also* Erin.
Ehran, Eiran.
Erasmus Greek: worthy of love.
Diminutives: Ras, Rasmus.
Erastus Greek: the loving one.
Diminutive: Rastus.
Ercole *See* Hercules.
Erdem Turkish: virtuous.

Erdleigh/Erdley *See* Eardley.
Erebus Greek: the mythological god of darkness.
Ereminio *See* Erminio.
Eren Turkish: a saint.
Erhan Turkish: a brave soldier or ruler.
Erhard Teutonic: strong and honourable.
Erhart.
Eric Old Norse: an all-powerful ruler.
Eerik (Finnish), *Eero* (Finnish), *Eirik* (Norwegian), *Erich* (German), *Erick, Érico* (Portuguese), *Erik* (Swedish), *Eriks* (Russian), *Erix, Erkki* (Finnish), *Eurico* (Portuguese).
Diminutives: Ric, Rick.
Ericson The son of Eric.
Erichsen, Erichson, Ericsen, Ericssen, Ericsson, Erixen, Erixon.
Erie *See* Eyrie.
Eriha Maori form of Elijah.
Erik/Eriks *See* Eric.
Erin Irish Gaelic: from Ireland. More commonly a girl's name.
Eran, Erran, Errin.
Erith Old English: from the gravelly landing place. An English placename.
Erix *See* Eric.
Erixen/Erixon *See* Ericson.
Erkki A Finnish form of Eric.
Erki.

Erland Old Norse: a foreigner, a stranger.
Erle *See* Earl.
Ermanno *See* Herman.
Erminio Italian: from an old Roman name.
Ereminio.
Ernest Teutonic: the serious, earnest one.
Earnest, Ernesto (Italian, Spanish), *Ernests* (Slavic), *Erno* (Finnish), *Ernst* (German).
Diminutives: Ern, Ernie, Erny.
Erno Finnish form of Ernest.
Ernst German form of Ernest.
Erol Turkish: a brave man. Also a form of Errol.
Eron/Erron *See* Aaron.
Eros Greek: the god of love.
Erran/Errin *See* Erin.
Errol Scottish: from an old family name. *See also* Earl.
Arrol, Arroll, Erill, Erol, Erroll, Erryl, Eryl.
Erskine Scottish Gaelic: from the heights.
Eruera Maori form of Edward.
Ervan/Ervin/Ervyn *See* Irving.
Erwin *See* Irwin.
Eryx Greek: a mythological figure.
Esau Hebrew: the hairy one. The son of Isaac and brother of Jacob in the Bible.
Esbern Old Norse: a divine bear. A Danish name.
Esben, Esbjörn (Swedish).

Eseia Welsh form of Isaiah.
Eser Turkish: achievement. Also a girl's name.
Esidor/Esidore *See* Isidore.
Esmond Old English: the gracious or handsome protector.
Esmonde, Esmund, Esmunde.
Esprit French from Latin: wit, lively intelligence or spirit.
Espree, Esprie.
Esra *See* Ezra.
Essex Old English: the Saxons from the east. An English county.
Essien African: the sixth, or sixth child.
Essian.
Este Italian: from the east.
Estes.
Estéban Spanish form of Stephen.
Estivo Italian: summer, or of the summer.
Etana Hawaiian: strong.
Etera Maori form of Ezra.
Ethan Hebrew: steadfast, or long-lived. A biblical name.
Aithan, Aithen, Eathan, Eathen, Eitan (Jewish), *Etan, Ethen.*
Ethelred Teutonic: a noble counsellor.
Étienne French form of Stephen.
Eton *See* Eaton.
Ettore *See* Hector.
Etu Native American: of the sun.
Etzel Teutonic: the noble one.
Edsel.
Euan *See* Ewan.
Euclid Greek: true glory. The name of a Greek geometrician.
Euclyd.
Eudo Greek: fortunate.
Yudo.
Eugene Greek: the noble, or well-born one.
Eugean, Eugen (German), *Eugène* (French), *Eugenio* (Italian, Spanish), *Eugenius, Eugeniuse, Eugeniusz* (Slavic), *Evgeni, Evgeniy, Evgeny, Jeno* (Hungarian), *Yevgeni* (Russian), *Yevgeny* (Russian).
Diminutive: Gene.
Eumann *See* Edmund.
Eunan Irish Gaelic: the name of an early saint.
Euphemios Greek: the masculine form of Euphemia, meaning of good reputation.
Efim (Russian), *Yefim* (Russian).
Eurico *See* Eric.
Eurig Welsh: golden.
Euro Aboriginal: the sun.
Euroa Aboriginal: the joyful one.
Eurus Greek: the god of the east wind.
Eurwyn Welsh: fair and golden.
Eusebios Greek: pious and respectful. The name of a 4th-century Christian historian.
Eusebio (Italian, Portuguese, Spanish), *Eusebius.*
Eustace Greek: fruitful, or steadfast.
Eustice, Eustis.
Eustathios *See* Efstathios.

Eustratios Greek: the right path. The name of a 9th-century saint.
Efstratios, Efstratius, Eustratius.
Diminutives: Stratis, Strato, Stratos, Stratus.

Evan Welsh: well-born. *See also* Bevan, Ieuan, John and Owen.
Evann, Evarn, Evin, Evyn.

Evander Greek: a good man. A mythological character.
Diminutive: Vander.

Evangelos Greek: the evangelist.

Eveleigh *See* Everley.

Evelyn English: from an old surname. Primarily a girl's name.
Evelin, Evelino.

Ever Middle English: always; at all times.

Everard Old English: as strong or brave as a boar. *See also* Eberhard.
Evered, Everet, Everett, Everey, Evert (German), *Every, Evrard* (French), *Evrett.*

Everdene Old English: the valley of the wild boar.
Everdean, Everdeen, Everden, Everdine.

Everest The name of the world's highest mountain.

Everet/Everett *See* Everard.

Everey/Every *See* Everard.

Everild *See* Averell.

Everley Old English: from the place of the wild boar.
Eveleigh.

Everton Old English: the town of the wild boar.
Everten, Evertyn, Evverton, Evvertyn.

Evgeni/Evgeniy/Evgeny *See* Eugene.

Evin/Evyn *See* Evan.

Evrard *See* Everard.

Evrett *See* Everard.

Ewald Teutonic: he who rules by the law.

Ewan Scottish Gaelic: possibly meaning born of the yew tree.
Euan, Ewen, Ewin, Uan.

Ewart Old English: an ewe herder.
Ewert.

Ewing Old English: a friend of the law.

Exavier *See* Xavier.

Exeter A city in Devon, England, located on the River Exe.

Exodus Middle English from Greek: to leave or go out. The second book of the Old Testament.
Exodos.

Exton Old English: from the ox farm.
Exten, Extyn.

Eynon *See* Ennion.

Eyre Teutonic: an eagle's nest.

Eyrie Middle English: an elevated nest or position.
Erie.

Eysteinn Norwegian: a lucky stone.
Eystein, Oeystein, Oeysteinn.

Eyvind/Eyvindur *See* Eivind.

Ezekiel Hebrew: God strengthens, or the strength of God. One of the

books of the Bible.
Ezequiel (Spanish).
Diminutives: Zeik, Zeke.
Ezel Hebrew: a juniper tree.
Ezera Hawaiian form of Ezra.
Ezio Latin: like an eagle.
Ezra Hebrew: the helper. A prophet in the Bible.
Esra, Etera (Maori), *Ezera* (Hawaiian), *Ezrah, Ezri.*
Ezri *See* Ezra.

F

Faber *See* Fabron.
Fabian Latin: the bean grower.
Fabiano (Italian), *Fabien* (French), *Fabio* (Italian, Portuguese, Spanish), *Fabius.*
Fabio/Fabius *See* Fabian.
Fabrice Latin: a craftsman.
Fabricio (Spanish), *Fabricus, Fabrizio* (Italian).
Fabron French: a little blacksmith.
Faber.
Facundo A Spanish name of uncertain meaning.
Fadi Arabic: a saviour.
Fadil Arabic: the generous or distinguished one.
Fadl.
Fáelán Irish Gaelic: a little wolf
Faolán.
Fagan Gaelic: the little fiery one.
Fagin.
Fahd Arabic: a leopard.
Fahim Arabic: a good scholar.
Fain/Faine *See* Fane.
Fainton/Faineton *See* Faneton.
Fairfax Old English: the one with beautiful hair.
Fairfaks.
Fairley Old English: a clearing in the woods. Also a girl's name.
Fairleigh, Fairlie, Fairly.
Fairuz/Fairouz *See* Feroz.
Faisal Arabic: a wise judge.
Faysal.
Faiz Arabic: victorious.
Feiz.
Falcon Old French: a bird of prey. *See also* Falkner.
Falkon.
Falconer *See* Falkner.
Falk Yiddish: the falcon.
Falkner Old French: a falconer, or falcon handler. *See also* Falcon.
Falconer, Faulkner.
Fallon Irish: a leader. Also a girl's name.
Fallan, Fallen, Fallyn.
Fanahan Irish Gaelic: a white hound; the name of a saint.
Fannahan.
Fane Old English: eager or glad.
Fain, Faine, Fayn, Fayne, Fein, Feine.
Faneton Old English: the town of the eager or glad one.
Fainton, Faineton, Fayneton,

Faynton, Feinton.
Faolán *See* Fáelán.
Faran/Faren/Farin *See* Farran.
Farand Teutonic: attractive or pleasant.
Farant, Farend, Farent, Farrand, Farrant, Farrend, Farrent.
Farasi Swahili: a horse.
Farid Arabic: unique or unrivalled.
Fareed.
Faris The angel of the night.
Fares, Farres, Farris.
Farley Old English: from the fern clearing.
Farleigh.
Farman Old Norse: a traveller or hawker.
Farndon Old English: the hill of ferns.
Farnden.
Farnell Old English: from the hill of ferns.
Farnall, Farnill.
Farnham Old English: from the place of ferns.
Farnley Old English: from the fern meadow.
Fernleigh, Fernley.
Farook Arabic: one who can distinguish right from wrong.
Farooq, Farouk, Faruq.
Farquhar Scottish Gaelic: the dear one.
Farran Old French: a journey or venture.
Faran, Faren, Farin, Farren,
Farrin.
Farrand/Farrant/Farrend *See* Farand.
Farrell Celtic: the valorous one.
Farrel, Pharrel, Pharrell.
Farres/Farris *See* Faris and Ferris.
Faru Swahili: a rhinoceros.
Faruq *See* Farook.
Faulkner *See* Falkner.
Faunus A Roman god of woodlands and forests.
Faun, Faunal, Faunis.
Faust Latin: the fortunate one.
Fausto (Italian).
Fauzi *See* Fawaz.
Favian Latin: understanding.
Favio.
Fawaz Arabic: successful.
Fauzi, Fawwaz, Fawz, Fawzi.
Fawzan Arabic: the victor.
Fayn/Fayne *See* Fane.
Fayneton/Faynton *See* Faneton.
Fayrouz *See* Feroz.
Faysal *See* Faisal.
Feargal/Feargall/Fearghal *See* Fergal.
Fearghas/Feargus *See* Fergus.
February Latin: the second month of the year. From februare, Latin for purification.
Febrero (Spanish), *Februar* (Danish, German), *Februari* (Swahili), *Février* (French).
Fedele *See* Fidel.
Federico *See* Frederick.
Feenix *See* Phoenix.
Fein/Feine *See* Fane.

Feinton *See* Faneton.
Feiz *See* Faiz.
Felan *See* Phelan.
Felice/Feliciano/Felicien/Felicio *See* Felix.
Feliks *See* Felix.
Felipe Spanish form of Philip.
Felix Latin: fortunate, lucky.
Felic, Felice (Italian), *Feliciano* (Italian, Spanish), *Felicien, Felicio, Feliks* (Polish), *Felise, Felixe, Feliz, Felizio.*
Felton Old English: from the farm in the field.
Fenix *See* Phoenix.
Fenlon Irish: son of the fair one.
Fenn Old English: a marsh or fen.
Fenris Old Norse: a wolf.
Fenrir.
Fenton Old English: from the marshlands.
Faneton, Feinton.
Fenwick Old English: from the farm in the marshland.
Fenwicke, Fenwyck, Fenwycke.
Feodore *See* Theodore.
Ferdaus *See* Firdos.
Ferdinand Teutonic: prepared for the journey; an adventurer or traveller.
Ferdinando (Italian), *Fernán* (Spanish), *Fernance, Fernand* (French), *Fernande, Fernando* (Spanish), *Hernando* (Spanish).
Diminutives: Ferd, Ferdie.
Ferenc Hungarian form of Francis.
Diminutives: Feri, Ferko.
Fergal Irish Gaelic: a man of valour. *See also* Friel.
Feargal, Feargall, Fearghal, Fearghall, Fergall, Firgal, Firgall, Firghal, Firghall, Firghil, Firghill.
Fergan Probably a form of Fergal or Fergus.
Fergus Gaelic: the chosen man, or a man of vigour. *See also* Ferguson.
Fearghas (Gaelic), *Feargus.*
Diminutive: Fergie.
Ferguson Gaelic: the son of Fergus.
Feri/Ferko *See* Ferenc.
Fermin Basque form of Firmin.
Fernán/Fernance/Fernand/Fernando *See* Ferdinand.
Fernleigh/Fernley *See* Farnley.
Feroz Arabic: victorious and successful.
Fairouz, Fairuz, Fayrouz, Feroze, Firoz, Firoze, Firuz.
Ferrand Old French: a grey-haired man.
Ferran.
Ferrato Italian form of Ferro.
Ferrer Old French: the blacksmith.
Ferrar.
Ferric *See* Ferro.
Ferris Gaelic: a rock. A form of Peter.
Farris.
Ferro Latin: like iron.
Ferrato (Italian), *Ferric, Ferruccio* (Italian), *Ferrucio* (Italian), *Feruccio.*
Festus Latin: steadfast.

Fetu Samoan: a star. The god of the night sky.
Février The French name for February.
Fiachra Irish Gaelic: a raven.
Fiacre.
Fiberte *See* Filbert.
Fidel Latin: faithful.
Fedele (Italian), *Fidele, Fidelio, Fidelis.*
Fielding Old English: a field dweller.
Field, Fielder.
Fife Scottish: a man from the region of Fife.
Fyfe.
Figaro Latin: daring, cunning.
Filbert Teutonic: very bright.
Fiberte, Filiberto (Italian), *Philbert.*
Filep Hungarian form of Philip.
Filib/Filip/Filippo *See* Philip.
Finan *See* Finian.
Finbar Irish Gaelic: fair-headed.
Findlay/Findley *See* Finlay.
Fineas/Finneas *See* Phineas.
Fingal Scottish Gaelic: the fair stranger.
Fingall.
Diminutive: Finn.
Finian Irish Gaelic: fair or white. The name of a saint.
Finan, Fineen, Finnian.
Finlay Scottish Gaelic: the fair warrior.
Findlay, Findley, Finley, Finnlay.
Diminutives: Fin, Finn.
Finn Irish Gaelic: the white or fair one. Old Norse: a man from Finland. Also a diminutive of names such as Fingal and Finlay.
Fionn, Fynn.
Finnegan Irish Gaelic: fair.
Finegan.
Fintan Irish Gaelic: the name of several Irish saints.
Fiorello Italian: the masculine form of Fiorella, meaning a little flower.
Firdos Arabic: paradise.
Ferdaus, Firdaus.
Fire English from Greek: heat, energy and passion.
Fyre.
Firgal/Firghal/Firghil *See* Fergal.
Firmin Latin: steadfast and firm.
Fermin (Basque), *Firman.*
Firoz/Firoze/Firuz *See* Feroz.
Firth Old English: of the woodland.
Frith.
Fisk/Fiske *See* Fysk.
Fitch Old French: a lance or spear.
Fitz Old French: a son. Also a diminutive of names such as Fitzgerald and Fitzjames.
Fitzgerald Old French: the son of Gerald.
Fitzhugh Old French: the son of Hugh.
Fitzjames Old French: the son of James.
Fitzpatrick Old French: the son of Patrick.

Fitzroy Old French: the son of the king.
Fiyero The name of a character in the musical *Wicked*.
Flae/Flai/Flaie *See* Flay.
Flame Middle English: something that burns or blazes.
Flaime, Flaym, Flayme.
Flanagan *See* Flannan.
Flanders Old French: the submerged land. A region of north-west Europe.
Flannders.
Flannan Irish Gaelic: ruddy, or red-haired.
Flann, Flanagan.
Flannery Irish Gaelic: the red one. Also a girl's name.
Flanary, Flanery, Flannary, Flanner.
Flavian Latin: golden-haired.
Flavien (French), *Flavio* (Italian), *Flavius.*
Flavio/Flavius *See* Flavian.
Flay Middle English: to strip or criticise.
Flae, Flai, Flaie, Flaye.
Flaym/Flayme *See* Flame.
Flax Middle English: a plant name.
Flaxen.
Fleance Celtic: the rosy one.
Fleming Old French: a man from Flanders.
Flemming (Scandinavian).
Fletcher Old French: an arrow maker.
Diminutive: Fletch.
Flin/Flinn *See* Flynn.

Flinders From Matthew Flinders, the renowned 19th-century navigator and explorer.
Flynders.
Flint Old English: a hard stone.
Flindt, Flynt.
Flintoff Old English: the place of flints.
Flintof, Flintofft, Flintoft, Flyntof, Flyntoff, Flyntoft.
Florian Latin: a flower, blooming. The masculine form of Flora.
Florean, Florencio (Italian, Spanish), *Florent* (French), *Florizel, Floro* (Italian, Spanish), *Florus.*
Floribert French/German: a bright flower.
Floyd *See* Lloyd.
Flynders *See* Flinders.
Flynn Irish Gaelic: the red-haired one.
Flin, Flinn, Flyn, Phlyn, Phlynn.
Flynt *See* Flint.
Flyntoff/Flyntoft *See* Flintoff.
Folant Welsh form of Valentine.
Folchard Teutonic: of the brave people.
Folkard, Folkhard, Folkert (Dutch).
Folcmar Teutonic: of the famous people.
Folkmar, Folmer.
Fontaine/Fontayne *See* Fountain.
Fonz/Fonzie *See* Alphonso.
Forbes Scottish Gaelic: a placename.
Ford Old English: from the ford or

river crossing.
Forde.
Forester Old French: a forester or gamekeeper.
Forrester.
Forrest Old French: a forest dweller.
Forest.
Forster *See* Foster.
Fortescue Old French: a strong shield.
Fortunato Latin: the fortunate one.
Fortunatu, Fortune.
Foster Old English: a foster parent. Old French: a shearer.
Forster.
Fotis Greek: light.
Fotios, Photios, Photis.
Fouad Arabic: the beloved one.
Fuad.
Fountain Old French: a spring or fountain.
Fontaine (French), *Fontayne, Founten, Fountin, Fountyn.*
Fourneaux *See* Furnell.
Fox Middle English: a fox.
Foxe, Foxx.
Frain/Fraine *See* Frayne.
Franc/Francesco *See* Francis.
Francilo Spanish form of Francis.
Francis Latin: from France, or a free man.
Ferenc (Hungarian), *Franc* (Slavic), *Francesco* (Italian), *Francilo* (Spanish), *Francisco* (Spanish), *Franciscus, Franciszek* (Slavic), *Franco* (Italian), *François* (French), *Franjo* (Slavic), *Frans* (Scandinavian), *Frantisek* (Slavic), *Franz* (German), *Werahiko* (Maori).
Diminutives: Chico, Cisco, (Spanish), France, Frank, Franki, Frankie, Paco (Spanish), Pancho (Spanish).
Franco/François *See* Francis.
Franjo Slavic form of Francis.
Frank Teutonic: a member of the tribe of the Franks. Also a diminutive of Francis and Franklin.
Franki/Frankie *See* Francis.
Franklin Old French: a free citizen.
Franklen, Franklyn.
Diminutive: Frank.
Frans/Franz *See* Francis.
Frantisek Slavic form of Francis.
Frase/Fraze *See* Phrase.
Fraser Old French: a strawberry, or from a Norman family name.
Frasier, Frazer, Frazier.
Fray *See* Frey.
Frayne Old French: an ash tree. Old English: a stranger.
Frain, Fraine, Frayn, Freyne.
Frazer/Frazier *See* Fraser.
Fred/Freddie/Freddy Diminutives of Alfred, Frederick and Wilfred.
Frederick Teutonic: a peaceful ruler.
Bedrich (Czech), *Bedros, Federico* (Italian, Spanish), *Frederic, Frédéric* (French), *Frederik* (Danish), *Fredric, Fredrick, Fredrik* (Swedish), *Freidreich, Freidrich, Frideric, Friderich, Friderick, Friderik,*

Friedrich (German), *Friedreich*.
Diminutives: Fred, Freddie, Freddy, Frits, Fritz (German).
Freeman Old English: a freeborn man.
Freitag The German name for Friday.
Fremont Teutonic: the noble protector.
Frey Old Norse: the god of weather and fertility, and the patron of seafarers.
Fray, Freyr.
Freyne *See* Frayne.
Friday A 'day name', from an Old Norse word – literally the day of Freya, the Norse equivalent of the Roman goddess Venus.
Freitag (German).
Frideric/Friderick/Friderik *See* Frederick.
Friedrich German form of Frederick.
Friel A form of Fergal, meaning a man of valour.
Friele, Friels.
Frith *See* Firth.
Frits/Fritz *See* Frederick.
Frixo An unusual modern name.
Frixos.
Fuad *See* Fouad.
Fudo Japanese: the god of fire and wisdom.
Fuego Spanish: fire.
Fuller Old English: a fuller or cloth-thickener.
Fulton Old English: from the muddy place.
Furneaux *See* Furnell.
Furnell Old French: a furnace.
Fourneaux, Furneaux.
Furze Middle English: gorse.
Furse, Fursey, Furzey, Furzy.
Fyfe *See* Fife.
Fynn *See* Finn.
Fyodor Russian form of Theodore.
Fyre *See* Fire.
Fysk Middle English: a fish.
Fisk (Scandinavian), *Fiske, Fyske*.

G

Gabe/Gabi/Gabie *See* Gabriel.
Gable French: little Gabriel.
Gabor Hungarian form of Gabriel.
Gabriel Hebrew: a man of God. One of the archangels in the Bible.
Gabor (Hungarian), *Gabriele* (Italian), *Gabriello* (Italian), *Gavril* (Russian).
Diminutives: Gab, Gabbie, Gabe, Gabi, Gabie.
Gad Native American: a cedar tree.
Gaddiel Hebrew: God is my fortune. An Old Testament name.
Gadi, Gadiel.
Gael French form of Gale.
Gaelan/Gaelen/Gaelin *See* Galen.
Gaerloch *See* Gairloch.
Gaetano Italian: a man from Gaeta, an ancient Italian town.

Gaetan, Gaetane, Gayton.
Gage Old French: a pledge.
Gaile *See* Gale.
Gaindah Aboriginal: thunder. Also a girl's name.
Gainda, Gaynda, Gayndah.
Gair Irish Gaelic: short.
Gairloch Scottish Gaelic: the short loch or lake.
Gaerloch.
Gaius Latin: to rejoice.
Caius.
Gajendra Sanskrit: the lord of the elephants.
Galahad From a placename in the Bible. One of King Arthur's knights.
Galan *See* Galen.
Galbraith Scottish Gaelic: a stranger from England or Wales.
Galbraithe, Galbrayth, Galbraythe.
Gale Old French: gay, lively. More commonly a girl's name. *See also* Gaylord.
Gael (French), *Gaile, Gayle.*
Galen Greek: the calm one, or the helper.
Gaelan, Gaelen, Gaelin, Galan, Galeno (Spanish), *Galin, Galo.*
Galileo A man from Galilee. Also after the famous Italian scientist and astronomer.
Galil.
Gallagher Irish Gaelic: the foreign helper.
Gallard *See* Gaylord.
Galloway Gaelic: a stranger or foreigner.
Galway, Galwey.
Galo *See* Galen.
Galor *See* Gaylord.
Galton Old English: from the rented estate or farm.
Galvin Irish Gaelic: the bright one.
Galvan, Galven, Galvyn.
Galway/Galwey *See* Galloway.
Gamal *See* Jamal.
Gamaliel Hebrew: the recompense of God. A biblical name.
Gamel Scandinavian: the old one.
Gan Chinese: the adventurous one.
Ganan Aboriginal: from the west.
Gandolf Teutonic: the progress of the wolf.
Gandolph.
Ganesh Sanskrit: the lord of the hosts. The elephant-headed Hindu god of wisdom.
Ganesa.
Gannon Irish Gaelic: the little blond or fair one.
Ganymede Greek: a mythological youth.
Gara Irish Gaelic: a mastiff.
Garan/Garen/Garin *See* Garran.
Garath *See* Gareth.
Gardiner Old French: one who tends the garden.
Gardener, Gardner, Garner.
Gared Aboriginal: the south.
Garred.
Garek *See* Garrick.
Garen *See* Gary.

Gareth Welsh: gentle, or an old man.
Garath, Garrath, Garreth, Geraint (Welsh), *Gerens* (Cornish), *Geronte* (French).
Diminutive: Gary.
Garett *See* Garrett.
Garey *See* Gary.
Garfield Old English: from the triangular field.
Diminutive: Gary.
Gari/Garie *See* Gary.
Garisen/Garison *See* Garrison.
Garland Old French: a wreath or garland.
Garman Old English: the spearman.
Garmond Old English: a spear protector.
Garmon.
Garner *See* Gardiner.
Garnet Old French: dark red, from the colour of pomegranates. Also the name of a gemstone.
Garnett.
Garnham Old French: a man with a moustache.
Garnam, Garnon.
Garonne French: the rocky source of a river.
Garon, Garonn.
Garran Possibly a form of Gary.
Garan, Garen, Garin, Garren, Garrin.
Garrath/Garreth *See* Gareth.
Garred *See* Gared.
Garrett English from Old French: a spear warrior. *See also* Gerald and Gerard.
Garett, Garret, Garritt.
Diminutive: Gary.
Garrey *See* Gary.
Garrick Old English: a spear ruler.
Garek.
Garrie/Garry *See* Gary.
Garrison Middle English: a fortified place.
Garisen, Garison, Garrisen.
Garston *See* Garton.
Garth Old Norse: from the garden or enclosure.
Garton Old Norse: a dweller at the fenced farm.
Garston.
Garuda Indonesian: the messenger of the gods, similar to the Greek god Hermes and the Roman god Mercury.
Garvan *See* Garvin.
Garvey Gaelic: from the rough place.
Garvie.
Garvin Teutonic: a spear friend.
Garvan, Garvyn, Garwin.
Garwin *See* Garvin.
Garwood Old English: from the fir trees.
Gary English/Teutonic: a spearman. Also a diminutive of Gareth, Garfield and Garrett.
Garen, Garey, Gari, Garie, Garrey, Garrie, Garry.
Diminutives: Gaz, Gazza.
Gascoigne Old French: a native of

Gascony. *See also* Gaston.
Gascon (French), *Gascogne, Gascoign, Gascoin, Gascoine, Gascoyn, Gascoyne.*
Gasento *See* Jacinto.
Gaspar Persian: the master of the treasure. *See also* Caspar and Jasper.
Gaspard (French), *Gaspare* (Italian), *Gasparo* (Italian).
Gaston French: a man from the province of Gascony. *See also* Gascoigne.
Gastone.
Gatsby From F Scott Fitzgerald's classic novel *The Great Gatsby*.
Gatsbey, Gatsbi, Gatsbie, Gatzbey, Gatzbi, Gatzbie, Gatzby.
Gaurav Sanskrit: possibly meaning one who is proud.
Gautama Sanskrit: the original name of the Buddha.
Gotama.
Gautier *See* Walter.
Gavin Celtic: probably derived from Gawain.
Gavan, Gavejn, Gaven, Gawen (Cornish), *Ghavan, Ghaven, Ghavin.*
Gavril *See* Gabriel.
Gawain Celtic: a battle hawk; one of King Arthur's legendary knights. *See also* Gavin.
Gawen Cornish form of Gavin.
Gayadi Aboriginal: a platypus.
Gayadin.

Gayle *See* Gale.
Gaylord Old French: gay and lively, or a dandy. *See also* Gale.
Gallard, Galor, Gayler, Gaylor.
Gaynda/Gayndah *See* Gaindah.
Gayton English form of Gaetano.
Gaz/Gazza *See* Gary.
Gearald/Gearold *See* Gerald.
Gearalt Irish form of Gerald.
Gearoid Irish Gaelic form of Gerald.
Geary Old English: changeable.
Gearey.
Geb The earth god in Ancient Egyptian mythology.
Keb.
Gedeon *See* Gideon.
Geert Dutch form of Gerhard. *See* Gerard.
Gefell Welsh: a twin.
Geffrey/Geffroy *See* Geoffrey.
Geir Scandinavian: a spear. *See also* Gere.
Geirr.
Gelar Aboriginal: a brother.
Gemini Greek: a twin. The name of a zodiac sign and a constellation.
Geminie, Geminio, Geminius. Geminus.
Gene A diminutive of Eugene, but also used independently.
Genesis Middle English from Greek: the beginning or origin.
Genghis After Genghis Khan, the 12th-century Mongolian conquerer.
Cengiz (Turkish).
Genki Japanese: courage.

Gennaio Italian for January.
Gennaro.

Geoffrey Teutonic: divinely peaceful. Derived from Godfrey. See also Jefferson.
Geffrey, Geffroy (Old French), *Geoffory, Geoffree, Geoffrie, Geoffro, Geofrey, Jeffery, Jeffory, Jeffree, Jeffrey, Jeffri, Jeffrie, Jeffry, Jefri, Jeoffrey, Joffre, Joffrey, Sieffre* (Welsh).
Diminutives: Geof, Geoff, Jeff.

Geordan See Jordan.

Geordie A diminutive of George. Also a short form of Geordan (see Jordan).

George Greek: a farmer. St George is the patron saint of England.
Egor (Russian), *Georg* (German), *Georges* (French), *Georgi* (Russian), *Georgios* (Greek), *Giorgio* (Italian), *Goran* (Swedish), *Gorgi* (Slavic), *Hori* (Polynesian), *Igor* (Russian), *Iouri* (Russian), *Jerzy* (Polish), *Jiri* (Czech), *Joerg, Joji* (Japanese), *Jorgan, Jorge* (Portuguese, Spanish), *Jorgen* (Danish, Swedish), *Joris* (Dutch), *Jory* (Cornish), *Juergen, Juraj* (Slavic), *Jurgen* (German), *Jurgis* (Slavic), *Juri, Juris* (Latvian), *Jurrien* (Dutch), *Jyrki* (Finnish), *Keoki* (Hawaiian), *Siôr* (Welsh), *Yiorgos* (Greek), *Yorgan, Yorick* (Old English), *Yoriyos* (Greek), *Yuri* (Russian).
Diminutives: Djuka (Slavic), Djuro (Slavic), Geordie, Georgie, Gino (Italian).

Gera Hebrew: a biblical name of uncertain meaning.

Geraint See Gareth.

Gerald English from Old French: a spear warrior. See also Garrett and Gerard.
Gearald, Gearalt (Irish), *Gearoid* (Irish Gaelic), *Gearold, Geraldo* (Spanish), *Gerallt* (Welsh), *Geraud* (French), *Gerhold* (German), *Gerrald, Giraldo* (Italian), *Jerald, Jerold, Jerrald, Jerrold.*
Diminutives: Geri, Gerri, Gerry, Gery, Jerrie, Jerry.

Gerard English from Old French: a spear warrior, or brave spearman. See also Garrett and Gerald.
Geert (Dutch), *Gerardo* (Italian, Spanish), *Gerardus, Gerhard, Gerhardt* (German), *Gerrard, Gerrit* (Dutch), *Gert* (Dutch), *Jerard, Jerrard.*
Diminutives: Geri, Gerri, Gerry, Gery, Jerrie, Jerry.

Gerasimos Greek: the name of a 5th-century saint.
Gerasimus.

Geraud French form of Gerald.

Gere A modern name, possibly after actor Richard Gere.
Geir.

Geremie/Geremy See Jeremy.

Gerens See Gareth.

Gerhard/Gerhardt *See* Gerard.
Gerhold German form of Gerald.
Geri *See* Gerald and Gerard.
Germain French form of Germanus, meaning a brother. *See also* Jermaine. *Germaine, Germayn, Germayne, Germanus.*
German *See* Jarman.
Germyn *See* Jermyn.
Gerome/Geronimo *See* Jerome.
Geron An angel of prayer.
Geronte *See* Gareth.
Gerrald *See* Gerald.
Gerrard/Gerrit *See* Gerard.
Gerri/Gerry *See* Gerald and Gerard.
Gershom Hebrew: in exile, a stranger. A son of Moses in the Bible. *Gershon.*
Gert Dutch form of Gerard.
Gervase Teutonic: a spear servant. *Gervais* (French), *Gervaise, Gervasio* (Italian), *Gervis, Jarvis, Jervaise, Jervase, Jervis.*
Gerwyn Welsh: fair love.
Gery *See* Gerald and Gerard.
Gesar Sherpa/Tibetan: from the lotus temple.
Gethin Welsh: dark-skinned. *Gethen, Gethyn, Gethynn.*
Géza A Hungarian name of uncertain meaning.
Gezinus A Dutch name of uncertain meaning.
Ghassan Arabic: in the prime of youth.
Ghavan/Ghavin *See* Gavin.

Ghulam Arabic: a servant or a youth. *Gholam, Ghulaam, Gulam.*
Gi Korean: the brave one.
Giacinto *See* Jacinto.
Giacobbe Italian form of Jacob.
Giacomo Italian form of James.
Giallo Italian: yellow.
Gian An Italian form of John.
Giancarlo Italian: a combination of Gianni and Carlo (*see* Charles). *Gian-Carlo.*
Gianfranco Italian: Gianni and Franco (*see* Francis). *Gian-Franco.*
Gianin *See* John.
Gianluca Italian: A combination of Gianni and Luca (*see* Luke). *Gian-Luca.*
Gianmario Italian: Gianni and Mario (*see* Marius). *Gian-Mario.*
Gianni/Giannino Italian forms of John.
Gianpiero Italian: Gianni combined with Piero (*see* Peter). *Gian-Piero.*
Gib/Gibb *See* Gilbert.
Gibson Old English: the son of Gilbert.
Gideon Hebrew: the mighty warrior. A biblical name. *Gedeon.*
Gifford Teutonic: a gift.
Gijsbert Dutch form of Gisbert.
Gil A diminutive of Gilbert, etc.
Gilbert Teutonic: a bright or famous

pledge. *See also* Gibson, Gillet and Gisbert.
Gilberto (Italian, Portuguese, Spanish), *Gilburt, Guilbert* (French). *Diminutives:* Bert, Gib, Gibb, Gil, Gill.

Gilby Norse: a pledge.
Gilbey.

Gilchrist Gaelic: the servant of Christ.

Gilead Hebrew: an Old Testament placename.

Giles Greek: a kid, or young goat. *Gil* (Spanish), *Gilles* (French), *Gillis* (Danish, Dutch), *Gyles, Gylles, Jiles, Jyles, Jylles.*

Gilford Old English: by the ford. *Guildford.*

Gilles/Gillis *See* Giles.

Gillespie Scottish Gaelic: the bishop's servant.
Gillespey.

Gillet French: little Gilbert.

Gilmer Scottish Gaelic: a servant of the Virgin Mary.
Gilmore, Gilmour.

Gilroy Gaelic: a son of the red-haired man.

Gilson The son of Gil (Gilbert). *Gillsen, Gillson, Gilsen.*

Gino Italian: a diminutive of names such as Giorgio and Luigi.

Gioachino Italian form of Joachim.

Giordano *See* Jordan.

Giorgio Italian form of George.

Giovanni Italian form of John.

Giovedi The Italian name for Thursday.

Giraldo *See* Gerald.

Girolamo Italian form of Jerome.

Girra Aboriginal: a creek, or a tree.

Girvan Gaelic: the rough little one. *Girven, Girvin.*

Gisbert Probably a form of Gilbert, meaning a bright or famous pledge. *Gijsbert* (Dutch), *Gysbert.*

Giulio *See* Julius.

Giuseppe Italian form of Joseph.

Gladstone Old English: a bright rock.

Gladwin Old English: a bright or kind friend.

Glanville Old French: from the estate of oak trees.
Glanfield, Glanvill, Glenvill, Glenville.

Glaukon Greek: a bluish-green colour.
Glaucon.

Glen Cornish/Gaelic/Welsh: from the valley or glen.
Glenn, Glenne, Glyn, Glyne, Glynn.

Glendon Gaelic: from the fortress in the glen.
Glenden.

Glenroy The king of the glen.
Glennroi, Glennroy, Glenroi.

Glenvill/Glenville *See* Glanville.

Glover Old English: a glove-maker.

Glyn/Glyne/Glynn *See* Glen.

Goddard Old English: divinely

brave or strong.

Godfrey Teutonic: divinely peaceful. See also Geoffrey.
Godefroy (Old French), *Godfree*, *Godfrid* (Old Norse), *Godfrie*, *Godfried* (Dutch), *Godfry*, *Gottfried* (German).

Godwin Old English: a divine or good friend.
Goodwin.

Goker Turkish: a man of the sky.

Golding Old English: the son of the golden one.

Goldsmith Old English: a gold worker.
Goldsmithe, Goldsmyth, Goldsmythe.

Goldwin Old English: a golden friend.
Goldwinn, Goldwyn, Goldwynn.

Golfo Italian: a gulf.

Goliath Hebrew: revealing.

Gomer Hebrew: complete. Old English: good and famous.

Gomez Spanish: a man.

Gonzales Spanish: a wolf.
Gonzalo.

Goodluck After the Nigerian politician Goodluck Jonathan.

Goodwin See Godwin.

Goola Aboriginal: a kangaroo.

Goonal Aboriginal: a large lagoon.

Gopal Sanskrit: the cowherd.
Gopala, Gopaul.

Goran Swedish form of George. See also Gorran.

Gordan Slavic: dignified. See also Gordon.
Diminutive: Danko.

Gordian The name of three Roman emperors.

Gordon Scottish Gaelic: a placename, probably meaning from the great hill.
Gordan, Gorden, Gordyn.
Diminutives: Gordie, Gordy.

Gore Old English: from the triangular plot of ground.

Gorgi A Slavic form of George.

Gorm Norse: a serpent of war.

Gorman Teutonic: blue-eyed.

Goro Japanese: the fifth, or the fifth-born child.

Gorokan Aboriginal: the dawn.

Goron See Gorran.

Goronwy Welsh: a figure from Celtic mythology.

Gorran Cornish: a hero.
Goran, Goron, Gorron.

Gorwel Welsh: the horizon.

Gösta Swedish form of Gustav.

Gotama See Gautama.

Goth Middle English: a member of an early Teutonic race.
Gothe.

Gottfried See Godfrey.

Gough Welsh: red-haired.

Govad Persian: the wind.

Govinda Sanskrit: a cowherd, one who is good at finding cows.
Govind.

Gower Celtic: pure.

Gowon Nigerian: a rainmaker.

Graciano See Gratian.

Grady Irish Gaelic: illustrious, noble.
Graeden/Graedon *See* Greyden.
Graem/Graeme *See* Graham.
Graesan/Graesen/Graeson *See* Grayson.
Graham Old English: from the gravelly place or homestead. A common Scottish surname.
Graem, Graeme, Grahame, Graheme, Graiem, Graieme, Gram, Greyam, Greyem.
Grandville *See* Granville.
Granger Old English: a farmer.
Grainge, Grainger, Grange.
Granite An igneous rock.
Grant Old French: the large or tall one.
Grantlee, Grant-Lee, Grantleigh, Grantley.
Grantham Old English: from the big meadow.
Grantlee/Grantleigh/Grantley *See* Grant.
Granville Old French: from the big town.
Grandville, Granvil.
Gratian Latin: pleasing, or thankful.
Graciano (Spanish), *Gratien, Graziano* (Italian).
Gratton Old English: from the big hill.
Grattan, Gratten.
Gray/Graye *See* Grey.
Grayden/Graydon *See* Greyden.
Grayson Old English: the son of the bailiff.
Graesan, Graesen, Graeson, Graysan, Graysen, Greysan, Greysen, Greyson.
Grayston Old English: the grey stone.
Graystone, Greyston, Greystone.
Graziano *See* Gratian.
Greer *See* Grier.
Greg/Gregg *See* Gregory.
Gregan A surname; meaning unknown.
Gregory Greek: vigilant, watchful. The name of several early saints and popes.
Gregery, Greggery, Grégoire (French), *Gregor* (Scottish), *Gregorio* (Italian, Spanish), *Gregry, Greguska* (Czech), *Greig* (Scottish), *Grgur* (Slavic), *Grigor* (Welsh), *Griogair* (Scottish Gaelic), *Kerekori* (Maori).
Diminutives: Greg, Grega (Czech), Gregg.
Greig *See* Gregory.
Grenfell/Grenville *See* Greville.
Gresham Old English: from the grazing land.
Greville Old French: from a placename in Normandy.
Grenfell, Grenfelle, Grenvill, Grenville, Grevill.
Grey Old English: the grey-haired one.
Gray, Graye, Greye.
Greyam/Greyem *See* Graham.
Greyden Middle English: from the grey place.

Graeden, Graedon, Grayden, Graydon, Greydon.
Greysan/Greyson *See* Grayson.
Greystone *See* Grayston.
Grgur Slavic form of Gregory.
Grier A Scottish form of Gregoria. More commonly a girl's name.
Greer.
Griffin/Griffyn *See* Gryffyn.
Griffith Welsh: a powerful lord. *See also* Gryffyn.
Diminutive: Griff.
Grigor/Griogair *See* Gregory.
Griswold Teutonic: from the grey forest.
Grosvenor Old French: a great huntsman.
Grovener, Grovenor.
Grover Old English: from the grove of trees.
Grove, Groves.
Grozdan Slavic: grapes.
Gryffyn Cornish/Welsh: little Griffith.
Griffin, Griffyn, Gryffin.
Gub From an Irish Gaelic name meaning a smith.
Gubb.
Guba The Tibetan name for September.
Guenter *See* Gunther.
Guerrino Italian: of the war.
Guglielmo *See* William.
Guido *See* Guy.
Guilbert *See* Gilbert.
Guildford *See* Gilford.
Guilhelm/Guilherme/Guillaume/Guillermo *See* William.
Guin *See* Gwyn.
Gul Turkish: a rose.
Gulam *See* Ghulam.
Gulbahar Turkish: a spring rose.
Gulio *See* Julius.
Gulliver The surname of Jonathan Swift's protagonist in the novel *Gulliver's Travels*.
Gumnut A eucalyptus nut.
Gunar/Gunars/Gunnar *See* Gunther.
Gunjan Sanskrit: buzzing like a bee.
Gunnel The upper part of a boat or ship.
Gunnell.
Gunner A soldier; one who works with a gun.
Gunther Teutonic: a bold warrior. Generally a German name.
Guenter (German), *Gunar, Gunars, Gunnar* (Scandinavian), *Gunnars, Gunter.*
Guntur Indonesian: thunder.
Gur Hebrew: a lion cub.
Gurana Aboriginal: a bee or bees.
Gurbachan Sikh: one who abides by the word of the guru.
Gurdial A Sikh name of uncertain meaning.
Gurion Hebrew: of lion-like strength, or the place of God.
Gursewak A Sikh name of uncertain meaning.
Gurshan Sikh: finding refuge or

peace with the guru.
Gurshant, Gursharan.

Guru Sanskrit: a teacher or holy man.

Gurwar The Hindi name for Thursday.

Gus/Gussy Diminutives of names such as Angus, Augustus and Gustav.

Gustav Old Norse: the staff of the Goths.
Gösta (Swedish), *Gustaav, Gustaf* (Swedish), *Gustave* (English, French), *Gustavo* (Italian), *Gustavus.*
Diminutives: Gus, Gussy.

Guthrie Scottish Gaelic: from the windy place.
Guthry.

Guy Teutonic: the wide one, or from the wood.
Guido (Italian), *Guyon, Gvido, Gye, Veit* (Dutch), *Wye.*
Diminutive: Wyatt.

Guyra Aboriginal: a fishing place, or a white cockatoo. The name of a town in NSW.

Guyten/Guyton *See* Gyton.

Gvido *See* Guy.

Gvozden Slavic: as strong as iron.

Gwain/Gwaine *See* Gwyane.

Gwener The Welsh name for Friday and the planet Venus.

Gwilym Welsh form of William.
Guillym.

Gwinear Cornish/Welsh: the name of a saint.

Gwyane A combination of Gwyn and Wayne (a cart or wagon maker).
Gwain, Gwaine, Gwyaine.

Gwydion Welsh: the god of the sky and magic in Celtic mythology.

Gwydir Welsh: the name of a New South Wales river.

Gwyn Welsh: white, fair, or blessed.
Guin, Gwinn, Gwynn, Gwynne.

Gwynfor Welsh: from the fair place. Also a girl's name.
Gwynnfor, Gwynnfore.

Gyalpo Sherpa/Tibetan: the supreme ruler.

Gye *See* Guy.

Gyles *See* Giles.

Gysbert *See* Gisbert.

Gyton From the place of Guy.
Guyten, Guyton, Gyeten, Gyeton, Gyten.

Gyula Hungarian form of Julius.

H

Haakon *See* Hakon.

Haarlem *See* Harlem.

Habib Arabic: the beloved one.

Hadad Arabic: the virile one.
Haddad.

Hadan/Hadein/Haden/Hadin *See* Hayden.

Haddon Old English: from the

heathery hill.
Hadden.
Hadi Arabic: a guide or leader.
Hadley Old English: from the heathery field.
Hadlee, Hadleigh.
Hadrian *See* Adrian.
Hadwin Old English: a friend in battle.
Hadwyn.
Haemish *See* Hamish.
Hafiz Arabic: the guardian.
Hafez.
Hagen Irish Gaelic: little Hugh. *See also* Hakon.
Hagan, Haggan.
Hagley Old English: from the hawthorn-wood clearing.
Hagop Armenian form of Jacob.
Hakop.
Hague *See* Haig.
Hai Vietnamese: of the sea.
Haidar Arabic: a lion.
Haider.
Haig Old English/Teutonic: from the enclosure or paddock.
Hague, Haigh.
Haile After Haile Selassie, a former emperor of Ethiopia.
Hailes *See* Hales.
Hailey *See* Hayley.
Haimish *See* Hamish.
Haimon/Haimond *See* Hammond.
Haines Old English: from the fenced area.
Haiz/Haize *See* Haze.
Hakan Turkish: an emperor. *See also* Hakon.
Hakaraia Maori form of Zachary.
Hakim Arabic: wise and judicious.
Hakeem.
Hakon Old Norse: of noble birth.
Haakon, Hagen (Danish), *Hakan* (Swedish).
Hakop Armenian form of Hagop.
Hal Diminutive of Harold, Harry and Henry.
Halbert Old English: a brilliant hero.
Halcyon Greek: a kingfisher, or calm and peaceful.
Alcyon.
Halden Old English: one who is half Danish.
Haldan, Haldane, Haldene, Haldin.
Haldor Old Norse: the rock of Thor (the Norse god of thunder).
Halldor.
Hale Old English: the dweller in the nook.
Haleem *See* Halim.
Hales Old English: of the valley or enclosure.
Hailes, Hayles.
Haley Irish Gaelic: ingenious. *See also* Hayley.
Halley.
Halford Old English: from the ford in the nook.
Helford.
Hali Greek: from the sea.
Halie.

H – Boys

Halifax Old English: from the holy field. A city in northern England and a seaport in Canada.
Halim Arabic: gentle.
Haleem.
Hall Old English: from the manor house or hall.
Hallam Old Norse: the dweller at the rocks.
Hallum.
Hallbjörn Icelandic/Old Norse: the bear of the rock.
Halldor *See* Haldor.
Halley *See* Haley.
Hallstein/Hallsten *See* Halsten.
Haloke Native American: a salmon.
Halse Old English: from the neck of land.
Halsey.
Halstead Old English: the stronghold.
Halsted.
Halsten Old Norse: a rock.
Hallstein, Hallsten.
Halvard Old Norse: the defender of the rock.
Halvar, Halvor.
Hamal Arabic: as gentle as a lamb. The name of a star in the constellation of Aries.
Hamel.
Hamaliel The angel of the month of August.
Hamar Old Norse: ingenious, or a hammer (as in the hammer of the god Thor).
Hamelin/Hamelyn *See* Hamlin.

Hamen *See* Hamon.
Hamer *See* Hammer.
Hami The Maori form of Sam.
Hamid Arabic: the thankful one.
Hamed.
Hamilton Old English: from the crooked hill.
Hamis Swahili: born on a Thursday.
Hamish Scottish form of James.
Haemish, Haimish, Haymish, Heymish.
Hamlet Old English: from the enclosed land. The name of a famous Shakespearean play.
Hamlin Teutonic: from the small home.
Hamelin, Hamelyn, Hamlen, Hamlyn.
Hammer Middle English: a hammer-maker.
Hamer, Hammor, Hamor.
Hammond English from Old French: of the home.
Haimon, Haimond, Hammonde, Hamon, Hamond, Hamonde.
Hamon Greek: the faithful one. *See also* Hammond.
Hamen.
Hamor *See* Hammer.
Hampton Old English: from the river meadow.
Hampden.
Hamuera Maori form of Samuel.
Hamza Arabic: like a lion.
Hamzah.
Han Vietnamese: the ocean.

Hanan Hebrew: the gracious gift of God.
Handel Teutonic: little Hans (*see* John). The name of a famous German composer.
Hanford Old English: from the rocky ford.
Hani Arabic: the contented one.
Hank/Hanke Diminutives of Henry and John.
Hanley Old English: from the high clearing.
Hanleigh, Henleigh, Henley.
Hannes/Hans/Hansi *See* John.
Hannibal Phoenician: the famous general of Carthage (northern Africa) who crossed the Alps and invaded Italy. *See also* Annibale.
Hannon An English surname, probably derived from John or Johan.
Hannan.
Hannu Finnish form of John.
Hans Sanskrit: a swan. Also a German form of John.
Hansard Old French: a cutlass- or dagger-maker.
Hannsard.
Hansel A diminutive of Hans. *See* John.
Hansjoerg Teutonic: a combination of Hans and Joerg (George).
Hanson Old English/Teutonic: the son of Hans.
Hansen.
Hanuman Sanskrit: the Hindu monkey god.
Hao Chinese: good.
Hapu Polynesian: the name of a tribe.
Hara Aboriginal: the sky.
Harah.
Haral/Harald *See* Harold.
Haram Hebrew: a mountaineer.
Haran.
Harbard Old Norse: the grey-bearded one. The name of a boatman in Norse mythology.
Harbert *See* Herbert.
Harbhajan Sikh: one who is devoted to God.
Harcharan Sikh: one who takes shelter in the Lord.
Harsharan.
Diminutive: Harsh.
Harcourt Old English: the dweller at the falconer's cottage.
Harden Old English: from the valley of the hare.
Harding Old English: a brave warrior.
Hardwicke Old English: from the sheep farm.
Hardwick, Hardwyck, Hardwycke.
Hardwin Old English: a brave friend.
Hardwyn, Harwin.
Hardy Teutonic: bold, daring.
Hardey, Hardie.
Hare Maori form of Charles. *See also* Hari.
Harekrishna Sanskrit: Lord Krishna, a Hindu god.

Harekrish, Harkrishna.
Harel Hebrew: God's mountain.
Harendra Hindi: a combination of two Hindu gods, Hari (also known as Vishnu) and Indra.
Harinder (Sikh), *Harindra.*
Hareth Hebrew: a hill.
Harford Old English: the ford of the stag.
Hartford, Hertford.
Hargreave Old English: from the hare grove.
Hargrave, Hargreaves.
Hari Sanskrit: he who removes evil.
Hare.
Harian *See* Adrian.
Hariel The angel of science, the arts and tame animals.
Harin Nepali: a deer.
Harinder/Harindra *See* Harendra.
Harith Sanskrit: green.
Hariyo Nepali: green.
Harjit Sikh: victorious through God's grace
Harjeet.
Harlan Old English: from the rocky land. Generally an American name.
Harland, Harlen, Harlin, Harlon, Harlyn.
Diminutive: Lanny.
Harleigh/Harley/Harly *See* Arley.
Harlem A region of New York City.
Haarlem (Dutch).
Harlock Old English: a lock of grey hair.
Harlow Old English: from the fortified hill.
Harlowe.
Harlyn *See* Harlan.
Harman/Harmon *See* Herman.
Haro Japanese: the son of the wild boar.
Harold Old Norse: army power, or ruler of the army.
Arailt (Scottish Gaelic), *Haral, Harald* (Scandinavian), *Harrold, Herold.*
Diminutive: Hal.
Haroon/Haroun/Harun Arabic forms of Aaron.
Harper Old English: a harp player or maker.
Harri/Harrie/Harry Diminutives of Henry but also used as independent names. *See also* Harrison and Parry.
Harrington Old English: the place or farm of Harry (Henry).
Harington.
Harrison Old English: the son of Harry (Henry).
Harries, Harris.
Harsh/Harsharan *See* Harcharan.
Harsha Sanskrit: happiness.
Hart Old English: a stag or male deer.
Harte.
Hartleigh/Hartley *See* Arley.
Hartman Teutonic: the strong man.
Hartmann.
Hartmut Teutonic: one of brave mind.
Hartwell Old English: from the stag ford.
Hartwin Teutonic: a brave friend.

Hartwood Old English: from the forest of stags.
Haru Japanese: born in the spring.
Haruko Japanese: the firstborn.
Harvard The name of a famous US university.
Havard.
Harvey Breton: battle-worthy.
Harvie, Hervé (French), *Hervey.*
Diminutives: Harv, Harve.
Harwin *See* Hardwin.
Harwood Old English: from the wood of the hares.
Hasad Turkish: the harvest, or the reaper.
Hassad.
Hasani *See* Hussain.
Haseleigh/Haseley *See* Hazely.
Hasim Arabic: the decisive one.
Haslett Old English: from the hazel-tree wood.
Haslet, Haslit, Haslitt, Hazlet, Hazlett, Hazlit, Hazlitt.
Hassad *See* Hasad.
Hassan Arabic: handsome and good.
Hasan.
Hastings The name of an English town.
Hasu Japanese: a lotus flower.
Hauk/Hauke *See* Hawk.
Hauora Maori: lively.
Havard Norwegian: a high defender or guardian. *See also* Harvard.
Havelock Old Norse: sea sport.
Havelocke, Havlock.
Haven Old English: a place of refuge.
Havyn.
Haverley Old English: from the oat meadow.
Haverleigh, Haverly.
Havgan Celtic: white.
Havika Hawaiian: beloved.
Havlock *See* Havelock.
Havyn *See* Haven.
Hawk Middle English: a bird of prey.
Hauk, Hauke, Hawke.
Hawkesbury The name of a major Sydney river.
Hawley Old English: from the hedged meadow.
Hayden Old English: from the heathery hill. Also a modern girl's name.
Hadan, Hadein, Haden, Hadin, Hadon, Haydan, Haydn, Haydon, Haydyn, Heydan, Heyden, Heydon, Heydyn.
Haydn Teutonic: the heathen. The name of a famous Austrian composer. *See also* Hayden.
Haydyn.
Hayes Old English: from the hedged area.
Hayles *See* Hales.
Hayley Old English: a high clearing or meadow. More commonly a girl's name.
Hailey, Haley, Haylie.
Haymish *See* Hamish.
Hayward *See* Howard.
Haywood Old English: from the

fenced wood.
Heywood.
Hazan Turkish: the autumn.
Hazen.
Haze A type of mist.
Haiz, Haize, Hayz, Hayze.
Hazely Old English: a hazel meadow.
Haseleigh, Haseley, Hasely, Hazeleigh, Hazeley.
Hazem Arabic: firm, or strong.
Hazim.
Hazlet/Hazlett/Hazlitt *See* Haslett.
Headley *See* Hedley.
Healy Irish Gaelic: possibly meaning a descendant.
Healey, Heley, Hely.
Hearn Gaelic: the lord of the horses. *See also* Ahearn.
Hearne, Hern, Herne.
Hearst *See* Hurst.
Heath Old English: the heathland dweller.
Heathe.
Heathcliff English: from the cliffland heath. The hero of Emily Brontë's *Wuthering Heights*.
Heathcliffe.
Heathcote Old English: from the cottage on a heath.
Heathfield Old English: from the heather field.
Heaton Old English: a high place.
Hebbourn/Hebburn *See* Hepburn.
Hebert *See* Herbert.
Hector Greek: to hold fast. A Trojan hero in classical mythology.
Ettore (Italian), *Heitor* (Portuguese), *Hektor.*
Heddwyn Welsh: blessed peace.
Hedley Old English: a clearing in the heather.
Headley.
Heikki Finnish form of Henry.
Heikkinen Finnish: the son of Henry.
Heilyn Welsh: a steward.
Hein Dutch diminutive of Hendrik. *See* Henry.
Heinrich German form of Henry.
Heinz Diminutive of Heinrich. *See* Henry.
Heiron *See* Heron.
Heitor *See* Hector.
Heka A god in Egyptian mythology.
Helaku Native American: a sunny day.
Heley *See* Healy.
Helford *See* Halford.
Helios Greek: a mythological sun god. *See also* Hyperion.
Heli, Helio, Helius.
Hellas The Greek name for Greece.
Helliar/Helliard *See* Hillier.
Helmut Teutonic: a courageous protector.
Helmuth.
Hely *See* Healy.
Hema A figure in Polynesian mythology.
Heman Hebrew: faithful.
Hemant Hindi: winter.
Hemi Maori form of James.

Henare Maori form of Henry.
Henderson Old English from Teutonic: the son of Henry.
Hendon Old English: from the high place.
Henden, Henton.
Hendra Cornish: from the old farm.
Hendry.
Hendrick/Hendrik *See* Henry.
Hendrix After Jimi Hendrix, the legendary 1960s rock musician. Also possibly a form of Henry or Hendry.
Hendricks, Hendryx.
Hendry A form of Henry.
Hendree, Hendrey, Hendrie, Hentrey, Hentrie, Hentry.
Hendy Old English: the courteous one.
Henerik *See* Henry.
Henerik *See* Henry.
Henleigh/Henley *See* Hanley.
Hennessey Irish Gaelic: a descendant of Angus.
Hennesey, Hennessy, Hennesy.
Henning *See* Henry.
Henri/Henric/Henrik/Henrique *See* Henry.
Henry Teutonic: the ruler of the home or estate. The name of eight English kings. *See also* Harrison, Henderson, Hendry and Parry.
Eanraig (Scottish Gaelic), *Emre* (Turkish), *Enrico* (Italian), *Enrique* (Portuguese, Spanish), *Enriquez, Heikki* (Finnish), *Heinrich* (German), *Henare* (Maori), *Hendrick, Hendrik* (Dutch, Scandinavian), *Hendrikis, Hendry, Henerik* (Danish), *Henri* (French), *Henric, Henrik* (Hungarian, Scandinavian), *Henrique* (Portuguese), *Henryk* (Polish), *Hinrik* (Icelandic), *Indrek* (Estonian).
Diminutives: Hal, Hank, Hanke, Harri (Welsh), Harrie, Harry, Hein (Dutch), Heinz (German), Henning (Danish).
Henton *See* Hendon.
Hentrey/Hentrie *See* Hendry.
Hepburn Old English: a high burial mound.
Hebbourn, Hebbourne, Hebburn, Hebburne, Hepburne.
Heracles/Herakles *See* Hercules.
Herbert Teutonic: a bright warrior.
Harbert (Dutch), *Hebert, Heribert* (German).
Diminutives: Bert, Bertie, Herb, Herbie.
Hercules Greek: the glory of Hera. The exceptionally strong mythological hero and the name of a large constellation. *See also* Alcides.
Ercole (Italian), *Heracles, Herakles* (Greek), *Hercule* (French).
Heremaia Maori form of Jeremiah (*see* Jeremy).
Herewini Maori form of Selwyn.
Herman Teutonic: a man of the army.

Armand (French), *Armando*, *Armenio* (Portuguese), *Armin* (Dutch), *Armindo*, *Armond*, *Ermanno* (Italian), *Harman*, *Harmen*, *Harmon*, *Hermann* (German), *Hermanus*, *Hermon*.

Hermes Greek: the messenger of the gods.

Hermod The Norse messenger of the gods: the equivalent of Hermes and the Roman god Mercury.

Hermon *See* Herman.

Hermoso Spanish: handsome.

Hern/Herne *See* Hearn.

Hernando *See* Ferdinand.

Herod A name from the Bible, probably of Greek origin. *Herrod.*

Herold *See* Harold.

Heron Middle English: a waterbird. *Heiron, Herron.*

Herrick Old Norse: the army ruler. *Herrik.*

Herrod *See* Herod.

Hershel Jewish: a deer. *Herschel, Herschell, Herschelle, Hersh, Hershal, Hershall, Hershell, Hershelle, Heshel, Hirsh.*

Herst *See* Hurst.

Hertford *See* Harford.

Hervé/Hervey *See* Harvey.

Herwin Teutonic: a battle companion.

Hesham Arabic: generous.

Heshel *See* Hershel.

Hesketh Old Norse: from the horseracing track.

Hespero Greek: the evening star. *Hesperio, Hesperos.*

Heston Old English: the place in the brushwood. Also after the actor Charlton Heston. *Hesten.*

Heugh *See* Hugh.

Hew/Hewey/Hewie *See* Hugh.

Hewett Teutonic: little Hugh. *Hewat, Hewatt, Hewet, Hewit, Hewitt, Hewlett, Hewlitt.*

Hewlett/Hewlitt *See* Hewett.

Hewon *See* Huon.

Hewston *See* Houston.

Heydan/Heyden/Heydyn *See* Hayden.

Heymish *See* Hamish.

Heyward *See* Howard.

Heywood *See* Haywood.

Hiatt *See* Hyatt.

Hiawatha Native American: he who made the rivers.

Hickson The son of Hick (a form of Dick, a diminutive of Richard). *Hicksen, Hixen, Hixon.*

Hide *See* Hyde.

Hideyuki A Japanese name of uncertain meaning.

Hieronymus German form of Jerome.

Higashi Japanese: from the east.

Highton Old English: a high place. *Hyton.*

Higo Japanese: a willow tree.

Hilal Arabic: crescent-like, as in the new moon. *Hilali, Hilel.*

Hilary Latin: cheerful. More commonly a girl's name.
Ellery, Hilaire (French), *Hillary, Hillery, Ilar* (Welsh), *Ilario* (Italian).
Hildebrand Teutonic: a battle sword.
Hillard An English surname.
Hillary/Hillery *See* Hilary.
Hillel Hebrew: the praised one. A biblical name.
Hillier Old English: a roofer or tiler.
Helliar, Helliard, Hilliar, Hilliard, Hillierd.
Hilton Old English: from the farm on the hill.
Hylton.
Himawan An Indonesian name of uncertain meaning.
Himmat Arabic: ambitious or determined.
Himat.
Hines Old English: the son of a servant.
Hinz, Hinze, Hynes.
Hinrik Icelandic form of Henry.
Hinto Native American: blue.
Hinton Old English: from the high place or farm.
Hynton.
Hippolyte Greek: he who frees the horses.
Hiram Hebrew: exalted. A name from the Bible.
Hyram.
Hiran Hindi: a deer.
Hirohito Japanese: abundant benevolence.
Hirokazu Japanese: possibly meaning abundant harmony.
Hiroki Japanese: wide trees.
Hiroshi Japanese: generous.
Hiro.
Hiroyuki Japanese: abundant snow or abundant happiness.
Hirsh *See* Hershel.
Hirsi African: an amulet.
Hirst *See* Hurst.
Hito Japanese: the benevolent one.
Hiwa Hawaiian: jet-black, or choice. Also a girl's name.
Hixen/Hixon *See* Hickson.
Ho Chinese/Korean: goodness.
Hoa Vietnamese: the peace-lover.
Hoani Maori form of Johnny (*see* John).
Hobart/Hobarte *See* Hubert.
Hobie A character in the *Baywatch* TV series. Also the name of a small sailing catamaran (Hobie Cat).
Hobee, Hobey, Hobi, Hoby.
Hobson The son of Hobb, an archaic diminutive of Robert (meaning bright fame).
Hobbes, Hobbins, Hobbs, Hobsen.
Hoder A son of Odin and Freya in Norse mythology.
Hodur.
Hodge A diminutive of Roger, a famous spearman.
Hodges The son of Hodge.
Hodgeson, Hodgson.
Hoera Maori form of Joel.

Hogan Irish Gaelic: a youth.
Hohepa Maori form of Joseph.
Hohua Maori form of Joshua.
Hoku Hawaiian: a star.
Holbeck *See* Holbrook.
Holbrook Old English: from the brook in the valley.
Holbeck.
Holden Old English: from the deep valley.
Holger Old Norse: spear-like.
Holiday Old English: a holy or religious day.
Holliday.
Holland Old English: from the enclosed or sacred ground. A 'country name'.
Holand, Hollan.
Holleb Polish: dove-like.
Hollis Old English: from the grove of holly trees.
Holman Old English: a dweller in the hollow.
Holmes Old English: from the island in the river.
Holt Old English: a dweller in the wood.
Holz German: a wood.
Holtz.
Homayoun Persian: probably meaning royal.
Homer The name of a Greek poet, possibly meaning a pledge.
Hona Maori form of Jonah.
Hondo African: a warrior.
Hone Maori form of John.
Honon Native American: a bear.
Hopkin Welsh: the son of Robert.
Hopkins, Hopkyn, Hopkyns.
Hopper Old English: a dancer or leaper.
Horace Latin: from a Roman family name.
Horacio (Spanish), *Horas* (Welsh), *Horatio, Horatius, Horice, Orazio* (Italian).
Horatio/Horatius *See* Horace.
Horea Romanian: possibly from the name of a dance.
Horia.
Hori Polynesian form of George.
Horice *See* Horace.
Horomona Maori form of Solomon.
Horst German: from the wood or wooded hill.
Hortensio The masculine form of Hortense (a garden lover).
Horton Old English: from the grey or muddy place.
Horten.
Horus The Ancient Egyptian god of the sky, sun and light. He was represented as a falcon or a falcon-headed man.
Hosea Hebrew: salvation. *See also* Joshua.
Hota Native American: white.
Hotah.
Hotei The Japanese god of good luck and jollity.
Hotoroa Polynesian: a figure from legend.

Hoturoa.
Houghton *See* Hutton.
Houssam Arabic: a fine-edged weapon.
Husam.
Houston Old English: from the place of Hugh. The name of a city in Texas.
Hewston, Houstoun, Huston.
Howard Teutonic: the brave one, or the chief guardian.
Hayward, Heyward, Howerd.
Diminutives: Howey, Howie.
Howe Old Norse: a hillock or burial mound.
Howell Cornish/Welsh: the eminent one. *See also* Powell.
Howel, Hywel, Hywell.
Hsin Chinese: after an ancient dynasty.
Hu Chinese: a tiger. *See also* Hugh.
Huarahi Maori: a track or road.
Huatare Maori: the name of a famous chief.
Hubert Teutonic: a brilliant mind. *See also* Hugh.
Hobart, Hobarte, Huberte, Huburt, Huburte, Huppert (German).
Diminutives: Huey, Hughie.
Huckleberry A North American fruit-bearing plant. The name of the hero of Mark Twain's novel *Adventures of Huckleberry Finn*.
Huckelberry.
Diminutive: Huck.
Hudson Old English: the son of Hugh.
Huey A diminutive of Hubert and Hugh.
Hugh Teutonic: heart and mind. *See also* Hagen, Hubert and Hudson.
Heugh, Hew, Hu (Welsh), *Hughes, Hugo* (Dutch, German), *Hugues* (French), *Huw* (Welsh), *Ugo* (Italian).
Diminutives: Hewey, Hewie (Scottish), Hewey, Huey, Hughie.
Hughes *See* Hugh.
Huginn Old Norse: thought, or thoughtful. One of the ravens of the god Odin in Norse mythology. *See also* Munin.
Hugin.
Hugo/Hugues *See* Hugh.
Hula Hawaiian: the name of a dance. Native American: an eagle.
Huma Hindi: an eagle.
Humbert Teutonic: a famous warrior.
Humberto, Umbert, Umberto (Italian).
Hume Old English: from the island in the river.
Humphrey Teutonic: the protector of the peace.
Humfrey, Humfry, Humphery, Humphry.
Hunt/Hunte *See* Hunter.
Hunter Old English: the huntsman.
Hunt, Hunte, Hunts, Huntz, Huntze.
Huntley Old English: from the

hunter's meadow.
Huntleigh, Huntlie, Huntly.
Hunts/Huntz *See* Hunter.
Huon The name of a Tasmanian river and a type of tree.
Hewon.
Huppert *See* Hubert.
Hura Maori form of Judah.
Huriu Maori form of Julius.
Hurley Gaelic: the sea tide. Old English: a clearing in the woods.
Hurleigh, Hurlie, Hurly.
Hurricane English from Spanish: a violent storm.
Hurst Old English: a dweller in the wood.
Hearst, Herst, Hirst.
Husam *See* Houssam.
Hussain Arabic: the handsome little one.
Hasani, Husain, Husani (Swahili), *Husayn, Husein, Huseyin, Hussein, Usain, Ussain.*
Huston *See* Houston.
Hute Native American: a star.
Hutton Old English: from the farm on the hill.
Houghton.
Huw *See* Hugh.
Huxley Old English: the inhospitable place.
Huyu Japanese: born in winter.
Hyam Hebrew: life.
Chaim, Hyman.
Diminutives: Hy, Hymie.
Hyatt Old English: a high gate.

Hiatt.
Hyde Old English: a hide (an old measurement) of land.
Hide.
Hyeon A Korean name of uncertain meaning.
Hyllus A figure in Greek mythology.
Hyllas, Hylles, Hylus.
Hylton *See* Hilton.
Hyman/Hymie *See* Hyam.
Hymir Old Norse: the dark one. A mythological giant.
Hynes *See* Hines.
Hynton *See* Hinton.
Hyperion Greek: radiant. A god of the sun, also known as Helios.
Hyram *See* Hiram.
Hyrax Greek: a tail-less rabbit or coney-like African animal.
Hythe Old English: a landing place.
Hyth.
Hyton *See* Highton.
Hywel/Hywell *See* Howell.

I

Iagan *See* Egan.
Iago Spanish and Welsh forms of James. *See also* Santiago.
Yago.
Iaian/Iain Gaelic forms of Ian.
Ian Hebrew: God is gracious. A Scottish form of John.
Ean, Eian, Iaian (Gaelic), *Iain*

(Gaelic).
Iau The Welsh name for both Jove and Jupiter.
Ibrahim/Ibrahima *See* Abraham.
Ibsen Teutonic: the son of the archer.
Ibson, Ibsyn.
Icarus Greek: a legendary figure.
Icaros, Ikaros, Ikarus.
Ichabod Hebrew: the glory has departed.
Ichiro Japanese: the first, or firstborn son.
Icon Latin from Greek: a picture or image.
Ikon.
Iden Old English: prosperous.
Ido Hebrew: a name from the Bible.
Iddo.
Idris Arabic: a good man. Welsh: a fiery, impulsive lord.
Idwal Welsh: the lord of the wall or rampart.
Idwel.
Iefan *See* Ieuan.
Iestin/Iestyn Welsh forms of Justin.
Ieuan Welsh form of John. *See also* Evan and Owen.
Iefan, Ifan, Ioan, Iwan.
Ifan *See* Ieuan.
Ifor Welsh: a traditional name of uncertain meaning.
Iggi/Iggie/Iggy Diminutives of Ignatius.
Ignace/Ignacio *See* Ignatius.
Ignatius Latin: ardent, fiery.

Ignace (French), *Ignacio* (Spanish), *Ignacius, Ignacz, Ignasi* (Catalan), *Ignate, Ignates, Ignatious, Ignatz* (German), *Ignazio* (Italian), *Inacio* (Portuguese), *Inigo*.
Diminutives: Iggie, Iggie, Iggy, Nacho (Spanish), Nacio (Spanish).
Igor Scandinavian: a hero. Also a Russian form of George.
Ihaka Maori form of Isaac.
Ihakara Polynesian: the name of a great chief.
Ihi Maori: power.
Ihorangi Polynesian: rain.
Ijaz Arabic: a miracle.
Ikale Polynesian: an eagle.
Ikan Indonesian: a fish.
Ikaros/Ikarus *See* Icarus.
Ike/Ikey/Ikie *See* Isaac.
Ikon *See* Icon.
Ilai The sun god in the mythology of Sulawesi, an Indonesian island.
Ilan Hebrew: a tree.
Ilar/Ilario *See* Hilary.
Ilfryn An unusual Welsh name; of uncertain meaning.
Ilhami Turkish: inspiration.
Ilie Romanian form of Elijah.
Ilija/Iliya *See* Ilya.
Ilker Turkish: the first man.
Ilkin Turkish: the first.
Ilmarinen Finnish: a figure in mythology.
Diminutive: Ilmari.
Iltar Finnish: the evening.
Ilya Aboriginal: a snake. Also the

Russian form of Elijah.
Ilija, Iliya, Illya.
Imad Arabic: a pillar or support.
Imam Arabic: a religious leader.
Imants Latvian: the name of a national hero.
Immanuel *See* Emmanuel.
Imran Arabic: the exalted one.
Imraan.
Imre *See* Emery.
Inacio Portuguese form of Ignatius.
Inar *See* Einar.
Indi Aboriginal: far away, or in the past.
Indee, Indey, Indhi, Indhie, Indie, Indy.
Indiana The name of a US state. Also a girl's name.
Indianna.
Indra Sanskrit: the god of the atmosphere and sky.
Indrajit Sanskrit: the conqueror of Indra.
Indrajeet.
Indrek Estonian form of Henry.
Indri Maltese form of Andrew.
Indus The name of a major Asian river, and also a southern constellation.
Indy *See* Indi.
Ingbert *See* Ingobert.
Ingemar Old Norse: a famous son.
Ingmar.
Inger Norse: from the son's army.
Inglebert *See* Engelbert.
Inglis The Scottish form of the word English.
Ingles.
Ingo Teutonic: the masculine form of Inge (*see* Ingrid).
Ingobert The name of an Irish saint.
Ingbert (German).
Ingolf German/Scandinavian: a wolf ancestor.
Ingram Teutonic: the raven.
Ingvar Old Norse: a warrior.
Ingvars.
Inigo *See* Ignatius.
Inkata Aboriginal: an elder or wise man.
Innes Celtic/Gaelic: an island in the river, or from the island. *See also* Ennis.
Iniss, Inness, Innis.
Innocent Latin: harmless, innocent. The name of several saints and popes.
Innocenzo (Italian), *Innokenti* (Russian), *Inocencio* (Spanish).
Integro Italian: honest; a man of integrity.
Ioan *See* Ieuan.
Ioannes Greek form of John.
Iolo/Iolyn *See* Iorweth.
Ion Romanian form of John.
Iorweth Welsh: a handsome lord.
Iorwerth.
Diminutives: Iolo, Iolyn.
Iouri A variation of Yuri, the Russian form of George.
Ira Hebrew: watchful, vigilant. A biblical name.

Irakly A Georgian name of uncertain meaning.
Irakli.
Irawaru Polynesian: a figure from legend.
Ireland Old English: the land of the Irish.
Irfan Arabic: wisdom.
Irfaan.
Irin A mythological angel.
Iruka Japanese: the name of a lake.
Irvin/Irvine *See* Irving.
Irving Scottish: from a placename.
Earvin, Ervan, Ervin, Ervyn, Irvin, Irvine, Irvyn.
Irwin Old English: from the words boar and friend.
Erwin.
Isa Arabic/Sanskrit: a lord. *See also* Isaac and Isaiah.
Issa.
Isaac Hebrew: laughter, the laughing one. The son of Abraham in the Bible.
Ihaka (Maori), *Isaak* (German), *Isacco* (Italian), *Isak* (Swedish), *Isaki, Isazi, Ishac, Ishak, Issac, Itzaak, Itzick, Itzik, Izaac, Izaak* (Dutch), *Izac, Izzac, Yitzaak, Yitzak.*
Diminutives: Ike, Ikey, Ikie, Isa, Isi.
Isacco *See* Isaac.
Isador/Isadore *See* Isidore.
Isaiah Hebrew: God is salvation, or God is my helper. One of the prophets in the Bible.
Asiah, Eseia (Welsh), *Isaia, Isaya, Isayah, Iziah, Izaya, Izayah.*
Diminutive: Isa.
Isak Swedish form of Isaac.
Isander A character from Greek mythology.
Isaya/Isayah *See* Isaiah.
Isazi *See* Isaac.
Isha Sanskrit: a lord or master.
Ishac/Ishak *See* Isaac.
Ishan Sanskrit: a king. An alternative name for the Hindu god Vishnu.
Ishaan, Ishant
Ishmael Hebrew: The Lord will hear. The first son of Abraham in the Bible.
Ismael, Ismail.
Isidore Greek: the gift of Isis (an Egyptian goddess).
Esidor, Esidore, Isador, Isadore, Isidor (German), *Isidoro* (Italian, Spanish), *Isidoros* (Greek), *Isidro* (Spanish), *Izidor* (Slavic), *Izidors, Izydor* (Polish), *Izydors.*
Diminutives: Isi, Issy, Izzi, Izzie, Izzy.
Iskandar Arabic form of Alexander.
Iskander/Iskender Turkish forms of Alexander.
Islam Arabic: peace.
Ismael/Ismail *See* Ishmael.
Isora The Japanese god of the beach and seashore.
Isra Arabic: one of the journeys of Muhammad. Thai: free, or freedom.
Israa.

Israel Hebrew: the Lord's soldier.
Isreal, Isriel, Izrael, Izreal, Izriel.
Diminutives: Isi, Issy, Izzi, Izzie, Izzy.
Issa *See* Isa.
Issac *See* Isaac.
István Hungarian form of Stephen.
Italus Latin: a man of Italy.
Italo (Italian), *Italius.*
Ithneen The Arabic name for Monday.
Ithnayn.
Itvar The Urdu name for Sunday.
Itzaak/Itzick/Itzik *See* Isaac.
Iva *See* Ivar.
Ivan Slavic form of John.
Ivann, Ivon, Iwan, Yvan, Yvann.
Diminutives: Ivica, Ivo, Van, Vanya.
Ivar Old Norse: a battle archer.
Iva, Iver, Ivor.
Ivaylo A Slavic name that possibly means a wolf.
Ivailo.
Ives Old English: the little archer. The name of a saint.
Ivo (German, Slavic), *Yves* (French).
Ivica *See* Ivo.
Ivo Croatian: a diminutive of Ivan (*see* John). *See also* Ives.
Ivica.
Ivon *See* Ivan.
Ivor *See* Ivar.
Ivory Latin: white; like the tusks of an elephant.
Ivorie.
Iwan *See* Ieuan and Ivan.
Ix Mayan: a jaguar.

Iyad Arabic: support or strength.
Iyaad.
Iyar The second lunar month of the Hebrew calendar, corresponding to the zodiac sign of Taurus.
Ayaru (Babylonian).
Izaac/Izaak/Izac *See* Isaac.
Izaih/Izaya *See* Isaiah.
Izidor/Izidors *See* Isidore.
Izrael/Izriel *See* Israel.
Izumi Japanese: a placename.
Izydor/Izydors *See* Isidore.
Izzac *See* Isaac.
Izzat Power. The name of the Baha'i month encompassing 8–26 September, so suitable for a Virgo baby.
Izzi/Izzie/Izzy Diminutives of names such as Isidore and Israel.

J

Jaabir *See* Jabir.
Jaak *See* Jack.
Jaakko Finnish form of Jacob.
Diminutive: Jaska.
Jaap Dutch diminutive of Jacob.
Jaason *See* Jason.
Jaaved *See* Javed.
Jabari Swahili: the brave one.
Jabez Hebrew: sorrowful.
Jabir Arabic: the comforter.
Jaabir.

Jabiru Aboriginal: a stork.
Jabiroo.
Jabuk Aboriginal: an ox or bullock.
Jabulani African: one who is happy.
Jac *See* Jack.
Jace/Jacen *See* Jacey and Jason.
Jaceb *See* Jacob.
Jacek Polish form of Jacinto.
Jacey A modern name, probably derived from Jacob or Jason. Also a Native American name meaning the moon.
Jace, Jacee, Jacie, Jacy, Jasee, Jasey, Jasie, Jasy, Jaycee, Jayci, Jaycie.
Jacin *See* Jacinto and Jason.
Jacinto Spanish: hyacinth. The masculine form of Jacinta.
Gasento (Basque), *Giacinto, Jacek* (Polish), *Jacin, Jacint, Jacinth, Jacinthe, Jacynt, Jacynto.*
Jack A diminutive of John.
Jaak, Jac, Jak, Jaki, Joc, Jock (Scottish).
Diminutives: Jackie, Jacky, Jake.
Jackson Old English: the son of Jack.
Jacksen, Jacksyn, Jakson, Jaxen, Jaxon, Jaxson, Jaxxon, Jaxxyn, Jaxyn.
Jacob Hebrew: the supplanter; one who takes the place of another. A biblical name. *See also* James and Kobe.
Giacobbe (Italian), *Hagob* (Armenian), *Hakop* (Armenian), *Jaakko, Jaceb, Jaco* (Portuguese), *Jacobi, Jacobo* (Spanish), *Jacoby,*
Jacopo (Italian), *Jacques* (French), *Jaicob, Jaikob, Jakko, Jakob* (Dutch, German, Scandinavian), *Jakobus, Jakov* (Croatian), *Jakub* (Czech, Polish), *Jayceb, Jaycob, Jaykeb, Jaykob, Yacoub, Yago* (Spanish), *Yakobe, Yakov* (Hebrew, Russian).
Diminutives: Jaap (Dutch), Jaiki, Jake, Jaki, Jaque, Jaques, Jaska (Finnish), Jay, Jayk, Jayke, Jeppe (Danish).
Jacques French form of Jacob and James.
Jadan/Jaden *See* Jayden.
Jade Spanish: the green gemstone. More commonly a girl's name.
Jaid, Jaide, Jayd, Jayde.
Jadem *See* Jayden.
Jadon Hebrew: one who is thankful. An Old Testament name.
Jae *See* Jay.
Jaedan/Jaedon/Jaedyn *See* Jayden.
Jaeger Teutonic: a hunter.
Jager, Yaeger, Yager.
Jael Hebrew: to ascend. Also a girl's name.
Jaelan/Jaelen/Jaelyn *See* Jaylen.
Jaeleb *See* Jaleb.
Jaemes *See* James.
Jaesen/Jaeson/Jaesun *See* Jason.
Jafet Spanish form of Japhet.
Jagan An unusual modern name.
Jagen.
Jagdish Sanskrit: the ruler of the world.
Jager *See* Jaeger.

J – Boys

Jagger Middle English: a carter or hawker.
Jaggard.
Jago Cornish form of James.
Jahan Sanskrit: the world.
Jahmal *See* Jamal.
Jai/Jaie *See* Jay.
Jaicob *See* Jacob.
Jaid/Jaide *See* Jade.
Jaiden/Jaidin/Jaidon/Jaidyn *See* Jayden.
Jaietham/Jaiethan *See* Jaithan.
Jaiki/Jaikob *See* Jacob.
Jailan/Jailen/Jailyn *See* Jaylen.
Jaileb *See* Jaleb.
Jailon *See* Jalon.
Jaiman/Jaimen/Jaimon *See* Jamen.
Jaime/Jaimes *See* James.
Jairus Hebrew: a figure from the Bible.
Jaithan A modern name, derived from Jai.
Jaietham, Jaiethan, Jaitham.
Jak *See* Jack.
Jake/Jaki *See* Jack and Jacob.
Jakko/Jakob/Jakov/Jakub *See* Jacob.
Jakson *See* Jackson.
Jal Gypsy: a wanderer.
Jalan/Jalen/Jalin *See* Jaylen.
Jaleb A modern name, possibly a combination of Jay and Caleb.
Jaeleb, Jaileb, Jayeleb, Jayleb.
Jalil Arabic: majestic.
Jaleel.
Jalon A modern name, probably derived from Jay.
Jailon, Jaylon.
Jamaine/Jamayne *See* Jermaine.
Jamal Arabic: the handsome one.
Gamal, Jahmal, Jamaal, Jamahl, Jameel, Jamil, Jehmal, Jemahl, Jemal.
Jambo Swahili: a greeting; literally hello.
Jamboh.
Jamen A popular modern name, probably derived from James or Jay.
Jaiman, Jaimen, Jaimin, Jaimon, Jaman, Jamin, Jamon, Jayman, Jaymen, Jaymin, Jaymon.
James Hebrew: the supplanter. A form of Jacob. *See also* Seamus. *Diego* (Spanish), *Giacomo* (Italian), *Hamish* (Scottish), *Hemi* (Maori), *Iago* (Spanish, Welsh), *Jacques* (French), *Jaemes, Jago* (Cornish), *Jaime* (Spanish), *Jaimes, Jamez, Jaume* (Catalan), *Jaymes, Jaymez, Jeames, Kimo* (Hawaiian), *Seamus* (Irish), *Shamus* (Irish), *Yago* (Spanish).
Diminutives: Jamesey, Jamie, Jamiee, Jamo, Jay, Jayme, Jaymie, Jem, Jhim, Jhimmy, Jhimy, Jhyimy, Jim, Jimi, Jimmi, Jimmie, Jimmy.
Jamie/Jamiee Diminutives of James.
Jamieson Old English: the son of James.
Jameson, Jamison.
Jamil *See* Jamal.
Jamo *See* James.
Jamon *See* Jamen.

Jamshid Persian: a figure from mythology.
Jamshed.
Jamuni Hindi: purple.
Yamuni.
Jan Slavic and Scandinavian forms of John.
Janek, Janko (Slavic).
Janeiro The Portuguese name for January.
Janek/Janko *See* Jan, Janez and John.
Janesh Hindi: the lord of the people.
Janez A Slavic form of John.
Diminutive: Janko.
Jangal Hindi: a forest. *See also* Jungle.
Jangu Tibetan: a wolf.
Janick/Jannick Diminutives of Yann, the Breton form of John.
Janko *See* Jan and Janez.
Janos *See* John.
Jansen/Janson *See* Jensen.
January English from Latin: the first month of the year; named after Janus (*see* below).
Janeiro (Portuguese), *Januar* (German), *Januari* (Swahili), *Januarie, Januario, Januarius, Janvier* (French).
Janus Latin: the two-faced Roman god of doors and gates (beginnings and endings).
Januarius.
Janush *See* John.
Janvier The French name for January.
Japhet Hebrew: youthful. A son of Noah in the Bible.
Jafet (Spanish), *Japheth, Yaphet.*
Jaque/Jaques *See* Jacob.
Jarad/Jaradth *See* Jared.
Jaran *See* Jaron.
Jardine Old French: a garden.
Jardene.
Jareb Hebrew: he who maintains.
Jarib.
Jared Hebrew: a descendant of Adam in the Bible.
Jarad, Jaradth, Jaret, Jarid, Jarod, Jarrad, Jarred, Jarrid, Jarrod, Jarryd, Jaryed, Jered, Jeret, Jerid, Jerod, Jerrad, Jerred, Jerrod, Jharad, Jhared, Jharod, Yered (Hebrew).
Jarek Slavic: born in January.
Jarick, Jarik, Jarrick, Jarryck.
Jaremie/Jaremy *See* Jeremy.
Jaren/Jarin *See* Jaron.
Jaret *See* Jared and Jarratt.
Jarib *See* Jareb.
Jarid *See* Jared.
Jariel *See* Juriel.
Jarkko Finnish diminutive of Jorma (*see* Jeremy).
Jarlath Irish Gaelic: a leader or prince.
Jarman Celtic: a man from Germany.
German, Jarmen, Jerman, Jermyn.
Jarmil Czech: strong yet gracious.
Jarna Nepali: a waterfall.
Jarod *See* Jared.
Jaron A modern name, probably derived from Jared.
Jaran, Jaren, Jarin, Jarran,

Jarren, Jarrin, Jarron, Jarryn.
Jaroslav Slavic: the glory of spring. A popular Czech name.
Jaroslaw (Polish), *Yaraslau, Yaroslav.*
Jarrad *See* Jared.
Jarrah Aboriginal: a type of eucalyptus tree.
Jarra.
Jarran *See* Jaron.
Jarratt Teutonic: a spearman.
Jaret, Jarrett.
Jarrick/Jarryck *See* Jarek.
Jarrod/Jarryd/Jaryed *See* Jared.
Jarron/Jarryn *See* Jaron.
Jarvis *See* Gervase.
Jase *See* Jason.
Jasee/Jasey/Jasie *See* Jacey.
Jasiel A Polish placename.
Jasim Arabic: one who is great.
Jaska *See* Jaako.
Jason Greek: the healer. The mythological hero who retrieved the Golden Fleece.
Jaason, Jacen, Jacin, Jaesen, Jaesin, Jaeson, Jaesun, Jasen, Jasin, Jasun, Jaycen, Jaycin, Jaysen, Jaysin, Jayson, Jaysun.
Diminutives: Jace, Jayce, Jase.
Jasper Persian: the treasurer. The name of a gemstone. *See also* Caspar and Gaspar.
Jaspa, Jaspah, Jaspar, Jazpar, Jazper, Jesper (Danish).
Jassan Native American: a wolf.
Jasy *See* Jacey.

Jaume Catalan form of James.
Java An Indonesian island. Also a girl's name.
Djava, Javah.
Javaid *See* Javed.
Javan Hebrew: of the clay; an Old Testament name. Hindi: the young one.
Javen.
Javed Persian: eternal. A popular Muslim name.
Jaaved, Javaid, Jave, Javid.
Javier *See* Xavier.
Jaxom A name from the *Dragonriders of Pern* series of fantasy novels.
Jaxon/Jaxson/Jaxyn *See* Jackson.
Jay Old English: a bird. Sanskrit: victory. Also used a diminutive of Jacob, James and many names beginning with J.
Jae, Jai, Jaie, Jaye, Jayen, Jhae, Jhai, Jhaye, Ji, Jiah, Jie, Jy, Jye.
Jayant Sanskrit: victorious.
Jayanta.
Jayce/Jaycen *See* Jason.
Jaycee/Jaycie *See* Jacey.
Jaycob/Jayceb *See* Jacob.
Jayd/Jayde *See* Jade.
Jayden English: a popular modern name, derived from Jai or Jay.
Jadan, Jadem, Jaden, Jaedan, Jaeden, Jaedin, Jaedon, Jaedyn, Jaidan, Jaiden, Jaidin, Jaidon, Jaidyn, Jaydan, Jaydem, Jaydin, Jaydn, Jaydon, Jaydyn.

Jayeleb/Jayleb *See* Jaleb.
Jaygen Possibly a form of Jayden.
Jaygan.
Jayke/Jaykeb/Jaykob *See* Jacob.
Jaylath A modern name, derived from Jay.
Jayleth.
Jaylen A modern American name.
Jaelan, Jaelen, Jaelin, Jaelyn, Jailan, Jailen, Jailin, Jailyn, Jalan, Jalen, Jalin, Jalyn, Jaylan, Jaylin.
Jaylon *See* Jalon.
Jayman/Jaymen *See* Jamen.
Jayme/Jaymes/Jaymie *See* James.
Jaysen/Jayson/Jaysun *See* Jason.
Jazpar/Jazper *See* Jasper.
Jazz A musical genre. Also a girl's name.
Jaz, Jazze.
Jeames *See* James.
Jean French form of John.
Jed/Jedd Diminutives of Jedediah.
Jedediah Hebrew: beloved of God. A biblical name.
Jediah, Jedidiah.
Diminutives: Jed, Jedd.
Jeden Polish: the number one.
Yeden.
Jeera/Jeerah *See* Jirah.
Jeevan Sanskrit: life.
Jeff/Jeffery *See* Geoffrey.
Jefferson Old English: the son of Jeffrey. *See* Geoffrey.
Jeffers, Jeffson.
Jeffory *See* Geoffrey.

Jeffree/Jeffrey/Jefri *See* Geoffrey.
Jehan Old French form of John.
Jehosophat Hebrew: the Lord judges.
Jelani Swahili: the mighty one.
Jelaney, Jelanie.
Jelle Dutch: a diminutive of names such as Willem (*see* William).
Jem Diminutive of James and Jeremy.
Jemaine/Jemayne *See* Jermaine.
Jen Chinese: able.
Jenkin A diminutive of John.
Jenk, Jenking, Jenkings, Jenkins, Jenkinson, Jenkison, Jenks, Jenkyn, Jenkyns.
Jenks *See* Jenkin.
Jeno Hungarian form of Eugene.
Jens *See* John.
Jensen Scandinavian: the son of John (God is gracious).
Jansen, Janson, Jenson.
Jeoffrey *See* Geoffrey.
Jeppe Danish diminutive of Jacob.
Jerald *See* Gerald.
Jerara Aboriginal: falling water.
Jerard *See* Gerard.
Jered *See* Jared.
Jereme/Jeremie *See* Jeremy and Jerome.
Jeremiah/Jeremias *See* Jeremy.
Jeremy Hebrew: appointed by God. From the biblical name Jeremiah.
Geremie, Geremy, Heremaia (Maori), *Jaremie, Jaremy, Jereme, Jeremiah, Jeremias* (Dutch, German,

Spanish), *Jeremie, Jermiah, Jorma* (Finnish).
Diminutives: Jarkko (Finnish), Jem, Jerri, Jerrie, Jerry.
Jeret *See* Jared.
Jericho Arabic: possibly meaning the city of the moon.
Jeriko, Jerricho, Jerriko.
Jerid/Jerod *See* Jared.
Jermaine A modern form of Germain.
Jamain, Jamaine, Jamayn, Jamayne, Jemain, Jemaine, Jemayn, Jemayne, Jermain, Jermayn, Jermayne.
Jerman *See* Jarman.
Jermiah *See* Jeremy.
Jermyn Cornish: a saint's name.
See also Jarman.
Jernej Slovene form of Bartholomew.
Jeroen Dutch form of Jerome.
Jerold *See* Gerald.
Jerome Greek: a sacred or holy name.
Gerome, Geronimo (Italian), *Girolamo* (Italian), *Hieronymus* (German), *Jereme, Jeremie* (French), *Jeroen* (Dutch), *Jeronimo* (Spanish), *Jerrome.*
Diminutives: Jerri, Jerrie, Jerry.
Jeronimo *See* Jerome.
Jerrad/Jerrod *See* Jared.
Jerrald/Jerrold *See* Gerald.
Jerrard *See* Gerard.
Jerrawa Aboriginal: a goanna.
Jerri/Jerrie/Jerry Diminutives of Gerald, Gerard, Jeremy and Jerome.
Jerricho/Jerriko *See* Jericho.
Jerrome *See* Jerome.
Jervaise/Jervase/Jervis *See* Gervase.
Jerzy Polish form of George.
Jesaia/Jesaiah/Jesiah *See* Josiah.
Jeson A Filipino name of uncertain meaning.
Jesper *See* Jasper.
Jesse Hebrew: God's gift. Also a girl's name.
Jessee, Jessie, Jessy, Jezee, Jezie, Jezy, Jezzee, Jezzie, Jezzy.
Diminutive: Jess.
Jesús Hebrew: the saviour, or God is salvation. A variation of Joshua, and primarily a Spanish and Portuguese name.
Jet Latin: a black decorative material.
Jett, Jette, Jhet, Jhett, Jhette.
Jeth Sanskrit: the Hindu month of May/June, corresponding to the zodiac sign of Gemini.
Jett.
Jethro Hebrew: excellence. A biblical name.
Jethroe.
Jevan/Jevon Welsh forms of John.
Jewang Aboriginal: a star.
Jezee/Jezie/Jezy/Jezzy *See* Jesse.
Jhae/Jhai/Jhaye *See* Jay.
Jharad/Jhared *See* Jared.
Jhet/Jhett *See* Jet.
Jhim/Jhimmy/Jhyimy Diminutives of James.
Ji/Jiah/Jie *See* Jay.

Jibben English Gypsy: life.
Jigme Sherpa/Tibetan: one who does not fear.
Jiles *See* Giles.
Jim/Jimi/Jimmie/Jimmy Diminutives of James.
Jimeoin Irish: the name of a well-known comedian. Possibly a combination of Jim and Owen.
Jimoein, Jimowen, Jymeoin, Jymowen.
Jimiyu African: born in the summer.
Jimoh Swahili: born on a Friday.
Jimo.
Jimon *See* Djimon.
Jin Chinese: golden.
Jingara Aboriginal: a big mountain.
Jirah Nepali: the spice, cummin.
Jeera, Jeerah, Jirah.
Jiri Czech form of George.
Jiro Japanese: the second, or second son.
Jirra Aboriginal: a kangaroo.
Jirrah.
Jitender Sanskrit: the powerful conqueror.
Jitendra, Jitinder.
Jivanta Sanskrit: one who is long-lived.
Jivantah.
Jo *See* Joseph.
Joab Hebrew: praise the Lord.
Joachim Hebrew: established by God. The name of a king of Judah in the Bible.
Achim, Akim (Russian), *Gioachino* (Italian), *Joakim* (Scandinavian), *Joaquim* (Portuguese), *Joaquin* (Spanish), *Jochen* (German), *Jochim* (German), *Jochum.*
Joah Hebrew: a biblical name, possibly meaning a brother.
Joanan/Joannes/Joao *See* John.
Joaquim/Joaquin *See* Joachim.
Job Hebrew: the persecuted one. A name that is associated with patience.
Jobe, Jobi, Jobie, Jobst (German).
Jobson The son of Job.
Jobbins.
Jobst German form of Job.
Joc/Jock Scottish forms of Jack, a diminutive of John.
Jocelin Latin: the merry one. More commonly a girl's name.
Jocelyn, Joscelin, Joselin, Josselin (French).
Diminutive: Joss.
Jochen German form of Joachim.
Jochim/Jochum *See* Joachim.
Jody *See* Joseph.
Joe/Joey Diminutives of Joseph.
Joel Hebrew: the Lord is God. A name from the Bible.
Joell, Hoera (Maori), *Yoel.*
Joerg A form of George.
Joesef/Joesph *See* Joseph.
Joffre/Joffrey *See* Geoffrey.
Joh/Johan/Johann/Johannes *See* John.
Johar Hindi: a jewel.
John Hebrew: God is gracious.

J – Boys

See also Ian, Ieuan, Jack, Jenkin, Jonathan, Owen, Sean and Shane.
Bevan (Welsh), *Eoin* (Gaelic), *Evan* (Welsh), *Gian* (Italian), *Gianin*, *Gianni* (Italian), *Giovanni* (Italian), *Hannes*, *Hannu* (Finnish), *Hans* (German), *Hone* (Maori), *Ieuan* (Welsh), *Iohannes* (Latin), *Ioannes* (Greek), *Ion* (Basque, Romanian), *Ivan* (Russian, Slavic), *Jan* (Czech, Dutch, Polish, Scandinavian), *Janez* (Slavic), *Janos* (Hungarian), *Janush* (Slavic), *Jean* (French), *Jehan* (Old French), *Jens* (Danish, Norwegian), *Jevan* (Welsh), Jevon (Welsh), *Joanan, Joannes, Joao* (Portuguese), *Johan* (Scandinavian), *Johann* (German), *Johannes* (Dutch, German), *Jon* (Swedish), *Jone* (Polynesian), *Jonte, Jonty, Jowan* (Cornish), *Juan* (Spanish), *Juhani* (Finnish), *Sean* (Irish), *Shaan, Shane* (Irish), *Shaughn* (Irish), *Shaun* (Irish), *Shawn* (Irish), *Siôn* (Welsh), *Yahya* (Arabic), *Yann* (Breton), *Yannis* (Greek), *Yohan, Yohann, Zain, Zaine, Zane, Zayn, Zayne*.
Diminutives: Giannino (Italian), Handel (German), Hank, Hanke (German), Hansel (German), Hansi (German), Hoani (Maori), Jack, Jackie, Jacky, Janek (Slavic), Janick (Breton), Janko (Slavic), Jannick (Breton), Jenkin, Joc, Jock, Joh, Johnnie, Johnno, Johnny, Jonsi, Jonsie, Jonzi, Jonzie, Nino (Italian), Ninos, Vanya (Russian), Yanick (Breton), Yannick (Breton), Yianni (Greek), Yiannis (Greek).

Johnathan/Johnathon
See Jonathan.

Johnhenry A combination of John and Henry (ruler of the home or estate).
John-Henry.

Johnson English: the son of John. *See also* Jones.
Johnston, Jonson.

Joji Japanese form of George.

Jojo African: born on a Monday.

Joleon/Jolyon *See* Julian.

Jon A diminutive of Jonathan. *See also* John.

Jonah Hebrew: a dove; a man of peace.
Hona (Maori), *Jona, Jonas, Jonis, Yona* (Russian), *Yonah, Younus* (Arabic), *Yunis* (Arabic), *Yunus* (Arabic).

Jonaid *See* Junaid.

Jonas/Jonis *See* Jonah.

Jonathan Hebrew: God has given, or a gift of the Lord. The friend of David in the Bible. *See also* John.
Johnathan, Johnathon, Jonathon, Jonothon, Yonatan (Hebrew).
Diminutives: Johnny, Jon, Jonnie, Jonno, Jonny, Yoni (Hebrew).

Jones The son of John. *See also* Johnson.

Jonnie/Jonno/Jonny Diminutives

of Jonathan.
Jonothon *See* Jonathan.
Jonquil A 'flower name', from the Latin word for a reed.
Jonsi/Jonsie Diminutives of John.
Jonson *See* Johnson.
Jonty A form of John.
Jontee, Jonte, Jontey, Jonti, Jontie.
Jonzi/Jonzie Diminutives of John.
Joop *See* Joseph.
Joost *See* Justin.
Jora Hebrew: the autumn.
Jorah.
Joram Hebrew: the Lord is exalted.
Yoram.
Diminutives: Jori, Jorie, Jory, Jouri, Jourie.
Jordan Hebrew: flowing down, as in the River Jordan. Also a girl's name. *Geordan, Giordano* (Italian), *Jordaan* (Dutch), *Jordanis, Jordayn, Jordayne, Jorden, Jordin, Jordon, Jordyn, Jourdain* (French), *Jourdan, Yordan* (Bulgarian).
Diminutives: Geordie, Jordi, Jordie, Jordy, Jori, Jorie, Jouri, Jourie, Jud, Judd.
Jordayne *See* Jordan.
Jordi/Jordy/Jordyn *See* Jordan.
Jorens Old Norse: a laurel.
Yorens.
Jorgan/Jorge/Jorgen *See* George.
Jori/Jorie Diminutives of Joram and Jordan.
Joris Dutch form of George.
Jorma *See* Jeremy.

Jorney *See* Journey.
Jory Cornish form of George. Also a diminutive of Joram.
Josaia *See* Josiah.
Joscelin/Joselin *See* Jocelin.
José Spanish form of Joseph.
Joseph Hebrew: God shall add.
Giuseppe (Italian), *Hohepa* (Maori), *Joesef, Joesph, José* (Spanish), *Josef* (Czech, Dutch, German, Scandinavian), *Josephus* (Dutch), *Josif, Józef* (Polish), *Jozeph, Jozif, József* (Hungarian), *Jusuf, Osip* (Russian), *Yosef* (Hebrew), *Yusuf* (Arabic).
Diminutives: Beppe (Italian), Che (Spanish), Jo, Jody, Joe, Joey, Joop (Dutch), Józsi (Hungarian), Pepe (Spanish).
Joshua Hebrew: God is salvation. The biblical figure who led the Israelites to the Promised Land. *See also* Hosea and Jesús.
Hohua (Maori), *Joshuah, Jozua* (Dutch), *Yeshua* (Hebrew).
Diminutives: Josh, Joshi, Joshie, Joshy.
Josiah Hebrew: God heals. A biblical name.
Jesaia, Jesaiah, Jesia, Jesiah, Josaia, Josia, Josias.
Josif *See* Joseph.
Joss Chinese: fate. Also a diminutive of Jocelin.
Josse.
Josselin French form of Jocelin.

Joukahainen A figure from Finnish mythology.
Diminutive: Jouko.
Jourdain/Jourdan *See* Jordan.
Jouri/Jourie Diminutives of Joram and Jordan.
Journey Middle English: a voyage.
Jorney, Jurney.
Jove Another name for the Roman god Jupiter, the lord of the heavens, rain and the thunderbolt.
Jovi, Jovo (Welsh).
Jovi A form of Jove, but also from the name of a well-known rock singer (Jon Bon Jovi).
Jovie.
Jowan Cornish form of John.
Juwan.
Józef/Jozif/József *See* Joseph.
Jozua Dutch form of Joshua.
Juan Spanish form of John.
Djuan, Djuann, Juann.
Diminutive: Juanito.
Juba The Tibetan name for October.
Jubaa, Jubah.
Jud/Judd *See* Jordan and Judah.
Judah Hebrew: the praised one. A son of Jacob in the Bible.
Hura (Maori), *Jud, Juda* (Arabic), *Judas, Judd, Yehuda* (Jewish).
Diminutive: Jude.
Judas *See* Judah.
Jude *See* Judah.
Juergen *See* George.
Jueves The Spanish name for Thursday.

Juhani Finnish form of John.
Juiris *See* Juris.
Juke A Creole word meaning wicked. Best known as part of the word jukebox.
Julai *See* Julius.
Jules *See* Julian and Julius.
Julian English form of Julius. Suitable for a child born in July.
Joleon, Jolyan, Jolyon, Julien (French), *Julion, Julyan.*
Diminutive: Jules.
Julio *See* Julius.
Julion *See* Julian.
Julius Latin: a Roman family name, possibly meaning youthful. Suitable for a July baby. *See also* Julian.
Giulio (Italian), *Gulio, Gyula* (Hungarian), *Huriu* (Maori), *Julai* (Swahili), *Jules* (French), *Julian, Julio* (Spanish), *Juliusz.*
Diminutive: Yul.
Julyan *See* Julian.
Jumah Swahili: born on a Friday.
Juma, Jumaa, Jumaah.
Jumala The supreme god in Finnish mythology; the equivalent of the Roman god Jupiter.
Jumane Swahili: Tuesday.
Jumaane, Jumani, Jumanie.
Jumarat The Urdu name for Thursday.
Jun Chinese: the truth, or handsome. Japanese: truthful. Nepali: moonlight.
Junaid Arabic: a soldier or warrior
Jonaid, Junayd.

448

Jungay Aboriginal: the west wind.
Jungle From the Hindi word for a forest (*see* Jangal).
Junho Portuguese form of Junius.
Junichi Japanese: one who is obedient.
Junio/Junious *See* Junius.
Junior The young or younger one.
Junius Latin: born in June.
Junho (Portuguese), *Junio* (Spanish), *Junious*.
Jupiter Latin: a planet and the Roman god of the heavens, rain and the thunderbolt. Also known as Jove, and the equivalent of the Greek god Zeus.
Iau (Welsh), *Jupitor*, *Jupyter*.
Juraj A Slavic form of George.
Jurgen German form of George.
Jurgis A Slavic form of George.
Juri A form of George.
Jurie, *Juriel* (Spanish).
Jurian/Jurien *See* Jurrien.
Juriel The name of an archangel in Judaic tradition. *See also* Juri.
Jariel.
Juris Latvian form of George.
Juiris.
Jurney *See* Journey.
Jurrien Dutch form of George.
Jurian, *Jurien*, *Jurriaan*, *Jurrian*.
Juste/Justen *See* Justin.
Justice Middle English: rightness. *See also* Justin.
Justise, *Justyce*, *Justyse*.
Justin Latin: fair and just. *See also* Justice.
Iestin (Welsh), *Iestyn* (Welsh), *Joost* (Dutch), *Juste* (French), *Justen*, *Justinian*, *Justino*, *Justis*, *Justo* (Portuguese), *Justus*, *Justyn*, *Yestin* (Welsh).
Justis/Justo/Justus *See* Justin.
Justyce/Justyse *See* Justice.
Justyn *See* Justin.
Jusuf *See* Joseph.
Juwan *See* Jowan.
Jy/Jye *See* Jay.
Jyles/Jylles *See* Giles.
Jymeoin/Jymowen *See* Jimeoin.
Jyotis Sanskrit: light.
Jyrki Finnish form of George.
Jyrkki.

K

Kaa Swahili: a crab.
Kaamran *See* Kamran.
Kaani *See* Kani.
Kabir Arabic: the great one.
Kabeer, *Khabeer*, *Khabir*.
Kabu Aboriginal: three.
Kacey/Kacie *See* Casey.
Kade *See* Cade.
Kadel/Kadell *See* Cadell.
Kaden *See* Caden.
Kadenz *See* Cadenz.
Kadi The angel of Friday.
Kadir Arabic: powerful.
Kadar, *Kedar*, *Qadir*.
Kadish Aramaic: the holy one.

K – Boys

Kado Japanese: a gateway.
Kaede *See* Cade.
Kaeden *See* Caden.
Kael *See* Cale.
Kaelan/Kaelen/Kaelyn *See* Kalan.
Kaelem/Kaelum *See* Calum.
Kafka The surname of a famous Czech author (Franz Kafka), possibly meaning a bird.
Kaha Maori: strong.
Kahai The god of lightning in Hawaiian mythology.
Kahika Maori: white pine.
Kahlan/Kahlen/Kahlyn *See* Kalan.
Kahn *See* Khan.
Kahnay/Kahne *See* Kané.
Kaho Polynesian: an arrow.
Kahoku Hawaiian: a star.
Kahran *See* Karan.
Kahua Poynesian: the sea.
Kahukura Maori: a rainbow.
Kahurangi Maori: sky-blue.
Kahvan *See* Cavan.
Kai Danish: the earth. Hawaiian: of the sea. *See also* Kay and Ky. *Kaie.*
Kaid/Kaide *See* Cade.
Kaiden/Kaidyn *See* Caden.
Kaie/Kaii/Kaiis *See* Ky.
Kail/Kaile *See* Cale.
Kailash The name of a sacred mountain in Tibet.
Kailem *See* Calum.
Kailey *See* Caley.
Kain/Kaine *See* Kane.
Kainaan/Kainan *See* Canaan.

Kainoa A Hawaiian name of uncertain meaning.
Kaipo Hawaiian: a sweetheart.
Kairo Nepali: brown. *Cairo.*
Kaisey *See* Casey.
Kaj *See* Ky.
Kaka Maori: a native New Zealand parrot.
Kakariki Maori: green, or a lizard.
Kal *See* Calvin.
Kala Hawaiian: the sun. Sanskrit: black. Also the Javanese god of the ocean.
Kalahari The name of a desert in southern Africa. *Kahari.*
Kalan A modern name, probably from an Irish Gaelic word. *Caelan, Caelen, Caelyn, Calan, Calen, Calyn, Kaelan, Kaelen, Kaelyn, Kahlan, Kahlen, Kalen, Kalin, Kalyn, Kaylan, Kaylen, Kaylin, Khalan, Khalen, Khalyn.*
Kalani Hawaiian: of the heavens.
Kalbar Aboriginal: a star.
Kalden Sherpa/Tibetan: of the golden age.
Kale Hawaiian: strong and manly. *See also* Cale.
Kaleb *See* Caleb.
Kaleem *See* Kalim.
Kalem/Kalum *See* Calum.
Kalevi An unusual Finnish name.
Kaley/Kalie *See* Caley.
Kalfani Swahili: one who is destined

to rule.
Kalid *See* Khalid.
Kalil *See* Khalil.
Kalim Arabic: one who teaches or lectures.
Kaleem.
Kalimat Words. The name of the Baha'i month that encompasses 13–31 July, so suitable for a Cancer or Leo baby.
Kalin *See* Kalan.
Kalis A modern name of uncertain origin.
Kallis, Kaylis, Kelis.
Kallaghan/Kallahan *See* Callaghan.
Kallan/Kallen/Kallin/Kallyn *See* Callan.
Kalled/Kallid *See* Khalid.
Kallem/Kallum *See* Calum.
Kalm A form of calm, meaning peaceful and quiet.
Kalman Hungarian: the name of a 12th-century king.
Kalmann.
Kalmanu Native American: lightning.
Kalo Nepali: black.
Kala (Hindi).
Kalon Greek: handsome.
Kalong Japanese: a bat (the animal).
Kalos Greek: good.
Kalti Aboriginal: a spear.
Kalven/Kalvin/Kalvyn *See* Calvin.
Kama Thai: the golden one.
Kamal Arabic: perfection. Sanskrit: a lotus. The name of the Baha'i month that encompasses 1–19 August, so suitable for a Leo baby.
Cemal, Kamahl, Kamil, Kemal.
Kamar *See* Qamar.
Kambara Aboriginal: a crocodile. Also a girl's name.
Kambarah, Kambarra, Kambarrah.
Kamber Aboriginal: a spring.
Kamé Japanese: a tortoise, implying longevity.
Kami Aboriginal: a prickly lizard. Hindi: loving. Japanese: heavenly.
Kamil/Kamilo *See* Camille and Kamal.
Kamis/Kamisi *See* Khamisi.
Kamran Persian: successful or prosperous.
Kaamran, Kamuran (Turkish).
Kan Mayan: a lizard. Tibetan: the snow.
Kana Aboriginal: a hunting spear. Hawaiian: the name of a demigod.
Kanaan/Kanan/Kanen *See* Canaan and Kanan.
Kanaloa Hawaiian: the god of the deep ocean.
Kanan Hindi: a garden.
Kanaan.
Kane Irish Gaelic: warlike. *See also* Cathan.
Kain, Kaine, Kayn, Kayne, Khain, Khaine, Khane, Khayn, Khayne.
Kané Hawaiian: the god of artistic beauty.
Kahnay, Kahne, Kanye.
Kang Korean: powerful.

K – Boys

Kangi Native American: a raven.
Kani Aboriginal: a lizard.
Kaani, Kanni.
Kaniel Arabic: spear-like. Hebrew: a reed.
Kanji Japanese: the metal, tin.
Kanku Aboriginal: a boy.
Kano Japanese: the god of the waters.
Kanu Sanskrit: an alternative name for the god Krishna. Swahili: a wild cat.
Kanuha Hawaiian: the sulky one. Also a girl's name.
Kanye *See* Kané.
Kapena Hawaiian: a captain.
Kapil Sanskrit: the name of a rishi (a Hindu seer).
Kapono Hawaiian: righteousness.
Kappa Aboriginal: the moon. Greek: ten.
Kappi *See* Cappi.
Kapua Maori: a cloud.
Kapura Maori: fire.
Kara Maori: an old man.
Karan Sanskrit: a warrior.
Kahran.
Karangi Aboriginal: a duck.
Karem Aboriginal: the ocean.
Karey *See* Carey.
Kari Aboriginal: smoke. Old Norse: the god of the air.
Karie.
Karie *See* Kari and Carey.
Karif Arabic: born in the autumn.
Karim Arabic: noble and generous.
Kareem.
Karkat Sanskrit: a crab. The Hindi name for the zodiac sign of Cancer.
Kartak, Katak.
Karl/Karlo *See* Charles.
Karleton/Karlton *See* Carlton.
Karlis Latvian form of Charles.
Karma Sanskrit: fate or destiny. Sherpa/Tibetan: a star. Also a girl's name.
Karmah.
Karmichael *See* Carmichael.
Karmine/Karmino *See* Carmine.
Karnabie/Karnaby *See* Carnaby.
Karnak Sanskrit: of the heart.
Karo The name of a New Zealand tree.
Karol/Károly *See* Charles.
Karst A geological term that refers to limestone or dolomite landscapes.
Karste.
Karsten *See* Christian.
Kartak *See* Karkat.
Kartik Sanskrit: the Hindu month of October/November, corresponding to the zodiac sign of Scorpio.
Kary *See* Carey.
Kase *See* Case.
Kaseem/Kasim *See* Qasim.
Kasen Basque: a helmet.
Kasey/Kasie *See* Casey.
Kash/Kashe *See* Cash.
Kashmir The name of an Indian state.
Cashmir.
Kasimier/Kasimierz/Kasimir

See Casimir.
Kason Burmese: the month of April/May, corresponding to Taurus.
Kayson.
Kaspah/Kaspar/Kasper *See* Caspar.
Kaspian/Kaspien *See* Caspian.
Kassian/Kassius *See* Cassius.
Kassidy *See* Cassidy.
Kastor *See* Castor.
Katak *See* Karkat.
Kateb Arabic: a writer.
Kathan Aboriginal: a waterlily.
Kathel *See* Cathal.
Kato African: the second-born twin.
Kauariki A Polynesian name of uncertain meaning.
Kauri Polynesian: a New Zealand tree.
Kaushik Sanskrit: a name from Hindu legend.
Koushik.
Kav/Kavan/Kaven/Kavien *See* Cavan.
Kavanagh/Kavannah *See* Cavanagh.
Kawa Japanese: a river.
Kawau Maori: a figure from legend.
Kay Welsh: rejoiced in. The name of an Arthurian knight.
Cai (Welsh), *Caie, Kai, Kaie, Kaye.*
Kaya Turkish: a rock.
Kayce *See* Case.
Kaycee/Kaycie *See* Casey.
Kayd/Kayde *See* Cade.

Kayden/Kaydn *See* Caden.
Kaydenz/Kaydnz *See* Cadenz.
Kaylan/Kaylen/Kaylin *See* Kalan.
Kayleb *See* Caleb.
Kaylis *See* Kalis.
Kayn/Kayne *See* Kane.
Kayse *See* Case.
Kayson *See* Kason.
Kazar *See* Caesar.
Kazimierz/Kazimir *See* Casimir.
Kazuki Japanese: the shining one.
Kazumi Japanese: harmony.
Kazuo Japanese: a man of peace.
Keaghan *See* Keegan.
Keal/Keale *See* Keel.
Kealii Hawaiian: the chief.
Kean Irish Gaelic: ancient. *See also* Keane.
Cian, Cianan, Ciann, Ciian, Keon, Kiaan, Kian, Kiian.
Keane Old English: handsome and bold.
Kean, Keen, Keene, Kene.
Keanu Hawaiian: a sea breeze.
Keaneau.
Kearney Irish Gaelic: the victorious one.
Kearny.
Keat Old English: a shed or outhouse.
Keates, Keats.
Keaton Old English: the town of the outhouse.
Keaten.
Keb *See* Geb.
Kebi Aboriginal: the little one.
Kedar *See* Kadir.

K – Boys

Kedjo Ghanaian: born on a Monday.
Keeden Aboriginal: a name for the moon.
Keedin.
Keefe Irish Gaelic: handsome, noble. See also Keith.
Keef.
Keefer See Kiefer.
Keegan Irish Gaelic: fiery, or determined.
Keaghan, Keeghan.
Keel Middle English: part of a ship's hull.
Keal, Keale, Kele, Kiehl, Kiel, Kiele.
Keelan See Kelan.
Keeley Irish Gaelic: handsome. Also a girl's name.
Keely.
Kee-Lin Chinese: a little dragon.
Keelin, Keelyn.
Keen/Keene See Keane.
Keenan Irish Gaelic: little, or ancient.
Keenann, Keenen.
Keer See Keir.
Keeran See Kieran.
Keerang Aboriginal: the moon.
Kees Dutch diminutive of Cornelius.
Keeth/Keethe See Keith.
Kefar Hebrew: a town or settlement.
Kei Hawaiian: dignified or glorious; also a girl's name. Japanese: possibly meaning a blessing.
Keifer/Keiffer See Kiefer.
Keigh See Keith.
Keighley The name of a town in Yorkshire, UK. Also a possible variation of Keith.
Keighlee, Keighleigh, Keighly, Keithlee, Keithleigh, Keithley, Keithly.
Keiji Japanese: to lead cautiously.
Keiki Hawaiian: a boy or son.
Keir Celtic: dark. Scottish: probably from the surname Kerr.
Keer, Kheir, Khier, Kier.
Keiran/Keirren/Keiryn See Kieran.
Keirnan See Kiernan.
Keirsten Probably a variation of Keir, a Scottish surname.
Keirston, Kiersten, Kierston.
Keisuke An unusual name from Japan.
Keith Celtic: from the forest.
Keef, Keefe, Keeth, Keethe, Keigh, Keithe, Kieth, Kiethe.
Keithleigh/Keithley See Keighley.
Keiven See Kevin.
Kekipi Hawaiian: a rebel. Also a girl's name.
Kekoa Hawaiian: the brave one.
Kekona Hawaiian: a second (as in time).
Kekra Hindi: a crab.
Kelan Irish Gaelic: slender.
Keelan.
Kelby Old German: from the farm by the spring or ridge.
Kelbeigh, Kelbi, Kelbie, Kellbeigh, Kellbi, Kellbie, Kellby.
Keld See Kjell.
Kele See Keel.

Kelen *See* Kellan.
Kelevi Finnish: a hero.
Kelis *See* Kalis.
Kell Old Norse: from the well or spring. *See also* Kjell.
Kellan A modern name, probably derived from Kell or Kelly.
Kelen, Kelon, Kellen, Kellon.
Kellbeigh/Kellby *See* Kelby.
Keller Irish Gaelic: a little companion.
Kellett Old Norse: a slope with a spring.
Kellet.
Kellven/Kellvin *See* Kelvin.
Kelly Irish Gaelic: a warrior. Also a girl's name.
Kelley.
Kelon *See* Kellan.
Kelsey Old Norse: a dweller on the island or by the water.
Kelsea, Kelsee, Kelsi, Kelsie, Kelsley, Kelsy.
Kelso A Scottish town.
Kelt Greek: a Celtic person.
Celt.
Keltie From Latin: a Celtic person. Also a girl's name.
Celtee, Celtey, Celti, Celtie, Celty, Keltee, Keltey, Kelti, Kelty.
Kelton Old English: from the calf farm.
Kelten.
Kelvin English/Scottish: the name of a Scottish river.
Kellven, Kellvin, Kellvyn, Kelven, Kelvyn.

Kelynack Cornish: a grove of holly.
Kelynak, Kelynek.
Kem Gypsy: the sun.
Khem.
Kemal *See* Kamal.
Kemar *See* Qamar.
Kembell/Kemble *See* Kimball.
Kembla Aboriginal: many blessings.
Kemp Old English: a warrior or champion.
Ken Aboriginal: a lizard. Japanese: clear water. Also a diminutive of Kenneth.
Kenan Cornish: the name of a legendary Cornish king.
Kendall English: from the bright valley.
Kendal, Kendel, Kendell, Kendle, Kendyl.
Kenden/Kendon *See* Kenton.
Kendi Aboriginal: a frilled lizard.
Kendrick Celtic: a hill. Old English: royal power.
Kene *See* Keane.
Kenedy *See* Kennedy.
Keneil A combination of Ken and Neil (*see* Neal).
Keneal, Keneale, Kenneal, Kenneale, Kenneil.
Kenelm Old English: a brave helmet; a protector. The name of a saint.
Kenenisa An African name of uncertain meaning.
Keneth *See* Kenneth.
Kenichi Japanese: the healthy and strong one.

Kenji Japanese: the second, or second-born son.
Kenley Old English: from the royal meadow.
Kenn Celtic/Welsh: as clear as bright water.
Kennard Old English: bold and hardy.
Kenneal/Kenneil See Keneil.
Kennedy Irish Gaelic: an ugly head, or a helmeted chief.
Kenedy.
Kenneth Scottish Gaelic: handsome and fair, or born of fire.
Keneth, Kenneith, Kennet, Kennith, Kennyth.
Diminutives: Ken, Kennie, Kenny, Kent, Keny, Khen.
Kennett An English river and placename.
Kennet.
Kennie/Kenny Diminutives of Kenneth and other names beginning with Ken.
Kenning Old English: from the family farm.
Kennington.
Kennith/Kennyth See Kenneth.
Kenrick Old English: a bold ruler.
Kenrik, Kenwrick.
Kensey/Kensie/Kensy See Kenzie.
Kent Celtic: bright, white. The name of an English county and also a diminutive of Kenneth.
Kentt, Khent, Khentt.
Kenta A popular Japanese name, meaning health.
Kentish A man from the county of Kent.
Kenton Old English: from the royal manor or estate.
Kenden, Kendon, Kenten.
Kenver Cornish: a great chief.
Kenward Old English: a bold guardian, or a brave soldier.
Kenway.
Kenway See Kenward.
Kenwrick See Kenrick.
Kenwyn Cornish/Welsh: a splendid chief. The name of a saint.
Kenwin, Kenwinn, Kenwinne, Kenwyne, Kenwynn, Kenwynne.
Keny A diminutive of Kenneth.
Kenya An African country.
Kenyon Irish Gaelic: white- or fair-haired.
Kenzie A modern name; a diminutive of the popular Mackenzie.
Kensee, Kensey, Kensi, Kensie, Kensy, Kenzee, Kenzey, Kenzi, Kenzy.
Keoki Hawaiian form of George.
Keon See Kean.
Keoni Polynesian: the righteous one.
Kep Aboriginal: an arrow.
Kephas See Cephas.
Kerbie/Kerby See Kirby.
Kerbiejohn/Kerbiejon See Kirbyjohn.
Kerekori Maori form of Gregory.
Kereru Maori: a wood pigeon.
Kereteki Polynesian: a mythological

figure.
Kerey English Gypsy: homeward bound.
Keri, Kerie.
Keriaki/Keriakos *See* Kyriakos.
Kerian *See* Kieran.
Kerie *See* Kerry.
Kerigan *See* Kerrigan.
Kermit Manx Gaelic/Irish Gaelic: a free man.
Kern Irish Gaelic: the little dark one.
Kernick Cornish: from the little corner.
Kernow Cornish: a man from Cornwall.
Curnow.
Kerod *See* Kerrod.
Keron *See* Kieran.
Kerr Irish Gaelic: dark.
Kerrey/Kerri/Kerrie *See* Kerry.
Kerrian *See* Kieran.
Kerrigan Irish Gaelic: dark or swarthy.
Kerigan.
Kerrin *See* Kieran.
Kerrod A modern name, probably from Kerr.
Kerod.
Kerry Irish Gaelic: the dark one. The name of an Irish county.
Kerie, Kerrey, Kerri, Kerrie.
Kersen Indonesian: a cherry.
Kersey Cornish: a reed-fringed bog.
Kersley, Kersly, Kersy.
Kert/Kertis *See* Curtis.
Kerwin Irish Gaelic: the little black-haired one.
Kerwan, Kerwen, Kerwyn, Kirwan, Kirwin, Kirwyn.
Kesar Russian form of Caesar.
Kester Scottish form of Christopher.
Kestar.
Keston A placename from Kent, England.
Kesten, Kestin, Kestyn.
Kestrel Middle English: a small falcon.
Kestrell, Kestryl, Kestryll.
Ketah Nepali: a boy.
Keta.
Kevan/Keven *See* Kevin.
Keverne Cornish: the name of a saint and a placename.
Kevern.
Kevin Irish Gaelic: beloved, lovable.
Keiven, Kevan, Keven, Kevon, Kevyn.
Diminutive: Kev.
Kevon/Kevyn *See* Kevin.
Keyar Aboriginal: a lobster.
Keysar *See* Caesar.
Keyt/Keyte *See* Kite.
Khabeer/Khabir *See* Kabir.
Khain/Khane *See* Kane.
Khalan/Khalen *See* Kalan.
Khalid Arabic: eternal.
Kalid, Kalled, Kallid, Khaled.
Khalif Arabic: a successor.
Khalifa, Khaliph, Khalipha.
Khalil Arabic: a friend.
Kalil.
Khamisi Swahili: born on a Thursday.
Kamis, Kamisi, Khamis.

Khan Arabic: a prince or king.
Cahn, Kahn, Khanh.
Kharon *See* Charon.
Khayne *See* Kane.
Kheir/Khier *See* Keir.
Kheliya A Sri Lankan name of uncertain meaning.
Khem *See* Kem.
Khen *See* Kenneth.
Khent/Khentt *See* Kent.
Khi/Khie *See* Ky.
Khian *See* Kyan.
Khiden/Khidon *See* Kyden.
Khisen/Khison *See* Kyson.
Khobi/Khobie *See* Kobe.
Khonsu The Ancient Egyptian moon god.
Konsu.
Khoury Arabic: a priest.
Khristian *See* Christian.
Khurram A Pakistani name of uncertain meaning.
Khyan *See* Kyan.
Ki/Kie *See* Ky.
Kiaan/Kian *See* Kean and Kyan.
Kiaran *See* Kieran.
Kidd Middle English: a young goat.
Kid, Kidh, Kyd, Kydd.
Kiden/Kidon *See* Kyden.
Kiefer Irish Gaelic: pleasure, enjoyment.
Keefer, Keifer, Keiffer, Kief, Kieffer.
Kiehle/Kiel/Kiele *See* Keel.
Kier *See* Keir.
Kieran Irish Gaelic: dark or black. *Ciarán* (Irish), *Keeran, Keiran, Keiren, Keiron, Keirren, Keiryn, Kerian* (Irish Gaelic), *Keron, Kerrian* (Irish Gaelic), *Kerrin, Kiaran, Kieren, Kieron, Kieryn, Kiran, Kirran, Kirron, Kirryn, Kyeran, Kyran* (Irish Gaelic).
Kiernan Irish Gaelic: a form of Tiernan, meaning a lord.
Keirnan.
Kiersten/Kierston *See* Keirsten.
Kiet Thai: truthful or honourable.
Kieth/Kiethe *See* Keith.
Kifen/Kiff/Kiffen *See* Kyffen.
Kiian *See* Kean.
Kilab Arabic: a dog.
Kilby Old Norse: the farm of the nobleman.
Kilbey.
Kile *See* Kyle.
Kilima Swahili: a hill.
Killara Aboriginal: permanent, always there. The name of a Sydney suburb.
Killarney Irish Gaelic: the church of sloes. An Irish county.
Killian Irish Gaelic: the little warlike one.
Kilian.
Kilmeny A Scottish placename.
Kilmeney.
Kilpatrick Gaelic: from the church of St Patrick.
Kim Rudyard Kipling's hero in the novel of the same name. Vietnamese: the golden one. *See also* Kimball and Kimberley.

Kimmo (Finnish), *Kym*.
Kimba Aboriginal: a bushfire.
Kimbah, Kymba, Kymbah.
Kimball Celtic: a warrior chief.
Kembell, Kemble, Kimbal, Kimbel, Kimbell, Kimble, Kymbal, Kymball, Kymble.
Diminutives: Kim, Kym.
Kimberley Old English: from the meadow. More commonly a girl's name.
Kimberleigh, Kimberlin, Kimberly.
Diminutives: Kim, Kym.
Kimble *See* Kimball.
Kimi Finnish: the name of a well-known racing car driver (Kimi Raikkonen).
Kimmo Finnish form of Kim.
Kimo Hawaiian form of James.
Kimon *See* Cimon.
Kin Japanese: golden.
Kindin Basque: the fifth, or fifth child.
Kindred Affinity, as in a kindred spirit.
King English: a ruler, a sovereign.
Kinge, Kyng, Kynge.
Kingi An unusual Maori name.
Kingsley Old English: from the king's wood or meadow.
Kingslee, Kingsleigh, Kingslie, Kinsley.
Kingston Old English: from the king's farm.
Kinnara Thai: a figure from mythology who was half-man, half-bird.
Kinnard Irish Gaelic: from the high hill.
Kinsey Old English: a victorious king or prince.
Kinsley *See* Kingsley.
Kinta Native American: a beaver, implying one who is skillful.
Kintah.
Kio A modern name of uncertain meaning.
Kioh.
Kipling After Rudyard Kipling, a famous English novelist.
Diminutives: Kip, Kipp.
Kipp English: the dweller on the pointed hill. *See also* Kipling.
Kippax Middle English: the town in the ash trees.
Kiral Turkish: a chief or king.
Kiran Sanskrit: a ray of light.
See also Kieran.
Kirani, Kiranie, Kirran.
Kirby Teutonic/Old Norse: from the church village.
Kerbie, Kerby, Kirbie.
Kirbyjohn A combination of Kirby and John (God is gracious).
Kerbiejohn, Kerbiejon, Kirbiejon, Kirbyjon.
Kirill *See* Cyril.
Kirin Japanese: a mythological unicorn.
Kiritowha Maori form of Christopher.
Kirk Old Norse: a dweller by the

K – Boys

Kirkcaldy The name of a Scottish town.
Kirkaldy.
Diminutives: Kirk, Kirke.

church. Also a diminutive of names such as Kirkdale and Kirkland.
Kirke.

Kirkdale Old Norse: the valley of the church.
Diminutives: Kirk, Kirke.

Kirkland Old Norse: the church land.
Diminutives: Kirk, Kirke.

Kirkley Old English: from the church meadow.

Kirkwood Old English: from the church wood.

Kiron *See* Chiron.

Kirran/Kirron/Kirryn *See* Kieran.

Kirstur *See* Kistur.

Kirwan/Kirwin/Kirwyn *See* Kerwin.

Kishnu *See* Kislev.

Kishor Sanskrit: a young boy or a colt.
Kishore.

Kislev The ninth lunar month of the Hebrew calendar, corresponding to Sagittarius.
Kishnu (Babylonian).

Kistur English Gypsy: a rider.
Kirstur, Kystur.

Kit/Kitt Diminutives of Christian and Christopher.

Kitchener Old English: a kitchen worker. The name of a famous British soldier.
Kitchenor, Kitchiner, Kitchinor.

Kite Middle English: a type of hawk.
Keyt, Keyte, Kyte.

Kito Swahili: a jewel.

Kitto Cornish diminutive of Christopher.
Kittow.

Kiva Hebrew: protected.

Kiwi Maori: a native New Zealand bird.

Kiyoshi Japanese: the quiet one.

Kizil Turkish: red.

Kjell Scandinavian: from an Old Norse word meaning a kettle or helmet.
Keld, Kell, Kjeld.

Klaas/Klaes/Klaus *See* Nicholas.

Klae *See* Clay and Clayton.

Klaeton/Klaten/Klaton *See* Clayton.

Klaro *See* Claro.

Klaud/Klaude *See* Claude.

Klay/Klayten/Klayton *See* Clay and Clayton.

Kleat/Kleate/Klete *See* Clete.

Kleave/Kleaver *See* Cleave.

Kleavon/Klevon *See* Cleavon.

Klein Dutch/German: small, the little one.
Clein, Cline, Kline.

Klemens/Kliment *See* Clement.

Klent/Klenton *See* Clinton.

Kleon *See* Cleon.

Kleto/Klito *See* Cleto.

Kleve *See* Cleave.

Kline *See* Klein.

Klint/Klinton *See* Clinton.

Knight Old English: a mounted soldier.
Knights The son of a knight. *Knightson.*
Knox Irish Gaelic: from the hillock.
Knut Old Norse: a knot. The name of several Danish kings. *Canute, Knud, Knute.*
Koa Hawaiian: brave and fearless.
Kobal Possibly a variation of Kobe.
Kobe A popular modern name, particularly in the US. Probably derived from Jacob, meaning the supplanter. *Cobe, Cobee, Cobey, Cobi, Cobie, Coby, Khobee, Khobi, Khobie, Kobee, Kobey, Kobi, Kobie, Koby.*
Kobe-Lee A modern 'combination name'. *Cobe-Lee, Coby-Lee, Koby-Lee.*
Kobyfox An unusual modern name. *Cobefox, Cobifox, Cobyfox, Kobefox, Kobifox, Kobeyfox.*
Koda/Kodah *See* Coda.
Kodee/Kodie/Kody *See* Cody.
Kodzo *See* Kojo.
Koen/Kohan/Kohen *See* Cohen.
Kofi Ghanaian: born on a Friday.
Kogarah Aboriginal: place of the rushes.
Kohdi/Kohdy *See* Cody.
Koi Native American: like a panther.
Koiranah Aboriginal: an eagle.
Koji Japanese: abundance.
Kojo Ghanaian: born on a Monday. *Kodzo.*
Koki Aboriginal: the wind.
Kola/Kolah *See* Cola.
Kolbey/Kolby *See* Colby.
Kolet Aboriginal: a dove.
Kolli Aboriginal: water.
Koloman Turkish form of Colman (*see* Columba).
Koloona Aboriginal: a young man.
Kolt/Kolte *See* Colt.
Kolya Aboriginal: winter. Russian: a diminutive of Nikolai (*see* Nicholas).
Komang Balinese: the third-born child.
Kona Hawaiian: the south.
Konak Aboriginal: the earth.
Konan *See* Conan.
Kongo Japanese: a diamond.
Kongoni Swahili: a hartebeest, a large African antelope.
Konol Aboriginal: the sky.
Konrad German and Polish forms of Conrad.
Konstadene/Konstadine *See* Constantine.
Konstantin/Konstantyn *See* Constantine.
Konsu *See* Khonsu.
Koolyn Aboriginal: a black swan. *Koolin.*
Kooper *See* Cooper.
Koora Aboriginal: the day.
Koorong Aboriginal: a canoe, or a snake. *Korong.*
Koorosh *See* Kourosh.

Kootingal Aboriginal: a star.
Koray Turkish: the ember moon.
Korbin/Korbyn *See* Corbett.
Koree/Korey/Korie *See* Corey.
Korin *See* Corin.
Korley/Korleigh *See* Corley.
Kornel *See* Cornelius.
Koro The name of a Fijian island.
Koroit Aboriginal: a fire.
Korrin/Koryn *See* Corin.
Kort *See* Conrad and Curtis.
Korvin *See* Corbett.
Koshin The Japanese god of travellers and journeys.
Kosho A Japanese god who rules south and the colour red.
Kosi An African water god.
Kosmo *See* Cosmo.
Kosta/Kostadin/Kostandin *See* Constantine.
Kostas Greek form of Constantine.
Kostya *See* Constantine.
Kosuke Japanese: a clear inlet.
Kourosh Persian form of Cyrus.
Koorosh, Kurosh, Kurush.
Koushik *See* Kaushik.
Koventrie/Koventry *See* Coventry.
Kovit Thai: a specialist.
Kowan/Kowen *See* Cohen.
Kraig/Kraigh *See* Craig.
Kreon *See* Creon.
Kresimir Slavic: a combination of words meaning light and peace.
Kressley A modern American name, probably from Carson Kressley of the *Queer Eye* TV series.
Kreslee, Kresleigh, Kresley, Kresslee, Kressleigh.
Krikor An unusual Turkish name.
Kris A diminutive of Christian and Christopher.
Krishi Nepali: agriculture.
Krishna Sanskrit: dark or black. The name of a Hindu god.
Chrishna, Krishni, Krisna (Indonesian), *Krisnan.*
Krispen/Krispin *See* Crispin.
Kristen *See* Christian.
Kristian/Kristijan/Kristinn/Kristjan *See* Christian.
Kristo/Kristof/Kristoffer *See* Christopher.
Kriv An unusual Scandinavian name.
Kryv.
Kronos Greek: the god of time, fertility and agriculture; the equivalent of the Roman god Saturn.
Chronos, Cronos.
Kruise/Kruiz/Kruze *See* Cruise.
Krys/Krystof/Krystoff *See* Christopher.
Kuddus *See* Quddus.
Kudret Turkish: might or power.
Kuja Sanskrit: a name for the planet Mars.
Kujah.
Kukuwai Maori: swampy.
Kulan Aboriginal: a possum.
Kulapo Tongan: a fish.
Kulnura Aboriginal: the clouds.
Kuma Japanese: a bear.

Kumar Nepali/Sanskrit: a boy, a son.
Kumbha Sanskrit: an earthen jug or pitcher. The Hindi name for the zodiac sign of Aquarius.
Kumera Sanskrit: a god of war.
Kumo Japanese: a spider.
Kunal Sanskrit: a lotus.
Kunda Aboriginal: a dog.
Kundah.
Kundan Sanskrit: one who is pure.
Kupah *See* Cooper.
Kupe Polynesian: the name of a heroic explorer.
Kuper Yiddish: copper. Used to describe someone with copper-coloured or red hair.
Kura Polynesian: red. Also a girl's name.
Kuracca Aboriginal: a white cockatoo.
Kurma Sanskrit: a tortoise in Thai and Hindu mythology, implying longevity.
Kurosh/Kurush *See* Kourosh.
Kurria Aboriginal: a crocodile.
Kurt *See* Conrad and Curtis.
Kurtis/Kurtiss *See* Curtis.
Kurtlee/Kurtleigh/Kurtly *See* Curtleigh.
Kuruk Native American: a bear.
Kuruna Aboriginal: a spirit child.
Kushal Sanskrit: clever.
Kusha.
Kuti Aboriginal: a swan.
Kuya Aboriginal: a fish.
Kuyan Aboriginal: a honeybee.
Kwain/Kwaine *See* Quain.

Kwako Ghanaian: born on a Wednesday.
Kwaku.
Kwame Ghanaian: born on a Saturday.
Kwan Korean: strong.
Kwao Ghanaian: Thursday.
Kwasi Ghanaian: born on a Sunday.
Kwesi.
Kwayde/Kwayden/Kweyd *See* Quade.
Kwintyn *See* Quentin.
Kwodjo An African name of uncertain meaning.
Ky A popular modern name, probably an abbreviation of Kyle. *Cai, Caie, Kai, Kaie, Kaii, Kaiis, Kaj, Khi, Khie, Ki, Kie, Kya, Kyah, Kye, Kygh.*
Kyal/Kyall *See* Kyle.
Kyan A modern name, probably from Kian (*see* Kean), or a variation of Ky. *Khian, Khyan, Kian.*
Kyd/Kydd *See* Kidd.
Kyden A modern name derived from Ky. *Khiden, Khidon, Kiden, Kidon, Kyeden, Kyedon, Kydon.*
Kye/Kygh *See* Ky.
Kyel/Kyell *See* Kyle.
Kyenan/Kynan *See* Conan.
Kyffen A modern name, possibly from Kevin. *Kifen, Kiff, Kiffen, Kyfen, Kyff.*
Kyle Scottish Gaelic: from the narrow strait. The name of a Scottish region.

Cyal, Cyall, Cyel, Cyell, Cyle, Kile, Kyal, Kyall, Kyel, Kyell, Kylan, Kylen.

Kyloe Old English: from the cows' meadow.
Kylow, Kylowe.

Kym/Kymbal/Kymble *See* Kim, Kimball and Kimberley.

Kymba/Kymbah *See* Kimba.

Kyne Old English: royal.

Kyng/Kynge *See* King.

Kyran *See* Kieran.

Kyriakos Greek: of the Lord. The name of a Greek saint.
Ciriaco (Italian, Spanish), *Cyriac, Cyriacos, Cyriacus, Keriaki, Keriakos, Kyriacos, Kyriaki.*
Diminutive: Cyr.

Kyrie Greek: from the word kyrios, meaning O Lord.
Kyree, Kyri.

Kyron *See* Chiron.

Kyson Another 'Ky combination name' literally the son of Ky.
Khisen, Khison, Kyesen, Kyeson, Kysen.

Kystur *See* Kistur.

Kyte *See* Kite.

L

Laban Hebrew: white.
Lavan.

Labhras Irish Gaelic form of Laurence.

Lachhiman *See* Lakshman.

Lachlan Scottish Gaelic: from the land of the lochs.
Lachlane, Lachlann, Lachlin, Lachlyn, Lauchlan, Lauchlann, Laughlan, Laughlin, Lochlainn (Irish Gaelic), *Lochlan* (Irish Gaelic), *Lochlann* (Irish Gaelic), *Lockelan, Lockelin, Lockelyn, Locklan, Locklin, Locklyn, Loclan, Loclyn, Loughlin.*
Diminutives: Lachie, Lochie, Lochtie, Lockey, Lockie, Locky.

Lacy Old French: lace.
Lacey.

Ladd English: a page or attendant.

Ladislav Slavic: a glorious ruler, or glorious power. *See also* Vladislav.
Ladislao, Ladislas (Polish), *Ladislaus* (Polish), *Ladislo* (Italian), *Laszlo* (Hungarian), *Lazlo* (Hungarian).

Lado African: the second, as in the second son.

Lael Hebrew: belonging to God.
Lale.

Laertes Greek: a legendary figure.

Lafayette French: faith.

Lago Italian/Spanish: a lake.

Laibrook Old English: the path by the brook.
Laibrooke, Laybrook, Laybrooke.

Laidley Old English: from the water meadow.
Laidleigh, Laidlie, Laidly.

Laike *See* Lake.
Laiken/Laikin *See* Laykin.
Laiker *See* Laker.
Laine *See* Lane.
Laing/Lainge *See* Lang.
Laird Scottish Gaelic: a landowner, the lord of the manor.
Lairde.
Lais Arabic: a lion.
Laister *See* Lester.
Laiten/Laityn *See* Leighton.
Laith Arabic: a little lion.
Laithe, Layth, Laythe.
Laitham *See* Latham.
Lajos Hungarian form of Louis.
Lake Old English: the original meaning was a stream rather than a pool or pond.
Laike, Layke.
Laken/Lakin *See* Laykin.
Laker Old English: one who lives by a stream.
Laiker, Layker.
Laki Hawaiian: lucky.
Lakshan Sanskrit: one who aims well.
Laksh.
Lakshman Sanskrit: auspicious.
Lachhiman, Lakshmana, Laxman.
Lal Sanskrit: the beloved one.
Lalama Hawaiian: clever and daring.
Lale *See* Lael.
Lalit Sanskrit: fine or lovely.
Lalor *See* Lawler.
Lamar Teutonic: famous around the land.
Lamarr, Lemar, Lemarr.
Lamat Mayan: a rabbit.
Lamba Hindi: tall.
Lambert Teutonic: from the bright or famous land.
Lamberto (Italian), *Lambros, Lammert, Landbert.*
Lamech Hebrew: strong or powerful.
Lameck, Lamek.
Lamine An African name of uncertain meaning.
Lammert *See* Lambert.
Lamont French: the mount. Old Norse: a lawyer.
Lamond, Lammond, Lammont, Lammonte, Lamonte.
Lancaster Old English: a Roman settlement on the river.
Lancester, Lankaster, Lankester.
Lance Old French: a lance-bearer. *See also* Lancelot.
Launce.
Lancelot Old French/Old English: a spear or lance attendant. The most famous of King Arthur's knights.
Launcelot.
Diminutive: Lance.
Landbert *See* Lambert.
Landers Old French: a launderer.
Lander, Landor, Landors.
Diminutive: Lanny.
Landon Old English: from the long hill.
Landen, Langden, Langdon, Langston.
Landor/Landors *See* Landers.

L – Boys

Lane Old English: from the narrow road.
Laine, Layne.
Lang Teutonic: a tall man.
Laing, Lainge, Lange, Langue.
Langden/Langdon *See* Landon.
Langford Old English: from the long ford.
Langforde, Lansford, Lansforde.
Langi Polynesian: heaven.
Langley Old English: from the long meadow.
Langston Old English: the farm of the tall man. *See also* Landon.
Langworth Old English: from the long enclosure.
Lani Polynesian: the sky. Also a girl's name.
Lanyi.
Lankaster/Lankester *See* Lancaster.
Lann Celtic: a sword.
Lanny *See* Harlan and Landers.
Lansford *See* Langford.
Lanyi *See* Lani.
Lanyon Cornish: a cold pool or lake.
Lares A Roman god of the household.
Laris Latin: cheerful.
Lark Aboriginal: a cloud. English: a songbird.
Larke.
Larrie/Larry *See* Laurence.
Lars Scandinavian form of Laurence.
Larson Scandinavian: the son of Lars. *See also* Laurence.
Lascelles Old French: the hermitage or cell.
Laser A light-emitting device.
Lazer.
LaShawn American: a variation of Shawn (*see* Sean).
LaShaughan, LaShaun, LaShaune.
Lasota Slavic: a man of the mountains.
Lasse Finnish form of Laurence.
Laszlo Hungarian form of Ladislav.
Lazlo.
Latham Old Norse: from the barn.
Laitham, Laytham.
Latif Arabic/Sanskrit: kind and gentle.
Lateef.
Latimer Old French: an interpreter or teacher.
La Trobe The surname of the first lieutenant-governor of the state of Victoria.
LaTrobe, Latrobe.
Lauchlan/Lauchlann *See* Lachlan.
Laughlan/Laughlin *See* Lachlan.
Laughton *See* Lawton.
Launce *See* Lance.
Launcelot *See* Lancelot.
Laurans/Lauras *See* Laurence.
Laurence Latin: from the laurel tree, or crowned with laurels. *See also* Lawson.
Labhras (Irish Gaelic), *Lars* (Scandinavian), *Lasse* (Finnish), *Laurans, Lauras* (Lithuanian), *Laurens* (Dutch), *Laurent* (French), *Laurentius* (Dutch), *Lauri* (Finnish), *Laurier, Lavrenti* (Russian), *Lawrance,*

Lawren, Lawrence, Loren, Lorencio (Spanish), *Lorenz* (German), *Lorenzo* (Italian), *Lorin, Lorne, Lourenço* (Portuguese), *Lovrenc* (Croatian, Slovene).
Diminutives: Enzo (Italian), Larrie, Larry, Laurie, Laury, Lawrie, Lawry, Laz, Lenz (German), Lon, Lonnie, Lovro (Croatian, Slovene), Lowrey, Lowrie, Lowry, Rens (Dutch), Rense (Dutch), Renzo (Italian).

Laurie/Laurier *See* Laurence.

Lauriston The place or town of Laurence.
Lauristan, Lauristen.

Lavan *See* Laban.

Lavern French: spring-like, or from the alder tree.
LaVern.

Lavrenti Russian form of Laurence.

Lawford Old English: from the ford by the hill.

Lawler Irish Gaelic: the mumbler, the soft-spoken one.

Lawley Old English: from the meadow on the hill.

Lawn English from Old French: grass-covered land.
Lawne.

Lawrance/Lawren/Lawrence/Lawrie *See* Laurence.

Lawson Old English: the son of Lawrence or Laurence.
Lawsen, Lowsen, Lowson.

Lawton Old English: from the town on the hill.
Laughton.

Laxman *See* Lakshman.

Laybrook/Laybrooke *See* Laibrook.

Layke *See* Lake.

Layker *See* Laker.

Laykin Old English: from the little field or meadow.
Laiken, Laikin, Laken, Lakin, Leghken, Leghkin, Leykin.

Layland *See* Leland and Leyland.

Laylor *See* Lawler.

Layman *See* Lyman.

Layne *See* Lane.

Layster *See* Lester.

Layten/Layton *See* Leighton.

Layth/Laythe *See* Laith.

Laytham *See* Latham.

Laz Diminutive of Laurence.

Lazar/Lazare *See* Lazarus.

Lazarus Hebrew: God is my help. The man who Jesus raised from the dead in the Bible.
Eleazar (Hebrew), *Elezar* (Hebrew), *Lazar* (Hungarian, Slavic), *Lazare* (French), *Lázaro* (Spanish), *Lazhar, Lazrus, Lazzaro* (Italian).
Diminutive: Lazo (Slavic).

Lazenby Old Norse: the farm of the freed man.

Lazer *See* Laser.

Lazhar *See* Lazarus.

Lazlo *See* Laszlo.

Lazo Slavic diminutive of Lazarus.

Lazrus *See* Lazarus.
Lazzaro Italian form of Lazarus.
Lea *See* Lee.
Leaf Middle English: a 'plant name'. *See also* Leif.
Leafe.
Leal Old English: loyal and true.
Leam *See* Liam.
Leander Greek: the lion man. The name of a hero in Greek legend. *See also* Leo, Leonard, Leonidas and Lionel.
Léandre (French), *Leandro* (Italian, Spanish), *Leandros* (Greek).
Lear Teutonic: joyful, or from the sea. A Shakespearean character.
Llyr (Welsh).
Leath *See* Leith.
Leben Yiddish: life.
Lebron American: a name popularised by basketball player Lebron James.
LeBron, Lebronn, LeBronn, Lebronne, LeBronne.
Lech Polish: the name of the legendary founder of Poland.
Ledger Teutonic: probably from St Léger.
Lee Old English: a meadow or clearing.
Lea, Leigh.
Leeland *See* Leyland.
Leeno *See* Lino.
Leeroi/Lee-Roi/Leeroy *See* Leroy.
Leeston A modern name, derived from Lee. Also a girl's name.
Leesten, Leestyn, Leisten, Leiston, Leistyn.
Leeth *See* Leith.
Leeuwin Dutch: a lioness.
Lewin.
Leghken/Leghkin *See* Laykin.
Leghland *See* Leyland.
Lei Chinese: thunder.
Leicester *See* Lester.
Leif Old Norse: beloved, or a descendant, an heir.
Leaf, Leiv (Norwegian), *Lief, Liev.*
Leigh *See* Lee.
Leighland *See* Leyland.
Leighman Old English: from the meadow.
Leighmann, Leman, Lemann.
Leighton Old English: the dweller at the farm by the meadow.
Laiten, Laiton, Laityn, Layten, Layton, Leyten, Leyton, Lleyton.
Leiham/Leihem/Leihm *See* Liam.
Leisten/Leiston *See* Leeston.
Leith Scottish Gaelic: a broad river. A Scottish placename.
Leath, Leeth, Leithe.
Leiv Norwegian form of Leif.
Lejeune French: literally the young one.
Lek Thai: the little one.
Leka A popular Albanian name.
Leks *See* Lex.
Leland Old English: from the meadow-land.
Layland.

Leman/Lemann *See* Leighman.
Lemar/Lemarr *See* Lamar.
Lemuel Hebrew: devoted or consecrated to God. The first name of Gulliver, the hero of Jonathan Swift's *Gulliver's Travels*, and also a biblical name.
Len/Lennie/Lenny Diminutives of names such as Lennox and Leonard.
Lenan/Lenon *See* Lennon.
Lenard/Lennard/Lennart *See* Leonard.
Lennon Irish Gaelic: a little cape or cloak.
Lenan, Lennan, Lenon.
Lennor English Gypsy: springtime.
Lennox Scottish Gaelic: from a Scottish district, also a surname. *Diminutives:* Len, Lennie, Lenny.
Lenz Diminutive of Laurence.
Leo Latin: a lion, lion-hearted. *See also* Leander, Leonard, Leonidas, Leopold and Lionel.
Leon, Léon (French), *Léonce* (French), *Leoncio* (Spanish), *Leone* (Italian), *Leontes, Leonti* (Russian), *Leonzio* (Italian), *Leos* (Czech), *Lev* (Russian), *Levin*.
Leon/Léon/Leone *See* Leo.
Leonard Teutonic: as brave as a lion. *See also* Leander, Leo, Leonidas and Lionel.
Lenard, Lennard, Lennart (Scandinavian), *Léonard* (French), *Leonardo* (Italian, Portuguese, Spanish), *Leonato, Leonerd,*
Leonhard (German), *Leonid* (Russian), *Levon* (Armenian), *Linart* (Croatian), *Lyon*.
Diminutives: Len, Lennie, Lenny.
Leonardo *See* Leonard.
Léonce/Leoncio/Leone *See* Leo.
Leonel/Leonello *See* Lionel.
Leonerd/Leonhard *See* Leonard.
Leonid Russian form of Leonard.
Leonidas Greek: like a lion. *See also* Leander, Leo, Leonard and Lionel.
Leonilo Italian form of Lionel.
Leontes/Leonti *See* Leo.
Leonzio Italian form of Leo.
Leopard English from Greek: a wild cat.
Lepard, Leppard.
Leopold Teutonic: brave for the people, patriotic. The name of kings of Belgium and Bohemia.
Léopold (French), *Leopoldo* (Italian, Spanish).
Diminutive: Leo.
Leor A popular Israeli name.
Leos Czech form of Leo.
Lepus Latin: a hare. The name of a constellation in the Southern Hemisphere.
Leroy French: the king. A popular name in the USA. *See also* Elroy.
Leeroi, Lee-Roi, Leeroy, Lee-Roy, Leroi, Le-Roi, Le-Roy.
Lesleigh/Lesley *See* Leslie.
Leslie Scottish Gaelic: from an ancient surname. Also a girl's name, but this is usually spelt Lesley.

Lesleigh, Lesley, Lezleigh, Lezley, Lezlie.
Diminutives: Les, Lez.
Lester Old English: from the place-name Leicester, meaning a Roman site or fort.
Laister, Layster, Leicester, Leycester.
Letterio Italian: a name associated with St Maria of the Letter, the patron saint of Messina, Sicily.
Leura Aboriginal: lava. The name of a NSW town.
Lev *See* Leo.
Levander Old French: rising from the east, as in the sun.
Levent Turkish: like a lion.
Leverett Old French: a young hare.
Leverton Old English: from the farm of the rushes.
Levey *See* Levi.
Levi Hebrew: united.
Levey, Levy.
Levin *See* Leo.
Levison The son of Levi.
Leveyson, Levyson.
Levon Armenian form of Leon.
Lew/Lewes *See* Lewis.
Lewie Diminutive of Aloysius, Lewis and Louis.
Lewey, Lewy.
Lewin *See* Leeuwin.
Lewis An English variation of Louis. Also an anglicised form of the Welsh name Llewellyn.
Lewes, Lewys, Ludovic (Scottish).
Diminutives: Lew, Lewey, Lewie, Lewy, Louie.
Lewy/Lewys *See* Lewie and Lewis.
Lex A diminutive of Alexander.
Leks.
Lexil Probably a form of Lex.
Lexel, Lexell, Lexill, Lexyl, Lexyll.
Leycester *See* Lester.
Leykin *See* Laykin.
Leyland Old English: from the fallow land.
Layland, Leeland, Leghland, Leighland.
Leyman *See* Lyman.
Leyten/Leyton *See* Leighton.
Lez/Lezleigh/Lezley *See* Leslie.
Lhakpa Sherpa/Tibetan: born on a Wednesday.
Lhawang Sherpa/Tibetan: the powerful one.
Li Chinese: strength.
Lial/Liall *See* Lyle.
Liam Irish Gaelic: a short form of Uilleam. *See* William.
Leam, Leiham, Leihem, Leihm, Liamh, Lian, Liham, Lyam.
Liang Chinese: excellence.
Libero Italian: freedom.
Liberatore, Liberio (Portuguese), *Liberty, Lyberio, Lybero.*
Liberty *See* Libero.
Libra Latin: a pair of scales. The name of a zodiac sign.
Libri, Librius, Librus.
Lief/Liev *See* Leif.
Liel/Liell *See* Lyle.
Liham *See* Liam.

Liko Hawaiian: a bud.
Lilburn An English placename.
Lillburn.
Lim A popular Korean name.
Limerick The name of a county in Ireland. Also a type of humorous verse.
Lin Burmese: bright.
Linart Croatian form of Leonard.
Linas *See* Linus.
Lincoln Old English: the settlement at the lake or pool. The name of an English city.
Lind/Lindan/Linden *See* Lyndon.
Lindberg Teutonic: the hill of the lime trees.
Lindell Old English: from the valley of lime trees.
Lyndell.
Lindeman The name of a Queensland island and a well-known Australian winemaking family. Of German origin.
Lindesay *See* Lindsay.
Lindfield Old English: the lime-tree field. The name of a Sydney suburb.
Linfield, Lyndfield, Lynfield.
Lindley Old English: from the lime-tree meadow.
Lindon *See* Lyndon.
Lindsay Scottish: from an old surname. Also a girl's name.
Lindesay, Lindsey, Lindsy.
Lineham *See* Lyneham.
Linford Old English: from the lime-tree ford.

Lynford.
Link Middle English: a bond or connection.
Linke, Lynk, Lynke.
Links/Linkse *See* Lynx.
Linley Old English: from the field of flax. Also a girl's name.
Linleigh, Lynleigh, Lynley.
Lino Portuguese and Spanish forms of Linus.
Leeno.
Linton Old English: from the flax farm or enclosure.
Linten, Lynten, Lynton.
Linu Hindi: a lily.
Linus Greek: flaxen-haired.
Linas, Lino (Portuguese, Spanish), *Lynas, Lynus.*
Linwood Old English: a lime-tree wood.
Lynwood.
Linx/Linxe *See* Lynx.
Lionel Old French: a young lion. *See also* Leander, Leo and Leonard.
Leonel, Leonell, Leonello (Italian), *Leonilo, Lionell, Lyonel, Lyonell.*
Liron Hebrew: my song.
Lyron.
Lisle *See* Lyle.
Lister Old English: one who dyes fabric.
Lyster.
Liston An English placename.
Listen, Listyn.
Litton Old English: from the place

on the river.
Lytton.
Livingston Old English: a dear friend's place.
Livingstone.
Livio Italian: one who is resentful.
Ljubo/Ljubomir *See* Lubomir.
Llewellyn Welsh: lion-like, a leader or ruler. *See also* Lewis.
Lewis, Llewellen, Llewhellyn, Llywelyn.
Diminutives: Lleu, Llew, Lyn, Lynn.
Lleyton *See* Leighton.
Lloyd Welsh: grey-haired.
Floyd, Llwyd (Welsh), *Loyd.*
Lluís Spanish form of Louis.
Llyndan/Llynden/Llyndon *See* Lyndon.
Llyr Welsh form of Lear.
Lobo Spanish: a wolf. *See also* Lupus.
Lobsang Sherpa/Tibetan: the kind-hearted one.
Loch Scottish Gaelic: a lake.
Diminutives: Lochie, Lochtie.
Lochie/Lochtie *See* Lachlan and Loch.
Lochinvar Scottish Gaelic: the hilltop loch or lake.
Lockinvar, Lokinvar.
Lochlainn/Lochlan/Lochlann *See* Lachlan.
Lochsley/Locksley *See* Loxley.
Locke Old English: from the stronghold.
Lock.
Lockelan/Lockelin/Lockelyn *See* Lachlan.
Lockey/Lockie/Locky *See* Lachlan.
Locklan/Locklin/Locklyn *See* Lachlan.
Lockwood Old English: from the enclosed wood.
Lockyer Old English: a locksmith
Lockyear.
Loclan/Loclyn *See* Lachlan.
Lodewijk/Lodewikus *See* Louis.
Lodge Old French: a hut or cottage.
Lodg, Lodj, Lodje.
Lodovico *See* Louis.
Loftus Old Norse: a house with a loft.
Lofthouse.
Logan Scottish Gaelic: a little hollow.
Loha Nepali: like iron.
Loic A French form of Louis.
Lok Chinese: happiness.
Loki Old Norse: the mythological god of fire. He was known for being a trickster, and represented change and disruption.
Lokinvar *See* Lochinvar.
Loksley *See* Loxley.
Loman Irish Gaelic: enlightened. The name of several early Irish saints.
Lomax An English surname, meaning the retreat by the pool.
Lomas.
Lombard Latin: long-bearded.
Lon/Lonnie Diminutives of

Alphonso and Laurence.
Lonato Native American: flint.
London The capital of England.
Londen, Londin.
Long Chinese: a dragon.
Longino Italian: from Longinus, the name of an early saint.
Longinus.
Lonsdale Old English: the valley of the River Lune. An English placename.
Lorand/Lorant Hungarian forms of Roland.
Lorcan Irish Gaelic: a fierce little one.
Loren/Lorencio/Lorenz/Lorenzo *See* Laurence.
Lorimer Old French: a spur-maker.
Lorimar, Lorrimar, Lorrimer.
Lorin *See* Laurence.
Loring Teutonic: a man from Lorraine, a former French province (now part of Alsace-Lorraine).
Lorne English/Scottish: from a placename in Scotland. *See also* Laurence.
Lorn.
Lorrimar/Lorrimer *See* Lorimer.
Lote A Fijian name, well known due to rugby player Lote Tuqiri.
Loti.
Lothair/Lothar/Lothario *See* Luther.
Lou/Louie *See* Lewis and Louis.
Loudon A Scottish placename, possibly meaning a low valley.
Loudan, Louden, Lughdan,
Lughden, Lughdon.
Loughlin *See* Lachlan.
Louis Teutonic: a famous warrior. The name of sixteen French kings. *See also* Lewis.
Lajos (Hungarian), *Lewis, Lluís* (Spanish), *Lodewijk* (Slavic), *Lodewikus* (Slavic), *Lodovico* (Italian), *Loic* (French), *Ludi* (Swiss), *Ludovic* (Scottish), *Ludovicus* (Dutch), *Ludvig* (Scandinavian), *Ludvik* (Czech), *Ludwig* (German), *Ludwik* (Polish), *Luigi* (Italian), *Luis* (Portuguese, Spanish), *Luiz* (Portuguese), *Luthais* (Scottish Gaelic).
Diminutives: Gino (Italian), Lewie, Lewy, Lou, Louie, Ludo (Dutch, Scottish Gaelic).
Louka/Loukah *See* Luke.
Lourenço Portuguese form of Laurence.
Lovel/Lovell *See* Lowell.
Lovemore Old English: from love's moor.
Lovemoor.
Lovrenc Croatian and Slovene forms of Laurence.
Diminutive: Lovro.
Lowan Aboriginal: a mallee fowl.
Lowell Old French: a little wolf.
Lovel, Lovell, Lowel.
Lowrey/Lowrie/Lowry Diminutives of Laurence.
Lowsen/Lowson *See* Lawson.

Loxley Old English: the place of a lock of hair.
Lochsley, Locksley, Loksley.

Loxton Old English: the town of a lock of hair.
Loxten.

Loyal Old French: true, faithful.
Loyale.

Loyd *See* Lloyd.

Lubomir Slavic: excellence.
Ljubomir, Lubomer, Lubomyr.
Diminutives: Ljubo, Lubo.

Luc/Luca/Lucais/Lucas *See* Luke.

Lucan *See* Lucian.

Lucian Latin: light. *See also* Luke.
Lucan (Irish), *Lucentio, Luciano* (Italian, Portuguese, Spanish), *Lucias, Lucien* (French), *Lucio* (Italian, Spanish), *Lucius, Lukan, Luzio* (Italian).
Diminutives: Luce, Lukey.

Lucio/Lucius *See* Lucian.

Lucretius Latin: gain. An early Roman poet.

Ludi Swiss form of Louis.

Ludlow Old English: from the prince's hill.

Ludo Dutch and Scottish Gaelic diminutives of Louis. Italian: light or brightness.

Ludomir Slavic: the peaceful one.
Ludomer, Ludomyr.

Ludovic *See* Lewis and Louis.

Ludvig/Ludvik/Ludwig/Ludwik *See* Louis.

Luger German: a type of gun.
Lugar.

Lugh Irish Gaelic: the name of a mythological sun god.
Luw.

Lughdan/Lughdon *See* Loudon.

Luigi/Luis/Luiz *See* Louis.

Luka/Lukah/Lukan *See* Lucian and Luke.

Lukas/Lukasz *See* Luke.

Luke Greek: a man from Lucania. One of Christ's apostles, the author of the third book of the New Testament. *See also* Lucian.
Louka, Loukah, Luc (French, Welsh), *Luca* (Italian), *Lucah, Lucais* (Scottish), *Lucas, Luka* (Russian), *Lukah, Lukan, Lukas* (German, Swedish), *Lukasz* (Polish), *Ruka* (Maori).
Diminutive: Lukey.

Lukener A form of Luke.
Luckner.

Lukey *See* Lucian and Luke.

Lund *See* Lunt.

Lundy French: born on Monday. The name of an island off the coast of England.
Lundi (French), *Lunedi* (Italian), *Lunes* (Spanish).

Lunedi/Lunes *See* Lundy.

Lunt Old Norse: from the sacred wood.
Lund.

Lupus Latin: a wolf. *See also* Lobo.
Lupe, Lupinus, Lupo (Hawaiian, Italian).

Lute Middle English: a stringed musical instrument.
Luthais Scottish Gaelic form of Louis.
Luther Old French: a lute player. Teutonic: a famous warrior.
Lothair, Lothaire, Lothar (German), *Lothario* (Italian).
Luw *See* Lugh.
Lux Latin: light.
Luzio *See* Lucian.
Lyall/Lyel/Lyell *See* Lyle.
Lyam A variation of Liam. *See* William.
Lyberio/Lybero *See* Libero.
Lycidas Greek: the son of the wolf.
Lyford Old English: from the ford where flax grows.
Lyforde.
Lyle Old French: from the island.
Lial, Liall, Liel, Liell, Lisle (French), *Lyal, Lyall, Lyel, Lyell.*
Lyman Old English: a man from the meadow or valley.
Layman, Leyman.
Lyn/Lynn Diminutives of the Welsh name Llewellyn.
Lynas *See* Linus.
Lyndan/Lynden *See* Lyndon.
Lyndell *See* Lindell.
Lyndfield/Lynfield *See* Lindfield.
Lyndon Old English: from the hill of the lime trees.
Lind, Lindan, Linden, Lindon, Llyndan, Llynden, Llyndon, Lyden, Lydon, Lyndan, Lynden.
Lyneham Old English: from the flax meadow.
Lineham, Lynham.
Lynford *See* Linford.
Lynk/Lynke *See* Link.
Lynleigh/Lynley *See* Linley.
Lynten/Lynton *See* Linton.
Lynus *See* Linus.
Lynwood *See* Linwood.
Lynx English from Greek: a North American wild cat. The name of a constellation.
Links, Linkse, Linx, Linxe, Lynxe.
Lyon A form of Leon. *See* Leonard.
Lyonel/Lyonell *See* Lionel.
Lyons The son of Lyon or Leon. *See* Leonard.
Lyron *See* Liron.
Lysander Greek: the liberator.
Lyster *See* Lister.
Lytton *See* Litton.

M

Maag *See* Magh.
Maaka Maori form of Mark.
Maanu *See* Manu.
Maardi *See* Mardi.
Maart The Dutch name for March.
Maarten Dutch form of Martin.
Mabon Welsh: a son.
Mac Scottish: the son of; a diminutive of names beginning with Mac. *See also* Mack.
Mc.

Macalla Aboriginal: the full moon.
Maccalla.

Macarius Latin: blessed.
Macharios, Makarios (Greek).

Macarthur Scottish Gaelic: the son of Arthur.
McArthur.

Macauley Irish and Scottish Gaelic: the son of Olaf.
McAulay, McAuley.

Macbeth A Scottish name, best known from the Shakespearean play of the same name.
McBeth.

McCall Scottish Gaelic: son of the warlike one.
Maccall.

McCartney Scottish Gaelic: the son of Arthur.
Macartney, McArtney.

McClelland Scottish Gaelic: the son of the follower of St Fillan.
McClellan.

Macdonald Scottish Gaelic: the son of Donald.
Macdonnell, MacDonnell, McDonald, McDonnell.

McDougall Irish and Scottish Gaelic: the son of Dougall.
McDougal, McDowall, McDowell.

Mace Middle English: the name of a spice.
Maice, Mayce, Mayse.

McEwan Scottish Gaelic: the son of Ewan.
McEwen, McEwing.

Macey Old English: little Matthew. Also a girl's name.
Macy.

McFarlane Scottish Gaelic: a common surname.
Macfarlan, Macfarland, Macfarlane, McFarlan, McFarland, McFarlane.

McGill *See* Magill.

MacGregor Scottish Gaelic: the son of Gregor or Gregory.
McGregor.

Macha Nepali: a fish.

Machanu Thai: a half-fish mythological figure.

McHardy Scottish Gaelic: the son of Sloe.
MacHardie, MacHardy, McHardie.

Macharios *See* Macarius.

Machi The Swahili name for March.

Macho Spanish: manly or virile.
Matcho.

Maciej Polish form of Matthew.

McInnes Scottish Gaelic: the son of Angus.
Macinnes.

McIntosh Scottish Gaelic: son of the chieftain.
MacIntosh, Mackintosh.

Mack Scottish: a diminutive of Mac names.
Mac.

Mackay Gaelic: son of the fiery one.
Magee, Makay, McKay.

McKenna Irish Gaelic: the son of Ken or Kenneth. Also a girl's name.
Mackenna, MacKenna, Makenna.

Mackenzie Scottish Gaelic: the son of the handsome one. *See also* Kenzie.
MacKensie, MacKenzie, McKenzie, Mekenzee, Mekenzie.

Macklin Irish Gaelic: possibly the Irish form of MacLean.
Macklan, Maklan, Maklin.

McLaren Scottish Gaelic: the son of Laurence.
Maclaren.

Maclean Scottish Gaelic: the son of the follower of St John.
Maclaine, MacLaine, Maclayne, McLaine, McLane, McLean.

Macleod Scottish Gaelic: the son of the ugly one.
McCleod.

McMahon Irish Gaelic: the son of the bear.
MacMahon.

McNicol Scottish Gaelic: the son of Nicholas.
MacNichol, MacNicol, McNichol.

McPherson Scottish Gaelic: the son of the parson.
Macpherson, MacPherson.

Macquarie Scottish Gaelic: the son of Godfrey.
McQuarie.

McTavish Scottish Gaelic: the son of Thomas, a twin. *See also* Tavish.
MacTavish.

Macy *See* Macey.

Maddoc/Maddock/Maddox *See* Madoc.

Madison Old English: the son of Maud or Matthew. Also a girl's name.
Maddison.

Madoc Old Welsh: fortunate. The name of a saint.
Maddoc, Maddock, Maddox, Madog, Madok (Cornish), *Maedoc, Maidoc.*

Madron Latin: a nobleman. A Cornish placename and the name of a saint.

Maedoc *See* Madoc.

Maehe Maori: the month of March.

Maeson *See* Mason.

Maex A diminutive of Maximilian and Maxwell.

Magdi *See* Majid.

Magee *See* Mackay.

Maggio *See* Maios.

Magh Sanskrit: the month of February.
Maag.

Maghnus Irish Gaelic form of Magnus.

Magill Scottish Gaelic: son of the stranger or servant.
McGill.

Magni Old Norse: the son of Thor, the Norse god of thunder.
Magny.

Magnus Latin: the great one. Generally a Scandinavian name.

Maghnus (Irish Gaelic), *Magnuss*, *Mànas* (Scottish Gaelic), *Manus* (Irish), *Mogens* (Danish).

Magus Greek: a magician or priest.

Maha A Buddhist name, meaning great, or the great one.

Mahal Hindi: a palace.

Mahdi Arabic: one who is guided.

Mahé French: the main island of the Seychelles.

Mahela An unusual name from Sri Lanka.

Mahendra Sanskrit: the great god Indra (the god of the sky). *Mahindra, Mohinder.*

Mahesh Sanskrit: a great ruler.

Mahfuz Arabic: one who is safe-guarded. *Mahfouz.*

Mahinda Sanskrit: of the earth. *Mahin.*

Mahindra See Mahendra.

Mahir Hebrew: industrious.

Mahlon See Marlon.

Mahmood Arabic: praiseworthy. See also Muhammad. *Mahmud, Mehmed* (Turkish), *Mehmet* (Turkish).

Mahomet/Mahommed See Muhammad.

Mahon Irish: a bear.

Mahsen/Mahson See Mason.

Mahsood See Masud.

Maice See Mace.

Maidoc See Madoc.

Maik/Maikel Dutch forms of Mike and Michael.

Maine The name of a US state. *Main, Mayn, Mayne.*

Maios Greek: the month of May. *Maggio* (Italian), *Maio* (Portuguese), *Mayo* (Spanish).

Maison See Mason.

Maitland Old French: from the meadow land.

Maji Swahili: water.

Majid Arabic: the illustrious one. *Magdi, Majeed, Majed, Majd, Majdi.*

Major Middle English: greater, larger or superior. *Majors.*

Maka Aboriginal: a small fire. Maori: the name of a South Island (New Zealand) chief and a form of Mark. *Makah.*

Makaha Hawaiian: fierce.

Makai Hawaiian: towards the sea.

Makani Hawaiian: the wind. The name of a storm god.

Makar Sanskrit: a crocodile, from Makara, the Hindi name for Capricorn.

Makarios See Macarius.

Makay See Mackay.

Makenna See McKenna.

Makis Greek form of Michael.

Maklan/Maklin See Macklan.

Mako The name of a shark.

Makoa Maori/Polynesian: either a form of Maaka (Mark), or from Maka.

Makoto Japanese: honest and sincere.
Maks/Makswell *See* Maximilian and Maxwell.
Maksim *See* Maximilian.
Maksym.
Makya Native American: the eagle hunter.
Mal Diminutive of Malcolm, Malden and other names.
Malachi Hebrew: the messenger of the Lord. A prophet in the Bible. *Malachai, Malachidiel, Malachy, Malaki, Malchi* (French).
Malachite Greek: a green mineral, used for making jewellery. *Malakite.*
Malakee/Malaki *See* Malachi.
Malakite *See* Malachite.
Malara The morning star (Venus) in New Guinea legend.
Malawi Native American: flaming. Also the name of an African country.
Malchi French form of Malachi.
Malcolm Scottish Gaelic: a follower of St Columba, known as the dove. *Malcom.*
Diminutive: Mal.
Malden Old English: from the hill with a monument. *Maldon.*
Diminutive: Mal.
Mali Hindi: a gardener.
Malik Arabic: the master or king. *Maleek, Malek.*
Malin Old English: a little warrior.
Malise Scottish Gaelic: the servant of Jesus.
Mallee Aboriginal: scrubland. *Malley, Mallie.*
Mallory Old French: unlucky. Also a girl's name. *Malory.*
Malo French: the name of a saint. Hawaiian: the winner.
Malone Irish Gaelic: a devotee of St John.
Malu Aboriginal: thunder. *Maloo.*
Malvern Old Welsh: the bare hill.
Malvil/Malville/Malvin/Malvyn *See* Melville.
Malvolio A character in Shakespeare's *Twelfth Night.*
Mamdouh Arabic: the praised one. *Mamdooh, Mamdou, Mamduh.*
Mamo Hawaiian: yellow.
Mamoru Japanese: the earth.
Manaia Maori: a seahorse.
Mànas *See* Magnus.
Manchu Chinese: pure.
Mandel Jewish: a little man. Teutonic: an almond.
Mandir Hindi/Nepali: a temple.
Mandu Aboriginal: the sun.
Manel Catalan form of Manuel (*see* Emmanuel).
Manfield Old English: from the communal field.
Manfred Teutonic: a man of peace. *Manfredo* (Italian), *Manfrid, Manfried* (German).
Mangal Sanskrit: born on a Tuesday.

Also a name for the planet Mars. *Mangalvar* (Urdu).
Mani Aboriginal: a creek. Sanskrit: a jewel. Also the name of a Norse moon god.
Manjano Swahili: yellow.
Manley Middle English: brave and manly. *Manly.*
Manmohan Sanskrit: one who is pleasing.
Mannie/Manny *See* Emmanuel.
Manning Old English: the man.
Mannix Irish Gaelic: a little monk. *Mannex, Mannox.*
Mano Hawaiian: a shark.
Manoel *See* Emmanuel.
Manoj Sanskrit: born of the mind. *Manoth.*
Manolis Greek: possibly a form of Emmanuel.
Manraj Sanskrit: probably meaning a great mind.
Mansa African: a king.
Mansell An English surname, possibly meaning a person from Le Mans, France. *Mansel.*
Mansfield Old English: the field by the hill.
Manson Literally the son of a man. *Mansan, Mansen.*
Mansoor Arabic: victorious. *Mansour, Mansur.*
Mantra Sanskrit: a prayer or incantation. Can also be a girl's name.
Manu Polynesian/Samoan: the man of the birds. Sanskrit: one who is wise. *Maanu.*
Manuel The angel of the zodiac sign of Cancer. Also the Spanish form of Emmanuel. *Manuelle, Menuel.*
Manus Irish form of Magnus.
Manzano Spanish: an apple tree.
Manzo Japanese: the third son.
Maqbul Arabic: one who is approved. *Maqbool.*
Marack/Marak *See* Marrick.
Marama Polynesian: the moon man.
Maran *See* Maren.
Marat A Russian and French name, after Jean-Paul Marat, a scientist and physician.
Marathon The name of a Greek town.
Marawa A spider god in Melanesian legend.
Marc/Marcel/Marceli/Marcelinho/Marcello *See* Mark.
March Latin: a month name, from Mars, the Roman god of war. *See also* Mardi, Mark and Mars. *Maart* (Dutch), *Machi* (Swahili), *Maehe* (Maori), *Marco* (Portuguese), *Mart* (Turkish), *Martios* (Greek), *Marts* (Danish), *Marz* (German), *Marzo* (Italian, Spanish), *Mawrth* (Welsh).
Marchant *See* Merchant.

Marcial *See* Martial.
Marcin Polish form of Mark.
Marco/Marcos/Marcus *See* Mark.
Marconi Italian: after the wireless telegraph inventor, Guglielmo Marconi.
Mardi French: Tuesday, after Mars, the Roman god of war.
Maardi, Mardy, Martedi (Italian), *Martes* (Spanish).
Marduk The chief Babylonian sun god.
Marek *See* Mark.
Maren Basque: from the sea. *See also* Marion.
Maran, Marin, Maron.
Marian/Mariano/Marianus *See* Marion and Marius.
Marick *See* Marick.
Marien *See* Marion.
Marijan Slavic: a form of Marianus (*see* Marius).
Marik Czech form of Mark.
Marin *See* Maren and Marino.
Marinko A diminutive of Marino.
Marino Latin: of the sea. Masculine form of Marina.
Mariano (Spanish), *Marin* (Slavic), *Marinus* (Dutch).
Diminutives: Marinko (Slavic), Rino (Italian), Rinus (Dutch).
Marinus Dutch form of Marino and Marius.
Mario *See* Marius.
Marion Old French from Latin: little Mary. Most often a girl's name.
Maren, Marian, Marien.
Marius Latin: virile; the warlike one. From a Roman family name. *See also* Mark and Martin.
Marian (Polish), *Mariano* (Italian, Spanish), *Marianus, Marijan* (Slavic), *Marinus* (Dutch), *Mario* (Italian, Spanish), *Mariusz* (Polish).
Diminutive: Rinus (Dutch).
Marjan Swahili: coral.
Mark Latin: from Marcus, which relates to Mars, the god of war. One of the four New Testament envangelists. *See also* Marius, Mars and Martin.
Maaka (Maori), *Maka* (Maori), *Marc* (French, Welsh), *Marcel* (French), *Marceli* (Polish), *Marcelinho* (Portuguese), *Marcell* (German, Hungarian), *Marcelli, Marcellin* (French), *Marcellino* (Italian), *Marcello* (Italian), *Marcellus* (French), *Marcelo* (Portuguese), *Marcin* (Polish), *Marcius, Marco* (Italian, Spanish), *Marcos* (Portuguese), *Marcus, Marek* (Czech, Polish), *Marik* (Czech), *Markku* (Finnish), *Marko* (Slavic), *Markos* (Greek), *Markus* (German), *Marsel, Marsell, Marshello, Marzell* (German).
Markham Old English: the homestead by the boundary.
Markku/Marko/Markos/Markus *See* Mark.

Marland Old English: from the lake land.
Marlee/Marleigh *See* Marley.
Marlen *See* Marlon.
Marley Old English: from the pleasant meadow.
Marlee, Marleigh, Marli, Marlie, Marly.
Marlin The name of a fish. *See also* Marlon.
Marlon Old French: a little hawk.
Mahlon, Marlen, Marlin.
Marlow Old English: from the lake or pond.
Marlowe.
Marly *See* Marley.
Marmaduke Irish: the servant of Madoc.
Diminutive: Duke.
Marmion French: the tiny one.
Maron Greek: a character from Greek mythology. *See also* Maren and Marron.
Maroo *See* Maru.
Maroon English from French: a 'colour name'. *See also* Marron.
Marquis French: a nobleman.
Marques, Marquest, Marquist.
Marrick Old Norse: from the ridge.
Marack, Marak, Marick, Marrack, Marrak.
Marriott A diminutive of Mary (a bitterly wanted child).
Marriot.
Marron Aboriginal: a leaf. French: brown, or a chestnut. Spanish: brown.
Maron.
Marroo Aboriginal: black.
Mars Latin: the Roman god of war (the equivalent of the Greek god Ares) and the ruler of the zodiac sign of Aries. *See also* March, Marius, Mark and Martin.
Marz, Mawrth (Welsh).
Marsden Old English: from the valley boundary.
Marsel/Marsell *See* Mark.
Marsena Persian: dignified.
Marsh Old English: from the marshy land.
Marshall Teutonic: a horse-keeper, or a steward.
Marshal, Marshel, Marshell.
Marshel/Marshell *See* Marshall.
Marshello *See* Mark.
Marsland Old English: marshy land.
Marston Old English: the place by the marsh.
Marsten.
Mart *See* March and Martin.
Mártan Irish Gaelic form of Martin.
Martedi/Martes *See* Mardi.
Martel A diminutive of Martin.
Martell.
Marten *See* Martin.
Marthavan A Sri Lankan name of uncertain meaning.
Marti Aboriginal: a rock. Also a diminutive of Martin.
Martial Middle English: brave or warlike. From Mars, the Roman

god of war.
Marcial (Spanish), *Martialis*.

Martin Latin: of Mars, the Roman god of war. *See also* Marius and Mark.
Maarten (Dutch), *Mártan* (Irish Gaelic), *Marten, Martien, Martijn* (Dutch), *Martino* (Italian), *Martinus, Martius, Marton* (Hungarian), *Martti* (Finnish), *Martyn, Merten* (German), *Morten* (Danish). *Diminutives:* Mart, Martel, Martell, Marti, Martie, Marty.

Martineau French: either a form of Martin, or from martinet, meaning a disciplinarian.

Martios/Marts *See* March.

Marton Hungarian form of Martin.

Martti Finnish form of Martin.

Marty/Martyn *See* Martin.

Martyr Someone with strong convictions.

Maru Aboriginal: black. Polynesian: the god of war.
Maroo.

Marv/Marvi/Marvin/Marvyn *See* Mervyn.

Marwen An unusual name, possibly a form of Marvin. *See* Mervyn.
Marwenn, Marwin, Marwinn.

Marwood Old English: from the large wood.

Marz/Marzo *See* March and Mars.

Marzell German form of Mark.

Masa Japanese: good.

Masahiro Japanese: goodness.

Masaki Japanese: true happiness.
Masaaki.

Mascot Something that brings good luck.
Mascott, Mascotte.

Masen *See* Mason.

Masih Arabic: a messenger.
Maseeh, Massih.

Maslin Old French: a twin.
Maslinn, Mazlin, Mazlinn.

Mason Old French: a stonemason.
Maeson, Mahsen, Mahson, Maisen, Maison, Masen, Maysen, Mayson, Mehsen, Mehson.

Massih *See* Masih.

Massimo/Massimiliano *See* Maximilian.

Masud Arabic: the fortunate one.
Mahsood, Masoud, Mesut (Turkish).

Mat/Mata *See* Matthew.

Matai Maori: to gaze out to sea.

Matangi Samoan: the wind.
Matagi.

Matareka Polynesian: the one with a smiling face.

Matari Aboriginal: a man.

Matcho *See* Macho.

Matej Slavic form of Matthew.
Maté, Matja.

Mateo/Mateus/Mateusz *See* Matthew.

Mathias/Mathieu/Mathiu/Matias *See* Matthew.

Matic A Slavic form of Matthew.

Matiu Maori form of Matthew.
Matja *See* Matej.
Matko Slavic diminutive of Matej (*see* Matthew).
Mato *See* Matu.
Maton A diminutive of Mat or Matt (*see* Matthew).
Matton.
Matong Aboriginal: strong or great.
Matrix A scientific and mathematical term, meaning what gives form or origin to something.
Matriks.
Mats *See* Matthew.
Matthew Hebrew: a gift of God. One of the twelve apostles and the author of the first book of the New Testament. *See also* Macey and Madison.
Maciej (Polish), *Mata* (Scottish Gaelic), *Matej* (Slavic), *Mateo* (Spanish), *Mateus* (Portuguese), *Mateusz* (Polish), *Mathew, Mathias, Mathieu* (French), *Mathiu, Matias* (Spanish), *Matic* (Slavic), *Matiu* (Maori), *Matja* (Slavic), *Mats* (Swedish), *Matteo* (Italian), *Mattew, Matthaios, Mattheus, Matthias, Matti* (Finnish), *Matz* (German).
Diminutives: Mat, Matko (Slavic), Maton, Matt, Matte (German), Matti, Mattie, Matton, Matty, Thies (Dutch), Thijs (Dutch).
Matti/Mattie/Matty *See* Matthew.
Matton *See* Maton and Matthew.

Matu Native American: a brave warrior. Polynesian: the north wind. *Mato.*
Matya Aboriginal: bold or brave.
Matz German form of Matthew.
Maui Polynesian: a legendary hero. The name of a Hawaiian island.
Maunga Maori: a mountain.
Maurese *See* Maurice.
Mauri Finnish form of Maurice.
Maurice Latin: dark-skinned, like a Moor. *See also* Morrison.
Maurese, Mauri (Finnish), *Mauricio* (Spanish), *Maurise, Mauritz, Maurizio* (Italian), *Mauro* (Italian), *Maurycy* (Slavic), *Merrick* (Welsh), *Meurig* (Welsh), *Morice, Moritz* (German), *Moriz* (Russian), *Morrell, Morrice, Morris, Morriss, Morse, Muiris* (Irish).
Diminutives: Maurie, Maury, Mo, Moe, Morey, Morrie, Morry.
Mauro Italian form of Maurice.
Maverick American: a dissenter or a loner.
Mawgan Cornish: the name of a saint.
Mawnan Cornish: a placename and the name of a saint.
Mawrth The Welsh name for March and Mars.
Mawson The surname of a famous Antarctic explorer (Sir Douglas Mawson).
Mawsen.

Max A diminutive of Maximilian and Maxwell.

Maxence A modern name, derived from Max.
Maxsence.

Maxey Old English: from the island of Magnus. *See also* Maximilian and Maxwell.

Maxim/Maxime *See* Maximilian.

Maximilian Latin: the greatest.
Maksim (Russian), *Maksym*, *Massimiliano* (Italian), *Massimo* (Italian), *Maxim*, *Maxime* (French), *Maximilien* (French), *Maximillian*, *Maximillien*, *Maximo*, *Maximus*, *Maxium*.
Diminutives: Maex, Maks, Max, Maxey, Maxi, Maxx, Maxy.

Maxwell Scottish Gaelic: from the stream of Magnus.
Makswell.
Diminutives: Maex, Maks, Max, Maxey, Maxi, Maxx, Maxy.

Maxy *See* Maximilian and Maxwell.

Mayce *See* Mace.

Mayer *See* Meir.

Mayn/Mayne *See* Maine.

Maynard Teutonic: strong and brave.
Meinard (German).

Mayo Spanish for the month of May (*see* Maios).

Mayon Sanskrit: the black god.

Mayse/Maysen/Mayson *See* Mace and Mason.

Mazhar Turkish: one who is honoured.
Mazher.

Mazin Arabic: rain clouds.
Mazen.

Mazlin/Mazlinn *See* Maslin.

Mc names – *See* Mac.

Mead Old English: from the meadow.
Meade.

Meadows Old English: from the meadow.
Meddowes, Meddows.

Mearann Aboriginal: to call.

Medhat *See* Midhat.

Medi The Welsh name for September.

Medway Old English: the way of the meadow.

Medwin Old English: a friend from the meadow.
Medwinn, Medwyn, Medwynn.

Mefin/Mefyn Welsh forms of Mervyn.

Mehill Albanian form of Michael.

Mehmed/Mehmet Turkish forms of Mahmood.

Mehsen/Mehson *See* Mason.

Meic/Meical Welsh forms of Mike and Michael.

Meilyr Welsh: a man of iron.

Meinard *See* Maynard.

Meine Dutch/German: the strong one.
Diminutive: Menno.

Meir Hebrew: one who gives light.
Mayer, Meier, Meyer, Myer.

Meirion Welsh: a traditional name of uncertain meaning.

Meka Hawaiian: the eyes.
Mekari Aboriginal: new.
Mekenzee/Mekenzie *See* Mackenzie.
Mel A diminutive of names such as Melville and Melvin.
Melan Greek: the dark or black one. The masculine form of Melanie.
Mellan.
Melburn Old English: from the millstream.
Melbourn, Melbourne, Milbourn, Milbourne, Milburn.
Melchior Persian: the king of the city. One of the three Magi in the Bible.
Melchor, Melek (Jewish).
Meldrum Scottish Gaelic: from the bare ridge.
Melldrum.
Melek *See* Melchior.
Melford Old English: from the ford by the hill.
Mellan *See* Melan.
Mellor/Melor *See* Mylor.
Melrose Old English: from the bare moor.
Melton Old English: from the middle farm.
Melten.
Melville Old French: from the bad or poor settlement.
Malvil, Malvill, Malville, Malvin, Malvyn, Melvil, Melvill, Melvin, Melvyn.
Diminutive: Mel.
Melvin/Melvyn *See* Melville.

Memphis The Ancient Egyptian capital and a city in Tennessee, the USA. Also a girl's name.
Memphys.
Menachem Hebrew: the comforter. An Old Testament name.
Menahem, Menchem, Mendel.
Menadue Cornish: from the dark hill.
Mendel *See* Menachem.
Mendoza Basque: a mountain.
Menelaus A king of Sparta in Greek legend. The name of a character in Shakespeare's *Troilus and Cressida*.
Menno *See* Meine.
Mensa African: the third, or third-born son
Mensah.
Mentor Greek: a counsellor or advisor. The name of a wise old man in Greek mythology.
Mentu The falcon-headed Ancient Egyptian god of war.
Menu The Baltic god of the moon.
Menulis.
Menuel *See* Manuel.
Menzies Scottish: a well-known surname.
Merak Arabic: the loin of the bear. A star in the constellation of Ursa Major, the Great Bear.
Mercer Old French: a merchant.
Merchant Old French: a trader.
Marchant.
Mercher *See* Mercury.
Mercredi French: Wednesday;

literally Mercury's day.
Mercoledi (Italian).

Mercury Latin: the Roman messenger of the gods.
Mercher (Welsh), *Mercurino, Mercurio, Mercutio*.

Meredith Old Welsh: a lord. Also a girl's name.
Meredeth, Meredyth, Merideth, Meridith, Meridyth.

Mereki Aboriginal: a peacemaker.

Merewyn *See* Mervyn.

Merfyn Welsh form of Mervyn.

Merick/Merik *See* Merrick.

Merivale Old English: a pleasant valley. Also a girl's name.

Merle Old French: a blackbird. More commonly a girl's name.

Merlin Old Welsh: from the fort by the sea, or the falcon. The legendary magician from the court of King Arthur.
Merlyn, Myrddin.

Merren/Merrin *See* Merryn.

Merrick Welsh form of Maurice.
Merick, Merik, Merrik, Meyrick.

Merrill Old English: the son of Muriel.
Merrell, Merril, Meryll.

Merryn Cornish: the name of a saint and a village. Also a girl's name.
Merren, Merrin, Meryn.

Merten *See* Martin and Merton.

Merton Old English: the place by the lake.
Merten.

Merv/Mervi *See* Merville and Mervyn.

Merville Possibly from Mervyn.
Mervil, Mervill, Mervyl, Mervyll, Mervylle.
Diminutives: Merv, Mervi.

Mervyn Old English: a famous friend. *See also* Marwen.
Marvin, Marvyn, Mefin (Welsh), *Mefyn* (Welsh), *Merewyn, Merfyn* (Welsh), *Mervin, Merwin, Merwyn, Myrven, Myrvin*.
Diminutives: Marv, Marvi, Merv, Mervi.

Merwin/Merwyn *See* Mervyn.

Meryll *See* Merrill.

Meryn *See* Merryn.

Mesut Turkish form of Masud.

Metin Turkish: strong.

Meurig Welsh form of Maurice.

Meyer Teutonic: a farmer. *See also* Meir.

Meyrick *See* Merrick.

Mial/Miall *See* Myall.

Mica Latin: the name of a mineral.

Micah A Hebrew form of Michael, mentioned in the Bible.
Mika (Maori).

Miceal *See* Michael.

Michael Hebrew: like the Lord. One of the archangels in the Bible. *See also* Mitchell.
Maikel (Dutch), *Makis* (Greek), *Mehill* (Albanian), *Meical* (Welsh), *Micah* (Hebrew), *Miceal, Michail* (Russian), *Michal* (Czech, Polish),

Michalis (Greek), *Michall*, *Micheál* (Scottish Gaelic), *Michel* (French), *Michele* (Italian), *Michelin*, *Michell* (Cornish), *Michiel* (Dutch), *Miguel* (Portuguese, Spanish), *Mihael* (Slavic), *Mihai* (Romanian), *Mihail* (Romanian), *Mihalis* (Greek), *Mihaly* (Hungarian), *Mihangel* (Welsh), *Mihovil* (Slavic), *Mika* (Finnish), *Mikael* (Swedish), *Mikaere* (Maori), *Mikail*, *Mikall*, *Mikel* (Slavic), *Mikele*, *Mikelis* (Latvian), *Mikell* (Scandinavian), *Mikhael*, *Mikhail* (Russian), *Mikkel* (Danish), *Mikko* (Finnish), *Miko* (Slavic), *Miquel* (Catalan), *Mitchel*, *Mitchell*, *Myall*, *Mychal*, *Mychael*, *Mykel*, *Mykell*, *Mykle*.
Diminutives: Maik (Dutch), Meic (Welsh), Mick, Micke (Scandinavian), Mickey, Mickie, Micky, Micko, Mike, Mikey, Mikie, Mikkeli, Mischa (Russian), Mishka (Russian), Miska (Hungarian), Misko (Slavic), Mitch, Myke, Myki, Mykie, Mykje, Quelo (Catalan).

Michal/Michall *See* Michael.

Michel/Michele/Michelin/Michell *See* Michael.

Michelangelo Italian from Hebrew: Michael the angel. The name of a legendary artist (Michelangelo Buonarroti).
Mikelangelo.

Michio Japanese: strong.

Mick/Mickey/Micko *See* Michael.

Midas Greek: a legendary figure who transformed all that he touched into gold.

Midgee Aboriginal: an acacia.
Midjee.

Midhat Arabic: commendation.
Medhat.

Midnight Literally the middle of the night.
Midnite.

Midwinter The middle of winter. Also a girl's name.
Midwynter.

Mieczyslaw Polish: the glory of the sword.

Miguel *See* Michael.

Mihael/Mihaly *See* Michael.

Mihai/Mihail Romanian forms of Michael.

Miharo Polynesian: a wanderer.

Mihovil Slavic form of Michael.

Mika Maori form of Micah. *See also* Michael.

Mikael/Mikail/Mikall *See* Michael.

Mikaere Maori form of Michael.

Mike/Mikel/Mikey *See* Michael.

Mikelangelo *See* Michelangelo.

Mikhael/Mikhail *See* Michael.

Miki Aboriginal: the moon. Japanese: a tree.

Mikkel/Mikkeli/Mikko *See* Michael.

Miklós/Mikulas Czech forms of Nicholas.

Miko Slavic form of Michael.
Mikolaj Polish form of Nicholas.
Miku Aboriginal: red.
Milan Czech: the favoured or beloved one. *See also* Milos.
Milad.
Diminutives: Mile, Milenko.
Milbourn/Milbourne/Milburn *See* Melburn.
Mile/Milenko Diminutives of Milan.
Miles Latin: a soldier. Teutonic: merciful.
Milles, Myles, Mylles.
Diminutives: Milo, Mylo.
Milford Old English: from the ford by the mill. A Welsh and New Zealand placename.
Millard Old English: the mill-keeper.
Millward.
Miller Old English: a grain-grinder or miller.
Millar, Milner.
Millhouse Old English: the house of the miller.
Milhouse.
Millthorpe Old English: the mill at the farm or village.
Milthorpe.
Millward *See* Millard.
Milne Old English: at the mill.
Miln, Myln, Mylne.
Milner *See* Miller.
Milo *See* Miles.
Miloje Slavic: one who is dear or gracious.
Diminutives: Milojica, Milojka.
Milorad Slavic: gracious care.
Diminutive: Rade.
Milos Czech: one who is loved or favoured. *See also* Milan.
Milosz (Slavic).
Miloslav Czech: one who is favoured by glory.
Miloslaw (Polish).
Milovan Slavic: one who is loved or caressed.
Milton Old English: from the town with a mill, or the middle farm.
Millton, Myllton, Mylton.
Diminutives: Milt, Mylt.
Milu The Polynesian god of the underworld.
Milutin Slavic: the dear one.
Mimas Greek: a satellite of the planet Saturn.
Min Burmese: a king.
Minar Aboriginal: a mark.
Ming Chinese: the name of a dynasty.
Mingan Native American: a grey wolf.
Mingma Sherpa/Tibetan: born on a Tuesday.
Minh Vietnamese: bright and clear.
Minik Greenlandic: possibly meaning whale oil.
Minos Greek: the son of Zeus in Greek mythology.
Miquel Catalan form of Michael.
Miran Slavic: the peaceful one.
Mirek A diminutive of Vitomir.

Mirko A diminutive of Miroslav.
Mirco (Italian).
Miro Aboriginal: a throwing stick. See also Miroslav and Vitomir.
Miron See Myron.
Miroslav Slavic: great glory.
Diminutives: Mirko, Miro.
Mirrabook Aboriginal: the constellation of the Southern Cross.
Mirza Sanskrit: a prince.
Mirzah.
Misbah Arabic: a lamp or light.
Mischa/Mishka See Michael.
Miska Hungarian: a diminutive of Mihaly (*see* Michael).
Misko Slavic diminutive of Mihael or Mihovil (*see* Michael).
Mitch Diminutive of Michael and Mitchell.
Mitcham Old English: from the large homestead.
Mitchell Old English: big. Also a form of Michael.
Mitchel, Mitchyl, Mitchyll, Mytchel, Mytchell.
Diminutives: Mitch, Mytch.
Mitford Old English: the ford where rivers meet.
Mithra Sanskrit: the Hindu and Persian god of the sun, the opposite of Varuna, god of the moon.
Mithras, Mitra.
Mitiaro Polynesian: the face of the ocean.
Mitja/Mitya Diminutives of Dmitri and Dmitriy, Russian forms of Demetrius.
Mladen Slavic: the young one.
Mo/Moe Diminutives of Maurice.
Moala Fijian: the name of a volcano.
Moana Maori/Polynesian: the sea or ocean. Also a girl's name.
Mochi Japanese: the full moon.
Modesto Italian: the masculine form of Modesty, meaning the moderate or modest one.
Modeste (French), *Modesty.*
Modred See Mordred.
Modris Latvian: alert.
Moffatt Scottish Gaelic: from the long plain.
Moffett, Moffitt.
Mogens See Magnus.
Mogo Aboriginal: a stone axe.
Mohamad/Mohamed/Mohammed See Muhammad.
Mohan Sanskrit: the bewitching one.
Mohanan, Mohin.
Mohandas Sanskrit: the servant of Mohan.
Mohd A diminutive of Muhammad.
Mohinder See Mahendra.
Mohit Sanskrit: attractive.
Mohsen/Mohsin See Muhsin.
Moises Portuguese form of Moses.
Mojo African-American: a magic charm bag.
Mojoe, Mojow, Mojowe.
Moke Hawaiian form of Moses.
Mokhtar See Mukhtar.
Moki Aboriginal: cloudy.
Moko Polynesian: a mythological

lizard god.
Mokoiro Polynesian: a mythological figure.
Molloy Irish Gaelic: a venerable chieftain.
Monaro A New South Wales placename, probably from an Aboriginal word.
Monash The surname of a famous Australian military commander.
Monasch, Monasche, Monashe.
Monday English from Latin: the day of the moon.
Mondai, Mondaie, Montag (German).
Mondo Swahili: a serval cat.
Mondrian After Piet Mondrian, an early 20th-century Dutch artist.
Mondriaan.
Monro/Monroe *See* Munro.
Monsa Native American: the shaft of an arrow.
Monsah.
Montag *See* Monday.
Montague Old French: from the pointed hill.
Montagu.
Diminutives: Monte, Montey, Monty.
Montana Latin: from the mountains. The name of a US state.
Monte Italian: a mountain. *See also* Montague, Montgomery and Montmorency.
Montel (Spanish), *Montes* (Italian), *Montez* (Spanish).

Montefiore Italian: a mountain of flowers.
Montego Spanish: mountainous.
Montel/Montes/Montez *See* Monte.
Montey/Monty Diminutives of Montague, Montgomery and Montmorency.
Montfort English from French: the fort on the hill.
Montforte, Mountfort, Mountforte.
Montgomery Old French: from the hill of the powerful man.
Montgomerie.
Diminutives: Monte, Montey, Monty.
Monti Aboriginal: a stork.
Montmorency Old French: from the hill of Maurentius.
Diminutives: Monte, Montey, Monty.
Montrose Scottish Gaelic: the moor on the cape.
Moorak Aboriginal: a mountain.
Morak.
Morado Spanish: the colour violet.
Moran A common Irish surname.
Morandoo Aboriginal: the sea.
Morandu.
Morant After 'Breaker' Morant, a famous Boer War soldier.
Moray *See* Murray.
Morcum Cornish: from the valley near the sea.
Morcom, Morcomb, Morcumb.
Mordaunt Old French: vehement or sarcastic.

Mordant.
Mordecai Babylonian or Hebrew: a biblical name.
Mordekai.
Mordred Teutonic: brave counsel. The name of an Arthurian knight.
Modred.
Moren A Welsh name of uncertain meaning.
Moreton *See* Morton.
Morey A diminutive of Maurice.
Morfil Welsh: a whale.
Morgan Welsh: the bright sea. Also a girl's name.
Morgen, Morgwn.
Morgen German: the morning. Also a form of Morgan.
Morgwn *See* Morgan.
Morice/Moritz/Moriz
See Maurice.
Morland Old English: from the moors.
Moreland.
Morley Old English: from the clearing on the moor.
Morleigh, Morly.
Morlo Welsh: a seal.
Morné An unusual South African name.
Mornay.
Moroccan A person from Morocco.
Morocan, Morokan, Morokkan.
Morocco An unusual 'country name'.
Moroco, Morokko, Moroko.
Moroko Aboriginal: the sky. *See also* Morocco.

Moroto Polynesian: the name of a god.
Morrell *See* Maurice.
Morrice/Morrie/Morry
See Maurice.
Morris/Morriss *See* Maurice.
Morrison Old English: the son of Maurice.
Morson.
Morrissey English from Irish Gaelic: the son of Muiris (Maurice).
Morse *See* Maurice.
Morson *See* Morrison.
Mort Middle English: stumpy. Also a diminutive of Mortimer and Morton.
Morten *See* Martin and Morton.
Mortimer Old French: from the still or stagnant water.
Mortemer, Mortemor, Mortemore, Mortimor, Mortimore.
Diminutives: Mort, Morty.
Morton Old English: from the settlement on the moor.
Moreton, Morten.
Diminutives: Mort, Morty.
Morven Gaelic: a Scottish region. Also a girl's name.
Morvan.
Morville Middle English/French: the town on the moor.
Morvill.
Moses Egyptian: probably meaning delivered or saved. The biblical patriarch who led the Israelites out of Egypt.

Amoho (Maori), *Moises* (Portuguese), *Moisey* (Russian), *Moishe* (Yiddish), *Moke* (Hawaiian), *Mose* (German) *Mosese* (Tongan), *Moshe* (Jewish), *Mosheh* (Hebrew), *Moss*, *Mouses*, *Mozes* (Dutch), *Musa* (Arabic). *Diminutives:* Mose, Moze.

Moshe Jewish form of Moses.

Mosi Swahili: the firstborn. Also a girl's name.

Mosman An English surname, probably derived from Moses. *Mossman.*

Moss See Moses.

Mostafa See Mustafa.

Mostyn Welsh: from the field of the fortress.

Motega Native American: an arrow.

Moto Aboriginal: a black snake.

Mountford English from French: from the ford on the hill. *Mounteford, Mountforde, Mountiford.*

Mountfort/Mountforte See Montfort.

Moustafa/Moustapha See Mustafa.

Moverley Old English: a clearing. *Moverly.*

Mowan Aboriginal: the sun.

Mowbray An English surname. *Mowbrae, Mowbrai.*

Mowgli The main character in Rudyard Kipling's *The Jungle Book*.

Moxham The son of Mog or Mox, old diminutives of Margaret.

Moxon.

Moze/Mozes See Moses.

Muammar Arabic: one who is long-lived.

Muata Native American: the sixth, as in sixth child.

Mubarak Arabic: blessed, fortunate.

Muhammad Arabic: the praised one. *See also* Mahmood. *Mahomet, Mahommed, Mohamad, Mohamed, Mohammed, Muhamad, Muhamed, Muhammed. Diminutives:* Mohd, Muhd.

Muhd A diminutive of Muhammad.

Muhsin Arabic: benevolent. *Mohsen, Mohsin.*

Muir Scottish: the moor.

Muiris Irish form of Maurice.

Mukhtar Arabic: the chosen one. *Mokhtar.*

Mulatu An unusual African name.

Mulga Aboriginal: an acacia.

Mullion Aboriginal: an eagle. Also a Cornish placename. *Mullian, Mullyan.*

Mundara Aboriginal: thunder. Also a girl's name. *Mundarra.*

Mundil Aboriginal: the night. *Mundill.*

Munga Hindi: coral.

Mungarry Aboriginal: an eaglehawk.

Mungo Scottish Gaelic: a dear friend. *Mungoe.*

Munin One of Odin's ravens in Norse mythology. *See also* Huginn.

Muninn.
Munir Arabic: bright, or shining.
Muneer.
Muniz Arabic: friendly.
Munis.
Munji Aboriginal: lightning.
Munro Irish Gaelic: from the mouth of the River Roe, in Ireland.
Monro, Monroe, Munroe.
Muraca Native American: a white moon.
Muraco.
Murali Sanskrit: a flute.
Murat Turkish: a desire or wish.
Murdad The angel of the month of July.
Murdo *See* Murdoch.
Murdoch Scottish Gaelic: a mariner.
Murdo, Murdock.
Muri Aboriginal: the sun.
Murihiku Maori: the Southland of New Zealand.
Murphy Irish Gaelic: a warrior of the sea.
Murphey.
Murray Scottish Gaelic: from the land by the sea. Derived from the region of Moray.
Moray, Murrey, Murry, Mury.
Musa Arabic: a form of Moses. Nepali: a rat.
Musaa, Muscat.
Muscat The capital of Oman and also a type of sweet wine.
Muskat.
Mustafa Arabic: the chosen one.
Mostafa, Moustafa, Moustapha, Mustapha.
Musumba African: the name of a city in the Republic of the Congo.
Myall Aboriginal: wild, or an acacia tree. Also a form of Michael.
Mial, Miall, Myal.
Mychal/Mychael *See* Michael.
Myer *See* Meir.
Myke/Myki/Mykie/Mykje Diminutives of Michael.
Mykel/Mykle *See* Michael.
Mykola Slavic form of Nicholas.
Myles/Mylles/Mylo *See* Miles.
Myllton/Mylt/Mylton *See* Milton.
Myln/Mylne *See* Milne.
Mylon American: a modern name.
Mylor Celtic: a Cornish placename.
Mellor, Melor.
Myrddin *See* Merlin.
Myron Greek: fragrant. From myrrh, an aromatic shrub.
Miron.
Myrven/Myrvin *See* Mervyn.
Mytchel/Mytchell *See* Mitchell.

N

Naaman Hebrew: pleasant.
Naazim *See* Nazim.
Nabil Arabic: noble.
Nabeel.
Nachman *See* Nahum.
Nacho/Nacio *See* Ignatius.
Nada Sanskrit: the Hindu thunder

god, the equivalent of the Norse god Thor.
Nadal Spanish form of Natale.
Nadim Arabic: a friend.
Nadeem, Nadhim.
Nadir Arabic: precious, rare.
Nadeer, Nader.
Na'eem *See* Naim.
Naftali/Naftaly *See* Naphtali.
Naga Malay/Thai: a mythical dragon or serpent.
Nagar Sanskrit: a settlement or town.
Nagin Urdu: a snake.
Nageen.
Nago Tibetan: black.
Nahoa Hawaiian: bold and defiant.
Nahum Hebrew: the comforter.
Nachman, Naham, Nahman, Naum (Russian).
Naim Arabic: peaceful.
Na'eem.
Nairn Scottish Gaelic: the dweller by the alder tree. A placename.
Nairne.
Nait/Naite *See* Nathan and Nathaniel.
Najib Arabic: the noble one.
Najeeb, Nayeeb, Nayib, Nayibe.
Naljor Tibetan: holy.
Nalong Aboriginal: the source of the river.
Nalu Hawaiian: an ocean wave.
Nam Vietnamese: from the south.
Nambur Aboriginal: a tea-tree.
Namgyal Sherpa/Tibetan: the sky king.
Namid Native American: a dancer.

Namir Hebrew: like a leopard.
Namoi Aboriginal: an acacia tree.
Nanda Sanskrit: joy.
Nandi Hindi: a mythological bull.
Nansen Danish: the son of Nancy.
Naoki Japanese: an honest tree.
Naoto Japanese: the honest one.
Naphtali A name from the Old Testament.
Naftali, Naftaly.
Napier The name of a New Zealand city.
Napoleon Greek: a new city.
Narayan Sanskrit: the son of man.
Narain.
Narcissus Greek: a flower. The name of the youth in Greek mythology who fell in love with his own reflection.
Narciso (Spanish).
Nardin A flowering plant of the valerian family.
Nardu Aboriginal: a plant with edible seeds.
Nardoo.
Narendra Sanskrit: a mighty man.
Naren.
Naresh Sanskrit: a lord or king.
Narrah Aboriginal: black, or the sea.
Narra.
Narrie Aboriginal: a bushfire.
Narri.
Narsingh Sanskrit: a lion among men.
Naseeb *See* Nasib.
Naseer *See* Nasir.

Nash Old English: at the ash tree.
Nashe.
Nashat Arabic: happiness.
Nashoba Native American: a wolf.
Nasi Hebrew: a prince.
Nasib Arabic: noble.
Naseeb.
Nasim Arabic: a gentle wind.
Nasir Arabic: the helper or supporter.
Naseer, Nassar, Nasser, Nazir, Nazr, Nizar.
Nason A variation of the popular name Mason.
Nasen, Naysen, Nayson.
Nasrullah Arabic: with the help of Allah.
Nasralla, Nasrallah, Nasrulla.
Nat/Nate *See* Nathan and Nathaniel.
Natale Italian: born at Christmas. *See also* Noel.
Nadal (Spanish), *Natal* (Spanish), *Natalino* (Italian), *Natalio* (Italian).
Natan Aboriginal: a fig-tree.
Nataniel *See* Nathaniel.
Nathan A modern form of Nathaniel.
Natham, Nathel, Nathon.
Diminutives: Nait, Naite, Nat, Nate, Nayt, Nayte.
Nathaniel Hebrew: a gift of God. The name of a biblical prophet.
Nataniel, Nathanael, Nathanial.
Diminutives: Nait, Naite, Nat, Nate, Nayt, Nayte.
Nathel *See* Nathan.

Nattai Aboriginal: water.
Naum *See* Nahum.
Navajo Native American: the name of a tribe.
Navaho.
Navin Sanskrit: a beginning.
Nawang Sherpa/Tibetan: the possessive one.
Nayden Bulgarian: one who is found.
Nayeeb/Nayib/Nayibe *See* Najib.
Naysen/Nayson *See* Nason.
Nayt/Nayte *See* Nathan and Nathaniel.
Nazarene An inhabitant of Nazareth, a town in Israel.
Nazareno, Nazarino, Nazario (Italian), *Nazzarene, Nazzareno* (Italian), *Nazzarino* (Italian), *Nazzario.*
Diminutive: Rino (Italian).
Nazim Arabic: an organiser.
Naazim, Nazm.
Nazir/Nazr *See* Nasir.
Neal Irish Gaelic: the champion. *See also* Nelson and Niles.
Neale, Neall, Neel, Neele, Neil, Neild, Neile, Neill, Nial, Niall (Gaelic), *Niel, Niele, Njal, Njale, Njall, Njalle.*
Nealson *See* Nelson.
Neave Old English: a nephew.
Neve.
Neco A diminutive of Nicholas.
Nectario/Nectarios *See* Nektarios.
Ned/Neddie/Neddy *See* Edward.
Nedelko Slavic: born on a Sunday.

Nedele (Czech), *Nedeljko.*
Nedup Sherpa/Tibetan: he who possesses sacred things.
Neel/Neele *See* Neal.
Neelo/Neeloh *See* Nilo.
Neemia Polynesian form of Nehemiah.
Nehemiah Hebrew: the consolation of the Lord.
Neemia (Polynesian), *Nemiah.*
Nehru Sanskrit: after Jawaharlal Nehru, a former Indian Prime Minister.
Neifion The Welsh name for Neptune.
Neil/Neild/Neile/Neill *See* Neal.
Neko A diminutive of Nicholas.
Nekoda Hebrew: an Old Testament name.
Nektarios Greek: like nectar. The name of a saint.
Nectario, Nectarios, Nektario.
Nelson English: the son of Neal or Neil. Also after the famous British admiral, Lord Nelson.
Nealson, Nelsen, Nielsen, Nielson, Nilson.
Nemanja Slavic: the name of a 12th-century Serbian king.
Nemenja.
Nemesio Italian/Spanish: from the Greek goddess Nemesis.
Nemesius.
Nemiah *See* Nehemiah.
Nemo Greek: a man from the glen.
Nenad Slavic: one who is unexpected.

Neo From the Greek word neos, meaning new. African: a gift.
Neoh, Nio, Nioh.
Neot The name of an English saint.
Neptune Latin: a planet and the Roman god of water and the sea, similar to the Greek god Poseidon.
Neifion (Welsh).
Nerang Aboriginal: little.
Nereus Greek: a legendary sea god, represented as old and wise.
Nereo (Italian), *Nerio.*
Nero Latin: dark, or black-haired.
Nesbitt Old English: a bent nose.
Nesbit.
Nestor Greek: wisdom.
Nestore.
Nev A diminutive of Neville and Nevin.
Nevada Spanish: snow. The name of an American state.
Nevan/Neven *See* Nevin.
Neve *See* Neave.
Neville Old French: from the new town or settlement.
Nevel, Nevell, Nevil, Nevile.
Diminutive: Nev.
Nevin Irish Gaelic: the servant of the saints.
Nevan, Neven, Nevins, Nevy, Niven, Nivens, Nives.
Diminutive: Nev.
Newbold Old English: from the new building.
Newell Old English: from the new hall.

Newall.
Newland Old English: newly acquired land.
Newlyn Celtic: the dweller at the new pool.
Newlin, Newlinn, Newlynn.
Newman Old English: the newcomer.
Newry Irish Gaelic: a placename, meaning the yew tree at the head of the strand.
Newrey, Newrie.
Newton Old English: from the new town or estate.
Newten.
Ngaio Maori: a native New Zealand tree. More commonly a girl's name.
Ngaru Polynesian: a hero.
Ngaro.
Ngawari Maori: the patient one.
Nial/Niall *See* Neal.
Nic *See* Dominic and Nicholas.
Nicander Greek: a man of victory
Nicandor, Nicandro (Italian).
Nicholas Greek: the victory of the people. *See also* Colin and Nixon. *Miklós* (Czech), *Mikolaj* (Polish), *Mikulas* (Czech), *Mykola* (Slavic), *Nichol, Nicholaos, Nicholos, Nickolas, Nickollas, Niclas, Nicol* (Scottish), *Nicola* (Italian), *Nicolaas, Nicolae, Nicolas* (Spanish), *Nicolino* (Italian), *Nicolo* (Italian), *Nicolos, Niculae, Niels* (Danish), *Niklas, Niklaus* (Scandinavian), *Nikola* (Slavic), *Nikolai* (Russian), *Nikolaos* (Greek), *Nikolas, Nikolaus* (German), *Nikolay* (Russian), *Nikos* (Greek), *Nils* (Norwegian, Swedish).
Diminutives: Claus (Dutch, German), Cole, Klaas (Dutch), Klaes (Frisian), Klaus (Danish, German), Kolya (Russian), Neco, Neko, Nic, Nico (Italian), Nick, Nickie, Nicko, Nicky, Nik, Niko, Nique.
Nichols the son of Nicholas.
Nicholds, Nicholls, Nicholson.
Nick/Nickie/Nicky *See* Dominic and Nicholas.
Nicko/Nickolas/Nickollas *See* Nicholas.
Nickson *See* Nixon.
Nico *See* Nicholas and Nicodemus.
Nicodemus Greek: the conqueror for the people.
Nicodeemus, Nicodeme (French), *Nikodeemus* (Finnish), *Nikodemus.*
Diminutives: Nico, Teemu (Finnish).
Nicol/Nicola/Nicolas/Nicolino/Nicolo *See* Nicholas.
Niculae *See* Nicholas.
Nidal Arabic: a contest or struggle.
Nidaal.
Niel/Niele *See* Neal.
Niels *See* Cornelius and Nicholas.
Nielsen/Nielson *See* Nelson.
Nigel Latin: dark, black-haired.
Nigell, Nijel, Nijell, Nygell.
Nik/Niklas/Niklaus *See* Nicholas.

Nikita Russian: unconquerable.
Niko *See* Nicholas.
Nikodeemus/Nikodemus *See* Nicodemus.
Nikolai/Nikolaus/Nikolay *See* Nicholas.
Nikos Greek form of Nicholas.
Nilam Hindi: a sapphire.
Niles An unusual name, probably a form of Neil or Neal.
Nilles, Nyles, Nylles.
Nilo Nepali: blue.
Neelo, Neeloh, Niloh.
Nils *See* Nicholas.
Nilson *See* Nelson.
Nima Sherpa/Tibetan: born on a Sunday. Also a girl's name.
Nimbin Aboriginal: a pointed rock. A NSW placename.
Nymbin.
Nimish Sanskrit: fast; a split-second.
Nimrod Hebrew: valiant, or a great hunter. A biblical name.
Ninian Gaelic: the name of a 5th-century saint.
Ninja A Japanese fighter or warrior.
Ninjah.
Nino/Ninos Diminutives of the Italian names Gianni and Giovanni. *See* John.
Nio/Nioh *See* Neo.
Nioka Aboriginal: green hills.
Niord *See* Njord.
Nique A diminutive of Nicholas.
Niran Thai: eternal.
Nirmal Sanskrit: pure or clear.
Nirmalya.
Nirvan From nirvana, the Buddhist and Hindu word for a heavenly state.
Nirvana, Nirvann.
Nisan The first month of the Hebrew calendar, associated with spring and corresponding to the zodiac sign of Aries.
Nisannu.
Nishan Armenian: a sign.
Nishi Japanese: from the west.
Nitin Sanskrit: master of the right path.
Nitish.
Nitro From nitrogen, a gaseous element.
Nitroe, Nitrow, Nitrowe.
Niven/Nivens/Nives *See* Nevin.
Nixon Old English: the son of Nicholas.
Nickson.
Nizar *See* Nasir.
Njal/Njall *See* Neal.
Njord Old Norse: a sea god.
Niord.
Noah Hebrew: rest, comfort. A biblical figure.
Noa, Noha.
Noal/Noale *See* Noel.
Noam Hebrew: pleasant.
Noble Latin: famous, noble.
Nobel.
Nodar A Georgian name of uncertain meaning.
Noel Old French: Christmas.

See also Natale.
Noal, Noale, Noël, Noele, Nowell.
Noga Hebrew: a star.
Nogah.
Noha *See* Noah.
Noko Aboriginal: water.
Nolan Irish Gaelic: famous, a champion.
Noland, Nolen.
Noor *See* Nur.
Nooroo Aboriginal: dark.
Norbert Teutonic: light or brilliance from the north.
Norbu Sherpa/Tibetan: a precious gem.
Nord *See* North.
Norden Teutonic: the north.
Nordan.
Norfolk The name of an English county and an island off the east coast of Australia.
Noriaki Japanese: bright law.
Norman Teutonic: a man from the north. *See also* Norris.
Normand, Normann.
Diminutives: Norm, Normie, Normy, Norrie.
Norrie *See* Norman.
Norris From the same root as Norman.
Noris.
North Old English: one who lives to the north.
Nord (German), *Northe.*
Northcliff Old English: from the north cliff.
Northcliffe.

Northcote Old English: from the northern cottage.
Northcott.
Northrop Old English: from the northern farm.
Norton Old English: from the northern farm or town.
Norten.
Norville Old English: from the northern estate or farm.
Norvel, Norvil.
Norvin Old English: a friend from the north.
Norvyn, Norwin, Norwyn.
Norwell Old English: from the north spring or well.
Norwin/Norwyn *See* Norvin.
Norwood Old English: from the northern forest.
Notaku Native American: a growling bear.
Notu A magical white tortoise in Philippine mythology.
Notus Greek: the mythological god of the south wind.
Nouri/Nouriel *See* Nuriel.
Novak Slavic: new.
Novac, Novack.
November From the Latin word for nine (November was originally the ninth month of the year).
Novemba (Swahili), *Novembre* (French, Italian), *Novembro* (Portuguese).
Nowell *See* Noel.
Nowra Aboriginal: a black cockatoo.

A town in NSW.
Nowrah.
Nudgee Aboriginal: a green frog.
A Queensland placename.
Nui Polynesian: many, or large.
Nukuhia Maori: increase.
Numa Latin: divine force.
Numair Arabic: a panther.
Nuncio Italian: a messenger.
Nunzio.
Nunga Aboriginal: the daytime.
Nur Arabic: light. Hebrew: fire.
Noor, Nuri.
Nuren Arabic: light.
Nuriel Arabic: light, or a flame.
Nouri (Hungarian), *Nourie*,
Nouriel.
Nuru Swahili: born in the daytime.
Nyani Swahili: a monkey or baboon.
Nyati Swahili: a buffalo.
Nyawi Aboriginal: the sun.
Nyauwe, Nyauwi, Nyawe.
Nye *See* Aneurin.
Nygell *See* Nigel.
Nyles *See* Niles.
Nymbin *See* Nimbin.
Nyoka Swahili: a snake.
Nyuki Swahili: a bee.
Nyusi Swahili: black.

Oak Old English: a 'plant name'.
Oake.
Oakes Middle English: the dweller by the oak trees.
Oakley Middle English: one who lives at the oak-tree meadow.
Oakly, Okely.
Oata Polynesian: a shadow.
Oaten Old English: probably an anglicised form of Otto, meaning prosperous. *See also* Ottiwell.
Oates, Oatten, Oten.
Oba African: a king.
Obah.
Obadiah Hebrew: the servant of God.
Obadias, Obediah.
Oberon A character in William Shakespeare's *A Midsummer Night's Dream. See* Auberon.
Obert Teutonic: wealthy and bright.
Obrad Slavic: one who is happy.
O'Brien Irish Gaelic: a descendant of Brian or Brien.
O'Brian.
Ocean Middle English: of the sea.
Oceanis, Oceano, Oceanus.
Octavius Latin: eight, or the eighth-born.
Octave (French), *Octavian*,
Octavio, Octavus, Ottavio (Italian).
October From octo, the Latin word for eight (October was originally the eighth month).
Octobre (French), *Oktoba* (Swahili),
Oktober (Dutch, German, Norwegian),
Ottobre (Italian).
Odell Old Norse: wealthy.
Odern Aboriginal: by the sea.

Odilo The name of an early French saint.
Odillo.
Odin Old Norse: the Scandinavian god of war.
Othen, Othin, Wodan (German), *Woden, Wotan* (German).
Odion African: the firstborn twin.
Odolf Teutonic: a noble wolf.
Odulf.
O'Donnell Irish Gaelic: a descendant of Donald.
O'Donell, O'Donnel.
Odran Irish Gaelic: pale green.
Odren, Odrin.
Oeystein/Oeysteinn *See* Eysteinn.
Ofydd Welsh form of Ovid.
Ogai A popular Japanese name.
Ogden Old English: from the valley of oak trees.
Ogdan, Ogdon.
Ogilvie Celtic: from the high hill.
Ogilvy.
Oglesby Old English: awe-inspiring.
Ognyan Bulgarian: one who is fiery.
Ognian.
Ogun Nigerian: the god of war.
Ohio Native American: a beautiful river. The name of a US state.
Ohtis *See* Otis.
Oisín *See* Ossian.
Okapi Swahili: an African deer-like animal that is related to the giraffe.
Oke Hawaiian form of Oscar.
Okely *See* Oakley.
Okon African: born during the night.
Okto Greek: eight.
Otto (Italian).
Oktoba/Oktober *See* October.
Okuri Native American: a bear.
Olaf Old Norse/Scandinavian: a descendant.
Olafur (Icelandic), *Olav, Olavi* (Finnish), *Ole* (Danish, Norwegian), *Olin* (English), *Olof, Olov.*
Oldree/Oldrey/Oldrie *See* Aldrey.
Oldric/Oldrich *See* Aldrich.
Ole Danish and Norwegian forms of Olaf.
Oleg Russian: the name of an early prince of Kiev.
Olegs.
Olek/Oleksander *See* Alexander.
Olin *See* Olaf.
Oliver Latin: an olive tree or branch; a symbol of peace.
Oliverio (Spanish), *Oliviae, Olivier* (French), *Oliviero* (Italian), *Olliver, Ollivier.*
Diminutives: Oli, Ollie, Olly.
Olmo Italian: an elm tree.
Olof/Olov *See* Olaf.
Omaka Maori: the place where the stream flows.
Omar Arabic: flourishing, long-lived.
Omer, Umar.
Omolara African: born at night-time.
Onak Aboriginal: the earth.
Onan Turkish: prosperous.
Ondray/Ondré/Ondrej *See* Andrew.

One *See* Onne.
O'Neil Irish Gaelic: a descendant of Neil.
O'Neal, O'Neale, O'Neall, O'Neill.
Onepu Maori: sand.
Onix *See* Onyx.
Onne Dutch: one who yields.
One, Onno.
Onofrio An Italian name, possibly meaning the peaceful one.
Onofre, Onofri, Onofrios.
Onslow An English surname of uncertain meaning.
Onslowe.
Onur Turkish: honour.
Onuris The ancient Ancient Egyptian god of hunting and the sky.
Onyx Greek: a semi-precious stone.
Ónix (Spanish).
Ora Polynesian: life.
Orad Aboriginal: earth.
Oram Old English: from the enclosure by the riverbank.
Oran Irish Gaelic: pale-skinned.
Oren, Orin, Orran, Orren, Orrin.
Orazio Italian form of Horace.
Orban Hungarian form of Urban.
Orchard Old English: a place where trees are grown.
Orcheard, Orchird.
Ordway Old English: the spear fighter.
Oreb Hebrew: black, or a raven.
Orev, Orreb.
Oregon The name of a US state.
Oregan.
Orel Russian/Slavic: an eagle. Swiss: a form of Aurelius.
Oren Hebrew: a pine tree. Welsh: orange. *See also* Oran.
Orestes Greek: a man of the mountain. A hero of Greek mythology.
Oreste (Italian).
Orev *See* Oreb.
Orfeo Italian form of Orpheus.
Orford Old English: a dweller at the ford.
Orforde.
Orhan Turkish: a great leader.
Orien Latin: from the east.
Orian.
Orin *See* Oran.
Oriol Catalan/Spanish: a golden bird.
Oriole.
Orion Greek: the son of light. The name of a constellation.
Orix *See* Oryx.
Orjan Scandinavian: a farmer.
Orlan Old English: from the pointed land.
Orland.
Orlando Italian form of Roland. The name of Shakespeare's hero in *As You Like It*.
Ormond Old English: a spearman.
Orman, Ormand, Ormon, Ormonde, Ormont, Ormonte.
Ornette An unusual modern American name.
Ornet, Ornett.
Oro Polynesian: the Tahitian god of

war and peace. Spanish: golden.
Oroiti Polynesian: the slow-footed one.
Orpheus Greek: a name from ancient mythology.
Orfeo (Italian), *Orphée* (French).
Orran/Orren/Orrin *See* Oran.
Orreb *See* Oreb.
Orsino *See* Orson.
Orson Old French (from Latin): a little bear.
Orsino, Orso, Urson.
Orton Old English: from the farm by the river.
Orville Old French: from the golden place or town.
Orvil, Orvill.
Orvin Old English: a spear friend.
Orvon, Orvyn.
Oryx Greek: a large African antelope.
Orix.
Osama *See* Usama.
Osbert Old English: divinely bright or famous.
Osborn Old English: a divine warrior.
Osborne, Osbourne, Osburn, Osburne.
Oscar Old English: a divine spearman.
Auska, Auskah, Auskar, Oke (Hawaiian), *Osca, Oscah, Oscer, Osgar* (Scottish Gaelic), *Oska, Oskah, Oskar* (German), *Oskari* (Finnish), *Osker.*
Diminutives: Okko (Finnish), Ossi, Ossie, Oz, Ozzie.

Oscuro Italian: dark.
Osgar *See* Oscar.
Osgood Old Norse: a pagan god.
O'Shea Irish Gaelic: a descendant of the dauntless one.
O'Shay.
Osip *See* Joseph.
Osiris Ancient Egyptian: the god of fertility, life, death and rebirth.
Oska/Oskar/Oskari/Osker *See* Oscar.
Osler Old French: a bird-catcher.
Ozler.
Osman Arabic: an Ottoman Turk, or a servant of God.
Ousman, Ozman, Usman, Uzman.
Osmar Old English: divinely glorious.
Ozmar.
Osmond Old English: a divine protector.
Osmonde, Osmont, Osmonte, Osmund, Osmunde.
Osric Old English: a divine ruler.
Osrich, Osrick, Osrik, Ozric, Ozrich, Ozrik.
Ossi/Ossie Diminutives of Oscar.
Ossian Irish Gaelic: a little deer or fawn. A warrior-poet in Irish mythology.
Oisín.
Osten/Ostin/Ostyn *See* Austin.
Oster Teutonic: east, or from the east.
Ostern Teutonic: Easter-time.
Ostoja A Slavic name of uncertain meaning.
Oswald Old English: divinely

powerful.
Osvaldo (Italian, Spanish), *Oswaldo*, *Oswallt* (Welsh), *Ozbay*, *Ozbej* (Slavic).

Oswin Old English: a friend of God, or a divine friend.
Oswen, *Oswyn*.

Otama Aboriginal: a porpoise.

Otello/Othello Italian forms of Otto.

Oten *See* Oaten.

Othen/Othin *See* Odin.

Othmar *See* Ottmar.

Otho *See* Otto.

Otis Greek: keen of hearing.
Ohtis.

Ottavio *See* Octavius.

Otter Old Norse: a mythological figure who was turned into an otter.
Ottar.

Ottiwell Old English: probably an anglicised form of Otto, meaning prosperous. *See also* Oaten.
Ottewell, *Ottewill*, *Ottiwill*.

Ottley Old English: from the meadow of the prosperous one.
Otleigh, *Otley*, *Ottleigh*.

Ottmar Teutonic: happy fame.
Othmar.

Otto Teutonic: rich, prosperous. *See also* Okto.
Otello (Italian), *Othello* (Italian), *Otho*.

Ottobre The Italian name for the month of October.

Otway Teutonic: fortunate in battle.
Ottway.

Ouranius/Ouranos/Ouranus *See* Uranius.

Ouray Native American: an arrow.

Ousman *See* Osman.

Ove A popular Scandinavian name.
Uwe.

Ovid Latin: a ram. The name of a famous Roman poet.
Ofydd (Welsh), *Oviedo* (Spanish).

Owain/Owayne *See* Owen.

Owen Welsh: well-born. Also a Welsh form of John (*see* Bowen, Evan and Ieuan).
Eoin (Irish Gaelic), *Owain*, *Owayn*, *Owayne*.

Oxford Old English: from the ford of the oxen. An English university city.
Oxforde.

Oxley Old English: from the meadow of the ox.
Oxlea, *Oxleigh*, *Oxlie*, *Oxly*.

Oxton Old English: from the ox enclosure.
Oxten.

Oz/Ozzie Diminutives of Oscar.

Ozbay/Ozbej *See* Oswald.

Ozgur Turkish: free. Also a girl's name.
Ozger.

Ozias *See* Uzziah.

Ozkan A Turkish name of uncertain meaning.
Ozcan.

Ozler *See* Osler.

Ozman *See* Osman.

Ozmar *See* Osmar.
Ozric/Ozrik *See* Osric.
Ozuru Japanese: a stork, implying longevity.

P

Paaveli/Paavo Finnish forms of Paul.
Pablo Spanish form of Paul.
Pacifico Spanish from Latin: peaceful.
Paco Native American: a gold eagle. Also a Spanish diminutive of Francis.
Paddy *See* Patrick.
Padget/Padgett *See* Page.
Padme Sanskrit: a lotus.
Padm, Padman.
Padraig/Padrig/Padruig *See* Patrick.
Page French: a young attendant or page. Also a girl's name.
Padget, Padgett, Paget, Paige.
Paige *See* Page.
Paine Old French: a countryman.
Payne.
Pakaa Hawaiian: the god of the wind.
Paka, Pakah.
Palaki Polynesian: black.
Palani Hawaiian: a free man.
Palauni Polynesian: brown.
Palmer Old English: a palm-bearing pilgrim.
Palmiro Latin: born on Palm Sunday.
Palmyro.

Pan The Greek god of nature.
Panagiotis Greek: all holy.
Panagiotes, Panayiotis, Panayotis.
Diminutives: Panagis, Panos.
Pancho Spanish diminutive of Francis.
Pancras Greek: all-powerful. The name of an early saint.
Pandit Hindi: a wise man or teacher.
Pangali Aboriginal: the eldest son.
Pankaj Sanskrit: a lotus flower.
Pankaja.
Panos *See* Panagiotis.
Pantelis Greek: he who helps everyone.
Paolo Italian form of Paul.
Paora/Paoro Maori forms of Paul.
Papa Polynesian: the earth.
Paques French form of Pascal.
Para Hindi: the metal, mercury.
Parah, Parra, Parrah.
Paradorn An unusual name from Thailand.
Paraone Maori: brown.
Paresh Sanskrit: the supreme lord.
Paride Italian form of Paris.
Paris Greek: a character in Greek mythology. The name of the French capital.
Paride (Italian), *Parris, Parrys, Parys.*
Park Old English: from the park.
Parke.
Parker Old English: the park-keeper.
Parkin Old English: little Peter.

Parminder Sanskrit: the god of gods, or supreme god.
Parminda, Parmindar, Perminda, Permindar, Perminder.

Parnell Latin: from the Greek word for a stone. The name is therefore related to Peter.
Parnel, Pernel, Pernell.

Parr Old English: a dweller by the cattle pen.

Parra/Parrah *See* Para.

Parri Aboriginal: a stream.

Parris/Parrys *See* Paris.

Parrish Old English: from the church parish.
Parish.

Parry Welsh: the son of Harry.

Parsefal/Parsifal *See* Percival.

Parvez/Parviz *See* Pervez.

Parys *See* Paris.

Pasang Sherpa/Tibetan: born on a Friday. Also a girl's name.

Pascal Latin: born at Easter.
Paques (French), *Pascalle, Paschal, Paschalis* (Greek), *Pascoe* (Cornish), *Pascual* (Spanish), *Paskal, Paskale, Pasqua* (Italian), *Pasquale* (Italian).
Diminutive: Pasqualino (Italian).

Pascoe Cornish form of Pascal.

Paskal/Paskale *See* Pascal.

Pasqua/Pasquale/Pasqualino *See* Pascal.

Pat A diminutive of Patrick.

Patariki Maori form of Patrick.

Patcharin A Thai name of uncertain meaning.

Patek Czech: Friday.

Paterson The son of Pat or Patrick.
Patersen, Pattersen, Patterson, Pattisen, Pattison.

Paton *See* Payton.

Patonga Aboriginal: a small wallaby.

Patric/Patrice/Patricio *See* Patrick.

Patrick Latin: noble, well-born. The patron saint of Ireland. *See also* Paterson.
Paaveli (Finnish), *Padraig* (Irish Gaelic), *Padrig, Padruig* (Scottish Gaelic), *Patariki* (Maori), *Patric, Patrice* (French), *Patrich, Patricio* (Portuguese, Spanish), *Patrik, Patritzio* (Italian), *Patritzo* (Italian), *Patrizio* (Italian), *Pavlis, Pavol.*
Diminutives: Paddy, Pat, Patsy, Ric, Rick.

Patterson/Pattison *See* Paterson.

Patton Old English: a warrior.
Patten.

Patu Polynesian: a weapon.

Paul Latin: small. *See also* Pollock.
Paavo (Finnish), *Pablo* (Spanish), *Paolino* (Italian), *Paolo* (Italian), *Paora* (Maori), *Paoro* (Maori), *Paula* (Tongan), *Paule, Paulino* (Portuguese, Spanish), *Paulinus, Paulis, Paull, Paulle, Paulo* (Portuguese), *Paulot* (French), *Pavel* (Polish, Russian, Swedish), *Pavils* (Latvian), *Pavliv* (Ukrainian), *Pavlo* (Ukrainian), *Pavlos* (Greek), *Pavlov* (Russian),

P – Boys

Pavol (Slovak), *Pawel* (Slavic), *Pol* (Irish Gaelic).
Diminutives: Paulie, Pauley.
Pavel/Pavlos/Pavlov/Pavol See Paul.
Pavo Latin: a peacock. The name of a small constellation.
Pavonis.
Pax Latin: peace.
Paxton Old English: from the estate of the warrior.
Paxten.
Payne See Paine.
Paytah Native American: fire.
Payton Old English: a dweller on the warrior's farm.
Paton, Payten, Peyton.
Peadar Irish and Scottish Gaelic forms of Peter.
Pearce See Peter.
Pearson See Pierson.
Peco See Pico.
Peder/Pedr/Pedro See Peter.
Pedrek/Pedrog See Petroc.
Pedrie See Petrie.
Peers See Piers.
Peeter See Peter.
Peetu Finnish: possibly a form of Peter.
Pegasus Greek: a winged horse in classical mythology. The name of a northern constellation.
Pek Slavic: a baker.
Pekelo Hawaiian: a stone.
Pekka A Finnish diminutive of Peter.
Pekko The ancient Estonian and Finnish god of crops.
Peko.
Peko See Pekko and Pico.
Pelagio Greek: from the sea.
Pelagius, Pelagos.
Pell Old English: a scarf.
Pelle Swedish diminutive of Per (*see* Peter).
Pelton Old English: from the farm by a pool.
Pellton, Pelten.
Pema Sherpa/Tibetan: a lotus. Also a girl's name.
Pemba Sherpa/Tibetan: born on a Saturday.
Pembe Swahili: white, like ivory.
Pembeh.
Pemberton Old English: the barton (barley field or farm) by a hill.
Pembarton.
Pembroke Celtic: from the headland. A Welsh county.
Pencast Cornish form of Pentecost.
Pendragon Celtic: the head of the dragon. The name of King Arthur's father.
Penglaze Cornish: a green headland.
Penglase.
Penjor Sherpa/Tibetan: the wealthy one.
Penley Old English: from the enclosed meadow.
Penlea, Penlee, Penleigh.
Penn Old English: an enclosure or pen.
Penrice Cornish: from the end of

the ford.
Penryce.
Penrith Welsh: the main ford.
Penrithe, Penryth, Penrythe.
Penrod Teutonic: a famous commander.
Penrose Cornish/Welsh: the end or top of the moor.
Penroze.
Pentecost Greek: born at Pentecost, the fiftieth day (or seventh Sunday) after Easter, generally falling mid-May to mid-June and suitable for a Gemini baby.
Pencast (Cornish), *Pentecoste.*
Pentheus Greek: the fifth, or the fifth son.
Penwyn Welsh: the fair-haired one.
Pepe Spanish diminutive of José. *See* Joseph.
Pepin Teutonic: the petitioner, one who seeks a favour.
Per Scandinavian form of Peter.
Peral Spanish: a pear tree.
Peran *See* Piran.
Percival Old French: to pierce the valley. One of the knights of Arthurian legend.
Parsefal, Parsifal, Perceval.
Diminutives: Perce, Percy.
Percy A Norman surname and a diminutive of Percival.
Persey, Pursey.
Pere Catalan form of Peter.
Peregrine Latin: a stranger or pilgrim. A type of falcon.

Peregrin, Peregryn.
Diminutive: Perry.
Perez Hebrew: to blossom. Also a Spanish surname, meaning the son of Pedro (Peter).
Peretz.
Pericles Greek: the name of an ancient political leader.
Periclis.
Permindar/Perminder *See* Parminder.
Pernel/Pernell *See* Parnell.
Pero Slavic diminutive of Petar (*see* Peter).
Perran/Perren/Perrin *See* Piran.
Perro Spanish: a dog.
Perry Old English: from the pear tree. Also a diminutive of Peregrine.
Perrey, Perri, Perrie.
Perseus A hero in Greek mythology, best known for rescuing the maiden Andromeda from a sea monster. The name of a northern constellation.
Persey *See* Percy.
Perth Celtic: a thornbush thicket. The name of cities in Scotland and Western Australia.
Perun Slavic: a god of thunder.
Perunn, Perunu.
Pervez Persian: the fortunate one.
Parvez, Parviz, Pervaiz, Perviz.
Pervis *See* Purvis.
Petar A Slavic form of Peter.
Peter Greek: a stone or rock. One of Christ's apostles. *See also* Ferris, Parkin, Parnell, Peterson, Petrie

and Pierson.
Peadar (Irish and Scottish Gaelic), *Pearce, Peder* (Danish, Norwegian), *Pedr* (Welsh), *Pedro* (Spanish), *Peeter, Per* (Scandinavian), *Pere* (Catalan), *Petar* (Slavic), *Petera* (Maori), *Peteris, Petero, Petr* (Czech), *Petri* (Basque, Finnish), *Petrika* (Albanian), *Petros* (Greek), *Petrou, Petrov* (Russian), *Petrovich* (Russian), *Petur* (Icelandic), *Pierce, Pierino, Piero* (Italian), *Pierre* (French), *Piers, Piet* (Dutch), *Pietari* (Finnish), *Pieter, Pietro* (Italian), *Piotr* (Slavic), *Pita* (Maori, Tongan), *Pyotr* (Russian), *Pyrs* (Welsh).
Diminutives: Pekka (Finnish), Pelle (Swedish), Pero (Slavic), Pete, Petey, Petya (Russian), Pierrick (Breton), Pierrot (French), Tika (Albanian).

Peterson The son of Peter. *See also* Pierson.
Peters, Petersen.

Petniunas A Lithuanian name of uncertain meaning.

Petr/Petri *See* Peter and Petrie.

Petrie Scottish Gaelic: a form of Peter.
Pedrie, Petre, Petri, Petry.

Petrika Albanian form of Peter.
Diminutive: Tika.

Petroc Cornish/Welsh: the name of a Celtic saint.
Pedrek, Pedrog, Petrock, Petrok.

Petros Greek form of Peter.
Petrou/Petrov/Petrovich *See* Peter.
Petya Russian diminutive of Peter.
Peverall French: a piper.
Peveral, Peverel, Peverell, Peveril, Peverill.

Peyton *See* Payton.

Phagun Sanskrit: the Hindu month of February/March, corresponding to the zodiac sign of Pisces.
Phalgun.

Pharaoh An Ancient Egyptian king.
Pharoah.

Pharrel/Pharrell *See* Farrell.
Phebus *See* Phoebus.
Phelan Irish Gaelic: as brave as a wolf.
Felan.

Phelps Old English: the son of Philip.
Philbert *See* Filbert.
Philemon Greek: loving.
Philo.

Philip Greek: a lover of horses. One of the New Testament apostles. *See also* Phelps and Phillips.
Felipe (Spanish), *Filep* (Hungarian), *Filib* (Scottish Gaelic), *Filip* (Polish), *Filippo* (Italian), *Philipp, Philippe* (French), *Phillip, Pilib* (Irish Gaelic), *Piripi* (Maori).
Diminutives: Phil, Phillie, Philly, Pino (Italian), Pip.

Phillips Old English: the son of Philip.
Philips.

Philo *See* Philemon.

Phineas Egyptian: the Nubian (a dark-skinned person). Hebrew: an oracle; an Old Testament name.
Fineas, Finneas, Phinehas, Phinnaeas, Phinnaeus, Phinneas.

Phintso Sherpa/Tibetan: prosperity.

Phiper *See* Piper.

Phlyn/Phlynn *See* Flynn.

Phoebus Greek: bright or radiant, like the sun. The masculine form of Phoebe.
Phebus.

Phoenix Greek: the legendary bird that rose again from its own ashes. The name of a southern constellation.
Feenix, Fenix, Pheonix.

Photios/Photis *See* Fotis.

Phrase English from Latin: a sequence of words.
Frase, Fraze, Phraze.

Phunahele Hawaiian: the favourite.

Phurba Sherpa/Tibetan: born on Thursday.

Phyper *See* Piper.

Pias English Gypsy: fun.

Pickford Old English: from the ford at the peak.

Pico A Spanish name of uncertain meaning.
Peco, Peko, Piko.

Pierce A form of Peter.
Pyrs (Welsh).

Pierino/Piero/Pierre *See* Peter.

Pierpont French: a stone bridge.
Pierrepont.

Pierrick Breton diminutive of Pierre (*see* Peter).

Pierrot French diminutive of Pierre.

Piers *See* Peter.
Peers.

Pierson English: the son of Peter. *See also* Peterson.
Pearson.

Piet/Pietari/Pieter/Pietro *See* Peter.

Pietrantonio Italian: a combination of Peter and Anthony.

Piko Maori: to bend. *See also* Pico.

Pikuwa Aboriginal: a saltwater crocodile.

Pilib Irish Gaelic form of Philip.

Pilot English from French: a guide or leader.
Pilote (French), *Pilott, Pilotte, Pylot, Pylott, Pylotte.*

Pim Dutch: a diminutive of Willem (*see* William).

Pindan Aboriginal: a desert.

Pindari Aboriginal: from the high ground.

Pine Middle English: a coniferous tree.
Pyne.

Pino Italian: a pine tree. Also a diminutive of names such as Filippo (*see* Philip).

Pinon Native American: a star or a constellation.

Pinterry Aboriginal: a star.

Pinto Spanish: piebald or mottled, like a pinto horse.
Pintoe, Pintoh, Pintow.

P – Boys

Piotr A Slavic form of Peter.
Pip Diminutive of Philip.
Piper English: a pipe player.
Phiper, Phyper, Pyper.
Pipiri Polynesian: the equivalent of the star Castor, in the constellation of Gemini.
Piran Cornish: a saint's name.
Peran, Perran, Perren, Perrin, Pirran.
Pirate Middle English: one who plunders at sea.
Pyrate.
Piripi Maori and Tongan forms of Philip.
Pirrin Aboriginal: a cave.
Pisces Latin: the fishes. The last sign of the zodiac.
Pita Maori form of Peter.
Pital Nepali: brass.
Pitney Old English: preserving one's island.
Pitt Old English: from the hollow.
Pius Latin: pious, devout. The name of several popes.
Pious.
Placido Latin: serene, untroubled. A Spanish name.
Placide.
Plata Spanish: silver.
Plato Greek: broad-shouldered.
Platt Old French: from the flat land or plateau.
Pluto Latin: the mythological god of the underworld; also the name of a planet.

Pol Irish Gaelic form of Paul.
Polaris Latin: the North Star, part of the constellation of Ursa Minor, the Little Bear.
Pollock Old English: little Paul.
Pollux Greek: a crown. Along with Castor, this star forms part of the constellation of Gemini.
Polo After Marco Polo, the legendary 14th-century explorer, or from a game played on horseback.
Polona Aboriginal: a hawk. Also suitable for girls.
Pomare Polynesian: the name of a hero.
Pomeroy French: from the apple orchard.
Pompey A character in Shakespeare's *Measure for Measure*.
Pondeli The Czech name for Monday.
Pons See Pontius.
Pontius Latin: the fifth.
Pons.
Poojan Sanskrit: one who worships.
Pujan.
Porfirio Greek: a purple stone.
Porphyre (French).
Porter French: the gatekeeper.
Poseidon The Greek god of the seas, who rode a chariot pulled by golden seahorses. The equivalent of the Roman god Neptune.
Potitio Italian: from Potitus, a Catholic saint.
Pouaka Maori: a box.
Poutini Polynesian: greenstone.

Powell Welsh: the son of Howell.
Powys Welsh: a man from Powys, a Welsh county.
Prabhat Sanskrit: the dawn.
Pradeep Sanskrit: a light or lantern.
Pradip.
Prageeth A Sri Lankan name of uncertain meaning.
Prakash Sanskrit: light, or famous.
Pramana Indonesian: wisdom.
Pramod Sanskrit: happiness.
Pranav Sanskrit: a sacred word.
Pranab.
Praneet Sanskrit: modest.
Pranit.
Prasad Sanskrit: brightness, or a blessing.
Prashanth Sanskrit: the silent or peaceful one.
Pravat Thai: a lover of history.
Praveen Sanskrit: expert or skilled.
Pravin.
Praza Czech: a man from Prague.
Preben Danish: of the battle.
Predrag Slavic: one who is very precious.
Prem Sanskrit: love.
Prentice Old English: an apprentice or learner.
Prentiss.
Prescott Old English: from the priest's house.
Prescot, Prestcott.
Presley Old English: from the priest's meadow.
Preslee, Presleigh, Preslie, Presly.

Preston Old English: from the priest's farm or town.
Presten, Prestin, Prestyn.
Priam Greek: a mythological king of Troy.
Price Welsh: the son of the loving man.
Pryce, Prys, Pryse.
Prideaux Old French: near the water.
Priestley Old English: the priest's clearing or meadow.
Priestleigh, Priestly.
Primo Latin: the firstborn son.
Prince Latin: the first in rank.
Printz, Printze, Prynce.
Prior Latin: the head of a monastery or priory.
Pryor.
Prize Middle English: a reward.
Pryse, Pryze.
Probert Welsh: the son of Robert.
Proctor Latin: the administrator or manager.
Procter.
Prometheus Greek: forethought.
Prosper Latin: fortunate, prosperous.
Prospero (Italian, Portuguese, Spanish) – a character in Shakespeare's play *The Tempest*.
Proteus Greek: changeable. A sea god in Greek mythology.
Provis Old French: a steward.
Provost.
Pryce *See* Price.
Pryderi Welsh: to care for.

Prynce *See* Prince.
Pryor *See* Prior.
Prys/Pryse/Pryze *See* Price and Prize.
Przemyslaw Slavic: one who is ingenious.
Przemek, Przemko, Przemo, Przemysl (Polish), *Przemyslav.*
Diminutives: Przemek, Przemko.
Publio Portuguese/Spanish: a modern form of Publius, a Latin name meaning public.
Puké Maori: a hill.
Puranga Aboriginal: grey.
Purcell Old French: a piglet.
Purcel.
Puriri Maori: the name of a New Zealand tree.
Pursey *See* Percy.
Purvis Old French: the purveyor, or provider.
Pervis, Purves.
Pylot/Pylott *See* Pilot.
Pyne *See* Pine.
Pyotr Russian form of Peter.
Pyper *See* Piper.
Pyrate *See* Pirate.
Pyrs Welsh form of Pierce. *See* Peter.

Q

Qadir *See* Kadir.
Qamar Arabic: of the moon.
Kamar, Kemar.
Qasim Arabic: one who shares or distributes.
Kaseem, Kasim, Qaseem, Qassem.
Quade A modern name, possibly of Gaelic origin. Occasionally given to girls.
Quaden, Quaid, Quaide, Quaiden, Quayd, Quayde, Quayden, Qwad, Qwade, Qwaden, Qwaid, Qwaide, Qwaiden, Kwayd, Kwayde, Kwayden, Kweyd, Kweyde, Kweyden.
Quadrat *See* Qudrat.
Quadri Latin: four, or the fourth.
Quaid/Quaiden *See* Quade.
Quaife Old French: a cap maker or seller.
Quaif.
Quaile Manx Gaelic: the son of Paul. Also a girl's name.
Quail, Quale, Quayl, Quayle.
Quain Old French: the clever one.
Kwain, Kwaine, Quaine, Quane, Quayn, Quayne.
Quamby Aboriginal: a shelter or camp.
Quandong Aboriginal: a native peach tree.
Quant Old French: clever or crafty.
Quante.
Quarto Latin: the fourth, or fourth child.
Quartz Greek: a silicon-based mineral that comes in many varieties and colours.
Quarz.

Quashi African: born on a Sunday. Also a girl's name.
Quattro Italian: four.
Quayde/Quayden *See* Quade.
Quayl/Quayle *See* Quaile.
Quayn/Quayne *See* Quain.
Quddus Arabic: most holy.
Kuddus, Qudus.
Qudrat Power. The Baha'i month that encompasses 4–22 November, so suitable for a Scorpio baby.
Quadrat.
Quelo Catalan diminutive of Miquel (Michael).
Quemby/Quenby *See* Quimby.
Quennel French: the one who lives by the little oak tree.
Quennell, Quinnel, Quinnell.
Quentin Latin: the fifth, as in the fifth-born child.
Kwintyn (Polish), *Quent, Quenten, Quenton, Quint, Quinten, Quintin, Quinton.*
Quest Middle English: a search or pursuit.
Queste.
Quetil Old French: a sacred cauldron.
Quetel.
Quetzal A Central American bird.
Quetzall, Quezal, Quezall.
Quidam Latin: a certainty.
Quiddam.
Quigley Irish Gaelic: a spinning distaff.
Quill Middle English: a feather or an old-fashioned pen.
Quiele, Quil, Quille.
Quillan Irish Gaelic: a cub.
Quilliam Manx Gaelic form of William.
Quilter Old French: a quilt-maker.
Quimby Old Norse: from the woman's estate.
Quemby, Quenby, Quinby.
Quincy French/Latin: from the fifth son's estate.
Quincey.
Quinlan Irish Gaelic: well-shaped, athletic.
Quinlann.
Quinn Irish Gaelic: wise and intelligent.
Quin, Quinne, Quyn, Quynn, Quynne.
Quinnell *See* Quennel.
Quinney Manx Gaelic: the son of the crafty one.
Quint/Quinten/Quintin/Quinton *See* Quentin.
Quintrell An English/French surname, probably related to Quentin.
Quintral, Quintrall, Quintrel.
Quintus Latin: fifth, as in the fifth child.
Quirce Spanish: the name of a 4th-century martyr.
Quiric Greek: born on a Sunday. Also a girl's name.
Quirino Italian form of Corin.
Quirinus A Roman god of war.

Quong Chinese: bright.
Quon.
Quoyle A character in the popular book *The Shipping News*.
Quoil, Quoile, Quoyl.
Quynn/Quynne *See* Quinn.
Qwade/Qwaden/Qwaide *See* Quade.

R

Ra The Ancient Egyptian sun god, whose symbols were a falcon and scarab (sacred beetle). Aboriginal: the sun. Polynesian: a sun god. Tibetan: a goat.
Raaid Arabic: a leader or guide.
Raamazan *See* Ramazan.
Rab/Rabbie Scottish diminutives of Robert.
Rabi Arabic: springtime.
Rabih.
Rad Old English: a counsellor. Also a diminutive of Slavic names that begin with Rad.
Radd.
Radanek *See* Radko.
Radar A detection system that uses electromagnetic waves.
Raydar.
Radborne Old English: from the red brook or stream.
Radbourn, Radbourne, Radburn.
Radcliffe Old English: from the red cliff.
Radcliff, Redcliff, Redcliffe.
Rade A diminutive of Slavic names such as Milorad and Radomir.
Radec/Radek/Radenko *See* Radko.
Raden *See* Raiden.
Radford Old English: from the red ford.
Redford.
Radhakrishnan Sanskrit: A combination of Radha and Krishna, important figures in Hindu mythology.
Radik *See* Radko.
Radike A Fijian name of uncertain meaning.
Radimir *See* Radomir.
Radko Czech: joyful.
Radost (Slavic), *Raiko* (Bulgarian), *Rajko* (Slavic), *Rayko* (Bulgarian). *Diminutives:* Radanek, Radec, Radek, Radenko, Radik, Rado.
Radley Old English: from the red meadow.
Radlee, Radleigh.
Radnor Old English: from the red shore. A town in Wales.
Rado *See* Radko.
Radomir Slavic: joyful peace.
Radimir.
Radoslav Slavic: joy and glory.
Radoslaw (Polish).
Radovan Slavic: one who is joyful.
Radvan.
Rae/Raey *See* Ray and Raymond.
Raebon *See* Raybon.

Raeburn/Raeburne *See* Rayburn.
Raeford/Raeforde *See* Rayford.
Raemond/Raemund *See* Raymond.
Raex *See* Rex.
Raf/Rafa/Rafael/Rafal *See* Raphael.
Rafe An alternative form and pronunciation of Ralph. *See also* Raphael.
Raffe, Raif, Raife, Raiff, Raiffe.
Raff/Raffaele/Raffaello/Raffhael/Rafhael *See* Raphael.
Rafferty Irish Gaelic: prosperous.
Rafi Arabic: the exalted one.
Raffi.
Rafiq Arabic: a companion, a friend.
Rafik, Rafiki.
Rafu Japanese: a net.
Raghnall *See* Ronald.
Raghu Sanskrit: one who is swift.
Raginald *See* Reginald.
Raglan The name of a Welsh town.
Rhaglan.
Ragnar *See* Rayner.
Ragnulf Old Norse: a wolf-like warrior or adviser.
Renouf (Old French).
Rago African: a ram.
Rahm/Rahma *See* Rama.
Rahman Arabic: merciful.
Rahim.
Rai Japanese: trust.
Raibeart Scottish Gaelic form of Robert.
Raiden Japanese: the god of thunder.
Raden, Rayden.
Raif/Raife/Raiff/Raiffe *See* Rafe.

Raihan *See* Rayan.
Raiko A Bulgarian form of Radko.
Raimo/Raimond/Raimondo *See* Raymond.
Raine Old German: advice, decision. Also a girl's name.
Rain, Rayne, Rein, Reine, Rhain, Rhaine, Rhane.
Rainer/Rainier *See* Rayner.
Rainford Old English: a powerful ford.
Rainsford, Raisford.
Rainger *See* Ranger.
Raj Sanskrit: a king.
Raja, Rajah, Rajan.
Rajani Sanskrit: night.
Rajat Sanskrit: silver, or a pearl.
Rajendra Sanskrit: a mighty king.
Rajit Sanskrit: one who is decorated.
Rajiv Sanskrit: a lotus flower.
Rajko Slavic form of Radko.
Rajkumar Sanskrit: a prince.
Rajnish Sanskrit: the lord of the night.
Rajneesh, Rajnesh.
Raju Sanskrit: prosperity.
Raka Polynesian: a legendary wind god.
Rakah.
Rakaia Polynesian: the name of an early convert to Christianity.
Rakaunui Maori: the full moon.
Rakesh Sanskrit: the lord of the full moon.
Rakin Arabic: firm and steady.
Rakeen.

R – Boys

Rakitha A Sri Lankan name of uncertain meaning.
Raleigh Old English: from the meadow of the roe deer.
Rawleigh, Rawley, Rawly.
Ralph Old English: the counsel of the wolf; meaning a fearless adviser. See also Rolf and Rudolph.
Rafe, Ralf, Ralphed, Raoul (French), *Raul* (Italian), *Raúl* (Spanish).
Ralston Old English: a dweller on Ralph's farm or estate.
Rama Sanskrit: pleasing. An alternative name for the Hindu god Vishnu.
Rahm, Rahma, Ram, Ramachandra, Ramah, Raman.
Ramazan Arabic: another name for the sacred Muslim month of Ramadan.
Raamazan, Ramzan.
Rambert Teutonic: mighty and brilliant.
Ramelan Indonesian: a prophecy.
Rameses Ancient Egyptian: born of the sun.
Ramesis, Ramses, Ramsis.
Ramesh Sanskrit: an alternative name for the Hindu god Vishnu.
Ramesha, Romesh.
Rami Arabic: one who throws.
Ramy.
Ramiro Spanish: a great judge or adviser.
Ramón/Ramone See Raymond.
Ramsay Old English: an island of wild garlic. Most commonly a Scottish name.
Ramsey, Ramzay, Ramzey, Ramzy.
Ramsden Old English: the ram's valley.
Ramses/Ramsis See Rameses.
Ramy See Rami.
Ramzay/Ramzey See Ramsay.
Ranald See Ronald.
Rand/Rande/Randie Diminutives of Randolph.
Randal/Randall/Randell See Randolph.
Randhir Sanskrit: brave.
Randolph Old English: a wolf-like shield. See also Rendell.
Randal, Randall, Randell, Randolf, Randyl, Randyll. Diminutives: Rand, Rande, Randie, Randy.
Randy/Randyl See Randolph.
Ranen Hebrew: he who sings with joy.
Ranga Sanskrit: another name for the god Vishnu.
Rangadas, Ranganath.
Rangan Sanskrit: a flower.
Ranger Old French: the keeper of the forest.
Rainger.
Rangi Aboriginal: a beach. Polynesian: heaven.
Raniera Maori form of Daniel.
Raniero Italian form of Rayner.

Ranjit Sanskrit: delight.
Ranjiv Sanskrit: victorious.
Rankin Old English: a little shield.
Rankyn.
Ranko Slavic: one who is early.
Ransford Old English: from the ford of the raven.
Ransley Old English: from the meadow of the raven.
Ranslee, Ransleigh.
Ransom Old English: a warrior's son.
Ranulf Old Norse: wolf-like advice.
Ranulph.
Raouf *See* Rauf.
Raoul French form of Ralph.
Rapata Maori form of Robert.
Raphael Hebrew: God heals, or healed by God. The angel of healing and one of the four archangels in the Bible.
Rafael (German, Portuguese, Spanish), *Rafaele, Rafaelle, Rafal* (Polish), *Raffaele* (Italian), *Raffaelle, Raffaello* (Italian), *Raffhael, Rafhael.*
Diminutives: Raf, Rafa, Rafe, Raff.
Raqi Arabic: one who is educated or superior.
Raqib Arabic: the observer.
Raqibul.
Rarmian An unusual name of uncertain meaning.
Ras/Rasmus *See* Erasmus.
Rashid Arabic: the well-guided one; a director.
Raschid, Rashad, Rasheed, Rashed.

Rastafarian A member of a Jamaican cult that believes in black supremacy.
Rustafarian.
Diminutive: Rasta.
Rastislav Slovak form of Rostislav.
Rastus *See* Erastus.
Rata Maori: friendly. Polynesian: the name of a great chief.
Ratan *See* Ratna.
Rateb Arabic: from a surname.
Rati Nepali: the night.
Ratko Slavic: of the battle.
Ratna Sanskrit: a jewel.
Ratan, Ratnam.
Rato Nepali: red.
Rauf Arabic: the compassionate one.
Raouf.
Rauiti Maori: a small leaf.
Raul *See* Ralph.
Rauman/Raumano *See* Roman.
Raupo Maori: a bullrush.
Raven Middle English: a bird name.
Ravi Sanskrit: of the sun.
Ravid Hebrew: the wanderer.
Ravinder Old French: a mountain stream.
Ravindra Sanskrit: the lord of the sun.
Raviv Hebrew: rain.
Raviwar The Hindi name for Sunday.
Ravivara.
Rawan Aboriginal: the rain.
Rawdon Old English: the rough hill.
Rawden.
Rawiri A Maori form of David.
See also Rewi.

Rawleigh/Rawley/Rawly
See Raleigh.
Rawson Old English: the son of the little wolf.
Rawsen.
Ray Old French: a king. See also Raymond, Rex and Roy.
Rae, Raey, Raye, Rea, Reay, Rey, Reye.
Rayan Arabic: sustenance, or favoured by God.
Raihan, Rayhaan, Rayhan.
Raybon English from Old French: the good king.
Raebon, Reabon, Reybon.
Rayburn Old English: from the brook of the deer.
Raeburn, Raeburne, Rayburne.
Raydar See Radar.
Rayden See Raiden.
Rayford English from Old French: the king's ford.
Raeford, Raeforde, Rayford, Reaford, Reaforde, Reyford, Reyforde.
Rayhaan/Rayhan See Rayan.
Rayko A Bulgarian form of Radko.
Raymond Teutonic: a wise or mighty protector.
Raemond, Raemund, Raimo (Finnish), *Raimond, Raimondo* (Italian), *Ramón* (Spanish), *Ramone, Raymon, Raymund, Réamann* (Irish Gaelic), *Reamonn* (Scottish Gaelic), *Redman, Redmond* (Irish), *Redmund, Romone.*
Diminutives: Rae, Raey, Ray, Raye, Raym, Rea, Reay.
Raynard See Reynard.
Rayne See Raine.
Rayner German: a wise warrior.
Ragnar (Scandinavian), *Rainer* (German), *Rainerio* (Spanish), *Rainier* (French), *Raniero* (Italian), *Raynar, Raynor, Reiner, Reinier* (Dutch), *Reyner.*
Raynold See Reynold.
Rayworth A form of Ray.
Raziel Hebrew: the secrets of God. The name of an angel who reveals heavenly secrets and knowledge of the future.
Razvan A Romanian name of uncertain meaning.
Rea See Ray and Raymond.
Reabon See Raybon.
Read Old English: red-haired.
Reade, Reed, Reede, Reid, Ried.
Reading Old English: son of the red-headed one.
Redding.
Readon A form of Reid.
Readan, Readen, Reedan, Reeden, Reedon, Reidan, Reiden, Reidon, Riedan, Rieden, Riedon.
Readthorn Old English: a red thorn.
Readthorne, Redthorn, Redthorne.
Reaford/Reaforde See Rayford.
Reagan/Reagen See Regan.
Réamann Irish Gaelic form of Raymond.

Reamonn Scottish Gaelic form of Raymond.
Rearden/Reardon *See* Riordan.
Reave/Reaves *See* Reeve.
Reay *See* Ray and Raymond.
Rebel Latin: the rebellious one. Also a girl's name.
Recep A Turkish name of uncertain meaning.
Rechab Hebrew: the horse rider.
Red Often a diminutive, but can be used as a proper name.
Redd.
Redcliff/Redcliffe *See* Radcliffe.
Redding *See* Reading.
Redford *See* Radford.
Redman/Redmond/Redmund *See* Raymond.
Redthorn *See* Readthorn.
Reece *See* Rhys.
Reed/Reede *See* Read.
Reedan/Reedon *See* Readon.
Reef An unusual modern name.
Reefe, Rif, Ryf.
Reegan *See* Regan.
Reeve Old English: a steward.
Reave, Reaves, Reeves, Reive, Reives, Reve, Reves.
Regan Irish Gaelic: the descendant of a king. Also a girl's name.
Reagan, Reagen, Reegan, Rehgan, Rehgen, Reigan, Reigen, Rhegan.
Regin Old Norse: a blacksmith; a figure from mythology.
Reginald Old English: a wise and powerful ruler. *See also* Reynold and Ronald.
Raginald (Teutonic), *Reginauld, Regnauld, Rheinallt* (Welsh), *Rignold.*
Diminutives: Reg, Reggie.
Reginos *See* Riginos.
Régis French: a ruler or king.
Regis.
Regnauld *See* Reginald.
Rehgan/Rehgen *See* Regan.
Rehua Polynesian: a god of the stars.
Reid *See* Read.
Reidan/Reiden/Reidon *See* Readon.
Reidar Scandinavian: probably meaning a warrior.
Reigan/Reigen *See* Regan.
Reiley/Reilly *See* Riley.
Rein/Reine *See* Raine.
Reinald/Reinaldo *See* Reynold.
Reiner *See* Rayner.
Reinhard/Reinhardt *See* Reynard.
Reinhold *See* Reynold.
Reis/Reise *See* Rhys.
Reive/Reives *See* Reeve.
Reks *See* Rex.
Remi/Remie Diminutives of Remington. *See also* Rémy.
Remigius/Remigijus *See* Rémy.
Remington Old English: from the farm of ravens.
Diminutives: Remi, Remie.
Remo *See* Remus.
Remus Latin: fast. In legend, one of the brothers who founded Rome. *See also* Romulus.
Remo (Italian).

Rémy French from Latin: an oarsman.
Remi, Remie, Remigius (Latin),
Remigijus (Lithuanian).
Renaldo Spanish form of Ronald.
Renard/Renaud *See* Reynard.
Renato/Renault *See* René.
Rendell A diminutive of Randolph or Reynold.
Rendall, Rendle, Rendoll.
René Latin: reborn.
Renato (Italian, Portuguese, Spanish), *Renault*.
Renfred Old English: mighty but peaceful.
Renfrew Celtic: from the still river.
Reni/Renie *See* Renny.
Rennard *See* Reynard.
Renny Irish Gaelic: small but powerful. Also a girl's name.
Reni, Renie, Rennie.
Renouf *See* Ragnulf.
Rens Dutch diminutive of names such as Laurentius.
Rense.
Renshaw Old English: from the forest of the ravens.
Renton Old English: the farm of the powerful one.
Renten.
Renzo A diminutive of Lorenzo. *See* Laurence.
Reo/Reon *See* Rio.
Repton The name of a town in Derbyshire, England.
Ret/Rett *See* Rhett.
Reuben Hebrew: behold, a son. One of Jacob's sons in the Bible.
Reubin, Reuvin, Ruben, Rubens (Portuguese), *Rubin, Rueben*.
Diminutives: Rube, Ruby.
Reuel Hebrew: a friend of God.
Ruel.
Reuvin *See* Reuben.
Reve/Reves *See* Reeve.
Revel Old French: a rebel, or one who makes merry. Also a girl's name.
Revell, Revelle, Revil, Revill, Reville.
Revere Latin: to regard with respect.
Revie Hebrew: Wednesday.
Revi.
Revil/Revill/Reville *See* Revel.
Rewa Polynesian: slender.
Rewi A Maori form of David. *See also* Rawiri.
Rex Latin: a king. *See also* Ray and Roy.
Raex, Reks, Rexim, Rexx.
Rexford English from Latin: the ford of the king.
Rey/Reye *See* Ray and Reynard.
Reybon *See* Raybon.
Reyford/Reyforde *See* Rayford.
Reynard Teutonic: brave, or a fox.
Raynard, Reinhard (German), *Reinhardt* (German), *Renard, Renaud* (French), *Rennard, Rynehard, Rynehart.*
Diminutives: Rey, Reye.
Reyner *See* Rayner.
Reynold Old English: a wise and

powerful ruler. *See also* Reginald, Rendell and Ronald.
Raynold, Reinald, Reinaldo, Reinhold (German), *Reynald, Reynaldo, Reynaud* (French).
Rez Hungarian: red-haired, or like copper.
Reza Arabic: satisfaction.
Riza.
Rhaglan *See* Raglan.
Rhain/Rhane *See* Raine.
Rhauri/Rhuarie *See* Rory.
Rheece/Rhees/Rheese *See* Rhys.
Rhegan *See* Regan.
Rheinallt Welsh form of Reginald.
Rhett Possibly a form of Rhys, but most likely invented by Margaret Mitchell for her character Rhett Butler in *Gone with the Wind*.
Ret, Rett, Rhet.
Rhian/Rhien *See* Ryan.
Rhisiart Welsh form of Richard.
Rhly *See* Riley.
Rhobert *See* Robert.
Rhod/Rhodd *See* Roderick and Rodney.
Rhodas *See* Rodas.
Rhoderic/Rhoderick *See* Roderick.
Rhodes Greek: the place of roses. The name of an Aegean island.
Rhodas, Rodas (Spanish), *Rodes*.
Rhodney *See* Rodney.
Rhodri Welsh: the ruler of the wheel.
Rhodrie, Rhodry.
Rhori/Rhorie/Rhory *See* Rory.
Rhudd Welsh: red.
Rudd.
Rhun Welsh: grand.
Rhyce *See* Rhys.
Rhydderch Welsh form of Roderick.
Rhyden *See* Ryden.
Rhydwyn Welsh: a dweller by the white ford.
Rhylee/Rhyley/Rhylie *See* Riley.
Rhyll The name of a Welsh town.
Rhyl, Ryl, Ryll.
Rhys Welsh: ardent.
Reece, Rees, Reese, Reis, Reise, Rheece, Rhees, Rheese, Rhyce, Rhyse.
Rian/Riann *See* Ryan.
Ric A diminutive of names such as Eric, Patrick and Richard.
Ricard/Ricardinho/Ricardo *See* **Richard**.
Richard Teutonic: brave and strong. The name of three English kings.
Rhisiart (Welsh), *Ricard, Ricardinho* (Portuguese), *Ricardo* (Spanish), *Ricarrdo, Riccardo* (Italian), *Richerd, Rickard, Rickert, Rikard* (Scandinavian), *Rikhard* (Finnish), *Rikhart* (Dutch), *Rikkard* (Finnish), *Riqard, Riquard, Rykard, Ryszard* (Slavic). *Diminutives:* Dick, Dickie, Dicky, Ric, Rich, Richie, Rick, Rickee, Rickie, Ricky, Rico (Spanish), Rik, Rikk, Riku (Finnish), Riq, Rique, Ritchie, Ryk.
Richman Old English: a powerful protector.

Richmond.
Rick/Rickard/Rickie/Ricky *See* Richard.
Ricker Old English: a powerful army.
Rickert *See* Richard.
Ricks/Rickson *See* Rix.
Rico Spanish: prosperous. *See also* Richard.
Rider Old English: a horseman or knight.
Ryder.
Ridge Old English: a ridge or long hill.
Ridges, Rydge, Rydges.
Ridgeway Old English: from the ridge road.
Ridgway.
Ridgley Old English: from the meadow's ridge.
Ridgleigh.
Ridley Old English: from the cleared wood.
Ridleigh, Ridlie, Ridly.
Riduan/Ridwan *See* Rizwan.
Ried *See* Read.
Riedan/Rieden *See* Readon.
Rieuwert Dutch: one who gives good counsel.
Ruerd, Rurd, Ruurd.
Rif *See* Reef.
Rigby Old English: the valley of the ruler.
Rigel Arabic: a foot. The brightest star in the constellation of Orion, marking the figure's left foot.
Rigg Old English: from the ridge.
Rig.
Riginos The name of a Greek saint.
Reginos.
Rignold *See* Reginald.
Rik/Rikard/Rikhard *See* Richard.
Riki Maori: small.
Riku Finnish diminutive of Rikhard (*see* Richard).
Riley Irish Gaelic: valiant. Old English: a rye meadow. Also a modern girl's name.
Reiley, Reilly, Rhly, Rhylee, Rhyley, Rhylie, Rily, Rylea, Rylee, Ryley, Ryly.
Rimu Polynesian: a tree. Also a girl's name.
Rinaldo Italian form of Ronald.
Rinchen *See* Rinzen.
Ring Old English: a ring.
Ringo Japanese: an apple. Old English: a bell-ringer.
Rinjin Japanese: the god of the oceans, similar to the Roman god Neptune.
Rinjen.
Rinky A modern Japanese name.
Rino Italian diminutive of names such as Marino and Nazzarino (*see* Nazarene).
Rinus Dutch diminutive of Marinus (*see* Marino) or Marius.
Rinzen Sherpa/Tibetan: the holder of intellect. Also a girl's name.
Rinchen.
Rio Spanish: a river.
Reo, Reon, Rion.

Riordan Irish Gaelic: a royal poet.
Rearden, Reardon.
Rip Diminutive of Ripley.
Ripley Old English: from the shouter's meadow.
Diminutive: Rip.
Riq/Riqard/Rique *See* Richard.
Rishi Sanskrit: a sage or saint.
Risley Old English: from the brushwood meadow.
Risleigh, Rizleigh, Rizley.
Risto Finnish diminutive of Kristo (*see* Christopher).
Riston Old English: from the brushwood farm.
Ritchie *See* Richard.
Ritter Teutonic: a knight.
Rive French: a riverbank.
Riven Middle English: to split apart.
Rivven.
River English from Old French: a river or waterway.
Rivers.
Rix Old English: the son of Richard.
Ricks, Rickson, Rixon.
Riyad Arabic: a garden.
Riyaad, Riyadh.
Riza *See* Reza.
Rizleigh/Rizley *See* Risley.
Rizwan Arabic: satisfaction.
Riduan, Ridwan, Rizwaan.
Roach/Roache *See* Roche.
Roald Old Norse: a famous ruler. A Norwegian form of Ronald.
Roal, Roel, Roeld.
Roan *See* Rowan.

Roarke Irish Gaelic: a famed ruler.
Rorke, Rourke, Ruark.
Robben/Robbin/Robbyn/Roben *See* Robin.
Robert Teutonic: famous, or bright fame. *See also* Hobson, Hopkin, Probert, Robertson and Robinson.
Raibeart (Scottish Gaelic), *Rapata* (Maori), *Rhobert* (Welsh), *Robbert, Roberto* (Italian, Spanish), *Rupert* (German).
Diminutives: Bert, Bob, Bobbie, Bobby, Rab (Scottish), Rabbie (Scottish), Rob, Robbie, Robby, Robi, Robin, Robyn.
Robertson The son of Robert.
Robi A diminutive of Robert.
Robin Originally a diminutive of Robert.
Robben, Robbin, Robbyn, Roben, Robyn.
Robinson English: the son of Robert or Robin.
Robis, Robison, Robson.
Robyn *See* Robin.
Roc/Roca *See* Rock.
Rocco Teutonic: to rest.
Rocko, Rocky, Roco, Rokko, Roko, Roque (Spanish, Portuguese).
Roche Old French: a rock.
Roach, Roache, Roch.
Rochester Old English: a rocky fortress, or camp on the rocks.
Rossiter.
Rock Old English: from the rock.
Roc, Roca (Spanish), *Rocke.*

R – Boys

Rocket English from French: a firework or missile.
Rockett, Roquet (French), *Roquett.*
Rockley Old English: from the rocky meadow.
Rockleigh, Rocklie.
Rocko/Rocky *See* Rocco.
Rockwell Old English: from the rocky well or spring.
Rod/Rodd/Roddie/Roddy *See* Roderick and Rodney.
Rodas/Rodes *See* Rhodes.
Rodda A Cornish surname.
Rodderic/Roddric/Roddrick *See* Roderick.
Roddman *See* Rodman.
Roddney *See* Rodney.
Roden Old English: from the valley of the reeds.
Rodan, Rowdan, Rowden.
Rodeney/Rodeny *See* Rodney.
Roderick Teutonic: a renowned ruler. *See also* Broderick.
Rhoderic, Rhoderick, Rhydderch (Welsh), *Rodderic, Rodderick, Roddric, Roddrick, Roderic, Roderich* (German), *Roderigo, Rodrick, Rodrigo* (Italian, Portuguese, Spanish), *Rodrigue* (French), *Rurik* (Russian, Scandinavian).
Diminutives: Rhod, Rhodd, Rick, Ricky, Rod, Rodd, Roddie, Roddy, Rui (Portuguese), Ruy (Portuguese).
Rodge/Rodger *See* Roger.

Rodman Teutonic: a famous hero.
Roddman.
Rodney English: from an old surname.
Rhodney, Roddney, Rodeney, Rodeny, Rodnee, Rodnie, Rodny.
Diminutives: Rhod, Rhodd, Rod, Rodd, Roddie, Roddy.
Rodolf/Rodolfo/Rodolphe *See* Rudolph.
Rodrick *See* Roderick.
Rodrigo/Rodrigue *See* Roderick.
Rodwell Old English: from the Christian's well.
Roe *See* Rowe.
Roel/Roeld *See* Roald, Roelof and Rowell.
Roeland Dutch form of Roland.
Roelof Dutch form of Rudolph.
Diminutive: Roel.
Roff/Roffe *See* Rolf.
Rogan Irish Gaelic: the red-haired one.
Rogen.
Rogelio Spanish: a famous soldier.
Rojelio.
Roger Teutonic: a famous spearman or warrior.
Rodger, Rogerio (Spanish), *Rogero, Rogier* (Dutch), *Rojer, Rudiger* (German), *Ruggero* (Italian), *Ruggiero* (Italian), *Rutger* (Dutch).
Diminutives: Hodge, Rodge, Rog.
Rohan Sanskrit: ascending. *See also* Rowan.

Rohen.
Rohit Hindi: red.
Roi/Roie/Roice *See* Roy, Royce and Royston.
Roial/Roiale/Roialle *See* Royal.
Rois/Roise *See* Royce.
Rojelio *See* Rogelio.
Rojer *See* Roger.
Rojo Spanish: red.
Rokko/Roko *See* Rocco.
Roland Teutonic: from the famed land.
Lorand (Hungarian), *Lorant* (Hungarian), *Orlando* (Italian), *Roeland* (Dutch), *Rolan* (Russian), *Rolande, Rolando, Rolant* (Welsh), *Roldan* (Spanish), *Rowland, Rowlande.*
Diminutives: Roley, Rollo.
Roldan Spanish form of Roland.
Roley *See* Roland and Rowley.
Rolf Teutonic: the famous wolf. *See also* Ralph and Rudolph.
Roff, Roffe, Rolfe, Rolph, Rolphe.
Roller One who rolls.
Rollin A form of Roland; probably an archaic diminutive.
Rollins, Rollinson.
Rollo *See* Roland.
Rolph/Rolphe *See* Rolf.
Roly *See* Rowley.
Romain/Romaine *See* Roman.
Roman Latin: a citizen of Rome.
Rauman, Raumano, Romain (French), *Romaine, Romane, Romano* (Italian), *Romanus* (Slavic), *Romas* (Portuguese), *Romayn, Romayne.*
Romas Portuguese form of Roman.
Romayn/Romayne *See* Roman.
Rome A man from Rome.
Romare (Italian).
Romeo Latin: a pilgrim to Rome. A famous Shakespearean character.
Romesh *See* Ramesh.
Romney Welsh: a curving river. A placename from Kent, England.
Romolo Italian form of Romulus.
Romone *See* Raymond.
Romulus Latin: one of the legendary brothers who founded Rome. *See also* Remus.
Romolo (Italian), *Romuald.*
Ron A diminutive of Ronald and other Ron names.
Ronald Old English: a wise and powerful ruler. *See also* Reginald, Reynold, Roald and Ronson.
Raghnall (Irish), *Ranald, Renaldo* (Spanish), *Rinaldo* (Italian), *Roald* (Norwegian), *Ronalde, Ronaldo* (Portuguese).
Diminutives: Ron, Ronnie, Ronny.
Ronan Irish Gaelic: a little seal (the animal).
Ronin.
Rondell American: possibly a form of Ron.
Rondel, Rondelle.
Rongo Maori/Polynesian: the god of rain and fertility.
Roni Hebrew: my joy.

Ronin *See* Ronan.
Ronit Hebrew: a song. Irish Gaelic: prosperity.
Ronnie/Ronny Diminutives of Ronald and other Ron names.
Ronson Old English: the son of Ronald.
Rooney Irish Gaelic: red-haired.
Roonee, Rooni, Roonie, Roony.
Roosevelt Dutch: from the rose field.
Roper Old English: a rope-maker.
Roque Portuguese and Spanish forms of Rocco.
Roquet/Roquett *See* Rocket.
Rorke *See* Roarke.
Rory Irish Gaelic: the red king.
Rhauri, Rhaurie, Rhori, Rhorie, Rhory, Rorey, Rorie, Ruairi, Ruari, Ruaridh.
Roscislaw Polish form of Rostislav.
Roscoe Old Norse: from the deer forest.
Rosco, Rosko, Roskoe.
Rosell/Roselle *See* Rozelle.
Roshan Persian: splendid; one who emanates light. Also a girl's name.
Rosko/Roskoe *See* Roscoe.
Roslin Old French: the small red-haired one.
Roslyn, Rosselin, Rosslin, Rosslyn.
Rosmer Danish: a seahorse, or from the sea.
Rozmer.
Ross Scottish Gaelic: from the headland or peninsula. *Rosse.*
Diminutives: Rossi, Rossie.
Rossario Italian: a male form of Rosa, meaning a rose.
Rosselin/Rosslin/Rosslyn *See* Roslin.
Rossiter *See* Rochester.
Rosso Spanish: red.
Rostam Iranian: a figure from Persian legend.
Roustam, Rustam.
Rostislav Slavic: a glorious usurper. *Rastislav* (Slovak), *Roscislaw* (Polish).
Roswald Teutonic: a mighty horse. *Roswell.*
Rothwell Old Norse: from the red well or spring.
Roudolf/Roudolph *See* Rudolph.
Rouen The name of a city in northern France.
Rourke *See* Roarke.
Rouse *See* Rowse.
Rouslan *See* Ruslan.
Roustam *See* Rostam.
Routledge *See* Rutledge.
Rove Middle English: to wander.
Rover Old English: a roofer, or one who roves.
Rowan Irish Gaelic: the little red-haired one. Can also be a girl's name.
Roan, Rohan, Rohen, Rowen, Ruwan, Ruwen.
Rowdan/Rowden *See* Roden.
Rowe Old English: either a hedgerow

or the rough one.
Roe, Row, Wroe.
Rowell Old English: from the deer spring.
Roel.
Rowland *See* Roland.
Rowley Old English: from the rough meadow.
Roley, Roly, Rowleigh, Rowlie, Rowly.
Rowse Cornish: from the heathland.
Rouse.
Rowson Old English: the son of the red-haired man.
Rowsan.
Roxbury Old English: from the rock fortress.
Roxburgh.
Diminutive: Rox.
Roy Old French: a king. Scottish Gaelic: the red one. Also a diminutive of Royce, Royston and other similar names. *See also* Ray and Rex.
Roi (French), *Roie, Roye.*
Royal Middle English: one who is kinglike.
Roial, Roiale, Roiall, Roialle, Royale, Royall, Royalle.
Royce Old English: the son of the king.
Roice, Rois, Roise, Royse.
Diminutives: Roi, Roy, Roye.
Roydon Old English: from the hill of rye.
Royde, Royden.

Royns *See* Ryence.
Royse *See* Royce.
Royston Old English: an English placename.
Roylsten, Roylston, Roysten.
Diminutives: Roi, Roy, Roye.
Rozelle More commonly a girl's name but sometimes used for boys by African-Americans.
Rosell, Roselle, Rozell.
Rozmer *See* Rosmer.
Rua Maori: a lake.
Ruadh Irish Gaelic/Scottish Gaelic: the red one (as in red-haired).
Diminutive: Ruadhan.
Ruairi/Ruari/Ruaridh *See* Rory.
Ruanaku Polynesian: a legendary figure.
Ruark *See* Roarke.
Ruben/Rubens/Rubin *See* Reuben.
Rudd *See* Rhudd.
Rudi *See* Rudolph.
Rudiger German form of Roger.
Rudolph Teutonic: a famous wolf. *See also* Ralph and Rolf.
Rodolf (Dutch, German), *Rodolfo* (Italian, Spanish), *Rodolphe* (French), *Roelof* (Dutch), *Roudolf, Roudolfe, Roudolph, Roudolphe, Rudolf* (Scandinavian, Slavic).
Diminutives: Dolf, Dolph, Roel (Dutch), Rudi, Rudy, Ruedi, Ruud (Dutch).
Rudra The Hindu god of storms, wind and lightning.
Rudy *See* Rudolph.

R – Boys

Rudyard Old English: from the red enclosure.
Rueben See Reuben.
Ruedi See Rudolph.
Ruel See Reuel.
Ruerd See Rieuwert.
Rufford Old English: from the rough ford.
Rufus Latin: red-haired.
Ruggero/Ruggiero Italian forms of Roger.
Rui Portuguese diminutive of Rodrigo (see Roderick).
Ruy.
Ruka Maori form of Luke.
Rukh Nepali: a tree.
Rumford Old English: from the wide ford.
Rune Old Norse: secret lore.
Rupe Polynesian: the brother of Maui, a legendary hero.
Rupert See Robert.
Rurd See Rieuwert.
Rurik Russian and Scandinavian forms of Roderick.
Ruric.
Ruru Maori: a New Zealand owl.
Rush Old English: a marshy plant. Also a diminutive of Rushford.
Rusch, Rusche, Rushe.
Rushdi Arabic: one who follows the right path.
Rushdie.
Rushford Old English: from the ford with rushes.
Rushforde.

Diminutive: Rush.
Ruskin Teutonic: the small red-haired one.
Ruslan Turkish: like a lion.
Rouslan, Ruzlan.
Russ A diminutive of Russell.
Russell Old French: with red hair.
Diminutives: Russ, Rustie, Rusty.
Russet Middle English: a reddish-brown colour.
Russett.
Rustafarian See Rastafarian.
Rustam See Rostam.
Rustie/Rusty See Russell.
Ruston Old English: the farm in the brushwood.
Rustan, Rusten, Rustin.
Rutger See Roger.
Rutherford Old English: from the cattle ford.
Rutland Old Norse: from the stump land.
Rutledge Old English: from the red pool.
Routledge.
Rutley Old English: from the stump meadow.
Rutleigh.
Ruud Dutch diminutive of Rudolph.
Ruurd See Rieuwert.
Ruwan/Ruwen See Rowan.
Ruy See Rui.
Ruzlan See Ruslan.
Ry/Rye Diminutives of names such as Rylan and Ryman.
Ryan Irish Gaelic: a little king.

Rhian, Rhien, Rian, Riann, Ryann, Ryen, Ryenn, Ryhan, Ryhen, Ryon.

Rycroft Old English: from the rye field.

Ryden Old English: from the place of rye.
Rhyden.

Ryder *See* Rider.

Rydge/Rydges *See* Ridge.

Ryen *See* Ryan.

Ryence Celtic: a Welsh king in Arthurian legend.
Royns, Ryens, Ryons.

Ryf *See* Reef.

Ryhan/Ryhen *See* Ryan.

Ryk/Rykard *See* Richard.

Ryl/Ryll *See* Rhyll.

Rylan Old English: from the rye land.
Ryland, Rylen, Rylon.
Diminutives: Ry, Rye.

Ryle Old English: from the hill of rye.

Rylea/Rylee/Ryley/Ryly *See* Riley.

Ryman Old English: a rye seller.
Diminutives: Ry, Rye.

Rynehard/Rynehart *See* Reynard.

Ryo Japanese: well-built.

Ryon *See* Ryan.

Ryons *See* Ryence.

Ryszard Slavic form of Richard.

Ryton Old English: from the rye farm.
Ryten.

Ryu Japanese: a dragon.

Saabih Arabic: one who arrives in the morning.

Sábado *See* Sabbath.

Saban *See* Saben.

Sabas/Sabath/Sabato *See* Sabbath.

Sabastain/Sabastian/Sabastyan *See* Sebastian.

Sabbath Hebrew: born on the Sabbath (Saturday in the Jewish religion; Sunday to Christians).
See also Saturday.
Sábado (Portuguese, Spanish), *Sabas* (Hebrew), *Sabath, Sabatino, Sabato* (Italian), *Sabbaton* (Greek), *Shabbat* (Hebrew).

Saben Latin: a Sabine man (from central Italy).
Saban, Sabian, Sabin, Sabino.

Saber *See* Sabre.

Sabian/Sabin/Sabino *See* Saben.

Sabir Arabic: the patient one.

Sabiti African: born on a Sunday.

Sabre French: sword-like.
Saber.

Sacha *See* Alexander and Sasha.

Sacharias A combination of Sacha and Zacharias.
Sasharias.

Sachel/Sachell *See* Satchel.

Sacheverell Old French: a leap of the young goat.

Sachiel The angel of water and Thursday.

Sachin Hindi: pure existence. The name of a famous Indian cricketer (Sachin Tendulkar).
Sachio Japanese: fortunate.
Sadik Arabic: truthful or faithful. *Sadiki, Sadiq.*
Sadwyn The Welsh name for Saturday and the planet Saturn.
Saeth Welsh: an arrow.
Safari Swahili: an adventurous expedition. Also a girl's name. *Safarie, Safari, Saffari, Saffarri.*
Safed Hindi: white.
Safford Old English: from the willow ford.
Safwat Arabic: possibly meaning the chosen one.
Sage Old French: wise. Also the name of a herb. *Saige, Sayge.*
Sagi Aramaic: mighty, or strong.
Sagittarius Latin: an archer. A zodiac sign. *Sagittario, Sagittarios.*
Sahal Native American: a falcon. *Sahale.*
Sahen Hindi: a falcon.
Sahir Hindi: a friend.
Saige *See* Sage.
Sail Middle English: to travel by sea. *Saile, Sale, Sayl, Sayle.*
Sailor Middle English: one who sails. *Sailer, Sayler, Saylor.*
Saimoni A Polynesian form of Simon.
Saka Swahili: a hunter.
Sakari Finnish form of Zachary.
Sakda Thai: power.
Sakeel *See* Shakil.
Sakelarios A Greek name of uncertain meaning.
Sakima Native American: a king.
Sal A diminutive of Salvador and other Sal names.
Saladin *See* Salah.
Salah Arabic: good, righteous. *Saladin, Saleh.*
Salama *See* Salim.
Sale *See* Sail.
Saleel *See* Salil.
Saleem/Salem *See* Salim.
Saleh *See* Salah.
Salif A West African name of uncertain meaning. *Saleef.*
Salil Sanskrit: water. *Saleel.*
Salim Arabic: safe, secure. *Salama, Saleem, Salem, Selim.*
Salisbury Old English: the fort by the willow pool.
Salman/Salomo/Salomon *See* Solomon.
Salter Old English: a salt seller.
Salton Old English: from the place in the willows.
Salvador Spanish from Latin: a saviour. *See also* Saviour. *Salvarie, Salvator* (Polish), *Salvatore* (Italian), *Salvidor, Salvitore.*

Diminutive: Sal.
Salvidor/Salvitore *See* Salvador.
Sam Korean: an achievement. Also a diminutive of Samson and Samuel.
Samaki Swahili: a fish.
Samak (Thai), *Samakah* (Arabic).
Samani Polynesian: like a salmon.
Samedi The French name for Saturday.
Sami Arabic: the elevated one.
Samir Arabic: a pleasant companion.
Sameer.
Sammie/Sammy Diminutives of Samson and Samuel.
Samson Hebrew: of the sun, or a strong man. A biblical name.
Sampson, Sansom, Sanson, Sansone (Italian).
Diminutives: Hami (Maori), Sam, Sammie, Sammy.
Samstag The German name for Saturday.
Samuel Hebrew: asked of God; a name from the Bible. *See also* Saul and Shem.
Hamuera (Maori), *Samual, Samuale, Samuele, Samuil* (Russian), *Shmuel* (Hebrew).
Diminutives: Hami (Maori), Sam, Samm, Sammie, Sammy.
San Korean: a mountain.
Sanah Sanskrit: one who is loved.
Sana.
Sanborn Old English: from the sandy brook.
Sanchai A Thai name of uncertain meaning.
Sancho Spanish: truthful and sincere.
Sanctus Latin: holy or saintly.
Sanctius.
Sandalfon Hebrew: the angel of prayer and birds.
Sandberg A Swedish surname.
Sandeep Sanskrit: power or strength.
Sandheep, Sandhip, Sandip.
Sanders Old English: the son of Alexander.
Sander, Sanderson, Saunder, Saunders, Saunderson.
Sandesh Sanskrit: a message.
Sandford *See* Sanford.
Sandi/Sandie/Sandy *See* Alexander.
Sandip *See* Sandeep.
Sandon Old English: from the sandy hill.
Sanden, Santen, Santon.
Sandor Hungarian diminutive of Alexander.
Sanford Old English: from the sandy ford.
Sandford.
Sani Sanskrit: the Hindi name for the planet Saturn.
Sanivara The Hindi name for Saturday.
Shanwar.
Sanjay Sanskrit: triumphant.
Sanjiv Hindi: long-lived, or a good man.
Sanjeev.
Sankara Sanskrit: auspicious.

Sansom/Sanson/Sansone *See* Samson.
Santen *See* Sandon.
Santiago Spanish: of St James. *See* Iago. *Diego.*
Diminutives: Thiago, Tiago.
Santo Italian and Spanish forms of Santos. Also the Cornish diminutive of Alexander.
Santon *See* Sandon.
Santos Spanish: of the saints. *See also* Toussaint.
Santo (Italian, Spanish), *Sanzio* (Italian).
Santoso Indonesian: peaceful.
Sanzio *See* Santos.
Saqil *See* Shakil.
Sarad Sanskrit: the Hindi name for autumn.
Sharad (Urdu).
Sarat Sanskrit: a sage.
Sarath.
Sardis Latin: carnelian, a semi-precious stone.
Sardius.
Sarfraz Arabic: one who holds his head high.
Sarfaraz.
Sargent Old French: a military officer.
Sargant, Sarjant, Sarjent, Sergeant, Sergent.
Sargon Persian: the sun prince.
Sarjant/Sarjent *See* Sargent.
Sarju A Sanskrit name of uncertain meaning.
Sarkir A Turkish name of uncertain meaning.
Sarkis Armenian: a shepherd or protector.
Sarngin Sanskrit: an archer.
Sasa Russian form of Sasha.
Sasha A Russian diminutive of Alexander.
Sacha (French), *Sasa* (Russian), *Sascha* (German), *Sasho* (Slavic), *Zascha, Zasha.*
Sasharias *See* Sacharias.
Sasho Slavic form of Sasha.
Sasso Italian: a stone or rock.
Satchel Middle English: a bag, often used for carrying books.
Sachel, Sachell, Satchell.
Satish Sanskrit: Lord Shankar, another name for the Hindu god Shiva.
Satordi The Basque name for Saturday.
Satoshi Japanese: the wise one.
Saturday Middle English from Latin: a day name, literally Saturn's day. *See also* Sabbath.
Sadwyn (Welsh), *Samedi* (French), *Samstag* (German), *Sanivara* (Sanskrit), *Satordi* (Basque), *Saturni, Saturnin, Saturnus, Shanwar* (Sanskrit), *Shavato* (Greek), *Sobota* (Czech, Polish), *Zadornin* (Basque).
Saturn English from Latin: the Roman god of agriculture; also a planet name. *See also* Sani and

Saturday.
Sadwyn (Welsh), *Saturne, Saturni, Saturnin, Saturnino, Saturninus, Saturnius, Saturno, Saturnus.*

Satyr Greek: a mythical forest god, with the legs, ears and horns of a goat.

Saul Hebrew: asked for, or prayed for; a name from the Bible. *See also* Samuel.
Saule, Sawyl (Welsh).

Saunders/Saunderson *See* Sanders.

Sava Slavic: the name of an Eastern European river.

Savan *See* Sawan.

Savas Turkish: warlike.

Saviero Italian form of Xavier.

Savigny A French placename.

Saville Old French: from the willow estate.
Savile, Savill.

Savin Latin: a cedar tree.

Saviour Middle English: one who rescues or saves. *See also* Salvador.
Savior.

Savitri The Hindu god of the morning and evening sun.

Savvas An unusual Greek name.
Savas.

Sawan Sanskrit: the month of August.
Savan.

Sawyer Old English: a sawer of wood.

Sawyl Welsh form of Saul.

Saxby Old Norse: from the farm of the short sword.

Saxon Old English: of the Saxons, or people of the sword.
Saxen, Saxin, Saxyn.

Saxton Old English: from the farm of the Saxon.

Saybo Tibetan: yellow.

Sayed Arabic: the lord or master.
Sayid, Sayyid, Seyed, Syed (Urdu).

Sayer Celtic: a carpenter.
Sayers, Sayre.

Sayge *See* Sage.

Sayl/Sayle *See* Sail.

Sayler/Saylor *See* Sailor.

Sayyid *See* Sayed.

Schaefer/Schaffer *See* Shaffer.

Schain/Schaine/Schein *See* Shane.

Schivas *See* Chivas.

Schwarz German: black.

Schylar/Schyler *See* Skyler.

Scipio Latin: a staff or walking stick.

Scorpius Greek: a scorpion. A constellation and a zodiac sign.
Scorpeo, Scorpio, Scorpios, Skorpio, Skorpios, Skorpius.

Scott Old English: from Scotland.
Scot, Scotte.
Diminutives: Scottie, Scotty.

Scout Middle English: one who observes and reports.
Scoutt, Scowt, Scowte.

Scully Irish Gaelic: a herald or town crier.
Sculley, Scullie, Skulley, Skullie, Skully.

Seabert Old English: sea glorious.
Sebert.
Seaborne Old English: the sea warrior.
Seaborn, Seabourne.
Seabrook Old English: from a brook by the sea.
Seabrooke.
Seager *See* Seger.
Seal Middle English: a hall, or a marine animal.
Seale, Seel, Seele, Sele.
Sealey Old English: blessed.
Sealy, Seeley, Seely.
Seamus Irish Gaelic form of James.
Seamas, Shamus, Shaymus.
Sean Irish Gaelic form of John.
See also Shane.
Shaan, Shaughan, Shaun, Shaune, Shawn, Shawne, Siôn (Welsh).
Seanan *See* Senan.
Seargeoh/Seargio *See* Sergius.
Searle Teutonic: an armed warrior.
Searl, Serle.
Seaton Old English: a place by the sea.
Seton.
Seb The Ancient Egyptian god of the earth. Also a diminutive of Sebastian.
Sebastian Latin: a man from Sebasta. The name of a 3rd-century saint.
Sabastain, Sabastian, Sabastyan, Sebastain, Sebastiano (Italian), *Sébastien* (French), *Sebastyan, Sebastyen, Sevastian* (Russian).
Diminutives: Bastian, Bastien, Seb.
Sebedeus Welsh form of Zebadiah.
Sebert *See* Seabert.
Sebo Hungarian: possibly meaning one who is revered.
Secil *See* Cecil.
Secundus Latin: the second child.
Secondo (Italian).
Sedgewick Old English: from the farm in the rushes.
Sedgwick.
Sedgley Old English: from the warrior's meadow.
Sedgeley, Sedgleigh.
Seel/Seele *See* Seal.
Seeley/Seely *See* Sealey.
Sef An Ancient Egyptian lion god.
Sefton Old English: the dweller at the place in the rushes.
Seger Old English: the sea warrior.
Seager, Segar.
Seido Japanese: bronze.
Seif Arabic: a holy sword, or the sword of religion.
Seiko Japanese: possibly meaning truth and force.
Seith/Seithe *See* Seth.
Selby Old Norse: from the willow farm. Also a modern girl's name.
Selbee, Selbeigh, Selbey, Selbie.
Seldon Old English: from the house on the hill.
Selden.
Sele *See* Seal.

Selig *See* Zelig.
Selim *See* Salim.
Selix A Georgian name of uncertain meaning.
Selwyn Latin: of the woods.
Herewini (Maori), *Selwin, Selwinn, Selwinne, Selwynn, Selwynne.*
Selyf Welsh form of Solomon.
Semi Latin: half.
Semie, Semih.
Semyon Russian form of Simon.
Senan Irish Gaelic: old, or wise. The name of a saint.
Seanan, Sinan.
Senior Middle English: one who is older or of higher rank.
Sennett Old English: bold in victory.
Sinnett, Sinnott.
Seppelt A German surname.
September English from Latin: from the word for seven or seventh (September was originally the seventh month of the year).
Septembra (Swahili), *Septembre* (French), *Setembro* (Portuguese), *Settembre* (Italian).
Septimus Latin: the seventh son.
Septimo.
Sequoia Native American: a large coniferous tree. Also a girl's name.
Sequoya.
Serafino Italian from Hebrew: the ardent one. The masculine form of Seraphina.
Serafine, Seraphine, Seraphino.

Seraj Arabic: a source of light.
Siraj.
Serdar *See* Sirdar.
Seren Welsh: a star.
Serren.
Sereno Italian: the serene and tranquil one. The masculine form of Serena.
Serene, Serino.
Serge/Sergei/Sergey/Sergeo *See* Sergius.
Sergeant/Sergent *See* Sargent.
Sergius Latin: a Roman family name.
Seargeoh, Seargio, Serge (French), *Sergei* (Russian), *Sergeo, Sergey, Sergi* (Spanish), *Sergie, Sergio* (Italian), *Sergiusz* (Slavic), *Sergiy* (Russian).
Serhat Turkish: a man of the frontier.
Serif *See* Sharif.
Serino *See* Sereno.
Serkan A Turkish name of uncertain meaning, possibly blood head.
Serkhan, Sirkan, Sirkhan.
Serle *See* Searle.
Serren *See* Seren.
Servet A Turkish name of uncertain meaning.
Sesil *See* Cecil.
Sesto Italian form of Sextus.
Setembro/Settembre *See* September.
Seth Hebrew: a biblical name meaning the appointed one; one of the sons of Adam and Eve. Sanskrit: a bridge. Also the Ancient Egyptian god of darkness.

S – Boys

Seith, Seithe, Set, Sethe.
Setiawan Indonesian: faithful.
Seto Nepali: white.
Seton *See* Seaton.
Sevastian *See* Sebastian.
Seven Middle English: an unusual 'number name'.
Severn The name of a British river.
Severo Italian: one who severe or rigid.
Severio, Severus, Severyn.
Seville A Spanish city.
Seward Old English: a sea defender.
Sexton Old French: a church official.
Sextus Latin: the sixth son.
Sesto (Italian).
Seyed *See* Sayed.
Seymour Old French: from a placename.
Seymore.
Shaahid *See* Shahid.
Shaan A form of Shane. *See also* John.
Shabbat *See* Sabbath.
Shabutu *See* Shevat.
Shackleton Old English: a farm on a strip of land. The surname of a famous Antarctic explorer.
Shade Middle English: comparative darkness. Also a girl's name.
Shady, Shadye, Shayde.
Shadi Arabic: a singer.
Shadow Middle English: a shaded area. A character in one of Shakespeare's plays.
Shadrach Hebrew: a name from the Old Testament.
Shadrack, Shadrak, Shedrach, Shedrack, Shedrak.
Diminutive: Shad.
Shadwell Old English: from the shady stream.
Shae *See* Shay and Shea.
Shaeden/Shaedon/Shaedyn *See* Shayden.
Shafan Hebrew: a coney or rabbit.
Shaffer English from German: a shepherd.
Schaefer, Schaeffer, Schafer, Schaffer, Shaefer, Shafer.
Shafiq Arabic: compassionate.
Shah Persian: the king.
Shahar Jewish: the dawn.
Shahid Arabic: a witness.
Shaahid, Shaheed, Shahed.
Shahin Persian: an eagle or falcon.
Shaheen.
Shahram A Persian name of uncertain meaning.
Shaka Zulu: the founder. Also the name of a Japanese god.
Shakil Arabic: handsome.
Sakeel, Saqil, Shakeel, Shaquil, Shaquille.
Shakir Arabic: the grateful one.
Shakur.
Shaldan/Shalden/Shaldon *See* Sheldon.
Shale Old English: a type of rock.
Shayle.
Shalom Hebrew: peace. *See also* Solomon.

Shamba Swahili: a farm.
Shamir Hebrew: as hard as flint.
Shamus *See* Seamus.
Shanahan Irish Gaelic: the wise one.
Shandy Old English: boisterous.
Shandey, Shandi, Shandie.
Shane A form of Sean. *See also* John.
Chayn, Chayne, Cheyn, Cheyne, Schain, Schaine, Schein, Scheine, Shaan, Shayn, Shayne, Sheyn, Sheyne.
Shani Hebrew: red.
Shankar Sanskrit: he who gives happiness.
Shanley Irish Gaelic: a venerable hero.
Shanleigh.
Shannon Irish: from the name of a river in Ireland. Also a girl's name.
Shannan, Shannen, Shannyn, Shanon, Shanyn.
Shanwar *See* Sanivara.
Shappa Native American: red thunder.
Shaquil/Shaquille *See* Shakil.
Sharad *See* Sarad.
Sharaf Honour. The name of the Baha'i month encompassing 31 December to 18 January so a suitable name for a Capricorn baby.
Sharif Arabic: the honourable one.
Charif, Serif (Turkish).
Sharma Sanskrit: giving protection.
Sharrod A modern name of uncertain meaning.
Shared, Sharod, Sharred.
Shashank A name from Hindu mythology; of uncertain meaning.
Shashi Sanskrit: like a moonbeam.
Shaughan/Shaun/Shaune Irish forms of Sean.
Shaugnessy Irish Gaelic: a common surname.
Shaugnessey, Shaunessey, Shawnesey, Shawnessey.
Shavar Hebrew: a comet.
Shavato The Greek name for Saturday.
Shaw Old English: from the grove of trees.
Shawe.
Shawn/Shawne *See* Sean.
Shawnesey *See* Shaughnessy.
Shay Tibetan: crystal. *See also* Shea.
Shae, Shaye.
Shayde *See* Shade.
Shayden A combination of Shane or Shay and Hayden.
Shaeden, Shaedon, Shaedyn, Shaydon, Shaydyn, Sheaden, Sheadon, Sheadyn.
Shayle *See* Shale.
Shaymus *See* Seamus.
Shayn/Shayne *See* Shane.
Shea Irish Gaelic: the stately one.
Shae, Shay.
Sheaden/Sheadyn *See* Shayden.
Shedrach/Shedrak *See* Shadrach.
Sheehan Irish Gaelic: peaceful.
Sheerbrook *See* Sherbrook.
Sheffield Old English: from the

crooked field, or the sheep field.
Shekhar Sansrkit: the ultimate, a peak.
Shikhar.
Shelby Old English: the dweller at the ledge estate.
Shelbee, Shelbi, Shelbie.
Sheldon Old English: from the steep valley.
Shaldan, Shalden, Shaldon, Sheldan, Shelden.
Shelley Old English: from the wood, or the meadow's edge. More commonly a girl's name.
Shelly.
Shelton Old English: from the place on the ledge.
Shelten.
Shem Hebrew: probably a variation of Samuel. The eldest son of Noah in the Bible.
Shemesh Hebrew: of the sun.
Shen Chinese: a deep thinker.
Sheng *See* Shing.
Shep Old English: one who keeps sheep.
Shepp.
Shepard Old English: a shepherd.
Sheperd, Shephard, Shepherd, Sheppard, Shepperd.
Sher Sanskrit: a lion.
Sheraga Aramaic: light.
Sherborne Old English: a clear stream.
Sherborn, Sherbourn, Sherbourne, Sherburn.
Sherbrook Old English: a bright stream or brook.
Sheerbrook, Sheerbrooke, Sherbrooke, Sherebrook, Sherebrooke.
Sheridan Irish Gaelic: the wild one. Also a girl's name.
Sheirdan, Sheirden, Sheriden, Sheridon, Sheridyn.
Sherlock Old English: fair-haired.
Sherlocke.
Sherman Old English: a wool-cutter.
Shermen, Shermin, Shermyn.
Sherwin Old English: a swift runner.
Sherwyn, Sherwynd.
Sherwood Old English: from the bright forest.
Sherwyn/Sherwynd *See* Sherwin.
Sheva *See* Shiva.
Shevat The eleventh lunar month of the Hebrew calendar, corresponding to the zodiac sign of Aquarius.
Shabutu (Babylonian).
Sheyn/Sheyne *See* Shane.
Shigeru Japanese: luxuriant.
Shihab Arabic: a shooting star.
Shikhar *See* Shekhar.
Shiloh Hebrew: a place of rest. A biblical placename.
Shilo, Shylo, Shyloh.
Shima Japanese: an island dweller.
Shimanu *See* Sivan.
Shimon *See* Simon.
Shinden Japanese: a temple.

Shine Middle English: a glow, or to excel.
Shyne.
Shing Chinese: a victory.
Sheng.
Shingo Japanese: the humble one.
Shinichi Japanese: one who is true.
Shinji Japanese: a true ruler.
Shino Japanese: a bamboo stem.
Shipley Old English: from the sheep pasture.
Shipleigh.
Shipton Old English: the dweller at the sheep farm.
Shiro Japanese: the fourth son.
Shiva Sanskrit: benign. An important Hindu god.
Sheva, Shiv, Shivendra, Shivesh, Shivraj, Siva.
Shivnarine Sanskrit, probably from Shiva.
Shlomo *See* Solomon.
Shmuel *See* Samuel.
Sho Japanese: to soar or fly.
Shou.
Shoda Japanese: a level field.
Shoden The Japanese name for Ganesh, the Hindu elephant-headed god of wisdom.
Sholto Scottish Gaelic: a sower of seed.
Shomari Swahili: forceful.
Shoreland Old English: the land by the shore.
Shorland.
Shreyas Sanskrit: fame, or goodness.
Shreyash.
Shusaku An unusual Japanese name.
Shwe Burmese: golden.
Shway.
Shyam Sanskrit: dark blue or black.
Shyama.
Shylo/Shyloh *See* Shiloh.
Shyne *See* Shine.
Siarl Welsh form of Charles.
Sibran Breton form of Cyprian, meaning a man from Cyprus.
Siddartha Sanskrit: one who has accomplished his goal. A name of the Buddha.
Sidell Old English: from the broad valley.
Sidall, Siddall, Siddel, Siddell.
Sidney Old English: from the riverside meadow. Old French: from St Denis.
Sidnee, Sidny, Sidonius (Slavic), *Sydnee, Sydnei, Sydney, Sydny.*
Diminutives: Sid, Syd.
Sidonius Slavic form of Sidney.
Sieffre Welsh form of Geoffrey.
Siegbert Teutonic: a bright or famous victory.
Diminutives: Siggy, Sigi.
Siegfried Teutonic: peace after victory.
Siegfrid, Sigfrid, Sigfried.
Diminutives: Siggy, Sigi.
Siemen Dutch form of Simon.
Siggy/Sigi Diminutives of names such as Siegbert and Siegfried.
Sigmund Teutonic: a victorious

protector.
Siegmund, Sigismund, Sigmond, Sigmunt, Zigmond, Zigmund, Zygmond, Zygmund, Zygmunt.

Sigurd Old Norse: a victorious guardian.
Zigurd.

Siimon *See* Simon.

Silas/Silus *See* Silvanus.

Silva/Silvan/Silvano *See* Silvanus.

Silvanus Latin: from the forest. *See also* Silvester.
Silas, Silus, Silva, Silvan, Silvano (Italian), Silvino (Portuguese), Silvio (Italian), Silvius, Sylvain (French), Sylvan, Sylvio.
Diminutive: Sly.

Silvester Latin: of the woods. *See also* Silvanus.
Silvestre (Spanish), Silvestro (Italian), Sylvere, Sylvester.
Diminutive: Sly.

Silvino/Silvio/Silvius *See* Silvanus.

Sim/Sims *See* Simon.

Simba *See* Simha.

Simeon The biblical form of Simon.

Simha Sanskrit: a lion. The Hindi name for the zodiac sign of Leo.
Simba (Swahili).

Simon Hebrew: the listener. *See also* Simpson.
Saimoni (Polynesian), Semyon (Russian), Shimon (Jewish), Siemen (Dutch), Siimon, Simeon, Simin, Simo (Finnish, Serbian), Simond, Simone (Italian), Simos,
Siomon (Irish Gaelic), Symin, Symon, Szymon (Polish), Ximen (Spanish), Ximenes (Spanish), Ximeno (Basque), Ximens (Spanish), Ximun (Basque).
Diminutives: Sim (Scottish Gaelic), Sime (Slavic) Sims, Sym, Syms.

Simos *See* Simon.

Simplice French: simplicity; one who is uncomplicated.

Simpson The son of Simon.
Simson.

Sinan *See* Senan.

Sinbad Teutonic: a sparkling prince.

Sinclair French: from St Clair.

Sindri Icelandic: the name of a figure in Norse legend.

Singh Sanskrit: a lion.
Singa, Singha (Indonesian).

Sinisa Slavic: a son.

Sinnett/Sinnott *See* Sennett.

Siomon Irish Gaelic form of Simon.

Sion Hebrew: one who is praised. Also a Welsh form of John and Sean (Siôn).
Syon.

Siôr Welsh form of George.

Siradanai An unusual name from Thailand.

Siraj *See* Seraj.

Sirdar Nepali: a leader or guide.
Serdar.

Sirius Greek: hot or scorching. The name of the brightest star in the sky, also known as the Dog Star.

Sirkan/Sirkhan *See* Serkan.
Sirroul A modern form of Cyril.
Sisay An Ethiopian name of uncertain meaning.
Sisi African: born on a Sunday.
Sisto *See* Sixtus.
Siva *See* Shiva.
Sivan The third lunar month of the Hebrew calendar, corresponding to the zodiac sign of Gemini.
Shimanu (Babylonian).
Sixtus Latin: the sixth.
Sisto (Italian), *Sixto*.
Sjeng A Dutch name of uncertain meaning.
Skeeter Old English: the fast one, or a swift, as in the bird.
Skeet.
Skelly Irish Gaelic: a storyteller.
Skelton Old English: from the place on the ledge.
Skene Scottish Gaelic: a bush.
Skipper Dutch: a ship's captain.
Diminutives: Skip, Skipp.
Skirnir Old Norse: the shining one. A mythological figure.
Skorpio/Skorpios/Skorpius *See* Scorpius.
Skulley/Skullie/Skully *See* Scully.
Skylar Dutch: a schoolmaster.
Schylar, Schyler, Skyler, Skylor.
Slade Old English: from the valley.
Slader *See* Slade and Slater.
Slaiter/Slaitor *See* Slater.
Slaney Irish Gaelic: a placename, meaning a river.
Slany.
Slatan *See* Zlatan.
Slate Middle English: a fine-grained rock.
Slayte.
Slater Middle English: one who works with slates.
Slader, Slaiter, Slaitor, Slator, Slatter, Slayter, Slaytor.
Slattery Irish Gaelic: strong or bold.
Slava Slavic: a form of Stanislav (*see* Stanislaus).
Slavah, Slavik, Slavko.
Slaven/Slavin *See* Slevin.
Slavko *See* Slava.
Slavoj Slavic: one who is famous.
Slawomir Slavic: great or famous peace.
Slavomir.
Slayte *See* Slate.
Slayter/Slaytor *See* Slater.
Slevin Irish Gaelic: the mountain climber.
Slaven, Slavin, Sleven.
Sloan Irish Gaelic: a warrior.
Sloane.
Slobodan Slavic: freedom.
Sly A diminutive of Silvanus and Silvester.
Smaragdos Greek: probably from a word meaning a green gem.
Smaragdus.
Smedley Old English: from the level meadow.
Smedly.
Smith Old English: a blacksmith.

Smithe, Smyth, Smythe.
Snape Old English: from the boggy patch.
Snare Middle English: a snare or trap.
Sneddon Old English: from the valley of the Snead.
Snedden.
Snowden Old English: from the snowy hill.
Snowdon.
Soames Old English: the homestead on the lake.
Soame.
Sobek The Ancient Egyptian crocodile god who was associated with the sun.
Sobota The Czech and Polish names for Saturday.
Socrates An ancient Greek philosopher.
Socratis.
Sohrab Persian: illustrious.
Sol Latin: the sun; the name of the Roman and Norse gods of the sun. Also a diminutive of Solomon.
Soll.
Solamh Gaelic form of Solomon.
Solly *See* Solomon.
Solomon Hebrew: wise and peaceful; a son of David in the Bible. *See also* Shalom.
Horomona (Maori), *Salman*, *Salomo* (German), *Salomon* (French, Spanish), *Selyf* (Welsh), *Shlomo* (Jewish), *Solamh* (Gaelic), *Solamon, Soloman, Suleiman* (Arabic), *Suleyman* (Turkish), *Sulieman, Zalman* (Yiddish), *Zalmen, Zelman.*
Diminutives: Sol, Solly, Zolli, Zollie, Zolly.
Solon Greek: the wise one.
Soma The Hindu warrior god of sacrifice, and also a Hindi name for the moon.
Som, Soman.
Somavar The Hindi name for Monday, literally the day of the moon.
Sombar (Nepali), *Somwar* (Hindi).
Diminutive: Som.
Somdev Sanskrit: the lord of the moon.
Somerby *See* Somerset.
Somerled Old Norse: the summer traveller. A Scottish name.
Somerset Old English: from the summer farm or settlement. The name of an English county.
Somerby.
Somerton Old English: from the summer town.
Sommerton.
Somerville Old English: from the summery hill.
Somervell, Sommerville.
Somwar *See* Somavar.
Sona Hindi: gold, or golden.
Sonah.
Sonam Sherpa/Tibetan: the fortunate one. Also a girl's name.

Sonchat A Thai name of uncertain meaning.
Sondre Norwegian: from the south.
Sondri, Sundri, Sundrie.
Soner Turkish: the last man.
Sonnet English from French: a type of poem. Also a girl's name.
Sonet, Sonnett.
Sonntag The German name for Sunday.
Sonny A diminutive for names beginning with Son.
Sono African: an elephant.
Sophocles Greek: the name of a classical dramatist.
Sorel/Sorell *See* Sorrell.
Soren Danish from Latin: the stern one.
Sorin, Sorren, Sorrin.
Sorin Romanian: of the sun. *See also* Soren.
Sorley Old Norse: the summer wanderer.
Sorlee, Sorleigh, Sorlie.
Sorrell Old French: bitter. A 'plant name'.
Sorel, Sorell, Sorrel.
Sorren/Sorrin *See* Soren.
Soul A modern name, meaning the soul or spirit.
Soule.
Southwell Old English: from the southern spring.
Sovan Cambodian: golden.
Soven.
Sparke Old Norse: the lively one.

Spark.
Sparrow Old English: a 'bird name'.
Sparo, Sparow, Sparowe, Sparro, Sparrowe.
Spartacus Latin: a man from the city of Sparta.
Spartaco.
Speck Middle English: the small or little one.
Specke, Spek.
Spencer Old French: a dispenser of provisions.
Spence, Spense, Spenser.
Spike Old English: a nail, or an ear of grain. Generally a nickname.
Spyke.
Spiridon Greek: of the soul or spirit.
Spiridone, Spiro, Spiros, Spyridon, Spyro, Spyros.
Sprig Middle English: a twig or small branch.
Sprigg, Sprigge.
Spyro/Spryos *See* Spiridon.
Squire Old French: a knight's attendant.
Stack Old Norse: a haystacker.
Stac, Stak, Stakk.
Stacy Latin: prosperous. Also a girl's name.
Stacey, Stacie.
Staffan Swedish form of Stephen.
Stafford Old English: from the ford by the landing place.
Staffard, Stafferd.
Stainlay/Stainley *See* Stanley.
Stainten/Stainton *See* Stanton.

Stak/Stakk *See* Stack.
Stamford/Stamforde *See* Stanford.
Stan A diminutive of Stanley and other names starting with Stan.
Stanbury Old English: from the stone fort.
Standen Old English: a dweller in the stony valley.
Standon.
Standish Old English: from the rocky pasture.
Stanfield Old English: from the stony field.
Standfield, Stansfield.
Stanford Old English: a dweller at the rocky ford.
Stamford, Stamforde, Stanforde.
Stanhope Old English: from the stony valley.
Stanislaus Slavic: the glorious ruler or government. *See also* Slava.
Stanislas, Stanislav (Czech, Russian), *Stanislaw* (Slavic).
Stanislav *See* Stanislaus.
Stanley Old English: from the stony meadow.
Stainlay, Stainley, Stanlay, Stanleigh, Stanlie, Stanly.
Diminutive: Stan.
Stansfield *See* Stanfield.
Stanton Old English: from the rocky farm or estate.
Stainten, Stainton, Stanten, Staunten, Staunton, Stenton.
Stanwick Old English: from the rocky village.
Stanwyck.
Star English: a star.
Starr.
Starbuck Old Norse: the stream in the sedges.
Staunten/Staunton *See* Stanton.
Stavrinos/Stavros Greek forms of Stephen.
Stean/Steane *See* Sten.
Steaphan Scottish Gaelic form of Stephen.
Stearn/Stearne *See* Sterne.
Stedman Old English: a farmer.
Steadman.
Steele Old English: like steel.
Steel.
Steen *See* Sten.
Steev/Steeve *See* Stephen.
Stefan/Stefano/Stefanos/Steffan/Steffen *See* Stephen.
Steffensen/Steffenson *See* Stevenson.
Stein/Steinar/Steiner *See* Sten.
Stelian/Stelios *See* Stylianos.
Stellan A Scandinavian name of uncertain meaning.
Sten Swedish: a stone. *See also* Stone.
Stean, Steane, Steen (Danish), *Stein* (German, Norwegian), *Steinar, Steiner* (Norwegian), *Stine.*
Stenton *See* Stanton.
Stepan *See* Stephen.
Stephen Greek: a crown or garland. *See also* Stevenson and Stinson.
Estéban (Spanish), *Étienne*

(French), *István* (Hungarian), *Staffan* (Swedish), *Stavrinos* (Greek), *Stavros* (Greek), *Steaphan* (Scottish Gaelic), *Stefan* (German, Polish, Russian, Scandinavian), *Stefano* (Italian), *Stefanos* (Greek), *Steffan* (Welsh), *Steffen*, *Stepan* (Czech, Russian), *Stephan* (German), *Stéphane* (French), *Stephano*, *Stephanus*, *Stevan*, *Steven*, *Stevin*, *Stiofan* (Irish Gaelic), *Tepene* (Maori), *Tipene* (Maori). *Diminutives:* Steev, Steeve, Steve, Stevey, Stevie.

Stephensen/Stephenson *See* Stevenson.

Sterling Old English: a little star, or a starling. *Stirling*.

Sterne Old English: austere, stern. *Stearn, Stearne, Stern*.

Stert *See* Sturt.

Stevan/Steve/Steven *See* Stephen.

Stevenson The son of Stephen. *Steffensen, Steffenson, Stephensen, Stephenson, Stevensen*.

Stevie/Stevin *See* Stephen.

Stewart Old English: a steward or keeper of a household. *Steward, Stuart. Diminutives:* Stew, Stewie, Stewy, Stu.

Stig Old Norse: the wanderer. *Stieg*.

Stiggur English Gypsy: a gate.

Stigur.

Stijn Dutch diminutive of names such as Augustijn and Constantijn.

Stiles *See* Styles.

Stiliyan *See* Stylianos.

Stine *See* Sten.

Stinson Old English: the son of Stephen, or the son of stone. *Stimson*.

Stiofan Irish Gaelic form of Stephen.

Stirling *See* Sterling.

Stockard An English surname.

Stockley Old English: a clearing with tree stumps. *Stockleigh*.

Stockton Old English: from the place near the tree trunk. *Stockten*.

Stoddard Old English: the horsekeeper. *Stoddart, Stodderd, Stoddert*.

Stojan *See* Stoyan.

Stoke Old English: from the settlement. *Stokes*.

Stone Middle English: a rock. *See also* Sten.

Stonewall Middle English: a wall made of stone.

Storey Old Norse: the large one. *Storee, Stori, Storie, Story*.

Storm Old English: a tempest. *Storme*.

Storr Old Norse: a great man.

Story Middle English: a tale or narrative. *See also* Storey.

Stover Old English: one who tends the stove.
Stovin.

Stowe Old English: from the place or religious site.
Stow.

Stoyan Slavic: to stay or stand.
Stojan.

Stradbroke The name of two islands in Moreton Bay, off Brisbane.
Stradbrook, Stradbrooke.

Strahan Scottish Gaelic: a little valley. A town in Tasmania.
Strachan, Straughan, Straun, Strawn, Struan.

Stratford Old English: from the ford on a Roman road. The name of an English city.

Strathmore Scottish Gaelic: a large valley.
Strathmoor, Strathmoore, Strathmor.

Stratis/Strato/Stratos Diminutives of Eustratios.

Stratton Old English: from the place on a Roman road.
Strattan, Stratten.

Straun/Strawn *See* Strahan.

Streda The Czech name for Wednesday.

Stroud Old English: the overgrown marshland.

Struan *See* Strahan.

Stu/Stuart *See* Stewart.

Sturt Old English: from the promontory.
Stert.

Styles Old English: from the stile.
Stiles.

Stylianos Greek: from stylos, meaning a pillar. The name of a 7th-century saint.
Stelian (Romanian), *Stiliyan* (Bulgarian).
Diminutives: Stelios, Stylios.

Styx Greek: an underworld river in classical mythology.

Subhi Arabic: early in the morning.
Subi.

Sudi Swahili: luck.

Suffield Old English: a dweller in the southern field.

Sufyaan Arabic: a shipbuilder.
Sufian, Sufyan.

Sujan Sanskrit: honest.

Sukarno A popular Indonesian name.

Sul The Welsh name for Sunday.

Suleiman/Sulieman *See* Solomon.

Suleyman Turkish form of Solomon.

Sulgwyn Welsh: born on Whit Sunday.

Sullivan Irish Gaelic: the black-eyed one.
Sullavan, Sullaven, Sulliven.

Sultan Arabic: a king or ruler. The name of the Baha'i month that encompasses 19 January to 6 February, so appropriate for an Aquarius child. *See also* Zoltan.

Sulwyn Welsh: the fair sun.

Suman Sanskrit: cheerful and wise.

Sumba The Tibetan name for the month of March.
Sumner Old French: the one who summons.
Sun Chinese: bending, or decreasing. Nepali: gold or golden.
Sundance An unusual name, probably from the movie *Butch Cassidy and the Sundance Kid*.
Sundar Sanskrit: handsome.
Sunday Old English: the day of the sun.
Sonntag (German), *Zondag* (Dutch).
Sundri/Sundrie *See* Sondre.
Sungur Nepali: a pig.
Suran The name of a town in Iran.
Suranjan Sanskrit: one who is pleasing.
Surendra Sanskrit: another name for the god Indra.
Suren, Suresh.
Surt Old Norse: black. A fire giant in Norse mythology.
Surya Sanskrit: the sun. The name of a Javanese sun god.
Suria.
Susila Indonesian: a person of good character.
Susilo.
Sutcliffe Old English: from the south cliff.
Sutcliff.
Sutherland Old Norse: from the southern land.
Sutton Old English: the dweller at the southern farm or town.
Sutten.
Svatoslav Slavic: bright glory.
Sven Old Norse: a youth.
Svein (Norwegian), *Svend* (Danish).
Svenbjörn Old Norse: Sven and Björn (a bear).
Sverre Norwegian: the wild one.
Svetozar Slavic: radiant; a shining light.
Svetoslav.
Diminutive: Svetko.
Swain Old English: a swineherd. Old Norse: youthful.
Swaine, Swayn, Swayne.
Swami Sanskrit: a religious teacher.
Swaraj Sanskrit: freedom.
Sweeney Irish Gaelic: the little hero.
Sweeny.
Swindon Old English: from the hill of the pigs. An English city.
Swinden, Swinten, Swinton.
Swinford Old English: the pig ford.
Swithin Old English: strong. The name of an English saint.
Swithun.
Sycamore Greek: a 'tree name'.
Sydenham Old English: from the wide river meadow.
Sydnei/Sydney/Sydny *See* Sidney.
Syed Urdu form of Sayed.
Sykes Old English: at the stream or gully.
Sylvain/Sylvan/Sylvio *See* Silvanus.
Sylvere/Sylvester *See* Silvester.

Sym/Syms Diminutives of Simon.
Symin/Symon *See* Simon.
Syon *See* Sion.
Syrus *See* Cyrus.
Szymon Polish form of Simon.

T

Taal *See* Tal.
Taavi Finnish form of David.
Tab/Tabb *See* Tabor.
Tabari Arabic: a historian.
   Tabarie.
Tabetu *See* Tevet.
Tabib Turkish: a physician.
Tábo Aboriginal: a snake.
Tabor Persian: a drum or drummer.
   Taber.
   Diminutives: Tab, Tabb.
Tabris The angel of free will.
Tabulum Aboriginal: my home.
   Tabulam.
Tad Irish Gaelic: a poet or philosopher. *See also* Teague.
   Tadgh, Tadhg, Tydhg.
Tad/Tadd/Taddeo/Tadeo *See* Thaddeus.
Tadashi Japanese: a faithful servant.
Taden A modern name, probably derived from the very popular Jaden.
   Tadan, Taedan, Taeden, Taidan, Taiden, Taihdan, Taihden, Taydan, Tayden.

Tadeusz Polish form of Thaddeus.
Tadi Native American: the wind.
Tadj/Tadji *See* Taj.
Tadzi Native American: the moon.
Tae *See* Taye.
Taedan/Taeden *See* Taden.
Tael African: green.
   Taele, Tayl, Tayle.
Tafari African: the awesome one.
Taffy Welsh diminutive of David.
Tag Teutonic: the day.
   Tage (Danish), *Tago* (Spanish)
   Tahg, Tajo (Spanish).
Taggart Gaelic: a priest.
Tagore Bengali: a lord. *See also* Thakur.
Tagu Burmese: the month of March/April, corresponding to the zodiac sign of Aries.
Taha Polynesian: one, or the firstborn.
Tahg *See* Tag.
Tahi Hawaiian: a mythological figure.
Tahir Arabic: pure and virtuous.
Tahj/Tahji *See* Taj.
Tahki *See* Taiki.
Tahl *See* Tal.
Tahmoor Aboriginal: a bronze-wing pigeon.
Tahn *See* Tan.
Tahnee *See* Tane.
Tahshi *See* Tashi.
Tahu A Polynesian name of uncertain meaning.
Tai Polynesian: the ocean. Thai: the south. Vietnamese: the talented one. *See also* Tye.

Taie.
Taiaha Maori: a long club.
Taidan/Taiden/Taihden *See* Taden.
Taiki Japanese: a big tree.
Tahki, Taki.
Tailer/Tailor *See* Taylor.
Taimurz *See* Teimuraz.
Taine *See* Tane.
Taiondai *See* Tyondai.
Tait/Taite *See* Tate.
Taiwo African: the firstborn twin.
Taj Hindi: the crowned one.
Tadj, Tadji, Tahj, Tahji, Taji.
Tajo *See* Tag.
Taka Japanese: a hawk.
Takao Japanese: possibly meaning respectful.
Takashi Japanese: praiseworthy.
Takawai Maori: a gourd or calabash.
Takeshi Japanese: bamboo, or a warrior.
Takeishi.
Taki *See* Taiki.
Takoda Native American: the friend of all.
Takuma Japanese: a pioneer of the truth.
Takumi.
Tal German: a valley. Hebrew: rain, or dew. Nepali: a lake.
Taal, Tahl.
Talan A modern name of uncertain meaning. Possibly based on Kalan.
Talen, Talon, Tallan, Tallen, Tallon, Taylan.
Talata Arabic: born on a Tuesday.
Also a girl's name.
Talatah.
Talbot Old French: from the valley.
Talbott.
Talen *See* Talan.
Talfryn Welsh: from the top of the hill.
Taliesin Welsh: a radiant brow.
Tallan/Tallen/Tallon *See* Talan.
Tallis Persian: wise, learned.
Talis, Tallys, Talys.
Talon *See* Talan.
Talor *See* Taylor.
Talus A bronze giant in Greek mythology.
Talos.
Tam Vietnamese: the heart. Also a diminutive of Thomas.
Tama Polynesian: a boy or son.
Tamaiti Maori: a son.
Taman Slavic: black- or dark-haired.
Tamen, Tamin.
Tamas Hungarian form of Thomas.
Tamati Maori form of Thomas.
Tamba Aboriginal: an ibis. Hindi: copper.
Tambo Aboriginal: a fish. A Queensland placename.
Tame Maori form of Tommy (*see* Thomas).
Tamim Arabic: solid or well formed.
Tameem.
Tamir Hebrew: tall.
Tammiku The Finnish name for January.
Tamiku.

Tammuz The Babylonian name for Adonis, a handsome youth in Greek mythology. Also the fourth lunar month of the Hebrew calendar, corresponding to the zodiac sign of Cancer.
Thammuz.
Tamus *See* Thomas.
Tan Vietnamese: fresh. Welsh: fire.
Tahn.
Tana/Tanay *See* Tane.
Tanapun A Thai name of uncertain meaning.
Tancred Teutonic: a thoughtful adviser.
Tane Polynesian: the name of a god of light.
Tahnee, Taine, Tana, Tanay.
Tanekaha Polynesian: a pine tree.
Tane Mahuta Maori: the god of the forest.
Tangaroa Polynesian: a god of the sea.
Tango The Tibetan name for January.
Tangohia Maori: to take hold of.
Tangwyn Welsh: peace.
Tani Japanese: from the valley.
Taniel Armenian form of Daniel.
Tanner Old English: a tanner or leather worker.
Tano Ghanaian: a river.
Tanzil Arabic: a revelation.
Tanzeel.
Tapanui Maori: the name of a New Zealand town.
Tapio Finnish: a figure from mythology.
Tara Sanskrit: the shining one.
Taran Sanskrit: heaven. Welsh: thunder.
Taranis, Taranu, Taren, Tarin, Tarran, Tarranis, Tarren, Tarrin, Tharan, Tharen, Tharin.
Taras Ukrainian: rebellious.
Tarasios.
Tarcisio An unusual Italian name.
Tarchisio, Tarchizio, Tarcizio.
Taree Aboriginal: a wild fig. A New South Wales town.
Tarek/Tareq *See* Tariq.
Taren/Tarin *See* Taran.
Targan Aboriginal: white.
Tariel The angel of summer.
Tariq Arabic: the night visitor.
Tarek, Tareq, Tarik.
Tarki Aboriginal: a perch (a fish).
Tarkin/Tarkyn *See* Tarquin.
Tarmo Finnish: one who is energetic.
Tarn Old Norse: a mountain pool.
Tarne.
Taro Japanese: the firstborn son.
Tarquin Latin: the name of two early Roman kings.
Tarkin, Tarkyn, Tarquinn.
Tarran/Tarranis/Tarren/Tarrin *See* Taran.
Tarrant Old English: from the name of a river.
Tarrent, Terrant, Terrent.
Tarro Aboriginal: a stone.
Tarrynce *See* Terence.
Tarun Sanskrit: young, tender.

Tashi Sherpa/Tibetan: prosperity. Also a girl's name.
Tahshi.

Tashretu *See* Tishri.

Tasman After Tasmania and Abel Tasman, the Dutch explorer who 'discovered' Tasmania.
Tazman.

Tatanka Native American: a black buffalo.

Tate Old Norse: jolly, cheerful. *See also* Tatum.
Tait, Taite, Tayt, Tayte.

Tatsu Japanese: a dragon.
Tatsuo, Tatsuro.

Tatsuya Japanese: the accomplished one.

Tatum Old English: from Tate's homestead.
Tatom.
Diminutive: Tate.

Taunton The name of a town in Somerset, England.
Taunten.

Taurean A suitable name for a boy born under the zodiac sign of Taurus.
Taure, Tauri, Taurian, Taurinos, Taurinus, Tauros, Taurus.

Tavas Hebrew: a peacock.

Tavi Jewish diminutive of David.

Tavish Scottish Gaelic: a twin; a form of Thomas. *See also* McTavish.
Tavis.

Tawa Native American: the sun.

Tawanda An unusual name from Zimbabwe; of uncertain meaning.

Tawhaki The Maori god of thunder and lightning.
Tawaki.

Tawhero Polynesian: a tree.

Tawhiri Polynesian: a tempest.

Tawhirimatea Maori: the god of the winds.

Taye A modern American name.
Tae, Tay.

Tayl/Tayle *See* Tael.

Taylan *See* Talan.

Taylor Old French: the tailor.
Tailer, Tailor, Talor, Tayler.

Taymuraz *See* Teimuraz.

Tayt/Tayte *See* Tate.

Taz Persian: a shot of liquor, or a goblet.
Tazz.

Tazman *See* Tasman.

Teague Irish Gaelic: a poet or philosopher. *See also* Tad.
Teage, Teigue, Tighe.

Teal English: a waterbird.
Teale.

Team Middle English: a group of people.
Teame, Teem, Teme.

Tean Cornish: a placename, from the Isles of Scilly.
Tehan.

Te Aroha Polynesian: the man of the long string.

Tecwyn Welsh: white, fair.

Ted/Teddie/Teddy *See* Edward, Theobald and Theodore.

Tedrich *See* Theodoric.
Teejae/Teejai/Teejay *See* Tejay.
Teem *See* Team.
Teemu Finnish: a diminutive of Nikodeemus (*see* Nicodemus).
Tehan *See* Tean.
Teigr Welsh form of Tiger.
Teigue *See* Teague.
Teimuraz Georgian: from a Persian name meaning a shah.
Taimurz, Taymuraz, Teymuraz.
Teirnan/Teirnon *See* Tiernan.
Teizo A popular Japanese name.
Tejas Sanskrit: brilliance.
Tejay An unusual name, based on the letters T and J.
Teejae, Teejai, Teejay, Tejae, Tejai.
Tekea Polynesian: a man of the sharks.
Teks *See* Tex.
Tel A diminutive of Terence.
Telek Polish: like iron.
Telemachus Greek: a distant fighter.
Telemachos.
Telford Old French: an iron-cutter.
Telfer, Telfor, Telfour, Telfourd.
Teman Hebrew: on the right-hand side, or from the south.
Tembo Swahili: an elephant.
Teme *See* Team.
Temel Turkish: fundamental.
Tempe A Sydney suburb, named after a valley in Greece.
Tempest Middle English: a storm.
Tempestt.
Templar Old French: a knight.
Templer.
Temuera Maori: after Temuera Morrison, a New Zealand actor.
Ten Japanese: the sky.
Tendai Southern African: be thankful.
Tenison *See* Tennyson.
Tennessee The name of a US state. Also a girl's name.
Tenessee, Tennesee.
Tennille The name of city in Georgia, the USA. More commonly a girl's name.
Teneal, Teneale, Teneel, Teneele, Tenille, Tenneal, Tenneel, Tenneele, Tenniel.
Tennyson Old English: the son of Dennis.
Dennison, Tenison, Tennison, Tenyson.
Tentagel/Tentagil *See* Tintagel.
Tenzing Sherpa/Tibetan: the holder of religion.
Tenzin.
Teo/Teodor/Teodosio *See* Theodore.
Teodulo Spanish from Greek: a slave of god.
Theodoulos.
Teofilo/Teofilio Portuguese and Spanish forms of Theophilus.
Tepene A Maori form of Stephen.
Te Ra Maori: the sun.
Terach Hebrew: possibly meaning a wild goat.
Terac, Terah, Terak.
Teran/Teren *See* Terran.
Terance *See* Terence.

Te Ranginui Maori: the sky father.
Terell/Terill *See* Terrell.
Terence Latin: smooth and polished.
Tarrynce, Terance, Terencio (Spanish), *Terenz* (German), *Terrance, Terrence, Thierry* (French), *Torrance, Torrence*. *Diminutives:* Tel, Terrie, Terry.
Tereus A king of Thrace in Greek legend.
Tero Finnish diminutive of Antero (*see* Andrew).
Terran Latin: the earth.
Teran, Teren, Terra, Terrano, Terren, Terreno (Italian).
Terrance/Terrence *See* Terence.
Terrant/Terrent *See* Tarrant.
Terrell Teutonic: belonging to Thor, the Norse god of thunder and lightning.
Terell, Terelle, Terill, Terille, Terrel, Terrelle, Terril, Terrill, Terrille, Terryl, Terryll, Terrylle, Teryl, Teryll, Terylle.
Terrie/Terry *See* Terence and Theodoric.
Tertius Latin: the third, or third child.
Tertio.
Teryl/Terylle *See* Terrell.
Tetsu Japanese: philosophy.
Tetsuya Japanese: the arrow of philosophy.
Teuton A person of German origin.
Tevet The tenth lunar month of the Hebrew calendar, corresponding to the zodiac sign of Capricorn.
Tabetu (Babylonian).
Tevin An African-American name of uncertain meaning, made popular through singer Tevin Campbell.
Teven, Tevenn, Tevinn, Tevvin, Tevvinn, Tevyn, Tevynn.
Tewart *See* Tuart.
Tewe A Maori or Polynesian name of uncertain meaning.
Tewesday/Tewsday *See* Tuesday.
Tex American: from Texas.
Teymuraz *See* Teimuraz.
Thabo Southern African: joy.
Thaddeus Greek: courageous. A biblical name.
Taddeo (Italian), *Tadeo* (Spanish), *Tadeusz* (Polish), *Thadeus*. *Diminutives:* Tad, Tadd, Thad.
Thai Thai: a free man. Vietnamese: many.
Thain/Thaine *See* Thane.
Thaksin Thai: probably meaning right-handed.
Taksin.
Thakur Sanskrit: a lord. *See also* Tagore.
Thakar, Thakir, Thakhor, Thakor, Thakore.
Thammuz *See* Tammuz.
Than Burmese: a million. An auspicious 'number name'.
Thanh (Vietnamese).
Thane Old English: a landholding soldier. Also a Scottish clan

chieftain.
Thain, Thaine, Thayn, Thayne.
Thanos Greek: noble.
Tharan/Tharen/Tharin *See* Taran.
Thatcher Old English: one who thatches roofs.
Thayn/Thayne *See* Thane.
Theano Greek: a divine name.
Themistocles Greek: the glory of the law.
Theo *See* Theobald, Theodore and Theodoric.
Theobald Teutonic: a bold leader of the people.
Thibault (French), *Tibald, Tibold* (German), *Tiobóid* (Irish Gaelic), *Tybalt.*
Diminutives: Ted, Teddie, Teddy, Theo.
Theodore Greek: the gift of God.
Feodore, Fyodor (Russian), *Teodor, Teodosio* (Italian, Spanish), *Theodor* (German), *Theodoros, Theodorus, Theofore, Theorodus, Todor* (Slavic), *Tudor* (Welsh).
Diminutives: Ted, Teddie, Teddy, Teo, Theo.
Theodis Greek: God's gift to the world.
Theodoric Teutonic: the ruler of the people. *See also* Derek.
Tedric, Thierry (French).
Diminutives: Terrie, Terry, Theo.
Theodoulos *See* Teodulo.
Theofore *See* Theodore.
Theon Greek: godly.

Theophilus Greek: one who is loved by God.
Teofilio, Teofilo, Theophile, Theophilos.
Theorodus *See* Theodore.
Theron Greek: the hunter.
Theros Greek: summer.
Theseus Greek: a hero of Greek legend.
Thiago A diminutive of Santiago.
Thian Vietnamese: smooth.
Thien.
Thibault French form of Theobald.
Thierry French form of Terence and Theodoric.
Thies/Thijs Dutch diminutives of Matthew.
Thilo German: a diminutive of names beginning with Diet (*see* Dieter).
Thomar Aboriginal: a small river.
Thomas Greek: a twin. One of the twelve apostles in the Bible. *See also* Tomkin.
Tamas (Hungarian), *Tamati* (Maori), *Tamus, Tavis* (Scottish Gaelic), *Tavish* (Scottish), *Thomasz, Thomaz, Toman* (Czech), *Tomas* (Czech, Irish and Scottish Gaelic, Spanish), *Tomasz* (Polish), *Tomaz* (Slavic), *Tomik* (Czech), *Tommaso* (Italian), *Tomo* (Slavic), *Tomos* (Welsh), *Toms* (Latvian), *Toomas* (Estonian), *Tuomas* (Finnish).
Diminutives: Tam (Scottish), Tame (Maori), Thom, Tom, Tomek

(Polish), Tommie, Tommo, Tommy, Toss.
Thor Old Norse: the god of thunder and lightning in Norse mythology. *See also* Torvald and Tory.
Thord (Norwegian), *Thorin*, *Thorr*, *Tor*, *Torben* (Danish), *Tord* (Norwegian), *Tore*.
Thorald Old Norse: ruling in the manner of Thor.
Thorburn Old Norse: Thor's warrior.
Thoreau Old French: thunder and water.
Thorhammer Scandinavian: the hammer of Thor.
Thorrhammer.
Thorin *See* Thor.
Thorleigh/Thorley *See* Thornley.
Thormund Old English: Thor's protection.
Thormond, Thurmond, Thurmund.
Thorn Old English: a prickle or sharp part of a plant.
Thorne.
Thornley Old English: from the thorny clearing.
Thorleigh, Thorley, Thornleigh, Thurleigh, Thurley.
Thornton Old English: from the place among the thorns.
Thornten.
Thorpe Old English: from the farm village.
Thorp.
Thorstan/Thorsten *See* Thurstan.
Thorvald *See* Torvald.

Thoth An Ancient Egyptian god, similar to the Roman god Mercury.
Thu Vietnamese: born in the autumn.
Thurleigh/Thurley *See* Thornley.
Thurmond/Thurmund *See* Thormund.
Thursday Middle English: the day of Thor, the Norse god of thunder and lightning.
Thursdae, Thursdai, Thursdaie, Torstai (Finnish).
Thurso A Scottish placename.
Thurstan Old English: Thor's stone.
Thorstan, Thorsten, Thorston, Thursten, Thurston, Thurstone.
Thye *See* Tye.
Thyer *See* Tyer.
Tiago A diminutive of Santiago.
Tiare Maori form of Charles.
Tiba Native American: grey.
Tibah.
Tibald/Tibold *See* Theobald.
Tiberius Latin: after the River Tiber.
Tibor (Hungarian).
Tibor *See* Tiberius.
Tie *See* Tye.
Tien Chinese: heavenly. Vietnamese: the first. Also a girl's name.
Tieondai *See* Tyondai.
Tiernan Irish Gaelic: a lord.
Keirnan, Kiernan, Teirnan, Teirnon, Tierney, Tiernon, Tirnan.
Tierney Irish Gaelic: the descendant of a lord.
Tiarney.
Tieson *See* Tyson.

Tiger From a Middle English word (tigre). The name of a well-known golfer (Tiger Woods).
Teigr (Welsh), *Tiga, Tigah, Tigar, Tigre, Tigris, Tigro, Tigryi, Tygar, Tyger, Tygre.*

Tighe *See* Teague.

Tika *See* Petrika.

Tiki Polynesian: one who is fetched, as in a spirit after death.

Tilar/Tiler *See* Tyler.

Tilford Old English: from the good man's ford.
Tilforde.

Tilman Old English: a tiller or a tile-maker.
Tillman.

Tim/Timmie/Timmy *See* Timothy.

Timaeus/Timaios Greek forms of Timothy.

Timana A Maori name of uncertain origin.

Timin Arabic: a mythological sea serpent.

Timo Dutch and Finnish forms of Timothy.

Timofei *See* Timothy.

Timon Greek: a reward, an honour.
Tymon.

Timor Malay: the east.

Timoteos Estonian form of Timothy.

Timothy Greek: honouring God, or honoured by God.
Timaeus (Greek), *Timaios* (Greek), *Timo* (Dutch, Finnish), *Timofei* (Russian), *Timoteo* (Italian, Spanish), *Timoteos* (Estonian), *Timothée* (French), *Timotheus* (Dutch), *Timoti* (Maori), *Tymothy.*
Diminutives: Tim, Timmie, Timmy, Tym.

Timoti Maori form of Timothy.

Tinan *See* Tynan.

Tino Italian: a diminutive of names such as Celestino and Valentino.

Tintagel Celtic: a Cornish placename; the supposed location of King Arthur's legendary castle.
Tentagel, Tentagil, Tintagil.

Tiobóid Irish Gaelic form of Theobald.

Tipene Maori form of Stephen.

Tir *See* Tyr.

Tiran/Tiren/Tiron *See* Tyran.

Tirnan *See* Tiernan.

Tirol *See* Tyrol.

Tise/Tison *See* Tyson.

Tishri The seventh lunar month of the Hebrew calendar, corresponding to the zodiac sign of Libra.
Tashretu (Babylonian).

Titan A giant in Greek mythology. A satellite of the planet Saturn.
Tytan.

Titian/Titiano/Titianus *See* Tiziano.

Tito/Titos *See* Titus.

Titus Latin: an old Roman name.
Tito (Italian, Portuguese, Spanish), *Titos* (Greek), *Tytus* (Polish).

Tivon Hebrew: a nature lover.

Tiziano Italian: of the Tizia people, a Roman family.
Titian, Titiano, Titianus, Tizian.

Tjaard Dutch: one who watches the people.
Tjeerd.

Toa Maori: a champion; the brave one.

Tobee/Tobey *See* Tobias.

Tobias Hebrew: God is good. A biblical name.
Tobee, Tobey, Tobi, Tobia, Tobiah, Tobie, Tobin, Toby, Tobyn, Tohbee, Tohbey, Tohbi, Tohbie, Tohby, Topia (Maori).

Tobie/Tobin/Toby/Tobyn *See* Tobias.

Todd Old Norse from Latin: a fox or foxhunter.
Tod.

Todor A Slavic form of Theodore.

Toft Old English: from the site of the building.
Tofte.

Togar Aboriginal: smoke, or smoky.

Togo An African country, officially known as the Togolese Republic.

Tohbee/Tohbi/Tohby *See* Toby.

Tolga Turkish: a helmet.

Tolland An English surname, possibly meaning the land on the river.
Toland.

Tolv Swedish: twelve.

Tom A diminutive of Thomas. Tibetan: a bear.
Tame (Maori), *Tomi, Tommie, Tommo, Tommy, Twm* (Welsh).

Toman/Tomas/Tomasz/Tomaz *See* Thomas.

Tome English from Greek: a volume, or section of a book.

Tomek A Polish diminutive of Tomasz (*see* Thomas).

Tomi Japanese: red. Also a form of Tom.

Tomik A Czech form of Thomas.

Tomio Japanese: one who is treasured.

Tomislav Slavic: the name of an early Croatian king.

Tomkin Old English: little Tom or Thomas.
Tomkins, Tomkyn, Tomkyns, Tomlin, Tomlins, Tomlyn, Tomlyns, Tompkin, Tompkins, Tompkyn, Tompkyns.

Tomlin/Tomlyn *See* Tomkin.

Tommaso/Tomo/Tomos/Toms *See* Thomas.

Tommie/Tommo/Tommy *See* Tom and Thomas.

Tompkin/Tompkins/Tompkyn *See* Tomkin.

Tona The Aztec sun god.

Toney Aboriginal: thunder. *See also* Anthony and Tony.

Tongatea Polynesian: a man from Tonga.

Tony A diminutive of Anthony.
Toney, Toni, Tonie.

Toomas Estonian form of Thomas.

Topaz Greek: the name of a

gemstone, often yellow-coloured.
Topaze, Topazio, Topazo.
Topher Diminutive of Christopher.
Topi African: an antelope.
Topia Maori form of Tobias.
Tor Celtic: a rock.
Tor/Tord/Tore *See* Thor.
Torben Danish form of Thor.
Torbjörn Old Norse: the bear of Thor.
Torcall *See* Torquil.
Torey *See* Tory.
Tori/Torie *See* Tory.
Torin Gaelic: the chief.
Torinn, Toryn, Torynn.
Tor-Ivar Scandinavian: a combination of Tor and Ivar (a battle archer).
Torkel/Torkell *See* Torquil.
Tormey Irish Gaelic: a thunder spirit.
Torquil Scottish Gaelic from Old Norse: Thor's cauldron.
Torcall (Gaelic), *Torkel* (Swedish), *Torkell, Torkelle, Torquill, Torquille.*
Torr Old English: from the tower.
Torrance/Torrence *See* Terence.
Torrens Probably an Irish surname; the name of a South Australian suburb, river and lake.
Torres Spanish: from the towers. The name of an Australian strait.
Torrington An English surname, derived from either Thor or tor (a hill).
Torington.

Torstai The Finnish name for Thursday.
Toru Japanese: the sea.
Torvald Old Norse: Thor the ruler.
Thorvald, Trudeau (Old French).
Tory Irish Gaelic: a placename, meaning a tower-like rock. Old Norse: a form of Thor.
Torey, Tori, Torie.
Toryn/Torynn *See* Torin.
Toshiro A popular name in Japan.
Toss A diminutive of Thomas.
Toussaint French: all the saints. *See also* Santos.
Tovi Modern Hebrew: good.
Tov, Tovee, Tovey, Tovie, Tovy.
Townley Old English: from the town meadow.
Townleigh.
Townsend Old English: from the town's end.
Townshend.
Townson A son of the town.
Towneson, Townesen, Townsen.
Tozer Old English: one who combs wool.
Track Middle English: a path or trail.
Trac, Tracke, Trak, Trakk.
Tracy Old French: from a placename. More commonly a girl's name.
Tracey.
Trae *See* Trey.
Trafford Old English: a ford in the valley.
Trafferd.

Traherne Welsh: of iron strength.
Trahearne, Trahern, Trehearn, Trehearne, Treherne.
Trai Vietnamese: a pearl.
Trait French: a distinguishing quality or feature. Also a form of Trey.
Trai, Traie.
Trajan The Anglicised name of a Roman emperor, Traianus.
Trak/Trakk *See* Track.
Tran Vietnamese: a family name.
Travance A combination of Travis and Vance (a thresher).
Travence.
Travers *See* Travis.
Travis Old French: from the crossing or crossroads.
Travers.
Traylor Old French: a hunter or tracker.
Trayler.
Tre A form of Trey. Also the beginning of many Cornish names such as Trethowan and Trevena, meaning a homestead, farm or place (pronounced 'truh').
Treat Middle English: something that brings pleasure.
Treate, Treet, Trete.
Treffon/Trefon *See* Tryphon.
Trefor *See* Trevor.
Trefusis Cornish: a placename.
Trehearn/Trehearne/Treherne *See* Traherne.
Treigh *See* Trey.

Trelawney Cornish: from the church village.
Treleaven Cornish: from the level homestead.
Treleven.
Trell American: a modern name of uncertain meaning.
Trel, Trelle.
Tremayne Cornish: from the place of the stone or rock.
Tremain, Tremaine, Tremayn.
Trengrove Cornish: from the homestead of the smith.
Trent English: the name of a river.
Trenton.
Tresco Cornish: a placename, one of the Isles of Scilly.
Trethowan Cornish: from the farm by the sandhills.
Treve/Trever *See* Trevor.
Trevelyan Cornish: from the farm at the mill.
Trevelyn, Trevilyn.
Trevena Cornish/Welsh: a homestead on the hill. Also a girl's name.
Treveena, Treveenah, Trevenah, Trevenna, Trevennah, Trevina, Trevinah.
Trevor Welsh: from the large village.
Trefor (Welsh), *Treve, Trever.*
Diminutive: Trev.
Trey Middle English: three, or the third child.
Trae, Trait, Tre (Swedish), *Treigh, Treye.*
Tribe Middle English: a group of

people with common customs and traditions.
Tryb, Trybe.

Trick Middle English: a roguish prank.
Tricke, Trik, Trikk, Trikke, Trique, Tryk, Trykk, Trykke.

Triffon/Trifon *See* Tryphon.

Trigg Old Norse: the faithful or trustworthy one.
Trig, Trigge.

Trinidad Spanish: a Caribbean island.

Trinity Latin: a trio or triad, as in the Holy Trinity. Also a girl's name.
Trini, Trinitey, Trynity.

Trip Middle English: a journey.
Tripp, Trippe.

Trique *See* Trick.

Tristain/Tristam/Tristan/Tristyn *See* Tristram.

Tristram Celtic: the noisy one.
Dristan, Dristin, Drostan, Drystan, Tristain, Tristam, Tristan, Tristen, Tristian, Tristin, Triston, Tristrand, Tristyn, Trystan (Cornish, Welsh).

Triton A Greek sea god who was half-man, half-fish.
Tryton.

Troi/Troie *See* Troy.

Troilus A Trojan prince in Greek legend.
Troylus.

Trowbridge Old English: from the wooden bridge.

Troy Old French: from a placename. Also the name of an ancient city in Asia Minor.
Troi, Troie, Troye.

Trudeau Old French form of Torvald.

Truman Old English: a trusty or faithful man.
Trueman.

Trump Old French: a trumpeter.
Trumpe, Trumper.

Trung Vietnamese: the loyal one.

Tryb/Trybe *See* Tribe.

Trygve Norwegian: trustworthy.
Tryggve (Swedish), *Tryggvi* (Icelandic).

Tryk/Trykk *See* Trick.

Trynity *See* Trinity.

Tryphon Greek: the name of an early saint.
Treffon, Trefon, Triffon, Trifon, Tryffon, Tryfon.

Trystan *See* Tristram.

Tryton *See* Triton.

Tsamcho Sherpa/Tibetan: the last issue.

Tseten Sherpa/Tibetan: the defender of religion. Also a girl's name.

Tshering Sherpa/Tibetan: long life. Also a girl's name.

Tu Polynesian: the god of war.

Tuaka Maori: a legendary chief.

Tuart Aboriginal: a type of eucalypt.
Tewart.

Tucker Old English: a cloth-worker.

Tudfil/Tudful *See* Tydfil.

Tudor Welsh form of Theodore.
Tudur, Tudyr.

Tuesday Old English: the day of Tiw or Tiu, the Anglo-Saxon god of war and the sky and the equivalent of the Norse god Tyr. *See also* Tyr.
Tewesday, Tewsday.
Tueva Polynesian: a mourner.
Tui Maori: a honeyeater.
Tuki Aboriginal: a bullfrog.
Tuldar Aboriginal: a star.
Tulla *See* Tulloch.
Tullio Italian: a Roman family name.
Tullius, Tullus.
Tulloch Irish Gaelic: a placename, meaning a little hill.
Tulla.
Tully An Irish surname. Also a town in Queensland.
Tullee, Tulley, Tulli, Tullie.
Tulsa The name of a city in Oklahoma, the USA. Also a girl's name.
Tunc Turkish: bronze.
Tunu Native American: a deer.
Tuomas Finnish form of Thomas.
Tupac African: a warrior.
Tupak.
Tura Aboriginal: a spear.
Turgay Turkish: a lark (a bird).
Turi Polynesian: the name of a famous chief.
Turk A man from Turkey.
Turke.
Turner Old French: a lathe-worker.
Turpin Old Norse: a Finnish man of Thor.
Turro Aboriginal: fire.
Tuscan from Tuscany, a region of Italy.
Tutapu Polynesian: the name of a Tahitian deity.
Tuyen Vietnamese: angelic.
Twain Middle English: two. The surname of a famous author (Mark Twain).
Twaine, Twayn, Twayne.
Twm Welsh form of Tom.
Twyford Old English: from the double ford.
Twyforde.
Tyack Cornish: a farmer.
Tyak.
Tybalt *See* Theobald.
Tyce *See* Tyson.
Tycho Greek: he who hits the mark.
Tyco, Tyko.
Tydfil Celtic: the name of a Welsh saint.
Tudfil, Tudful.
Tydhg *See* Tad.
Tye Old English: from the enclosure. *See also* Tyer.
Tai, Taie, Thye, Tie, Ty, Tyh, Tyhe.
Tyer A variation of Tye.
Thyer, Tyher.
Tyeson *See* Tyson.
Tygar/Tyger/Tygre *See* Tiger.
Tyh/Tyhe *See* Tye.
Tyko *See* Tycho.
Tyler Old English: a tiler or tile-maker. Also a modern girl's name.

Tilar, Tiler, Tylar.
Tym/Tymothy *See* Timothy.
Tymon *See* Timon.
Tynagh Irish Gaelic: the name of an Irish village.
Tynah.
Tynan Gaelic: the dark one.
Tinan.
Tyne The name of an English river.
Tynne.
Tyondai A modern name, probably a form of Tye.
Taiondai, Tieondai, Tyeondai, Tyhondai.
Tyr The Norse god of war and victory; the equivalent of the Roman god Mars.
Tir.
Tyran An unusual modern name.
Tiran, Tiren, Tiron, Tyren, Tyron.
Tyrese African: a talented leader.
Tyrol An Austrian alpine region.
Tirol.
Tyron *See* Tyran.
Tyrone Irish: a county in Northern Ireland.
Tyson Old French: a firebrand. Can also be a girl's name.
Tieson, Tison, Tyeson.
Diminutives: Tise, Tyce, Tyse.
Tytan *See* Titan.
Tytus *See* Titus.

U

Uan *See* Ewan.
Udale/Udall *See* Udell.
Uday Sanskrit: accomplishment.
Udell Anglo-Saxon: from the valley of the yew trees.
Udale, Udall.
Udo German: prosperity, fortune. Japanese: a ginseng plant.
Udolf Old English: a prosperous wolf.
Ueli *See* Ulrich.
Uenuku Maori: a rainbow.
Uffo Teutonic: a wild bear.
Ufuk Turkish: the horizon.
Ugo Italian form of Hugh.
Ugur Turkish: a good sign or omen.
Uilleam Scottish Gaelic form of William.
Uilleag, Ulick.
Ukko A god of the sky and air in Finnish mythology.
Ulan African: the firstborn twin.
Uland Teutonic: the noble land.
Ulandi Aboriginal: a big tree.
Ulbrecht Teutonic: noble splendour.
Uldis Latvian form of Ulrich.
Ulf Swedish form of Wolfe.
Ulfred Old English/Teutonic: peace.
Ulises/Ulisse *See* Ulysses.
Ulivo Italian: the colour, olive.
Ulixes *See* Ulysses.
Ull The Norse god of skiers.
Ulli *See* Ulrich.
Ullo Hindi: an owl.
Ulo.

Ulmer Old English: a famous wolf.
Ulmar.

Ulrich Teutonic: a ruler.
Alric (German), *Uldis* (Latvian), *Ulric* (Old English), *Ulrick* (Scandinavian), *Ulrico* (Italian), *Ulryk* (Polish).
Diminutives: Ueli, Ulli, Utz (German).

Ultan Irish: from an old Gaelic name.

Uluka Sanskrit: an owl.

Ulysses Greek: the angry one, wrathful. The famous wanderer of Homer's Odyssey.
Ulises (Spanish), *Ulisse* (Italian), *Ulixes, Ulyses, Ulysse* (French), *Ulyxes.*

Umar *See* Omar.

Umbert/Umberto *See* Humbert.

Umbriel A satellite of the planet Uranus.

Umit Turkish: hope.
Umut.

Uno Latin: one, or the first child.

Unwin Old English: the enemy.
Unwyn.

Upendra Sanskrit: and other name for the god Vishnu.
Upender.

Upravda Slavic: the upright one.

Upton Old English: from the upper farm or town.
Upten.

Upwood Old English: from the forest on the hill.

Uralba Aboriginal: a place of quartz stones.

Uranius Greek: heavenly. The planet Uranus (or Ouranos) is the ruler of the zodiac sign of Aquarius.
Ouranius, Ouranos, Ouranus, Uranio (Italian), *Uranus.*

Urbain/Urbaine *See* Urban.

Urban Latin: a city dweller. The name of several early saints and popes.
Orban (Hungarian), *Urbain, Urbaine, Urbane, Urbano, Urvan* (Russian).

Urgyen Sherpa/Tibetan: the name of Tibet's greatest saint.

Uri/Urie *See* Uriah and Uriel.

Uriah Hebrew: God is light. A biblical name best known from the Charles Dickens character Uriah Heep in *David Copperfield. See also* Uriel.
Diminutives: Uri, Urie.

Urian *See* Urien.

Uriel Hebrew: light; the angel of light and prophecy. *See also* Uriah.
Uriele (Italian), *Uriell, Urielle.*
Diminutives: Uri, Urie.

Urien Welsh: of privileged birth, or born in the town.
Urian.

Uriz Aboriginal: a turtle.

Ursel Latin: a bear. The masculine version of Ursula.
Urs (German), *Ursell, Urshell, Ursus.*

Urson *See* Orson.
Ursus *See* Ursel.
Urvan *See* Urban.
Urvil Hindi: the sea.
Usaia/Usaiah *See* Uzziah.
Usain/Ussain *See* Hussain.
Usama Arabic: a lion.
Osama.
Usher Old French: an attendant or usher.
Ushnisha Sanskrit: a crown.
Usko Finnish: faith.
Usman *See* Osman.
Utah An American state.
Yutah.
Utu Polynesian: to return.
Utz *See* Ulrich.
Uwan Aboriginal: to meet.
Uwe *See* Ove.
Uyeda Japanese: from the rice field.
Uzi Hebrew: my strength.
Uziel/Uzziel *See* Uzziah.
Uzman *See* Osman.
Uzziah Hebrew: the power or strength of God.
Ozias, Usaia, Usaiah, Uziah, Uziel, Uzziel, Uzziyah.

V

Vachel Old French: a little cow, or one who raises cows.
Vachell.
Václav Czech form of Wenceslas.
Vadim *See* Vladimir.
Vail Old English: from the valley.
Vaile, Vale, Valle, Vayl, Vayle.
Valdemar Danish form of Vladimir.
Valdir Portuguese form of Walter.
Vale *See* Vail.
Valentine Latin: strong and healthy. The name of a 3rd-century saint.
Folant (Welsh), *Valentin* (Danish, French, Swedish), *Valentino* (Italian), *Vallentin, Vallentine, Walenty* (Polish).
Diminutives: Tino (Italian), Val.
Valerian Latin: strong and powerful. A 'herb name'.
Valery (French).
Valery *See* Valerian.
Vali A son of Odin in Norse mythology. He was the god of vegetation and eternal light and renowned for his strength.
Valie.
Valin Hindi: a mighty warrior.
Valle *See* Vail.
Vallentin/Vallentine *See* Valentine.
Vallis Old French: the Welshman.
Valon A Slavic name of uncertain meaning.
Vallon.
Valroy A 'combination name'
Valroi, Valroie, Valroye.
Valter *See* Walter.
Valu Polynesian: the eighth child.
Vamana Sanskrit: deserving praise.
Van Dutch: from or of. Generally a prefix to a surname, but also used as a first name. Also a diminutive

of Ivan, and a popular Vietnamese name.
Vance Old English: a thresher.
Vander From Greek: an archer. Also a diminutive of Evander.
Vane *See* Venn.
Vangelis Greek: possibly from Evangelos, the evangelist.
Vanya Russian: a diminutive of Ivan. *See also* John.
Varad Hungarian: from the fortress.
Varaha An incarnation, in the form of a boar, of the important Hindu god Vishnu.
Varanger Old French: a sailor.
Varant An Armenian name of uncertain meaning.
Varden Old French: from the green hills.
Vardon, Verden, Verdon.
Varian Latin: the changeable one.
Varick Icelandic: a sea drifter. Teutonic: a protecting ruler.
Varic, Varik.
Varley An English surname, possibly a variation of Farley (from the fern clearing).
Varlee, Varlei, Varleigh, Varli, Varlie, Varlli, Varllie, Varlly, Varly.
Vartan Armenian: a rose.
Varuna Sanskrit: the god of water and the night sky. Also a Balinese wind god.
Varun, Waruna.
Vasant Hindi: born during the spring.
Vasco Portuguese/Spanish: the name of a 15th-century explorer (Vasco da Gama).
Velasco (Spanish).
Vasek Czech: victorious.
Vasik, Vassek, Vassik.
Vasily A form of Basil, meaning royal or kingly. *See also* Vassos.
Vasil, Vasile, Vasiley, Vasili, Vasilis (Greek), *Vasiliy* (Russian), *Vasilly, Vassilios* (Greek), *Vassilis* (Greek), *Vassily, Wassily, Wasyl.*
Diminutives: Vaschka, Vasilo, Vaska (Russian), Vasso.
Vassos Greek: regal.
Vasos.
Vasudeva Sanskrit: the father of the god Krishna.
Vaughan Welsh: small.
Vaun, Vaune, Vawn, Vawne.
Vayl/Vayle *See* Vail.
Vayu The Hindu god of the air and wind, who carries a thunderbolt.
Ved Sanskrit: knowledge.
Veet *See* Vit.
Veit Dutch form of Guy.
Vekoslav Slavic: eternal glory.
Velasco *See* Vasco.
Vendelin Czech form of Wendell.
Venerando Italian: one who is worthy of veneration.
Venero.
Venerdi Italian: Friday, the day of Venus.
Vendredi (French), *Viernes* (Spanish).
Venkatesh Sanskrit: another name

for the god Vishnu.
Venkatesha.

Venn Old English: from the marsh or fen.
Vane, Ven, Venne.

Vennard An English surname.

Venton Old English: a place in a marsh or fen.
Vennten, Vennton, Venten.

Ventry The name of an Irish village.
Ventrey.

Verano Spanish: summertime.

Verde Italian: green.
Verdey, Verdi, Verdie, Verdy.

Verden/Verdon *See* Varden.

Verdun A town in northern France.

Vere Latin: faithful and loyal.

Vered Hebrew: a rose.

Verell/Verill *See* Verrell.

Verge Middle English: a rim or edge.
Virge.

Vergil *See* Virgil.

Verlon *See* Vernon.

Verner/Verners *See* Vernon and Warner.

Vernon Latin: spring-like.
Verlon, Vern, Vernard, Vernarde, Verne, Verner, Verners.

Verrell French: honest.
Verell, Verill, Verrall, Verrill.

Vesak Sanskrit: the Hindu month of April/May, corresponding to the zodiac sign of Taurus.
Besak, Besakh, Vesakh.

Veselin Slavic: the cheerful one.
Veselko.

Vic/Vick *See* Victor.

Vicent/Vicente *See* Vincent.

Victor Latin: the conqueror. *See also* Vincent.
Victoras, Victorio, Viktor (Czech, German, Polish, Scandinavian), *Vitorio, Vittore* (Italian), *Vittorino, Vittorio* (Spanish), *Wiktor* (Polish). *Diminutives:* Vic, Vick.

Vidal *See* Vitale.

Vidar Old Norse: the name of a Norse god, known for his silence and solitude.

Vidas A form of Vitale.

Vidor Hungarian: cheerful.

Vidya Sanskrit: knowledge.

Viernes *See* Venerdi.

Viggo Scandinavian: one who fights.

Vijay Sanskrit: victory.

Vijendra Sanskrit: the victorious one.

Vikenti/Vikentije *See* Vincent.

Vikesh Sanskrit: the moon.

Viking Icelandic: an ancient Scandinavian warrior.

Vikram Sanskrit: valour or bravery.

Viktor *See* Victor.

Vilem/Vilhelm *See* William.

Vilis Latvian form of William.

Vilko *See* William.

Villiers English from French: from the farm or estate.
Viliers.

Vilmos Hungarian form of William.

Vimal Sanskrit: pure.

Vincent Latin: conquering. *See also* Victor and Vinson.
Vicent (Catalan), *Vicente* (Spanish), *Vikenti* (Russian), *Vikentije* (Slavic), *Vincens* (German), *Vincenso* (Italian), *Vincente* (Italian), *Vincentio*, *Vincenzo* (Italian), *Visant* (Breton), *Vyncent*.
Diminutives: Vin, Vince, Vinnie, Vynce.
Vincenzo *See* Vincent.
Vinden Possibly a variation of Vinson.
Vindin, Vindon, Vindyn, Vinten, Vintin, Vinton, Vintyn.
Viner Old French: a vineyard worker or dweller.
Vyner.
Vinicio Italian/Spanish: from a Latin word meaning wine.
Vinicius.
Vinnie A diminutive of Vincent.
Vinod Sanskrit: one who is pleasing.
Vinson Old English: the son of Vincent. *See also* Vinden.
Vinsen.
Vinten/Vinton *See* Vinden.
Viorel Romanian: a bluebell.
Virendra Sanskrit: a brave lord.
Virender, Virendranath.
Virge *See* Verge.
Virgil Latin: the name of a famous Roman poet.
Vergil, Virgile (French), *Virgilio* (Italian, Spanish).
Virgo Latin: a virgin. A constellation and one of the zodiac signs.
Virginis, Virgoe.
Virode Thai: the light.
Virote Thai: outstanding.
Visa A Finnish name of uncertain meaning.
Visant Breton form of Vincent.
Vishnu Sanskrit: the protector. An important Hindu god.
Visvaldis Latvian: one who rules.
Vsevolod (Russian).
Vit Slavic: a diminutive of Vitus and other Vit names.
Veet.
Vita *See* Vitus.
Vitale Latin: lively. *See also* Vitus and Vivian.
Vidal, Vidas, Vital, Vitali (Russian), *Vitalij, Vitalis, Vitaliy, Vitas, Vito, Vytas* (Slavic), *Witali* (Slavic).
Vitas A form of Vitale.
Vitek A diminutive of Vitomir.
Vitezslav Slavic: glorious or valiant.
Viteslav.
Vito *See* Vitale.
Vitomir Slavic: a peaceful ruler.
Witomir (Polish).
Diminutives: Mirek, Miro, Vitek, Vito.
Vitorio/Vittore/Vittorio *See* Victor.
Vitus Latin: life; the name of a Sicilian child saint. *See also* Vitale and Vivian.
Vita.
Diminutives: Veet, Vit.
Vivaldo Italian: one who dominates the will.

Vivek The masculine form of Viveka, meaning lively.
Vivec.

Vivian Latin: lively. *See also* Vitale, Vitus and Vivek.
Vyvyan.

Vjekoslav Slavic: from a glorious age.
Diminutive: Vjeko.

Vlad *See* Vladimir and Vladislav.

Vladimir Slavic: a powerful ruler. Generally a Czech or Russian name.
Vadim (Russian), *Valdemar* (Danish), *Vladamir, Vlademir, Vladimiro* (Italian), *Vladimirs, Vladmir, Waldemar* (Dutch, German, Scandinavian), *Waldermar, Waldomar* (Teutonic), *Wladimir.*
Diminutives: Vlad, Vlado, Waldo (Teutonic).

Vladislav Slavic: a glorious ruler. *See also* Ladislav.
Vladyslav.
Diminutives: Vlad, Vlado.

Vlado A diminutive of Vladimir.

Vlastislav Slavic: the glorious homeland.
Vlastimil.

Voj/Vojan Diminutives of Voj names.

Vojislav Slavic: a famous warrior.
Diminutives: Voj, Vojan.

Vojtech Slavic: an eager warrior.
Diminutives: Voj, Vojan.

Volcan *See* Vulcan.

Voldemar A Slavic name that is related to Vladimir.
Voldemars, Woldemar.

Volf Jewish form of Wolfe.

Volkan *See* Vulcan.

Volker German: the army of the people.

Volney Teutonic: of the people.

Vortigern Celtic: a great king.

Vrischik The Sanskrit name for the zodiac sign of Scorpio.

Vrisha Sanskrit: a bull. The name for the zodiac sign of Taurus.

Vuc Slavic: a wolf.
Vuk.

Vulcan The Roman god of fire and metalworking, after whom volcanoes are named.
Volcan, Volkan (Turkish), *Vulkan.*

Vulpe Latin: a fox.

Vyasa Sanskrit: the arranger.

Vynce/Vyncent *See* Vincent.

Vyner *See* Viner.

Vytas Slavic form of Vitale.

Vytautas Lithuanian: the name of national hero, possibly meaning one who sees the people or nation.

Vyvyan Cornish: from an old surname. Also a form of Vivian.

W

Waclaw Polish form of Wenceslas.

Wade Old English: a wanderer, or from the river crossing.
Waide, Wayde.

Wafiq Arabic: a friend or companion.
Wafeeq.
Wagner Dutch: a wagon driver or wagonmaker.
Wagoner.
Wahib Arabic: the generous one.
Waiariki Maori: hot springs.
Waide *See* Wade.
Waihanga Maori: a builder.
Wain/Waine/Wainwright
See Wayne.
Waitangi Maori: the signing place of the 19th-century treaty between the Maori and British.
Waite Old English: a watchman or guard.
Waitoa Maori: the name of a New Zealand town.
Wajih Arabic: one who is honoured.
Wajeeh, Wajiha.
Wakelin An English surname.
Wakeling.
Wakeman Old English: a watchman.
Wal A diminutive of Walter.
Walby Old English/Old Norse: the farm by the ancient wall.
Walcha Aboriginal: the sun. A New South Wales placename.
Waldemar/Waldermar *See* Vladimir.
Walden Old English: from the valley in the forest.
Waldon.
Waldir A German form of Walter.
Waldo/Waldomar *See* Vladimir.
Walenty *See* Valentine.
Walford Old English: from the ford over the stream.
Walid Arabic: the newborn boy.
Waleed.
Walker Old English: a fuller; one who thickens cloth.
Walla Aboriginal: rain.
Wallah.
Wallace Old French: a foreigner, particularly a Welshman.
Wallis, Walsh, Welch, Welsh.
Wallis *See* Wallace.
Wallison The son of Wallis.
See Wallace.
Wallisen.
Wally A diminutive of Walter.
Walmer Old English: the pool of the Welsh.
Walmond Teutonic: the mighty protector.
Walpole Old English: from the pool by the ancient wall.
Walsh *See* Wallace.
Walter Teutonic: a mighty ruler.
See also Watkin.
Gautier (French), *Valdir* (Portuguese), *Valter* (Scandinavian), *Waldir* (German), *Waltern, Walther* (German), *Wata* (Maori), *Wolter* (Dutch).
Diminutives: Wal, Wally, Walt, Wat, Watt.
Walton Old English: from the farm or town of the foreigners.
Walwyn Old English: a powerful friend.
Walwin.

Wandelin *See* Wendell.
Wanderlei A Brazilian name of uncertain meaning.
Wang Chinese: kingly.
Wangdi Sherpa/Tibetan: he who possesses power.
Warburton Old English: from the fortress town.
Ward Old English: a guard or watchman.
Warde, Warden.
Wardell Old English: from the valley of the River Wear.
Wardale, Wardelle.
Warden *See* Ward.
Warfield Old English: the field by the stream.
Warka Aboriginal: a tortoise.
Warley Old English: from the cattle pasture.
Warleigh.
Warmund Old English: a loyal protector.
Warman, Warmond.
Warner Teutonic: the protecting army or warrior.
Verner (Scandinavian), *Verners*, *Werner* (German).
Diminutives: Wessel (German), Wetzel (German).
Warra Aboriginal: water.
Warrain Aboriginal: belonging to the sea.
Warraine, Warrane, Warrayne.
Warral Aboriginal: honey, or a honeybee.

Warren Old English/Old French: the game-park keeper.
Warrran, Warrand, Warrend, Warrenne.
Diminutives: Waz, Wazza.
Warrick *See* Warwick.
Warrigal Aboriginal: wild, or a dingo.
Warringa Aboriginal: the sea.
Warringah.
Warrington Old English: the place or farm at the weir.
Warington.
Warrun Aboriginal: the sky.
Warton Old English: a lookout point.
Waruna *See* Varuna.
Warwick Old English: from the dairy farm at the weir.
Warrick.
Waseem *See* Wasim.
Washi Japanese: an eagle.
Washington Old English: from the settlement of the Wassa family.
Wasim Arabic: the handsome one.
Waseem.
Wassily/Wasyl *See* Vasily.
Wat/Watt Diminutives of Walter.
Wata Maori form of Walter.
Watkin Old English: the son of Walter.
Watkins, Watson.
Watson *See* Watkin.
Wattan Native American: black.
Waveney The name of a river in Suffolk, England.
Waverney.

Waverley Old English: from the village of the aspen trees.
Waveley, Wavely, Waverly.
Wayan Balinese: the firstborn child.
Wayde *See* Wade.
Wayland Old English: from the land by the crossroads or roadway.
Waylan, Waylen, Waylend, Waylon, Waylond.
Wayman Old English: a man of the way or path.
Wayne Old English: a cart- or wagon-maker. Actor John Wayne made this popular as a first name.
Wain, Waine, Wainwright, Wayn.
Waz/Wazza *See* Warren.
Wazir Arabic: a minister.
Wazeer, Wazire, Wazyr, Wazyre.
Webb Old English: a weaver.
Webbe, Webber, Weber, Webster.
Webber/Weber/Webster *See* Webb.
Wednesday Middle English: the day of Odin, also known as Woden or Wotan.
Wednesdai, Wensdai, Wensday.
Welby Old English/Old Norse: from the farm by the spring.
Welbeigh.
Welch *See* Wallace.
Weldon Old English: from the hill with a spring.
Welden.
Welford Old English: from the ford by the willows.
Wella Cornish diminutive of William.
Wellard *See* Willard.

Wellington Old English: from the rich man's farm.
Wells Old English: from the spring or well.
Welles.
Welsh *See* Wallace.
Wen Chinese: cultured or ornamental.
Wenceslas Slavic: great glory.
A 10th-century Bohemian saint.
Václav (Czech), *Waclaw* (Polish), *Wenceslaus, Wenzel* (Czech, German).
Wendell Teutonic: a wanderer.
Vendelin (Czech), *Wandelin, Wendall, Wendel, Wendelin.*
Diminutive: Dell.
Wendron Cornish: a placename.
Wenlock Old Welsh: from the holy monastery.
Wenlok.
Wensdai/Wensday *See* Wednesday.
Wensley Old English: from Woden's clearing.
Wensleigh, Wenslie, Wensly.
Wentworth Old English: the estate of the white-haired one, or a winter estate.
Wentworthe.
Wenzel *See* Wenceslas.
Werahiko Maori form of Francis.
Werner *See* Warner.
Wes *See* Wesley.
Wesley Old English: from the west meadow. A name sometimes given in honour of the founder of the Methodist church, John Wesley.

Wesleigh, Weslie, Wesly, Wezley.
Diminutives: Wes, Wez.
Wessel German diminutive of Werner (*see* Warner).
Westholme English from Old Norse: the western hill or river flat.
Westholm.
Westleigh Old English: from the western wood or clearing.
Westley, Westlie, Westly.
Weston Old English: from the western farm or town.
Westwood Old English: from the wood to the west.
Westy One who comes from the west.
Westie.
Wetherby Old English: from the sheep farm.
Wetzel German diminutive of Werner (*see* Warner).
Weylin Celtic: the son of the wolf.
Weymouth Old English: the mouth of the River Wey. A town in Dorset.
Wez/Wezley *See* Wesley.
Whatitiri Maori: thunder.
Whatu Maori: the pupil of the eye.
Wheatley Old English: from the wheat meadow.
Wheatleigh, Wheatlie, Wheatly.
Wheeler Old English: a wheel-maker.
Whero Maori: red.
Whetu Polynesian: a star.
Whitby Old English: the white town. A town in Yorkshire.
Whitbeigh, Whitbey.
Whitcombe Old English: from the wide valley.
Whitcomb.
Whitfield Old English: the white field.
Whitford Old English: from the white ford.
Whitforde.
Whitley Old English: the white meadow or clearing.
Whitleigh, Whitly.
Whitman Old English: the white man.
Whitmore Old English: from the white moor.
Whitmer.
Whitney Old English: from the white island. Also a girl's name.
Whitny, Witney.
Whitson Old English: a white stone.
Whitsun.
Whittaker Old English: the white field.
Whitaker.
Wickham Old English: from the meadow homestead.
Wykeham.
Widald *See* Witold.
Wiktor Polish form of Victor.
Wil *See* William.
Wilari Aboriginal: a star.
Wilber/Wilbert *See* Wilbur.
Wilbey/Wilby *See* Willoughby.
Wilbur Old English: the resolute one.
Wilber, Wilbert, Wilburt.

Wilcox A diminutive of William. *See also* Wilkins, Williams, Willis and Wilson.
Wilcocks, Wilcoxe, Wilcoxx, Wilcoxxe.

Wilder Old English: one who is wild.
Wylder.

Wiley *See* Wylie.

Wilford Old English: the ford in the willows.
Wilforde.

Wilfred Teutonic: desirous of peace, a peacemaker.
Wilfrid, Wilfried (German).
Diminutives: Fred, Freddie, Freddy, Wilf.

Wilhelm/Wilhelmus *See* William.

Wiliam *See* William.

Wilkes/Wilkie *See* William.

Wilkins The son of William. *See also* Wilcox, Williams, Willis and Wilson.
Wilkin, Wilkinson.

Will A diminutive of William.

Willard Old English: resolute and brave.
Wellard, Willerd.

Willbey/Willby *See* Willoughby.

Willem Dutch form of William.

Willi/Willie Diminutives of William.

William Teutonic: a strong and resolute protector. Introduced to England by the Normans in the 11th century. *See also* Wilcox, Wilkins, Williams, Willis, Wilmer, Wilmot and Wilson.
Guglielmo (Italian), *Guilhelm, Guilherme* (Portuguese), *Guillaume* (French), *Guillermo* (Spanish), *Gwilym* (Welsh), *Quilliam* (Manx Gaelic), *Uilleam* (Scottish Gaelic), *Vilem* (Czech), *Vilhelm* (Scandinavian), *Vilis* (Latvian), *Vilko, Vilmos* (Hungarian), *Wilhelm* (German), *Wilhelmus* (Dutch), *Wiliam, Wilkes, Wilkie, Willem* (Dutch), *Willum, Wiremu* (Maori), *Wollem, Wullem.*
Diminutives: Bill, Bille, Billie, Billy, Jelle (Dutch), Liam (Irish Gaelic), Lian, Lyam, Pim (Dutch), Wella (Cornish), Wil, Wilkin, Will, Willi (German), Willie, Wills, Willy, Wim (Dutch, German).

Williams The son of William. *See also* Wilcox, Wilkins, Willis and Wilson.
Williamson.

Willis The son of William. *See also* Wilcox, Wilkins, Williams, and Wilson.
Willison, Williss, Wills.

Williston From the town or place of Willis.
Willisten.

Willoughby Old Norse/Old English: from the farm by the willows.
Wilbey, Wilby, Willbey, Willby.

Wills A diminutive of Willis, Wilson and other names.

Willum *See* William.

Willy A diminutive of William.
Wilman Old English: a man from the willows.
Willman.
Wilmer Teutonic: famously resolute. From a similar origin to that of William.
Wilmot Teutonic: of resolute mind. Originally a diminutive of William.
Wilny Native American: a flying eagle.
Wilney.
Wilson Old English from Teutonic: the son of William. *See also* Wilcox, Wilkins, Williams and Willis.
Willson.
Wilstan Teutonic: from the stone of the wolf.
Wilsten, Wilston, Wylstan, Wylsten, Wylston.
Wilton Old English: from the farm by the stream.
Wylton.
Diminutive: Wilt.
Wim A diminutive of William.
Win Cambodian: bright.
Winchester Old English: a Roman site. A city in Hampshire, southern England.
Windsor Old English: from the riverbank or landing place.
Winsor, Winzor.
Winford/Winforde *See* Wynford.
Winfred Old English: a friend of peace. The masculine form of Winifred.
Winfrid, Winfried (German).
Wing Chinese: glory.
Winslow Old English: from a friend's hill.
Winslowe.
Winston Old English: from a friend's estate or town.
Winstone, Wynston, Wynstone.
Winter Old English: born in the winter months.
Winters, Wynter, Wynters.
Winthrop Old English: from a friend's village.
Winton Old English: from a friend's farm.
Winten, Wynten, Wynton.
Winzor *See* Windsor.
Wirake Aboriginal: a friend.
Wiraki.
Wiremu Maori form of William.
Wirrin Aboriginal: a tea-tree.
Wistan *See* Wystan.
Witali Slavic form of Vitale.
Witi Maori: wheat.
Witney *See* Whitney.
Witold Polish: the ruler of the woods.
Widald (Teutonic).
Witomir Polish form of Vitomir.
Witton Old English: a farm by the wood.
Witten.
Wladimir *See* Vladimir.
Wodan/Woden *See* Odin.
Woldemar *See* Voldemar.
Wolfe Teutonic: wolf-like, courageous. *See also* Wolfram.

Ulf (Swedish), *Volf* (Jewish), *Wolf* (German), *Wulf, Wulfe*.
Wolfgang Teutonic: the advancing wolf.
Wolfram Teutonic: the wolf raven. *Wulfram*.
Diminutives: Wolf, Wolfe, Wulf, Wulfe.
Wollaston/Wollstone *See* Woolston.
Wollem *See* William.
Wolter Dutch form of Walter.
Wonga Aboriginal: a native pigeon.
Woodburn Old English: from the stream in the wood. *Woodbourn, Woodbourne, Woodburne*.
Woodley Old English: the meadow or clearing in the forest. *Woodleigh*.
Woodrow Old English: from the row of houses in the wood. *Diminutive:* Woody.
Woodstock Old English: a place in the woods.
Woodward Old English: a forester, a forest guardian.
Woody Diminutive of Woodrow and similar names.
Woolston Old English: the town by the spring. *Wollaston, Wollastone, Wollston, Wollstone, Woolstone*.
Woorak Aboriginal: honeysuckle, or from the plain.
Woorin Aboriginal: the sun.
Worcester Old English: a Roman site. The name of an English city.
Wotan German form of Odin.
Wren Old English: a tiny bird. *Wrenn*.
Wright Old English: a carpenter or craftsman.
Wroe *See* Rowe.
Wulf/Wulfe/Wulfram *See* Wolfe and Wolfram.
Wullem *See* William.
Wullun Aboriginal: blue sky.
Wyatt/Wye *See* Guy.
Wyber Old English: a battle fortress. *Wybar, Wybrew*.
Wyburn Old English: a battle hero. *Wyborn, Wyborne, Wyburne*.
Wycliff Old English: from the cliff of the warrior. *Wyclef, Wycleff, Wycliffe, Wyeclef, Wyecleff*.
Wykeham *See* Wickham.
Wylder *See* Wilder.
Wylie Old English: wily or beguiling. *Wiley*.
Wylstan/Wylston *See* Wilstan.
Wylton *See* Wilton.
Wyman Old English: a warrior.
Wyn Native American: the first, or firstborn son. *See also* Wynn.
Wyndham Old English: from the battle protector's homestead.
Wynford Welsh: from the white ford. *Winford, Winforde, Wynforde*.
Wynn Welsh: the fair or blessed one. *Wyn, Wynne*.

Wynstan *See* Wystan.
Wynston/Wynstone *See* Winston.
Wynten/Wynton *See* Winton.
Wynter/Wynters *See* Winter.
Wystan Old English: the battle stone.
Wistan, Wynstan.

X

Xander A diminutive and variation of Alexander. *See also* Zander.
Xahnder.
Diminutives: Xan, Xahn.
Xannan/Xannon *See* Zannon.
Xanthus Greek: golden-haired.
Xanthios, Xanthius, Xanthos, Zanthius, Zanthos, Zanthus.
Xaver *See* Xavier.
Xavier Arabic: bright. Spanish: of the new house.
Exavier, Javier (Portuguese, Spanish), *Saviero* (Italian), *Xaver* (German), *Xaviar, Xaviero* (Italian), *Zavier.*
Diminutives: Xavi, Zavi.
Xelio *See* Zelio.
Xenophon Greek: strange voices, or strong sounding.
Zenophon.
Xenos Greek: a stranger.
Xeno, Xenon, Zeno, Zenon, Zenos.
Xerxes Persian: a king or ruler. The name of a famous Persian king.
Zerxes.
Ximen/Ximenes/Ximens Spanish forms of Simon.
Ximeno/Ximun Basque forms of Simon.
Xolani Southern African: peace.
Xylon Greek: from the forest.
Zylon.

Y

Yaakov *See* Yakov.
Yacoub *See* Jacob.
Yaeger/Yager *See* Jaeger.
Yael Hebrew: a wild goat; an Old Testament name. Also a girl's name.
Yago Tibetan: good. Also a Spanish form of Jacob and James.
Yahya Arabic: God is gracious. A form of John.
Yahyaa, Yaya.
Yail/Yaile *See* Yale.
Yakez Native American: the heavens.
Yakim Hebrew: God will establish.
Yakeem.
Yakir Hebrew: one who is loved.
Yakobe *See* Jacob.
Yakov The modern Jewish and Russian forms of Jacob.
Yaakov.
Yale Old English: from the corner of the land. Teutonic: the one who pays.
Yail, Yaile.
Yama Japanese: a mountain. Sanskrit: the Hindu god of the setting sun.
Yamma.

Yamal Hindi: a twin.
Yampi Aboriginal: fresh water.
Yamuni *See* Jamuni.
Yana Native American: a bear.
 Yanah, Yanna, Yannah.
Yance/Yancey *See* Yancy.
Yancy Native American: the Englishman. The word later became Yankee.
 Yance, Yancee, Yancey, Yancie.
Yaniv Hebrew: one who prospers.
Yann Breton form of John.
 Diminutives: Janick, Jannick, Yanick, Yannick.
Yanna/Yannah *See* Yana.
Yannick *See* Yann.
Yannis Greek form of John.
Yao Ghanaian: Thursday's child.
Yaphet *See* Japhet.
Yaraslau *See* Jaroslav.
Yardan Arabic: a king.
 Yarden.
Yardley Old English: from the enclosed meadow.
 Yardlee, Yardlie, Yardly, Yeardlee, Yeardley, Yeardlie, Yeardly.
Yaron Hebrew: one who sings.
Yaroslav *See* Jaroslav.
Yarran Aboriginal: an acacia tree.
Yarto Aboriginal: the wind.
Yasin Turkish: lightning.
Yasir Arabic: wealthy.
 Yasar, Yaseer.
Yasu Japanese: peaceful.
Yasuhiro Japanese: abundant honesty.

Yasushi Japanese: peaceful and honest.
Yates Middle English: the keeper of the gates.
Yavuz Turkish: the stern one.
Yawar Arabic: possibly meaning an assistant.
Yazid Arabic: ever increasing.
Yeardley/Yeardlie/Yeardly *See* Yardley.
Yeden *See* Jeden.
Yefim Russian form of Euphemios.
Yefrem Russian form of Ephraim.
Yehuda *See* Judah.
Yehudi Hebrew: praise to the Lord.
Yelgun Aboriginal: the sun.
Yen Vietnamese: the calm or peaceful one.
Yered Hebrew form of Jared.
Yerin Aboriginal: a boy.
Yervant An Armenian name of uncertain meaning.
Yeshe Sherpa/Tibetan: the wise one.
Yeshua Hebrew: a form of Joshua, meaning God is salvation.
 Yeshna.
Yestin Welsh form of Justin.
Yevgeni/Yevgeny *See* Eugene.
Yhuko Aboriginal: the sun.
 Yuko.
Yianni/Yiannis Greek forms of John.
Yigael Hebrew: God will redeem.
 Yigal.
Yileen Aboriginal: a dream.
Yin Chinese: silvery.
Yiorgos A Greek form of George.

Yitzaak/Yitzak *See* Isaac.
Ynyr Welsh: honour.
Yo Chinese: bright. Japanese: sunshine.
Yoel *See* Joel.
Yogesh Sanskrit: one of the names of the god Krishna.
Yohan/Yohann *See* John.
Yoland From Greek: a violet.
Yona Native American: a bear. Also a Russian form of Jonah.
Yonah.
Yonatan Hebrew: the original form of Jonathan.
Diminutive: Yoni.
Yong Chinese/Korean: the brave one.
Yoram *See* Joram.
Yordan Bulgarian form of Jordan.
Yorens *See* Jorens.
Yorgan *See* George.
Yorick Old English: a form of George.
Yoriyos A Greek form of George.
York Celtic: the farm of the yew tree. Old English: a boar farm.
Yorke.
Yosef *See* Joseph.
Yoshi Japanese: good. Also a girl's name.
Yoshihiro Japanese: widespread goodness.
Yoshikazu Japanese: possibly meaning harmony.
Yoshinori Japanese: probably meaning a good rule or ceremony.

Youcef *See* Yusuf.
Younus An Arabic form of Jonah.
Yousaf/Yousef *See* Yusuf.
Yovel Hebrew: the horn of a ram.
Yoval.
Yu Chinese: like jade. Tibetan: the gemstone, turquoise.
Yuan Chinese: the original.
Yucel Turkish: the sublime one.
Yuksel.
Yudo *See* Eudo.
Yuka Aboriginal: a tree.
Yukio Japanese: a boy of the snow.
Yuko *See* Yhuko.
Yul *See* Julius.
Yule Old English: born at Christmas.
Yules.
Yuma Native American: the son of a chief.
Yunis/Yunus Arabic forms of Jonah.
Yuri Aboriginal: to hear. Also a Russian form of George.
Yuroka Aboriginal: the sun.
Yurung Aboriginal: the rain.
Yusuf Arabic form of Joseph.
Youcef, Yousaf, Yousef, Yusef.
Yutah *See* Utah.
Yuto Japanese: tenderness.
Yuuto.
Yuval Hebrew: rejoicing.
Yuvel.
Yvan/Yvann *See* Ivan.
Yves French form of Ives.

Z

Zaac/Zaak *See* Zachary and Zack.
Zab/Zabulon *See* Zebulun.
Zac/Zach *See* Zachary.
Zacarias Spanish form of Zachary.
Zachary Hebrew: the Lord has remembered. *See also* Zack.
Hakaraia (Maori), *Sakari* (Finnish), *Zacarias* (Spanish), *Zachariah*, *Zacharias* (German), *Zachariasz* (Polish), *Zacheus*, *Zackary*, *Zackery*, *Zahari* (Bulgarian), *Zaharias*, *Zakar* (Russian), *Zakaria* (Arabic), *Zakarias* (Swedish), *Zakariya* (Arabic), *Zakary*, *Zakiah*, *Zakir* (Arabic), *Zaxaria*, *Zaxariah*, *Zaxarias*, *Zecharia*, *Zechariah*.
Diminutives: Zac, Zach, Zack, Zak.
Zachriel The angel of memory.
Zack A diminutive of Zachary, but used increasingly as a separate name.
Zaac, Zaak, Zac, Zach, Zak, Zaki, Zakk, Zakki, Zec, Zech.
Zackary/Zackery *See* Zachary.
Zacoda A modern made-up name, based on Zac.
Zackoda, Zakoda.
Zadok Hebrew: just, righteous.
Zadoc.
Zadornin The Basque name for Saturday.

Zaeden/Zaedon *See* Zayden.
Zafar Arabic: the triumphant one.
Zafiro Spanish: a sapphire.
Zaffire, Zaffiro, Zafire, Zafirio, Zafirios (Greek), *Zafiris* (Greek), *Zapphire, Zapphiro.*
Zage A modern made-up name, possibly a form of Sage.
Zaige, Zayge.
Zahari/Zaharias *See* Zachary.
Zahavi Hebrew: golden.
Zaheer *See* Zahir.
Zahi Arabic: brilliant or beautiful.
Zahir Arabic: shining, radiant.
Zaheer.
Zahn *See* Zan and Zander.
Zaid *See* Zayed.
Zaiden/Zaidon *See* Zayden.
Zaige *See* Zage.
Zain/Zaine Forms of Zane. *See* John.
Zak/Zakaria/Zakarias/Zakary *See* Zachary.
Zakar Russian form of Zachary.
Zaki Arabic: pure. *See also* Zack.
Zakiah/Zakk/Zakki *See* Zachary and Zack.
Zakir An Arabic form of Zachary.
Zakoda *See* Zacoda.
Zale Old English: to sell, or a salary.
Zales.
Zalman/Zalmen *See* Solomon.
Zamael The angel of joy and Tuesday.
Zaman Arabic: probably meaning time or an era.
Zamir Hebrew: a songbird.
Zan A short form of Zander (and

Z – Boys

see Alexander).
Zahn.
Zander A diminutive and variation of Alexander. *See also* Xander.
Diminutives: Zahn, Zan.
Zane *See* John.
Zaniel The angel of Monday and the zodiac sign of Libra.
Zannon A modern name, probably from Zan.
Xannan, Xannen, Xannin, Xannon, Xannyn, Zannan, Zannen, Zannin, Zannyn.
Zanthius/Zanthos/Zanthus *See* Xanthus.
Zappa Italian: the surname of legendary 1960s and 1970s musician, Frank Zappa.
Zappah.
Zapphire/Zapphiro *See* Zafiro.
Zared Hebrew: an ambush.
Zareth.
Diminutive: Zar.
Zareh Armenian: the name of a legendary king.
Zarif Arabic: one who moves gracefully.
Zareef, Zarife.
Zarko Slavic: zealous.
Zascha/Zasha *See* Sasha.
Zavi/Zavier *See* Xavier.
Zaxaria/Zaxariah/Zaxarias *See* Zachary.
Zayd/Zayde *See* Zayden and Zayed.
Zaydan Arabic: growth. *See also* Zayden.

Zayden A modern name, probably derived from Zavier and Jayden.
Zaedan, Zaeden, Zaedon, Zaidan, Zaiden, Zaidon, Zaydan, Zayde, Zaydon, Zeydan, Zeyden, Zeydon.
Zayed Arabic: abundance.
Zaid, Zayd, Zeid, Zeyd.
Zayge *See* Zage.
Zayit Hebrew: an olive.
Zayn Arabic: beautiful. Also a form of Zane (*see* John).
Zayne A form of Zane (*see* John).
Zbigniew Slavic: to get rid of anger. A common Polish name.
Diminutive: Ziggy.
Zdenek Slavic form of Dennis.
Zdravko Slavic: healthy.
Zdrawko.
Zdzislav Czech: he who creates glory.
Zdzislaw (Polish).
Zealot Latin from Greek: one who is enthusiastic.
Zeb *See* Zebadiah and Zebulun.
Zebadiah Hebrew: a gift of the Lord.
Sebedeus (Welsh), *Zebadee, Zebedee, Zebediah.*
Diminutive: Zeb.
Zebulun Hebrew: exaltation, or the dwelling place. One of the sons of Leah and Jacob in the Bible.
Zabulon, Zebulon.
Diminutives: Zab, Zeb.
Zec/Zecariah/Zechariah

See Zachary.
Zeco *See* Zeko.
Zedekiah Hebrew: the justice of the Lord.
Diminutive: Zed.
Zeeki *See* Zeki.
Zeeland The name of a Dutch province.
Zealand.
Zeeman Dutch: a sailor or seaman.
Zeheb Turkish: gold.
Zeid *See* Zayed.
Zeik/Zeke Diminutives of Ezekiel.
Zeki Turkish: intelligent.
Zeeki, Zekie, Ziki, Zikie.
Zeko A modern name, probably from Zeke (*see* Ezekiel).
Zeco, Zico, Ziko.
Zelig Jewish: blessed, fortunate.
Selig.
Zelio A Brazilian name of uncertain meaning.
Xelio.
Zeljko Slavic: one who wishes.
Zelko.
Zelman *See* Solomon.
Zelotes Greek: zealous.
Zelus.
Zen Japanese: the name of a Buddhist sect. Also a girl's name.
Zenn.
Zenas Greek: living.
Zenden A modern name, probably based on Zen.
Zendan, Zendin, Zendon, Zendyn.
Zenith Middle English from Arabic: the highest point; the culmination.
Zenithe, Zenyth, Zenythe.
Zennor Cornish: a placename. Also a girl's name.
Zeno/Zenon/Zenos *See* Xenos.
Zenophon *See* Xenophon.
Zephaniah Hebrew: hidden by God.
Zephania.
Diminutive: Zeph.
Zephyr Greek: a breeze. A form of Zephyrus, the god of the west wind in mythology. Also a girl's name.
Zephir.
Zero Italian: a 'number name'.
Zeroun Armenian: a sage.
Zerun.
Zerxes *See* Xerxes.
Zethus A son of Zeus in Greek mythology, the strong and warlike twin brother of Amphion.
Zethos.
Zeus Greek: the father of the gods, or living. The ruler of the heavens in ancient Greek mythology.
Zeviel Hebrew: God's gazelle.
Zeyd *See* Zayed.
Zeyden/Zeydon *See* Zayden.
Zhen Chinese: precious.
Zhi/Zhie *See* Zi.
Zhiv/Zhivko *See* Ziv.
Zi An unusual, and very brief, modern name.
Zhi, Zhie, Zie, Zy, Zye.
Zia Arabic: splendour.
Ziya.
Zico/Ziko *See* Zeko.

Zidane After the famous French soccer player Zinedine Zidane.
Zidaine, Zidayne.
Ziggy *See* Zbigniew.
Zigmond/Zigmund *See* Sigmund.
Zigurd *See* Sigurd.
Zike An unusual modern name.
Zyke.
Ziki/Zikie *See* Zeki.
Zin A Burmese name of uncertain meaning.
Zinan Japanese: the second, or second son.
Zingaro Italian: a gypsy.
Zinzan Of uncertain meaning. The name of a former New Zealand rugby player (Zinzan Brooke).
Zio Italian: an uncle.
Zion A hill in Jerusalem, the site of a holy temple. Also a name for the Jewish people.
Zyon.
Zircon Persian: a 'mineral name'.
Zirkon.
Ziv Hebrew: full of life.
Zhiv, Zhivko (Slavic), *Zivan, Zivar, Ziven* (Polish), *Zivko* (Slavic), *Zivomir* (Slavic), *Zivorad* (Slavic), *Zivu* (Slavic).
Ziya *See* Zia.
Zlatan Slavic: golden.
Slatan.
Zoa A Burmese name of uncertain meaning.
Zodiac Greek: the circle of the astrological signs.
Zodiak.
Zola After Emile Zola, a 19th-century French author, or possibly a version of the girl's name Zoë.
Zolah.
Zolli/Zollie/Zolly Diminutives of Solomon.
Zoltan Arabic: a ruler or sultan. A popular Hungarian name.
See also Sultan.
Zommer German: summer.
Zomer.
Zondag The Dutch name for Sunday.
Zoran Slavic: of the dawn.
Zoren, Zorin, Zorran, Zorren, Zorrin.
Zordan Probably a combination of Zoran and Jordan.
Zorden, Zordin, Zordon, Zordyn.
Zoroaster Persian: a golden star.
Diminutives: Zoro, Zorro.
Zorra Spanish: a fox.
Zorro *See* Zoroaster.
Zouhad An Arabic name of uncertain meaning.
Zuhad.
Zowie The made-up name of singer David Bowie's son.
Zowi.
Zubin Hebrew: the exalted one.
Zuba, Zuben.
Zuma The surname of a South African president (Jacob Zuma).
Zumah.
Zuriel Hebrew: God is my foundation.
Zy/Zye *See* Zi.

Zygmond/Zygmund/Zygmunt
See Sigmund.
Zyke *See* Zike.

Zylon *See* Xylon.
Zyon *See* Zion.

Names by Ethnic Origin

The following lists feature 10,000 names categorised by their ethnic origins or usage. Please refer to the main A–Z listings for meanings, and note that some of these names are listed under others – for example, Edvard is under Edward.

There are also many non-Aboriginal Australian names scattered throughout the book. For some ideas, see *Names for Australians* on pages 16–17.

	Page		Page
Aboriginal	587	Hungarian	605
African	588	Italian	605
American	590	Japanese	607
Arabic	590	Maori	608
Armenian	592	Native American	609
Asian	592	Persian/Iranian	609
Baltic	593	Polynesian	610
Basque	593	Portuguese/Brazilian	611
Celtic	593	Romanian	611
Dutch	596	Sanskrit/Hindi/Sikh	611
Finnish/Estonian	596	Scandinavian	613
French	597	Slavic	615
Gaelic	598	Spanish	618
German/Teutonic	601	Tibetan/Sherpa	619
Greek	602	Turkish	620
Hebrew/Jewish/Yiddish	603		

ABORIGINAL

Boys

Adoni, Akama, Allambee, Allunga, Amaroo, Apari, Araluen, Aroona, Arunta, Bahloo, Balonne, Balun, Banjora, Baradine, Bardo, Baree, Barega, Bareki, Baringa, Barti, Baru, Barwon, Belar, Benalla, Berrigan, Berrima, Berringar, Biloela, Bilyana, Bilyarra, Bindar, Bombala, Booral, Booran, Boree, Borun, Bowral, Brolga, Burnu, Burnum, Burra, Burrill, Calca, Callan, Ceduna, Chubie, Cobar, Colane, Collin, Coombah, Coorain, Cooran, Coorong, Cooyong, Corowa, Cowan, Cullya, Currumbin, Daku, Dalo, Dalyo, Darel, Derain, Derrilin, Dheran, Dili, Doongara, Dorak, Dougan, Dural, Erad, Euro, Euroa, Gaindah, Ganan, Gared, Gayadi, Gelar, Girra, Goola, Goonal, Gorokan, Gurana, Guyra, Hara, Ilya, Indi, Inkata, Jabiru, Jabuk, Jarrah, Jerara, Jerrawa, Jewang, Jingara, Jirra, Jungay, Kabu, Kalbar, Kalti, Kambara, Kamber, Kami, Kana, Kani, Kanku, Kappa, Karangi, Karem, Kari, Kathan, Kebi, Keeden, Keerang, Kembla, Ken, Kendi, Kep, Keyar, Killara, Kimba, Kogarah, Koiranah, Koki, Kolet, Kolli, Koloona, Kolya, Konak, Konol, Koolyn, Koora, Koorong, Kootingal, Koroit, Kulan, Kulnura, Kunda, Kuracca, Kurria, Kuruna, Kuti, Kuya, Kuyan, Leura, Lowan, Macalla, Maka, Mallee, Malu, Mandu, Mani, Marron, Marroo, Marti, Maru, Matari, Matong, Matya, Mearann, Mekari, Mereki, Midgee, Miki, Miku, Minar, Miro, Mirrabook, Mogo, Moki, Monti, Moorak, Morandoo, Moroko, Moto, Mowan, Mulga, Mullion, Mundara, Mundil, Mungarry, Munji, Muri, Myall, Nalong, Nambur, Namoi, Nardu, Narrah, Narrie, Natan, Nattai, Nerang, Nimbin, Nioka, Noko, Nooroo, Nowra, Nudgee, Nunga, Nyawi, Odern, Onak, Orad, Otama, Pangali, Parri, Patonga, Pikuwa, Pindan, Pindari, Pinterry, Pirrin, Polona, Puranga, Quamby, Quandong, Ra, Rangi, Rawan, Tábo, Tabulum, Tahmoor, Tamba, Tambo, Taree, Targan, Tarki, Tarro, Thomar, Togar, Toney, Tuart, Tuki, Tuldar, Tura, Turro, Ulandi, Uralba, Uriz, Uwan, Walcha, Walla, Warka, Warra, Warrain, Warral, Warrigal, Warringa, Warrun, Wilari, Wirake, Wirrin, Wonga, Woorak, Woorin, Wullun, Yampi, Yarran, Yarto, Yelgun, Yerin, Yhuko, Yileen, Yuka, Yuri, Yuroka, Yurung.

Girls

Adelong, Akala, Alba, Algita, Alinga, Alkina, Alkira, Alli, Allirea, Allora, Allunga, Amarina, Anka, Apanie, Araluen, Arika, Arinya, Arnurna, Aroona, Arora, Babinda, Bakana, Bambra, Bami, Bandera, Barina, Beela, Beeree, Bega, Beltana, Berimilla, Berri, Bertana, Biara, Billa, Binda, Bindi, Bingarra, Binya, Birra, Bombala, Boorah, Broula, Bunda, Bundarra, Bunjil, Burilda, Calca, Calleen, Camira, Cardinia, Carina,

Cawana, Coolah, Coorah, Coreen, Corella, Corowa, Cowra, Cullya, Culmara, Curra, Darri, Derrilin, Dimana, Eerin, Ekala, Elanora, Ellin, Elouera, Endota, Euroka, Gaindah, Galinda, Gareema, Garriwa, Gedala, Gemalla, Gheera, Ghera, Gilah, Gilba, Girra, Girraween, Godarra, Gongora, Gulara, Gunida, Gurley, Guyra, Gwandalan, Gymea, Hanya, Hara, Iloura, Iluka, Ingah, Iona, Ira, Irinka, Ita, Jannali, Jedda, Jerula, Jiba, Jili, Jirra, Jiruna, Jular, Junee, Kadee, Kadina, Kadla, Kadli, Kaiya, Kalari, Kali, Kalina, Kalinda, Kaliya, Kalla, Kallang, Kalpara, Kalyan, Kama, Kamarah, Kamballa, Kambar, Kami, Kanandah, Kandelka, Kara, Karalta, Kareela, Karla, Karri, Karuah, Kata, Katina, Katyin, Kawana, Keina, Keira, Kembla, Kena, Kiah, Kiama, Kiara, Kiata, Kiki, Killara, Kilpanie, Kimba, Kindilan, Kinka, Kirra, Kiwa, Koko, Kokora, Kolora, Kolya, Koolyn, Koora, Koorine, Kooya, Kora, Korana, Korra, Kulka, Kumbelin, Kuna, Kunama, Kunara, Kunika, Kupala, Kurria, Kwinana, Kyeema, Kylie, Lakari, Lalirra, Lamilla, Lark, Layaleta, Leena, Leewana, Leita, Lemana, Lerra, Leura, Lirra, Liya, Loorea, Lowanna, Lowitja, Lurnea, Macalla, Magura, Maiya, Malla, Mallana, Mallee, Malya, Mani, Manilla, Mankara, Manoora, Manya, Mara, Marama, Marda, Marinna, Marlee, Marna, Marree, Marron, Mathoura, Mayrah, Meera, Mega, Melinga, Mereki, Merinda, Merri, Merrigal, Merriwa, Meta, Miah, Miandetta, Milina, Mincarlie, Mingara, Minkie, Minore, Minta, Miriyan, Mirrabooka, Mirria, Mirrin, Moira, Moona, Morang, Moree, Morilla, Munda, Mundara, Murna, Murrami, Myee, Myndee, Myndie, Myuna, Nadda, Naliandrah, Nama, Namaga, Namoi, Nana, Nandalie, Nara, Narang, Narara, Naretha, Narooma, Naya, Nepelle, Nerida, Niangala, Niley, Noora, Numira, Nunda, Nunkerie, Nuta, Nyrang, Oba, Olba, Olono, Oola, Orana, Oura, Padulla, Pallano, Pambula, Pangari, Paringa, Patya, Pengana, Perkanna, Peta, Pierah, Pilar, Pinterry, Pinyali, Pitta, Polona, Pretella, Quarallia, Queenida, Quoba, Raja, Rata, Rikkara, Riyala, Roka, Shara, Taldra, Talia, Tallara, Tamba, Tarana, Taranna, Tarcoola, Tarni, Taronga, Tarra, Tathra, Tatya, Thala, Tharah, Tinar, Tindarra, Tingira, Tinka, Tirranna, Tiwa, Toora, Tuki, Turella, Tya, Uka, Ularit, Ulla, Umina, Undurra, Uralla, Uuna, Wala, Wanda, Wanya, Waratah, Warrah, Warrina, Wayamba, Weema, Welya, Wilga, Willa, Wincey, Winta, Wirrah, Wirruna, Woora, Wyuna, Yagoona, Yamba, Yandina, Yani, Yara, Yaralla, Yarrah, Yelka, Yeran, Yeranda, Yileen, Yilla, Yindi, Yonga, Yooralla, Yoorana, Yuki, Yuku, Yungara, Yunta, Yurrah.

AFRICAN

General – Boys
Ade, Ajala, Ameki, Angat, Asamoah, Asbel, Bayanda, Bheki, Bizu, Chad, Chidozie, Cola, Danladi, Dereb, Djimon, Dukale, Ebo, Edu, Essien,

Hirsi, Hondo, Jabulani, Jimiyu, Jojo, Kalahari, Kato, Kenenisa, Kenya, Kola, Kosi, Kwodjo, Lado, Lamine, Malawi, Mansa, Mensa, Morné, Mulatu, Musumba, Neo, Oba, Odion, Okon, Omolara, Quashi, Rago, Sabiti, Salif, Shaka, Sisay, Sisi, Sono, Tael, Tafari, Taiwo, Tawanda, Tendai, Thabo, Togo, Topi, Tupac, Tyrese, Ulan, Xolani, Zuma.

General – Girls
Abayomi, Amadika, Aminatta, Asmara, Ayanna, Baba, Beoline, Cola, Dalma, Damola, Dilla, Eba, Ebele, Efia, Epua, Faithi, Gabourey, Hasana, Jala, Jendaya, Kamaria, Kambiri, Kanika, Kenda, Kenya, Keshia, Kimana, Kinay, Lula, Mafata, Malawi, Mandela, Mandisa, Marula, Mashona, Miriamu, Neela, Nyala, Pita, Poni, Quashi, Seble, Shaka, Shona, Sosina, Syda, Tale, Tanaka, Tanisha, Thandi, Wangari, Yola, Zamunda, Zenani, Zethu, Zimba, Zindzi.

Egyptian – Boys
Aker, Ammon, Anubis, Apis, Atum, Geb, Heka, Horus, Keb, Khonsu, Mentu, Moses, Onuris, Osiris, Phineas, Ra, Rameses, Seb, Sef, Seth, Sobek, Thoth.

Egyptian – Girls
Ammut, Arish, Edjo, Hathor, Hoda, Isis, Kiki, Kiya, Neith, Sekhmet.

Ghanaian – Boys
Bobo, Kedjo, Kodzo, Kofi, Kojo, Kwako, Kwame, Kwao, Kwasi, Tano, Yao.

Ghanaian – Girls
Aba, Abina, Adzo, Afi, Ajua, Akosua, Aku, Ama, Ashanti, Awusi, Ayao, Ekua, Esi, Kakra, Kobla, Kofi, Kwabena, Kwame, Ya.

Nigerian – Boys
Agu, Ajani, Akin, Azi, Boseda, Daren, Edu, Gowon, Ogun.

Nigerian – Girls
Abeo, Adeola, Akila, Alika, Apara, Ayoka, Dumaka, Jumoke, Oba, Onaedo, Taiwo, Toyin, Ulu.

Swahili – Boys
Abasi, Alhamisi, Aprili, Ashon, Bahari, Bakari, Chui, Desemba, Duma, Farasi, Faru, Februari, Hamis, Husani, Jabari, Jambo, Januari, Jelani, Jimoh, Julai, Jumah, Jumane, Kaa, Kalfani, Kanu, Khamisi, Kilima, Kito, Kongoni, Machi, Maji, Manjano, Marjan, Mondo, Mosi, Nuru, Nyani, Nyati, Nyoka, Nyuki, Nyusi, Okapi, Pembe, Safari, Saka, Samaki, Shamba,

Shomari, Simba, Sudi, Tembo.

Swahili – Girls
Adia, Alhamisi, Almasi, Bahari, Bahati, Barika, Dalila, Duma, Emba, Februari, Fedha, Feruzi, Hadiya, Hasina, Ieshia, Ijumaa, Jabali, Jamila, Januari, Julai, Jumaa, Juni, Kaa, Kasa, Kidani, Kima, Leta, Lulu, Machi, Madini, Mahindi, Majani, Maji, Majivu, Mamba, Manjano, Marini, Marjani, Masika, Mosi, Myika, Nyani, Nyati, Nyika, Nyoka, Oktoba, Paka, Pembe, Ramla, Safari, Samaki, Sanura, Shani, Simba, Suka, Sukari, Tisa, Twiga, Winda, Zalika, Zawadi, Ziwa, Zumaradi, Zuri.

AMERICAN

Boys
Alamo, Arizona, Baratunde, Bershawn, Boston, Bud, Buzz, California, Chilli, Cleavon, Cleveland, Colorado, DeMarcus, Denver, DeReese, DeShawn, Devonte, Dime, Duane, Dwayne, Eldene, Harlan, Harvard, Indiana, Jaylen, Kobe, Kressley, LaShawn, Lebron, Leroy, Maine, Maverick, Memphis, Mojo, Montana, Mylon, Nevada, Oregon, Ornette, Rondell, Rozelle, Taye, Tennessee, Tennille, Tevin, Tex, Trell, Tulsa, Utah.

Girls
Alaska, Autumn, Beyoncé, Birdie, California, Chanda, Channette, Chilli, Chima, Cyreta, Denver, Destiny, Divonne, Dixie, Exene, Georgia, Indiana, Jearl, Jolene, Kalisha, Kedra, Keisha, Kenisha, Lacena, Ladene, Ladonna, Lakeisha, Lakena, Laneka, LaRhonda, Latasha, Latoya, Lavelle, Laverne, Lavonne, Louisiana, Maine, Marshevet, Memphis, Montana, Monyetta, Naleya, Navana, Nevada, Philadelphia, Rielle, Shenay, Suellen, Takeisha, Taleisha, Tanedra, Taneka, Tekiya, Tennessee, Tennille, Tonique, Tulsa, Tupelo, Utah, Velma, Wyomia, Yetunde.

ARABIC

Boys
Abboud, Abdul, Abdullah, Abdulmajid, Adnan, Ahmed, Ajmal, Akbar, Akil, Akmal, Akram, Aladin, Alem, Ali, Altair, Amal, Amer, Amin, Amir, Anas, Ansari, Anwar, Arsalan, Asad, Ashfaq, Ashraf, Asif, Asim, Aslan, Awad, Azadeh, Azim, Aziz, Badar, Bashir, Basim, Bilal, Birjis, Borak, Coman, Dabir, Danesh, Daoud, Daud, Dawud, Ebrahim, Fadil, Fahim, Faisal, Faiz, Farid, Farook, Fawaz, Feroz, Firdos, Fouad, Ghassan, Ghulam, Habib, Hadad, Hafiz, Hakim, Halim, Hamal,

Hamid, Hamza, Hani, Haroun, Harun, Hasim, Hassan, Hazem, Hesham, Hilal, Himmat, Houssam, Hussain, Ibrahim, Idris, Imam, Imran, Irfan, Iskandar, Islam, Isra, Iyad, Jabir, Jalil, Jamal, Jasim, Kabir, Kadir, Kalim, Kamal, Kamar, Karif, Karim, Khalid, Khalif, Khan, Khoury, Latif, Mahdi, Mahfuz, Mahmood, Mahommed, Majid, Malik, Mamdouh, Mansoor, Maqbul, Masud, Merak, Misbah, Muammar, Mubarak, Muhammad, Muhsin, Mukhtar, Munir, Muniz, Musa, Mustafa, Nabil, Nadim, Nadir, Najib, Nashat, Nasib, Nasim, Nasir, Nasrullah, Nidal, Nuren, Nuriel, Omar, Osama, Osman, Qamar, Qasim, Rabi, Rafi, Rafiq, Rahman, Ramazan, Rami, Raqi, Raqib, Rashid, Rauf, Rayan, Reza, Rizwan, Rushdi, Sabir, Sadik, Safwat, Salah, Salim, Sami, Samir, Sarfraz, Sayed, Seif, Shafiq, Shahid, Shakil, Sharif, Suleiman, Sultan, Tahir, Tamim, Tanzil, Tariq, Umar, Usama, Wafiq, Wahib, Wajih, Wasim, Wazir, Yahya, Yardan, Yasir, Yawar, Younus, Yunus, Yusuf, Zafar, Zahir, Zakaria, Zaki, Zakir, Zaman, Zarif, Zayed, Zayn, Zia, Zoltan, Zouhad.

Girls

Abia, Adara, Adiba, Adila, Adiva, Afifa, Aisha, Akila, Alima, Aliya, Almira, Alzena, Alzubra, Amala, Amani, Ambara, Amina, Amira, Anan, Arwa, Asima, Asira, Asiya, Asma, Asra, Atika, Atiqa, Atiya, Ausma, Azima, Aziza, Azra, Azusa, Bahaar, Basimah, Bathshira, Benazir, Bibi, Boshra, Dalia, Dara, Fadia, Fadila, Fahima, Fairuz, Faiza, Farah, Farida, Farzana, Fatima, Fazila, Firuza, Ghada, Ghazal, Golzadeh, Gulzaar, Habiba, Hadara, Hadiya, Hadya, Hagir, Hakima, Hala, Halima, Hamida, Hana, Hanan, Hayat, Hayfa, Hoda, Houria, Hushniya, Hussana, Huwaida, Iman, Isra, Jadida, Jala, Jalila, Jamal, Jamila, Jehan, Jumah, Jumana, Junna, Kabira, Kalila, Kamilah, Karida, Karima, Khadija, Khalida, Latifa, Layla, Leila, Lulu, Maha, Majida, Malika, Manal, Martiza, Marwah, Marya, Maryam, Marzia, Masuma, Maysa, Meissa, Muna, Munira, Nabila, Nada, Nadima, Nadira, Nafisa, Najam, Najiba, Najila, Naseem, Nasiba, Natiqa, Nazima, Nida, Nilufar, Noor, Oma, Omaira, Qadira, Qamra, Rabia, Radhia, Rafiqa, Rana, Raniya, Rashida, Raya, Rida, Rihana, Roya, Sabira, Sabiya, Safia, Safura, Sahar, Sakinah, Salima, Samina, Samira, Sana, Sara, Sarwat, Sausan, Sawsan, Shabana, Shafiqa, Shahana, Shahar, Shahina, Shahira, Shaila, Shakira, Shamal, Shamarra, Shameeka, Sharifa, Shazia, Shula, Soheila, Suad, Tahira, Takia, Tamima, Tarana, Tasnim, Timna, Ula, Ulima, Vega, Wafiqa, Wahiba, Wahida, Wajiha, Walida, Wasima, Xaviera, Yasmeen, Yasmin, Yusra, Zada, Zahia, Zaina, Zara, Zarifa, Zaynab, Zohra, Zulema.

ARMENIAN

Boys
Ara, Armen, Atom, Hagob, Hakop, Levon, Nishan, Sarkis, Taniel, Vartan, Yervant, Zareh, Zeroun.

Girls
Ankine, Anoush, Araxia, Arkina, Avan, Elmas, Gadar, Lucine, Perouze, Siran, Siranouche, Zagir.

ASIAN

Chinese – Boys
Bo, Chan, Chang, Chen, Cheung, Chung, Gan, Hao, Ho, Hsin, Hu, Jen, Jin, Joss, Jun, Kee-Lin, Lei, Li, Liang, Lok, Long, Manchu, Ming, Quong, Shen, Sheng, Shing, Sun, Tien, Wang, Wen, Wing, Yin, Yo, Yong, Yu, Yuan, Zhen.

Chinese – Girls
An, Bai, Bic, Bo, Chen, Chow, Chu, Chun, Guan-yin, Heshu, Hoong, Hua, Hweiling, Jie, Jin, Jun, Kuan-Yin, Lee, Li, Lian, Lien, Li-Li, Lin, Ling, Mee, Mei, Mei-Lin, Mei-Ling, Mei-Yu, Meizhen, Mengtao, Ming, Qing, Shuang, Shui, Tao, Tien, Tu, Ushi, Xiang, Xiaoli, Xingxing, Yang, Yi, Yin, Yu, Yue, Ziang.

Indonesian – Boys
Aman, Amat, Andian, Budi, Chahaya, Dian, Garuda, Guntur, Himawan, Ikan, Ilai, Java, Kersen, Pramana, Ramelan, Santoso, Setiawan, Singha, Sukarno, Susila.

Indonesian – Girls
Arti, Asri, Atika, Atin, Bali, Cahaya, Dewi, Indara, Kade, Lastri, Luspida, Madura, Manyura, Melati, Merpati, Niluh, Rukmini, Ruksha, Sujatmi, Tuti, Yarni.

Korean – Boys
Bae, Chin, Dae, Gi, Ho, Hyeon, Kang, Kwan, Lim, Sam, San, Yong.

Korean – Girls
Cho, Dae, Eun, Jin, Jing, Kyon, Song, Soo, Sun, Yon.

Thai – Boys
Agkarajit, Aran, Aroon, Chet, Danai, Isra, Kama, Kiet, Kinnara, Kovit, Kurma, Lek, Machanu, Naga, Niran, Paradorn, Patcharin, Pravat, Sakda,

Samak, Sanchai, Siradanai, Sonchat, Tai, Tanapun, Thai, Thaksin, Virode, Virote.

Thai – Girls
Amara, Isra, Kanya, Kedsarin, Lawan, Mali, Mayoree, Noilani, Noppawan, Nya, Pensiri, Phailin, Pramsiri, Premrudee, Puntira, Ratana, Sirikit, Solada, Suchin, Sumalee, Sunee, Tamarine, Tasanee, Tida, Vanida, Yanisa.

Vietnamese – Boys
Anh, Bay, Binh, Chau, Dinh, Duc, Hai, Han, Hoa, Kim, Minh, Nam, Tai, Tam, Tan, Thai, Thanh, Thian, Thu, Tien, Trai, Tran, Trung, Tuyen, Van, Yen.

Vietnamese – Girls
Am, An, Anh, Bian, Cai, Cam, Chau, Kim, Lan, Le, Nu, Tam, Tan, Thanh, Thao, Tien, Xuan.

BALTIC

Boys
Algirdas, Andris, Imants, Juris, Karlis, Lauras, Menu, Mikelis, Modris, Pavils, Petniunas, Remigijus, Toms, Uldis, Vilis, Visvaldis, Vytautas.

Girls
Aija, Aldona, Alena, Ane, Antonya, Ausma, Baiba, Daila, Ginta, Gundega, Laima, Lauma, Liga, Magryta, Milda, Mirdza, Ona, Reda, Saule, Velta, Vija, Zenta, Zuzanna.

BASQUE

Boys
Aitor, Aritz, Benat, Edur, Eguzki, Fermin, Gasento, Ion, Kasen, Kindin, Maren, Mendoza, Petri, Satordi, Ximeno, Ximun, Zadornin.

Girls
Alaia, Birkita, Eguzkine, Katalin, Kattalin, Maren, Naiara, Satordi, Sorkunde, Unda, Ximena.

CELTIC

General – Boys
Aland, Anlon, Annan, Anwell, Anyon, Ardan, Arthur, Banen,

Banquo, Belenus, Beltane, Bran,
Brent, Brian, Brice, Brone, Cadman,
Caedmon, Caradoc, Carey,
Carnarvon, Carney, Celt, Conall,
Corey, Cymbeline, Dallas, Deverell,
Devin, Doane, Druce, Druid,
Dunham, Ennis, Farrell, Fleance,
Gavin, Gawain, Gower, Gwydion,
Havgan, Innes, Jarman, Keir, Keith,
Kelt, Keltie, Kendrick, Kent, Kimball,
Lann, Newlyn, Ogilvie, Pendragon,
Perth, Renfrew, Ryence, Sayer, Tor,
Tristram, Tydfil, Vortigern, Weylin,
York.

General – Girls
Affrica, Alma, Amena, Anwen,
Arduina, Arianrhod, Armelle,
Arthura, Beltane, Binnie, Boann,
Briana, Bridget, Brigantia, Bryce,
Bryher, Carey, Cordelia, Corey,
Dallas, Deirdre, Duessa, Enid,
Ennis, Epona, Gryffyn, Imogen,
Innes, Keitha, Keltie, Kendra, Kenna,
Maura, Melora, Pixie, Rowena,
Sabrina, Tristanne, Ula, Vanora.

Breton – Boys
Devi, Harvey, Jannick, Pierrick,
Sibran, Visant, Yann, Yannick.

Breton – Girls
Aamor, Aliciedik, Alodia, Harried,
Joyce, Kaer, Nolwenn, Tereza, Yannah.

Cornish – Boys
Austell, Brae, Bray, Brea, Breok,
Budock, Cardew, Carew, Carey,
Carleon, Carlin, Carlyon, Carne,
Corin, Crantock, Cubert, Curnow,
Daveth, Denzil, Derrick, Derry,
Dhu, Diggory, Ellery, Ennor, Gawen,
Gerens, Glen, Gorran, Gryffyn,
Gwinear, Hendra, Howell, Jago,
Jermyn, Jory, Jowan, Kelynack, Kenan,
Kenver, Kenwyn, Kernick, Kernow,
Kersey, Keverne, Kitto, Kittow,
Lanyon, Madok, Madron, Mawgan,
Mawnan, Menadue, Merryn, Michell,
Morcum, Mullion, Mylor, Pascoe,
Pencast, Penglaze, Penrice, Penrose,
Petroc, Piran, Rodda, Rouse, Rowse,
Santo, Tean, Tintagel, Tre, Trefusis,
Trelawney, Treleaven, Tremayne,
Trengrove, Tresco, Trethowan,
Trevelyan, Trevena, Trystan, Tyack,
Vyvyan, Wella, Wendron, Zennor.

Cornish – Girls
Beryan, Bronnen, Caja, Cara,
Carleon, Carlin, Carlyon, Colenso,
Demelza, Ebrel, Ennor, Genowefa,
Gweniver, Gwennap, Jennifer, Kaja,
Kayna, Kenwyn, Kerensa, Lamorna,
Lowenna, Mabyn, Marya, Melloney,
Melwyn, Merryn, Morenwyn, Morva,
Morwenna, Nessa, Pascoe, Penaluna,
Pencast, Rosen, Rosenwyn, Rosevear,
Roskear, Rozen, Talwyn, Tamsin,
Tean, Tegen, Tregenna, Tregenza,
Trelise, Tressa, Trevena, Ula, Ursell,
Verran, Wenna, Wynne, Vyvyan,
Zelah, Zennor.

Welsh – Boys

Adda, Aeron, Afon, Alawn, Aled, Alun, Alun-Wynn, Amaethon, Ambr, Andreas, Aneurin, Angwyn, Arian, Arthes, Athan, Auryn, Awst, Awstin, Baez, Bartholomeus, Beda, Bedward, Bedwyr, Berwyn, Bevan, Beynon, Bledig, Bledri, Bowen, Brecon, Brenin, Breok, Broderick, Brychan, Bryn, Brynmor, Cadell, Cadog, Cadogan, Caerwyn, Cai, Caradoc, Cardew, Carwyn, Cesar, Cigfran, Cledwyn, Clorian, Cochrane, Collen, Colomen, Conway, Conwil, Conyn, Copor, Cranog, Creighton, Crisiant, Cynfor, Cystennin, Dafad, Dafydd, Dai, Derren, Derwen, Derwent, Dewi, Dhu, Dinsdale, Dolffin, Draig, Dyfan, Dylan, Edryd, Efydd, Eleias, Elfed, Elfynian, Emlyn, Emrys, Emyr, Ennion, Eseia, Eurig, Eurwyn, Evan, Folant, Gareth, Gefell, Geraint, Gerallt, Gerwyn, Gethin, Glen, Goronwy, Gorwel, Gough, Griffith, Grigor, Gryffyn, Gwener, Gwilym, Gwinear, Gwydion, Gwydir, Gwyn, Gwynfor, Harri, Heddwyn, Heilyn, Hopkin, Horas, Howell, Hu, Huw, Hywel, Iago, Iau, Idris, Idwal, Iestin, Iestyn, Ieuan, Ifan, Ifor, Ilar, Ilfryn, Ioan, Iorweth, Jevan, Jevon, Jovo, Kadell, Kay, Kenn, Kenwyn, Llewellyn, Lloyd, Llwyd, Llyr, Luc, Lyn, Mabon, Madoc, Malvern, Marc, Mawrth, Medi, Mefin, Mefyn, Meic, Meical, Meilyr, Meirion, Mercher, Meredith, Merfyn, Merlin, Merrick, Meurig, Mihangel, Moren, Morfil, Morgan, Morlo, Mostyn, Myrddin, Neifion, Nye, Ofydd, Oren, Oswallt, Owain, Owen, Parry, Pedr, Pembroke, Penrith, Penrose, Penwyn, Petroc, Powell, Powys, Price, Probert, Pryderi, Pyrs, Raglan, Rheinallt, Rhisiart, Rhobert, Rhodri, Rhudd, Rhun, Rhydderch, Rhydwyn, Rhyll, Rhys, Rolant, Romney, Ryence, Sadwyn, Saeth, Sawyl, Sebedeus, Selyf, Seren, Siarl, Sieffre, Siôn, Siôr, Steffan, Sul, Sulgwyn, Sulwyn, Taffy, Talfryn, Taliesin, Tan, Tangwyn, Taran, Tecwyn, Teigr, Traherne, Tomos, Trefor, Trevor, Trystan, Tudor, Twm, Urien, Vaughan, Wenlock, Wynford, Wynn, Yestin, Ynyr.

Welsh – Girls

Aderyn, Aerona, Almedha, Alwin, Ambr, Anchoret, Aneira, Angharad, Angwen, Arianrhod, Arianwen, Artha, Arwen, Awena, Awsta, Aylwen, Berwyn, Bethan, Bethwynn, Beti, Betrys, Betsan, Blenn, Blodwen, Branwen, Brean, Briallen, Bronwen, Bryn, Cadi, Caillin, Carryl, Carys, Catrin, Ceinwen, Ceridwen, Claerwen, Copor, Crisiant, Delwyn, Delyth, Derryn, Derryth, Dilys, Dolffin, Dylan, Ebril, Efa, Eiddwen, Eira, Eirian, Eiriol, Eirwen, Elen, Eleri, Eluned, Elwyn, Emrallt, Esyllt, Eurwen, Ffion, Gaenor, Gaynor, Gladys, Glen, Glenda, Glenys, Guinevere, Gwen, Gwendolen, Gwener, Gwenfra, Gwenfrewi, Gwenfrynne, Gwenllian, Gwenllyn, Gwinau, Gwladus, Gwladys, Gwyn, Gwyneth, Gwynfor, Hafwen, Heledd, Heulwen, Isolde, Jennifer, Kenwyn, Keyna, Llawella, Llyn, Lowri, Mabli, Mabyn, Mair, Mairwen, Mali, Marged, Margred, Megan, Meinwen, Melva, Melyn, Melys, Meredith,

Mererid, Merlyn, Modlen, Morgan, Morgwn, Morwenna, Morwyn, Moryn, Myfanwy, Nerys, Nesta, Nimue, Olwen, Orena, Owena, Perl, Quendryth, Rhiannon, Rhianwen, Rhonda, Rhonwen, Rhosyn, Rhyll, Sadwyn, Saffir, Seirian, Seiriol, Serena, Sian, Siôna, Sioned, Sula, Tegan, Tegwen, Teigra, Tirion, Trevena, Valmai, Winifred, Wynne.

DUTCH

Boys
Adrianus, Andreas, Arend, Arje, Arjen, Armin, Arne, Arnoldus, Augustijn, Barend, Bartholomeus, Baue, Bazel, Benedikt, Bruin, Carel, Claus, Constantijn, Cornelis, Daneel, De Witt, Dirk, Douwe, Edmond, Folkert, Geert, Gerrit, Gert, Gezinus, Gijsbert, Gillis, Godfried, Haarlem, Harbert, Hein, Hendrik, Hugo, Izaak, Jaap, Jakob, Jan, Jelle, Jeremias, Jeroen, Johannes, Joop, Joost, Jordaan, Joris, Josef, Josephus, Jozua, Jurrien, Karel, Kees, Klaas, Klein, Laurens, Laurentius, Leeuwin, Ludo, Ludovicus, Maart, Maarten, Maik, Maikel, Marinus, Martijn, Meine, Menno, Michiel, Mozes, Onne, Piet, Pim, Reinier, Rens, Rense, Rieuwert, Rikhart, Rinus, Rodolf, Roel, Roeland, Roelof, Rogier, Roosevelt, Ruerd, Rurd, Rutger, Ruud, Schuyler, Siemen, Sjeng, Skipper, Skylar, Stijn, Thies, Thijs, Timo, Timotheus, Tjaard, Tjeerd, Van, Veit, Waldemar, Wagner, Wilhelmus, Willem, Wim, Wolter, Zeeland, Zeeman.

Girls
Alletta, Aniek, Anneka, Anneke, Anneloes, Ans, Antje, Barta, Bartha, Bartholomea, Bendikta, Brandy, Cato, Cornelietta, Dorothea, Doutzan, Doutzen, Elf, Elsje, Francina, Geerta, Gerdina, Gesina, Gezina, Gisela, Gratia, Griet, Grieta, Grietha, Hendrika, Janneke, Jannike, Jantine, Jantje, Johanna, Juli, Jutte, Katrien, Katrine, Lene, Maaike, Margriet, Marieke, Mariet, Marja, Marjolein, Marleis, Marlies, Marlika, Marloes, Mechteld, Mechtilda, Meike, Mieke, Miep, Mies, Miesje, Renske, Saskia, Schuyler, Sien, Sieneke, Skylar, Sofie, Willeke.

FINNISH/ESTONIAN

Boys
Ahti, Antero, Antti, Arttu, Artu, Arvo, Eerik, Eero, Eetu, Eliel, Elokuu, Ensio, Erkki, Erno, Hannu, Heikki, Heikkinen, Ilmarinen, Iltar, Indrek, Jaakko, Jarkko, Jaska, Jorma, Joukahainen, Jouko, Juhani, Jumala, Jyrki, Kalevi, Kelevi, Kimi, Kimmo, Kristo, Lasse, Lauri, Markku, Martti, Matti, Mauri, Mika, Mikko, Nikodeemus, Okko, Olavi, Oskari, Paaveli, Paavo, Peetu, Pekka, Pekko, Petri, Pietari, Raimo, Rikhard, Rikkard, Riku, Risto, Sakari, Simo, Taavi, Tammiku, Tapio, Tarmo,

Teemu, Tero, Timo, Timoteos,
Toomas, Torstai, Tuomas, Ukko,
Usko, Visa.

Girls
Aili, Aino, Anu, Aseri, Dorotea,
Eila, Erja, Hilkka, Ilma, Inari, Inkeri,
Irja, Kaisa, Kalaa, Kuusi, Kylli,
Leea, Maarit, Maimu, Marit, Marja,
Marketta, Meri, Merja, Orvokki,
Piltti, Piritta, Pirjo, Pirkko, Puna,
Rikka, Satu, Senja, Sirkka, Soila,
Tammiku, Tapania, Tarja, Teija,
Torsta, Venla.

FRENCH

Boys
Aamadou, Abbe, Abbot, Acelin,
Achille, Adolphe, Adrien, Aimé,
Aimon, Alain, Alexandre, Algernon,
Alphonse, Ambroise, Anastase,
André, Ange, Ansel, Antoine,
Armand, Armistead, Armour,
Arnaud, Arnett, Arras, Arsène,
Artus, Aubert, Aubin, Audric,
Auguste, Aurele, Aurélien, Avent,
Avril, Baptiste, Barnabé, Basile,
Batiste, Baudile, Baudouin, Beau,
Benoit, Blaisot, Bleu, Brunet,
Camille, Caton, Césaire, Chrétien,
Christophe, Clément, Conrade,
Corneille, Cyprien, Cyrille, Danton,
Dauphin, Davide, Didier, Dominique,
Donatien, Dubois, Duval, Edgard,
Edmond, Édouard, Émile, Étienne,
Eugène, Evrard, Fabien, Fabron,
Fernand, Février, Flavien, Florent,
Fontaine, François, Frédéric, Gael,
Gaspard, Gaston, Gautier, Georges,
Geraud, Germain, Geronte,
Gervais, Gilles, Grégoire, Guilbert,
Guillaume, Gustave, Henri, Hercule,
Hervé, Hilaire, Hugues, Ignace,
Jacques, Janvier, Jean, Jehan, Jeremie,
Josselin, Jourdain, Jules, Julien,
Juste, Lafayette, Lascelles, Laurent,
Lazare, Léandre, Léon, Léonard,
Léopold, Levander, Lionel, Lisle,
Loic, Louis, Luc, Lucien, Lundi,
Malchi, Malo, Marat, Marc, Marcel,
Mardi, Marion, Marquis, Martineau,
Mathieu, Maxime, Michel, Modeste,
Nicodeme, Nöel, Octave, Olivier,
Orphée, Paques, Paris, Patrice, Paulot,
Philippe, Pierre, Pierrot, Pilote,
Prideaux, Rainier, Raoul, Régis, Rémy,
Renaud, Renouf, Rive, Rodolphe,
Rodrigue, Roi, Romain, Roquet,
Sacha, Sagan, Salomon, Samedi,
Sébastien, Serge, Simplice, Stéphane,
Sylvain, Thibault, Thierry, Timothée,
Toussaint, Trudeau, Ulysse, Valentin,
Valery, Virgile, Yves, Zidane, Zola.

Girls
Adèle, Adrienne, Agate, Agathe,
Agnies, Aimée, Alacoque, Alette,
Alexandrine, Alize, Alsace,
Amandine, Ambre, Amélie,
Amorette, Amour, Anastasie, Ancelin,
Andrée, Ange, Angelique, Annetta,
Anselme, Antoinette, Aravane,
Arette, Armynel, Athalie, Athène,
Audrée, Auguste, Aurélie, Aurore,
Aveline, Avril, Azura, Barbe, Belle,

Benoite, Bérengère, Berthe, Bijou, Blanche, Bleu, Brabazon, Brigitte, Briolette, Briot, Brunetta, Calais, Calandre, Calanthe, Camille, Candide, Caresse, Carole, Cartier, Cassandre, Cécile, Céline, Cerise, Chamonix, Chanel, Chantal, Chardonnay, Cher, Chic, Chiffon, Chimene, Christelle, Ciel, Claire, Claudette, Cleanthe, Clothilde, Coco, Colette, Colombe, Cordélie, Cosette, Cyrille, Danette, Délice, Denise, Desirée, Dior, Dominique, Doré, Dorothée, Douce, Edwige, Elbertine, Eleonore, Elise, Elle, Emeraude, Émilie, Esmé, Esprit, Estée, Estelle, Étienette, Étoile, Eudocie, Eugénie, Fabienne, Fanchon, Félicité, Fernande, Finesse, Flavie, Fleur, Flore, Fontaine, Francine, Françoise, Fréderique, Garance, Gazelle, Genevieve, Georgette, Germaine, Ghislaine, Gigi, Gisèle, Hélène, Henriette, Hilaire, Honore, Huguette, Irène, Isabeau, Isaure, Jacinthe, Jehanne, Jeudi, Jeune, Joelle, Jolie, Josée, Juillet, Juliette, Laure, Léonne, Liliane, Lionelle, Lisette, Lourdes, Luce, Lucienne, Ludivine, Lydie, Lys, Madelon, Manon, Marcelle, Margot, Marianne, Marielle, Marine, Marjolaine, Martine, Mathilde, Matisse, Mélisande, Micheline, Mietta, Mignon, Mireille, Monet, Monique, Moreau, Mystique, Nadine, Nanette, Nanon, Narcisse, Nathalie, Nicolette, Ninon, Nouvelle, Octavie, Odette, Odile, Olympe, Ophélie, Oriane, Paradis, Pascale, Patrice, Paulette, Perette, Régine, Réjeanne, Rémy, Renée, Rochelle, Rosette, Rosine, Rouge, Sabine, Sebastienne, Segolene, Seraphine, Sévérine, Simonette, Solange, Suzette, Sybille, Tatienne, Terezon, Tifaine, Toinette, Trisette, Vedette, Véronique, Vevette, Victorine, Violette, Virginie, Voile, Xavière, Yolande, Yseult, Yvette, Yvonne, Zélie, Zenobie.

GAELIC

General – Boys
Abboid, Adhahm, Alan, Bearnard, Blaine, Brae, Breck, Camden, Cane, Carvel, Christie, Christy, Corey, Corlett, Culley, Dacey, Daibhidh, Dalgleish, Delaney, Dhugald, Donnelly, Dougal, Duffy, Dugan, Dunbar, Eoin, Fagan, Fergus, Ferris, Galloway, Galway, Garvey, Gilchrist, Gilroy, Girvan, Glen, Glendon, Hearn, Hurley, Iain, Innes, Kermit, Kilpatrick, Macauley, McDougall, Mackay, Morven, Niall, Ninian, Peadar, Quaile, Quilliam, Quinney, Ruadh, Solamh, Taggart, Torcall, Torin, Tynan.

General – Girls
Alauda, Armorel, Cailin, Catriona, Ceilidh, Corey, Corlette, Culley, Dacey, Danu, Delaney, Edana, Fenella, Fergine, Fiona, Flanna, Glen, Innes, Maidie, Mairead, Malise, Malvina, Morven, Muirne, Muriel, Quaile, Sorcha.

Irish – Boys

Adhamh, Aguistin, Ahearn, Aidan, Ailfrid, Ailin, Aillen, Alphonsus, Alroy, Alsandair, Ambros, Anntoin, Ardal, Arlen, Artur, Athlone, Barry, Bartle, Beagan, Beattie, Bécan, Benen, Blaney, Brady, Branagh, Branduff, Breandan, Brendan, Brian, Brodie, Brogan, Brosnan, Byrne, Caley, Callaghan, Canice, Carden, Carey, Carlin, Carrick, Carroll, Casey, Cash, Cashel, Cassidy, Cathal, Cathan, Cathmor, Cavan, Cavanagh, Cian, Cianan, Ciarán, Cillian, Clancy, Cleary, Cluny, Colm, Colum, Columba, Conan, Conlan, Conn, Connaught, Connery, Connolly, Connor, Conroy, Conway, Cormac, Corrigan, Costello, Creagh, Cregan, Crevan, Cronan, Cuan, Cuin, Cumal, Curran, Daley, Dara, Darby, Darragh, Declan, Dempsey, Dermot, Derry, Desmond, Devlin, Dolan, Domhnall, Donagh, Donahue, Donal, Donegal, Donn, Donovan, Dooley, Doone, Doran, Dorsey, Dow, Driscoll, Duane, Durack, Eamonn, Eden, Egan, Eimar, Enda, Enos, Eoghan, Eoin, Erin, Eunan, Fáelán, Fallon, Fanahan, Fenlon, Fergal, Fiachra, Finbar, Finian, Finn, Finnegan, Fintan, Flanagan, Flannan, Flannery, Flynn, Gair, Gallagher, Galvin, Gannon, Gara, Gearalt, Gearoid, Grady, Gub, Hagen, Haley, Healy, Hennessey, Hogan, Hurley, Ingobert, Jarlath, Jimeoin, Kalan, Kane, Kean, Kearney, Keefe, Keegan, Keeley, Keenan, Kelan, Keller, Kelly, Kennedy, Kenyon, Kerian, Kermit, Kern, Kerr, Kerrigan, Kerry, Kerwin, Kevin, Kian, Kiefer, Kieran, Kiernan, Killarney, Killian, Kinnard, Knox, Kyran, Labhras, Lawler, Lennon, Liam, Limerick, Lochlainn, Lochlan, Loman, Lorcan, Lucan, Lugh, McKenna, Macklin, McMahon, Maghnus, Mahon, Malone, Mannix, Manus, Mártan, Molloy, Moran, Muiris, Munro, Murphy, Neal, Nevin, Newry, Nolan, O'Brien, O'Donnell, Odran, O'Neil, Oran, O'Shea, Ossian, Padraig, Patrick, Phelan, Pilib, Pol, Quigley, Quillan, Quinlan, Quinn, Rafferty, Raghnall, Réamann, Redmond, Regan, Renny, Riley, Riordan, Roarke, Rogan, Ronan, Ronit, Rooney, Rory, Rowan, Ryan, Scully, Seamus, Sean, Senan, Shanahan, Shane, Shanley, Shannon, Shaugnessy, Shaun, Shawn, Shea, Sheehan, Sheridan, Siomon, Skelly, Slaney, Slattery, Slevin, Sloan, Stiofan, Sullivan, Sweeney, Tad, Tadgh, Teague, Tiernan, Tierney, Tiobóid, Tomas, Tormey, Tory, Tulloch, Tully, Tynagh, Tyrone, Ultan, Ventry.

Irish – Girls

Aidan, Aideen, Aigneis, Ailis, Aine, Aingeal, Aiofe, Aiveen, Alana, Allsun, Ashling, Athea, Augusteen, Aurnia, Avoca, Aylice, Bairbre, Berneen, Bevin, Biddy, Blaine, Blinnie, Boann, Brady, Breda, Brenda, Brenna, Bríd, Bridget, Bridie, Briege, Brighid, Brodie, Brona, Bryna, Cairine, Cait, Caitlin, Caitrin, Caley, Caoimhe, Cara, Caragh, Carden, Carey, Carleen, Carlin, Casey, Cassidy, Ceara, Ciara, Clancy, Clare, Clodagh, Cloneen, Colleen, Crida, Crístíona, Cushla, Dairine, Daley, Darby, Deirdre,

Dervla, Donla, Doone, Duana, Dymphna, Edel, Eibhlin, Eileen, Eilis, Eily, Eister, Eithne, Emer, Ena, Enda, Erin, Etain, Evaleen, Fallon, Fennagh, Fidelma, Fina, Fiona, Flannery, Grainne, Grania, Hibernia, Ierne, Illona, Ireland, Ita, Kathleen, Kayley, Keeley, Kelly, Kennedy, Kerry, Keverne, Kevine, Kiana, Kiara, Kiera, Kyna, Léan, Luiseach, MacKenna, Maeve, Maidie, Maire, Mairead, Mairin, Maureen, Mavourneen, Moira, Mona, Muirenn, Muiriol, Murphy, Myrna, Nano, Neala, Nevan, Niamh, Nola, Nuala, Onóra, Oonagh, Orla, Orna, Ossia, Queenan, Quinn, Quishla, Raghnailt, Renny, Riley, Riona, Róisín, Ronan, Rory, Rosaleen, Rosheen, Rowan, Ryan, Sabia, Saoirse, Saraid, Shane, Shannah, Shannon, Sheehan, Sheila, Shelagh, Sheridan, Shevaun, Síle, Sinéad, Siobhán, Slaney, Sloan, Sweeney, Talulla, Tara, Teague, Tierney, Torin, Treasa, Tullia, Tully, Tynan, Úna, Vevila, Yootha.

Scottish – Boys

Abernethy, Adair, Adhamh, Ailbert, Ailean, Aindréas, Airlie, Alasdair, Alasdhair, Alastair, Allister, Angus, Arailt, Argyll, Arran, Artair, Athol, Baird, Balfour, Ballantyne, Beathan, Benneit, Berridge, Blair, Bowie, Boyd, Buchan, Buchanan, Cailean, Calum, Cameron, Campbell, Chalmers, Chivas, Clunes, Clyde, Cormag, Craig, Cunningham, Dalziel, Diarmad, Donalbain, Donald, Douglas, Drew, Duff, Duncan, Dundas, Dundee, Dunmore, Eachan, Eanraig, Eideard, Elgin, Ellar, Errol, Erskine, Euan, Eumann, Ewan, Farquhar, Fife, Filib, Fingal, Finlay, Forbes, Gairloch, Galbraith, Gillespie, Gilmer, Gordon, Graeme, Gregor, Greig, Griogair, Guthrie, Hamish, Hewie, Iagan, Ian, Inglis, Irving, Jock, Keir, Kelso, Kelvin, Kenneth, Kester, Kilmeny, Kirkcaldy, Kyle, Lachlan, Laird, Leith, Lennox, Leslie, Lindsay, Loch, Lochinvar, Logan, Lorne, Loudon, Lucais, Ludo, Ludovic, Luthais, Mac, Macarthur, Macbeth, McCall, McCartney, McClelland, Macdonald, McEwan, McFarlane, MacGregor, McHardy, McInnes, McIntosh, Mack, Mackenzie, McClaren, Maclean, Macleod, McNicol, McPherson, Macquarie, McTavish, Magill, Malcolm, Malise, Mànas, Mata, Maxwell, Meldrum, Menzies, Micheál, Moffatt, Montrose, Moray, Morven, Muir, Mungo, Murdoch, Murray, Nairn, Nicol, Osgar, Padruig, Perth, Petrie, Rab, Raibeart, Ramsay, Reamonn, Ross, Roy, Scott, Sholto, Sim, Skene, Somerled, Steaphan, Strahan, Strathmore, Tam, Tavis, Tavish, Thane, Thurso, Tomas, Torquil, Uilleam.

Scottish – Girls

Adair, Aileen, Ailsa, Ainsley, Aisleen, Alexina, Annella, Atholene, Barabal, Bearnas, Beitris, Blair, Bonnie, Cairistìona, Caledonia, Cameron, Donalda, Edmé, Euna, Fife, Finlay, Fiona, Greer, Grier, Grizel, Hughina, Iona, Isbel, Iseabail, Isla, Kerrera, Kirstie, Kyla, Kyle, Leith, Lesley,

Lilias, Lindsey, Lorna, Lorne, Mackenzie, Mackinley, Maclean, Maidie, Mairead, Maisie, Morag, Moray, Morven, Muireall, Nairne, Neilina, Nora, Norma, Raghnaid, Rona, Senga, Seònaid, Sheena, Shona, Sìleas, Siubhan, Siùsan, Skye, Vaila, Zena.

GERMAN/TEUTONIC

Boys
Adolf, Alberich, Albrecht, Alfons, Alric, Andreas, Anselm, Anton, Arne, Arno, Aronne, August, Axel, Bach, Bauer, Benedikt, Berlin, Bernhard, Berthold, Bismarck, Blassius, Braun, Bruno, Burkhard, Carl, Carsten, Christoph, Claudius, Claus, Dannel, Dedrick, Detlef, Diesel, Dieter, Dietrich, Dionysus, Dolf, Dorf, Eduard, Egon, Einstein, Engelbert, Erich, Ernst, Eugen, Evert, Februar, Floribert, Folchard, Franz, Freitag, Friedrich, Fritz, Georg, Gerhardt, Gerhold, Gottfried, Gunther, Handel, Hanke, Hans, Hansel, Hansi, Heinrich, Heinz, Helmut, Heribert, Hermann, Hieronymus, Holz, Horst, Hugo, Huppert, Ibsen, Ignatz, Immanuel, Ingbert, Ingolf, Isaak, Isidor, Ivo, Jakob, Jeremias, Jobst, Jochen, Jochim, Johann, Johannes, Josef, Jurgen, Karl, Karsten, Kasimir, Kaspar, Klaes, Klaus, Klein, Klemens, Konrad, Konstantin, Kurt, Lenz, Leonhard, Leopold, Lorenz, Lothar, Ludi, Ludwig, Lukas, Manfried, Marcell, Markus, Marzell, Matte, Matz, Meinard, Meine, Menno, Merten, Meyer, Morgen, Moritz, Mose, Nikolaus, Nord, Norden, Oskar, Oster, Ostern, Otto, Rafael, Rainer, Reiner, Reinhardt, Reinhold, Roderich, Rodolf, Roland, Rolf, Rudiger, Rupert, Salomo, Sascha, Schwarz, Siegfried, Stefan, Stein, Tal, Terenz, Theodor, Thilo, Tibold, Udo, Ulrich, Urs, Utz, Viktor, Vincens, Volker, Waldemar, Waldir, Walther, Wenzel, Werner, Wessel, Wetzel, Widald, Wilfried, Wilhelm, Willi, Winfried, Wodan, Wolf, Wolfgang, Xaver, Zacharias, Zommer.

Girls
Ada, Adelheid, Adriane, Agathe, Agnethe, Alda, Alena, Alvara, Amalie, Anja, Anke, Annali, Annegrete, Anneliese, Annerl, Anschau, Antonie, Arilda, Arnika, Auguste, Axelle, Bärbel, Beatrix, Benedikta, Berlina, Berta, Bertrude, Brigitte, Bruna, Brunhilde, Cacelie, Dorothea, Edeline, Eleonore, Elfriede, Elke, Eloise, Elrica, Else, Erda, Erika, Erma, Felicie, Franziska, Freide, Frieda, Friederike, Fritzi, Gabriele, Gerde, Gerlinde, Gertrud, Gisela, Gratia, Greta, Gretchen, Grete, Gretel, Griselda, Grit, Hanne, Hannelore, Hanni, Hansine, Hedwig, Heidi, Heike, Helene, Helma, Helmine, Henrike, Hermine, Hilde, Hildegard, Idette, Ilse, Imke, Irma, Johanna, Julianna, Jutta, Karlotte, Karoline, Katherina, Kathri, Katja, Katrien, Katrine, Klara, Klarissa, Konstanze, Kristel, Leisel, Lene, Liesl, Lila, Lilie, Lora, Lore, Lorelei,

Luana, Luise, Lulu, Luzie, Madlena, Magda, Margaretha, Margret, Mariane, Marla, Marlene, Marthe, Matilda, Meike, Minna, Mitzi, Monika, Nixie, Odile, Philippine, Raine, Rebekka, Renate, Romy, Roswitha, Ruperta, Rut, Sara, Sascha, Sibylle, Silke, Steffi, Stephanine, Susanne, Tabea, Tala, Tamara, Tanja, Theresia, Traudl, Uda, Uli, Ulrike, Uschi, Ute, Vala, Valda, Veronike, Viktoria, Wanda, Werna, Wesselina, Wilhelmine, Zerlina, Ziska, Zommer.

GREEK

Boys

Abraxas, Acastus, Achelous, Achilles, Actaeon, Adelpho, Adonis, Adrastos, Aeneas, Aeolus, Aesop, Agamemnon, Ajax, Alekos, Alexandros, Alexios, Alfa, Almo, Ampelios, Amphion, Anastasios, Anatolios, Andis, Androcles, Andronikos, Angelos, Antares, Anteros, Apollo, Apostolos, Aquila, Arcadio, Arcas, Archimedes, Arcturus, Ares, Argos, Argyro, Arion, Aristedes, Aristomenes, Aristotle, Arseni, Artemas, Artemisios, Athanasius, Athos, Atlas, Atticus, Avel, Avram, Bacchus, Basileos, Belen, Boreas, Cadmus, Castor, Centauri, Charon, Chiron, Christos, Chrysander, Cimon, Cleon, Corvus, Corydon, Cosmo, Creon, Cygnus, Cyrano, Daedalus, Damon, Darius, Deimos, Delius, Demas, Demetrios, Demos, Diomedes, Doric, Draco, Efstathios, Efthimios, Endymion, Eneas, Eon, Erasmus, Erastus, Erebus, Eros, Eryx, Euclid, Eudo, Euphemios, Eurus, Eusebios, Eustratios, Evander, Evangelos, Fotis, Galen, Ganymede, Georgios, Gerasimos, Halcyon, Hamon, Hector, Helios, Hellas, Herakles, Hermes, Hespero, Hippolyte, Homer, Hyllus, Hyperion, Icarus, Ioannes, Isander, Isidoros, Jason, Kalon, Kalos, Kosmo, Kostas, Kronos, Kyriakos, Laertes, Leandros, Leonidas, Linus, Lycidas, Lysander, Makarios, Makis, Manolis, Markos, Maron, Martios, Mentor, Michalis, Midas, Mimas, Minos, Myron, Narcissus, Nektarios, Nemo, Neo, Nereus, Nestor, Nicander, Nicodemus, Nikolaos, Nikos, Notus, Orestes, Orion, Orpheus, Otis, Panagiotis, Pancras, Pantelis, Paris, Paschalis, Pavlos, Pegasus, Pelagio, Pericles, Perseus, Petros, Philemon, Philo, Phoebus, Phoenix, Plato, Porfirio, Poseidon, Priam, Prometheus, Proteus, Quiric, Riginos, Sakelarios, Savvas, Sirius, Smaragdos, Socrates, Solon, Sophocles, Spiridon, Stavros, Stefanos, Stylianos, Talus, Telemachus, Tereus, Thaddeus, Thanos, Theano, Theodis, Theodore, Theon, Theophilus, Theron, Theros, Theseus, Timaios, Timon, Titos, Triton, Tryphon, Tycho, Ulysses, Uranius, Vangelis, Vasilis, Vassos, Xanthus, Xenophon, Xenos, Xylon, Yannis, Yianni, Yiorgos, Yoriyos, Zafirios, Zelotes, Zenas, Zethus, Zeus.

Girls

Acantha, Achilla, Adara, Adelpha, Adonia, Adrastea, Aëdon, Aegea, Agapé, Aglaia, Aikaterini, Akesa, Alala, Alastrina, Alatea, Alcestis, Alcina, Aldara, Aleka, Alethea, Aleydis, Aliki, Alpha, Althea, Altheda, Aludra, Alysia, Alyssa, Amalthea, Amaranth, Amaryllis, Aminta, Ananke, Andrea, Andromache, Andromeda, Angeliki, Annys, Anteia, Anthela, Anthoula, Antigone, Anusia, Aphrodite, Apollonia, Ara, Arachne, Araminta, Arcadia, Areta, Arethusa, Argiro, Ariadne, Arista, Artemis, Arva, Aspasia, Astrea, Atalanta, Athanasia, Athena, Attica, Aura, Basilia, Calandra, Calantha, Calista, Callidora, Callisto, Caloris, Calypso, Canace, Candia, Carmé, Cassandra, Castalia, Ceto, Charis, Charisma, Chloris, Chrisoula, Chrysilla, Circe, Cleantha, Clio, Clymene, Clytie, Constatina, Cosima, Cynara, Cynthia, Cyriaca, Dacia, Damaris, Danaë, Delia, Delta, Demetria, Desma, Despina, Diantha, Dido, Dione, Dirce, Dora, Dyna, Dysis, Echo, Efstathia, Egeria, Ekaterini, Elara, Electra, Elefteria, Eleni, Elma, Elpis, Endocia, Enora, Enyo, Eolanda, Eos, Eranthe, Erato, Ercilia, Ersa, Euclea, Eudocia, Eulalia, Euphemia, Euphrasia, Europa, Eurydice, Eustacia, Euterpe, Evadne, Fereniki, Fotini, Gaia, Galatea, Haidee, Halcyone, Hariklia, Haroula, Hebe, Helianthe, Hemera, Hera, Hero, Hestia, Hippolyta, Ianthe, Ileana, Iolanthe, Iphigenia, Ithaca, Jacinda, Jocasta, Kalika, Kalliope, Koren, Krystalia, Kyria, Kyriaki, Kyriakoula, Leda, Lefki, Leto, Louiza, Lycoris, Lydia, Lyris, Lystra, Marianthi, Maroulla, Medea, Medusa, Melantha, Melina, Metaxia, Metis, Myra, Naida, Nestor, Nike, Niki, Niobe, Nova, Nymphea, Nyssa, Oceana, Pallas, Panagiota, Pandia, Pandora, Paraskeve, Parthenia, Penelope, Persephone, Phaedra, Pherenike, Philantha, Philomena, Phoebe, Psyche, Renya, Reveka, Rhea, Rheta, Roula, Scylla, Semele, Sinope, Smaragda, Sofi, Sotiria, Stamatina, Stavroula, Stefania, Styliani, Sybil, Syna, Syntyche, Tasoula, Tethys, Thais, Thea, Theftera, Themis, Theophania, Theophilia, Thera, Thetis, Tola, Toula, Tryna, Tyro, Vasiliki, Xanthe, Xenia, Xylia, Zafera, Zenobia, Zeta, Zeva, Zocha, Zoë.

HEBREW/JEWISH/YIDDISH

Boys

Abaddon, Abba, Abdiel, Abel, Abiel, Abijah, Abir, Abisha, Abner, Absalom, Adam, Adar, Adin, Adir, Adlai, Adon, Adriel, Ahab, Aharon, Akiva, Aleph, Almon, Alon, Alvah, Amal, Amiel, Amin, Amirov, Amon, Amos, Anno, Aram, Aran, Ardon, Ari, Ariel, Armon, Arvad, Asa, Asher, Ashur, Atarah, Avan, Avi, Avidan, Aviel, Aviv, Avner, Avrom, Avron, Azariah, Azriel, Azzan, Barak, Baruch, Belshazzar, Binyamin, Boaz, Cain, Caleb, Canaan, Cohen, Dagan, Dani, Dar, Dathan, Doron, Dov, Dror,

Dudi, Eden, Edom, Ehud, Eitan, Elam, Elan, Eldad, Eleazar, Eli, Eliyahu, Elkan, Elul, Emek, Enoch, Enos, Eran, Esau, Ethan, Ezel, Ezra, Falk, Gadiel, Gamaliel, Gera, Gershom, Gideon, Goliath, Gomer, Gur, Gurion, Hanan, Haram, Harel, Hareth, Heman, Hershel, Hillel, Hiram, Hosea, Hyam, Ichabod, Ido, Ilan, Ira, Ishmael, Israel, Itzik, Iyar, Jabez, Jadon, Jael, Jairus, Japhet, Jareb, Jaron, Javan, Jedediah, Joab, Joah, Jora, Joram, Jordan, Kaniel, Kefar, Kislev, Kiva, Kuper, Laban, Lael, Lamech, Leben, Leor, Levi, Liron, Mahir, Mandel, Meir, Melek, Menachem, Micah, Moishe, Mordecai, Moshe, Naaman, Nahum, Namir, Nekoda, Nimrod, Nisan, Noah, Noam, Noga, Nur, Oreb, Oren, Perez, Ranen, Ravid, Raviv, Raziel, Rechab, Reuben, Reuel, Revie, Roni, Ronit, Sabas, Sandalfon, Seth, Shadrach, Shafan, Shahar, Shalom, Shamir, Shani, Shavar, Shem, Shemesh, Shevat, Shimon, Shlomo, Shmuel, Sion, Sivan, Tal, Tamir, Tavas, Tavi, Teman, Terach, Tevet, Tishri, Tivon, Tovi, Uriel, Uzi, Vered, Volf, Yael, Yakim, Yakir, Yakov, Yaniv, Yaron, Yehuda, Yehudi, Yered, Yeshua, Yigael, Yonatan, Yoni, Yosef, Yovel, Yuval, Zadok, Zahavi, Zalman, Zamir, Zared, Zayit, Zebulun, Zelig, Zeviel, Ziv, Zion, Zubin, Zuriel.

Girls

Abelia, Abera, Abigail, Abijah, Abilene, Abra, Adah, Adalia, Adama, Adar, Adara, Adiel, Adina, Adira, Afina, Afraima, Ahuda, Ahuva, Aliya, Aliza, Alona, Aluma, Amana, Amaris, Amira, Amita, Amora, Anat, Anya, Aphra, Arda, Ardath, Ariel, Ariella, Ariza, Arna, Arona, Asenath, Asera, Asher, Ashira, Asisa, Atarah, Athalia, Atira, Avel, Avera, Avia, Avirit, Aviva, Ayala, Ayelet, Ayla, Azaria, Azelias, Bathsheba, Batsheva, Behira, Beila, Bena, Bethany, Bethel, Bethesda, Bethia, Bethulah, Beulah, Bina, Brina, Carmel, Carna, Cassia, Cayam, Cayla, Charna, Chava, Chaya, Dalit, Dara, Delilah, Derora, Devash, Devora, Dinah, Diza, Dodie, Eden, Elan, Elana, Eliora, Elula, Endora, Esara, Frayda, Freyde, Fruma, Gada, Gali, Galia, Galya, Gana, Gavrila, Gelila, Geola, Geva, Gilana, Golda, Gurit, Hadassa, Hagar, Haifa, Hannah, Hava, Haya, Hepzibah, Hinda, Hulda, Ilana, Imber, Inbar, Irit, Jada, Jael, Jaffa, Janna, Jarah, Jemima, Jerusha, Jonina, Jora, Jordan, Kaila, Katriel, Kefira, Kelila, Keren, Kerith, Keturah, Kezia, Lariel, Leah, Lemuela, Levana, Lewanna, Lilith, Livana, Liviya, Luz, Madrona, Mahalia, Mahira, Malkah, Mara, Marganit, Mariamne, Masada, Maven, Mehitabel, Menorah, Menuha, Merab, Merkaba, Michal, Moriah, Naomi, Nasia, Nava, Nili, Nira, Nisana, Nitza, Nizana, Noa, Nuria, Nurit, Odelia, Ofira, Ophrah, Orinda, Orli, Orna, Ornice, Ozora, Panina, Pazia, Perez, Rahel, Raiza, Ravia, Rena, Rifka, Rinat, Rivka, Ruth, Sabas, Sabra, Salome, Samara, Samaria, Sana, Sarina, Sasona, Sela, Semira, Shabbat, Shaina, Shani, Sharon, Sheni, Shevat, Shifra, Shiloh, Shimona, Shimrit, Shira, Shoshana, Shulamit, Simcha, Sivanah, Talia, Talma, Talya, Tamar, Tameka,

Tammuza, Tarah, Teveta, Thirza, Timora, Tishra, Tivona, Torah, Tuvia, Udiya, Uma, Varda, Yael, Yakira, Yarkona, Yehudit, Yona, Yovela,
Zahava, Zaneta, Zara, Zaria, Zayita, Zazu, Zelah, Zerah, Zeresh, Zeva, Zillah, Zilpah, Zion, Ziona, Zippora, Ziva, Zofeya, Zulema.

HUNGARIAN

Boys
Akos, Andras, Antal, Arpad, Atalik, Ballas, Bela, Bendek, Bertalan, Bodi, Dezso, Ferenc, Feri, Ferko, Filep, Gabor, Géza, Gyula, Henrik, Imre, István, Janos, Jeno, József, Józsi, Kalman, Károly, Krisztian, Lajos,

Laszlo, Lazar, Lazlo, Lorand, Lorant, Marcell, Marton, Mihaly, Miska, Nouri, Orban, Rez, Sandor, Sebo, Tamas, Tibor, Varad, Vidor, Vilmos, Zoltan.

Girls
Aniko, Aranka, Babara, Bodi, Dorottya, Edit, Erzsebet, Erzsi, Eszter, Hedviga, Ildiko, Ilka, Ilona, Ilonka, Iren, Jola, Jolan, Jolanka, Juli,

Magdolna, Margit, Marica, Panna, Piri, Piroska, Prioska, Rez, Rezia, Roskia, Terezia, Tizane, Veronika, Vilma, Zigana, Zizi, Zsa Zsa.

ITALIAN

Boys
Abramo, Achilleo, Adamo, Adan, Adolfo, Adriano, Agapito, Agnello, Agostino, Alberico, Alberto, Albino, Alcide, Aldo, Alessandro, Alessio, Alfio, Alfonso, Allighiero, Aloisia, Alto, Amadeo, Ambrogio, Amerigo, Amores, Ampelio, Anatolio, Andrea, Angelo, Aniello, Annibale, Antonio, Aquilino, Arduino, Argento, Ariosto, Aristede, Arnoldo, Aronne, Arsenio, Artemio, Arturo, Attilio, Aurelio, Baldassare, Bartolomeo, Battista, Benedetto, Beniamino, Benvolio, Beppe, Bernardo, Biaggio, Bianco, Calogero, Calvino, Camillo, Candelario, Candido, Carlo, Carmine, Celestino, Celso, Cesare, Ciriaco, Cirino, Ciro, Claudio, Cleto, Concetto, Corrado, Cosimo,

Costantino, Costanzo, Cristiano, Cristoforo, Damiano, D'Angelo, Daniele, Dante, Delfino, Demetrio, Desiderio, Dino, Domenico, Donatello, Edgardo, Edmondo, Edoardo, Eliseo, Elmo, Emanuele, Emidio, Emilio, Ennio, Enrico, Enzo, Ermanno, Erminio, Ernesto, Ettore, Eugenio, Eusebio, Fabiano, Fabio, Fabrizio, Fausto, Fedele, Federico, Feliciano, Ferdinando, Ferrato, Filippo, Flavio, Florencio, Floro, Francesco, Franco, Gabriele, Gaetano, Galileo, Gaspare, Gerardo, Geronimo, Gervasio, Giacobbe, Giacomo, Giancarlo, Gianfranco, Gianluca, Gianmario, Gianni, Gianpiero, Gilberto, Gino, Gioachino, Giordano, Giorgio, Giovanni,

Giraldo, Girolamo, Giulio, Giuseppe, Graziano, Guglielmo, Guido, Gustavo, Ilario, Ignazio, Isacco, Italo, Jacopo, Ladislo, Lazzaro, Leandro, Leonardo, Leonzio, Letterio, Libero, Livio, Lodovico, Lorenzo, Lothario, Luca, Luciano, Ludo, Luigi, Marcello, Marco, Marconi, Mario, Martino, Massimo, Matteo, Mauro, Michelangelo, Michele, Mirco, Modesto, Natale, Nazario, Nicandro, Nico, Nicola, Nino, Oliviero, Onofrio, Orazio, Orlando, Otello, Ottavio, Paolino, Paolo, Paride, Pasquale, Patrizio, Piero, Pietrantonio, Potito, Quirino, Raffaele, Raniero, Raul, Remo, Renato, Renzo, Riccardo, Rinaldo, Rino, Roberto, Rodolfo, Rodrigo, Romano, Romare, Rossario, Ruggiero, Salvatore, Sansone, Santo, Saviero, Sereno, Sergio, Silvano, Simone, Stefano, Taddeo, Tarcisio, Terreno, Tino, Tito, Tommaso, Ugo, Ulisse, Ulrico, Umberto, Valentino, Vicente, Vincenzo, Vinicio, Vittore, Xaviero, Zingaro.

Girls

Addolorata, Adriana, Agata, Agnese, Agnola, Agostina, Alba, Alessandra, Alisa, Allegra, Amadora, Amalina, Amata, Ambra, Angelina, Angiola, Angiolina, Aniela, Annata, Annica, Annunziata, Antonella, Arancia, Arcangela, Armani, Armonia, Assunta, Batista, Bellino, Benedetta, Bianca, Bicetta, Brigida, Cadenza, Calogera, Capri, Cara, Carezza, Carita, Carlina, Carlotta, Carmela, Cassina, Caterina, Celestina, Cettina, Chiara, Cinzia, Clelia, Collina, Concetta, Consolata, Cristina, Delfina, Domenica, Donatella, Dorotea, Edda, Edita, Elda, Eleganza, Elena, Eleonora, Elettra, Elisa, Elisabetta, Emilia, Enrica, Enza, Ersilia, Esterre, Felicita, Filippa, Fiore, Fiorella, Fiorenza, Fontana, Franca, Francesca, Gabriella, Gaetana, Gala, Ghita, Gia, Giacinta, Giacomina, Giada, Gianina, Gigliola, Ginevra, Gioconda, Gioia, Giorgetta, Giovanna, Giuditta, Giulia, Giuseppa, Grazia, Graziella, Honorata, Ignazia, Imelda, Ippolita, Isabella, Jacobella, Jolanda, Lauretta, Letizia, Letteria, Lia, Lonzina, Lorenza, Luce, Lucia, Luciana, Luigina, Luisa, Luzia, Maddalena, Madonna, Mafalda, Majella, Marchesa, Margherita, Mariella, Marietta, Marta, Mercede, Milana, Mimi, Mirella, Modesto, Natalina, Neroli, Nicetta, Nicla, Olimpia, Orazia, Oriana, Ortense, Ottavia, Ottobra, Paola, Pasqua, Patrizia, Pazienza, Perlita, Phebe, Pia, Pietra, Quirina, Rachele, Raula, Renata, Romina, Rosa, Rosetta, Rosina, Rosmunda, Rossella, Santa, Santina, Serafina, Siena, Silvana, Simonetta, Solidea, Sonata, Sorella, Speranza, Stefania, Sveva, Tarcisia, Tathiana, Teodora, Teresina, Tosca, Traviata, Trieste, Trinita, Valeria, Vanni, Velia, Venera, Venezia, Venturina, Verona, Vincenza, Viola, Virna, Vitalia, Vittoria, Viviana, Zingara, Zita.

JAPANESE

Boys
Akemi, Akeno, Akihiro, Akira, Akiyama, Amida, Asa, Botan, Chiko, Dai, Daido, Daisuke, Denzo, Ebisu, Fudo, Genki, Goro, Haro, Haru, Haruko, Hasu, Hideyuki, Higashi, Higo, Hiro, Hirohito, Hirokazu, Hiroki, Hiroshi, Hiroyuki, Hito, Hotei, Huyu, Ichiro, Iruka, Isora, Izumi, Jiro, Joji, Jun, Junichi, Kado, Kalong, Kamé, Kami, Kanji, Kano, Kawa, Kazuki, Kazumi, Kazuo, Kei, Keiji, Keisuke, Ken, Kenichi, Kenji, Kenta, Kin, Kirin, Kiyoshi, Koji, Kongo, Koshin, Kosho, Kosuke, Kuma, Kumo, Makoto, Mamoru, Manzo, Masa, Masahiro, Masaki, Michio, Miki, Mochi, Naoki, Naoto, Nishi, Noriaki, Ogai, Ozuru, Rafu, Rai, Raiden, Ringo, Rinjin, Rinky, Ryo, Ryu, Sachio, Satoshi, Seido, Seiko, Shaka, Shigeru, Shima, Shinden, Shingo, Shinichi, Shinji, Shino, Shiro, Sho, Shoda, Shoden, Shusaku, Tadashi, Taiki, Taka, Takao, Takashi, Takeshi, Takuma, Takumi, Tani, Taro, Tatsu, Tatsuya, Teizo, Ten, Tetsu, Tetsuya, Tomi, Tomio, Toru, Toshiro, Udo, Uyeda, Washi, Yama, Yasu, Yasuhiro, Yasushi, Yo, Yoshi, Yoshihiro, Yoshikazu, Yoshinori, Yukio, Yuto, Zen, Zinan.

Girls
Ai, Aiki, Aiko, Akako, Aki, Akiko, Akina, Akira, Amaya, Aneko, Anzu, Asa, Asahi, Asuka, Atsumi, Aya, Ayame, Ayumi, Azami, Azusa, Bato, Chie, Chika, Chiyo, Chiyoko, Chizu, Chizuko, Cho, Dai, Eiko, Emiko, Eriko, Etsu, Etsuko, Fuki, Fukiko, Fuyu, Fuyoko, Gen, Gin, Gwatan, Hama, Hana, Hanako, Hanka, Haru, Haruka, Haruko, Hasuko, Hatsu, Hatsuko, Hidé, Hideyo, Hikaru, Hina, Hiroko, Hisako, Hoshi, Ichiko, Iku, Ima, Inari, Isako, Ishi, Izanami, Junko, Kagami, Kaiko, Kame, Kameko, Kami, Kana, Kané, Kaoru, Katsuko, Kaya, Kayoko, Kazu, Kazuko, Kazumi, Keiko, Kichi, Kiji, Kiku, Kimi, Kimiko, Kin, Kinu, Kira, Kita, Kiyo, Kiyoko, Kiyomi, Kohana, Koko, Kuma, Kumi, Kumiko, Kuri, Kyoko, Machiko, Madoka, Maeko, Maiko, Maki, Mariko, Masa, Masako, Matsu, Matsuko, Mayu, Megumi, Meiko, Michiko, Midori, Mika, Miki, Miko, Minami, Mineko, Minoru, Mirai, Misayo, Mitsuko, Miwako, Miya, Miyuki, Mochi, Moeka, Momo, Momoko, Moriko, Mura, Murasaki, Myo-Jo, Nami, Naoki, Naoko, Nara, Narada, Nari, Nariko, Natsu, Natsuki, Natsumi, Nishi, Nobuko, Nori, Nyoko, Ohara, Oki, Ran, Reiko, Ren, Riko, Rokuko, Rumi, Ruri, Ryoko, Sachi, Sachiko, Sada, Sakana, Sakuko, Sakura, Saori, Sato, Satomi, Satu, Sayo, Sayoko, Seki, Sen, Setsuko, Shiho, Shika, Shima, Shina, Shiori, Shizu, Shoko, Sugi, Suki, Sumi, Sumiko, Suri, Suzu, Suzuki, Suzuko, Taka, Takara, Taki, Tama, Tamami, Tamiko, Tani, Taniko, Tazu, Tera, Tetsu, Toku, Tomi, Tomiko, Tomoko, Tora, Toshi, Toshia, Tuki, Umeko, Umiko, Uzume, Yachi,

Yachiko, Yasu, Yoi, Yoko, Yori, Yoshi, Yumiko, Yuna, Yuri, Yuriko, Zen.
Yoshiko, Yukari, Yuki, Yukiko, Yumi,

MAORI

Boys

Ahi, Akuhata, Amiri, Amoho, Amokura, Anaru, Ani, Aperahama, Araketenara, Arama, Arana, Arapata, Arapeta, Arapeti, Arawa, Aroha, Atonio, Epeha, Eriha, Eruera, Etera, Hakaraia, Hami, Hamuera, Hare, Hauora, Hemi, Henare, Heremaia, Herewini, Hoani, Hoera, Hohepa, Hohua, Hona, Hone, Horomona, Huarahi, Huatare, Hura, Huriu, Ihaka, Ihi, Kaha, Kahika, Kahukura, Kahurangi, Kaka, Kakariki, Kapua, Kapura, Kara, Karo, Kauri, Kawau, Kerekori, Kereru, Kingi, Kirimei, Kiritowha, Kiwi, Kukuwai, Maaka, Maehe, Maka, Makoa, Manaia, Matai, Matiu, Maunga, Mika, Mikaere, Moana, Murihiku, Ngaio, Ngawari, Nui, Nukuhia, Omaka, Onepu, Paoro, Paraone, Patariki, Petera, Piko, Piripi, Pita, Pouaka, Puké, Puriri, Rakaunui, Raniera, Rapata, Rata, Rauiti, Raupo, Rawiri, Rewi, Riki, Rongo, Rua, Ruka, Ruru, Taiaha, Takawai, Tamaiti, Tamati, Tame, Tane Mahuta, Tangohia, Tapanui, Tawhaki, Tawhirimatea, Temuera, Tepene, Te Ra, Te Ranginui, Tewe, Tiare, Timana, Timoti, Tipene, Toa, Topia, Tuaka, Tui, Uenuku, Waiariki, Waihanga, Waitangi, Waitoa, Wata, Werahiko, Whatitiri, Whatu, Whero, Wiremu, Witi.

Girls

Ahorangi, Akenehi, Amiria, Ane, Ani, Anihera, Aniwaniwa, Aperira, Arihana, Aroha, Ataahua, Ata Marama, Atarau, Awatea, Awhina, Ehetera, Ekore, Emere, Erihapeti, Haki, Hana, Harata, Hariata, Harikoa, Heni, Hera, Hihiria, Hikitia, Hikurangi, Hinengaro, Hira, Hiria, Hoki, Hotoke, Huhana, Huia, Humarie, Hune, Hura, Huria, Huriana, Hurihia, Ihipera, Iriaka, Irihapeti, Iwi, Kahu, Kaku, Kanapa, Kararaina, Karewa, Kataraina, Kea, Kereru, Kerewin, Keri, Koanga, Kopu, Kori, Kowhai, Kuine, Kuku, Kura, Maata, Mahia, Makarena, Makareta, Maku, Mana, Manawa, Manawaroa, Mangu, Marama, Mareikura, Marie, Marika, Mata, Mei, Mereanna, Miriama, Miromiro, Moana, Moata, Moe, Moerangi, Moetuma, Mokai, Moko, Muka, Nanaia, Nga, Ngahere, Ngahiwi, Ngahuia, Ngahuru, Ngaio, Ngaire, Ngoikore, Nikau, Nyree, Ohorere, Okeroa, Omaka, Otira, Pani, Pania, Pare, Parirau, Peata, Piki, Pipi, Pounamu, Puna, Pupuhi, Putiputi, Ra, Rahera, Rangi, Rangimarie, Rata, Raukura, Reka, Rere, Riana, Rima, Ripeka, Roimata, Rona, Rongo, Rongopai, Ruhia, Ruiha, Rutu, Tahuri, Taimana, Tamahine, Tangiwai, Tapora, Tarati, Te Atawhai, Te Awatea, Teina, Temepara, Te Paea, Tepora, Te Puna, Terehia, Tia, Tiaki, Tihi, Tui, Tumanako, Turuhira, Uaina,

Waimarama, Waipounamu, Waipuna, Weka, Whetu, Whetuaroha, Whetumarama, Whina, Wikitoria, Wini.

NATIVE AMERICAN

Boys
Adita, Ahmik, Anoke, Apache, Ayani, Chaska, Cherokee, Cheyenne, Chula, Dakota, Dyami, Elan, Elsu, Etu, Gad, Haloke, Helaku, Hiawatha, Hinto, Honon, Hota, Hula, Hute, Jacey, Jassan, Kalmanu, Kangi, Kinta, Koi, Kuruk, Lonato, Makya, Malawi, Matu, Mingan, Monsa, Motega, Muata, Muraca, Namid, Nashoba, Navajo, Notaku, Ohio, Okuri, Ouray, Paco, Paytah, Pinon, Sahal, Sakima, Sequoia, Shappa, Tadi, Tadzi, Takoda, Tatanka, Tawa, Tiba, Tunu, Wattan, Wilny, Wyn, Yakez, Yana, Yancy, Yona, Yuma.

Girls
Abequa, Ahawi, Alaqua, Aponi, Aqueena, Awanata, Awandela, Awenita, Bena, Buffy, Chapa, Chenoa, Cheyenne, Chu, Dakota, Dyani, Elan, Eyota, Haloke, Halona, Hausu, Isi, Jacey, Judi, Kai, Kasa, Kasha, Kateri, Kinta, Kiona, Koko, Lupetu, Lusela, Magena, Maka, Malawi, Malila, Nascha, Nashota, Neka, Nepa, Niabi, Nita, Nokomis, Nuna, Odina, Olathe, Onata, Onawa, Onida, Opa, Pakuna, Pana, Pelipa, Poloma, Sakara, Sapata, Sequoia, Shada, Shappa, Shumana, Sora, Tain, Takenya, Tala, Tallulah, Taluta, Tasida, Tayanita, Tenaya, Tiba, Tuwa, Utina, Waneta, Winema, Winona, Wyanet, Yana, Zuni.

PERSIAN/IRANIAN

Boys
Aban, Atar, Azadeh, Azamat, Babak, Bahram, Caspar, Cyrus, Darius, Gaspar, Govad, Homayoun, Izzat, Jamshid, Jasper, Javed, Kalimat, Kamal, Kamran, Kourosh, Marsena, Melchior, Mithra, Parvez, Pervez, Quadrat, Roshan, Rostam, Sargon, Shah, Shahin, Shahram, Sharaf, Sohrab, Sultan, Suran, Tabor, Tallis, Taz, Teimuraz, Xerxes, Zerxes, Zircon, Zoroaster.

Girls
Alá, Aravane, Arezou, Asma, Azura, Baha, Banu, Clorinda, Cyra, Elika, Esta, Golnar, Hengameh, Jalal, Jamal, Jasmine, Kamal, Keshvar, Kira, Kismet, Lilac, Mahsa, Marsena, Nahid, Nasrin, Nilufer, Noor, Nur, Pari, Parisa, Parvin, Pashmina, Perizada, Persia, Persis, Roqia, Roshan, Roxana, Sadira, Satarah, Shahnaz, Shiraz, Shirin, Simin, Soheila, Soraya, Souzana, Suri, Tala, Vashti, Yalda, Zenda, Zuleika.

POLYNESIAN

General – Boys
Aikane, Alika, Alipate, Amama, Anaru, Arana, Ariki, Atea, Atiu, Hapu, Hema, Hori, Hotoroa, Ihakara, Ihorangi, Ikale, Irawaru, Jone, Kaho, Kauariki, Kauri, Keoni, Keretiki, Kupe, Kura, Langi, Lani, Lote, Makoa, Manu, Marama, Maru, Matareka, Matu, Maui, Miharo, Milu, Mitiaro, Moana, Moko, Mokoiro, Moroto, Neemia, Ngaru, Nui, Oata, Ora, Oro, Oroiti, Palaki, Palauni, Papa, Patu, Pipiri, Pomare, Poutini, Ra, Radike, Raka, Rakaia, Rangi, Rata, Rehua, Rongo, Ruanaku, Rupe, Saimoni, Samani, Taha, Tahu, Tai, Tama, Tane, Tanekaha, Tangaroa, Tawhero, Tawhiri, Te Aroha, Tekea, Tewe, Tiki, Tongatea, Tu, Tueva, Turi, Tutapu, Utu, Valu, Whetu.

General – Girls
Angarua, Apakura, Aroha, Atanua, Atarapa, Ature, Dorit, Elka, Hapai, Hariata, Hika, Hina, Hina-Uri, Hine, Hinemoa, Hiriwa, Hoku, Hula, Ina, Inas, Ira, Kaniva, Kanoa, Kearoa, Kini, Kiri, Kiwa, Kohia, Kono, Kura, Lali, Lani, Laione, Latai, Lona, Losa, Mahina, Mahuika, Mahuru, Maili, Makala, Makana, Makani, Marama, Maru, Maweke, Mere, Meri, Moana, Moetuma, Naia, Nanala, Nani, Oliana, Onike, Puatara, Ra, Rangi, Rehua, Rewa, Rimu, Rongo, Ruange, Salote, Samoa, Sina, Tahiti, Tai, Taka, Tapairo, Tara, Taranga, Tarita, Tautiti, Tavake, Te Mira, Tongatea, Turua, Ulani, Umei, Vana.

Hawaiian – Boys
Ailani, Aka, Akamu, Alemana, Amana, Amoka, Anakoni, Analu, Asera, Bane, Edega, Edwada, Eleu, Eneki, Etana, Ezera, Havika, Hiwa, Hoku, Kahai, Kahoku, Kai, Kainoa, Kaipo, Kala, Kalani, Kale, Kana, Kanaloa, Kané, Kanuha, Kapena, Kapono, Kealii, Keanu, Kei, Keiki, Kekipi, Kekoa, Kekona, Keoki, Kimo, Koa, Kona, Laki, Lalama, Liko, Lupo, Makaha, Makai, Makani, Malo, Mamo, Mano, Maui, Meka, Moke, Nahoa, Nalu, Oke, Pakaa, Palani, Pekelo, Punahele, Tahi.

Hawaiian – Girls
Ailani, Aka, Akamai, Akela, Alamea, Alana, Alani, Alaula, Aliikai, Alika, Aloha, Alohi, Anani, Anela, Aolani, Derya, Eleu, Enaki, Ewalani, Gladi, Haimi, Halia, Hanai, Hiwa, Hiwakea, Hoala, Iniki, Inoki, Iokina, Iolana, Iona, Ipo, Kahili, Kaikala, Kailana, Kailani, Kailmana, Kaimana, Kala, Kalama, Kalani, Kalea, Kalei, Kalena, Kaloni, Kamea, Kanani, Kani, Kanuha, Kapua, Kawena, Keala, Kei, Keilani, Kekipi, Keona, Kiele, Kilia, Kina, Kolohe, Kona, Lahela, Laka, Lanai, Lanikais, Lea, Lei, Leilani, Lilia, Lilo, Lokelani, Loni, Luana, Malana, Malia, Malina, Mana, Meli, Miki, Miliani, Momi, Nalani, Noe, Noelani, Nohea, Okalani,

Olena, Palila, Pele, Pualani, Pualena, Puanani, Puna, Roselani, Uilani, Ululani, Wailana, Wanika.

PORTUGUESE/BRAZILIAN

Boys
Abril, Adao, Alexio, Amarildo, Amaro, Armenio, Belém, Belo, Benvindo, Branco, Brasiliano, Carlos, Davi, Demetre, Dimas, Domingo, Duarte, Enrique, Erico, Eusebio, Fabio, Gilberto, Guilherme, Heitor, Henrique, Inacio, Jaco, Janeiro, Jesús, Joao, Joaquim, Jorge, Junho, Justo, Leonardo, Liberio, Lino, Lourenço, Luciano, Luis, Luiz, Manoel, Marcelinho, Marcelo, Marco, Marcos, Mateus, Miguel, Moises, Patricio, Paulino, Paulo, Prospero, Publio, Rafael, Renato, Ricardinho, Rodrigo, Romas, Ronaldo, Roque, Rubens, Rui, Ruy, Silvino, Teofilio, Tito, Valdir, Vasco, Wanderlei, Xelio, Zelio.

Girls
Almada, Belém, Cacilda, Catarina, Cintia, Cristina, Dores, Edite, Elena, Elzira, Eufemia, Graça, Isaura, Jaçana, Judite, Madeira, Mafalda, Margarida, Marilia, Noemia, Roseta, Teresinha, Terezinha, Vidonia, Xiomara, Xuxa, Zeffa, Zuza.

ROMANIAN

Boys
Alexandru, Costin, Dragos, Dumitru, Horea, Ilie, Ion, Mihai, Mihail, Razvan, Sorin, Stelian, Viorel.

Girls
Arina, Doina, Dolina, Ileana, Raluca, Rodica, Sorina, Viorica.

SANSKRIT/HINDI/SIKH

Boys
Abhijit, Adil, Agni, Ajay, Akash, Alok, Amar, Ambar, Amit, Amrit, Anand, Anil, Anish, Ankit, Ankur, Ankush, Anup, Arjun, Arun, Arvan, Arvind, Ashad, Ashish, Ashok, Ashwin, Atish, Avatar, Azad, Balin, Bharat, Bhavin, Bhima, Bilawal, Brahma, Buddha, Chaitanya, Chaman, Chand, Chandan, Chandi, Chandra, Chetan, Dalajit, Damodar, Darshan, Daru, Deepak, Deo, Dev, Devdan, Devendra, Devkumar, Dhani, Dhanu, Dharma, Dhiren, Dilip, Din, Dinesh, Drona, Durga, Gajendra, Ganesh, Gaurav, Gautama, Gopal, Govinda, Gunjan, Gurbachan,

Gurdial, Gursewak, Gurshan, Guru, Gurwar, Hanuman, Harbhajan, Harcharan, Harekrishna, Harendra, Hari, Harinder, Harith, Harjit, Harsha, Hemant, Hiran, Indra, Indrajit, Isa, Ishan, Jagdish, Jahan, Jamuni, Janesh, Javan, Jayant, Jeevan, Jitender, Jivanta, Jyotis, Kala, Kamal, Kami, Kanan, Kanu, Kapil, Karan, Karma, Karnak, Kaushik, Kiran, Kishor, Krishna, Kumar, Kumera, Kunal, Kundan, Kurma, Kushal, Lakshan, Lakshman, Lal, Lalit, Mahendra, Mahesh, Mahinda, Mali, Mandir, Mangal, Mani, Manmohan, Manoj, Manraj, Mantra, Manu, Mayon, Mirza, Mithra, Mohan, Mohandas, Mohit, Murali, Nada, Nanda, Nandi, Narayan, Narendra, Naresh, Narsingh, Navin, Nehru, Nilam, Nimish, Nirmal, Nirvan, Nitin, Padme, Pandit, Pankaj, Paresh, Parminder, Poojan, Prabhat, Pradeep, Prakash, Pramod, Pranav, Praneet, Prasad, Prashanth, Praveen, Prem, Radhakrishnan, Raghu, Raj, Rajani, Rajat, Rajendra, Rajit, Rajiv, Rajkumar, Rajnish, Raju, Rakesh, Rama, Ramesh, Randhir, Ranga, Rangan, Ranjit, Ranjiv, Ratan, Ratna, Ravi, Ravindra, Raviwar, Rishi, Rohan, Rohit, Rudra, Sachin, Safed, Sahen, Sahir, Salil, Sanah, Sandeep, Sandesh, Sani, Sanivara, Sanjay, Sanjiv, Sankara, Sarad, Sarat, Sarju, Sarngin, Satish, Savan, Savitri, Seth, Shankar, Shanwar, Sharma, Shashank, Shashi, Sher, Shiva, Shivnarine, Shreyas, Shyam, Siddartha, Simha, Singh, Soma, Somavar, Somdev, Sona, Sujan, Suman, Sundar, Suranjan, Surendra, Surya, Swaraj, Taj, Tara, Taran, Tarun, Tejas, Thakur, Uday, Upendra, Ushnisha, Valin, Vamana, Varaha, Varuna, Vasant, Vasudeva, Vayu, Ved, Venkatesh, Vesak, Vidya, Vijay, Vijendra, Vikesh, Vikram, Vimal, Vinod, Virendra, Vishnu, Vrisha, Vyasa, Yamal, Yogesh.

Girls

Adya, Ahimsa, Ajala, Ajaya, Akasha, Alaka, Amara, Ambar, Ambika, Amirtha, Amisha, Amrita, Anala, Ananda, Ananya, Anchala, Anila, Anisha, Anjali, Ankita, Ansha, Ansuya, Antara, Anudhi, Anuradha, Anushka, Apsara, Aruna, Arundhati, Arusha, Asha, Ashada, Ashima, Ashna, Ashwina, Avani, Avara, Ayushi, Bahara, Bala, Bina, Brishti, Candi, Chakra, Chameli, Chandra, Chitra, Corah, Damayanti, Daya, Dayanita, Deepika, Devaki, Devi, Devika, Devisingh, Dhani, Dhara, Dharma, Drishti, Drissa, Durga, Ellora, Esha, Eshana, Gita, Gopi, Guri, Harpreet, Harshita, Haryana, Hasika, Hawa, Hema, Hemanta, Himanshi, Hira, India, Indira, Indrani, Indred, Ishana, Jamuni, Janisha, Jarita, Jasvinder, Jaya, Jena, Jyoti, Kali, Kalinda, Kalpana, Kalyani, Kama, Kamala, Kanitha, Kanti, Kanya, Karma, Kashmira, Kavita, Kerala, Kerani, Kiran, Komala, Krishna, Krita, Kumari, Kumuda, Lakshmi, Lakya, Lalita, Leela, Madhuri, Mahesa, Mahima, Makali, Mala, Malati, Malika, Mandala, Mandara, Mangala, Mani, Manjula, Mantra, Marakata, Masara, Matrika, Meena, Meera, Mehadi, Mela,

Mohana, Mridula, Muniamma, Nadira, Naina, Nalika, Nalini, Naresha, Nata, Navya, Naya, Nidra, Nila, Nirma, Nirvana, Nisha, Orissa, Padma, Pahala, Pameela, Pandita, Panita, Panna, Parmita, Parvati, Poonam, Prabhawati, Pradeepa, Prakriti, Pranita, Prasana, Prasheila, Pratibha, Pratika, Preeti, Prema, Priya, Purnima, Pushpa, Rachana, Radha, Radhika, Rajani, Rajiva, Rajkumari, Rani, Ranjani, Rati, Ratna, Ratri, Ravia, Rekha, Renuka, Reshma, Rohana, Roopa, Rukmini, Ruma, Rupa, Rupali, Sagara, Sahira, Sameera, Samiya, Sandhya, Sangita, Sania, Sanskrity, Sarala, Sari, Sarisha, Sarna, Saroja, Satya, Saura, Savitri, Serai, Shakti, Shakuntala, Shalini, Shameena, Shantala, Shanti, Sharmila, Shashi, Sheela, Shefali, Shera, Shilpa, Shivali, Shivani, Shobana, Shreya, Shyamala, Sindhuja, Sita, Sitara, Soma, Sona, Sonal, Sujata, Sulakshana, Sundar, Sunita, Supriya, Surata, Surya, Susheela, Susmita, Sutra, Swati, Taja, Talika, Tara, Tarika, Trishna, Uma, Urmila, Usha, Vandana, Varana, Varuna, Vasanti, Veda, Veena, Vidya, Vimala, Vinita, Vipasha, Vrinda, Yamini, Yamuna, Yantra, Yogita, Yosana, Zeenat.

SCANDINAVIAN

General – Boys
Aage, Aegir, Algot, Alvis, Amund, Anders, Anker, Arne, Arve, Asgard, Ask, Askel, Aslak, Bain, Balder, Bengt, Björn, Bo, Bodil, Borg, Bragi, Brander, Dack, Dagfinn, Dain, Daven, Davin, Dyre, Edvard, Egil, Einar, Elvig, Elvis, Emanuel, Erland, Fenris, Fisk, Flemming, Frans, Frey, Gamel, Garth, Geir, Godfrid, Gorm, Gunnar, Gustav, Hakon, Haldor, Hallbjörn, Halsten, Halvard, Hamar, Harald, Harbard, Hendrik, Henrik, Hermod, Hoder, Holger, Huginn, Hymir, Igor, Ingemar, Inger, Ingolf, Ingvar, Ivar, Jakob, Jan, Jensen, Joakim, Johan, Jorens, Josef, Kari, Karl, Kelsey, Kirk, Kjell, Knut, Konstantin, Kristoffer, Kriv, Lars, Larson, Leif, Lennart, Loki, Ludvig, Magni, Magnus, Mani, Micke, Mikell, Munin, Niklaus, Njord, Odin, Olaf, Orjan, Ove, Per, Ragnar, Ragnulf, Ranulf, Regin, Reidar, Rikard, Rudolf, Rune, Rurik, Sigurd, Skirnir, Starbuck, Stefan, Stellan, Stig, Surt, Sven, Svenbjörn, Thor, Thorald, Thorhammer, Torbjörn, Tor-Ivar, Torvald, Tyr, Ull, Ulrick, Vali, Valter, Verner, Vidar, Viggo, Viktor, Vilhelm, Waldemar.

General – Girls
Agnethe, Alfhild, Amalia, Anja, Anjah, Anneli, Anneliese, Annot, Asta, Asther, Astrid, Berit, Birgit, Birgitta, Birgitte, Bodil, Brenda, Brigitta, Dagmar, Dagna, Disa, Eir, Elisabet, Embla, Erika, Freya, Fulla, Gerd, Gerda, Gudrid, Gudrun, Gulla, Gunda, Gunnhild, Guri, Haldana, Hedda, Hedvig, Hedy, Heidrun, Heike, Hela, Helga, Helmi, Helmie,

Henrike, Hjördis, Hulda, Ida, Idona, Inge, Ingrid, Janne, Jannike, Johanna, Jord, Kalinn, Karita, Karolina, Katrina, Kelda, Kirby, Kirsten, Klara, Lene, Linnea, Lise, Liv, Marte, Maybritt, Mia, Nanna, Nissa, Noomi, Nora, Norna, Ola, Pernille, Petronilla, Quenby, Rakel, Ran, Rigmor, Rinda, Ronalda, Runa, Rut, Sieglinde, Sif, Signy, Sigourney, Sigrid, Sigrun, Siri, Skade, Sonja, Sonje, Sunna, Tekla, Thora, Thorberta, Thordis, Tove, Tyra, Ulla, Ulrike, Vaila, Vanja, Veronika, Viktoria, Viveka, Volva.

Danish – Boys
Aren, Christer, Denmark, Diederik, Esbern, Frederik, Gillis, Hagen, Henerik, Henning, Jens, Jeppe, Jesper, Jorgen, Kai, Klaus, Knut, Kristen, Marts, Mikkel, Mogens, Morten, Nansen, Niels, Ole, Peder, Preben, Rosmer, Soren, Steen, Svend, Tage, Torben, Valdemar, Valentin.

Danish – Girls
Agneta, Aleksia, Benedikte, Bente, Birte, Dorete, Else, Helle, Iben, Jonna, Juni, Jytte, Karen, Kathrina, Kristen, Lene, Lone, Lykke, Magdalone, Malene, Margrethe, Mia, Petrine, Saffi, Sofie, Soren.

Icelandic – Boys
Arni, Eyvindur, Eldur, Hallbjörn, Hinrik, Kristinn, Olafur, Petur, Sindri, Tryggvi, Varick, Viking.

Icelandic – Girls
Artis, Björk, Brynhildur, Dalla, Falda, Lilija, Rindill, Sula, Svana, Unna, Valdis.

Norwegian – Boys
Aksel, Bergen, Bjarne, Eirik, Eivind, Eysteinn, Havard, Jens, Leiv, Nils, Oeystein, Ole, Peder, Roald, Sondre, Stein, Steiner, Svein, Sverre, Thord, Tord, Trygve.

Norwegian – Girls
Aleksia, Andras, Anitra, Gro, Guro, Kelsey, Kjersti, Magna, Mette, Silje, Sofia, Solrun, Solveig, Vika.

Swedish – Boys
Adolphus, Alfonso, Alvar, Alvars, Boel, Christer, Erik, Esbjörn, Fredrik, Goran, Gösta, Gustaf, Hakan, Isak, Jorgen, Jon, Kristian, Lukas, Mats, Mikael, Nils, Pavel, Pelle, Sandberg, Staffan, Sten, Tolv, Torkel, Tre, Tryggve, Ulf, Valentin, Zakarias.

Swedish – Girls
Agda, Angelika, Annika, Anouska, Barbro, Britt, Dahlia, Elin, Freja, Greta, Gunilla, Henrika, Juli, Karin, Katarina, Kerstin, Kolina, Kristina,

Lova, Lovisa, Mai, Malin, Margit, Marna, Mia, Ronja, Saga, Sofia, Solvig, Svea, Vendela.

SLAVIC

General – Boys
Alojz, Anatolij, Andon, Andraz, Andrej, Antun, Atanasij, Benydykt, Blaz, Bogdan, Boguslaw, Bojan, Boleslav, Boris, Borlslav, Bozek, Bozidar, Branislav, Branko, Bratislav, Bronislav, Budimir, Casimir, Cedomir, Damir, Danijel, Danko, Darko, Davor, Dejan, Dinko, Djuka, Djuro, Dragan, Dragisha, Dragomir, Dragutin, Drazen, Ernests, Eugeniusz, Franc, Franciszek, Franjo, Gordan, Gorgi, Grgur, Grozdan, Gvozden, Ivan, Ivaylo, Ivo, Izidor, Jakov, Jan, Janek, Janez, Janko, Janush, Jarek, Jaroslav, Jernej, Juraj, Jurgis, Karlo, Kresmir, Kristijan, Kristof, Ladislav, Lasota, Lazar, Lazo, Leopold, Linart, Lodewijk, Lodewikus, Lovrenc, Lovro, Lubomir, Ludomir, Marijan, Marin, Marinko, Marko, Matej, Matic, Matja, Matko, Maurycy, Mihael, Mihovil, Mikel, Miko, Miloje, Milorad, Miloslav, Milosz, Milovan, Milutin, Miran, Mirek, Mirko, Miro, Miroslav, Misko, Mladen, Mykola, Nedelko, Nemanja, Nenad, Nikola, Novak, Obrad, Oleksandr, Ondrej, Orel, Ostoja, Ozbej, Pavliv, Pavlo, Pavol, Pawel, Pek, Pero, Perun, Petar, Piotr, Predrag, Przemyslaw, Rad, Rade, Radomir, Radoslav, Radost, Radovan, Rajko, Ranko, Rastislav, Ratko, Romanus, Rostislav, Rudolf, Ryszard, Sasho, Sava, Sergiusz, Sidonius, Sime, Simo, Sinisa, Slava, Slavko, Slavoj, Slawomir, Slobodan, Stanislaus, Stanislaw, Stojan, Svatoslav, Svetozar, Taman, Taras, Todor, Tomaz, Tomislav, Tomo, Upravda, Valon, Vekoslav, Veselin, Vikentije, Vit, Vitek, Vitezslav, Vitomir, Vjekoslav, Vlad, Vladimir, Vladislav, Vlado, Vlatislav, Vojislav, Vojtech, Voldemar, Vuc, Vytas, Wenceslas, Witali, Yaroslav, Zarko, Zbigniew, Zdenek, Zdravko, Zdzislav, Zeljko, Zhivko, Zivomir, Zivorad, Zivu, Zlatan, Zoran.

General – Girls
Ajla, Aleksija, Alenka, Ana, Anastasija, Anastazia, Anca, Ancika, Andreja, Aneta, Anjela, Anka, Antonetta, Barbica, Bijana, Bisera, Blazena, Bogdana, Bojana, Borislava, Bosiljka, Bozena, Bozka, Branka, Bronislava, Bronya, Cecilija, Chesna, Cilka, Cvetka, Dana, Danika, Darija, Darinka, Darja, Divna, Dobrila, Dominika, Donka, Dorothea, Dragana, Dragica, Dura, Dzenita, Dzintra, Evana, Florinka, Fryderyka, Gorana, Gordana, Gorica, Grozda, Halyna, Ilija, Ioana, Irena, Iskra, Iva, Ivana, Iveta, Ivka, Jadranka, Jarka, Jarmila, Jaroslava, Jasenka, Jasna, Jelena, Jovana, Jovanka, Jozefa, Julijana, Jurisa, Kateryna, Katra, Katica, Katina, Kisa, Klara, Klimentina, Kresimira, Lada, Lala,

Leokadia, Leposava, Lida, Ljerka,
Ljubica, Luba, Lubica, Lubov, Lucija,
Ludmila, Ludowicka, Ludwika, Mari,
Marica, Marija, Marika, Marusa,
Maruska, Masa, Mateja, Mila,
Milada, Milica, Milojka, Miloslava,
Mira, Mirana, Miriana, Mirijana,
Mirjana, Miroslava, Mladenka,
Monika, Morana, Morela, Nadia,
Neda, Nevena, Nika, Nikolinka,
Ojdana, Olena, Olesia, Orlenda,
Orysia, Otylia, Rada, Radinka,
Radmilla, Reza, Rozina, Rusalka,
Ryba, Ryszarda, Saba, Sanja, Senka,
Serbia, Slavena, Slavica, Slobodanka,
Smiljana, Snezana, Sobena,
Stanislava, Stefka, Suska, Sveta,
Svetlana, Trajanka, Velika, Verra,
Vesela, Vesna, Victorija, Vijoleta,
Vilia, Vivijana, Vladimira, Vladislava,
Vlasta, Wioletta, Wirginia,
Wladyslawa, Yaroslava, Zeineb,
Zinka, Zivka, Zlata, Zofja, Zora,
Zorka, Zuzu.

Bulgarian – Boys
Atanas, Danail, Dimitar, Nayden,
Ognyan, Raiko, Rayko, Stiliyan,
Yordan, Zahari.

Bulgarian – Girls
Elitsa, Oana, Roumiana, Sesil,
Tezzhan, Yoana.

Czech – Boys
Bedrich, Bohumil, Danek, Dominik,
Dusan, Eduard, Greguska, Jakub,
Jan, Jarmil, Jaroslav, Jiri, Josef, Kafka,
Kamil, Karel, Kazimir, Kornel,
Krystof, Leos, Ludvik, Marek,
Marik, Michal, Miklós, Mikulas,
Milad, Milan, Mile, Milenko, Milos,
Miloslav, Nedele, Patek, Petr, Pondeli,
Praza, Radek, Radenko, Radko, Rado,
Sobota, Stanislav, Stepan, Streda,
Toman, Tomas, Tomik, Václav, Vasek,
Vendelin, Viktor, Vilem, Vladimir,
Wenzel, Zdzislav.

Czech – Girls
Alena, Anastazie, Andela, Anezka,
Barbora, Blanka, Dana, Daniela,
Dorota, Dusana, Fiala, Frantiska,
Gabriele, Hana, Ivana, Ivanka, Iveta,
Jana, Jitka, Johana, Judita, Kamila,
Katerina, Katerine, Lenka, Libuse,
Lida, Marcela, Malenka, Marjeta,
Matylda, Mila, Milena, Mirka,
Moravia, Nedele, Pateka, Pavla,
Pondela, Radka, Raina, Ratka, Rayna,
Rusalka, Ruzena, Sarka, Sobota,
Streda, Svetla, Trava, Verushka, Viera,
Zelenka, Zofie, Zuzana.

Polish – Boys
Andrzej, Antoni, Artek, Aurek,
Bartek, Blazej, Bogumil, Branislav,
Bronislav, Brunon, Casimir, Czeslaw,
Dobry, Dominik, Donat, Feliks, Filip,
Henryk, Holleb, Izydor, Jacek, Jakub,
Jan, Jaroslaw, Jasiel, Jeden, Jerzy, Józef,
Karol, Kasper, Kazimierz, Konrad,
Konstantyn, Kornel, Kwintyn,
Ladislas, Ladislaus, Lech, Ludwik,
Lukasz, Maciej, Marcin, Marceli,

Marek, Marian, Mariusz, Mateusz,
Michal, Mieczyslaw, Mikolaj,
Miloslaw, Olek, Oleksander, Pavel,
Przemysl, Radoslaw, Rafal, Roscislaw,
Salvator, Stefan, Szymon, Tadeusz,
Telek, Tomasz, Tomek, Tytus, Ulryk,
Viktor, Waclaw, Walenty, Wiktor,
Witold, Witomir, Yeden, Zachariasz,
Zbigniew, Zdzislaw, Ziggy, Ziven.

Polish – Girls
Agata, Agnieska, Aliaksandra, Alicja,
Aloyza, Anastazja, Ancela, Aniela,
Anusia, Basia, Berta, Blanka, Brygida,
Cecylia, Clemenza, Daniela, Danuta,
Dorosia, Dulcyna, Edyta, Eudoksya,
Ewa, Frydryka, Gabriela, Gosia,
Halina, Hania, Helenka, Henryka,
Iga, Imber, Inocenta, Jadwiga, Jadzia,
Jakuba, Jana, Janina, Jolanta, Kamila,
Karolina, Kazimiera, Klaudia,
Klementyna, Krystyna, Ksenia, Lidia,
Lucya, Martyna, Matylda, Melka,
Miloslawa, Natasza, Nimfa, Rachela,
Raina, Rayna, Renia, Roza, Rula,
Salomea, Stefania, Teodora, Tresna,
Ulryka, Urszula, Valeska, Zadora,
Zofia, Zosia, Zula, Zuzanna.

Russian – Boys
Afanasiy, Agai, Akelin, Akim,
Alexandr, Aleksandr, Alexei, Anatoly,
Artyom, Avel, Baran, Boris, Danil,
Danya, Demyan, Diaghilev, Dmitri,
Edvard, Efim, Egor, Eriks, Fyodor,
Gavril, Georgi, Igor, Ilya, Innokenti,
Iouri, Ivan, Kesar, Kirill, Kliment,
Kolya, Konstantin, Kostya, Lavrenti,
Leonid, Leonti, Lev, Luka, Maksim,
Marat, Michail, Mikhail, Mischa,
Mishka, Mitja, Moisey, Moriz, Naum,
Nikita, Nikolai, Nikolay, Oleg, Orel,
Osip, Pavel, Pavlov, Petrov, Petya,
Pyotr, Rolan, Rurik, Samuil, Sasha,
Sasa, Semyon, Sergei, Sevastian,
Stanislav, Stefan, Stepan, Timofei,
Urvan, Vadim, Vanya, Vasiliy, Vasily,
Vaska, Vikenti, Vitali, Vladimir,
Vsevolod, Yakov, Yefim, Yefrem,
Yevgeni, Yona, Yuri, Zakar.

Russian – Girls
Agafya, Agnessa, Agrafena, Akilina,
Aleksandra, Alexdra, Alina, Alla,
Alyona, Anastasia, Anastasiya,
Anninka, Annuschka, Arina,
Borislava, Csarina, Darya, Dzidra,
Ekaterina, Elisavetta, Eudokhia,
Evgeniya, Evva, Fedora, Feodora,
Franka, Galina, Guinara, Gulfiya,
Inna, Irina, Irisa, Iroda, Ivanna, Julya,
Kaleria, Katenka, Katerine, Katusha,
Katya, Kisa, Lada, Lara, Larissa,
Luba, Lyudmila, Magdalina, Mariya,
Masha, Matrona, Mavra, Mischa,
Modest, Nadejda, Nadezhda, Nadya,
Nastasia, Nastya, Natalya, Natasha,
Nika, Nikita, Nina, Nonna, Oksana,
Olga, Olien, Orlenda, Paraska,
Pavlovna, Petenka, Petrova, Petya,
Pievitza, Praskovya, Raisa, Revekka,
Roksana, Rusalka, Ruslana, Sasha,
Savina, Serafima, Sofya, Sonya,
Stasya, Svetlana, Taisiya, Talia, Talya,
Tamara, Tanya, Tatyana, Tetiana,
Tsarina, Ulrika, Ulyana, Valentina,
Vanja, Vanka, Varvara, Vasilisa, Vera,
Viktoriya, Volga, Yekaterina, Yelena,
Yelizaveta, Yeva, Yevgenia, Yuliya,
Zenovia, Zoia.

SPANISH

Boys

Abad, Abran, Abril, Adan, Adriano, Agapito, Agustin, Albino, Albizo, Alejandro, Alejo, Alfredo, Alonso, Alvarez, Amado, Amarillo, Amigo, Amor, Amparo, Anatolio, Andres, Angelino, Anselmo, Antonio, Aragon, Arnaldo, Arturo, Augustino, Aureliano, Azafrán, Azul, Basilio, Baudilio, Bautista, Benigno, Benito, Bernabe, Bernardo, Blanco, Caballo, Calvino, Cariño, Carlos, Carmesi, Carmine, Casimiro, Cedro, Che, Ciriaco, Cisco, Claro, Claudio, Cleto, Cobre, Condor, Constantino, Cordero, Cortez, Cristóbal, Cruz, Custodio, Darien, Delfino, Demetrio, Desiderio, Dia, Diablo, Diego, Diez, Dimas, Domingo, Dorado, Edgardo, Edmundo, Eduardo, Efrain, Eliseo, Eloy, Emilio, Enero, Enrique, Ernesto, Estéban, Eugenio, Eusebio, Ezequiel, Fabio, Fabricio, Facundo, Febrero, Federico, Feliciano, Felipe, Fernán, Fernando, Florencio, Floro, Francilo, Francisco, Fuego, Galeno, Geraldo, Gerardo, Gil, Gilberto, Gomez, Gonzales, Graciano, Gregorio, Guillermo, Hermoso, Hernando, Horacio, Iago, Ignacio, Inocencio, Isidoro, Jacinto, Jacobo, Jafet, Jaime, Jeremias, Jeronimo, Jesús, Joaquin, Jorge, José, Juan, Jueves, Julio, Junio, Juriel, Lago, Lázaro, Leandro, Leonardo, Leoncio, Leopoldo, Lino, Lluís, Lobo, Lorencio, Luciano, Lunes, Manuel, Manzano, Marcial, Marco, Mariano, Martes, Marzo, Mateo, Matias, Mauricio, Mayo, Miguel, Montel, Montez, Morado, Nacio, Nadal, Narciso, Natal, Nemesio, Nevada, Nicolas, Oliviero, Ónix, Oriol, Oro, Osvaldo, Oviedo, Pablo, Pacifico, Paco, Pancho, Pascual, Patricio, Paulino, Pedro, Pepe, Peral, Perez, Perro, Pico, Pinto, Placido, Plata, Prospero, Publio, Quirce, Rafael, Rainerio, Ramiro, Ramón, Raúl, Renaldo, Renato, Ricardo, Rico, Rio, Roberto, Roca, Rodas, Rodolfo, Rodrigo, Rogelio, Rogerio, Rojo, Roldan, Roque, Rosso, Sábado, Salomon, Salvador, Sancho, Santiago, Santos, Sergi, Silvestre, Tadeo, Tago, Teodosio, Teodulo, Teofilio, Terencio, Timoteo, Tito, Tomas, Torres, Ulises, Vasco, Velasco, Verano, Vicente, Viernes, Vinicio, Virgilio, Vittorio, Xavier, Ximen, Ximenes, Yago, Zacarias, Zafiro, Zorra.

Girls

Abril, Adella, Adoncia, Agueda, Aguila, Alameda, Alatea, Aldonza, Alegria, Alejandra, Aletta, Allegra, Almena, Alondra, Altamira, Amalina, Amalita, Amaranta, Amata, Amatista, Ampelia, Ana, Anabel, Angelita, Anica, Anita, Annonciada, Arabela, Arantxa, Armada, Asela, Auristela, Azucena, Barba, Bautista, Beatriz, Belita, Belize, Benicia, Benigna, Blanca, Bonita, Brigida, Buena, Calandria, Camila, Caridad, Carilla, Carlota, Carmelita, Carmen, Carmina, Carmine, Caro, Catalina, Catalonia, Catina, Chabeli, Charina, Charo, Chiquita, Clarisa, Clarita,

Clementina, Colina, Concepción, Consuela, Corazón, Custodia, Dali, Damita, Delfina, Delma, Desirita, Dia, Diera, Dolores, Dominga, Dorotea, Duena, Dulcinea, Elbertina, Eldora, Elena, Encina, Engracia, Enrica, Esmeralda, Esperanza, Estefania, Estrella, Eufemia, Eusebia, Evita, Fabiola, Felicidad, Felipa, Francisca, Gitana, Gracia, Graciela, Guadalupe, Havana, Hermila, Hermosa, Hilaria, Idalia, Imelda, Immaculada, Imperio, Inca, Inocencia, Isabella, Isaura, Isla, Ivelisse, Ivis, Jacinta, Jessenia, Jesúsa, Jimena, Jorgelina, Josefina, Joya, Juanita, Judita, Jueva, Julietta, Julita, Junio, Lana, Latoya, Leanor, Leocadia, Leticia, Lila, Lima, Lirio, Loida, Lola, Lolita, Lona, Lourdes, Lucia, Lucrecia, Luisa, Luisana, Lupe, Luzanne, Macarena, Madalena, Madra, Maite, Majorana, Malaya, Manuela, Manyana, Marambra, Marcelle, Margarita, Maribel, Marieta, Marijosé, Mariposa, Mariquita, Marisol, Marta, Mercedes, Milagros, Montserrat, Naranja, Natividad, Nazaret, Nevada, Nieves, Nimfa, Nina, Nita, Nohemi, Nuria, Ofelia, Olalla, Onil, Ónix, Pacienca, Paloma, Paquita, Pascuala, Pasena, Paulina, Paz, Pepa, Pepita, Pera, Perez, Perla, Pia, Piedra, Pilar, Pimienta, Pina, Primavera, Prisca, Puma, Querida, Quirina, Ramona, Raquel, Rebeca, Ria, Rica, Roca, Rosa, Rosario, Rosita, Rossana, Rubi, Salvadora, Santina, Savanna, Seda, Segovia, Serafina, Sevilla, Solana, Soledad, Susana, Tango, Teodora, Teresita, Tierra, Trinidad, Tulipan, Valeriana, Ventura, Veracruz, Vina, Violante, Violeta, Vitoria, Xaviera, Xiomara, Yamila, Ynes, Ynez, Yolandita, Ysabel, Zafira, Zita, Zonda, Zuela.

TIBETAN/SHERPA

Boys
Bala, Chamba, Chembo, Chewang, Chola, Chungda, Dawa, Dhondup, Dorjee, Dru, Dzong, Gesar, Gyalpo, Jangu, Jigme, Kailash, Kalden, Kan, Karma, Lhakpa, Lhawang, Lobsang, Mingma, Naljor, Namgyal, Nawang, Nedup, Nima, Norbu, Pasang, Pema, Pemba, Penjor, Phintso, Phurba, Ra, Rinzen, Saybo, Shay, Sonam, Sumba, Tashi, Tenzing, Tom, Tsamcho, Tseten, Tshering, Urgyen, Wangdi, Yago, Yeshe, Yu.

Girls
Ajala, Amala, Ani, Chamba, Chiru, Choden, Dawa, Dechen, Diki, Dolkar, Dolma, Garma, Guba, Juba, Karma, Kesang, Lhakpa, Lhamu, Lobsang, Nago, Nima, Palam, Pasang, Pema, Rinzen, Sangmu, Sera, Shay, Shiba, Sonam, Tango, Tashi, Tseten, Tshering, Yangchen, Yangzom, Yu.

TURKISH

Boys
Abi, Adem, Akar, Alp, Altan, Altun, Artan, Asil, Asker, Aslan, Ata, Aydin, Babar, Baghatur, Baris, Bedir, Berk, Berkant, Berker, Bora, Bulut, Cagatay, Cahil, Can, Cengiz, Coskun, Deniz, Derya, Direnc, Duman, Duygu, Ediz, Emin, Emre, Engin, Erdem, Eren, Erhan, Erol, Eser, Goker, Gul, Gulbahar, Hakan, Hasad, Hazan, Ilhami, Ilker, Ilkin, Iskander, Iskender, Kamuran, Kaya, Kiral, Kizil, Koloman, Koray, Krikor, Kudret, Levent, Mart, Mazhar, Mehmed, Mehmet, Mesut, Metin, Murat, Onan, Onur, Orhan, Osman, Ozgur, Ozkan, Recep, Ruslan, Sarkir, Savas, Serhat, Serif, Serkan, Servet, Sirkan, Soner, Suleyman, Tabib, Temel, Tolga, Tunc, Turgay, Turk, Ufuk, Ugur, Umit, Umut, Usman, Volkan, Yasin, Yavuz, Yucel, Zeheb, Zeki.

Girls
Adana, Ajda, Alma, Anka, Asli, Aygul, Ayla, Aylin, Ayse, Aysel, Aysen, Aysu, Aysun, Banaz, Basak, Belgin, Bercu, Berna, Bilge, Cagla, Canan, Cansu, Cari, Ceren, Deniz, Dilara, Duygu, Ebru, Ece, Eda, Ekin, Elif, Elmas, Emel, Emine, Esen, Eser, Esin, Ferida, Fidan, Gizem, Gonca, Gozde, Gulistan, Hande, Harika, Havva, Hazan, Ipek, Irmak, Izel, Karli, Kelebek, Magali, Meryem, Muge, Mukaddes, Nergis, Nesrin, Nilufer, Nuray, Nurcan, Ozge, Ozgur, Ozlem, Pembe, Pinar, Resmin, Saril, Sebnem, Sema, Sevil, Simge, Su, Suna, Suvla, Tulay, Tulip, Yagmur, Yesim, Yeter, Yildiz, Yonca, Zerdali, Zerrin, Zeynep.

Your favourite names

www.ingramcontent.com/pod-product-compliance
Lightning Source LLC
Chambersburg PA
CBHW060358230426
43663CB00008B/1309

9781425722222